The Genius of Christ

A Global Academic Publishing Book

Studies in Contemporary Philosophical Theology

ʻAbbās Maḥmūd al-ʻAqqād

The Genius of Christ

Translated and edited by

F. Peter Ford, Jr.

SUNY
PRESS

Translated from 'Abbās Maḥmūd al-'Aqqād, *'Abqariyyat al-Masīḥ* (second edition of *Ḥayāt al-Masīḥ*) by F. Peter Ford, Jr.

Cover illustration by Dana Starkey.

Library of Congress Cataloging-in-Publication Data

'Aqqād, 'Abbās Maḥmūd, 1889-1964.
[Ḥayāt al-Masīḥ. English]
The genius of Christ / 'Abbās Maḥmūd 'Aqqād ; translated and edited by F. Peter Ford, Jr.
p. cm. — (Studies in contemporary philosophical theology ; 1)
ISBN 1-58684-104-1 (pbk. : alk. paper)
1. Jesus Christ—Islamic interpretations. 2. Islam—Relations—Christianity. 3. Christianity and other religions—Islam. I. Ford, F. Peter, 1953- II. Title. III. Series.
BP172 .A6513 2001
297.2'4—dc21

2001005943

For information, contact
State University of New York Press, Albany, NY
www.sunypress.edu

ANNOUNCEMENT

This series, entitled *Studies in Contemporary Philosophical Theology* (SCPT), focuses on original contributions of contemporary thinkers on philosophical theology in purely philosophical as well as in monotheistic and other religious traditions. The editors and external referees evaluate each manuscript for originality of scholarship and the philosophical and/or religious significance of its content. No censorship is exercised that might arrest either a departure from a philosophical or religious creed or silences the expression of support for established orthodoxy. The publications express solely the positions of the authors, and being diverse, cannot reflect the views of either the editors or home institutions. The editors are pleased and privileged to be instrumental in documenting some dimensions of the creative thought of the contemporary era. In addition, the editors wish to express their gratitude for support from the sponsoring institutions and to Ali A. Mazrui (the Director of *Institute of Global Cultural Studies* at Binghamton University) and to the administrators at Brigham Young University.

Parviz Morewedge
Institute of Global
Cultural Studies
Binghamton University

Daniel C. Peterson
Center for the Preservation
of Ancient Religious Texts
Brigham Young University

For Patty,
who taught me the meaning
of honest dialogue

Contents

SECTION THREE: APPENDIXES

Foreword

The main portion of this book is a translation of an Arabic work extolling the person and mission of Jesus, whose life and teachings form the foundation of the Christian faith. That its author was a Muslim, and one who wrote several other books in defense of his own faith, may seem strange for Christian readers who know little about Islam. Yet Muslim readers will hardly find this remarkable. In concert with their holy book, the Qur'ān, Muslims have consistently regarded Jesus as one of the most esteemed of a long line of prophets. Like most Christians, they believe that he was born of the Virgin Mary, performed many miracles, and, most importantly, was called by God to be the bearer of divine revelation to the Jews.

On the other hand (and again, following the Qur'ān), Muslims have departed from certain traditional Christian beliefs about Jesus. In particular, they have rejected any divine status for Jesus himself, and have denied the historicity, as well as the theological necessity, of his crucifixion. As a result, Muslims have produced a large body of literature which portrays their own distinctive understanding of Christ. This literature developed in various forms, such as traditional sayings from the prophet Muḥammad, scholarly commentaries on Qur'ānic passages about Jesus, or mystical reflections of the Sufi's. In addition, a number of medieval apologetic works openly attacked Christian beliefs about Jesus, and this polemical approach (which was countered with equal antagonism among Christian writers) has unfortunately characterized most Muslim writing on the subject into the modern period. In the twentieth century, a few Muslim authors have tried to offer a more positive approach to the subject, even attempting to bridge the gap between the divergent views of Christians and Muslims. Yet such works have generally relied on traditional Islamic sources, with little acknowledgment, much less dependency, on the sources revered by Christians. Indeed, they generally uphold a popular belief about the Bible, long held among Muslims, that its text is unreliable, having been "corrupted" at some stage of its formation or transmission.

What is remarkable, then, about this particular book is that its author virtually ignores the Islamic literature about Jesus, and instead draws almost exclusively from the New Testament, especially the four Gospels. Furthermore, he makes extensive use of modern Western scholarship concerning various issues surrounding the person and ministry of Jesus. This is not to say that he has succeeded in "bridging the gap"; while his portrayal of Christ pushes the boundaries, his presentation remains within the scope of a distinctly Islamic perspective. Nevertheless, he offers a vigorous affirmation of Jesus' teaching and personality which he believes to be instructive for all people in all times. The result is a work that is unique in both its positive exposition of Jesus as well as its positive appreciation for the Gospels.

The author of this unusual book was 'Abbas Maḥmūd al-'Aqqād (1889-1964), who remains, among Arabs, one of the most well-known and well-loved modern Egyptian writers.

Raised in Aswan with little formal education, he nevertheless became a self-taught intellectual and a prominent poet, journalist and author. He lived in a turbulent period of Egyptian history, during the first half of the twentieth century when the country was struggling to gain independence from British domination. A fervent nationalist, al-'Aqqād supported the cause for liberal democracy; but he disavowed the secular approach espoused by some. At the same time, he criticized the religious traditionalists whom he felt were stifling modern progress. He was an apologist for an orthodox yet revitalized Islam which would provide the framework for social and political reforms.

Al-'Aqqād's primary contribution to the cause of reform was through literature. A prolific writer, he authored over a hundred books and several thousand articles. He also read avidly from Western literature, particularly in English, and he sought to convey its insights to the Egyptian populace along with his own critical review. His books included many biographical studies of both historical and contemporary personalities. Among these, his most enduring and best known works cover the lives of Muḥammad and other prominent figures of Islamic history; since the most important of these bear the title *'Abqarīyat* . . . [The Genius of . . .], these books comprise what has been popularly known as the "*'Abqarīyah*" series.

'Abqarīyat al-Masīḥ [The Genius of Christ] was an important contribution to this series. It focuses on the religious and social conditions surrounding Jesus' ministry and on the essence and significance of his teaching. Al-'Aqqād highlights Jesus' ethical instruction, the opposition he faced, and the inner conflicts with which he struggled as a prophet. The book is a penetrating investigation of both the call *to* Jesus into a universal mission, and the call *by* Jesus into a universal compassion. Like his other "biographical" works, it is a study of a personality rather than a biography *per se*. As a result, readers familiar with the Bible will find that several details of the life of Christ are bypassed. Indeed, Jesus' miracles are set aside by al-'Aqqād as irrelevant to his purpose, while the events of his trial and crucifixion are considered to lie outside the realm of history. Al-'Aqqād's approach is thus selective in its use of the Gospels, and this has been criticized by a number of Western Christian reviewers. Yet his purpose was not to appease Christian readers, or even to promote Muslim-Christian dialogue. It seems that his primary intention was to call his own Muslim compatriots to heed the teaching of one of their most eminent prophets, to follow Jesus' call to brotherly love rather than follow rigid traditional religion or self-promoting secularism. While such an understanding of Jesus' mission is not absent from the Islamic tradition, al-'Aqqād instead turned to the Christian Gospels. It is true that he did not accept these documents categorically. Yet his tacit recognition of their validity goes far beyond what most Muslims would advocate, and it marks a dramatic departure from other Muslim works about Jesus. His book is in fact a significant contribution to dialogue, and nearly half a century after its appearance, it can continue to be profitable for Muslim and Christian readers alike.

'Abqarīyat al-Masīḥ was first published in Cairo in 1953. Five years later, al-'Aqqād produced a second edition in which new material was added which especially dealt with the Dead Sea Scrolls. The title was also changed at that time to *Ḥayāt al-Masīḥ* [The Life of Christ], although the substance of the book was left intact. (The change in title was evidently an editorial decision.) The book has undergone several printings and was most recently pub-

lished in 1996 as a slightly revised version of the second edition; this is referred to here as the "third" edition, or "ed. 3," and it forms the basis for this translation. For any who wish to consult the Arabic text, page references to ed. 3 are provided in italicized brackets on the inside edge of the header throughout the translation. Meanwhile, references to the book itself in the Introduction and Notes utilize its original title, since that much more appropriately reflects the theme of the work, and since al-'Aqqād would have probably preferred to retain it.

The book was reportedly well-received in Egypt (among both Muslims and Christians), in other Arab countries, and in Pakistan, where it was translated into Urdu. Its reception in the West, however, has thus far been limited to scholars able to read Arabic and willing to wrestle with al-'Aqqād's arduous style. It is hoped that this translation into English, though far from perfect, will result in the wider circulation that the original work deserves — something which al-'Aqqād himself would certainly have wanted.

The present edition, however, is much more than a translation of al-'Aqqād's text. The extensive Introduction provides background material for a more beneficial understanding of the book. A review is first made of the wider context of how Muslims have regarded Jesus and the Gospels throughout their history. This especially applies to modern Arab Muslim works about Christ, most of which al-'Aqqād probably knew. Next, an overview is furnished of al-'Aqqād's more immediate context, including the sociopolitical environment in which he lived, the main features of his own life, and the vast amount of literature which he produced. The third chapter of the Introduction provides a general assessment of *The Genius of Christ.* The translation proper is accompanied by numerous endnotes. These serve a variety of functions: important terminology is noted; sources for al-'Aqqād's quotations or allusions are supplied and discussed; and commentary is made on general issues as well as specific points raised by al-'Aqqād, with references given to modern secondary sources where a subject can be explored in more detail. Finally, the Appendixes deal with issues of secondary relevance to the translation.

This material was originally produced as a Ph.D. dissertation (Temple University, 1998). It has been slightly revised, particularly with regard to the format of the chapters, such that the arrangement now more accurately reflects that of the Arabic text. Also, I have removed most of the numerous notes to textual discrepancies among the various Arabic editions that were published. (See Appendix A for a discussion of these editions.)

I am very grateful to a large number of people who assisted me, especially in identifying sources and locating relevant materials. These are too numerous to mention here. However, special thanks must be made to Mahmoud Ayoub (the chair of my review committee) for guiding me through the dissertation process; and to Yahya Hendi, Nasser Lutfi and Oddbjørn Leirvik for reviewing the accuracy of the translation and helping me sort through a wealth of Arabic materials.

F. Peter Ford, Jr.
Khartoum
May, 2001

Abbreviations

Books of the Bible

Old Testament:

Gen.	Genesis
Ex.	Exodus
Lev.	Leviticus
Num.	Numbers
Dt.	Deuteronomy
Josh.	Joshua
Judg.	Judges
1, 2 Sam.	1, 2 Samuel
1, 2 Kg.	1, 2 Kings
1, 2 Chr.	1, 2 Chronicles
Ezr.	Ezra
Neh.	Nehemiah
Est.	Esther
Job	Job
Ps.	Psalms
Pr.	Proverbs
Eccl.	Ecclesiastes
Song	Song of Songs
Isa.	Isaiah
Jer.	Jeremiah
Lam.	Lamentations
Ezk.	Ezekiel
Dan.	Daniel
Hos.	Hosea
Joel	Joel
Amos	Amos
Obad.	Obadiah
Jonah	Jonah
Mic.	Micah
Nah.	Nahum
Hab.	Habakkuk
Zeph.	Zephaniah
Hag.	Haggai
Zech.	Zechariah
Mal.	Malachi

New Testament:

Mt.	Gospel of Matthew
Mk.	Gospel of Mark
Lk.	Gospel of Luke
Jn.	Gospel of John
Acts	Acts of the Apostles
Rom.	Romans
1, 2 Cor.	1, 2 Corinthians
Gal.	Galatians
Eph.	Ephesians
Phil.	Philippians
Col.	Colossians
1, 2 Ths.	1, 2 Thessalonians
1, 2 Tim.	1, 2 Timothy
Titus	Titus
Phile.	Philemon
Heb.	Hebrews
Jas.	James
1, 2 Pet.	1, 2 Peter
1, 2, 3, Jn.	1, 2, 3 John
Jude	Jude
Rev.	Revelation

Reference Works

ABD *The Anchor Bible Dictionary*. Edited by David Noel Freedman. 6 vols. New York: Doubleday, 1992.

DCE	*A Dictionary of Christian Ethics.* Edited by John Macquarrie. London: SCM Press, 1967.
DJG	*Dictionary of Jesus and the Gospels.* Edited by Joel B. Green, Scot McKnight, and I. Howard Marshall. Downers Grove, IL: InterVarsity Press, 1992.
EI[1]	*The Encyclopaedia of Islam,* 1st ed. Edited by M. T. Houtsma et al. 8 vols. Leiden: E. J. Brill, 1913-36, with Supplement, 1938.
EI[2]	*The Encyclopaedia of Islam,* 2d ed. Edited by H. A. R. Gibb et al. 9 vols. to date. Leiden: E. J. Brill, 1960-.
EJ	*Encyclopaedia Judaica.* Edited by Cecil Roth. 16 vols. Jerusalem: Keter Publishing House, 1971.
ER	*The Encyclopedia of Religion.* Edited by Mircea Eliade. 16 vols. New York: Macmillan, 1987.
Loeb	Loeb Classical Library. (See *References Cited* for publication details on individual classical authors.)
OCD	*The Oxford Classical Dictionary,* 2d ed. Edited by N. G. L. Hammond and H. H. Scullard. Oxford: Clarendon Press, 1970.
ODCC	*The Oxford Dictionary of the Christian Church,* 2d ed. Edited by F. L. Cross and E. A. Livingstone. Oxford: Oxford University Press, 1974.

Other Abbreviations

Ar.	Arabic
AV	the Authorized (King James) Version of the Bible
ch.	chapter(s)
ed. 1, 2, 3	the first, second or third edition of the printed text of *'Abqarīyat al-Masīḥ* (see Appendix A)
Gk.	Greek
Heb.	Hebrew
lit.	literally
LXX	the Septuagint (the standard ancient Greek translation of the Hebrew Bible)
ms., mss.	manuscript(s)
MT	the Masoretic Text of the Hebrew Bible
NT	New Testament
OT	Old Testament
pl.	plural
RSV	the Revised Standard Version of the Bible
sg.	singular
v., vv.	verse(s)
VD	the Van Dyck Arabic version of the Bible (see Appendix C)
=	indicates parallel passages among the Synoptic Gospels (Matthew, Mark and Luke)

Transliteration

Arabic

Arabic transliteration generally follows the Library of Congress standards as set forth in *Library of Congress Romanization Tables and Cataloging Policies*, compiled by Sally C. Tseng (Metuchen, NJ: Scarecrow Press, 1990), 5-19. Consonants are rendered as follows:

ب	*b*	ز	*z*	ف	*f*
ت	*t*	س	*s*	ق	*q*
ث	*th*	ش	*sh*	ك	*k*
ج	*j*	ص	*ṣ*	ل	*l*
ح	*ḥ*	ض	*ḍ*	م	*m*
خ	*kh*	ط	*ṭ*	ن	*n*
د	*d*	ظ	*ẓ*	ه	*h*
ذ	*dh*	ع	ʻ	و	*w*
ر	*r*	غ	*gh*	ي	*y*

Additional Notes:

1. In names of authors from Egypt (but not for the titles of their books), "g" is used instead of "j."
2. Initial *hamzah* is not transliterated; otherwise it is represented by an apostrophe.
3. *Tā' marbūṭah* is usually rendered as "h." If it appears in the first word of a genitive construct, or after an *alif,* it is rendered as "t."
4. A slash is used in the rare instance when two separate consonants might be confused for a digraph, e.g., *s/h.*
5. Short vowels are as follows: a, i and u.
6. Long vowels are as follows: *ā* (for both *alif* and *alif maqṣūrah), ī, ū, ay* and *aw.*
7. The definite article is always *al-*, even if followed by a "sun letter."
8. Inseparable prepositions and conjunctions are joined by a hyphen to what follows; the *al-* form of the definite article is retained. E.g., *wa-al-bāb.* But note the exception for the preposition *li-* plus the definite article: *lil-bāb.*

Biblical Languages

The transliteration of Hebrew, Aramaic and Greek words follows the customary practice used in most scholarly biblical works, such as *The Anchor Bible Dictionary*.

SECTION ONE

INTRODUCTION

Jesus and the Gospels in Arab-Islamic Thought

The Qur'ānic Basis

The intellectual and literary context for all Muslim writing about Jesus must of necessity begin with the Qur'ān, the foundation for Islamic faith in general.[1] There, Jesus is mentioned in a few dozen passages, primarily with regard to his role as one of the many prophets who appeared prior to Muḥammad and who taught the unity of God and how to worship Him properly. Yet in many respects Jesus is elevated in the Qur'ān above all other prophets, such that Muslims have almost universally considered him to be second in esteem only to Muḥammad. Jesus was set apart from birth through the miraculous conception of his mother Mary, a virgin chosen by God for this role because of her purity and humble submission (3:42-47, 19:16-26).[2] At the outset he was designated a prophet of God, appointed to proclaim a scripture to the people of Israel (e.g., 19:30). In addition to his special title of "Messiah" (Ar. *al-Masīḥ*, e.g. 3:45), he is uniquely designated as God's "word" (*kalimatuhu*) and "a spirit from Him" (*rūḥ minhu*, 4:171). To convince those who doubted his prophethood, Jesus performed many miracles through the power and permission of God, especially healing the sick and raising the dead (3:49, 5:110). Although the people to whom he was sent rejected his message and plotted against him, God would not allow them to succeed (3:52-54).

However, many passages in the Qur'ān regarding Jesus are presented in opposition to certain views espoused by Jews and Christians of that time and locality. The well-known passage regarding the attempted crucifixion of Jesus actually appears as a criticism against the Jewish nation which boasted of that deed:

> And because of their saying: We slew the Messiah Jesus son of Mary, Allah's messenger — They slew him not nor crucified, but it appeared so unto them; and lo! those who disagree concerning it are in doubt thereof; they have no knowledge thereof save pursuit of a conjecture; they slew him not for certain, but Allah took him up to Himself. Allah was ever Mighty, Wise. (4:157-58)

There are certain aspects of this passage which have been variously interpreted by Muslims, such as the meaning of "it appeared so unto them," and the matter of when and how God "took him up to Himself." Nevertheless, Muslims have almost universally regarded this passage as an explicit denial that Jesus was crucified or killed by the Jews.[3]

Other passages denounce Christian claims regarding the divinity of Jesus, the Trinity, or Jesus as God's Son. These concerns are best viewed together within the general intent of the Qur'ān to elucidate a sharp distinction between God and Jesus.[4] Perhaps the most explicit verse, which happens to deal with all three issues, is 4:171:

> O People of the Scripture! Do not exaggerate in your religion nor utter aught concerning Allah save the truth. The Messiah, Jesus son of Mary, was only a messenger of Allah, and His word which He conveyed unto Mary, and a spirit from Him. So believe in Allah and His messengers, and say not "Three" — Cease! (it is) better for you! — Allah is only One God. Far is it removed from His transcendent majesty that He should have a son. . . .

It has been suggested that the Christian claims which are in view in passages such as this were in fact not those of orthodox Christianity, but that they rather represented current sectarian beliefs.[5] Whether or not that is the case, a clear line of distinction is drawn with regard to traditional Christian doctrine about Christ. The "basic issue is the Qur'ānic insistence on the radical Otherness of God . . . in relation to Jesus, and therefore the absolute necessity of an uncompromising differentiation between them."[6]

Thus the composite picture of Jesus in the Qur'ān (as well as of Christianity in general), with respect to the doctrines held by Christians, is, "in a word, ambivalent," or "a sort of dialectical approach."[7] Certain Christian beliefs about Jesus are maintained, while others are renounced. David Kerr has outlined a summary of the Qur'ānic view of Christianity, devised primarily by a Muslim colleague, in which sixteen points of affirmation are contrasted with their parallel points of rejection. For example, the Qur'ān recognizes Jesus as the son of Mary, while it disavows any notion of him as the "Son of God"; the fact of Jewish opposition to Jesus is acknowledged, while his crucifixion by them is repudiated; there is an assertion of Jesus' designation as "Messiah," but a denial of the implications of this title in Christian theology.[8]

A similar dialectical approach of affirmation/rejection is present in the Qur'ān regarding the Christians' scripture.[9] On the one hand, Jesus is said to have received revelation from God designated as "the Scripture" (*al-Kitāb*, 19:30) and "the Gospel" (*al-Injīl*, 5:46). This Gospel is affirmed to be in harmony not only with previous scriptures (especially the *Tawrāt*, the scripture of the Jews), but also with the Qur'ān itself (5:46, 3:3). The Christians are said to be in possession of this Gospel and thus are among "the People of the Scripture" (*ahl al-Kitāb*, 5:68, 7:157). Muslims are commanded to affirm its authenticity and reliability (29:46, 10:95).

On the other hand, Christians are criticized in the Qur'ān, along with Jews, for not regarding their own scriptures with proper esteem. They quarrel among themselves and discredit each other's scripture (2:113). Jews in particular are charged with having "altered" or "corrupted" (*yuḥarrifūna*) their scripture (2:75, 4:46), an allegation which was later to be applied to Christians as well. Meanwhile, certain Christians are said to have forgotten part of their scripture and hidden other parts (5:14-15). It should also be observed that the Qur'ān speaks of only the one Gospel; there is no recognition of the presence of four Gospels as documents which contain much more than the words of Jesus and which were written in a language other than what he spoke. The perceived discrepancy among Muslims between the scripture which Jesus left and the book which the Christians possess was later to fuel charges of textual corruption.

The Qur'ān's perception of Jesus and the Gospels is thus inextricably bound with its understanding of Christian doctrine and practice concerning them, at least as expressed at that time. Jesus himself and the Gospel he proclaimed are explicitly affirmed within specific parameters based on the Qur'ānic concepts of the unity of God and the prophethood of his messengers. But Christian claims which exceed those parameters are soundly denounced. Since the Qur'ān subsequently became the foundation for virtually all Muslim thought regarding Jesus and the Gospels, this pattern of affirmation/rejection was to continue throughout the history of Islam. As will be seen, 'Abbās Maḥmūd al-'Aqqād gave far more emphasis to the affirmation side while hardly ever referring to the Qur'ānic data concerning Jesus; yet his presentation nevertheless falls within the confines delineated by the Qur'ān.

The Classical Period

While a review of the context of any contemporary Arabic-Muslim work concerning Jesus must begin with the Qur'ān, it must continue with the vast corpus of Islamic literature which developed over the centuries concerning Jesus, as well as concerning Christians and their beliefs. This literature in turn can only be understood in the context of the vicissitudes of Muslim relations with Christians since the rise of Islam. Most of what was written by Muslims (as well as by Christians) grew out of a mutual misunderstanding of the other's religion and mistrust of the other's community. Works which try to cover this subject can at best provide an outline of the main themes and key writers concerned.[10] Here, only brief references can be made to a few of the more important issues and authors dealing specifically with Jesus and/or the Gospels. For the sake of structure, various genres of literature are considered (*ḥadīth* and *tafsīr*, historical and apologetic, Shī'ī and Ṣūfī), but it must be noted that there is considerable overlap among these.

The word *ḥadīth* (pl. *aḥādīth*) refers to an account of something Muḥammad said or did, but it can also include something said or done in his presence which he tacitly approved. These accounts were passed on over time, eventually gaining an authority second only to that of the Qur'ān. Although the large majority of such accounts were later considered to be spurious, Muslim scholars set precise standards whereby the authenticity of individual units were judged on the basis of the credibility of the chain of transmitters that passed on the *ḥadīth*. Many *aḥādīth* which were considered genuine were gathered into large collections; six of these attained "canonical" status, the most authoritative being those by Muḥammad ibn Ismā'īl al-Bukhāri (d. 256/870) and Muslim ibn al-Hajjāj al-Qushayrī (d. 261/875). Meanwhile, many other "weak" *aḥādīth* continued to flourish.

A sizable number of *ḥadīth* accounts focus on Jesus, although the majority of these are said to have originated from companions of Muḥammad who were converts from Christianity rather than Muḥammad himself. Many of these accounts deal with the physical appearance of Jesus, his meritorious behavior, and especially his teachings. They often reflect material present in the Gospels, and undoubtedly this was frequently the source for such traditions.[11] Even if the authenticity of certain accounts might be questioned, they nevertheless reflect views that had developed within the early Muslim community.

The *tafsīr* ("interpretation") literature consists of the large works of commentary on the Qur'ān by some of Islam's most distinguished scholars. Foremost in the field were Muḥammad ibn Jarīr al-Ṭabarī (d. 310/923), the first great commentator who set the stage for virtually all later writers; Abū al-Qāsim al-Zamakhsharī (d. 538/1144, renowned despite his Mu'tazalī outlook) who wrote with careful analysis and rationalism; Fakhr al-Dīn al-Rāzī (d. 606/1209), a brilliant philosopher whose massive work is convoluted with intertwined arguments; and 'Imād al-Dīn ibn Kathīr (d. 774/1373), a conservative jurist who carefully relied on a variety of historical sources and whose work is today perhaps the most widely used of the classical commentaries.[12] Many *aḥādīth* are found in the *tafsīr* literature, where they served to offer background or explanatory information about a particular Qur'ānic text. Often several conflicting accounts appear simultaneously (along with their alleged transmitters), leaving the reader to decide which one might be the most authentic.

Commentators such as these sought to elucidate verses dealing with Jesus in an affirmative manner, while remaining within the bounds of orthodox Islam as they understood it. Frequently this also entailed criticism of prevailing Christian beliefs while remaining silent concerning phrases that could possibly be rendered in a manner compatible to those same doctrines. For example, when each of these commentators (as well as others) analyzed passages that reproach Christian claims to Jesus as the Son of God, they routinely granted to Jesus this title in a limited, metaphorical sense, while accusing Christians of taking the phrase literally. At the same time, however, they were unable to explain the nature of God's role in the miraculous conception of Jesus in terms that would have been consistent with the Islamic emphasis on God's transcendence.[13]

Another example of such affirmation/rejection is the Qur'ānic record of Jesus' miracles. Al-Rāzī relates his discussion with a Christian who claimed that these demonstrated the divinity of Jesus. Al-Rāzī argues against this, claiming that such miracles are not equivalent with God's creation, and that other prophets such as Moses performed similar miracles. Their purpose, he says, was rather to distinguish Jesus as a prophet appointed by God.[14] This point is also emphasized in the *tafsīr* literature with respect to the statement in 3:49 and 5:110 that Jesus "created" or "fashioned" birds from clay; the verb (*khalaqa*) is otherwise attributed in the Qur'ān (in the positive sense) only to God, but here the commentators seek to limit the strictly creative aspect of the word.[15]

Naturally, the passage concerning the crucifixion of Jesus (4:157-58), with its apparently explicit denial of its historicity, provided ample opportunity to reject a primary Christian contention. The issue for the interpreters was not the death of Jesus; other passages which speak of Jesus being "received" by God (3:55 and 5:117, with the verb *tawaffā*) were generally understood to refer to his death at some time or another.[16] Nor was the issue whether or not a crucifixion took place; it was assumed that such an event did occur. Rather, what they denied was the claim that it was Jesus who was crucified. However, this still left them to explain the meaning of the phrase "but it appeared so unto them" (*wa-*

lākin shubbiha lahum). Here, most commentators proposed an explanation in which someone else was killed instead of Jesus, drawing from various *ḥadīth* reports to this end. The account preferred by al-Ṭabarī was that when the Jews came to seize Jesus, God cast his likeness upon all the disciples around him; in confusion, the Jews took and crucified one of them, thinking they had killed Jesus himself. Later commentators, however, preferred accounts which indicated that one of the disciples had volunteered to be killed in place of Jesus (so Ibn Kathīr); others opted for a punishment-substitution view, whereby the man killed was either the Jew sent to seize Jesus, or was Judas Iscariot (the view most commonly held among Muslims today). But not all commentators took an approach involving substitution: al-Zamakhsharī questioned it for grammatical reasons, and al-Rāzī rejected it on philosophical grounds, although neither scholar was clear as to what he believed actually happened.[17]

One other prominent theme about Jesus in the *ḥadīth* and *tafsīr* literature is that of his return, or more properly, his future "descent." Although there is no clear reference to this event in the Qur'ān, the *ḥadīth* collections include a large number of accounts which incorporate a variety of details. It is said that Jesus will return to the earth at the end of time, when he will smash all symbols of the cross, kill any swine and abolish the *jizyah* (the poll-tax levied on non-Muslims living in Muslim territory); he will establish peace, confirm Islam, and kill the *Dajjāl* (the Deceiver or Antichrist) and his followers. Some reports state that he will remain on the earth for forty years, after which he will die and be buried by the Muslims. The accounts include certain conflicting details: some say he will descend at Damascus, others at Jerusalem; some say he will lead the Muslims in prayer, others that he will decline to do so in deference to the previously chosen leader.[18] Many of these *aḥādīth* were also utilized by the *tafsīr* commentators in their explanations of verses which possibly allude to a return by Jesus.[19] It is clear from these accounts that Jesus' return to earth was affirmed in a manner parallel to Christian belief, but with a distinctly Muslim orientation.

These views of Jesus found in the *ḥadīth* and *tafsīr* literature demonstrate that Muslims were willing to accept a considerable amount in common with Christians, but that limits were set by the Qur'ān beyond which they would not venture. It is worth mentioning here briefly that all of these themes are raised by al-'Aqqād in his book; and, while he deals with the issues rather differently, he shares with the classical commentators both their willingness to affirm much about Jesus held by Christians and their persistence in maintaining the discussion within parameters which are distinctly Islamic.[20]

In other genres of literature where Jesus is depicted, various authors were dependent to a large extent on their knowledge of and attitude towards the Gospels. Muslim historians who covered pre-Islamic times often felt free to draw from material found in the Gospels and other Christian sources when discussing the origins of Christianity. This trend is especially evident in Aḥmad ibn Wāḍiḥ al-Ya'qūbī (d.284/895), who devotes considerable space to the birth narratives, the teaching ministry and even the crucifixion of Jesus basically as found in the Gospels. He includes the names of the twelve disciples, summarizes the Sermon on the Mount (Mt. ch. 5-7), and quotes the "Prologue" of the Gospel of John

(1:1-18); yet only rarely does he display his Muslim bias.[21] Such detail is not found among the historians who followed him. Al-Ṭabarī (the commentator mentioned above who also wrote a mammoth work of history) seems not to have had direct knowledge of the Gospels, drawing instead from Muslim tradition concerning Jesus. His successor, ʻAlī ibn Ḥusayn al-Masʻūdī (d. 345/956), presents some material from the Gospels and Christian apocryphal works mingled with that from Muslim sources. And ʻAbd al-Raḥmān ibn Khaldūn (d. 808/1406), regarded as the Muslim world's most astute historian, offered nothing of consequence that was new.[22] However, ʻAlī ibn al-ʻAsākir (d. 571/1176), who wrote his *Tārīkh Madīnat Dimashq* [History of Damascus] at the time of the Crusades, included an extensive biography of Jesus. He was clearly familiar with the Gospels, but he drew from them, along with *aḥādīth* and other traditions, in a manner which emphasized the ascetic character of Jesus.[23]

The extensive apologetic literature need not be covered here in detail, for almost all of it is polemical in nature. The purpose of these authors was to refute Christian claims about Jesus, most often by discrediting the Christians' Bible. Qur'ānic charges of "corruption" *(taḥrīf)* or other mishandling of previous scriptures (see above) were frequently invoked against Christians as well as Jews. Some accused them of concealing what they knew to be within their texts; others asserted that they had altered the texts themselves; still others considered the distortion to be one of faulty interpretation.[24]

This last approach was adopted by one of the earliest of these authors, ʻAlī ibn Rabbān al-Ṭabarī (d. 240/855), in his work *Al-Radd ʻalā al-Naṣārā* [Refutation of the Christians]. A convert from Christianity at age seventy, ʻAlī al-Ṭabarī was thoroughly familiar with the Bible, and he accepted its content at face value. But he utilized it as a proof text against Christian beliefs, stating that neither Jesus nor his disciples had ever claimed he was God, and that his birth and miracles proved nothing regarding divinity.[25]

A very different approach from ʻAlī al-Ṭabarī's *Al-Radd ʻalā al-Naṣārā* is found in a tract with the same title, and written at about the same time, by one of Islam's most famous classical authors, ʻAmr al-Jāḥiẓ (d. 255/869). This work is primarily a scathing attack on the social position of the Christians of his day, but it includes a condemnation of their claim that Jesus is the Son of God. This was based on al-Jāḥiẓ' belief that the four Gospels were completely unreliable, and that their authors may even have deliberately deceived their readers.[26]

A more eclectic approach was taken by ʻAbd al-Jabbār ibn Aḥmad (d. 416/1025), the chief *qāḍī* (judge) of Rayy (modern Teheran). In one of his works, Christians are criticized for deviating significantly from the teachings of Jesus. A number of passages from the Gospels are used in support of his arguments, while other passages are considered forgeries or interpreted metaphorically. Thus, the traditional Muslim view of Jesus remains the standard. He also draws from the apocryphal gospels, e.g., as proof that Judas Iscariot was crucified in place of Jesus. In his view, those primarily responsible for the corruption of Jesus' religion were the apostle Paul and the Roman Emperor Constantine.[27]

The classical writer most adamantly opposed to the text of the Bible was ʻAlī ibn Aḥmad ibn Ḥazm (d. 456/1064). A convinced literalist, he attacked all schools of thought which made interpretations of the Qur'ān based on either reason or metaphor. In his attack on Christianity, he painstakingly identified contradictions in the Bible, and so denounced it as completely corrupted and unreliable. Christian beliefs about Jesus were thus ridiculed as absurd. Although Ibn Ḥazm left his mark on Muslim apologetic literature, few followed his virulent approach. Rather, the scholar who became the most prominent in the field of apologetics was Taqī al-Dīn ibn Taymīyah (d. 728/1328). His massive *Al-Jawāb al-Saḥiḥ li-Man Baddala Dīn al-Masīḥ* [The Correct Response to Those who Changed the Religion of Christ] was a veritable "Summa" of all that Muslims had written on Christianity, and it set the standard for all subsequent writing as well. His view of the Bible is a mediating one, courteous yet cautious. The text, he argued, can be considered essentially reliable, but not without corruption. Moreover, he did not believe it to be authentic revelation. But the main problem for Ibn Taymīyah was the manner in which the Bible had been interpreted by Christians; he especially criticized the doctrines of the Trinity and the incarnation. In any case, the primary emphasis of his work was the superiority of Islam — including its traditional view of Jesus.[28]

The polemical attitude which pervades most of the classical apologetic literature is significant for our study precisely because of its absence in al-'Aqqād's book on Jesus. Thus, it is important to consider one other, rather different approach seen in the writings attributed to the renowned theologian Abū Ḥāmid Muḥammad al-Ghazālī (d. 505/ 1111). He made a number of references in his works to Jesus and to Christianity, though he was not inclined to go into great detail. The one exception is a work purported to be his but which was probably written by one of his disciples: *Al-Radd al-Jamīl li-Ilāhīyat 'Īsā bi-Ṣarīḥ al-Injīl* [The Excellent Refutation of the Divinity of Jesus from what is Manifest in the Gospel]. The author accepts the Christian scriptures as authentic, although only the words of Jesus as recorded in the Gospels are discussed. Various sayings are treated differently: those implying his humanity are taken literally, while those implying his divinity are understood metaphorically. Though the book may not have come from the pen of al-Ghazālī, it may well reflect his own views. Perhaps more pertinent to al-'Aqqād's approach is another, authentic work, his *Iḥyā' 'Ulūm al-Dīn* [The Revitalization of the Religious Sciences], in which he seeks to harmonize the formal elements of Islam with the mystical. This work includes a large number of sayings attributed to Jesus, and while these are drawn from Muslim tradition rather than the Gospels, distinct echoes of the latter are present throughout. The sayings especially render a note of austerity and asceticism — significant given al-Ghazālī's pilgrimage into Ṣūfism later in life.[29]

This leads us into a brief consideration of classical Shī'ī and Ṣūfī literature which often displayed a willingness to venture beyond the traditional Islamic picture of Jesus. Shī'ī commentaries on the Qur'ān are generally quite similar to their Sunnī counterparts regarding passages on Jesus, although one distinct feature concerning his return is his subordinate role to that of the Mahdī, whom "Twelver" Shī'īs believe will be the Twelfth Imām. However, some of the Shī'ī *ḥadīth* literature gives special emphasis to Jesus as the exemplar of piety, love and austerity, an image not far from that found in Christian piety. At the same time, the *ḥadīth* accounts stress the humanity of Jesus; he is even warned by God against overstepping the limits placed on him.[30]

This moderate extension of the traditional view of Jesus contrasts with a fascinating and unique account found in the writings of "The Brethren of Purity" *(Ikhwān al-Ṣafā')*, a tenth-century sect which was probably part of the Ismā'īlī branch of Shī'ī Islam. It contains a long summary of the life of Jesus, who is pictured as an itinerant preacher in a manner not unlike that found in the Synoptic Gospels. But most interesting in this work is Jesus' prediction to his disciples that he is to return to the "Father," followed by a brief account of his crucifixion and the empty tomb. Thus, this group was willing to accept the historicity of Jesus' death on the cross, although this was probably understood in Neoplatonic terms, that of his soul's release when the prison of his body died.[31]

The picture of Jesus the ascetic and the model of piety incorporated in some Shī'ī literature was carried further in varying degrees by Ṣūfī writers. The more conservative were the Ṣūfī commentators; although they sought for an esoteric meaning to the text of the Qur'ān, this was generally supplemental to the standard, "external" understanding of the text, and so their comments added little to the accounts of Jesus found in the standard *tafsīr* writings. At the other extreme were more speculative writers such as Muḥyī al-Dīn ibn al-'Arabī (d. 638/ 1240). His references to Jesus are rather cryptic, but it is clear that for him, Jesus was a unique figure from conception as "a spirit from God." He believed that Jesus, like a few other prophets, transcended history, continuing to influence great spiritual leaders. In this regard, Ibn al-'Arabī referred to Jesus as "the Seal of the Saints," a term parallel to Muḥammad's title "the Seal of the Prophets." However, it was probably the Ṣūfī poets who best encapsulated the mystical sentiment for Jesus. For example, Jalāl al-Dīn al-Rūmī (d. 672/1273) saw himself as one of the clay birds into whom Jesus breaths life and whom he sends flying away. He is "the Beloved" who continues to revive the dead and heal the sick.[32]

We shall later see that al-'Aqqād spoke well of the Ṣūfī perspective; furthermore, in *'Abqarīyat al-Masīḥ* he not infrequently lapses into mystical reflection concerning Jesus. Nevertheless, he should probably be placed somewhere between the Shī'ī/Ṣūfī approach and that of al-Ghazālī. As for the classical Islamic literature in general, although there is no evidence that any of it directly influenced al-'Aqqād's writing about Christ, there is no doubt that he was quite familiar with its enormous legacy.

Modern Arabic Works Before 1953

It is commonly held that creative Muslim thinking declined significantly beginning with the fifteenth century. While a general perspective such as this can certainly be debated, it would seem to be valid with respect to Islamic writing about Jesus. In any case, virtually nothing new was produced in the centuries following Ibn Taymīyah's monumental work.

In the late nineteenth century, Muslims began to respond intellectually to the advent of the modern era (see the first section of the following chapter). In the Arab world, this included a growing recognition of and response to Christianity, and this in turn produced several significant works concerning Jesus leading up to al-'Aqqād's publication in 1953 of *'Abqarīyat al-Masīḥ.*[33] Initially, Christianity was viewed as inextricably tied to Western civilization. The negative response to what was perceived as Western imperialism governed the perspective of Christianity. This can be seen especially in the writings of the three successive figures who were the most prominent in the Arab world as exponents of reform based on Islam: Jamāl al-Dīn al-Afghānī (d. 1897), Muḥammad 'Abduh (d. 1905), and Rashīd Riḍā (d. 1935). The important sociological roles played by these men will be discussed in the next chapter; here, we focus here on what they had to say about Jesus and the Gospels.

In fact, al-Afghānī wrote nothing about Christianity *per se*, referring to it only in connection with his arguments against Western imperialism. In one tract, for example, he lists Christians among the various communities who have held to false religious beliefs, since they maintain such doctrines as the Trinity, the cross, and the resurrection.[34]

Muḥammad 'Abduh, however, dealt to some extent with the subject of Christianity. His views are especially important here because of the high esteem in which he was held by al-'Aqqād. In all his writings, 'Abduh's primary concern was Islam: its reformation in the modern world, and its defense against attacks from the West. He believed that Christianity had deviated from the teachings of Jesus and instead had aligned itself with Western civilization. In his most systematic work, *Risālat al-Tawḥīd* [Discourse on Unity], 'Abduh argues that Islam is the pinnacle of human history and the only religion truly based on reason; as such, its reform must also stem from reason. Christianity *per se* is not dealt with here; Jesus is mentioned only twice, listed among the other great prophets who had faithfully carried out their divine mission. However, Gaudeul observes that the book "never seems to forget the presence of Christian readers. Reform of Islam is not envisioned for its own sake only, but seeks to ensure that Christians will never again find reasons for criticizing Islam."[35]

The one work in which 'Abduh focuses on Christianity is his *Al-Islām wa-al-Naṣrānīyah ma' al-'Ilm wa-al-Madanīyah* [Islam and Christianity with regard to Science and Civilization].[36] This is actually a collection of articles which first appeared in the periodical founded by 'Abduh, *Al-Manār al-Islāmī* [The Islamic Beacon]; they were written in response to a Syrian Christian's claim that Islam (among other religions) impeded the progress of free thought and expression. 'Abduh contends that it is Christianity that is built on irrational principles, whereas Islam is the religion of reason. He lists six of these irrational principles, which in turn are derived primarily from the sayings of Jesus as found in the Gospels. For example, Christianity elevates the power of its church leaders, based on the disciples' authority given by Jesus "to bind and to loose"; it promotes withdrawal from the world, based on such teachings of Jesus as "do not be anxious about tomorrow"; and it encourages division among Christians, based on Jesus' statement, "I have not come to bring peace, but a sword."[37] Later in the book, 'Abduh briefly elucidates the Muslim view of Jesus as "the spirit of God and his word," and his messenger sent to the Israelites; as such, Jesus promoted the use of human reason rather than its suspension.[38] While it is clear that 'Abduh views Christianity as a distortion of the real Jesus, i.e., the Jesus of Islam, it must also be recognized that he has failed to understand properly the way in which Jesus has been interpreted by Christians.[39] What is not clear in this book, however, is 'Abduh's view of the Gospels, and whether or not they reliably convey the true words of Jesus. He constantly emphasizes that a particular saying, which subsequently led to the faulty basis of Christianity, is rendered "according to what is found in the Gospel";[40] from this it might be inferred that the Gospels themselves present an unreliable picture of Jesus. However, this matter requires the investigation of another work of 'Abduh's, namely his commentary on the text of the Qur'ān.

In fact, the *Tafsīr al-Qur'ān al-Ḥakīm*[41] (or *"Tafsīr al-Manār"* as it has customarily been called) was primarily the work of 'Abduh's disciple, Rashīd Riḍā. The commentary had begun with 'Abduh's lectures on the Qur'ān at al-Azhar University; these were then edited and published by Riḍā (with 'Abduh's approval) in the *Al-Manār* journal. But these lectures covered only a small portion of the Qur'ān, ending part way through the fourth *sūrah.* After further editing, Riḍā then incorporated the lectures into a separate work, extending the material with his own commentary into the ninth *sūrah;* usually, he made note of the views which were distinctly 'Abduh's.[42] Although references to Christianity in this major work are almost wholly Riḍā's,[43] there are two important statements made by 'Abduh which illuminate his view of the Gospels. The first is near the end of his comment on 3:78, concerning those who "distort" *(yalwūna)* the scripture with their tongues. 'Abduh includes in this group the Christians who had applied a literal meaning to such sayings of Jesus as "Son of God" and "Father"; instead, he claims, Jesus meant these to be understood "figuratively" *(majāzīyan).*[44] 'Abduh implies here that the text in which these sayings are found is accurate; only the interpretation was faulty. Even more clear is a parenthetical remark in his comment on 2:185: "We see that in the Gospels the disciples of Christ themselves did not understand everything that he told them, . . . yet we believe these to be the authentic Gospel *(al-Injīl al-ḥaqīqī).*"[45] Thus, despite the uncertainty apparent in his book on Christianity, it is evident from his commentary that 'Abduh did not accept the belief common among Muslims that the actual text of the Gospels (or of the Bible as a whole) had been corrupted, at least concerning the words of Jesus. The problem, as he saw it, lay rather in the way Christians had interpreted these words.

It is doubtful that 'Abduh would have applied his blanket statement concerning the Gospels to historical accounts such as the crucifixion (his own commentary stopped short of the key passage of the Qur'ān in 4:157). Yet his perspective is significant in that no other Arab-Muslim author for the next half century followed a similar approach — until al-'Aqqād produced his *'Abqarīyat al-Masīḥ.* Indeed, the most prominent example of those who took a more polemical view of the Gospels and of Christian beliefs about Jesus was none other than Rashīd Riḍā. The *Al-Manār* Commentary is replete with remarks of his against the doctrines of the Trinity and incarnation. According to Riḍā, the original Gospel was subject to alteration due to the moral lapse of the Christians, such that the only value of the Gospels as they presently exist is their prediction of Muḥammad. Not only is the notion of Jesus' crucifixion absurd (Riḍā promotes the view that Judas Iscariot was crucified in his place), but the Christian interpretation of redemption through the cross defies all rational understanding.[46]

Riḍā has more to say about the Christian scripture in another of his own works, *Shubuhāt al-Naṣārā wa-Ḥujaj al-Islām* [The Ambiguities of the Christians and the Proofs of Islam].[47] There, he claims that the Gospels are a mixture of the true gospel revealed to Jesus and whatever the human authors chose to add by way of history or stories. The problem is that "we have no criterion (*furqān*) by which we might distinguish those precepts which were originally revealed from what has been combined (*mazaja*) with them during their composition"; but in any case, "we reject as false whatever is contrary *(khālafa)* to the Qur'ān." [48] Thus the Sermon on the Mount is most likely authentic, but there is much that cannot be considered reliable. Later in the book, he refers to the process of mixing as one of "changing, substituting and corrupting *(al-taghyīr wa-al-tabdīl wa-al-taḥrīf).*" [49]

It was also Riḍā who was responsible for making known to the Arab world the so-called "Gospel of Barnabas." This document is stylized as a first-century "Gospel," purportedly written by Barnabas, who is depicted as one of Jesus' disciples. Yet the work presents a distinctively Islamic perspective of Jesus: in it, Jesus explicitly denies that he is the Son of God; he foretells the coming of Muḥammad by name; and he escapes crucifixion when Judas Iscariot is substituted in his place. In fact, the "Gospel of Barnabas" stems from the sixteenth century, the oldest extant version being a medieval Italian manuscript now housed in Vienna. This manuscript became the basis for an English translation in 1907 by Lonsdale and Laura Ragg, who undertook the project in order to expose its dubious character.[50] Riḍā, however, was much more ready to treat the document as genuine, since it clearly served to substantiate his arguments against the claims of Christians. In 1908, he arranged for the translation of the English version into Arabic by a Syrian Christian; he wrote a Preface in support its authenticity, and he was the first Arab writer to refer to it.[51] This Arabic version of the "Gospel of Barnabas" immediately gained popularity, and it continues to draw widespread acceptance among Arabic speaking Muslims today. Indeed, al-'Aqqād remains one of the very few Muslims who have publicly cast doubt on this document as a reliable source about Jesus (see pp. 54-55).

Other examples of Arabic-Muslim literature which were written during this period and which dealt with Christianity reflected Riḍā's critical approach, especially works produced by those associated with his *al-Manār* school. One of these, Muḥammad Tawfīq Ṣidqī, made violent attacks against Christian beliefs in several writings, even maligning the picture of Jesus presented in the Gospels.[52] However, it was a work not directly associated with Riḍā which was to gain the greatest influence for years to come: *Muḥāḍarāt fī al-Naṣrānīyah* [Lectures on Christianity] by Muḥammad Abū Zahrah.[53] This book seeks to demonstrate that the chain of transmission for the gospel as it was revealed to Jesus was broken at several points during the history of the church; the New Testament and later church councils distorted the authentic picture of Jesus, and this was only recovered centuries later by the Qur'ān. The author, who was a professor at al-Azhar University, claims to be writing impartially. Yet despite his reference to a few Christian secondary sources in Arabic, he relies almost exclusively on traditional Muslim works such as those by Ibn Ḥazm and Ibn Taymīyah, and on the "Gospel of Barnabas." He also depends heavily on the popular Arabic version of a nineteenth-century polemical work from India called *Iẓhār al-Ḥaqq* [Demonstration of the Truth], which sought to prove that the Bible was corrupted and had been abrogated.[54] Abū Zahrah thus provided a source book for an ongoing critical attitude towards Christianity among Arab Muslims; the fact that it has been reprinted several times is evidence of the popularity it has achieved.[55]

In fact, the years preceding al-ʿAqqād's writing of *ʿAbqarīyat al-Masīḥ* saw only a single work which can be said to have attempted a more irenic approach to Jesus and the Gospels, i.e., *Al-Masīḥ ʿĪsā bin Maryam* [The Messiah, Jesus the Son of Mary] by ʿAbd al-Ḥamīd Gūdah al-Saḥḥār.[56] This is an interesting biographical venture, blending material from the Gospel accounts into a rather traditional Muslim view of Jesus. That the work remains distinctively Muslim is clear in the author's primary dependence on the Qur'ān: its quotations preface nearly every chapter, accounts unique to the Qur'ān are included (Jesus' speaking from the cradle and making birds from clay), and Jesus is portrayed emphatically denying any claim to divinity. In particular, al-Saḥḥār's account of the crucifixion has Jesus escaping the crowd of soldiers while Judas is crucified in his place (willingly, in contrition for his evil deed). On the one hand, al-Saḥḥār makes free use of accounts found in the Gospels without denying their validity; on the other hand, he is quite selective in his approach (Jomier goes as far as charging him with "manipulation"[57]), and one can only assume that he would deny any validity to the remainder of the Gospels.

Although al-Saḥḥār was not as renowned as al-ʿAqqād, both of them were popular writers of biographies. It is quite possible that al-Saḥḥār's book served to encourage al-ʿAqqād concerning his own study of Christ, in both a positive and a negative sense. Three points of comparison are especially instructive. First, both authors devote considerable space early in their books to the background of Jesus' ministry. However, al-ʿAqqād discusses, in a more academic manner, the broader context of Jewish sects and pagan society, whereas al-Saḥḥār stays closer to home with an imaginative portrayal of Jesus' family life in Nazareth, including pilgrimages to Jerusalem. Second, both authors emphasize the centrality of the kingdom of God in Jesus' teaching. But while al-ʿAqqād reiterates that this kingdom was "not of this world," al-Saḥḥār describes it in rather this-worldly terms with its own law and state. Third, both authors view the end of Jesus' ministry as one of crisis in which the antagonism of his enemies develops to a climax, and both recognize Jesus' submission to the will of God concerning this in the Garden of Gethsemane. Where they differ is in the final outcome of Jesus' ministry. Al-Saḥḥār regards it to have ended in defeat, even though Jesus himself was raised to heaven: "So Jesus left, without establishing truth on the earth, vanquished by his enemies" (lit., "his enemies broke him [*kasarahu*]").[58] Instead, says al-Saḥḥār, God sent another (i.e., Muḥammad) who would be victorious in establishing the truth. In contrast, al-ʿAqqād chooses not to elaborate on how the crisis was resolved; at the same time, he claims that Jesus' ministry was indeed victorious through the subsequent spread of the gospel throughout the world.

Modern Arabic Works Since 1953

The modern Arabic works considered thus far are significant because they pre-date the first edition of *'Abqarīyat al-Masīḥ*. Undoubtedly al-'Aqqād was familiar with most if not all of them; yet he chose to pursue his own course with an approach far more positive than any of them. But in order to appreciate the full context of his book, subsequent works about Jesus must also be briefly considered, with some comparison to his.

The first of these, published the very next year, is also often regarded as the most significant work of this genre. *Qaryah Ẓālimah* [A Wrongful Village], whose title is a reference to Jerusalem at the time of the crucifixion, was penned by the Cairo medical doctor Muḥammad Kāmil Ḥusayn.[59] This book was well-received in Egypt and won the Egyptian State Prize for literature in 1957; it also quickly won recognition from a number of Western scholars.[60] The book is neither biography nor fiction, but rather an imaginative portrayal of the people who were involved in the events surrounding the crucifixion of Jesus. While leaving open the question of what actually happened regarding the crucifixion itself, the author has no doubt concerning the people's *intention* to carry through with it (an approach very similar to al-'Aqqād's). He explores the way in which individuals, despite their recognition that a particular action is wrong, allow themselves to go along with the majority in performing that action while seeking to justify their own minor role. Thus the work is an astute analysis and condemnation of communal sin as well as individual participation within it. Reference is also made in the book to Jesus' instruction that his disciples reject violence, refrain from intervening, and allow God to fulfill his purpose. Certainly, it is significant that Ḥusayn chose a dominant Christian theme (Jesus' crucifixion) in order to explore a more broadly human ethical issue (communal guilt), and it is this fact that has captured the attention of Western Christian reviewers. Nevertheless, the book as a whole is not about Jesus (who is present only behind the scenes) or even about Christianity. Thus its significance for Muslim-Christian dialogue, though genuine, should not be overestimated.[61]

Indeed, it is in another work of Ḥusayn's where we find a discussion which can be considered more relevant here. In his book *Al-Dhikr al-Ḥakīm* [The Judicious Reminder],[62] Ḥusayn deals directly with the question of the authenticity of the Bible, and in particular the Gospels. He asserts that the Old and New Testaments are quite distinct from the *Tawrāt* and *Injīl* referred to in the Qur'ān. The latter were actual texts "revealed" *(awḥa)* directly to Moses and Jesus, whereas, he claims, Jews and Christians have not maintained this view concerning the scriptures they possess. Rather, they say that the two Testaments are the records of "inspired saints" *(qiddīsīn mulhamīn)* who wrote with conviction and pure intentions. This view, according to Ḥusayn, is one with which Muslims can agree. He goes on to argue that the corruption of the previous scriptures mentioned in the Qur'ān had applied only to the people of Muḥammad's time, and here he includes the Christians of Arabia along with the Jews. This corruption referred, in part, to the apocryphal Gospels that were prevalent among the Christians then. However, he contends that the four canonical Gospels contain portions of the original *Injīl* revealed to Jesus. Thus, it is incumbent on Muslims to study these Gospels and to "extract" *(yastakhlisu)* the actual words Jesus spoke, with the understanding that nothing authentic will contradict the Qur'ān. When Ḥusayn follows such a procedure, he finds that Jesus never called himself the "Son of God," and that his reference to God as "Father" was probably only a term of respect. Ḥusayn's remarks in this work are thus among the most bold in offering a limited approval of the biblical text, while remaining firmly within an Islamic perspective. They do much to encourage a more positive view of the Gospels than has been the case among most Muslim writers, past and present, and they probably come closest to the approach actually pursued by al-'Aqqād.

Another important work, which also takes a similar view of the Gospels, is *Ma' al-Masīḥ fī al-Anājīl al-Arba'ah* [With Christ in the Four Gospels] by Fatḥī 'Uthmān.[63] First published in 1961, this lengthy biography of Jesus (running more than four hundred pages of small print in the second edition) is an intentional effort towards building more positive relations between Muslims and Christians. To do this, 'Uthmān examines the Gospels rather than traditional Islamic sources:

> The reader will observe that this book is based on the Gospels as they now exist concerning its discussion of Christianity. I intend to speak about Christianity from the perspective of its own adherents, while also demonstrating, both to Muslims and to Christians, that . . . the existing Gospels include areas which can encompass both groups, and which call us to do what we all know is right and to refrain from what is reprehensible.[64]

The book goes on to portray Jesus as an eloquent teacher who sought to reform Judaism by establishing a more ethically based law. Thus, of all the modern Arabic-Muslim works on Jesus, 'Uthmān's is the most analogous, both in content and in attitude, to al-'Aqqād's *'Abqarīyat al-Masīḥ.* Three areas in particular are worthy of comparison. First, both authors make extensive reference to the Gospels, as well as to contemporary Western sources. In the latter case, however, 'Uthmān's book is limited to modern works which have been translated into Arabic, whereas al-'Aqqād almost exclusively utilizes works in English. On the other hand, 'Uthmān provides more complete and accurate footnotes to his sources. Second, 'Uthmān's work is more properly a biography and is more systematically organized with regard to the themes of Jesus' teaching. Al-'Aqqad's book is better regarded as a "study" in which he delves more deeply into the heart of Jesus' message, as well as the context into which it came and the impact which it originally made. Third, al-'Aqqād purposefully leaves aside issues of controversy between Muslims and Christians; in contrast, 'Uthmān, in an effort to face the issues of division realistically, deems it necessary to delineate the major differences of belief between the two groups in his last chapter. There he clearly rejects, among other things, the crucifixion of Jesus both as a historical event and as a means of salvation; al-'Aqqād, as noted above, does not directly resolve the matter. In conclusion, Goddard is undoubtedly correct in stating that 'Uthmān's book, while a marked improvement over that by al-Saḥḥār, still falls short of al-'Aqqād's penetrating analysis; furthermore, it is regrettable that no positive work of this kind has since appeared in the Arab world.[65]

A few other works may be mentioned, however, which offer a fairly positive view of Jesus by way of locating common ground between Muslims and Christians. Khālid Muḥammad Khālid finds several points of contact between Jesus and Muḥammad (as well as with other teachers of truth such as Socrates and the Buddha) in his book *Ma'an 'alā al-Ṭarīq: Muḥammad wa-al-Masīḥ* [Together on the Road: Muḥammad and Christ].[66] Stress is laid on the social teaching of the two prophets (brotherly love, freedom of conscience, etc.), as well as similar experiences between them (e.g., both encountered plots against their lives by the Jews). Other aspects of their careers which cannot be so easily compared are left aside.

A book offering a similar approach is *Dīn Allāh Wāḥid: Muḥammad wa-al-Masīḥ Akhawān* [The Religion of God is One: Muḥammad and Christ are Brothers], by Maḥmūd Abū Rayyah.[67] This work actually has little to say about Jesus except by way of arguing forcefully for more positive relations between Muslims and Christians. Since there is, in the author's view, an essential unity between the three monotheistic religions, quotations from the Bible are presented merely to demonstrate this assertion.

One other comparative work is unique in its approach: *Yasū' al-Masīḥ wa-al-Imām 'Alī, bayn al-Injīl wa-al-Qur'ān wa-al-'Aql* [Jesus Christ and Imām 'Alī in the Gospel and the Qur'ān and Reason], by Muḥammad 'Ārif Muṣṭafā Fahmī.[68] Picking up on a *ḥadīth* in which 'Alī is likened to Jesus, the author compares a number of incidents between their careers, and also examines a few similarities in their teachings. For example, just as 'Alī was rejected by the Kharijites, so was Jesus rejected by the Jews. Although it is unclear in his book whether or not Fahmī is a Shī'ī, he is clearly sympathetic to the less extreme Shī'ī views.[69] He also includes a short chapter on Ṣūfism, in which he identifies Jesus as a Ṣūfī based on the purity of his motives, his renunciation of worldly gain and marriage, and his "remembrance" *(dhikr)* of God.[70] This book thus offers a point of contact with al-'Aqqād who, while never expressing such views directly, would have concurred with them to some extent.

Mention should also be made of a form of literature quite different from that of *'Abqarīyat al-Masīḥ*, but which frequently displays positive overtones regarding Jesus and Christianity, that of fiction. In particular, the sufferings and even the crucifixion of Jesus have been explored through this medium by authors such as Nagīb Maḥfūẓ, Iḥsān 'Abd al-Quddūs, Ṣalāḥ 'Abd al-Ṣabūr, and Fatḥī Riḍwān. While these authors remain essentially within a Muslim framework, they are yet able to see, as did Muḥammad Kāmil Ḥusayn, a measure of significance in the cross of Christ as a symbol of the darker side of human behavior.[71] Comparable sentiments can be found in modern Arabic-Muslim poetry as well.[72]

In contrast, several other Arabic-Muslim works which post-date al-'Aqqād's book are more inimical towards Christianity. Because of their later date and rather polemical stance, only a few of these are noted here. Their significance lies mostly in the disturbing trend which they seem to be re-establishing in the Arab world. For example, in *Da'wat al-Ḥaqq aw al-Ḥaqīqah bayn al-Masīḥīyah wa-al-Islām* [The Call of Truth, or the Truth between Christianity and Islam],[73] Manṣūr Ḥusayn 'Abd al-'Azīz argues forthrightly against the crucifixion and incarnation of Christ. Convinced that the Islamic position renders the Christian position completely false, he builds up his case based on his reinterpretation of the biblical record. One particular point of this argument should be noted here, that the substitution of Judas in the crucifixion was in fact God's answer to Jesus' prayer in the Garden of Gethsemane, in which Jesus requested that the evil deed about to happen be taken away from him. In fact, al-'Aqqād also implies that Jesus' prayer in Gethsemane, a request to be relieved of the impending "cup" of suffering, was answered favorably by God. However, al-'Aqqād has no inclination to argue the point or to spell out its details.[74]

Other works follow an approach similar to that of 'Abd al-'Azīz. In his book *Al-Masīḥ fī al-Qur'ān wa-al-Tawrāt wa-al-Injīl* [Christ in the Qur'ān, the Torah, and the Gospel],[75] 'Abd al-Karīm al-Khaṭīb points to the inconsistencies of the Bible as an indication of the error of Christian doctrines and the sole validity of the Muslim position. At least the author was willing to make a written response to a Western Christian who had reviewed his book, although it served only to accentuate his conviction that the only authentic witness to Jesus is the Qur'ān as traditionally interpreted.[76] Aḥmad Shalabī, a respected scholar on Islamic history, produced a volume on Christianity as part of his series on comparative religion.[77] Yet it is little more than a rehearsal of the themes present in Abū Zahrah's earlier book: the original message of Jesus was corrupted in the development of church history, especially through the teaching of Paul who even influenced the writing of the Gospels.

The most recent Arabic work considered here uses essentially the same argument as that found in Shalabī, but with a different approach: *Al-Masīḥ fī Maṣādir al-'Āqā'id al-Masīḥīyah* [Christ in the Sources of Christian Beliefs], by Aḥmad 'Abd al-Wahhāb.[78] The author reviews a number of Western Christian scholarly works in order to demonstrate that they testify to the historical corruption of the gospel as it had been taught by Jesus. In his list of sources examined, he includes (in addition to some rather dubious books) such well-known Christian scholars as C. H. Dodd, F. C. Grant, and Adolf Harnack. A perusal of the text, however, reveals that 'Abd al-Wahhāb has selected only the more "critical" statements of these authors. Perhaps more telling of his approach is an addition to his list which appears in the English edition: *The Myth of God Incarnate.*[79] Thus, although this work is apparently the only other Arabic book which makes extensive use of Western Christian sources written in English, 'Abd al-Wahhāb's purpose for doing so is quite different from al-'Aqqād's.

These works of a more polemical nature are only a few of the many which have appeared in the modern Arabic-speaking world. Since they are generally more recent than the few positive books concerning Jesus and Christianity, it would seem that they exemplify an approach which has become characteristic of Arabic-Muslim writing on these themes. Goddard suggests that the problem is that such authors have "neither the means nor the will" to make a genuine effort at understanding Christianity.[80] One can only hope that the more positive works will also become the more popular.

Contemporary Arab Scholars and the West[81]

For many Arab Muslims, the effort to understand Christianity and to offer a sympathetic response has developed only through a careful study of the Christian faith combined with extensive contact with Western Christians.[82] In order to provide a balanced overview, we conclude with remarks on a few Arab-Muslim scholars who, through prolonged dialogue with Western Christianity, have in recent years offered fresh examples of an Islamic view of Jesus which encompass some appreciation for the Christian perspective.[83]

The Algerian scholar Ali Merad, while studying in France, came under the influence of Louis Massignon, the Catholic Islamicist who sought for a Christian recognition of Islam. Merad's article "Le Christ selon le Coran,"[84] was initially an address given by invitation at the Pontifical Institute of Arabic and Islamic Studies. In it he maintains that Muslims have not sufficiently recognized the especially high esteem afforded to Jesus in the Qur'ān itself. Through a careful examination of passages about Jesus, Merad concludes that these negate any notion of divinity concerning Jesus. But simultaneously, he understands the Qur'ān to confer on him a "suréminence" by which it recognizes his extraordinary character and mission. He focuses on the titles which the Qur'ān applies to Christ, especially the unique expressions *kalimah* [Word] and *rūḥ* [Spirit]. He also notes that the word *bashar* [mortal human] is not among these:

> In this respect, it is remarkable that at no time is the term *bashar* applied to Christ. And yet, it seems obvious that this would have been the best argument to weaken the notion of Christ's divinity and to put him forward under the guise of an ordinary mortal.[85]

Merad further states that the Qur'ān categorically denies the crucifixion of Jesus and does not promote any concept of redemption; yet he sees in this negation a demonstration of God's triumphal affirmation of Jesus' unique status.

The second example here is the late Mohamed al-Nowaihi who, in his position as Professor of Arabic Language and Literature at the American University in Cairo, studied the manner in which contemporary Christians as well as Muslims have expressed religious themes in symbolic fashion. He observed that the cross of Jesus is sometimes employed in modern Arabic literature, not because writers believe in its historicity, but because it communicates figuratively truths they wish to convey. In his article "The Religion of Islam: A Presentation to Christians," al-Nowaihi expressed a genuine appreciation for the concept of redemption in Christianity, a theme he dealt with further in a subsequent unpublished address.[86] He believes that the Qur'ān, while in opposition to this doctrine as developed in Christianity, nevertheless includes certain elements which are congenial to this concept, such as its portrayal of God's sorrow because of human sin. Although he tacitly accepts the traditional denial of the crucifixion, he also finds meaning in the harsh treatment and rejection Jesus experienced: "So the promised victory of right over wrong . . . is not automatic: it demands much struggle and sacrifice on the part of the prophets. Hence all prophets may be considered in this sense Redeemers."[87]

Final consideration here is given to Mahmoud Ayoub, an Islamic scholar whose early education in Lebanon was in a Christian school and who later studied Christian theology at Harvard; today he is at the forefront among Muslims seeking to foster positive relations with Christians. Among his many works, he often refers to the same themes of Jesus' eminence and the redemptive quality of his mission. And, like Merad and al-Nowaihi, his arguments are consciously formulated in the broader context of the Qur'ān. For Ayoub, "the Jesus of the Qur'ān and later Muslim piety is much more than a mere human being."[88] Furthermore,

> [Islam] denies the divinity of Christ, but without denying his special humanity. . . . [It] denies the expiatory sacrifice of Christ on the Cross as a ransom for sinful humanity, but again denies neither the actual death of Christ nor his general redemptive role in human history.[89]

Elsewhere, Ayoub refers to Jesus as "Miracle," a divine sign (*āyah*) demonstrating God's infinite mercy and power. The miracles Jesus performed, he explains, brought healing and salvation, and in this sense, Jesus is also "the Savior of us all."[90] However, it is Ayoub's unconventional perspective of the crucifixion which has especially attracted the attention of Christian reviewers. Although he nowhere passes judgment on the historicity of Jesus' death on the cross, he claims that the Qur'ānic verse in question (4:157) should be understood as a statement of theology rather than of history. What this passage denies, he asserts, is "the power of men to vanquish and destroy the divine Word." In a manner reminiscent of Muḥammad Kāmil Ḥusayn, Ayoub concludes that the crucifixion constitutes "an accusation or judgment against the human sin of pride and ignorance."[91] Such perspectives, found frequently in Ayoub's writings, serve to narrow the gap considerably between Muslim and Christian perspectives of Jesus.

The themes about Jesus put forward by these contemporary Arab scholars are generally absent in al-'Aqqād's writings. Although he promotes the uniqueness of Christ's humanity along the lines of Merad and Ayoub, al-'Aqqād would not have accepted the more broad-minded views noted here regarding the redemptive role of Jesus or the historicity of his crucifixion. These more recent developments have been formed, in part, from substantial dialogue with contemporary Western Christianity. Al-'Aqqad did not enjoy the same privilege, except by means of his extensive reading of Western literature. His own background and context, as will be seen in the next chapter, was less conducive to a more personal interaction. Yet this fact makes his own perspective of Jesus all the more remarkable. It is a perspective which, under other circumstances, might well have progressed in a manner similar to that observed among these recent authors.

Al-'Aqqād in His Context

The Development of Modern Egypt to 1964

It is impossible to understand any major literary figure apart from the socio-political environment in which that person was raised. This is certainly the case for 'Abbās Maḥmūd al-'Aqqād, who sought to interact, primarily through his writing, with his Egyptian context in the political, social and religious spheres. The first half of the twentieth century (the period in which he flourished) was a turbulent era during which Egypt emerged from its Ottoman legacy and British domination into a tenuous independence. We begin, then, with an outline of the major events and personalities concerned with that period, focusing on those who, like al-'Aqqād, led the search for a successful coalescing of their religious heritage with the realities of modern society.

The formative features of Egyptian history leading up to the early twentieth century must first be recognized. The year 1798 is usually regarded as the beginning of the modern era for Egypt. Prior to that date, its people had been living a medieval existence while the rulers of the Mamlūk dynasty struggled among themselves for power. The Ottomans had conquered Egypt in 1517, but by the end of the eighteenth century their authority had diminished significantly. Suddenly Napoleon Bonaparte landed at Alexandria in July 1798 and invaded Cairo. His interest in Egypt itself was minimal; the reasons for his expedition had more to do with political opportunism in France's struggle against Britain. The French presence there lasted only a few years, but from then on, the West would become an important factor in Egypt's development.[1]

The British, who had formed an uneasy alliance with the Ottomans, ousted the French in 1802 and then departed themselves the following year. In the confusion that followed, neither the Ottoman overlords nor the factious Mamlūks could gain control. Rather it was Muḥammad 'Alī (d. 1849), an Albanian officer in the Ottoman forces, who seized power with the aid of the religious leadership, defeated his political rivals, and emerged by 1812 as sole ruler under nominal Ottoman oversight. He then embarked on a number of reforms patterned after Western standards, including an organized political administration, a disciplined military and a state-run system of education. Agriculture, commerce, industry and communications were also modernized. Although a short period of stagnation followed his death, reforms were rejuvenated under the more progressive members of his family, especially his grandson Ismā'īl (d. 1895). In his vision to transform Egypt into a virtual European state, he instituted a railway system, irrigation, and the construction of the Suez Canal (completed 1869).[2]

Meanwhile, the thrust into modernism precipitated by these dramatic changes posed a significant challenge for traditional Islamic religion. The majority of the *'ulamā'* (religious scholars) resisted any parallel transformation in doctrine or practice. However, one person in particular began to grapple with how religion might be adapted in order to keep pace with reforms in other areas, and his ideas were to influence many others in subsequent years. Rifā'ah Rāfi' al-Ṭahṭāwī (d. 1873) had been sent as a student to Paris for five years by Muḥammad 'Alī, and this experience profoundly affected him. Upon his return in 1831 he promoted the adoption of certain reforms, patterned after the French, in the spheres of culture, education and science. These could be done, he felt, without harm to religion, which simply needed to undergo a kind of renewal *(tajdīd)* which allowed a degree of acceptable innovation *(bid'ah).* He wrote extensively on these themes, utilizing a traditional Islamic style, yet arguing that reason was an essential complement to religion.[3]

Shortly after al-Ṭahṭāwī's death, there was a breakdown of the Egyptian financial system. This, combined with a general discontent, led in 1882 to a mutiny of army officers, known as the 'Urābī Revolt. This in turn led to British intervention, primarily in order to preserve the Suez Canal. The British had been reluctant to occupy Egypt and had intended to withdraw when the situation stabilized, but they were to remain in control for several decades. This was due at first to the need to deal with the Mahdist uprising in Sudan which had begun in 1881, but as their jurisdiction of the area continued it became increasingly difficult to pull out. Throughout its occupation, the British sought to establish a degree of Egyptian self-government while retaining stability through their own influence and control. An Egyptian constitution was written in 1883 which called for an elected General Assembly under the titular authority of the Ottoman Khedive. But the British selected the government ministers and then provided them with British "advisors" who were the true power-brokers. Under British auspices, Egyptian finances were stabilized, the military reorganized, and economic and industrial development promoted — especially through public works such as the Aswan Dam (completed 1902).[4]

This Western encroachment into the traditional Arab-Islamic world produced an inevitable reaction. One of the leading figures of this response was Jamāl al-Dīn al-Afghānī (d. 1897). Although probably born in Iran (despite his name), he traveled throughout the Islamic world advocating political unity among Muslims in order to confront the dangers of Western imperialism. He was an imposing man, confrontational with the political and religious establishment, yet displaying a charismatic appeal among the populace. While solidarity against Western hegemony was his primary goal, he believed that Islamic renewal would be the principal means to this end. This, for al-Afghānī, required nothing less than the Islamic equivilent of the Protestant Reformation. Going beyond al-Ṭahṭāwī, he called for a revival of *ijtihād* (independent judgment) which would reassert the core of Islamic religion while cleansing it of the accretions of traditionalism which inhibited proper reform. Naturally, this brought him in direct conflict with the *'ulamā'* who, perhaps rightly, questioned his religious sincerity. Although his lofty goals were never realized and his influence eventually waned, he made a profound impact on prominent intellectuals who came after him.[5]

Al-Afghānī's chief disciple and collaborator in many of his exploits was Muḥammad 'Abduh (d. 1905). The two met in 1869 while 'Abduh was a student at al-Azhar. Disillusioned by the academic approach to religious studies, 'Abduh was drawn by al-Afghānī's novel interpretations of the Qur'ān with respect to the contemporary situation. In 1882,

'Abduh resisted British intervention in Egypt and was sent into exile. He joined al-Afghānī in Paris, where together they published a periodical directed against the British occupation. However, when 'Abduh was allowed to return to Egypt in 1888, he adopted a somewhat different approach in which he no longer sought to confront the British. Instead he focused on the reform of religion itself. 'Abduh more than al-Afghānī saw the potential value of Western ideas and technology, but he felt that these were leading Muslims away from their faith. The primary fault in his view was due more to traditional Islam than to the West. In particular, education had become polarized between traditional religious and modern secular perspectives. Education, he believed, needed to become integrated so that religion and science could be recognized as mutually compatible. Indeed, one of 'Abduh's major points was the concord between Islam and reason, a theme he developed from al-Afghānī (and al-Ṭahṭāwī before him). Reason and revelation coincided, he claimed, so that the veracity of Islam could be demonstrated by rational proofs. Religious principles should be adapted by means of *ijtihād* in order to formulate an Islamic law appropriate for the times which would be the basis for a modernized, yet truly Muslim society. 'Abduh earned great respect among his compatriots, but his ideas tended to be more theoretical than practical, and they were open to various interpretations.[6] Nevertheless, the influence of his governing principle — the compatibility of reason and religion — can clearly be seen in the writings of al-'Aqqād.

While 'Abduh changed his position regarding British control from opposition to reluctant cooperation, a younger generation began to make its voice heard. The benefit of a modern Western-style education and the exposure to nationalist ideas from elsewhere in the Arab world led to various responses. As discontent rose, the British began to allow for more political expression, which in 1907 took the form of political parties. The People's Party was led by Aḥmad Luṭfī al-Sayyid (d. 1963), a follower of 'Abduh. He utilized 'Abduh's ideas, except that he rejected religion as a basis for politics and advocated a moderate nationalism in cooperation with the British. Opposing al-Sayyid was Muṣṭafā Kāmil (d. 1908), who founded the Constitutional Reform Party, and who demanded immediate British withdrawal. He tried, somewhat unsuccessfully, to reconcile al-Afghānī's concept of pan-Islamic unity with an ardent Egyptian nationalism.[7]

Kāmil's goals, and party, were short-lived due to his death in 1908 and the outbreak of World War I. During the war, Britain retained a tight control on Egypt, which it used as its main base of operations in the Middle East. But following the war, events in Egypt came to a crisis. In 1918 Sa'd Zaghlūl (d. 1927), another prominent follower of 'Abduh, emerged as the popular leader. He led a "delegation" *(wafd)* before the British High Commissioner, requesting a hearing in London where demands for independence were to be presented. When Britain refused and Zaghlūl was deported from Egypt, a popular revolt spread throughout the country, fueled by a crippled economy. The British then tried to compromise with Zaghlūl and his Wafd Party, but he held to his demands. In 1922, Britain finally declared independence for Egypt, except that matters such as the Canal, defense and the control of Sudan were to be discussed further.

While this was a significant retreat for the British, they were to retain a measure of control for several decades through the resident High Commissioner and several advisors. A local monarchy and Parliament were established. But the king had limited popular support and the Parliament was beset with divisions and unable to exert much power. Initially the Wafd Party was dominant, but it was weakened when several other parties originated as breakaway movements. Eventually, consensus among the various parties led to a treaty with Britain in 1936. This called for a military alliance and cooperation in foreign affairs, while Britain would retain control of the Canal for twenty years. Nevertheless, British influence in Egyptian affairs continued to be a reality and actually increased during the Second World War. Following the war, nationalism again came to the fore. A revolution broke out in 1952 ending in a military coup led by Jamāl 'Abd al-Nāṣir (d. 1970), and the complete withdrawal of the British by 1956. 'Abd al-Nāṣir directed a socialist government which centralized political and economic power. Although Islam was declared the state religion in the 1964 constitution, Egypt had essentially become a secular state.[8]

During this period, two prominent figures advocated a firm religious foundation for the ongoing social and political development. Rashīd Riḍā (d. 1935), a Syrian by birth, had been 'Abduh's chief disciple; he continued to promote his mentor's ideas, but channeled into a more conservative line. He felt that 'Abduh had compromised too much, and so took a more rigid stand against the influx of Western ideas. Religious reform was the key, and for this he renewed al-Afghānī's call for pan-Islamic unity, which 'Abduh had set aside. Simultaneously, he developed a concept of 'Abduh's which would serve as the basis for this reform: a return to the pristine religion of Muḥammad and his companions (together known as the *salaf* or "ancestors"). Riḍā also rejected 'Abduh's view of reason as complementary to revelation, believing that this would allow reason to supersede the sharī'ah (law) as the basis for ethics. Riḍā gained a following, known both as the *salafīyah* movement and as the *Al-Manār* school (named after the periodical he had founded with 'Abduh). But in the end, Riḍā's views were too rigid and idealistic and were generally ignored by conservatives and liberals alike.[9]

Al-Afghānī, 'Abduh and Riḍā were primarily theoreticians. They gained many followers and sought to promote reform, but made few actual changes in the way Egyptian society was developing. While those involved in the political structure wrangled among themselves, the masses of people felt that they were left without clear direction. Sensing this problem, an ordinary school teacher named Ḥasan al-Bannā (d. 1949) began a local network of social action in the Canal Zone, and in 1928 this became a grass roots movement known as *Ikhwān al-Muslimīn,* the Muslim Brothers. Al-Bannā drew his ideas from all three earlier reformists, but he simplified them by promoting a return to the basic Islamic sources of Qur'ān and sharī'ah. He combined this with energetic programs in education and social work at the local level but was reluctant to get involved in the political structure. Al-Bannā believed that modernization was acceptable, but only on the basis of strict Islamic principles. He initially argued for an Islamic "order" *(al-niẓām al-Islāmī),* and later an Islamic state. This call, plus a growing militant activism following World War II, brought condemnation from the government in 1948. Nevertheless, the movement's wide appeal has made it a major component of Egyptian society ever since.[10]

Somewhat parallel to the more direct religious approach, which was rather antithetical to the secular political system, was a liberal intellectual stream which sought to offer the ideological basis for the ongoing political and social changes that were actually taking place. This stream was represented by several prominent writers, including al-'Aqqād, who cultivated the medium of print in order to address a growing literate class. Most of these writers had received a Western education and had been associated with Luṭfī al-Sayyid's more moderate political agenda. They combined a variety of methods, such as journalism, translation, and writing (both scholarly and popular), in order to promote Western ideals in the spheres of history, culture, education, etc.

Foremost among these was Ṭāhā Ḥusayn (d. 1973), whose disenchanting experience as a student at al-Azhar was made famous through an autobiographical work. Later he earned two doctorates in classical Islamic literature, became a professor and department head at Cairo University, and eventually served as Minister of Education. Muḥammad Ḥusayn Haykal (d. 1956) studied law in Paris and, after practicing law in Egypt, went on to found his own political party and daily newspaper; these combined ideological reform with a practical moderation in politics. Tawfīq al-Ḥakīm (d. 1987) also went to Paris to study law but rejected that field. He instead became a literary artist, producing dozens of plays, novels and stories. Ḥusayn, Haykal and al-Ḥakīm together formed what is known as the "French school" of writers, reflecting both their education and their inspiration. Al-'Aqqād was part of the "English school" which included, among others, his frequent colleague Ibrāhīm 'Abd al-Qādir al-Māzinī (d. 1949). Al-Māzinī, along with al-'Aqqād, began a new trend in Arabic poetry, and he also produced novels and stories.[11]

It has often been observed that many of these individuals (including al-'Aqqād) made a distinct shift in their writing during the 1930's and 1940's to specifically Islamic themes. Prior to this date, their emphasis was on science and reason as the basis for a progressive society rather than religion. As Cachia notes, none of these writers

> ever renounced or denounced Islam, but they confined it to the role which they perceived Europeans had assigned to their religion: it was to be a matter between the individual and his God, but not the arbiter of public affairs. . . . Yet beginning in 1933, those very modernists produced a number of more sympathetic works that may broadly be called Islamic.[12]

Certainly one of the reasons for this shift was the felt need to counter the attacks being made against Islam, and especially its Prophet, by Christian missionaries; Haykal explicitly stated this with regard to his own biography of Muḥammad.[13] But there was also some recognition of the need to accommodate to a revival of public sentiment for religion. This had been expressed not only by the growing popularity of the Muslim Brothers, but also by the uproar caused by Ṭāhā Ḥusayn's 1926 publication of a book on pre-Islamic poetry, in which he undercut traditional interpretations of the Qur'ān.[14] In Safran's view, the shift to Islamic themes represented a surrender of the rationalistic approach to social progress. For him, it was merely an attempt to appease the populace by providing a religious alternative.

Rather, we should understand this situation, with Charles Smith and Cachia, as one in which the writers sought to express their ideas in new ways that would meet the aspirations of the people, and to demonstrate that the best qualities of their religious heritage were compatible with modern ideals.[15]

Al-'Aqqād's Islamic writings did not begin to appear until the 1940's, but he certainly had a role to play in this effort to re-interpret religion in the light of modern realities. Before examining the manner in which he did this, we must consider the main features of his life in the political, social and literary context just outlined.

A Sketch of al-'Aqqād's Life

It is unfortunately the case that 'Abbās Maḥmūd al-'Aqqād is virtually unknown in the West outside the circle of specialists who deal with modern Arabic literature. This is partly due to the fact that, in contrast to some of his contemporaries,[16] only two of his books have been translated into Western languages.[17] In addition, and again in contrast to several of his contemporaries,[18] no Western author has endeavored to write a biography of al-'Aqqād. Indeed, one is hard pressed to locate so much as an outline of al-'Aqqād's life published in English. The most extensive overview given is by Louis Awad, but this covers only six pages and is marred by some technical inaccuracies.[19] Shorter summaries are given by Safran and Badawi, and in *The Encyclopaedia of Islam.*[20] In addition, brief reviews of al-'Aqqād's life, which draw from a number of Arabic sources, are found in two unpublished works.[21] In Arabic, however, the picture is entirely different, for al-'Aqqād has been held in high esteem in Egypt as one of that country's foremost contemporary authors. Many of his compatriots have written about his life and literary career: the standard bibliographic work on al-'Aqqād by Ḥamdī al-Sakkūt lists no less than sixty-one books devoted solely to al-'Aqqād, and 209 others which include a chapter about him.[22]

Al-'Aqqād also produced two autobiographical works which were published shortly after his death in 1964, bearing the brief titles *Anā* [Myself] and *Ḥayāt Qalam* [The Life of a Pen].[23] His close friend Ṭāhir al-Ṭanāḥī, who wrote a foreword in both books, explains that al-'Aqqād had already written several articles of an autobiographical nature when, as early as 1946, he began planning to include these along with new material in a full-length autobiography. It was to be entitled simply *"'Annī"* [About Myself], and would contain two parts, dealing first with his personal life, then with his involvement in politics and political writing. He continued writing segments of this work until his death, after which al-Ṭanāḥī incorporated all the material into two books. *Anā* and *Ḥayāt Qalam* are thus equivalent to the two parts of the originally planned work.[24]

The sketch of al-'Aqqād's life which follows is a composite picture drawn from the English works mentioned above, al-'Aqqād's two autobiographical books, and the biographical sections of Shawqī Ḍayf's *Ma' al-'Aqqād* [With al-'Aqqād].[25] Since the details of this outline are generally common to more than one of these sources, references are given only for quotations or specific points.

Al-'Aqqād was born June 28, 1889 in Aswan, a conservative city in upper Egypt. His parents, both of Kurdish descent, were devout Muslims, and they passed on a strong religious heritage to their children. At an early age, al-'Aqqād developed an interest in politics, literature and writing. Even before he started primary school at age seven, he was reading his father's magazines, which included the periodical published by al-Afghānī and 'Abduh. At eight he began to accompany his father (a minor civil servant) to meetings dealing with such matters as the 'Urābī Revolt and famous Islamic personalities. He began composing poetry at ten and also started a student paper. Meanwhile, he learned English through his contacts with Westerners and through reading English books and magazines. Although Aswan is the most distant from Cairo among Egypt's principle cities, hundreds of British were living there for the construction of the Aswan Dam, and the city attracted many European tourists as well. Thus he had considerable exposure to the Western frame of mind; in his words, "I saw East and West meet in Aswan, and gradually I witnessed European culture in all its variety and from every angle."[26]

One particular childhood experience made a lasting impression on him. In 1902, Muḥammad 'Abduh was in Aswan for the dedication of the completed Dam, and while there he paid a visit to al-'Aqqād's class at school. When the teacher asked al-'Aqqād to read one of his compositions for the Shaykh, 'Abduh is reported to have said, "This boy especially deserves to become a writer someday."[27] 'Abduh was to become the single most important personality for al-'Aqqād. "In my opinion," he later claimed, "Muḥammad 'Abduh is the greatest man to have appeared in Egypt or its neighbors in the last five centuries; he has made the most powerful impact on my life."[28]

The following year al-'Aqqād completed his primary education and began secondary school. However, this was cut short by his move to Cairo in 1905 to seek employment. Although this was the extent of his formal education, he never ceased to collect books and be an avid reader for the rest of his life. For a few years he worked at a number of government and teaching jobs while writing minor pieces for newspapers and magazines. His first chance at professional journalism came in 1907 when Muḥammad Farīd Wajdī, a reform-minded student of 'Abduh, started his own newspaper *(Al-Dustūr)* and invited the young al-'Aqqād to serve as co-editor.[29] Al-'Aqqād immersed himself in this opportunity, attacking politicians and orientalists alike whom he regarded as blocking the way of genuine reform. But the paper failed in 1909, and al-'Aqqād returned to Aswan, dejected and in poor health.

For the next two years he experienced a serious depression, during which he even contemplated suicide. His religious faith was shaken by Darwinism, and he expressed his pessimistic outlook through poetry and in his first book, *Khulāṣat al-Yawmīyah* [Synopsis of a Diary],[30] in which he claimed that the moral behavior of humanity was no better than that of beasts. The book earned him a measure of success, but he continued to struggle for professional recognition and, with it, financial stability. During the 1910's, he moved between Cairo, Aswan and Alexandria, taking various civil service and editorial positions while he continued to write poetry and produce a few books. His greatest accomplishment in this period was his collaboration with al-Māzinī and 'Abd al-Raḥmān Shukrī (d. 1958) in establishing the "Dīwān School" of poetry and literary criticism, which would eventually set the standard for modern Arabic poetry. Inspired by the English Romantic poets, the group advocated the organic unity of the poem, the need for a poet to be faithful to himself and his age, and especially the role of the imagination. Al-'Aqqād and al-Māzinī in particular were sharply critical of popular contemporary poets who, they claimed, merely mimicked the classical poets without any expression of feeling appropriate to modern times.[31]

Politically, al-'Aqqād was an ardent nationalist. Following World War I, he avidly supported Sa'd Zaghlūl and participated in the popular revolt. Zaghlūl took a liking for al-'Aqqād and invited him to contribute regularly to the official newspaper of the Wafd Party, *Al-Balāgh,* and then to become its editor. In this capacity he finally gained recognition and influence as a journalist. Safran believes that at this stage in his career, his meager formal education served to his advantage: "it gave his columns an engaging tone of enthusiasm and excitement at new discoveries and turned them into journeys of self-education in which al-'Aqqād served his readers as guide."[32] He was also appointed to Parliament in 1925 as a delegate of the Wafd Party. Yet he did not always tow the party line. For example, when the Wafd denounced Ṭāhā Ḥusayn's 1926 book criticizing traditional Qur'ānic interpretation, al-'Aqqād defended his colleague's right to freedom of expression even though he himself felt Ḥusayn had gone too far in his critical analysis of the Qur'ān.[33] A few years later al-'Aqqād experienced his own altercation with higher authorities, when he was imprisoned in 1930 for nine months after making critical statements against the king in one of his books as well as in Parliament.

Following his term in prison, al-'Aqqād became increasingly pessimistic concerning politics. In 1938 he left the Wafd Party and joined one of the many breakaway groups, the Sa'dist Front; he wrote articles for its newspaper and served as one of its senators. But after a few years he abandoned political structures altogether and, as noted by Allen, he "became essentially a one-man party."[34] Meanwhile, he was horrified at the rise of Fascism in Europe and in 1940 wrote two books against Hitler and the Nazis. In mid-1942, as the German army advanced on Alexandria, it appeared that Egypt would be occupied by the Germans. Al-'Aqqād fled to Khartoum out of fear of reprisal for his books; but allegations in the Sudanese press against his integrity in this excursion prompted him to return after a few weeks.[35]

Al-'Aqqād had gradually become more skeptical of the way in which Egypt was developing. According to Safran, his turn to religious themes in his writing was reactionary and unsuccessful.[36] Yet this view does not appreciate the genuine commitment to Islam evident in al-'Aqqād's works, and his conviction that religion spoke directly to the social problems of his day. In any case, this turn to religious themes in the 1940's began his most productive period of writing. From 1942-61, he published on average three books per year, one third of which dealt with some aspect of Islam. He became one of Egypt's most popular authors and was awarded the State Appreciation Prize for Literature in 1960. When failing health caught up with him and he died of a heart attack on March 12, 1964, he was given a state funeral in which he was eulogized by a large number of government and literary figures.

Al-'Aqqād's Literary Vocation

'Abbās Maḥmūd al-'Aqqād was certainly one of the most prolific writers of modern Egypt. Yet apparently the only survey of his works published in English is the one by Kermit Schoonover, and this is itself limited by its appearance only midway through al-'Aqqād's literary career.[37] Following a brief biographical synopsis, Schoonover lists forty-seven of al-'Aqqād's books, making no attempt to cover his many articles. Another survey in English can be found in Nijim's unpublished thesis, where some seventy-three titles are mentioned, interwoven in his short biography.[38]

Fortunately, the situation is much better in Arabic. Most important by far is the exhaustive coverage by al-Sakkūt: his two volume survey lists 105 prose works, eleven books of poetry, 137 individually published poems, fourteen co-authored works, fifty-two introductions to other books, translations of five non-Arabic works, and a staggering 5873 published articles.[39] Al-'Aqqād's complete works have also been printed in twenty-six large volumes.[40]

Another helpful bibliographic work, in which his books and a number of his articles are organized by category, is that of al-Ḥalwajī.[41] The breadth of al-'Aqqād's writing is evident in a simple listing of the topics covered there: Philosophy, Religion, Language, Arts and Literature, Social Sciences, Egypt and the Arab World, Biographies, and Music. The biographical studies in particular incorporate about thirty complete books on individual people.[42] Many of these concern the great figures of early Islamic history (to be discussed below), but many others are about prominent personalities in philosophy, the arts and statesmanship. As might be expected, works about those whom he most admired — al-Ghazālī,[43] Muḥammad 'Abduh[44] and Sa'd Zaghlūl — are numbered among them. But the diversity among these biographies as a whole is phenomenal: they include names such as Ibn Rūmī, Ibn Sīnā and Ibn Rushd; Shakespeare, Goethe and George Bernard Shaw; Francis Bacon, Benjamin Franklin, Sun Yat-sen, Gandhi and Hitler.

A few important trends in al-'Aqqād's writings can be noted, turning first to the poetry which he wrote throughout his career. Al-'Aqqād was fairly introspective as a poet; he dealt with topics that were important to him, including objects of nature, children, and the vicissitudes of romantic love. He also wrote on public themes, especially moral issues. He was usually quite direct in getting his meaning across, and he even sometimes supplied a prose explanation of his verse. While several poems are regarded as fine pieces of art, Badawi's opinion is that al-'Aqqād's poetry in general is not of high quality; much of it is also burdened by his sense that he was not sufficiently appreciated as a poet within his society.[45]

In his prose writing, al-'Aqqād lauded Arab culture as a heritage of which his fellow Egyptians could be proud. He even felt that modern Western society owed its best features to classical Arab civilization.[46] Yet he also recognized that there must be a transition into a new era, and he felt that certain traditional Arab mores had to give way to reform. Thus in the sphere of literature, as observed by Schoonover, al-ʻAqqād "fought for freedom; freedom from archaic style and freedom of thought and expression."[47] He believed that literature should not be bound by conventional forms, nor should it become the tool of political or personal ambitions. It should rather serve as the artistic expression of the author's personality — and here al-ʻAqqād was especially influenced by the English Romantic school.[48] This search for literary freedom was a principle which he invariably put into practice in his own writing. In the words of Gibb, al-ʻAqqād

> forged for himself a style which is peculiar in contemporary Arabic literature, a style which is elaborate and rather of a western type in texture, yet slightly archaic in language, and which demands the utmost concentration on the part of the reader.[49]

In the socio-political realm, al-ʻAqqād consistently battled for Egyptian self-identity; yet simultaneously, he welcomed Western ideas which would enable his own society to progress. To this end, he constantly read Western literature, and he was adept at synthesizing what he read and passing it on to his own readers, along with his critique. He promoted political ideologies which espoused freedom of conscience for the individual and was an ardent opponent of the fascist regimes of the 1930's.[50]

In the field of ethics, al-ʻAqqād attacked what he regarded as the traditional view of law which consisted merely of negative injunctions. Such an outlook, he believed, served only to shackle the human conscience. Both individuals and society must rise above this antiquated notion, and actively choose to follow laws which work for progress and freedom. Nevertheless, al-ʻAqqād could not bring himself to apply this concept in all areas, and his rigidly traditional view of women is perhaps a prime example.[51]

When al-ʻAqqād began writing on Islamic themes in the 1940's, his ideas about society and ethics were already well formed. Yet he found in religion a new basis for these ideas, and for the rest of his life he served his community as "a modern Muslim apologist," producing some twenty-five books dealing with Islam or religion in general.[52] Like his mentor ʻAbduh, al-ʻAqqād defended the faith as valid and rational for the modern era. People should exercise their free will, making full use of reason rather than blindly accepting religious tradition. ʻAbduh had taught that Islam requires people to think, and al-ʻAqqād reiterated this in his book *Al-Tafkīr: Farīḍah Islāmīyah* [Reflection: A Duty of Islam].[53] Al-ʻAqqād also claimed that Islam formed the foundation for all aspects of public life. He argued that there was nothing in Islam which was inconsistent with modernity, and that all social and political reforms could be carried out within an Islamic framework. He even claimed that it was Islam rather than the early Greek and Roman states which had espoused true democratic freedom.[54]

Al-ʻAqqād is also renowned for emphasizing the more internal aspects of religion, as has been noted by several of his students. He claimed that doctrine can be based solely on neither reason nor feelings, for in themselves these do not give a person any certainty about

God. One must also develop a "cosmic consciousness" *(wa'y kawnī)* in order to ascertain divine reality. But since that reality is ultimately hidden, al-'Aqqād frequently refers to it as *al-ghayb,* a Qur'ānic term designating all that is beyond human knowledge concerning God and His universe except for what is graciously revealed by Him.[55] This inward dimension of faith, as found especially in al-'Aqqād, has been summarized by one of his students in the expression *al-jawwānīyah* ("internalism").[56] It is hardly surprising, then, to find al-'Aqqād extolling the Ṣūfī approach to religion, although he is careful to caution against its excesses. He devotes a chapter to the topic of Ṣūfism in *Al-Tafkīr,* and also a chapter in his book *Allāh: Kitāb fī Nash'at al-'Aqīdah al-Ilāhīyah* [God: A Book concerning the Origin of Belief in the Divinity].[57] In this work, al-'Aqqād explores the concept of God evident in the various major religions and ideologies. The Ṣūfīs, he says, are especially attuned to divine reality through their possession of a "religious genius" *('abqarīyah dīnīyah).*[58]

In addition to expounding the attributes of Islam for his fellow Arab Muslims, al-'Aqqād believed it necessary to defend the faith against outside attacks. Several of his works explore the theme of revelation and prophetic activity, especially *Allāh, Ibrāhīm: Abū al-Anbiyā'* [Abraham: Father of the Prophets],[59] and *Maṭla' al-Nūr: Aw Ṭawāli' al-Ba'thah al-Muḥammadīyah* [The Dawning of the Light: The Preliminaries that Gave Rise to the Message of Muḥammad].[60] These books contain a distinct apologetic for the supremacy of Islam over other religions. Expanding on yet another concept of 'Abduh, al-'Aqqād regards the historical appearance of the world's religions to be a progressive process leading up to the advent of Muḥammad. The various religions are treated with respect, and as precursors to Islam they comprise a degree of truth. Yet they were always incomplete and in need of further revelation. Furthermore, the more advanced religions were those which appeared within the Semitic race, through prophets descended from Abraham. By all accounts, then, Islam is to be regarded as the pinnacle of divine activity among humanity.[61]

Al-'Aqqād's defense of his religion became more prominent, and more direct, in his later works on Islam. This is true especially of two books, *Ḥaqā'iq al-Islām wa-Abāṭīl Khusūmihi* [The Truths of Islam and the Lies of its Opponents] and *Mā Yuqāl 'an al-Islām* [What is Being Said about Islam].[62] Ḍayf states that these works were actually patterned after 'Abduh's *Al-Islām wa-al-Naṣrānīyah,* and that they were written "in refutation against the adversaries of Islam."[63] Al-'Aqqād was particularly concerned about criticisms against the faith made by Christian missionaries such as the American Samuel Zwemer. Such people, he claimed, had presented Islam out of context so as to distort the facts: faults were alleged which were unfounded and other faults, which might have some basis, were greatly exaggerated. On the other hand, al-'Aqqād was more willing than others to extend a measure of appreciation for the few orientalists whom he considered to be more balanced, such as Wilfred Cantwell Smith, Hamilton Gibb, and William Montgomery Watt.[64]

The "'Abqarīyah" Series

As several of his colleagues had done before him, al-'Aqqād produced a number of religious biographical studies; indeed, these form the majority of his works on religion, with fourteen titles on individual figures. First came his celebrated book on Muḥammad in 1942, and this was soon followed by similar studies on the Caliphs Abū Bakr, 'Umar and 'Alī (his work on the third Caliph 'Uthmān did not appear until some years later).[65] These were followed by books about other well-known personalities from the early Islamic period, namely (in order of their appearance): 'Ā'ishah, 'Amr ibn al-'Āṣ, Ḥusayn, Bilāl, Khālid, Fāṭimah and Mu'āwiyah.[66] These works were clearly his most popular, and several of them have since been incorporated into large single-volume collections.[67] The two other works in this category deal with prophets who pre-date Muḥammad, i.e., Abraham and Jesus. Al-'Aqqād had also planned to write books on Moses, Confucius and the Buddha, though he recognized that the latter two were involved in a different kind of mission from that carried out by the "Semitic" prophets;[68] however, he was not able to generate these before his death.

'Abqarīyat Muḥammad established the style which the rest of these works would follow. In his Preface, al-'Aqqād describes how the impetus for this book actually came from a discussion which took place thirty years previously. He was with a group of friends who had gathered to celebrate the Prophet's birthday, and the conversation turned to the treatise on Muḥammad written by the Scottish essayist Thomas Carlyle (d. 1881). After many in the group expressed appreciation for the positive comments Carlyle had made, one young fellow spoke up and, in an effort to appear intellectual, made critical remarks against the Prophet. The group rebuked him, but they also questioned why they should be content with a work written by a Westerner who did not really understand Muḥammad in the Muslim manner. Some of them then suggested that al-'Aqqād should write his own book about the Prophet "following the new approach" *('alā al-namaṭ al-ḥadīth),* presumably that of Carlyle. Al-'Aqqād agreed to produce one soon, but he did not accomplish this until thirty years later. He was glad for the insight and experience he had gained during the intervening period, but the book was nevertheless the fulfillment of his promise made then; it spoke to the issues which were raised at that time, since they continued to be relevant. Thus, his chapters on Muḥammad's military activities and on his married life are the longest, because these were the focus of the young man's remarks made that night.[69] Al-'Aqqād's comments here are important because they point both to the influence of Carlyle in his biographical writings, and to the apologetic concerns which are evident throughout these works.

The essay by Carlyle is important in its own right due to the generally positive attitude taken towards Muḥammad. It was the second of a series of lectures delivered in 1840 and published the following year as *On Heroes, Hero-Worship and the Heroic in History.*[70] The series as a whole included evaluations of Shakespeare, Luther, Rousseau, Napoleon and others. It dealt with a concept important to Carlyle: the impact of certain individuals who, despite their historical specificity, convey an authority which transcends history.[71] In the case of Muḥammad, Carlyle's conciliatory approach countered the polemical attitude which had long been current in the West. He was not the first to speak of Muḥammad as a great religious leader, and he was probably influenced by Goethe in this regard. But, as noted by Watt, "he was the first writer in either east or west to attempt to fathom the inner experience of the founder of Islam."[72] This novel approach gained widespread attention in the West, and Carlyle's work reached the Muslim world as well. Lines such as these undoubtedly struck a resonant chord with al-'Aqqād:

> That Mahomet's whole soul, set in flame with this grand Truth vouchsafed him, should feel as if it were important and the only important thing, was very natural. That Providence had unspeakably honoured him by revealing it, saving him from death and darkness; that he therefore was bound to make known the same to all creatures: this is what was meant by "Mahomet is the Prophet of God."[73]

Nevertheless, Carlyle's overall assessment is hardly without its points of contention for Muslims. He believed that what Muḥammad sensed as revelation actually derived from within himself, and that the result, which came to be the Qur'ān, was only "a wearisome confused jumble. . . . One feels it difficult to see how any mortal ever could consider this Koran as a book written in Heaven, . . . or indeed as a book at all."[74] Yet despite these negative comments, Carlyle's essay became the model for al-'Aqqād's own work on Muḥammad in which he praised the greatness of the Prophet, and in which the term "genius" (*'abqarīyah*) was virtually equivalent to Carlyle's "hero."

Unlike Carlyle, however, it is clear that al-'Aqqād simultaneously had an apologetic purpose to his book, directed at criticisms being leveled against Muḥammad. This is especially evident when he deals with Muḥammad's military activities. In the context of World War II, al-'Aqqād sought to discredit Western charges that Muḥammad had resorted to undue violence. Every incident involving his use of force, whether against the Meccans or prisoners of war or the Jews of Medina, is explained with moral justification. The Prophet did not impose Islam by force, he says, but merely established civil order and eliminated the obstacles which hindered its spread.[75] Yet in the Preface, al-'Aqqād explicitly denies that the book is "a defense [of Islam] or an argument against its opponents" (*difā'an 'anhu aw mujādalatan li-khuṣūmihi).*[76] One can only interpret this statement as an attempt to emphasize the book's positive focus on Muḥammad rather than its negative rejoinders against outside attacks. He seeks to recognize Muḥammad's "genius" in every respect, presenting him as the eloquent preacher, the ideal leader, the exemplary husband and father. But in the process of building up the Prophet as a supra-historical figure, al-'Aqqād has moved beyond Carlyle, often sacrificing historical objectivity.[77] The result might well be described, with Badawi, as "an exercise in hero-worship."[78]

In the same way that the word "genius" epitomizes for al-'Aqqād his sense of Muḥammad's greatness, the term is applied to several other figures as well, forming part of the title for his books on Abū Bakr, 'Umar, 'Alī and Khālid. Its absence from other titles, notably for his books on 'Uthmān and Mu'āwiyah, indicates that these figures did not possess the same stature for him. Although these two works are often treated as part of the *'Abqarīyah* series, they betray a "marked anti-Umayyad bias."[79] Al-'Aqqad states that Mu'āwiyah, for example, was certainly a capable leader but could not be described as "great" *('aẓīm).*[80] In his works on contemporary individuals as well, the term *'abqarīyah* is largely absent among the titles. However, his book *Tadhkār Gītā* [In Commemoration of Goethe], underwent a title change in the second edition, to *'Abqarīyat Gītā.*[81] In addition, and more importantly, the cognate *'Abqarī* ("genius" as a person rather than a quality) is part of the title for al-'Aqqād's book on 'Abduh.[82]

'Abqarīyat Muḥammad likewise formed the model for al-'Aqqād's methodology in the other Islamic *"'Abqarīyah"* works. This is made clear in the Preface of his book on Abū Bakr, where he deals at length with critical statements from Aḥmad Amīn, an Arab colleague. Amīn had claimed that *'Abqarīyat 'Umar,* which had appeared the previous year, was not sufficiently objective, since a biography should properly cover the person's faults as well as his virtues.[83] Al-'Aqqād replies that these works were not meant to be biographies as such. Rather, each book was a "portrait of the person's inner character" *(ṣūrah nafsīyah).*[84] This does not mean, he asserts, that the portrait is inaccurate; one must still be able to recognize the individual being described. He claims to strive for "reverence" *(tawqīr)* in his presentation while avoiding "embellishment" *(tajmīl).* If this means that certain faults of the person are overlooked, it is in order to provide a high moral standard to which his readers might aspire.[85]

Several of al-'Aqqād's students have also tried to explain the nature of these works. They are said to present a person's "genius" as a quality which lies within the individual himself, not within his great deeds; whatever he might have accomplished, his *intention* to serve humanity was paramount.[86] Thus the studies are not concerned with events and achievements surrounding the person, but seek to "personify" *(tushakhkhisu)* the merits of the individual.[87] Nevertheless, the superior character of these figures is such that they made a "decisive reverberation" in history; in this regard, even Ṭāhā Ḥusayn did not understand what his colleague meant by "genius."[88] Al-'Aqqād is thus described as an artist or poet who highlights the positive aspects of these great figures, yet without intentionally concealing their shortcomings.[89]

Al-'Aqqād continued to defend his approach despite occasional disapproval. Not long before his death, he responded to another critic who claimed that his *'Abqarīyah* series was neither scholarly nor historical. Al-'Aqqād could only refer to what he had written twenty years earlier in *'Abqarīyat al-Ṣiddīq,* repeating his description of each work as a *"ṣūrah nafsīyah"* rather than a historical biography.[90] Nevertheless, he could not avoid dealing with historical details, and on this count such criticism has considerable validity. Nijim mentions several examples of factual inaccuracies, blatant exaggerations, and assertions made without evidence among al-'Aqqād's books on Islam. Yet, he says, "al-'Aqqād has managed, notwithstanding his exaggerations and contradictions, to present an eloquent and incisive apology for Islam to those willing to accept his assumptions and conclusions."[91]

Indeed, the ongoing popularity of al-'Aqqād's books might well be considered the best evidence for the "success" of his approach. The high regard in Egypt for his works has been measured to some extent in surveys made by Nijim and Schoonover. According to Dār al-Ma'ārif, the one publisher who responded to Nijim's inquiry, more than 200,000 copies (total) of only six of al-'Aqqād's titles had been printed as of 1969; *'Abqarīyat al-Ṣiddīq* alone had gone through twelve impressions.[92] Schoonover's survey covered Arabic books in general which were considered to be the most significant as of 1952 (before several of al-'Aqqād's other popular books were published). He tabulated the results of his research into a list of the top forty titles, arranged in descending order of frequency with which each was mentioned. Books by al-'Aqqād appear six times, more than for any other author. These include *Allāh, 'Abqarīyat Muḥammad* and *'Abqarīyat 'Umar*. Interestingly, they all appear near the end of the list, and this fact, according to Schoonover,

> brought more comments than any other point. Some argue that, since [al-'Aqqād] has written a large number of good books, it is mathematically improbable for any one title to be selected enough times to cause his name to appear higher in such a poll. Others say that his somewhat unusual style has not been in his favor and coupled with this is the feeling that he has, in recent years, turned from the more vigorous creative writing to politics and to escapist pursuits among the heroes of Islam.[93]

Whatever may have been the reality at that time concerning the last two points, al-'Aqqād went on to establish a solid reputation as one of the twentieth century's most popular Egyptian authors. Perhaps the most significant tribute to his stature in the field of modern Arabic literature is the fact that, more than thirty years after his death, most of his books remain in print. In the most recent catalogue for Dār Nahḍat Miṣr, currently the principal publisher for al-'Aqqād, no less than seventy-six of his works are listed, including all of his books on Islam and religion in general.

One of these works, of course, is *Ḥayāt al-Masīḥ*, the title given for the second edition of *'Abqarīyat al-Masīḥ*. Now that the context for this book has been outlined (concerning both Jesus in Arab-Islamic thought, and al-'Aqqād's life and writings in general), we turn to an overview and assessment of this particular work.

An Assessment of The Genius of Christ

A Preliminary Note

Although the central thesis in *'Abqarīyat al-Masīḥ* is not stated at the outset, it becomes quite evident as the book progresses: the world of the first century had deteriorated, spiritually and socially, and was acutely in need of the mission of Jesus; to meet that need, Jesus directed his call of spiritual renewal and brotherly love first to the Jews, and then, when they rejected him, to humanity at large. To present his thesis, al-'Aqqād draws considerable material from the Bible, from classical writers such as Josephus and Philo, and from modern Western scholarship. An assessment of al-'Aqqād's work should properly include an evaluation of the manner in which he handles these sources. Yet such an evaluation is possible only to the degree that these sources can be identified, since al-'Aqqād rarely provides the information himself. References to quotations and allusions from biblical and classical material can generally be established, allowing for an appraisal of al-'Aqqād's treatment of such passages. But the same cannot be said concerning his use of modern secondary literature. As discussed more thoroughly later in this chapter, al-'Aqqād provides a direct reference to only a few of the undoubtedly numerous works he consulted. The books which he does cite span more than a century, making it virtually impossible to surmise what other works he might have utilized. Furthermore, the contents of his vast personal library, which probably contains many of these sources, currently remain inaccessible (see Appendix D).

Thus, much of our analysis of al-'Aqqād's claims can be made only in light of current scholarship on the issues involved. Critical evaluation, provided both in this chapter and in the notes to the translation, may often need to be understood as criticism of whatever sources lie behind such claims, and as an effort to provide more accurate information based on more recent scholarship. At the same time, it must be recognized that al-'Aqqād occasionally misreads or misapplies material from a source that is known. In other instances, he makes incorrect statements concerning facts which he should have been able to ascertain accurately from resources available to him. From a modern scholarly perspective, then, the value of this book is quite limited. The significance of this work lies rather in the author's attitude regarding a topic which has historically been a point of contention between Muslims and Christians.

An Analytical Synopsis of the Book

'Abqarīyat al-Masīḥ begins with a brief Preface which al-'Aqqād added for the second edition (see Appendix A). It serves to describe his larger intention of producing a number of books dealing with the major prophets of Islam, and to underscore that each of them participated in a common stream of prophetic mission designated by God. The Preface is followed by a short chapter called "The Blessed Tree"; since its purpose is to provide a poetic overture

to the book as a whole, it is designated as a "Prologue" in the translation.[1] Its title refers to the olive tree, a staple crop of the Middle East long cherished for its many benefits. The Prologue begins with a quotation from several passages of the Qur'ān in which the olive tree is mentioned as a blessing to humanity. Al-'Aqqād then applies this as a symbol of Christ and his mission: just as the "precious" and "revered" olive tree provides a variety of blessings, so Christ brought a message of light and goodness which blessed all people, and which especially influenced the mission of Muḥammad. This is probably the most "Islamic" portion of the book; the Qur'ān is quoted in only a few other places, and Muḥammad is mentioned directly only once again.[2] In other works al-'Aqqād develops the idea that Christianity paved the way for Islam;[3] but here he treats Christ and his mission on their own merits.

The flow of the book is somewhat interrupted, however, by the presence of the three chapters which were added in the second edition, and which together form Part One. Most likely they were placed here, rather than at the end of the book, because al-'Aqqād saw them as part of the wider context for the life and mission of Christ, dealt with in Part Two. This would especially apply to the first of these chapters, which deals with the Dead Sea Scrolls and their significance for the study of Christian origins. He explains that material dealing with the scrolls had not been available when he was first writing *'Abqarīyat al-Masīḥ*, and that the second edition was delayed until this could be incorporated. Al-'Aqqād is clearly caught up in the excitement of the potential significance of these discoveries, and also with the likely identification of the Qumran community with the Essenes. His conclusion, however, is that the Dead Sea Scrolls offer nothing that would change the focus of his book; indeed, coming as they do from a secluded and puritanical group, they only serve to confirm his central thesis that the world was in need of a mission precisely such as that brought by Christ.[4]

Although the discoveries of Wadi Qumran were the primary reason for updating his book, al-'Aqqād takes the opportunity to deal with two other current issues in ch. 2 and 3. He first considers the controversy surrounding the newly published Revised Standard Version [RSV] of the Bible. Conservative Christians had especially criticized the RSV rendition of Isa. 7:14, which is traditionally believed to be a prophecy of the Virgin Birth of Jesus. Instead of "a virgin shall conceive . . ." as found in the Authorized Version [AV], RSV reads "young woman." Al-'Aqqād had hoped that the discovery of a text of Isaiah among the Dead Sea Scrolls would have settled the matter in favor of the AV. Interestingly, he seems to affirm both the older reading as well as the traditional interpretation of the passage.

However, al-'Aqqād regards that issue as a minor one, and moves on to consider the large amount of recently published Western literature about Jesus. He focuses his attention on three works that rely heavily on speculative assumptions to maintain that only a strictly Jewish version of early Christianity had faithfully followed the teachings of Jesus. Al-'Aqqād's criticizes this view, claiming that the disciples and even Jesus himself had appropriately redirected their mission from the Jews to the Gentiles. Here he reiterates one of the main aspects of his central thesis, that the message of Christ was intended at an early stage for all people (this is the primary theme of ch. 19). Dismissing these books as containing nothing that would modify his views, al-'Aqqād ends his new material by introducing his readers to the remainder of the book, which comprises *'Abqarīyat al-Masīḥ* as it was originally written.

Part Two then picks up where the first edition had begun (following the Prologue). This section presents various aspects of the socio-historical context in which Christ, and his message, appeared. Its first three chapters begin, appropriately, with the Jewish religious context. Al-ʻAqqād discusses in ch. 4 how the concept of "the Messiah" had been only vaguely enshrined in other ancient religions, but had received its full development in Judaism. His treatment of the theme of "anointing" and God's "anointed one" (i.e., "Messiah") in the Old Testament reflects the more traditional Christian perspective which assumes a rather pervasive and monolithic messianic hope among the Jews of that time. Current scholarly opinion recognizes that the concept of "the Messiah" was actually not so prevalent, and that Jewish expectations for the future, which only sometimes included a messianic figure, varied considerably.

Al-ʻAqqād next considers the notion of prophecy in ancient Israel and its bearing on the Jewish expectation of a coming messenger from God (ch. 5). He seeks to explain to his readers why there existed such a great number of "prophets" in Israel, recognizing that Muslims attach great significance to this office and would understand prophets to have appeared only rarely in history. He claims that the term "prophet" is used more comprehensively in the Old Testament than in traditional Islamic usage, so that it includes not only the "great" prophets (i.e., those recognized as such in the Qur'ān), but also subsequent religious leaders who interpreted the words of their predecessors to the people. He compares this latter group to the jurists of Islam (religious scholars who interpret Islamic law), and thus he places them in a category with somewhat less status than true prophets. He thus imposes on the Old Testament material an artificial distinction between two levels of "prophet." His conclusion is that by the time Christ appeared, prophets in general (i.e., of lower rank) were not uncommon. But the Jews were especially looking for one of higher stature who would demonstrate the qualities of a true prophet.

A long chapter then follows describing the predominant Jewish sects of that time (ch. 6). Al-ʻAqqād devotes the first half to an overview of five major groups in Judaism (broadly defined, since they include the Samaritans). His presentation is informative and usually accurate. Regarding the Sadducees, he notes their aristocratic status and their conservative attitude toward religion in contrast to their liberal attitude toward Hellenistic culture. The Pharisees are recognized to have been generally popular and representative of Jewish society at large, though he could be more explicit concerning their adherence to oral tradition and ritual purity. Al-ʻAqqād is especially fascinated with the Essenes because of their contemplative lifestyle. The Zealots are properly depicted as extremist rebels, but the discussion of the Samaritans is problematic; his claim that they played a pivotal role in shaping the messianic expectations of the Jews in fact has no basis. The chapter continues with a discussion of other aspects of Jewish religion: the Temple, the priesthood, the Sanhedrin (the supreme Jewish council in Jerusalem), and the "Nazirites," individuals who dedicated themselves to holiness and service to God.[5] Al-ʻAqqād's arguments are sometimes speculative, but the purpose of this chapter is clear: none of the various facets of Jewish religious life in themselves could meet the inner, spiritual needs of the people; the Jews longed for something more which could not be found in their religion as they knew it.

Al-'Aqqād moves on to the wider context of Jesus' and his message in ch. 7, demonstrating that the Gentile world was equally in need of and ready for that message. Thus, the deterioration of Roman society was evidenced in the various slave uprisings of that period, as well as the growing disparity between rich and poor. In Palestine, the Jews suffered under the decadence of Herod's court and the burden of Roman taxation. Ch. 8 deals with the religious life of the Roman world in general.[6] Al-'Aqqād's focus here is on the influx of deities from the East, such as the Persian god Mithra and the Egyptian goddess Isis. He also mentions here the Jewish-Egyptian sect known as the Therapeutae. The attraction which these cults held for Westerners is proof for al-'Aqqād that the people's search for genuine faith could not be met by the world's religions. The same was true, he says in ch. 9, for the various systems of philosophy current in the Roman world at that time.[7] He first examines the major schools of Greek thought: the Pythagoreans, Epicureans, and Stoics. Al-'Aqqād then turns to the Jewish philosopher Philo of Alexandria, showing how he incorporated Greek ideas into his expositions on religion, while simultaneously elevating the traditional teachings of Judaism. Philo thus represents for al-'Aqqād the most sublime of the philosophical trends that helped to prepare the way for the mission of Christ.

Part Three continues to set the stage for al-'Aqqād's examination of that mission; it comprises a collection of essays which cover various historical factors with regard to Jesus. Ch. 10 deals with Galilee as the specific setting in which he lived and preached. Al-'Aqqād outlines its geography and history, noting the general aversion of Judean Jews towards the regions north of their border due to the influx of Gentiles there. At this point, he enters an area of controversy concerning the degree of the religious and cultural distinction between the Jews of Galilee and Judea. Al-'Aqqād adopts the common view that the Galilean Jews were seriously tainted by Gentile influence and thus rejected by Jews of the south, whereas more recent scholarship has recognized their loyalty to the faith of Jerusalem at the time of Christ, and even their general acceptance in Judea. Al-'Aqqād's perspective, however, better serves to bolster his thesis: the eclectic character of Galilee, including the tolerance and syncretism of its Jewish inhabitants, made it a more fitting place of origin for the mission of Jesus, since that mission was destined to move beyond traditional Judaism and into the world at large.

The theme of ch. 11, at least initially, reflects its title: "When Christ was Born." Al-'Aqqād begins by explaining the historical anomaly as to why the date of Jesus' birth is actually a few years prior to the start of the Christian era. After discussing the Roman census mentioned by Luke and the "star" of Bethlehem referred to in Matthew, he joins most scholars in holding the date of Jesus' birth to be 5 or 6 B.C.E. The bulk of this chapter, however, deals with the existence of Christ in history; the connection here with the chapter's title is perhaps best understood as an attempt to demonstrate the *fact* of Christ's birth. Al-'Aqqād is rather agitated concerning those whom he claims have doubted the actual historicity of Jesus. He counters such skepticism, first with a fine review of the bits of evidence from the historians Josephus, Tacitus and Suetonius. After submitting other arguments that point to the Jesus of history, such as the rapid emergence of Christianity, he concludes that the mission of Christ is completely logical within its historical setting.

With ch. 12, we finally arrive at a presentation of Christ himself. Until now, almost the only direct references to Jesus have been to a few of his sayings and to the event of his birth.[8] Here, al-ʻAqqād begins his "descriptive portrait" of Christ, rather inauspiciously, with a quotation from an apocryphal source allegedly describing Jesus' physical appearance. He recognizes the account as dubious, but nonetheless believes it to be indicative of what can be inferred from the biblical data. Fortunately he remains within the parameters of the Gospels as he mentions Jesus' eloquence in speech, his partiality for nature, and the attraction he held for women as a spiritual guide. He then considers Jesus' character: he was gentle in spirit, yet he did not hesitate to express his anger when it was called for, or to impose tough conditions for discipleship. This leads al-ʻAqqād into a fascinating portrayal of Jesus' own determination to remain true to his mission. The faithful messenger experienced the lot of all prophets, the necessity to speak the word of truth in the face of opposition and to "venture into the struggle" (*al-jihād,* p. 148) without reservation. Yet this necessarily involved an inner struggle as well, and al-ʻAqqād draws from the scene of Gethsemane to describe the temptation Jesus faced, either to shrink back from the ordeal or to demand assurance of a successful outcome. Jesus' victory in resisting either path, and his willingness to forge ahead and allow destiny to follow its course, characterizes for al-ʻAqqād his entire mission.

Part Four of *ʻAbqarīyat al-Masīḥ* forms the heart of the book, focusing on the essential message which Jesus proclaimed. The title of this section is simply "The Call" *(Al-Daʻwah);* while this term initially refers to the divine call to which Jesus himself responded, it primarily designates the call which Jesus issued to his Jewish listeners — disciples and opponents alike. Al-ʻAqqād asserts that this call had a universal dimension as well, and although its proclamation was ultimately carried out by Jesus' followers, it was prefigured in Jesus' own ministry. We are introduced to this broad theme in ch. 13. Al-ʻAqqād first rehearses his main thesis that the world was in need of this call because of the inflexible nature of society and religion, and how the message of brotherhood and peace came to meet that need. But naturally, it met with opposition; the Jews refused the invitation to the banquet (referring to Jesus' well-known parable), and the invitation instead went to others who "were more deserving of it" (p. 154). Jesus' mission thus involved "a change of course" or the start of a new "direction" (p. 155). The last word here is *qiblah,* normally the technical term for the direction in which Muslims face when at prayer. Al-ʻAqqād employs it here to indicate one's orientation towards the will of God. The change in direction not only represents the shift in the call of Christ from Jews to Gentiles, but also the shift in attitude for anyone who would follow that call, the choice that must be made between selfish ambitions and the way of God.

Ch. 14 elaborates on the radical nature of Christ's call in what is essentially a brief homily. One must make the same choice that Jesus made, renouncing the way of the world and seeking the more important things that last. One must "hate" family members but love one's enemies, a contradiction that is resolved only by following the new *qiblah.* People were surprised at the way Jesus accepted children, outcasts and sinners, and many criticized him for being oblivious to the social conventions of that day. But he had set his sights on the future, knowing that others would join him in his *qiblah.*

The title of ch. 15, "The Ordeals Incorporated in the Call," picks up on this idea of opposition to the message of Jesus. But the ordeal through which he passed was preceded by another ordeal experienced by John the Baptist, who is the focus of this chapter. Al-'Aqqād presents the announcement of John's birth, as found in Luke's Gospel and also in the Qur'ān. He then examines the Gospel material concerning John's austere lifestyle, his acerbic character, and his death at the hand of Herod Antipas. His message was one of judgment against ungodly deeds and attitudes among the Jews, a message, claims al-'Aqqād, that Jesus also preached, although his approach was somewhat different. Ch. 16 continues, then with the obstacles faced by Jesus in proclaiming his call. These are summed up in the word "law" — not just the law of Rome or even that of the Jewish authorities, but the entire fabric of society and religion which was at once stratified, inflexible and hypocritical. Jesus came neither to eliminate this "law" nor to add to it, but to bring about its required transformation. Part of that mission was his pronouncement of divine forgiveness, and this would become his "greatest offense" to the Jewish leaders (p. 168). Thus, when they compelled him to judge the woman caught in adultery, he sent her away without condemnation. He refused to be drawn into their traps concerning their law, for his "kingdom [was] not of this world . . . [and] had nothing to do with other kingdoms" (p. 170).

In contrast to that inflexible and hypocritical law, Jesus brought "the Law of Love" — the title and theme of ch. 17. The legalists of Jesus' day wanted only to show off their skill in dealing with the fine points of legal requirements. Their world focused on external matters and was thus opposed to the world of the conscience *(al-ḍamīr).* What, then, did Jesus mean when he said that he came not to abolish the law but to fulfill it, especially when his actions went against many of its stipulations? What Christ abolished, says al-'Aqqād, were the external aspects of the law, while he instituted the law of love which was the essence of the law itself, "the eternal principles on which the human conscience is based" (p. 172). He offers several examples, drawn mainly from the Sermon on the Mount, which show how the law of love and conscience was even more strict in its requirements. "For the conscience is first responsible for a person's intentions and thoughts, and only then for his deeds and encounters" (p. 176). It was the law as it was meant to be, yet radically opposed to the law as it existed; it was "new wine in an old wineskin" (p. 177).

This concept of an internal law of conscience also leads to a proper discernment of the stern ethical injunctions of Jesus (the subject of ch. 18). Al-'Aqqād believes that a more literal interpretation of his commands was appropriate for the original disciples who devoted themselves to propagating his call; but for ordinary folks who must live in the day-to-day world, Jesus' commands should be understood figuratively. Christ's main intention was to relocate ethics away from its dependence on inflexible rules to a new, more humane "center" (or "axis," *miḥwar*). The focus is to be a person's motives, not meticulous compliance to the law. "Thus a person should give out of love and from his own free will" rather than under compulsion (p. 182). This ethical relocation results in a completely new perspective regarding worldly concerns. A person might own many possessions, says al-'Aqqād, but this is permissible as long as that person serves God rather than those possessions; for the soul is more important than the world.

In his chapter on "The Kingdom of Heaven," al-'Aqqād elaborates an important element of his thesis which he has mentioned previously: that the call proclaimed by Jesus' was rejected by the Jews, and so became a universal call to all people (ch. 19). He begins with a pertinent comparison from early Islamic history: if the message of Muḥammad had been accepted by the Meccans at the outset, there would have been no *hijrah* or emigration to Medina, and the history of Islam would have been fundamentally altered. In the same way that the rejection of the Meccans served to advance the cause of Islam, so the rejection of Jesus' message by the Jews prompted its spread throughout the world. Thus al-'Aqqād views Jesus' mission as one that evolved from a call appropriately directed to the Jews alone, to a call which incorporated all of humanity. Here he has simplified the complex data of the Gospels, assuming that the Jewish response was negligible, and that Jesus unequivocally initiated a mission to the Gentiles. Yet if he overstates his case here, at least he captures some of the radical inclusiveness inherent in many of Jesus' sayings. Al-'Aqqād goes on to discuss Jesus' teaching about the kingdom of heaven, emphasizing its spiritual character and universal scope. Again, his selectivity of the biblical data is evident; he sets aside any future aspect of the kingdom as too ambiguous, and focuses on the present dimension of the kingdom and its immediate relevance to Christ's mission. For him, Jesus' self-designation as "the Son of Man" applies only to the here-and-now, and the "kingdom of the Son of Man" exists in this world as people conduct their lives in conformity to Jesus' commands. Such a mission, he says, could never have arisen among the pagan religions; its appearance among the Jews, and its subsequent rejection by them which led to its spread, could only have been arranged by Divine Wisdom.

The title of Part Five is simply *Adawāt al-Da'wah,* "The Tools of the Call." Having presented the heart of Jesus' message in Part Four, al-'Aqqād moves on to explore the means by which that call was proclaimed and propagated. The first and most important "tool" was the remarkable teaching ability of Jesus himself (ch. 20). The world's awareness of its need for Jesus' message was no guarantee that it would listen to his call. Crucial to its success was his ability to proclaim it effectively. Thus al-'Aqqād considers certain features of Jesus' teaching style, especially his use of parables. He believes that Jesus expressed these parables spontaneously, but only after they had formed and developed in his subconscious during periods of meditation. The second "tool" by which the call was proclaimed, and especially the means by which it spread throughout the world, was the "fidelity of the disciples" (ch. 21). Al-'Aqqād notes how they were called by the Master and trained by him, like military recruits, to carry on the mission after his own role would end. They became his special *"ummah"* or "community" (p. 201). They were ordinary men with their own frailties, and initially they misunderstood his role as Messiah, but they were faithful to their call. They accepted Jesus' instruction about self-denial and his warning of opposition. Then (without any reference here to how Jesus' own ministry ended), they were scattered throughout the world and proclaimed the same message, primarily among the Gentiles.

It is not until Part Six that al-'Aqqād examines the New Testament Gospels as sources for the life of Christ. Ch. 22 begins with a technical discussion concerning their nature as documents: their interrelationship, authorship, date of composition, etc. While the discussion reflects generally accepted scholarship on the subject, its brevity and complexity would probably leave most Muslim readers somewhat bewildered. Nevertheless, al-'Aqqād affirms the

Gospels as reliable records; discrepancies which are found among them, he claims, can generally be explained. Besides, his interest is in the "personality" of Christ rather than historical details. From this perspective, contradictions may even support the creditability of the Gospels, since it would be unusual if no contradictions at all were to surface in a careful investigation. Al-'Aqqād concludes the chapter with a digression, explaining why his work makes no reference to the miracles of Jesus. Drawing on an argument of al-Ghazālī, he notes that miracles cannot be explained on the basis of natural causes. He does not discount their authenticity, but neither does he regard them as necessary in order to explain or receive the truth of Christ's message. Miracles, of themselves, never led anyone to faith. In any case, the greatest miracle was the impact which Jesus had on history, despite his humble origins.

Ch. 23, the longest chapter of the book, is al-'Aqqād's attempt at an outline of Jesus' life based on the Gospels' record. It is only here that the work becomes biographical in nature (despite the title given to the second edition). However, the presentation is uneven; some aspects are considered at length, while others are mentioned briefly or not at all. After noting Jesus' birth, childhood and education (presumably in the local synagogue), al-'Aqqād focuses on the "turning point" of Jesus' career: his baptism by John, followed by his Temptation in the wilderness. Here, we are treated to a remarkable meditation concerning the inner struggles of Jesus, similar to al-'Aqqād's comments at the end of ch. 12. Jesus would not succumb to worldly expectations of messianic privilege, but would instead rest solely on divine assistance in order to carry out his mission; furthermore, Jesus would experience this kind of temptation — and victory — throughout his ministry. Christ thus embarked on his mission which, as al-'Aqqād had stated earlier, progressed from an ethnic to a universal call. Otherwise, little is said about what this mission entailed; the Gospel accounts of Jesus' ministry of healing and exorcism are completely ignored, as they are throughout the book. Instead, al-'Aqqād examines two of the titles which were ascribed to Jesus ("the Son of God" and "the Son of Man"), attempting to interpret them in a manner acceptable for Muslims.

From here, al-'Aqqād jumps directly to the end of Jesus' mission and his final confrontation with Jewish leaders. His last visit to Jerusalem for the Feast of Passover was necessarily public; going secretly might have avoided the impending crisis, but this would have discredited his mission. In describing Jesus' reliance on God in the face of opposition, al-'Aqqād again makes notes of his prayer in Gethsemane; here, he seems to refer to the arrest of Jesus which, in the Gospels, takes place immediately afterwards. But then he backs up and recounts only Jesus' entry into Jerusalem (which occurred earlier in the week) and his so-called cleansing of the Temple. For al-'Aqqād, it was this incident that prompted the Jewish authorities to take "immediate action"; yet he does not explain what that action might have been. Rather, he claims that at this point, "the role of history ends, and the role of faith begins" (p. 226). In al-'Aqqād's view, the Gospel accounts of the arrest, trial, crucifixion and resurrection cannot be trusted because of certain discrepancies. Instead, he turns to a report, related by the Aḥmadīyah leader Muḥammad 'Alī, indicating that Jesus traveled to India at the end of his mission in Palestine and died there. While al-'Aqqād makes no definitive judgment on the veracity of this account, he states that it "would be improper to neglect, since it deserves particular attention" (p. 227). In conclusion, he says, the way in which Jesus' life ended cannot be resolved with certainty; yet that by no means impinges on his affirmation of the genius of Christ and the universal nature of his call.

The Epilogue with which the book ends bears an independent character, and was reprinted on its own several times after the book was published. In it, al-'Aqqād explores what might transpire "if Christ were to return" to the world of today. To set the stage, he recounts a famous tale from Dostoyevski's *The Brothers Karamazov,* where Jesus suddenly yet peaceably arrives in fifteenth-century Seville. He is apprehended by "the Grand Inquisitor," who resents that Jesus has come to change the traditions of the church, claiming that the freedom of conscience offered by Jesus would create a grievous constraint for the people. In the same way, says al-'Aqqād, if Christ were to return at this time, "he would renounce many things which are being done today in his name. He would find scribes and Pharisees among his followers, and he would reproach them for their hypocrisy" (p. 230). Then has the message of Christ gone out in vain? No, he says; we must continue the struggle to gain complete freedom of conscience, and to put into practice the ideals taught by the religions, despite the ongoing presence of evil. Even if Christ came today and rectified many errors, it is up to humanity, with a conscience illuminated by religion, to carry on the task.

The Book's Reception in the Muslim World and the West

Several reviewers of *'Abqarīyat al-Masīḥ* have commented that when the book was published in 1953, it was well received in Egypt among both Muslims and Christians. Cragg relates a report that it sold 200,000 copies in the first nine months, while Schoonover claims the same figure for a period of only "a few weeks."[9] Although it is difficult to believe that the latter statement is accurate, clearly the book gained a wide hearing.[10] Al-'Aqqād himself, in the second edition published in 1958, offers his gratitude for the many expressions of appreciation from his readers (p. 86), and the revised work was subsequently reprinted several times by various publishers.

Nevertheless, the book did have its critics, also noted by al-'Aqqād in the second edition. On p. 80, he responds to objections that he was not sufficiently careful in describing the person of James, the brother of Jesus; he is evidently reacting here to the review written in English by Butrus 'Abd al-Malik.[11] Other readers felt that his positive approach made it sound like he had actually become a Christian, as he observes on p. 86.

It is also quite possible that the change of title for the second edition reflects some disapproval concerning the orientation of the book. In the case of *'Abqarīyat Muḥammad,* Louis Awad claims that al-'Aqqād had been severely criticized by orthodox Muslims who "could not quite reconcile the concept of individual genius to the concept of divine revelation".[12] Perhaps the same objection was being leveled at *'Abqarīyat al-Masīḥ,* either by Muslims or Christians or even both. Al-'Aqqād gives no indication on p. 86 as to why the change was made, and the new title — *Ḥayāt al-Masīḥ* [The Life of Christ] — hardly does justice to his approach. Furthermore, he purposefully left the main part of the book completely intact, and whenever he refers to the book by name in the new material, it is always as *'Abqarīyat al-*

Masīḥ. The impression made is that the change was not according to his wishes, and that it likely resulted from an editorial decision in response to some pressure.

In fact, outside of the reputed publication figures and al-'Aqqād's own comments, it is rather difficult to gauge objectively the reception of this book in the Arab world. Not a single Arabic review has been located, and among the many Arab works which were written about al-'Aqqād and his writings, only one has been found which offers a comment on *'Abqarīyat al-Masīḥ*. Muḥammad Khalīfah al-Tūnisī published a collection of excerpts from a variety of al-'Aqqād's writings; included there is a quotation from a series of articles which he had written in 1929 in response to Emil Ludwig's book about Jesus. In a footnote, al-Tūnisī mentions that al-'Aqqād had also written *'Abqarīyat al-Masīḥ*; he claims that it is better than Ludwig's book because of its more reverent approach and its attention to the context in which Christ lived.[13]

'Abqarīyat al-Masīḥ also reached the wider Arab-Islamic world, most notably through the Beirut edition of the revised work, published under the original title (see Appendix A). The book was not included in either of the single-volume collections of the *'Abqarīyah* series (i.e., *Al-'Abqarīyāt al-Islāmīyah* and *Islāmīyāt)*, but it was incorporated in al-'Aqqād's "Islamic Encyclopedia" *(Mawsū'at 'Abbās Maḥmūd al-'Aqqād al-Islāmīyah)*, and, of course, in his complete works. The book was also well received among Muslims of the Indian subcontinent. Asghar Ali Engineer, an Indian Muslim, includes a favorable discussion of *'Abqarīyat al-Masīḥ* in his survey of Muslim writings about Jesus.[14] Also, the second edition *(Ḥayāt al-Masīḥ)* was translated into Urdu and published in Lahore in 1965;[15] this is said to have been reprinted several times.[16]

In the West, al-'Aqqād's book has caught the attention of a number of scholars of Islam, primarily Christian, as might well be expected. However, most references are rather brief or are included in surveys of several Arabic-Muslim works about Jesus. Only two reviews in English are devoted solely to *'Abqarīyat al-Masīḥ*, and only one of these may be considered substantial. One would have expected to find in a journal such as *The Muslim World* something more than the mere page and a half notice by Butrus 'Abd al-Malik (to which al-'Aqqād responded as mentioned above). 'Abd al-Malik's judgment is primarily negative, his main criticism being that al-'Aqqād is evasive with regard to the significance of the crucifixion. Nevertheless, he says, "it deserves our attention and consideration."[17] The more extensive review was made by Kenneth Cragg, and this remains the best survey to date of this book in English. He credits al-'Aqqād for venturing into the world of the New Testament, one that is strange and forbidding to the average Muslim. He appreciates the author's emphasis on the first century context, the inner character of Jesus, and his internalization of the law. Yet he finds al-'Aqqād's presentation, focusing as it does on the teaching ministry of Christ, to be bereft of the heart of that ministry — the cross which it envisioned and exemplified. In the end, Cragg finds the work to be "disappointing," since it "leaves several unanswered questions and a great wistfulness for more."[18] Cragg's brief references to *'Abqarīyat al-Masīḥ* in subsequent writings offer the same mixed response.[19]

Reviews of the book in English are also incorporated in surveys made of several Muslim works about Jesus. Most notable is that of Leirvik, who draws attention to al-'Aqqād's understanding of "conscience,"[20] and Goddard, who emphasizes the influence on al-'Aqqād of "liberal Christian writers."[21] Both writers express appreciation for his profound sympathy with the Gospel presentation of Jesus, while also noting his insistence on remaining within a Muslim framework. Shorter English reviews, with variously mixed reactions, are noted in a few other works about Jesus in Islam.[22]

'Abqarīyat al-Masīḥ was also one of three Arabic-Muslim works on Christ (in addition to those of Shalabī and Khālid) which were considered in a 1991 Doctor of Missiology dissertation.[23] However, the presentation there is almost entirely a summary and translation of selected passages; comments are few, and footnotes are made only to biblical references.

A number of French Catholic scholars of Islam have likewise been drawn to al-'Aqqād's book. All of them express admiration for his break with the traditional polemical approach and his grasp of the message of Christ; but at the same time, they are disappointed that he cannot move closer to a Christian (and more specifically Catholic) view of the person and work of Jesus. The most extensive review in this group is by Georges Farès;[24] interspersed among a number of long quotations and a few digressions are several comments of appreciation. For example, "in his essay, al-'Aqqād has shown us, through his frequent and often quite meaningful reflections, that a non-Christian can assimilate for himself the mystery of Christ."[25] Yet he also faults the author's presentation as incomplete, focused only on ethical issues and not on Christ's real mission of salvation. Henri Teissier offers a similar mixed response in a review of this book along with two others; he notes several weaknesses, historical as well as theological, but he welcomes the definite "rapprochement" between the traditional Muslim idea of Christ and the authentic figure of Jesus (i.e., that which is found in the Gospels).[26] *'Abqarīyat al-Masīḥ* is evaluated by Georges Anawati in several places. One of these is a summary of the contents of the book with little comment.[27] Two other very similar discussions offer a brief critique. In them, al-'Aqqād is commended for his respect for the Gospels as authentic sources, but chided for using them only to examine Jesus' teachings while his miracles and crucifixion are left in the shadows.[28] Anawati also gives space to this work near the end of his entry on Jesus in *The Encyclopaedia of Islam*, where similar comments are made.[29] In a survey by Jacques Jomier, al-'Aqqād's book receives only brief consideration, and again he is faulted for the selective manner in which he uses only those passages which correspond with his thesis.[30] Gaudeul barely mentions this work, but he credits the books of al-'Aqqād and Ḥussayn as "signs of a positive change."[31] Also to be included here is the anonymous review of several works in the Catholic periodical *Encounter*; this simply provides a few remarks, both favorable and critical, drawn from the writings of Teissier and Jomier, along with a number of short, translated extracts from the book.[32] Most recently, Maurice Borrmans devotes a section of his book *Jésus et les musulmans d'aujourd'hui* to a discussion of *'Abqarīyat al-Masīḥ*.[33] Again, this is primarily a presentation of translated excerpts, drawn from the earlier review by Farès. His conclusion epitomizes to a large degree the perspective of the French Catholic school: While the Muslim reader receives a lesson about the human conscience, informed by Christ's teaching on the law of love and the kingdom of God, "the Christian reader can only be glad [in that], even as he regrets that the author has overlooked, intentionally or not, certain dimensions of Jesus' identity."[34]

Finally, *'Abqarīyat al-Masīḥ* is discussed in a few German writings. The essay *Jesus und der moderne Islam* by Abdel-Fattah el-Didi (a disciple of al-'Aqqād) is, despite its title, essentially a presentation of the main points of this particular book. Even as a Muslim, el-Didi considers it "unfortunate" that al-'Aqqād says so little about the end of Jesus' life.[35] The chapter in Wielandt on prophetic activity in the writings of al-'Aqqād includes an examination of this book's contribution to that theme.[36] She focuses on the author's concern to establish Jesus as a historical figure, but she overstates her case when she implies that this is the main purpose of his work. Another point is well-stated, that, in contrast to Rashīd Riḍā, al-'Aqqād was willing to rely on the Gospels as his primary historical source. The reason, states Wielandt, was that "he wished to extend proper reverence to a religious genius whom he had encountered more vividly in the New Testament than in the Qur'ān."[37] The more recent work by Schumann includes a chapter on *'Abqarīyat al-Masīḥ*. Most of it is a summary of its contents, but this is followed by some insightful remarks.[38] He points out, for example, that the traditional Muslim view about Christ's mission was that it was limited to the Israelites, whereas al-'Aqqād emphasizes its universal character. This perspective, he remarks, would be quite new for the Muslim reader. Schumann also notes al-'Aqqād's focus on the human conscience in relation to Jesus' message and his view that this has not been superseded even by Islam.[39]

Al-'Aqqād's book about Christ has thus generated a fair amount of interest, particularly among those who are looking for evidence of a more positive appreciation of Christianity among Muslim intellectuals. Almost everyone recognizes the significant manner in which this work is an indication of such evidence. Yet no one gives it unqualified approval. Some fault the book for technical inaccuracies, others for its incomplete presentation of Jesus' ministry. Most Christian reviewers, however, find the way in which al-'Aqqād sets aside the historicity and significance of the crucifixion to be disheartening. This is an issue which will be considered further at the end of this chapter.

Al-'Aqqād's Style and Use of Sources

For several reasons, *'Abqarīyat al-Masīḥ* presents the reader (and the translator!) with a text which is at once intriguing yet challenging. The observation which Gibb made concerning al-'Aqqād's writing in general can certainly be said of this work, that its style is "elaborate," "slightly archaic" and "demands the utmost concentration."[40] A few features which occur frequently might be noted: he is fond of the passive voice (which often can only be rendered by the active voice in translation); he regularly repeats a word or expression by using a synonym in a balanced fashion; and occasionally he becomes so involved with his discussion that he switches briefly from third to first person.[41]

Al-'Aqqād's positive attitude towards Ṣūfism and his recurrent attention to the internal aspects of religion often give a mystical tenor to his writing. This especially applies to his meditation on "The Blessed Tree" (the Prologue) and to his penetrating reflections on the inward struggles of Jesus. While this undoubtedly arises primarily from the author's own personality, perhaps this also represents further influence from 'Abduh; the style of the latter's *Al-Islām wa-al-Naṣrānīyah* is said to be "highly poetic and powerful,"[42] words which could frequently be applied to *'Abqarīyat al-Masīḥ.*

The terminology present in the book also calls for comment. Occasionally al-'Aqqād uses a classical expression;[43] there are instances where he makes a play on words;[44] and at times he uses innovative expressions not technically part of Arabic vocabulary.[45] There is repeated use of Islamic terminology; some are terms which are fundamental to the discussion, e.g., *qiblah* [the direction for prayer] and *miḥrāb* [prayer-niche] in ch. 14. Jewish religious leaders are often described as *fuqahā'* [jurists] who might issue a *fatwā* [legal opinion]. The words *nīyah* [intention] and *jihād* [struggle] frequently appear in discussions which deal with inner character. The "Sermon on the Mount" is called *al-khuṭbah 'alā al-jabal* rather than *al-maw-'izah 'alā al-jabal* as among Arab Christians.

Nevertheless, Christian terminology is also present. The disciples are generally (though not always) referred to as *al-talāmīdh,* as in the Arabic Bible, rather than by the Qur'ānic term *al-ḥawārīyūn.* The title *rasūl* [messenger, apostle] is used in the usual Christian sense for Paul and others. References to God as "Father" *(āb)* and to "the Holy Spirit" *(al-rūḥ al-qudus),* which appear in biblical quotations, are left intact without further discussion. Probably the most important observation in this regard is the manner in which al-'Aqqād refers to his main character. The name "Jesus" rarely appears; when it does, sometimes the Islamic form is given *('Īsā)* and sometimes the Christian form *(Yasū'),* although the latter is found almost exclusively with biblical quotations or summaries. Instead, the author consistently utilizes the title *al-Masīḥ.* Since this term is popular among both Muslims and Christians, al-'Aqqād has avoided criticism from either side on this major point. However, it might be noted that the Muslim salutation *('alayhi al-salām,* "peace be upon him") is sometimes employed, especially when he uses only a personal pronoun to refer to Christ.

The style of the book as a whole leaves the reader wondering about its organization. The addition of the three new chapters to the front of the book seems quite out of place; these would have been better placed at the back, or better still, worked into the original text. The various points of his thesis are not clearly stated at the beginning but emerge only through the course of his discussion. The movement from the context of Christ's call to its content is sufficiently clear; but the emphasis on message rather than events renders a secondary status to certain chapters. In particular, one might have preferred to find his discussion of the Gospels (ch. 22) near the beginning, since they form the basis on which the mission of Jesus is presented. Furthermore, the chronological outline of Jesus' life (ch. 23) appears more like an afterthought, where it might have better served as the initial framework in which to place his various sayings. As it is, there are serious gaps in the outline, while the book's quotations of what Jesus taught are frequently bereft of the important context in which they occur.

At the same time, al-'Aqqād is hardly oblivious to historical issues in *'Abqarīyat al-Masīḥ.* Whether his concern is the context, the person, or simply the message, he is fully aware that he is dealing with a personality who lived centuries ago. Thus he draws quite heavily on written sources, and it must be considered one of the most significant aspects of this work that the author, as a Muslim, chooses to utilize the Gospels rather than traditional Islamic material as the primary basis for a presentation about Jesus. Quotations from the Qur'ān are infrequent, despite their prominence in the Prologue. The longest excerpts have to do with the birth of John the Baptist (ch. 15), but these might well have been utilized precisely because of their general agreement with the biblical accounts, as an opportunity to incorporate some Islamic material without raising strong objections from Christian readers. A brief verse is mentioned at the beginning of ch. 19 with regard to the Meccans' rejection of Muḥammad's message. The only other Qur'ānic citations, and the only ones in the entire book which directly refer to Jesus, are in connection with al-'Aqqād's discussion about the end of Jesus' life, and his possible death in India.[46] Furthermore, the classical Islamic material on Jesus in the *ḥadīth, tafsīr* and historical sources are altogether ignored.

On the other hand, there are innumerable references to the Bible, and especially the Gospels.[47] Al-'Aqqād's own comment about this is probably not far from the truth: "we have opened the two Testaments at least a hundred times in order to investigate them in our research and to utilize them in our quotations" (p. 80). In the same paragraph, he refers to his use of the Arabic Bible. This source was undoubtedly the nineteenth-century translation produced by the American missionary Cornelius Van Dyck, and which has remained the standard Arabic Bible ever since.[48] Al-'Aqqād quotes this translation verbatim, or nearly so, in several places. Yet his citations, as Cragg notes, frequently evince "a certain casualness";[49] words are substituted, important phrases are omitted, and occasionally his rendition considerably alters the sense of the original text of VD. Obviously he read the biblical material carefully in preparation for writing a particular segment; but it would seem that when he later put pen to paper, often he simply relied on his memory without bothering to check the actual wording of the text.

In some cases, al-'Aqqād has apparently made his own translation into Arabic from an English version of the Bible.[50] Most likely this was the Revised Standard Version. This translation appeared in its complete form in 1952, just as al-'Aqqād was writing *'Abqarīyat al-Masīḥ;* but it is clear from his discussion at the beginning of ch. 2 that he had read the Old Testament as well as the New in that translation. Undoubtedly he was also familiar with the Authorized (King James) Version, and this may have been a source as well.[51] It should also be noted here that al-'Aqqād does not usually cite the location of a passage; at most, he indicates the name of the book and occasionally the chapter number as well.

In addition to the Bible, several other primary sources are mentioned by al-'Aqqād. There are a few quotations or discussions from some of his favorite classical Arab writers — al-Ghazālī, al-Jāḥiẓ and al-Ma'arrī.[52] Far more numerous are the references to a number of classical Greek and Latin authors, especially Josephus and Philo; it may well be that al-'Aqqād utilized standard English translations of their works, although in most cases he probably derived these quotations from English secondary sources. Again, however, details concerning the origin of a classical citation are never provided beyond the occasional reference to the title of a particular treatise.

'Abqarīyat al-Masīḥ is distinguished among Arabic-Muslim studies of Jesus by the author's frequent use of secondary sources, all of which (as nearly as can be determined) are English works written by Western scholars. In the first edition, al-'Aqqād identifies seven

such books either by author or title or both; unfortunately, he provides only scanty information, so that complete identification cannot always be made. Most of these works were written in the first half of the twentieth century, but some date as far back as 1836. The names of four other authors are mentioned in ch. 23 (p. 227), but these are much more difficult to identify. He also refers to the English translation of the Qur'ān by Muḥammad 'Alī in ch. 23 (p. 227), and, of course, to Dostoyevski's *The Brothers Karamazov* in the Epilogue (presumably he utilized the English translation here as well). The three more recent books about Jesus are discussed at length in the new material of the second edition (ch. 2 and 3).

Undoubtedly, al-'Aqqād utilized many other sources which he does not name. The clearest example is at the beginning of ch. 1, where he refers to a large, scholarly book on the Dead Sea Scrolls but makes no mention of its author or title.[53] In another instance, he gives a brief quotation about the language of Matthew's Gospel, but offers no clue as to where he found it (ch. 21, p. 205). His fondness for mentioning the etymology of certain terms, such as the Essenes (p. 98) or "the Son of Man" (p. 222), is surely further evidence for his dependence on scholarly works. The same can be said regarding his references to Western classical writers. Yet it is almost always impossible to identify his sources, even in cases where he has obviously taken over large segments of information, such as his elaborate discussion of Jesus' parables in ch. 20. It may well be that many of these works were part of his own personal library, said to have reached immense proportions for that time. This library is still intact and would presumably provide an excellent means for tracing many of these sources. Circumstances are such, however, that this library has remained almost completely inaccessible since his death in 1964 (see Appendix D for details).

Al-'Aqqād frequently utilized his sources well. Other times, however, his writing displays a casual approach towards his sources which is reflected in the numerous historical inaccuracies present in this book.[54] A few of these are fairly minor: e.g., Luke is said to have been one of Jesus' original disciples (p. 110); the reign of the Emperor Claudius is placed in the second century rather than the first (p. 138); and the description of Herod Antipas' death belongs instead to that of Herod Agrippa I (p. 113). Others might be considered more significant errors for which al-'Aqqād might well be responsible: a saying of John the Baptist is attributed to Jesus (p. 111); those who come to hear John are described as "Christians" (p. 163); and details of the various slave rebellions in the Roman Empire are confused (p. 107). In most cases, however, it is impossible to ascertain whether an inaccuracy or dubious claim should be traced to a faulty source, to al-'Aqqād's indiscriminate research, or to his own occasionally speculative reasoning.

Thus, the significance of al-'Aqqād's incorporation of a large number of scholarly Western sources in this book is marred by the less-than-scholarly manner in which he often utilizes those sources. Nevertheless, while he can and should be faulted on this count, it is probably best not to overstate the importance of this matter in evaluating the book as a whole. In the final analysis, historical events are not what al-'Aqqād wishes to emphasize, but rather the message of a particular person in history.

It remains to consider whether there might have been a specific source which influenced al-'Aqqād's overall perspective of Jesus and his mission. Certainly this cannot be found among the previously reviewed Arabic-Muslim works on Jesus which predate *'Abqarīyat al-Masīḥ,* such as those by Abū Zahrah or al-Saḥḥār. If anything, al-'Aqqād wrote his own study as an alternative approach to those more traditionally Islamic presentations. Despite the number of references in the book to Western secondary sources regarding specific points of the discussion, there is no clue which would indicate that a more general work on Jesus was in the background. It is true that there is a reference in ch. 18 to Albert Schweitzer, whose book *The Quest of the Historical Jesus* is well known.[55] However, al-'Aqqād's interest in the famous scholar/missionary has more to do with his ethical perspective than with his discussion about Jesus.[56] Schweitzer's view of Christ's mission was based on his "thoroughgoing eschatology," whereby Jesus preached the imminent arrival of God's kingdom and, when this did not happen, he tried to provoke its coming by sacrificing his own life. This approach contrasts sharply with the way in which al-'Aqqād minimizes the eschatological aspect of Jesus' message, making Schweitzer an unlikely candidate here.

A writer to be considered more seriously is Emil Ludwig, whose book about Jesus, like al-'Aqqād's, was less a biography and more a portrayal of the personality of Christ as a wise teacher.[57] This work, written by a non-specialist from a liberal perspective, emphasizes Jesus' growing sense of his messianic vocation and plays down the miraculous element in his ministry; these are features paralleled in *'Abqarīyat al-Masīḥ.* Ludwig had also written a series of biographical studies on historical figures, and al-'Aqqād apparently utilized his book on Napoleon in ch. 11 (p. 136). That al-'Aqqād was thoroughly familiar with Ludwig's book on Jesus is evidenced in a series of newspaper articles he had written in 1928-29 in response to this work.[58] These articles primarily deal with several topics which are taken up by al-'Aqqād more fully in his book, such as the existence of Christ in history and the title "the Son of Man." In the process of these discussions, however, al-'Aqqād criticizes Ludwig's work on several points. For example, he complains that Ludwig's picture of Christ is too bare and misses the element of majesty; also, Ludwig believes that Jesus the Jew preached only to Jews, whereas al-'Aqqād insists that his message was universal.[59] However, his main objection is that Ludwig wrote about Jesus the man without saying anything about Christ the messenger. At this point, al-'Aqqād makes a remarkable statement:

> The one who has the right to distinguish between these two approaches is the one who is able to introduce better evidence which deals entirely with "the Christ who came with a mission," and not merely with the man from his birth to the end of his days. Such a writer can fill in the empty gaps of that history and reconcile disparate perspectives and interpret what was previously lacking.[60]

It would seem, then, that more than twenty years prior to his writing *'Abqarīyat al-Masīḥ,* the idea of producing such a work was already in al-'Aqqād's mind. Such a long period of gestation cannot be considered unusual for him; as was previously noted, an even longer interval had been required for *'Abqarīyat Muḥammad.* In any case, the impact which Ludwig's book had on al-'Aqqād was clearly much more negative than positive, despite the claim to the contrary by some reviewers.[61] Although the impetus for al-'Aqqād's book about Jesus probably came from Ludwig, the influence for this work must be sought elsewhere.

The source for that influence is almost certainly a work which predates both those of Schweitzer and Ludwig, namely, *La vie de Jésus* by Ernest Renan; its English translation appeared the year before Ludwig's book.[62] The author was a French Catholic who sought to portray Jesus as a romantic revolutionary, yet one who was devoid of any supernatural traits. Based primarily on the Synoptic Gospels and his own imagination, Renan's biography is an attempt at a realistic, indeed vivid, account of Jesus' life. "Renan had written what was virtually a historical novel — not going beyond the materials in the Gospels . . . but always suggesting naturalistic explanations and employing a good deal of conjecture."[63] Evidence that al-'Aqqād knew of this work, and also thought highly of it, is another feature of his 1928-29 articles. In contrast to Ludwig, he states, "Renan is the most adept at creating stories and at combining the facets of the life of Christ in a manner which does not exclude research."[64] His only complaint is that Renan did not attempt to establish the historical existence of Jesus in his book; yet, he asserts, if Renan were alive today, he would most likely expand it to include this issue.[65]

These remarks strongly suggest that Renan's book made a significant impression on al-'Aqqād, one that was to be expressed in his own book several years later.[66] Indeed, many of the themes expressed by Renan also appear in *'Abqarīyat al-Masīḥ*. For example, Renan states that Jesus was born in Nazareth (rather than Bethlehem), was educated in the synagogue there, and grew up in Galilee where "the most diverse elements were seething."[67] He was extremely devout, such that "the highest consciousness of God which has existed in the bosom of humanity was that of Jesus"; this led him to proclaim "the kingdom of God" as an expression of "the revolution which he brought into the world."[68] As opposition grew, he reached out to the Samaritans and Gentiles, finally making a firm break with official Judaism.[69] It is this last point which perhaps is most important in the comparison; "the greatness of Jesus, for Renan, lies in his having given perfect, definitive expression to . . . a universal religion of the spirit, without rites, doctrine, or external forms."[70] The same could easily be said of al-'Aqqād.

Renan's influence on al-'Aqqād was important, but not controlling. Al-'Aqqād parts company with the French author at least regarding the end of Jesus' life, noting (in his Ludwig articles) that Renan accepts the crucifixion, though not the resurrection.[71] Also, al-'Aqqād's book is much less biographical and much more focused on the internal character of Jesus. Thus, although *'Abqarīyat al-Masīḥ* manifests a degree of dependence on Renan and other sources, the picture of Christ which al-'Aqqād paints is distinctly his own.

Al-'Aqqād's Portrait of Jesus

While *'Abqarīyat al-Masīḥ* is not a biography as such, al-'Aqqād expresses a particular concern with respect to the historicity of Jesus, wishing to counter any suggestion that he was not a historical figure. This concern initially surfaces briefly at the beginning of ch. 6, and later forms the main argument in the greater portion of ch. 11 (pp. 135-43). He also posits the questionable argument that the very existence of Jesus' "law of love and conscience" demonstrates the existence of the one who devised it; this law "[leaves] one convinced that it could not have been fabricated" (p. 173). A similar concern had been at the heart of al-'Aqqād's book *Ibrāhīm*, which was "devoted to proving the historicity of Abraham and his connection with the Ka'ba."[72] It may well be that his anxiety displayed there was carried over into *'Abqarīyat al-Masīḥ*, his only other work about a pre-Islamic prophet. In any case, he points the finger especially at those in the school of comparative religion, but he has misunderstood their approach. He believes that their arguments actually deny the historicity of Jesus, when in fact what they tried to demonstrate was that Jesus was merely one factor in the stream of people and events which shaped religion in general and Christianity in particular.

On this matter of the historical Jesus, al-'Aqqād might have done better to stay within the field of biblical studies; among biblical scholars, at least, no one has seriously denied the actual existence of Jesus in history. Rather, their overriding interest, since the end of the eighteenth century, has been with what can be known about his life from the Gospels, since these form virtually the only source for this knowledge. What many of these scholars have doubted is not the Jesus of history, but the Jesus of the Gospels, claiming that these documents tell us more about the doctrines of the early church than about what Jesus actually said and did. This has been the focus of the so-called "Quest of the Historical Jesus," an enterprise which has continued, off and on, up to the present day.[73]

Yet al-'Aqqād shows absolutely no interest in such a quest. Convinced that Jesus did exist, he goes on to accept the canonical Gospels, at least in principle, as reliable sources for his life. He insists that the disciples were not lying when they passed on the words of their Master (p. 208), and that there is no good reason to dismiss the authenticity of the Gospels, even though they were written some years after the fact and in several versions (p. 212). He is willing also to acknowledge the more common postulates of Gospel criticism, such as the existence of "Q" and the interdependence of the Synoptic Gospels (pp. 211-12), and the likelihood that a process of editing occurred in the organization of the parables and the Sermon on the Mount (p. 197).

Also important is what is missing in al-'Aqqād's comments about the Gospels. Nowhere does he give any indication that there was a process of *"taḥrīf"* whereby "corruption" occurred either in the text of the Gospels or in their interpretation. As was noted previously, this has been a common accusation in Muslim polemical works that deal with Jesus, modern as well as classical. Furthermore, *'Abqarīyat al-Masīḥ* contains no reference at all to the "Gospel of Barnabas," which had been promoted by Rashīd Riḍā as an authentic source and utilized by Abū Zahrah in his work about Jesus (see p. 12). In fact, in a subsequent article, al-'Aqqād explicitly rejects the "Gospel of Barnabas" as a reliable source for the life of Jesus.[74] On the one hand, he accepts Riḍā's assertion that the modern document has its origins in a "Gospel" which was attributed to Barnabas in early church tradition (a theory not generally accepted among scholars). However, he believes that the original text was later subjected to considerable alteration during the Middle Ages, thus rendering it unsuitable for historical study. As to the purpose of such alteration, al-'Aqqād's opinion is that this was deliberately made by a writer who wanted to stop the circulation of a document that had been rejected by the church, by conferring it with even greater suspicion. But he is also open to the possibility that it was the work of a Muslim convert who "wanted to bring the book more into line with his new-found faith."[75]

This is not to say that al-'Aqqād accepts the New Testament Gospels categorically. His rejection of the accounts concerning the arrest, crucifixion and resurrection of Jesus is clear evidence to the contrary; these cannot be regarded as historical, he says, but instead belong to "the role of faith" (p. 226). Undoubtedly, he would include in this category other passages which he mentions without comment, such as his reference to statements in Mark and John that point to the "divinity" or the "divine incarnation" of Jesus (p. 213). Furthermore, the discriminating manner in which he selects those texts which support his argument, while leaving aside other relevant material, indicates the ambivalent approach he actually demonstrates with regard to the Gospels. Ultimately, al-'Aqqād's view of the Gospels seems to follow that of his mentor Muḥammad 'Abduh, who had accepted the Gospels as "authentic," but claimed that certain statements in them were misunderstood by the disciples or misinterpreted by later Christians (see p. 12).

In the end, however, al-'Aqqād is not greatly concerned about this problem. His statement on p. 213 is especially revealing:

> We have relied on the Gospels in order to study the life of the Messenger . . . and we have not found any more trustworthy source than these. However, as we have examined them we have pursued a method different from that followed by those who emphasize the historicity of events and reports. . . . Rather, as we have compiled the various events and reports, we have inquired concerning what lies behind these which would elucidate the personality of the Messenger.

Since it is the personality of Christ which is most important for al-'Aqqād, what emerges from his study is a portrait of Jesus where many of the historical elements of the Gospels are either left in the background or ignored altogether.

Other aspects of a historical nature are discussed by al-'Aqqād but are treated in an inconsistent manner. A case in point concerns the birthplace of Jesus. The birth narratives of Matthew and Luke, despite their many differences, agree that Jesus was born in Bethlehem; yet most modern scholars regard Nazareth as the more likely place of Jesus' birth. Al-'Aqqād seems to favor the latter view, but not consistently. Although he gives attention to matters surrounding the *date* of Christ's birth (ch. 11, pp. 133-34), nowhere does he present a sustained discussion concerning the *place* where he was born. In fact, various comments throughout the book concerning this issue are contradictory. Several times in the earlier part of his book, he clearly states that Jesus was born in Galilee (pp. 109, 121 and 129. Apparently his assumption there is that Jesus' birthplace was Nazareth. Later, his discussion in ch. 11 is more ambiguous. The partial quotation there of Lk. 2:1-7 omits the reference to Bethlehem, yet the statement in the text that Mary gave birth in Judea is allowed to stand (p. 133). He then argues that Luke's reference to the census under Quirinius cannot be correct, but he implies that another census was responsible for bringing the family to Judea, where Jesus was born. Al-'Aqqād further complicates the matter in ch. 23. There (p. 217), he refers to the flight of the family from Bethlehem just before Herod slaughtered the infants, as recorded in Mt. 2:13-16. He assumes the veracity of the text, but states his puzzlement as to why the family was there at all, "since they were actually from Nazareth." Nevertheless, he later offers a novel explanation (p. 219): they would have traveled to Bethlehem specifically so that Jesus would be born there, thus fulfilling ancient prophecies concerning the birthplace of the Messiah! It is impossible to reconcile al-'Aqqād's inconsistency on this matter. He seems to want it both ways, to accept the biblical statements as far as he can while also acquiescing to scholarly opinion against the validity of certain points.[76]

Al-'Aqqād's approach also leads to his omission of several important features of Jesus' ministry as presented in the Gospels. What is particularly striking in his presentation is the paucity of interaction between Jesus and other people. Aside from a few references to the presence of the disciples or his opponents or some women, al-'Aqqād's portrait of Christ is mostly abstract. This contrasts sharply with the image of Jesus in the Gospels as one who is constantly on the move, mingling with the crowds, actively involved with admirers and adversaries alike. There, the bulk of Jesus' teaching is connected in some way with the people who surround him, and al-'Aqqād often diminishes the impact of his quotations of Jesus by ignoring the context in which those sayings occur. But the most obvious aspect of Jesus' ministry excluded by al-'Aqqād is his miracles. The constant reference in the Gospels to Jesus healing the sick, casting out demons, and feeding the multitudes is completely lacking in *'Abqarīyat al-Masīḥ*. Al-'Aqqād tries to explain his disregard for the miraculous in ch. 22 (pp. 214-15), where he claims that this is not a necessary factor in appreciating and accepting the message of Christ. In the Gospels, however, that message often goes hand in hand with Jesus' performance of miracles, which serve not only to illustrate but also to effect his teaching about divine forgiveness and reconciliation. Al-'Aqqād's approach was likely due to his desire to find acceptance within the rationalistic world view of modern society, an interest which is also manifest in other Arabic-Muslim works about Jesus.[77] The same tendency is found in many Western studies; yet it is an understatement to say that such an approach does not do justice to the full "genius" of Christ as found in the Gospels.[78]

Al-'Aqqād's rejection of the Gospel accounts concerning the end of Jesus' life is, of course, understandable for him as a Muslim, despite the desire among some reviewers to find a more congenial attitude. However, both the manner in which he discusses this topic and the solution which he proposes are noteworthy. On the one hand, his desire not "to stir up controversy in matters . . . not connected with [our] purpose" (p. 228) lead him to devote only as much space as is necessary to this issue. On the other hand, the substance of his remarks runs the risk of alienating those on both sides of the divide. Christian readers such as Cragg and Anawati find their frustration increased by the offhand manner in which he points out various discrepancies in a few Gospel passages, with no appreciation for how these have been dealt with by Christian scholars. Equally disappointing for them is the way in which al-'Aqqād ignores the many prior references to Jesus' passion in his sayings; this is especially true of al-'Aqqād's presentation of Peter's confession (pp. 203-204), where the Gospels go on to emphasize Jesus' prediction of his death.

However, orthodox Muslim readers, as well, are likely to be disconcerted with the report of Jesus' end which al-'Aqqād proposes in place of the Gospel accounts, that he traveled to India and died there (p. 227). This is the view held by the Aḥmadīyah sect of Islam, which also claims that Jesus was nailed to the cross but did not die there, that instead he lost consciousness and later revived. Most Muslims believe that Jesus was never placed on the cross, but that he was rescued by God from the attempted crucifixion and taken alive into heaven, and that at the end of time he will return to earth. In fact, years earlier in his 1928-29 Ludwig articles, al-'Aqqād had stated his preference for a view of Jesus' crucifixion which advocated a "swoon" theory, similar to that promoted by the Aḥmadīyah sect.[79] In *'Abqarīyat al-Masīḥ*, however, he is silent on this particular point, undoubtedly due to its controversial nature among Muslims and Christians alike.

Nevertheless, al-'Aqqād does not hide his partiality for that aspect in the Aḥmadīyah view related to Jesus' journey to India following the crisis in Jerusalem. While he does not categorically state his acceptance of this divergent view, his reference to a number of "historical" arguments put forward by the Aḥmadīyah leader Muḥammad 'Alī leaves no doubt that he finds it quite feasible. Again, al-'Aqqād had once before discussed at length the possible relationship between Jesus and India, of a different kind, in the fourth of his Ludwig articles, subtitled "Jesus in India."[80] This was a review of the thesis of Russian traveler Nicolas Notovitch, who claimed to have discovered evidence in Tibet that Jesus had journeyed to India as a young man, prior to his ministry in Palestine.[81] In the article, al-'Aqqād expresses doubt about the validity of this story, yet he is clearly intrigued by the possible connection of Jesus with the East. His silence in *'Abqarīyat al-Masīḥ* about this earlier connection with India apparently indicates that he no longer found it worthwhile. Instead, he suggests a connection dealing with the end of Jesus life which at least had been adopted by a minority group of fellow religionists.

Thus, these issues of a strictly historical nature are minimized by al-'Aqqād in favor of a perspective of Jesus which focuses on his message. For him, Jesus is fundamentally a prophet who came with a *da'wah* [call] or *risālah* [message or mission]. He sometimes refers to Jesus with the title of *rasūl* [messenger] in combination with another term reflective of the nature of that mission, e.g., *rasūl al-bashīr* [the messenger of good news] (pp. 157); *rasūl al-raḥmah* [the messenger of mercy] (p. 157); or *rasūl al-ikhā' wa-al-salām* [the messenger of brotherhood and peace] (p. 154). Other terms for Jesus also describe the *activity* of Jesus as a messenger, e.g., *al-murshid al-muṣliḥ* [the one who brought guidance and reform] (p. 174); or *al-mu'allim al-maḥbūb* [the beloved teacher] (p. 199).

Al-'Aqqād is keen to portray Jesus as a "messenger" in the fundamentally Islamic sense of the term. The message he taught could have come "only [through] those religions based on scriptures and on monotheism" (p. 191). Apparently, he felt that this idea was not sufficiently clear to his readers, such that he underscored it in his Preface added to the second edition: the prophetic mission was a "divine phenomenon" which "appeared among the nations only within the Semitic race" (p. 69), in accordance with the perspective of the Qur'ān. Yet nowhere does al-'Aqqād refer to this message as actual revelation from God. Indeed, direct references to God *(Allāh)* in *'Abqarīyat al-Masīḥ* are rare; far more common is his use of *al-ghayb*, indicative of a more remote sense of God's involvement (the word is here translated as "the Divine Mystery"). Like the Old Testament book of Esther, God seems to be relegated to the background. On the other hand, we need not go as far as Wielandt when she states that "prophetic activity is for him really no different from religious genius *('abqarīya)*," or that divine guidance was merely part of the historical process.[82] It is true that al-'Aqqād wishes to emphasize the human aspect in the prophetic role of Jesus as he delivers the urgent message, an emphasis which his more conservative compatriots would find inappropriate. Yet there is sufficient evidence of his assumption that Jesus is sent by divine will, to issue a call that is ultimately God's own invitation. The reality of the divine presence in Jesus' mission is perhaps most evident in al-'Aqqād's portrayal of the inner character of Christ. In addition to several references to Jesus' contemplative nature (e.g., pp. 146, 198), in two extended passages al-'Aqqād especially explores the struggle Jesus faced as he sought to determine the will of God (ch. 12, pp. 148-49; ch. 23, pp. 219-21).

So Christ sets out on his mission. Having chosen the divine *"qiblah"* [direction] in which he would head, he called others to reject selfish ambitions and embrace the same *qiblah*. Al-'Aqqād notes several factors which enabled his message to be effective, including the preparatory mission of John the Baptist (ch. 15), the exceptional ability of the Teacher (ch. 20), and the willingness of the disciples to be taught and trained for their own mission (ch. 21). But al-'Aqqād devotes the most amount of space to the essence of the message, the call itself. Jesus had come not to eliminate the existing Jewish law but to transform it; thus his call emphasized divine forgiveness and the inclusion of women (ch. 16). It focused on the internal dimension of the law in contrast to the external concerns current in the religion of the day; yet because his "law of love" went beyond mere duty, it was even more strict in what it required (ch. 17). He sought to relocate one's ethical center from outward observance to inward motivation (ch. 18); and he proclaimed the Kingdom of Heaven as a spiritual reality existing now in the world (ch. 19).[83]

Present throughout this discussion is the recurrent theme of the human conscience *(al-ḍamīr)*. Several times al-'Aqqād equates Jesus' law of love with the law of conscience (p. 172, etc.). For, he says, the true law of religion "consists of the eternal principles on which the human conscience is based" (p. 172). He also speaks of "the kingdom of the conscience, which lies in the depth of every heart, [which] is more lasting than the kingdoms of this world" (p. 182). And later in the Epilogue, he emphasizes that the quest for freedom of conscience is a never-ending struggle (p. 231). In this regard, al-'Aqqād develops an idea which he had introduced in his book *Allāh*. There he claimed that never before had a messenger raised the value of the human conscience as had Christ, and that Christianity was the first to establish the human conscience as the foundation for the worship of God; furthermore, this was a principle which Islam did not replace but only completed.[84] Nowhere does al-'Aqqād offer a definition of conscience; he seems to regard it as the basis by which a person or society is able to frame an ethical world view and then act on it. Then what is the role of revelation? His statement on p. 232 seems to relegate this to a secondary status: "the world's religions . . . are beneficial to the extent that they entrust values and incentives to the soul; they help people to the degree that they add their share concerning freedom of conscience." Schumann takes al-'Aqqād to mean that conscience is the "source of knowledge," and that the function of revelation is to preserve proper conduct and to strengthen one's faith in that knowledge. Thus, he says, al-'Aqqād's view is similar to 'Abduh's, where revelation has no dominant role to play but merely confirms what is already known.[85] However, Schumann's claim is surely an overstatement at least with regard to 'Abduh, who insisted that revelation was essential because human reason alone could not act as an infallible moral guide.[86] It is probably better in al-'Aqqād's case as well to recognize conscience and revelation going hand in hand, both equally necessary. His emphasis on conscience and his relative silence concerning revelation is rather meant to redress the imbalance he perceives in which religion is followed blindly without recourse to the benefits of reason and conscience.[87]

The blindness of religion as it existed in Jesus' day is another prominent theme in al-'Aqqād's presentation of the message of Christ. His repeated description of the Jewish law as inflexible, hypocritical, and purely external is doubtless rather lopsided; yet he does not far exceed what we find in the Gospels themselves, written as they were when Jewish opposition to the Christian movement continued unabated. His portrayal of Jesus' confrontation with the Jewish leaders and castigation of their traditional ways likewise captures something of the vehemence of his rebuke often found in the Gospels. Al-'Aqqād rightly perceives that this confrontation inevitably led Jesus into a clash with the Jewish religious authorities, and that this opposition continued to increase until it reached a climax during Jesus' last visit to Jerusalem. The manner in which that climax was resolved is, of course, markedly different between the Gospels and al-'Aqqād's version; but this certainly does not negate the intensity of the opposition which he describes.

Al-'Aqqād emphasizes this Jewish opposition partly because he sees in it the key to the transformation of Jesus' message from an exclusive call involving the Jews only, to a universal call that incorporated the Gentiles. Had the Jews welcomed his message, Christianity would have remained just another sect within Judaism, "an ethnic clique" (p. 186). Their rejection prompted Jesus to make the switch. Claiming that John the Baptist had already foreseen this (p. 163), al-'Aqqād focuses on the parable of the Great Banquet, where those who are summoned (the Jews) are rejected after having declined the offer, while those who actually come (the Gentiles) are welcomed (pp. 154-55, 186-87). He sees this parable as exemplary of the shift which Jesus himself made in his own ministry. However, al-'Aqqād fails to recognize that the parable actually envisions a significant response by the less fortunate Jews before the Gentiles are invited and respond (see p. 155, n. 19). Indeed, Jesus' entire ministry according to the Gospels was almost exclusively among his compatriots; the New Testament as a whole portrays the early church (ideally, and to a large extent in reality) as a community in which Jews and Gentiles were equal participants. As noted above (p. 43), al-'Aqqād has overstated his case with regard to the degree in which the Gentile mission was already being promoted by Jesus. Yet his point that such a mission was inherent in Jesus' message is well taken. Indeed, from the perspective of the Gospels, he is right to criticize contemporary authors who allege, at the other extreme, that Jesus had no intention of having his message spread beyond Israel (ch. 2 and 3).[88]

Certain other claims in *'Abqarīyat al-Masīḥ*, which might be questioned, would seem to coincide with al-'Aqqād's stress on Jesus' own mission to the Gentiles: that the Jews of Galilee were rather cosmopolitan, many of them being "Arabs" (p. 131), and that Jesus probably was conversant in Greek (p. 194). Cragg, in noting these features of the book, remarks, "it may be conjectured that he is perhaps anxious to minimize the Jewish elements to Jesus' background."[89] In any case, this focus of al-'Aqqād is the key to appreciating the considerable space which he devotes at the beginning of the book to the social, political and religious context in which Jesus lived and preached. His assessment of the Jewish environment begins on a fair note, with its expectation of the promised Messiah (ch. 4). One wonders, however, if his discussion of the many prophets who appeared in ancient Israel (ch. 5) is perhaps designed to make evident an ongoing resistance of the Jews to divine correction. But it is especially in his long review of the various sects in Judaism (ch. 6) where we see al-'Aqqād's thesis beginning to take form. Although the sects indicate for him that there was a longing for a new prophetic word, they basically serve to demonstrate the legalism and hypocrisy that for him typified Jewish religion in general. Their need for the new call was great; yet they were not able to recognize their need and respond to that call, entrenched as they were within their own tradition.

Al-'Aqqād finds it necessary as well to paint a comparably bleak picture of the Gentile world, one that was just as needy for the new call, yet one in which the response was destined to be positive. In fact, he sees the larger world environment as in many respects more needy than Israel. Roman society was stratified, with the lower class languishing while the upper class lived in decadent opulence (ch. 7). Some people sought vainly for inner peace through the various religions and philosophies of the time, while most settled for the lifeless rituals of pagan ceremonies (ch. 8 and 9). Such a stark portrayal might be considered exaggerated or even distorted by most contemporary historians; but for one such as al-'Aqqād who sought to analyze the very soul of a society, the gravity of this situation was all too evident.

Thus, both the Jewish and Gentile worlds were in need of a call such as that brought by Christ. Al-'Aqqād compares this situation to a disease requiring medicine; the patient may be in *need* of treatment, but not necessarily *ready* to request and receive it. At one point, al-'Aqqād states that this readiness to listen to Christ's message (in addition to standing in need of it) was true of Jews as well as Gentiles (p. 193). But that statement must be considered inconsistent with his general thesis that only the Gentile world responded to the call, because only it was ready to embrace it.[90]

This dichotomy between the reaction of the Jews and that of the Gentiles is carried into al-'Aqqād's remarks about how the message continued to spread through the disciples, after Jesus' role had ended. He admits that the Jews were included in the early mission of the church (pp. 85, 207), but he offers no indication that they made any significant response, as was indeed the case.[91] Nor does he recognize the continuity of the Jewish community beyond the fall of Jerusalem, for "within forty years," he says, "the religion of fanatical self-centeredness collapsed" (p. 228). Instead, al-'Aqqād emphasizes the early spread of Jesus' message among the Gentile world — and here he is more on track.[92] The disciples, having been trained by the Master, are scattered across the Roman Empire where they find their message well received (p. 207). The positive response among the Gentiles demonstrates for him the fact that Jesus actually existed and issued his call (pp. 138-39). Yet the disciples faced opposition as well, just as their Master had. It was incumbent on them that they take a more literal understanding of Jesus' ethical imperatives, since they had devoted themselves to the struggle (p. 180). Their willingness to suffer for the sake of their message was further evidence that they had received it directly from Christ and had been instructed by him to carry it among the Gentiles (pp. 85-86).

Throughout *'Abqarīyat al-Masīḥ*, we find a genuinely favorable attitude towards the disciples. They figure prominently, even though the focus of the book is on Jesus himself, because al-'Aqqād understands that they are intimately involved in his mission. He recognizes that they played an essential role in proclaiming the message to the Gentiles following the mission of Jesus. He even admires them for their depth of conviction and determination to persevere in the face of opposition: "We must pay attention to what they said and believe with their kind of faith" (p. 209). His commendation probably helps to explain the lack of any critical remarks against the disciples, as is often found in Muslim writings on Christianity, where they are sometimes blamed for misunderstanding or even falsifying the message of Jesus. Even Paul is mentioned a number of times by al-'Aqqād without any adverse criticism, despite the statement that he exercised "a degree of accommodation" so that the message could be more readily understood and received by Gentiles (pp. 207-208).[93]

However, there are also hints in the book of a rather different view of Christianity as it came to be expressed following the period of the disciples. Al-'Aqqād claims, for example, that as Gentiles joined the ranks of the faithful, they brought with them certain pagan beliefs and customs; he implies that, over time, this led to an inappropriate syncretism (p. 208). In another brief passage which anticipates his last chapter, he states that if Christ had returned to the earth a few generations later, he would have found it necessary to preach against the crude manner in which his ethical injunctions were being followed (p. 181). But perhaps the most revealing insight into al-'Aqqād's perspective on this issue can be found at the end ch. 20, in which the central role of Jesus himself with regard to his call is emphasized:

> For surely there is no message without a messenger; there is no way to establish Christianity apart from a Christ. The origin of that spiritual message must also be its essence and core, the fundamental basis of its power and effect. Whatever particulars go beyond the original messenger are but offshoots and additions. (p. 199)

Al-'Aqqād says nothing more in this book about what might have constituted those accretions to Jesus' teachings. In other works he is more clear, though still quite brief: there developed a belief in "the divine right of kings," leading to a misunderstanding of religious authority; Christian emperors began to mix politics and doctrine, causing hardship for the people; various schools of thought arose and fostered serious disputes about the unity of God as understood in the Gospels.[94] Yet despite his conviction that the church went astray in these matters, and that Islam came to re-establish proper belief in God and to carry religion to its highest point, al-'Aqqād displays remarkable reticence in offering criticism of the manner in which Christianity developed. This is due to his equally strong conviction that Christianity still preserved the essence of Jesus' message which even Islam has not superseded. One can still fully ascertain within the Gospels the eminent genius of Christ and the majestic power of his message — a message which, for al-'Aqqād, was as relevant for his own day as it was for the first century.

The Book's Contribution to Muslim-Christian Dialogue

There is no clear indication in *'Abqarīyat al-Masīḥ* as to why al-'Aqqād wrote this book. What *is* obvious is his fascination with the personality of Jesus, which went hand in hand with the message he taught. The new *qiblah* proclaimed by that prophet was a radical call to a devout way of life based on the will of God for humanity; but its appeal would have been drastically diminished were it not for the fact that Jesus himself had first chosen that *qiblah.* He struggled with the calling that had been destined for him; but emerging victorious, he called others to follow the same path and taught them how to remain faithful.

Undoubtedly al-'Aqqād sought to convey this personality primarily to his fellow Muslims. The prevalence of Islamic terminology, the occasional reference to passages from the Qur'ān, and above all the presentation of a Jesus who remains within the parameters of Islamic prophethood all point to a Muslim audience. Furthermore, he was writing (as he did with all his works) on a popular level; he did not bother to provide proper footnotes or to verify the accuracy of his statements. Yet, as one reviewer says, "what [the book] lacks in scholarship it makes up for by sympathy and warmth."[95] Jesus was a prophet, asserts al-'Aqqād, who continues to speak with authority and eloquence to the masses of today. At the same time, there is a word from Jesus to the religious elite in Islam who would emphasize rituals and interpretations which only serve to stifle true faith. It is clear that al-'Aqqād was no less patient with the merely external forms of his own religion than he found Jesus to be with his.

On the other hand, al-'Aqqād must certainly have had Christian readers in mind as well. His utilization of the Gospels as his primary source speaks volumes in this regard. Traditional Islamic interpretations of Jesus are all but abandoned while he instead borrows from Western scholarship. He has sought to avoid issues of controversy between the two faiths, and for the most part he has succeeded. He has thus endeavored, as a Muslim, to comprehend the founder of Christianity, and to appropriate for himself the substance of his life and teaching, from within a Christian framework. In the process, he has discovered much that he shares in common with Christian believers.

So it would seem that part of al-'Aqqād's purpose was to build a bridge across the Muslim-Christian divide: to help Muslims hear the Christ of the Gospels speaking to their own religious convictions, while also to help Christians appreciate the degree to which Islam can genuinely embrace the founder of their faith. Al-'Aqqād was probably all too aware of the dearth of existing material on Jesus from either side which sought to encourage a dialogue. Despite its weaknesses, *'Abqarīyat al-Masīḥ* succeeds in breaking new ground for interreligious conversation. Among the many points of contact in this regard, the following key issues that arise from this book, and which continue to be relevant, can be mentioned.

1. No other Muslim work about Jesus has focused on the New Testament Gospels as sources meriting general acceptance, as well as extensive utilization, as has *'Abqarīyat al-Masīḥ.* While al-'Aqqād's blanket recognition of their validity does not manifest itself completely, and although he frequently misreads or misapplies the biblical text, he has made a laudable effort at investigating for himself the Christian scripture with respect and even admiration. He has thus opened a door into a whole new world for Muslim readers. For the vast majority who have never been disposed to cross the divide into the alien environment of the Bible, al-'Aqqād's book provides an insightful, even if partial, representation. It is not only an invitation for them to move beyond this book and read the Gospels for themselves; it is also a challenge for them to move beyond al-'Aqqād's interpretation of Jesus and examine for themselves what the Gospel writers really have to say about the way Jesus understood and carried out his mission. But *'Abqarīyat al-Masīḥ* is equally a challenge to Christians, who are implicitly called upon to treat the scripture of Islam with comparable deference. Although Western scholarship has subjected the Qur'ān to intensive analysis, little effort has been made on the part of Christians to appropriate for themselves some measure of its religious, even spiritual, significance.[96]

2. In *'Abqarīyat al-Masīḥ,* al-'Aqqād demonstrates a remarkable grasp of the radical nature of Jesus' ethical teaching, which he highlights in contrast to conventional Jewish law. He emphasizes Christ's insistence that the essence of religion does not lie in external regulations, but in eternal principles:

> In fact, Christ fulfilled the established law, because he instituted the law of love; and the law of love goes beyond the established law. For that law had committed a person to carry out his duty. But love goes beyond duty; it does not wait to be commanded nor does it wait to be compensated. (p. 172)

It would seem that al-'Aqqād wished to apply this truth to the situation he found in the Egypt of his day. Over against Islamic traditionalism, on the one hand, and Western secularism on the other, he found that the message of Jesus as presented in the Gospels provided a solid religious foundation on which Muslims and Christians could together build a just and peaceful society. Yet this would require a drastic reorientation to the path of God by following the *qiblah* that Jesus introduced. Even though this is a distinctly Islamic term, its focus on prayer captures the sense of movement toward God through utter dependence on the divine will that is fundamental to both faiths. At the same time, al-'Aqqād recognizes in Jesus' call the necessity to respond wholeheartedly. His quotations and comments on various sayings of Christ in ch. 14 ("The Choice of Direction") could almost be read as a passionate plea for Christian discipleship. Following Jesus in his *qiblah* means counting the cost; "you [must] despise yourself and carry your cross" (p. 158 — a striking reference to Jesus' teaching given al-'Aqqād's dismissal of his crucifixion). Muslims and Christians have for some time recognized "ethics" as an appropriate arena for dialogue and cooperation; al-'Aqqād has given added depth to that exchange by focusing on Jesus as the one, for both groups, who provides the model and the mandate for doing the will of God.

3. "The Choice of Direction" (*Ikhtiyār al-Qiblah,* the title of ch. 14) not only epitomizes Jesus' call to others, but also the call which he himself answered. In this regard, al-'Aqqād's presentation of Christ includes a fascinating portrayal of his inner character. He claims that Jesus, like all true prophets, struggled within himself — and with God — concerning the nature and purpose of his mission. More than once, al-'Aqqād reflects on the Temptation of Jesus in the wilderness, where he explores the mystical depths of Jesus' soul as he wrestles with his divine calling. The specific temptations which Christ experienced there, he says, created for him an intense spiritual conflict:

> They leave him standing on the pinnacle of faith and on the brink of hell at the same moment. On the one side, he is enticed by a mission which focuses on the body, on authority, and on making deals in order to gain proofs and signs. On the other side, he is restrained by a mission which focuses on the spirit, on holiness, and on a conviction which does not make deals in order to gain a proof. (p. 220)

Here, we see Jesus the Ṣūfī, engaged in "spiritual exercises" (pp. 148, 220), plunging into the recesses of his conscience as he seeks to ascertain the will of God. Yet we also see Jesus the prophet, beset with the temptation to avoid the difficult and uncertain path, but emerging victorious through the struggle by way of his utter reliance on the God who is in control. Such a portrayal, despite its emphasis on human "genius" more than divine determination, lies firmly within the Muslim concept of prophethood. At the same time, al-'Aqqād has surely grasped here a fundamental dimension of the Jesus portrayed in the Gospels, who was "tempted in every way, just as we are" (Heb. 4:15).

4. Although al-'Aqqād parts company with the Christian faith regarding the crucifixion, as well as in his partiality for the belief that Jesus instead went to India, he still offers some points for discussion concerning the end of Jesus' mission. In the first place, he is fully in agreement with the Gospels that the opposition Jesus faced from the Jewish leaders reached its climax in his last visit to Jerusalem. He is also correct in observing that Jesus' "cleansing of the Temple" was a key event which induced the Jews into resolute action against him. But since al-'Aqqād insists that what happened next cannot be historically ascertained, dialogue on this issue cannot proceed at length from a historical perspective. Nevertheless, *'Abqarīyat al-Masīḥ* does provide material for considering the *theological* dimension of the cross. Prominent here are al-'Aqqād's references to Jesus' prayer, "Let this cup [of suffering] pass from me, oh Father! Yet may it be according to your will, not according to my will" (ch. 23, p. 224; see also in ch. 12, pp. 148-49). Although he is quite aware that this prayer occurred at

the end of Jesus' mission, al-'Aqqād does not mention the specific location and time. According to the Gospels, Jesus prayed these words during his intense inner struggle in the Garden of Gethsemane, which took place *after* the "role of history" ended for al-'Aqqād. Yet he sees in this prayer Jesus' determination to face the ultimate trial, one that the disciples would interpret as utter defeat, but one that God would bring to victory (pp. 224-25). On the one hand, he implies that God answered Jesus' prayer and indeed took away the cup of suffering (p. 149, n. 29). On the other hand, he seems to envision some kind of final confrontation not unlike that which the Gospels say actually took place, and which Christians have subsequently interpreted to be the heart of the Christian message. It can hardly be surprising that al-'Aqqād, as a Muslim, will not admit to the crucifixion as the incident by which God resolved the crisis. It must also be considered extraordinary that he has nevertheless recognized a measure of Christ's passion embodied in the Christian understanding of the crucifixion. Although the event of the cross is absent from *'Abqarīyat al-Masīḥ*, something of its essence still remains.

Al-'Aqqād readily admits that his book is not the final word regarding the person and message of Christ; "there is room for others to offer their own presentations and illuminations from various points of view" (pp. 227-28). Thus, he offers an invitation, evidently to both Muslims *and* Christians, to continue the conversation about the prominent role which Jesus has for Islam as well as for Christianity. Notwithstanding its limitations, *'Abqarīyat al-Masīḥ* continues to deserve consideration from readers who are willing to listen to each other — as well as to the book's main character.

SECTION TWO

TRANSLATION

Preface [1]

Whenever I would consider the list of books which I hoped to find time to write, I would rehearse in my mind some of my ambitions. One of these has been to study the history of the religious call as it was expressed in the missions of its greatest heralds in humanity: Abraham (the Friend of God), and his descendants Moses, Christ, and Muḥammad (peace be upon them).[2]

This divine phenomenon — the prophetic mission — was unique in humanity, something which appeared among the nations only within the Semitic race. That this was inevitable becomes clear from a study of the prophetic vocations which occurred among these Semitic nations.[3]

From a historical perspective, the reason for this occurrence is obvious to us through an extensive study of comparative religion. It is that the great prophetic vocations were linked to the trading towns, for these offered an intermediate environment between civilization and nomadic life. Such towns were Ur, Baalbek, Jerusalem, Mecca, Yathrib,[4] Madyan,[5] as well as the travel stops in the south of Palestine and the north of the Hejaz. The environment offered by these places regarding legislation was comparable neither to urban civilization, which operated according to the state system, nor to desert nomadic life, which operated according to the custom of blood revenge and subjugation. Rather, these trading towns were intermediate between the two extremes; in their case, it was necessary for laws to be determined at any given moment, so that the intricacies of mutual relations and the repeated visits of itinerant travelers would continue. From these travelers the townspeople gained revenue and sought transient entertainment. In the process, each of them endeavored to defeat his companion in the marketplace of give-and-take and in the arena of deception and pretense.

For this reason, the trading towns were looking for a source of guidance which was neither bureaucratic law, nor the revenge and mastery which occurred between usurper and usurped, aggressor and victim. Rather, this source was the prophetic guidance located within this intermediate environment. They were ready for this guidance with the kind of zeal found among those who live in the desert. They recognized that mutual agreement and the bond of trust were valuable for every far-reaching relationship, such as the relationship which linked the caravans as they traveled back and forth across great distances.

Thus I was rather fortunate, and quite happily so, to be guided to the wisdom of this phenomenon in my writing of the biographies of Abraham (the Friend of God), and of Muḥammad and Christ (peace be upon them). Each of these biographies appeared at an appropriate time, as is evident by how each has been well received. There was an intense desire for them not only on my part, but also in general among Arabic readers of various persuasions and creeds. It seems to us that this interest has been demonstrated by the reception of these three books — a reception which has surpassed that of any other recent book,[6] from what we have ascertained in the last few years.

The present edition of this book should have appeared before now. However, this most recent interval has been teeming with publications and archaeological reports to be considered,[7] and this is something which has delayed every historian of Christ and of the era in which he issued his call. Hopefully this renewed investigation will add to the historical study of the herald and his call. At least it can be expected to confirm some ancient matter which still requires either confirmation or revision.

Prologue

The Blessed Tree [1]

In the Name of God, the Gracious, the Beneficent[2]

> Allah is the Light of the heavens and the earth. The similitude of His light is as a niche wherein is a lamp. The lamp is in a glass. The glass is as it were a shining star. (This lamp is) kindled from a blessed tree, an olive neither of the East nor of the West, whose oil would almost glow forth (of itself) though no fire touched it. Light upon light, Allah guideth unto His light whom He will. And Allah speaketh to mankind in allegories, for Allah is Knower of all things. (*Sūrat al-Nūr* 35)[3]

> He it is Who produceth gardens trellised and untrellised, and the date-palm, and crops of divers flavour, and the olive and the pomegranate, like and unlike. Eat ye of the fruit thereof when it fruiteth, and pay the due thereof upon the harvest day, and be not prodigal. Lo! Allah loveth not the prodigals. (*Sūrat al-An'ām* 141)[4]

> He it is Who sendeth down water from the sky, whence ye have to drink, and whence are trees on which ye send your beasts to pasture. Therewith He causeth crops to grow for you, and the olive and the date-palm and grapes and all kinds of fruit. Lo! herein is indeed a portent for people who reflect. (*Sūrat al-Naḥl* 10, 11)[5]

> By the fig and the olive, by Mount Sinai, and by this land made safe. (*Sūrat al-Tīn* 1-3)[6]

> Let man consider his food: how We pour water in showers, then split the earth in clefts, and cause the grain to grow therein, and grapes and green fodder, and olive-trees and palm-trees, and garden-closes of thick foliage. (*Sūrat 'Abasa* 24-30)[7]

The "blessed tree" of revealed scripture is none other than the olive tree.[8] It is the tree of the everlasting sea, the tree of the Mediterranean basin upon whose shores human civilization originated and around which it turns unceasingly. Its height is a lofty five fathoms,[9] and it grows even beyond that. It can flourish for five centuries without becoming depleted.

It is a precious tree which provides sustenance by its fruit, the goodness of its nourishment which is craved by all. It is a favored tree which provides from its juice light, medicine, and perfume for hides.[10] From its wood it provides splints for broken bones,[11] designs for prayer niches, and supports for pulpits. From its leaves it provides wreaths for champions and heralds of glad tidings. Its blessing was evident among the ancient heroes who anointed themselves with its goodness, seeking strength of body and soul as they entered the contest and vied with each other. Its blessing was evident once again when they proclaimed peace, raising aloft the olive branch!

The olive tree has been revered because of the inspiration it bestows in temples and in hearts. It has been revered through the symbols produced by people's talents and ideas. For whatever people have longed for, they have found it symbolized in the grandeur and prestige of the olive tree. Whenever they mention some little pleasure, they speak of its grace. The olive tree has become the symbol for light, peace, goodness and prosperity. It is the source of sustenance whether in the desert or the metropolis. It is stored up for the present world as well as the world to come. It is utilized for the lamps in the niches used for prayer and praise. And they refer to the olive tree when they speak the most sacred of names, the very name of "Christ."

It so happened that this Olive Tree originated in Palestine and from there it spread to the gardens of the universe. In this way it bestowed its anointing authority[12] on the Faithful Messenger.[13] And so his message roamed wherever it would; beginning in heaven, its clear proclamation fulfilled its destination.

Thus the "olive tree," precisely because this blessed name goes back to the anointing and blessing which it bestowed, has become worthy of eternal bliss, full of green leaves for years and centuries.

Part One
The Discoveries of Wadi Qumran

Chapter 1

In Wadi Qumran[1]

It is said metaphorically at times that a certain event would come to pass whenever this or that well-known sign of the zodiac would appear. If we might be allowed to borrow such a manner of speaking, we would say that within the domain of religious thought, the few years preceding the middle of the twentieth century were a period overshadowed by the "sign" of the investigations and studies concerning the history of Christ. In particular, the scrolls which were discovered in early 1947, as well as the commentaries, debates and rejoinders which have ensued, have finally been brought together into a library brimming with religious and historical tomes. I now have in front of me an outline added to the end of one of these books which fills fifteen large pages.[2] This contains only the names of the books and articles dealing with these newly-discovered scrolls which have appeared since 1947, excluding books and articles by scholars who wrote about Christ apart from this subject, and who never intended to investigate these discoveries or to make a connection between them and their research on the life of Christ.

I am quite aware that the scrolls were discovered back in early 1947; but also that ongoing circumstances have prevented any research on them or any exploration of what is left. This is because they were discovered in Wadi Qumran which is part of Transjordan, and at that time the Palestinian problem had become very serious so that it precluded any peaceful research or safe exploration in that vicinity.[3] The news of these significant discoveries had not been followed up by any details or meaningful report, until after investigations on them and attention to their study had resumed around 1952; that was the year in which I first wrote my book concerning "the genius of Christ."[4]

When I learned about these scrolls from Wadi Qumran, I suspended the reprinting of this book until I could gain a sufficient opportunity to become acquainted with their contents. I had hoped to utilize whatever hidden treasures of history which they might yield from such an examination. For at that time these scrolls were said to have contained a complete book from the Old Testament, commentaries on other books, and a booklet full of commandments and instructions concerning proper behavior.[5] These were said to have originated among a religious group whose rites and religious observances were similar to those of the first Christians.

Thus there was a delay in the completion of the matter[6] which was subject to the outcome of my examination of the Wadi Qumran scrolls. But this did not necessarily prevent me from continuing with my research in the prophetic mysteries, such as those which arose in the eras of Abraham and of Moses. For us, the investigation into these mysteries concerning the era of Abraham begins at the very beginning, and it brings us close to the emergence, indeed the very earliest sources, of these mysteries. The study of the prophetic activity in the era of Moses introduces other eras of prophetic activity involving tens or even hundreds of prophets in succession. But the history of Moses might also be closely connected to the history of the Wadi Qumran scrolls, if indeed some of them contain, as has been claimed, books from the Hebrew Bible along with fragments from the five well-known books called "the Books of Moses."[7] The discovery of copies of these books, along with the resumption of their examination, had raised expectations among archaeologists and theologians. Because of this, I preferred to postpone the writing about Moses (peace be upon him),[8] and instead I began to write about Abraham, entitling my book about him "The Father of the Prophets." In fact I completed the details of my research, establishing decisively that the trading towns offered the best environment for the reception of the prophetic mission. For Abraham had successive relationships with each of the large trading towns of his time as he journeyed from Ur to the vicinity of Baalbek, Jerusalem and the towns along the route between Sinai and the Hejaz. These towns form a chain of clear witnesses which direct our attention to this truth, and their nearly equivalent representations reveal it with perfect clarity.[9]

As for the re-publication of this book, which I had placed in suspension as long as there were new resources calling for my investigation, this still depended, around the year 1953, on three concerns: most importantly, the scrolls of Wadi Qumran; and pertaining to them, the revised translations of the Old and New Testaments in Western languages; and also pertaining to them, an unceasing torrent of publications in that same year, offering both religious and non-religious reflections about Christ from a modern, post-World War II perspective.[10]

* * *

We had already read in journals and reports that the Wadi Qumran scrolls include the following: a complete copy of the book of Isaiah;[11] a legible, mostly intact copy of a commentary of the prophecies of Habakkuk (which subsequent events have confirmed); fragments from a commentary on the book of Micah;[12] a narrative entitled "The Story of the War between the Sons of Light and the Sons of Darkness";[13] hymns arranged for supplication and prayer;[14] an Aramaic copy of a book which was not among the authorized books of the Hebrew Bible;[15] miscellaneous scraps from diverse books appended to the Old Testament;[16] and a detailed copy of a book about proper behavior which was observed among the group of ascetics who had resided for some time in the secluded settlement of Wadi Qumran.[17] All of these scrolls had been placed in large clay jars, most of which were found in some adjacent caves, and it was obvious from this that they might contain deposits of this kind. The scrolls are generally considered to be of inestimable value by archaeologists, scholars of comparative religion, and a large number of theologians.

Now if anyone wanted to gain a thorough grasp of the books and reports which in the last five years have dealt with the scholarly questions concerning these scrolls, he would not be able to deal with them all, even if he were to devote all his time to this. It is sufficient for the Arab reader to know that these studies have investigated every aspect involved with the scrolls concerning matters of religion, philology, history, archaeology, chemistry and production. Not a single contemporary Western language is devoid of such studies. The investigations have dealt with questions of spelling and principles of writing, the combination of different dialects and languages, and the components of the paper, leather, ink and adhesive, as well as the drying process. They also deal with the names of key figures and matters concerning their titles, characteristics, and connections with national and tribal histories; matters of geography, meteorology and astronomy; the origins of the creeds and the rituals of the worship services. The studies deal with each period of time, whether it happened to be one that was original in itself or was borrowed from another, and they utilize only the technical terms which are associated with each specific period. The scope of the research extends to the outermost limits, even to constructing models of buildings and manufacturing earthen vessels. They cover such customs as eating, drinking, dress, dietary ingredients and crop yield. Estimates of the time in which these people lived vary from the fifth century B.C.E. to the first century C.E. And there has been no consensus in the research even after all of this accumulation and scrutiny and firm resolve to be precise.[18]

It is quite evident that we will never assimilate this deluge of publications which overflow with assumptions and contradictions. In any case, these studies present issues which must be either re-examined or relinquished, some of which must be treated skeptically, others favorably. We can never appreciate how much study and investigation would be required in order for us to retrieve something towards a new account of the history of Christ. However, we shall proceed to a particular matter mentioned in the more reliable books which discuss the main issues. It summarizes the heart and scope of the controversy concerning the ramification of every issue within these books. We have derived from this particular matter the essential point which we had sought ever since it had interested us. This essential point is that the novelty of the situation at that time was precisely in the work of Christ, that is, in his innovative victories in the spiritual world. For every comparison between him (peace be upon him) and the religious institutions before his time ends up with merely external similarities. Such comparisons do not point to anything prior to him which deserves credit for initiating the tenets of the religion which followed him.[19]

Among the conclusions given in most of these investigations and discussions, perhaps the one which has the most in its favor is that the residents of the Qumran community were a group of "Essenes."[20] This sect was one of those which were strict in their regard for religious regulations and which fully expected their immanent salvation when the promised Messiah would appear. This was the sect which we had mentioned in the first edition of *The Genius of Christ.* We said that its significance lay in being the Jewish sect which had most emphasized purification from the filth of greed and lust. We wrote then that "The Essene community was organized along three ranks. . . . Each person would take a one-time oath of fidelity, promising to preserve the secrecy of the group. He was prohibited from making any further oath, whether in sincerity or in pretense, for the rest of his life. . . . There was no leadership or domination among them. . . . Material possessions were for them the source of all evil; to take pleasure in them was to indulge in filth and treachery. . . . There was a brotherly association among them, and they used to journey together in pairs. . . . They believed in the Day of Judgment and in the Resurrection, and in the mission of the Messiah-Savior. They were convinced that salvation entailed a spiritual resurrection which would guide the people into a life of integrity and righteousness."[21]

We also spoke of the Essenes in the course of our discussion about a group in Egypt called the "Therapeutae."[22] We said that these Therapeutae might have been the mentors of the Jewish ascetics called "Essenes,"[23] as reported by certain historians. For we considered it most likely that the name given by the word *āsī* could have the meaning "physician," as this is comparable to the Greek word *therapeutai,* which can have the meaning "those who give medical treatment."[24]

* * *

If it is true that the group in Wadi Qumran was affiliated with the Essenes, then it is truer still that their secluded locality was none other than the desert in which both Christ and John the Baptist had taken refuge.[25] Indeed the novelty of the Qumran discovery is that it confirms the necessity of the mission of Christ. That is, it confirms the superiority of the messianic call for reforming the beliefs of the people, even though, as I had learned, such beliefs were in their most advanced and pure state among the followers of the Jewish sects prior to the first century B.C.E.[26]

The Essene writings which were found in the settlement of Qumran portray for us their organization as a group, their regulations concerning proper behavior, and the intensity of their aspiration to follow the religious ceremonies which had been handed down among their nation. However, they were still afflicted by the disease of the nation which had reached its peak during that period. This was the disease of rigidity concerning the literal interpretation of texts, and of the departure from the essence of doctrine and the core of faith. Indeed, the Essene sect itself demonstrated a greater need for reform than was the case for other more questionable or extremely obscure sects. For these latter experienced their reformation through those who were rightly guided[27] among the members of the existing religion, and every Jewish sect which deviated from the straight path found some who would correct it from those within the scope of Judaism who were knowledgeable of its orthodox standards. On the other hand, the need for reform was absolutely established whenever the sect had reached the limit of what it could attain, when it had depleted all capacity for its own refinement, purification, devotion and reflection, and yet after that it was incapable of providing its soul with what it yearned for and was in need of.[28]

Such was the sect of the Essenes, whatever its name or objective, revealed in the Wadi Qumran scrolls. It was prepared for the mission of Christ precisely in the way that a patient is prepared to receive his treatment or a disease its medication.[29] There is no doubt that the newly discovered scrolls will be a useful storehouse of information concerning this matter. But they will add nothing to our knowledge of the facts of Christ's mission, nor will they bring out for us anything new concerning this mission, other than the confirmation of its superiority and necessity in its time.[30] Whatever might have been the goal of the Essene sect, it continued to be, in its various manifestations, a remnant vigorously maintaining its legacy. It looked to its past, waiting and hoping for a new day in which it anticipated the savior who had been promised in the ancient prophecies.[31] The call of Christ was of necessity directed to this harmful affliction — the affliction of fundamentalism in worship ceremonies and texts. This mission taught the people what they needed to learn whenever they sank into the stagnant abyss of lifeless literalism and petrified formalities. It taught them that doctrine is a matter of the mind and the conscience, not one of literalism and formality. This was the mission of Christ in that era, which was contaminated as much by rigidity as by hypocrisy. For hypocrisy was in fact internally rigid, even while externally it was a façade.

Chapter 2

Evaluations on the Philosophy of History[1]

We now proceed from summarizing what has transpired from the recently-discovered scrolls to summarizing what has transpired in the discussion (or rather, the lengthy discussions) concerning the revised English translation of the Old and New Testaments.[2]

When we heard the news of this revised translation (after we had heard of the discovery of the scrolls), we had hoped that the loud clamor which arose concerning a particular passage in the Old Testament book of Isaiah would be restrained.[3] We had thought that those who worked on the revised translation would have referred to the new text in the Wadi Qumran scrolls, since Isaiah was found as a complete book among the scattered remnants comprised by the scrolls.[4] However, when we were informed with sufficient clarity of the work of the revisers, we found nothing in it which would indicate a relationship between the recent discoveries and the revision of the current translation,[5] particularly among the Old Testament books.[6] For a loud clamor had broken out, concerning this passage in Isaiah, between those who supported its revision and those who opposed it. This came as no surprise to the theologians, as if they had been unaware of the difference of opinion; yet they made no attempt to take sides with either of the opposing parties.

The argument in question has to do with a verse in the seventh chapter of Isaiah, translated as follows: ". . . The Lord himself will give you a sign. Behold, the virgin will become pregnant and will give birth to a son, and she will call his name Immanuel."[7] This passage appears in the revised English version with the phrase "a young woman" as an equivalent for the Hebrew word *'alāmah,* and the Greek word *bārānthūs* in the Septuagint.[8]

There is nothing new in this dispute, for it has always been present among the three schools of thought whose research revolves around the interpretation of what is meant by the "virginity"[9] of Mary, the mother of Christ (peace be upon him). Among the adherents of these Christian schools are those who interpret this as a Perpetual Virginity both before and after the birth of Christ. Others maintain that Mary's virginity existed prior to his birth, but that she later bore other sons as his brothers, and that allusions to them are echoed in the books of the New Testament. Still others go back to the Hebrew wording of this text and they do not speak of the word "Virgin" as noted above.[10] Those who advocate the Perpetual Virginity of Mary have responded to those who cite references to Christ's brothers in the New Testament, claiming that these are only paternal cousins, i.e. "brothers" having some relation to Joseph, Mary's fiancé.[11] And so this old-new dispute goes on.

We had been aware of the details of this dispute when we first wrote *The Genius of Christ,*[12] but we did not deal with it at that time. Nor did we deal with any of the research in regard to this, except what was firmly connected to the mission of Christ within the domain of spiritual guidance.[13]

Likewise, we had said nothing about the meaning of the phrase "the brother of the Lord" which is appended to the name of "James"[14] (equivalent to *Ya'qūb* in Arabic). We had written simply that he is "James the relative of Christ."[15] Some critics have assumed that we referred to him in this way because we had not examined the Arabic translation of the New Testament. They certainly have been quick to criticize this issue without any careful reflection. Although they think it virtually impossible, they would realize from reading *The Genius of Christ* that we have opened the two Testaments at least a hundred times in order to investigate them in our research and to utilize them in our quotations. The appropriateness of our discussion should now be clear concerning why this reference stands in spite of its weakness. Nor is there any need for us to express any opinion about the "misreading" of *Jayms* for the word *Ya'qūb,* or to settle the matter conclusively concerning this passing reference which has no valid place among the more important details of this book.[16]

Perhaps there is some compatibility of timing between the clamor over the revised translation and the clamor over the scrolls excavated from Wadi Qumran. The renewed discussion about the book of Isaiah finds itself in both of these commotions. Thus we were inspired to wait and see what was behind the clamor over the translation, just as we were inspired to wait and hear from those behind the clamor over the recently-discovered scrolls. We had thought that there might well be within these texts and documents some matter which should be reconsidered in the re-writing of *The Genius of Christ.* But without this appreciation for the scrolls, the dispute over the interpretation of the virginity of Mary would never by itself have been a reason for our waiting until after the end of the discussion. Since all sides of this dispute have been known for a long time, it was among those matters whose origins we could have investigated before re-writing this book about Christ.[17]

* * *

Nevertheless, after five years since the first edition appeared we now raise the question: Why do we have no qualms about proceeding with the re-publication of this book without first examining the latest books in Western languages about Christ and his mission? For these books have continued to appear one after another, and contemporary authors have reflected on this mission, both as it appeared in Christ's time and also in subsequent periods.

We proceeded slowly in the last five years with the publication of the current edition because we believed that the revised translation of the Bible might offer reasons which would require a re-examination and reconsideration of certain issues. So today we ask: do you think that even if we had been aware at that time of the pivotal issue in the clamor over the translation, that it was a recurring subject in a well-known problem — would this have been reason for us to take lightly the effusive deluge of books and reports written on a subject similar to ours, and from a perspective which interests us, whether their contents were in conformity or in contrast to our point of view?[18]

We believe that our work in examining only a portion of these books was sufficient for allowing our previous observations to stand as they are. Thus we can now publish this book again, at least being confident of the results of our perseverance. For if our examination of these recent books were to alter our views about any passage in this book, then it would have been appropriate to wait and gain the benefit. But if such an examination were to make no modification of our perspective, then our confidence is commendable, and we have neglected nothing because of this perseverance.

Fortunately, we can now say that our examination of these recent books was a very enjoyable reading experience. They please us as ordinary readers, and then also as authors. Within this literature there is the fat and the lean, the superior material and everything else, just as in all literature. But it is only right that we should be thankful for the good fortune in treating some of this material exhaustively. For the lean books are the kind whose leanness becomes evident when leafing through them after becoming acquainted with a few lines here and there. On the other hand, the fat books contain enough subject matter to compensate for whatever time and effort is expended by the reader.

It is possible for us to place these valuable books into two broad categories. One is the category of contemplation, including philosophical reflection and sentimental ideas. The other is the category of historical criticism and scientific analysis according to the principles of comparative religion.

With respect to the first category, the reader would undoubtedly be happy to learn about the opinion of the contemporary philosopher regarding the teachings of Christ as compared to the teachings of Nietzsche in the modern period; or to learn about his opinion regarding the teachings of Christ as compared to the teachings of Karl Marx and his followers the materialists. Or he might learn about the similar and contrasting aspects between the approach of Christ in reforming humanity and the approaches of the politicians and propagandists of society in recent centuries. Or he might learn about the eloquence of Christ's words at a time when they are being associated with the words of eloquent speakers among the masters of common rhetoric and conventional wisdom. These and similar issues form the central thesis in many of these contemporary books; occasionally there is some consistency in that their titles indicate their objectives. However, we do not believe that the research for this book of ours requires us either to expand on them or to condense them in summary fashion. The most we will say about them is that they are like various pictures of the same face but in many frames. Although there is no room here to summarize them, there is room for anyone who wishes to add to this literature.

On the other hand, the books which we place into the category of historical criticism and scientific analysis actually contain material of interest to the person who wishes to investigate the history of Christ's mission. They include studies which unquestionably deserve lengthy consideration and careful examination. Their entire subject matter should be encountered within its broad field and from all aspects. Yet no one is able to encounter this broad range unless he were fully prepared with respect to the sources and documents.

Because it would take so long, it would be useless to enumerate here the names of the works and the authors among these critical investigations. But after having become acquainted with some of this material, we found that something of their essence cannot escape the reader when he examines two books in particular. These two encompass all the contradictions and statements, which must become subject to either approval or rejection, found in all the studies. We refer to the two books, written in English, entitled *The Other Side of the Story* by Rupert Furneaux, and *The Nazarene Gospel Restored* by Robert Graves and Joshua Podro.[19]

We will set aside the fabricated conjectures which pervade these two books. For we ought to mention at the outset that they contain many conjectures and that now and then these go astray. The authors concede that they have forced these conjectures in order to complete the non-existent links in a particular chain of events. They formulated this chain from the remnants of documents which have been missing since the first century C.E., and from what their imaginations have produced to complete deficient passages which might be considered objectionable among the gaps in these documents.[20] We would not forget that one of these authors, Robert Graves, is a novelist. As such, he relies on his artistic creativity by which he accommodates his information into an orderly account of the story's features, and by which he perceives harmony among all kinds of personalities.

Graves had also written a novel on the same theme entitled *King Jesus,* in which he set forth in narrative fashion his theory about the historical nature of the life of Christ.[21] The gist of the theory is that Christ had grown up in the custody of a secretive group which had been working to hasten their salvation through the work of a king called "the Messiah."[22] He would come from among the descendants of David and would deliver God's chosen people. Graves further claimed that John the Baptist had been the one entrusted to choose the anticipated Messiah according to the signs which were preserved in the prophecies. Thus John had chosen him, pledging himself to him and paying him homage as "king" and Messiah, meaning someone anointed with sacred oil according to the ancient custom of choosing kings.[23] None of the leaders of the Temple had been aware of this secretive pledge, which combined an oath of fidelity along with one of obedience. So the overseers of the group took it upon themselves to fulfill this pledge, being wary of the authority of Rome and that of the Temple at the same time. Events then follow the course which we know from the Gospels, and Graves goes beyond them here and there, providing links which make the connection between the outward and inward aspects of history. The author put this all together from his documentary sources as well as from inspired imagination, i.e., his artful arrangement and presumed ideas. And perhaps he added here and there a segment drawn from authentic material.

We set aside these conjectures, putting as much effort in deleting them as the novelist did in adding them. However, we do not want to delete them whenever they leave behind a void which is even more likely to lead to confusion and indecision regarding the evidence.

The best of what remains after deleting these conjectures is that the Christian mission[24] after Christ derived from two centers.[25] One was under the leadership of James (i.e., *Ya'-qūb),* called "the brother of the Lord,"[26] who resided in Jerusalem. The other was under the leadership of Paul the apostle and his followers who resided outside of Palestine far from the authority of the Jewish Temple. The Jerusalem contingent was more inclined to comply with and aspire to the rituals of the Old Testament. They had a prominent standing in the Christian world, both within Palestine and beyond it throughout the Roman Empire. This is evident from the injunctions promulgated by the Jerusalem Christians and from the response against them from the Christians living outside of the city. All of these injunctions promoted the compliance to the Jewish rituals as they were presented in the Old Testament prophecies.

Leadership over the Christian world remained closely tied to this contingent residing in Jerusalem until the Temple was destroyed and the city was demolished, and the Christian community there was scattered across the regions of the Empire. The leadership of the mission then reverted to the contingent which had been working outside of Palestine, and this resulted in a large impact on the style of mission and on the choice of the means of persuasion. Thus there developed two different styles: preaching addressed to the Jews only, and preaching addressed to the Gentiles who had an aversion to the Jews. On the one hand, the matter was settled for the Jews that salvation would come from a single person within Israel, and that this deliverance was for themselves only. On the other hand, the outside world was in need of a messenger-savior who possessed divine characteristics which would be accepted by the Gentiles. By accepting these characteristics, they would not be bound by the conditions and tokens adhered to by those who clung to the letter of the law.[27]

Now the Gospels were being written at about the same time as when the Temple was destroyed, when the contingent residing in Jerusalem became scattered. The standards of the mission were made clear in these Gospels just as this mission was being taken over by those who proclaimed it in the Gentile world. But within the Gentile mission, the divine characteristic of Christ prevailed over any other characteristics which were heard within the Temple walls, before there was an urgent need to record the Gospels.[28] So these authors go to great lengths in repeating passages from the Gospels which demonstrate Christ's adherence to the books of the Torah, and how his exhortations to the disciples were in conformity with them according to the conventions of the Pharisees. The best known of these passages include what he says to the disciples and the crowds as found in chapter 23 of the Gospel of Matthew: "The scribes and the Pharisees sit on Moses' seat; so observe and learn[29] everything they tell you to observe. But do not practice their deeds; for they preach but they do not practice." From this passage they move on to what he says as found in chapter 5: "Do not think not that I have come to abolish the law or the prophets; I have come not to abolish but to fulfill. For truly I say to you, until heaven and earth pass away, not one letter or one dot will pass away from the law until all is accomplished." And from this to what he says as found in chapter 10: "Do not go anywhere among the Gentiles, and do not enter the town of the Samaritans, but go rather to the lost sheep of the house of Israel." And from this to what he says as found in chapter 15: "I was sent only to the lost sheep of the house of Israel."[30] And they go on to other sayings whose meaning is to be understood in a similar way to what is said in these passages, even though their explicit wording might not be understood as such.[31]

Chapter 3

Response and Critique [1]

It is our opinion that the authors who hold this theory can dispense with the trouble and inconvenience of re-interpreting the words of Christ, or of investigating hidden documents. Instead, they ought to limit themselves to establishing that the Christian mission[2] began by directing its message to the nation which was subject to the Torah and which expected the Messiah-Savior to appear from among its own people. They can also dispense with the trouble and inconvenience of trying to prove that those who carried out the mission to the Gentiles adopted a missionary method different from that agreed upon by the Jewish Christians who believed in the various prophecies which they read in their books; or of trying to prove that the messengers of the Christian mission to the Gentiles attributed characteristics to Christ which he did not attribute to himself according to his words as reported in the Gospels.[3]

There is no need for all of these authors to go to such trouble and inconvenience to contrive evidence concerning Christ from the substance of his sayings or from the hidden passages of forgotten documents. For these authors who hold such theories greatly overburden their proofs when they try to deny that the mission to the Gentiles had begun in the time of Christ; or when they try to deny that the disciples and apostles had learned from him that they were to include the Gentiles in this mission and that in the end they were not to restrict this mission to the Jews. There is nothing which is repeated more often in the passages of the Gospels, and in reasonably appropriate situations, than these reports. The Gospels present in these reports nothing but the natural outcome which is reinforced by the course of events, and from which the logic of things seeks its inspiration (as we say in our modern terminology). For what do we observe in the activity of Christ after his own people insisted on rejecting his call?[4] That he was re-directed by his mission to another group, and that he gave up his mission to the Jews and resolutely turned away from it; and that the disciples and apostles also turned away from that mission, and they were re-directed by it to the Gentiles rather than to Israel.[5]

The authors who hold this theory must surely be aware that the apostles who brought Christianity to the Gentiles were heralds who endured the greatest suffering for its sake. They were the ones who remained steadfast in this suffering after the heralds of Christianity who were in Jerusalem became scattered. It was incumbent on those who did this that they should believe the message to which they called others, and that their range of doctrine should not be such that they employ stratagems in order to entice their listeners, using some method which was not customary among the Jews. Whatever may have been the source of this doctrine, the apostles who proclaimed it to the Gentiles had accepted it before they called others to accept it, and they had confidence in it before they enabled others to have confidence in it.[6]

Moreover, we do not find it strange that these authors have provoked a commotion by their innovations. For in these they have relied on their "historical" documents or on their method of supplementing history by arranging artistic representations inspired by their natural disposition or their imagination. Nevertheless, we have considered the matter seriously regarding the picture of Christ's mission which had presented itself to us when we brought together our thoughts and findings for the writing of this book. Yet we conclude that these authors have given us no insight into a novel concept which might lead us to modify anything essential. Thus we now celebrate this re-publication as happily as when we first published it, having made no modification worth mentioning except by way of correcting some typographical and spelling errors.

We were already happy to encounter expressions of appreciation from our readers which gave us much delight. Indeed, anyone who has ventured to write specifically about this magnificent subject would be delighted with such acknowledgment. We are not aware that the procedure we followed in writing about Christ met with disapproval from anyone, which either the writer or the reader should regard as meaningful criticism. The only criticism to be found is from some who think that our writing about Christ required us to profess Christianity or to profess all its schools of thought at the same time. Yet when we wrote about Brahma, no one said that we should have been Brahmanists, or when we wrote about the religions of the world that we should have been converting from one religion to another.[7] If this were incumbent on anyone making such an investigation, then neither the histories of these religions nor of their heralds would be written, either by those who agree on the one religion or by those who do not.[8] If this were necessary, then only Easterners would write about the East and only Europeans about Europe. No one would write about the past except someone who experienced it, and no one would write about the future except someone who would be born within it. None of these supposed conditions are necessary in making any meaningful critical judgment.

In fairness to the large majority of readers, we would say that they are far more numerous, inasmuch as this minority of critics should be considered in comparison to the majority to be one in a thousand, let alone one in a hundred. However, the majority will encounter the minority in varying proportions within diverse branches of historical-religious studies. Thus, it may be that we wrote a discussion about the first four Caliphs[9] which did not please members of the Shī 'ites, while we wrote a discussion about Mu'āwiyah ibn Abū Sufyān[10] which did not please anyone else. But there is a lesson from such readers who find some things agreeable and other things incompatible: they would not be satisfied even if the writer provided them with a copy of what is already in their hearts and minds. As we have offered these readers the first edition of this book, so we now offer this second edition with the title *The Life of Christ,* seeking God's blessing.[11]

Part Two
The Messiah in History

Chapter 4

The Messiah

The science of comparative religion demonstrates the diffusion of belief in salvation and in the future appearance of a messenger-savior. It is evident from the beliefs of the American Indians that not a few tribes on both continents held to this belief.[1] This is not surprising, since the anticipation that things will get better is one of the roots of religion, and the hope for righteousness is one of the components of human life which the Creator placed in the conscience of all those He created. In this way, He provided the means by which they could search diligently for perfection and salvation from their shortcomings.

This hope would usually intensify when the need for it became stronger. Thus the early Egyptians looked for a savior who would deliver them after their ancient nation would come to an end. J. H. Breasted relates a story from a sage named Ipuwer who claimed that the promised savior "brings cooling to the flame; . . . he is the shepherd of all men. . . . he passes the day to gather his herds together. . . ."[2]

The Babylonians believed that the god Marduk would return to earth from time to time when he would quell any discord and purge the world of immorality.[3] The Zoroastrians[4] believed that a messenger from the god of light would appear every thousand years, sent in a human body. He was said to be Zarathushtra, the greatest messenger of the Zoroastrians, to whom they would refer concerning the details of their belief in the gods of light and darkness.[5] This belief in the continual reappearance of a special messenger remained alive even after Judaism, Christianity and Islam. Al-Jāḥiẓ[6] alludes to this in his reference to his teacher Ibrāhīm ibn Sayyār al-Naẓẓām[7] where he says, "The ancestors claim that every thousand years there appears a man who is unparalleled, and if this claim is true then al-Naẓẓām is this man for this millennium."[8]

However, the belief in the coming of a divine messenger specifically referred to as "the Messiah" was not known before the appearance of the Hebrew Bible, along with the interpretations and commentaries written on it found in the Talmud, Haggadah, etc.[9] The title itself can be traced to the religious ceremonies which are mentioned in the books of Genesis and Exodus, as well as subsequent prophetic books. Anointing[10] with blessed oil was one of the rites of consecration and reverence. This first appears in Genesis chapter 28, where it says that Jacob "rose early in the morning and took the stone which he had put under his head and set it up for a pillar and poured oil on the top of it. He called that place

Bethel," i.e., "House of God."[11]

In Exodus chapter 30 it says: "The Lord said to Moses, '. . . Take the finest spices . . . [and you shall make of these] a sacred anointing oil . . . and you shall anoint with it the tent of meeting and the ark of the testimony, and the table [and all its utensils, and the lampstand and its utensils, and the altar of incense, and the altar of burnt offering . . . .] You shall consecrate them, that they may be most holy; whatever touches them will become holy. And you shall anoint Aaron and his sons, and consecrate them, [that they may serve me as priests].'"[12]

Because of this, the priests and prophets were called "God's anointed ones." The Torah prohibited anyone from hurting them, as it says in the book of the Chronicles chapter 16: "Touch not my anointed ones, do my prophets no harm".[13] Whenever kings were crowned and allegiance was pledged to them, the first rite to be performed was anointing. Saul and David were among these "anointed ones."

The title of "the Messiah" was later applied figuratively to any "chosen one" or "expected one." Cyrus the Persian is called "a messiah" in Isaiah chapter 45, for God empowered him to destroy the enemies of Israel and to establish the rebuilding of the Temple.[14] Also, the entire nation of Israel was referred to as "messiah." This is evident in the Psalms, and it is mentioned in the prophet Habbakuk: "You went forth for the salvation of your people, for the salvation of your anointed one," i.e. the chosen people.[15]

References to an expected messenger bearing the name of "Messiah" are repeatedly found in Jewish instructional literature called "Haggadah." Sometimes this name is applied to Joseph and sometimes to Moses (peace be upon them).[16] Those who believe in the messianic message among Jews today continue to wait for a messiah in the form of a messenger-guide, or in the form of a blessed nation. This is because they do not profess belief in the mission of Jesus son of Mary (peace be upon them).

Belief in the expectation of the Messiah was at its height after the kingdom ruled by David's dynasty had disappeared and the first Temple had been destroyed. The people of Israel reverted to statements made by their prophets which promised the return of their king. These claimed that he would come as a prince from among the descendants of David himself; kings would submit to him and the nations would profess his authority. There was then a development concerning belief in the "Messiah"; rather than being characterized as a king, it was believed that he would be "the chosen one" or "the expected one" who would offer guidance and establish righteousness. This transformation reached a climax in several prophetic books, among them the book of Isaiah, which is distinguished from the others by its repetition of these promises. There the portrayal of this figure ranges from the description of his power, might and regal authority, to his gentleness, sacrifice, and endurance of the abhorrent things he must bear in the process of warning against judgment and preaching the good news. According to Isaiah chapter 53, the expected messenger is characterized as "despised and rejected by men, a man of sorrows and grief."[17] It says in Zechariah chapter 9 that he is "just and victorious, humble and riding on a donkey, the foal of a donkey."[18] Many passages also agree that the Messiah would be preceded by a forerunner who would announce his coming; this would be the prophet Elijah, resurrected from the dead.[19]

This development in the understanding of the messianic mission was related to the stages through which the Israelites lived in their ongoing history. Hope in the Messiah as King intensified whenever the empires who controlled Palestine were weak, whenever they had little care that revolt was possible and that the hope for independence among their subjects was becoming serious. But the people reverted to a hope in the Messiah as Guide whenever the authority of their conquerors was strong, and it was clear that the possibility of winning an assault through the strength of weapons was too unlikely. Thus the interpretation of the expected Messianic mission fluctuated between a conviction that the Jewish state would be restored and the belief that the Messiah would simply offer guidance to the people. Each alternative depended on the historical conditions at that time.

Thus when Palestine came into the possession of the Roman Empire in 65 B.C.E.,[20] hope in the restoration of the Jewish state began to diminish. It was replaced by the ongoing hope in the expected messenger-savior and the spiritual revival he would bring. This transformation was linked to two phenomena which at one time were associated together, but which diverged from each other and became mutually exclusive for all time. One of these phenomena was the authority of the Temple and its priests, which had increased significantly when Rome transferred on it the complete supervision of local affairs. The Temple became a refuge for all those eagerly waiting for a national leader who would oppose the foreign power over them. The other phenomenon was the longing for a spiritual awakening which existed in the hearts of many people. They were greatly inclined to rebel against the old way, believing that the revival would come from a source other than the remnants of the "Temple" with its inherited customs and traditions which had become rigid over time.[21]

So when the fulfillment of these things reached its appointed time, and the long-awaited inauguration of the Messianic mission drew near, the two camps faced each other, ready and waiting.

Chapter 5

Prophecy Among the Israelites

We will especially come to understand how the people of the first century were ready for a prophetic call if we acquaint ourselves with the conditions for prophecy among the Israelites at that time, when their number had increased significantly, and when the accomplishments of their leaders and the teachings among their tribes were quite diverse. For this subject concerning the conditions for prophecy among the Israelites is not one that usually comes to mind when we consider the historical setting of the great prophets, nor when we consider the situation of the various nations during the intervals between the appearance of these prophets in history.

We today are quite suspicious of anyone declaring a prophetic pronouncement. We certainly know that whoever makes a claim to prophecy in our time lays claim to an extraordinary phenomenon; such a person makes himself suspect among religious people, even more so than the irreligious or atheists. This is because the adherents of the various religions believe that prophecy has been terminated,[1] or that a new prophet would jeopardize their doctrines when he claims that he himself would teach them what they do not know from their books and from the sayings of their prophets. On the other hand, it is understood that the irreligious and atheists cannot be considered prophets, either today or at any other time.

We also know today that the intervals between Abraham and Moses, Moses and Jesus, and Jesus and Muḥammad (the blessings of God be upon them) each extended for hundreds of years. Concerning this duration it is our belief that the appearance of the prophets was a momentous occurrence which was not repeated in every generation, something which was not seen twice in a person's lifetime.[2]

We also know from the history of the great prophets that they undertook intimidating challenges, and their call led them along paths which were not easy to overcome. For they demolished idols and they refuted idle dreams. They changed the convictions which the nations had followed throughout the ages. They set up those with authority over these nations and they set up laws for those who ruled and for those who were ruled. Muḥammad and Moses (peace be upon them) operated like this, and whoever was entrusted with guidance issued his call in this manner. Each one faced hostility and hatred; he would thrust upon the people a new way, but they would not accept such an intrusion from anyone. They would pay no attention to anyone who came to them doing this except to harass him and set up obstacles in his path.

But when we consider the conditions for prophecy among the Israelites, it is necessary that we conceive of the matter along other lines. This is a case which differs from the above representation in every respect.

Among the distinctions which characterize the Israelite prophets, we should note first of all that their appearance among the people was hardly a rarity. There were no intervals of time between them, nor were such intervals an absolute necessity. There might be four hundred prophets living in the same period, as we see in the book of First Kings, where the king of Israel gathered together "the prophets, about four hundred men; and he asked them, 'Shall I go to battle against Ramoth-gilead?'"[3]

The status of the Israelite prophets is best characterized by a saying of the Prophet (i.e., Muḥammad, the blessings of God be upon him): "The scholars of my community are like the prophets of the children of Israel."[4] Thus the work of the prophet among the people of Israel was like the work of the jurist-scholar[5] in the Islamic community. It was not unusual that the prophets would be found speaking, sometimes about specific matters and sometimes about general concerns. Their appearance in the community was not to deny the validity of the previous prophets. Rather, they came to interpret the scriptures and to warn and prod the people into following the conventions which had been previously prescribed for them by Abraham, Moses and Jacob, as well as by others among the former prophets. They would teach from the books of the Old Testament about God's promise to Israel that he will raise up prophets like Moses and will put his word in their mouths (Deuteronomy 18). However, some of these prophets might speak a message which is not a divinely revealed word, and the people must then repudiate them. "And if you say in your heart, how will you know the word which the Lord has not spoken, then know that when the prophet speaks in the name of the Lord, and when it does not occur or come to pass, then this is a word which the Lord has not spoken; . . . do not be afraid of him."[6]

It was possible that the message spoken by certain prophets or the signs which they performed would sometimes prove to be true, but they would call the people to worship a lord other than the God of Israel. In this case, the people were not allowed to follow their commands. "If a prophet or someone with a vision arises among you, and gives you a sign or a wonder, you shall not listen to the word of that prophet or visionary if he calls you to worship other gods which you do not know and which you do not worship, even if the wonder or the sign proves to be true" (Deuteronomy 13).[7]

The prophetic message was not to be subject to the permission of those in authority, i.e., the princes or priests or elders who complied with the wishes of the tribe. Rather, when someone was completely certain of the inspiration which came to him, he would proceed to convey the revelation without ever being able to refrain his tongue. Thus Jeremiah says: "Oh Lord, you have persuaded me, and I have been convinced. You have prevailed upon me, and you have triumphed. I have become a laughingstock and an object of derision. . . . The word of the Lord has covered me with shame and disgrace. . . . I said, 'I will not mention him or speak in his name any more.' Yet there is in my heart as it were a burning fire confined within my bones. . . and I am not able to be silent" (Jeremiah 20).[8]

Frequently the prophet had to turn against his associates of the same period and contradict them by offering a different interpretation of the warning from his Lord. Thus Jeremiah says: "From the prophets of Jerusalem hypocrisy has gone forth into all the land. . . . Do not listen to the words of the prophets who prophesy to you, for they nullify your work, and they speak from visions of their own minds."[9] Or as Micaiah said to the king of Israel: "Behold, the Lord has put a lying spirit in the mouths of all these your prophets." When he had said this, he was opposed by Zedekiah the son of Chenaanah: "He struck Micaiah on the jaw and said to him, 'How did the spirit of the Lord pass from me to speak to you?'"[10]

A well-known feature concerning the prophets, as related in the books of the Hebrew Bible, was that the prophets of Israel used to seek a state of illumination, similar to that sought by Sūfīs and hermits (as we understand from what they have often stated). Such people would fast and keep night vigils; they would refrain from the superfluous matters of life and they would seek the seclusion of gardens and riverbanks. For example, Daniel says: "I ate no rich food, and no meat or wine entered my mouth, nor did I anoint myself for three full weeks. And in the twenty-fourth day of the first month, I was standing beside the great river, the Tigris; I lifted up my eyes and I looked."[11]

On the other hand, there were those prophets who made use of audible assistance in order to perceive the Spirit clearly and to seek inspiration from the Divine Mystery. We read in the book of First Samuel, "You will meet a band of prophets coming down from the high place. In front of them will be a lyre, tambourine, flute and lute, and they will be prophesying. Then the Spirit of God will descend upon you" (1 Samuel 9).[12] We also read in the book of Second Kings, "Elisha said, 'As the Lord of hosts lives, . . . now bring me a minstrel.' And when the minstrel played the lute, the hand of the Lord was upon him."[13]

For the most part, however, they would seclude themselves and withdraw to the riverbanks: "by the river Chebar [the heavens] were opened and I saw visions of God" (Ezekiel 1).[14]

It was not impossible that God might grant a suitable vision or a clear sign to someone who was not a prophet or who was outside the people of Israel. Such was the case when God inspired Abimelech and Balaam.[15] Despite their being Gentiles, these men were inspired that they might recognize the same truth given to the prophets and others whom God sent.

Most of those who heard the prophecies would ask for a sign by which they would know that the speaker was proclaiming a revelation from God. But such a request did not necessarily indicate true conviction and faith on their part. It was also possible that the prophet would be given permission to seek a sign, but he would carry out his search with so much diligence, that he would realize it was improper to put his Lord to the test by demanding such evidence for these signs (Isaiah 7).[16]

In any case, people would seek out the prophets and consult them before they would go to war or embark on a journey. Or, they would simply want to increase their knowledge so as to draw near to God. They hoped to be drawn up to the Divine Mystery that was concealed from the concerns of worldly folks who were immersed in the cares of life. Some of the prophets could even hear revelation by means of a loud voice and could perceive it as inspiration or guidance or a serviceable vision.

In general, whenever the people departed from the ancient traditions and turned away from the path of true worship which previous prophets had taught their ancestors, the prophets' message included more than simply a warning of punishment. What they proclaimed was neither an intrusion nor a strange innovation.[17] Nor were they in any danger by proclaiming such a message, except when they were in opposition to the kings and rulers, admonishing them for violating the law or the traditions handed down from their ancestors. Some of these kings and rulers would proceed to torture the prophet in order to prove to the people that he was deceitful and had not come from God. For the death of the false prophet was considered to be one of the indications that he was acting under false pretenses.[18]

We believe that we describe the situation accurately when we say that the Jewish people were in search of the prophets. They used to anticipate their coming, and they did not regard their appearance as an extraordinary or astonishing event, nor did they feel that its repetition was unusual.[19] As for the person who was ready to be a prophet, he would not dare to keep silent concerning the call entrusted to him. Its impulse would stir up his conscience and would press upon him day after day, until he became convinced that keeping silent would be rebelling against God's command and shrinking back from his will. And as soon as he was determined in his innermost being that his search for a sign was putting God to the test and displaying a weakness of faith, he would forsake the affairs which concerned him, and stirred up by the spirit of God, he would preach both warnings and glad tidings. After all of this, God would be sure to confirm the message of his prophet, both guiding him and guiding the people to him according to his will.

The first century was an era when people everywhere were anticipating the good news of God's call, like those who watch for a star to rise at its appointed time. When the promised messenger of good news would come, there is no doubt that they stood ready to heed his voice. There is likewise no doubt that the demonstration which they required in order to validate his prophecy was in proportion to how much benefit they hoped he would accomplish. The people would surely test him to the ultimate degree. They felt that it was too easy for impostors to make false claims; they were afraid that their hope would be nullified at a time when they yearned for such a hope. Thus there was an exceptional expectation for a prophet, and for those who entertained such a hope, this was dependent on an exceptional demonstration of his validity.

Chapter 6

Jewish Sects in the First Century

At the time when Christ was born, the Jewish world was comprised of various sects — each with its own doctrine concerning the expectation of the promised Messiah-Savior. An explanation of these sects is necessary in order to establish the position which this new belief held among the beliefs which preceded it in the Jewish milieu.

This explanation is also necessary from another aspect. From what we have seen, an even stronger reason for presenting this material is because of modern critics who have appeared since the eighteenth century. They have been so recalcitrant in their craving to produce criticism and to express skepticism, that they have surpassed doubts about texts and narratives and have doubted the existence of Christ himself.[1] They allege, for example, that he is simply to be included among the many legendary personalities. The allegations made by these critics fall down with nothing more than an acquaintance with the basic teachings of the ideologies which were recognized in the first century. For the call of Christ served to amend each one of these ideologies in one aspect or another. All together, these correctives marked a return to a single consolidation of their principles and ideals. These ideologies were in definite need of a "personality" which was independent of them all, one which could incorporate their rites and beliefs onto a single touchstone with a well-ordered system of thought and belief.

Among the religious sects which were recognized in the first century, it will be sufficient for us to discuss five of them: the Sadducees, the Pharisees, the Essenes, the Zealots, and the Samaritans. All of these five sects were important in the history of this era, for the strength of each depended on a particular characteristic which each displayed.

* * *

The Sadducees claimed that they were the successors of Zadok and his family who, it is reported in many places, assumed the priesthood at the time of David and Solomon.[2] This sect was important because of the central roles played by its adherents. In short, they supported the prevailing conservative attitude and the status quo, and they held positions of high standing and wealth. They were unrelenting in their denial of anything innovative or interpretive. Adhering to the old ways, they upheld the authority of the Temple and the priests. They accepted only the oldest books of the Hebrew Bible, namely the five books of Moses (peace be upon him), and they rejected anything else, especially what was handed down by oral tradition.[3]

In order to maintain the existing order, the Sadducees were prompted to follow a policy which was incompatible with their creed, as is evident from its requirements. Among the

Jews, they were the most inclined to adopt the Greek culture and lifestyle of the Roman milieu. It is reported that at that time a few of them held to some of the philosophical ideologies, such as that of the Epicurians.[4] It had become public knowledge in those days that this ideology promoted the sensuous enjoyment of luxury and comfort.

However, the Sadducees were actually true to their accustomed practice, one which is displayed by others like them in every age. For they preserved the order of society by maintaining firm control over it. Thus they enjoyed its pleasure and comfort, and they were quite accommodating to the political powers of the time, i.e., the Greeks and the Romans. Along these lines, it was incumbent upon them to believe that the earliest Jewish scriptures made no mention of the Resurrection or the Last Day, and that they credited to the righteous no life beyond this life. This was in contrast to the other sects which believed in the Resurrection and the Final Judgment.

The assault against Christ was led by two of the leading priests in the party of the Sadducees, Annas and Caiaphas.[5] There was nothing strange in this, since all of the Sadducees maintained the authority of the Temple and the existing social order. That is, they were not pleased with any rebellion or revolution.

The essence of Sadducean protocol was that they were literalists with regard to religious affairs, but they were quite open regarding matters of everyday life. They associated closely with foreigners rather than remaining segregated from them as was the practice of the rest of Jewish society. This was because the activities and positions of the Sadducees were closely connected to those who had authority.

* * *

Another sect which can be compared to the Sadducees was that of the Pharisees.[6] This group was more powerful than the Sadducees because of their great number and because their principles and ideas were widespread. They had a good reputation among the majority of the people, including those of the upper class who did not mingle with foreigners. This was in spite of the fact that very few of the Pharisees were among the ranks of the leaders and notables.

The name of the Pharisees comes from a Hebrew word which is nearly equivalent, both in pronunciation and meaning, to the Arabic word *"farz"* ["separation"]. Thus they were the "separated ones" or the "those who are set apart." Their opponents had applied this name to them in mockery and contempt, convinced that the Pharisees had separated themselves from their forebears and had seceded from the path of the first Israelites. However, the Pharisees had also applied this title to themselves with a different sense to the meaning "separated." They traced it back to an address from God to all the Israelites which is related in Leviticus chapter 20. There, God spoke to the people saying, "I have set you apart from the peoples, that you should be mine."[7] Thus the Pharisees viewed themselves as those who were set apart from others and who were therefore superior.[8]

Because of this, characteristics of pretension and arrogance were occasionally evident among the Pharisees, something which is found among any group that claims for itself a prerogative over other groups. Some of them became the target of criticism from Christ, who found fault with their show of self-reliance and pride.

Although they displayed this kind of pride, the Pharisees opposed another kind that derived from prestige and wealth, things which they detested in their opponents the Sadducees. The Pharisees rebelled against any "official" rule, whether it was present in the Temple or among the foreign authorities. They rejected the arbitrary control of the priests concerning religious rites and ceremonies, and at the same time they rejected the customs of the foreigners and of anyone who tried to imitate the power and domination of foreign leaders.

Their first uprising[9] had been one against foreign innovations which they rejected completely, and they had no tolerance for those Jews who accepted them. When king Antiochus commanded the Temple priest to sacrifice swine on its altar (in 168 B.C.E.), every one of them rose up in revolt. They offered themselves up to death by the hundreds and thousands because of their abhorrence of this sacrilege.[10] There was also an incident during the Roman period when the governor Petronius was amazed at how stubborn they were in their opposition to the Roman Empire, despite their weakness and its strength. He asked their leaders, "How can you think to fight against Caesar when you are not equal to his power?" And they answered, "We do not fight against Caesar, nor do we claim to be equal to his power. But without exception we would rather die than break the Jewish Law." And they bared their necks, ready to substantiate what they said.[11]

Some of the opposition of the Pharisees was in revolt against the arbitrary control of the Temple authorities, while they also desired to make accessible to the public the religious rites which had been confined to the niches of the Temple. These issues are what prompted them to perform these rites in houses, without the requirement that ordained priests be present; indeed, it was not long before they made from every house a temple of sacred rituals.[12] Thus, while they tended to be rather tolerant towards the people, their opposition to the "official" absolutism of the Temple made them more conservative than the existing conservatives.[13]

Nevertheless, most of the time the Pharisees avoided matters which were susceptible to opposition. Instead, they were more inclined to apply independent judgment and analogy.[14] That is, they tended to allow rational opinion to play a greater role regarding written provisions and conventional rules. For example, the Sadducees had insisted on upholding the law of "an eye for an eye and a tooth for a tooth,"[15] and they would not accept the payment of blood money as an alternative. In contrast, the Pharisees preferred to accept blood money along with a pardon of the offense instead of retaliation. The Sadducees also laid a greater emphasis on the material world and on practical principles, whereas the Pharisees emphasized spirituality and an introspective demeanor which focused on contemplation and meditation. But it was the Sadducees' denial of the Resurrection and of life after death which drew the most intense repudiation of the Pharisees against their opponents. All of this was the reason why the Pharisees, far more than the Sadducees, were anticipating the coming of salvation, or the Messiah-Savior, within the sphere of the Spirit, unfettered by the demands of crown and scepter.[16] In general, if the Sadducees are to be characterized as the "aristocrats," then those among the Jewish sects of that time who deserve to be described as the "democrats" are none other than the Pharisees.

The Pharisees of the first century were divided into two factions. One party followed the teachings of the sage Hillel, who had come to Palestine from Babylonia. This was the more liberal party and they favored friendly relations toward foreigners. The other party followed the teachings of the sage Shammai. They tended to be more reserved and narrow regarding foreigners, and they opposed those who sought the conversion of Gentiles into the Jewish religion.[17] The distinguishing feature of Hillel's teaching was a moderation between renunciation and gratification. One of his sayings which has been handed down states, "The more flesh, the more worms."[18] His rule concerning relations with others was that the entire law could be stated in a single injunction: "Do not do to someone else what you would hate to be done to you by him. Everything else among the revealed precepts is commentary and elaboration."[19] On the other hand, the sage Shammai could not quite master a moderation between renunciation and gratification. It is related that he used to work as a carpenter so that he could live on what he earned. It is also said that he was more zealous to stick to the old ways than he was to interpret the texts in a new fashion or without restriction.

Historians agree that those who taught Christ in his youth were most likely from the sect of the Pharisees.[20]

* * *

The third sect which we shall discuss, namely the Essenes,[21] was much less significant than the Sadducees or the Pharisees with regard to numbers. Yet they equaled the other two or even exceeded them in terms of vigor and influence, according to reports from those in the first century who wrote about this sect. Both the historian Josephus and the philosopher Philo estimated that their number did not exceed four thousand, most of them living in the south of Palestine.[22]

The source of their vigor was the stringent nature of their doctrine and the organization of their daily routine. More important than their vigor might well have been the example which they set. Although they were a sect which came from the heart of the Israelite community, they were independent with respect to their religious ceremonies, their observances, their ideas and their secret beliefs. They were close to becoming completely independent from the Temple because of their devotion to the Jewish religion and national identity. Had it not been that they still acknowledged the sacrificial offerings in the Temple, they would not even be counted among the Jewish sects. Nevertheless, they renounced the slaughtering of animals, and instead they presented only offerings from plants.

There are differences of opinion about the origin of the name of this sect. From the numerous suggestions, however, the most preferable one is that it comes from the word *"āsī"* which means "doctor" or "skilled physician" in Aramaic. This word conveys the same meaning in Arabic,[23] and indeed among the Semitic languages Aramaic is considered to be the closest to Arabic.[24] It is reasonable to believe that the adherents of this school were called Essenes because they were engaged in the healing of the spirit. They would call for the release of the sick through their prayers and invocations,[25] even as they would call upon their knowledge of the healing properties of drugs.[26]

The sect most likely originated in Alexandria in the second century B.C.E. It borrowed from the schools of Alexandria, taking over much from the secret religious organizations and some of the philosophical ideologies. For example, it adopted ideas from the school of Pythagoras, who forbade the slaughtering of animals, and who called for a life of asceticism and contentment with very little.[27]

It was forbidden for the followers of this sect to own two cloaks or pairs of sandals, or to participate in pleasures and unnecessary nourishment. Most of them lived a monastic way of life, except those who were permitted to be married and who were exempt from the shackles of reclusion and celibacy.

The Essene community was organized along three ranks. First was the rank of apprenticeship into which they received boys before they had reached puberty. The next rank comprised those who had taken the oath; following this oath they completed a year of spiritual exercises, being trained in the worship ceremonies and studying the secret teachings of the sect. The aspirant then moved to the rank of full membership, completing this stage in two years. He would then put on the emblem of the sect, a blue cloak and a sash, and he would carry an ax in his hand, representing the arduous labor now required of him.

Between the first and second stages, the members participated in a series of rites performed by the masters. These included ritual ablutions and the public recitation of some vows. Each person would take a one-time oath of fidelity, promising to preserve the secrecy of the group. He was prohibited from making any further oath, whether in sincerity or in pretense, for the rest of his life. After his ceremony, a member might be dismissed if he were to break his oath, and if one hundred of the brothers agreed that he was guilty. It was even possible for him to be sentenced to death if he went so far as to betray the community and repudiate the fundamental elements of the faith.

The ritual observances of the Essenes included the purification from ritual contamination, the recitation of prayers at daybreak, and the observance of rest on the Sabbath. There were some who on that day would not even allow themselves to wash off bodily impurities.

There was no leadership or domination among them, and slavery was forbidden. Their preference was to work in agriculture and handicraft. However, trade was considered repulsive and unbefitting in this sect, and carrying a weapon for fighting was the most repulsive of all.

Material possessions were for them the source of all evil; to take pleasure in them was to indulge in filth and treachery. Because of this, complete silence and remorse was predominant among them. The only pleasure which they allowed for themselves was of a spiritual nature; they sought to contact the spiritual world, to ascend to the most noble place of the heavenly realm, which is possible for the believer through worship, spiritual exercises, and devoted humility.

There was a brotherly association among them, and they used to journey together in pairs. Seldom would they be seen in the populated towns or in areas frequented by those who seek pleasure or an escape from solitude.

The Essenes believed in the Day of Resurrection and Judgment, and in the mission of the Messiah-Savior.[28] They were convinced that salvation entailed a spiritual resurrection which would guide the people into a life of integrity and righteousness. In their search for approval from God, they took their guiding principle from the prophet Amos, who used to teach the people that approaching God with justice and mercy was better than approaching him with sacrifices and offerings.[29]

* * *

It is not unlikely that the Zealots[30] (or the Galileans, i.e., followers of Judas the Galilean) were an extremist faction of the Essenes. For the Zealots followed the same path of asceticism and moderation, going beyond the Essenes by inciting activities which would lead to the fulfillment of the prophecies and the immanent arrival of the day of deliverance.[31]

The Zealots were the ones who organized bands of rebels in the year 6 or 7 B.C.E., in protest against the census issued by the Syrian governor Quirinius. They felt that under the census, the Jews would be counted as subjects of Caesar, or even his slaves who must yield to his domination. Their argument was that obedience to Caesar was to be classified under the worship of idols, and that to honor the census as if they were slaves of Caesar would be the same as apostasy from their faith.[32] On another occasion when Herod the king erected a statue of the eagle of Caesar above the Temple in Jerusalem, two Zealots went and forcibly pulled it down. They warned their brothers that whoever put it back in its place would be punished by death.[33]

Judas the Galilean, who had led the Zealots in rebellion during the year of the census, had died during that uprising along with his sons and relatives.[34] The Roman Empire became wary of dissension in this patch of land situated in the middle of three continents, and so it preferred to deal with the rebels with prudence and consideration. It did not try to control them by repression or domination, except when it felt that this policy of forbearance and toleration simply could not be maintained.[35]

* * *

The Samaritan sect was a result of intermarriage between Jews and Assyrians who were living in the old kingdom of Israel. It is said that the kings of Babylon sent Assyrian tribes into Palestine to inhabit the land in place of the Jewish tribes which had been banished to the area between the two great rivers; these Jews were thus called the Babylonian Exiles. It is then said that the Assyrian tribes intermarried with the Jews whom the Babylonians did not bring to their country along with the Exiles and who had been left behind. The result of this relocation and intermarriage was a blending of customs and religious practices.[36]

When the Jews of the Exile[37] returned to Palestine after the fall of Babylon, they refused to acknowledge the Samaritan rites which were at variance with their own traditions. They accused the Samaritans of idol worship, and they rejected their offer of collaboration in the rebuilding of the Temple.[38] The Samaritans then proceeded to build a temple for their own use at Gerizim, and they began to intentionally dishonor the Temple in Jerusalem. The Samaritans utilized their temple as the center toward which they prayed, the focus of their pilgrimage, and the place where they conducted their worship. It remained in competition to the Jerusalem Temple for about two hundred years, until the High Priest of Jerusalem, John Hyrcanus, destroyed it prior to 100 B.C.E. However, the Samaritans rebuilt their temple and it remained standing until the Romans destroyed it following the Samaritan revolt in the fifth century C.E.[39] After Vespasian had destroyed their city, he founded another one on its ruins which he named Neapolis (i.e., "the new city" or Nablus as it is known today).[40]

The remnants of the Samaritans continue to maintain their traditions. They rely on a copy of the Torah written in their language, and they do not recognize any book other than the five books known as the Books of Moses. The only center for worship which they profess is the area surrounding their destroyed temple at Gerizim. In the first century, the animosity between the adherents of the two temples was so great, that security was non-existent for any travel between Samaria and other towns. Any Jew, whether from the north or south, who dared to travel to Samaria exposed himself to humiliation and maltreatment.

It is certain that these Samaritans played a role in the development of the Messianic idea, that is, the concept of a coming salvation which would be established by the promised messenger.[41] This role goes back to the ancient struggle between the kingdom of Judah in the south and the kingdom of Israel which was inherited by the Samaritans. For the Samaritans traced their ancestry back to Jacob, insisting that only they deserved to be called "Israelites."

Now the people of the kingdom of Judah in the south believed that the expected king would rule from their capital, Jerusalem, and that this king would be one of the descendants of David. They were quite content in this belief, for this event would bring glory back to their nation and would make them the avenue of salvation. But the Samaritans in the north persisted in their animosity toward David and his descendants, and they stirred up the ancient struggle between the tribes. At the very least, they rejected the doctrine that salvation would come through a king from the royal family in Judah. In this manner they opened the way to belief in a spiritual salvation and in guidance from among the people themselves. As the appointed time for the Messianic mission drew near, the Samaritans had shaken up any trust which was placed either in the leaders of the southern Temple, or in anyone who might accept homage as a king.

* * *

In spite of what has just been said, the land was never devoid of people here and there who had renounced every one of the religious groups and withdrew from the world to live as hermits, isolated from the bustle of life. Such people gained respect from the rest of society, for they had lost trust in the propagandists who had become immersed in a world crowded with politicians and priests. One of these ascetics was Bannus, under whom the great historian Josephus had spent three years as a disciple.[42] This rebellious hermit lived in seclusion and ate whatever happened to come his way without his effort and without asking others. He was often engaged in self-purification with water and in self-discipline through spiritual exercises and recitation. There were numerous hermits similar to Bannus who followed his pattern of ritual seclusion and ablution. The most famous of these was John the Purifier,[43] known in the Gospels as John the Baptist.[44]

As for the position of the Temple with respect to these sects and factions, it played the familiar "official" role in society. That is, those responsible for the Temple had the role of trying to avoid any partiality to this or that group. They worked their hardest at gaining the trust of the people while not annoying the ruling authorities. But seldom does success in such a task come easily, especially in times when the people are restless and have aspirations and are fed up with the entire situation.

The Temple had originally been a tent when the Israelites were living in the desert. Back in those days, the people believed that God appeared in this tent to the prophets and priests. Later this tent was constructed with a wooden frame which could be dismantled and moved during their travels through the wilderness.[45] Afterwards, Solomon the Wise built his Temple to replace this tent or wooden tabernacle. It is said that he spent a hundred thousand talents of gold and a million talents of silver for building this Temple, besides what his predecessors and offspring had collected for it.[46] By the reckoning of today, his expenditures for this project amounted to a half billion Egyptian pounds, and that is less than what others have calculated, depending on how one estimates the value of the weight which was used in business transactions, whether official or unofficial.[47]

For a long time this Temple inspired tremendous reverence, while the powers of the priests and Temple authorities increased. After it had stood in its glory for more than four centuries, the Babylonians destroyed it. Then Cyrus the Persian ordered its reconstruction in 536 B.C.E.[48] Five centuries later King Herod renewed its construction and made further additions; this was completed, or nearly so, at the time of Christ's birth.[49]

However, as one era superseded another and the Roman Empire achieved domination over the offices of the priesthood, the Temple lost the level of its imposing influence which it had previously gained. At the beginning of the period of Christ, its authority was declining in actual fact while gaining prestige in outward appearance. It was declining because it was not based on the trust of the people; it was gaining prestige because it was the only refuge which remained for them following the end of the monarchy, and they had no hope in its restoration since by that time the Romans had vanquished both the East and the West.[50]

All of the tasks performed in the Temple were restricted to the members of the priesthood. This religious function was reserved for the descendants of Aaron or for those of his tribe, a position which none of the other Jewish tribes could occupy. Among their duties in the Temple were the leadership of the prayers and the issuing of decisions in matters of jurisprudence;[51] the presentation of sacrifices; the performance of the religious ceremonies for weddings and funerals;[52] and the care of the sacred vessels. The number of these priests had increased over time. Thus when the governor, Zerubbabel (meaning "born in Babylon"), returned from the region of Babylon, it is said that approximately 4300 priests came with him — and these did not include those who had previously returned or those who had stayed behind.[53] In addition, these priests had partitioned themselves into divisions, each responsible for the services a few days per month. They also divided among themselves the offerings and the salaries given to the Temple.

As time went on and the descendants of Aaron became numerous, there were thousands of them who had no education and no work. Although they took on the vocation of the priesthood and they divided the offerings among themselves, yet they did not participate in teaching the people or performing the prayers.[54] Alongside these were others who knew how to write; they made copies of the Scriptures but they did not have a share in the duties of the Temple, nor were they part of its system of offerings and endowments. These were known as the "Scribes" or the legal scholars of the faith.[55] All of them were from the Pharisees, since they were the ones who had accepted the more recent books as scriptural, relying on them in their religious observances and social behavior. As has already been mentioned, this was in contrast to the Sadducees, who restricted their canon to the five books of Moses, rejecting the subsequent prophetic books. Thus the Sadducees were not dependent on the group of Scribes and legal scholars.

By the time of the first century, many priests had their vocation in the priesthood, but they did not work in the Temple. And many Scribes and legal scholars participated in the religious sciences, but they were not counted among those who inherited the Temple leadership. Meanwhile, the people began to disregard the priests of the Temple concerning matters of religion, especially those which needed to be taught to them or which required authoritative decisions. Instead the people turned their attention to scholars who did not bear the legacy or the official stamp of the Temple; they looked to them concerning their questions about the difficulties of life, and they began to emulate their life-styles. In this way, the conventional position was stricken by a powerful blow and the way became clear for the religious call which was unaccompanied by the ritual of the priests and especially by the rites of the Temple.

At the time of Christ's birth, according to the best known accounts, the duties of the Temple were filtered through a sacred assembly designated as the "Sanhedrin." It consisted of seventy-one members, twenty-three of whom formed a special council. It was predominated by an official and traditional character. Its members had connections with state officials concerning public affairs, so that regulations were implemented and the law, both local and Mosaic, was observed.[56]

Concerning the origin of the Sanhedrin, its dignitaries customarily attempted to refer to the earliest period of Israelite history. They maintained that it was this council which is mentioned in the book of Numbers. As it says there, "The Lord said to Moses, 'Gather to me seventy men from the elders of Israel, those whom you know to be elders and officers of the people. Bring them to the Tent of Meeting, and they will stand there with you.

Then I will come down and speak with you, and I will take some of the spirit which is upon you and I will put it upon them. And they will bear the burden of the people along with you so that you will not bear it by yourself.'"[57]

However, historical sources, as well as sources in the Scriptures themselves, are devoid of any mention of the Sanhedrin except for a passing reference here and there. None of these are helpful for estimating the number of its members or for determining its claims and duties. From what can be ascertained beyond doubt, the council as it existed in the time of Christ was deprived of the right to judge capital offenses about forty years before the destruction of the Second Temple.[58] The Sanhedrin's most important legal decisions in the days of Christ were dependent on the consent of the Roman governor, who could confirm or revoke them at will.

When we consider the position of the Sanhedrin with respect to the good news of the expected Messiah, we can scarcely see any reason why that good news should have been welcomed by its members. This is because their authority was infused with the corruption of the entire period; they renounced any claim to goodness, and they brought accusations against those among the people who were upright in matters of religion. But at the same time the Sanhedrin could not alienate itself from this mission, because it was the only door of hope open to the expectant believers. The council was thus in the position of being fearful that what all the people hoped for would come true, but without its playing any role. It felt that it should be armed against the onslaught of this mission, ready to deal with the people's response to it and their imagined hope that it would circulate and become widespread. Indeed, as this mission spread out, it was not confined to the general populace, as was usually the case for that period. For it included legal experts, religious scholars and members of the educated class who also had misgivings about the priests; they did not fail to recognize that these priests had been corrupted and were corrupting others. Such are those who, at the end of time, will finally hear the warner's cry against them and will see the unfavorable balance of their account.[59]

* * *

Our discussion has dealt with the religious forces which had made a definite impact in the homeland of Christ (peace be upon him) just prior to his birth. But it would not be complete without some reference to the sect of the Nazirites or "the consecrated ones."[60] These people had given themselves, or they were presented by their families, to a life of holiness, of service to God, and of preaching about the appointed day, i.e., the day of salvation from injustice and oppression and of purification from sin.

These Nazirites were not a sect which displayed the type of social and ritual unity present in other sects. Rather each one individually dedicated himself, or his family dedicated him, apart from others. They had no association with any single group apart from their association to the community through their relatives.

The meaning of the word "Nazirite" in Arabic includes an element which has to do with military service, and it seems that this was borrowed from the concept of striving in the way of religion.[61] It is said that a man who dedicates himself to the army offers himself to be placed at the front of the ranks, where he might have to sacrifice his life. Perhaps part of his work was to warn[62] his people of the enemy and to keep them away from dangers and sudden attacks. No doubt a similar element revolves around the meaning of the Hebrew word despite the differences in letters and forms.[63]

The Nazirite, or "consecrated one," was not required to renounce the world and withdraw into seclusion from other people. However, he did practice a life of austerity. He was not permitted to drink wine or to defile his body through contact with the dead or with forbidden substances. He was required to let his hair grow long and not to cut it before the completion of his vow if this was for a limited period. An infant who had been consecrated before his birth would be under his vow for the duration of his life. It was said that the consecrated person who was still young was very much like a prophet; the prophet Amos said, as a spokesman for Yahweh the God of the Israelites: "And I raised up prophets from among you and Nazirites from your youths. . . . But you made the Nazirites drink wine and you charged the prophets to pretend that they are prophesying."[64] (The prophecy meant here is one of warning the people about what will take place.)

The number of Nazirites had increased just prior to the time of Christ's birth, for this had coincided with the end of the fourth millennium since the beginning of the world, according to Hebrew assessment. This was the appointed time in which the mission of the Messiah was anticipated, since they looked for him at the end of every thousand years. Others said that for God a day is like a thousand years, as is mentioned in the Psalms, and that the life span of the world is like a week for God: six of its "days" are completed in hardship and misery, but then the seventh comes like the Sabbath day, in rest and tranquillity. Then a period of goodness and peace would continue for a full thousand years before the world passed away. Westerners still refer to this as "the Millennium" and they apply this name to any era for which happiness and peace are promised.[65]

Some people supposed that the Resurrection would occur after seven thousand years from the beginning of the world. They would put off the coming of the kingdom of heaven on earth until the end of the sixth millennium, when the reign of the promised Messiah would prevail. But these were like others who were looking for a messenger from God whenever a thousand year span (as measured from the beginning of the world) would come to an end. Thus the beginning of the fifth millennium was an "anticipated" date; or we could say it was a "consecrated" one in which the number of Nazirites increased.[66] Perhaps they are to be considered as a kind of salvation army. Or perhaps destiny enabled one of them such that salvation would be accomplished by him.[67]

The important thing concerning the Nazirites with respect to Christ is that one of the few eminent personalities among them was John the Purifier (John the Baptist).[68] It was by him that Christ was baptized, i.e., he took an oath which was administered by John. Some historians also consider Christ to have been a Nazirite, but this matter is somewhat obscure because the words "Nazirite" and "Nazarene" are very similar expressions in Hebrew.[69] Some of these historians maintain that Christ did not come from Nazareth, even claiming that this town did not exist since it is never mentioned in the Old Testament.[70]

However, we believe that the best explanation is that Nazareth itself had been named *"Nadhīrah"* with the meaning of "vanguard."[71] This took place in former times when it stood on the borders of the land which the Hebrews had conquered. It was then a suitable outpost for reconnaissance, because from there one could see across the surrounding hills to Mt. Hermon, Mt. Carmel, and the plain known as the "pasture land of Ibn 'Āmir."[72] This explanation eliminates the difficulty which has presented itself especially to Western interpreters, and in particular those who pay attention only to the Greek language, which is that found in the Gospels. It is hardly surprising that these people have strayed in their pronunciation, since they have failed to distinguish between the reference to "the consecrated ones" and that to "the votive offering."[73] This is especially the case because the name of the town has been mispronounced by Hebrews and aliens throughout time, spoken sometimes with the letter *ṣād* and other times with *sīn.*

As we have already said, the Nazirites were not a unified sect. Rather, they were members of every school of thought which had room for youthful enthusiasm. It was this which made them a significant force, especially in the first century. They were altogether adolescents whose hearts were filled with hope and whose desires were fixed on reform. They believed themselves to be pioneers in calling others to the expectation of the promised Messiah, and they were waiting for his appearance when they would welcome him and turn their attention to him. But they were not comprised within a specific sect or a definite school.

Chapter 7

Political and Social Life in the First Century

Syria and Palestine were conquered for the Roman Empire by the distinguished leader Pompey, who had put an end to the third revolt of the slaves led by the famous Spartacus.[1] This defeat of Spartacus is considered to be one of the great events which added to Pompey's glory and immortalized his name among the Roman heroes. But the glory which such great events bestow on heroes and empires is not one which encompasses the common good. Now it was one of the marks of its power that the Roman Empire was capable of suppressing such an enormous uprising for which no equal is known among ancient slave rebellions. But undoubtedly alongside of these marks of power stood the contrasting marks of weakness. For it was only the presence of a terrible rift in the structure of the Empire that allowed a slave to gather together seventy thousand other slaves and with them to overwhelm the armies of Rome some three years.[2] And it was only because a rupture had occurred in the fabric of society that he could prevail over an army consisting of many times the number of oppressed slaves who regarded the glory of Rome with contempt and who risked their lives in order to bring it down to utter ruin.

Spartacus was from the people of Thrace, and he was not the first Eastern slave to rebel against the Roman Empire. Other slaves from Eastern countries preceded him in a rebellion in Sicily (143 B.C.E.). They were able to establish a rule on that island which lasted for ten years. This was the rebellion whose leader, Eunus, appeared to his followers in the form of a prophet sent to them by God, and as one who had been granted royal authority by Him. He was originally from Syria and many of his followers were Easterners.[3]

Other rebellions of this kind occurred, both before and after the rebellion of Eunus the Syrian, but none of them reached the same level of severity. Not one of them was devoid of a religious character conferred upon their leaders. There was one in Asia Minor which gave rise to a government calling itself "the Sun-State,"[4] the sun being a symbol indicating the worship of light and freedom. So this government established itself,[5] while the defeated rebels in Sicily were hung by the thousands on wooden crosses.[6]

This latent danger of uprisings from the slaves was not hidden to reformers among the Roman statesmen who lived shortly before the birth of Christ. These men wanted to reform the imperfections of society by returning to the law which would restrict how much a person could inherit and which would prohibit anyone from inheriting more than five hundred acres of land. Gaius Gracchus thought that he could deal with this blight by producing a new class of money changers and merchants; through them he could limit the influence of the aristocrats and unjust landowners. He and his brother were compelled to provide the destitute with food which the state sold for less than its value.[7]

However, the factors contributing to the state of decay in those days were deeper and more powerful than the factors leading to restoration and reform. In 104 B.C.E., Julius Philippus tried to organize the feudal estates through his agricultural legislation.[8] Cicero relates that he said in his "explanatory" address "that the landowners of the city of Rome are not more than two thousand."[9] This situation grew worse in the period of the celebrated Augustus, according to the descriptions found in historical works. Thus the colony in Africa passed into the hands of only six unjust landowners, yet it had thousands of oppressed slaves.[10]

The period of the celebrated Augustus was also the one in which Christ was born. It was during that time that Christ said, according to the account of his disciple[11] Matthew, that "Foxes have dens and the birds of the sky have nests, but the Son of Man has no place to lay his head."[12]

* * *

As a matter of fact, this period was made glorious through the power of the sword, more so than by any other human power. And from the power of the sword Rome took everything it could get: sweeping conquests along with a brazen authority which deterred its enemies and subdued those who rebelled against it. Rome thus developed complete reliance on this power, such that it became an indispensable support to the Empire. Its need for this power arrived at the point where it laid itself on the altar, surrendering its freedom and its honor. This power destroyed the Republic for the sake of the unrestricted imperialism of Caesar. Yet his position was elevated by that same power to the extent that he was worshiped as a deity. Caesar Augustus was thus given the title of a god, and it became an established practice that he was worshiped alongside of other gods.[13] He was also given a month of the year which is still known today by his name. After him, the periods of the militant Caesars followed one after the other. Trajan and Hadrian were such rulers, along with others who emulated them.[14] Eventually, these militant Caesars became a scourge upon their times.

Rome's chief pride had been its system of law and order. But then law perished with the coming of absolute authority, and order perished because of the deep disparity between the rulers and the ruled. On one side were wealth, luxury, and oppression; on the other were poverty, wretchedness, and degradation. Now states cannot have order along with an imbalance of the equilibrium in society. Even life itself can have neither order nor value when there is so much comfort that one gets weary of life, or when there is so much hardship that one resents life. It can truly be said that all of Rome conformed to what Christ said about the lost man who gained the world yet forfeited his soul;[15] he himself perished, and he caused others to perish as well.

The situation in Palestine immediately following its conquest by the Roman Empire was not settled quickly. This was because the struggle between the Romans and the Parthians[16] left that area without any stability for a period of twenty years. Opinion was divided in Palestine between the two empires; some sided with the Parthians and others with the Romans.[17] The bloodshed which occurred between the two parties became increasingly violent, and this resulted in fierce savagery among the religious dignitaries, not to mention the worldly dignitaries. An example of this deterioration occurred when those who supported the Parthians triumphed over those who supported the Romans in Jerusalem.[18] The supporters of the Parthians nominated Antigonus, the son of Aristobulus, to take over as the High Priest. This man seized his rival Hyrcanus with his hands and gnawed off his ear with his teeth.[19] He did this so as to prevent him from serving as a priest for the rest of his life, since it was forbidden for anyone to serve as a priest who was disfigured or had any bodily defect.[20]

* * *

In the southern desert of Palestine, there was a leader who was famous for his shrewdness and determination and who was at the head of the Idumean tribes.[21] Through his discernment and farsightedness, he realized that the balance in the struggle over Palestine would tip towards the Roman Empire. So he joined forces with Rome and defied death in his support for Rome. The Empire then rewarded him for his service by appointing him king over Judea, Samaria, and Galilee, where Christ was born.[22] He in turn rewarded Rome by consistently imitating Roman civilization. His shrewdness led him to outsmart both the religious and worldly authorities at the same time. Thus he went to great lengths in his zeal for Jewish concerns, although his tribe professed in Judaism only in order to indulge and cater to the Jews. He also went to great lengths in his imitation of Roman and Greek conventions concerning dress, houses, insignias and names. He took upon himself the completion of the Temple at his own expense. Moreover, he took it upon himself to make sure that those nominated as the leaders of the Temple would come from among his assistants who were "Romanized,"[23] if such an expression exists. Sometimes they would gloss over Herod's excessive imitation of the Romans, along with the offense which this posed to Hebrew customs, whenever he needed to reconcile the two opposing sides.

In spite of this exhausting effort at rapprochement between the two sides, when Herod died he was the object of the strongest indignation from those of his religion. It so happened that shortly before his death, a group of Zealots had rebelled against the buildings and monuments he had erected, intending to blot out any features of paganism which they contained. So Herod summoned them to court; he ordered his soldiers to carry him to the session, and there he condemned them to be burned alive![24] He also arrested the most popular leaders among the Jews and held them in custody. He charged his sister to kill them as soon as he died, before the announcement of his death was made public. In this way, the grief of the people would eliminate any joy in gloating over his misfortune. He would not provide them the joy which they were anticipating on that day.[25]

The trial suffered by the Jews was brought to a head when the country was partitioned among the three sons of Herod. Galilee — where Christ was born[26] — was allocated to Herod II Antipas, Judea to Archelaus, and the heights of Syria to Philip. Now state protocol required that the king go to Rome in order to receive his commissioning as a ruler from Caesar himself. It was this custom to which Christ alluded in his famous parable, related by the disciple[27] Luke, where the sense of what he says is: "A man of noble descent went to a distant region in order to receive royal authority for himself and then return. . . . But the people of his city hated him and they sent an embassy after him saying, 'We do not want him to be king over us.'"[28]

However, Caesar installed the three sons in their districts, and Palestine emerged as a country torn apart among the sons of Herod. This also occurred in the jurisdictions of the Nabateans and the Decapolis. Rome's intention in this fragmentation was to gratify itself by raising in each district a fear of the others and by coercing the rulers into rivalry. It also planned to use these districts together as a shield by which it could keep at bay incursions from the desert and the fury of the fanatics.[29]

* * *

In spite of the correction concerning the date of the year of Christ's birth, a subject which will be dealt with later,[30] the following argument will show that he was born amidst the effects of a devastating rebellion which broke out in the regions of Jewish Palestine in particular.[31] In this rebellion, the blood of thousands of Zealots and their followers was shed in vain, since they took to flight in the face of the Roman Empire. They were protesting against the order which was issued concerning the general census. This census was not naturally a sufficient cause for igniting the fire of rebellion among the members of a tranquil community. However, it did indeed ignite this fire because it stirred up two ancient problems which existed in Palestine, especially among the Israelites.[32]

The first problem was one of acknowledging a king other than Yahweh, whom the Jewish people believed to be the only God and king, and that allegiance by the people to anyone else represented infidelity and disloyalty. They believed that God punished those who committed these two sins by bringing them afflictions and tribulations, and that he would forgive these only after an atonement was presented which involved the loss of life and goods. So if a Jew were to profess in a king other than Yahweh or his chosen anointed ones,[33] he would be banished from the mercy of God, worthy only of torment and exclusion. The Jewish people regarded the census to be a prelude leading to the imposition of imperial domination over each one of them. They believed that it would place them in shackles as slaves to Caesar who would be required to worship him and to begin their prayers in his name.

Now the legal scholars among the Jews used to submit to being taxed. This tax was taken from them forcefully by means of a contract which made no distinction among individuals by name but was imposed in a general manner on the villages and provinces. However, in principle these scholars vehemently rejected paying this tax. They judged anyone who approved it or who cooperated in its collection as guilty of infidelity, and they expelled him from the community, along with anyone who associated or conversed with him. It was in reference to this matter that they contrived their plot against Christ; they would ask him in front of the crowd of people about whether or not the payment of the tax should be permitted. "They sent their disciples from the Herodians to him, saying 'Teacher, indeed you are true and you teach the truth, and you pay no attention to anyone because you do not regard the status of people. Tell us, then, what you think. Is it permissible to pay taxes to Caesar, or is it not permissible?'" Then he gave his famous response: "Show me the coin[34] for paying the tax!" He looked at a Roman denarius and he asked them, "Whose picture and inscription is this?" And when they answered him that it was Caesar's, he said to them, "Then give to Caesar what belongs to Caesar, and to God what belongs to God."[35] His answer silenced them, because they did not reject the presence of Roman currency along with Jewish currency. And if they insisted on their rights and condemned having to pay with this currency, they would also have been against earning it and accumulating it. In fact, they did earn and accumulate the Roman currency, with the exception of the Zealots among them. It was this group that rebelled when the general census was established.

The other problem which was stirred up due to the census being established had to do with the tax itself and the injustice of the tax collectors by virtue of their collecting it. For it meant that the Jews had to pay two taxes: the first one to the Temple,[36] and the other to the Empire. It is said in the Gospels that envoys from the Temple requested a tax from Christ and his disciples,[37] and that one time Christ (peace be upon him) was asked if he would pay the tax. Then he said to his disciple Simon, "What do you think, Simon? From whom do the kings of the earth take the tax and the tribute? From their sons or from foreigners?" The disciple said to him, "Only from the foreigners." Then Christ said, "Therefore the sons are free." But he returned to the matter at hand and ordered his disciple to make a payment of the tax, for himself as well as for those of the disciples who were with him.[38]

Paying both of these taxes was a burden beyond what the poor could manage. However, along with the injustice involved in the collection of the state tax, it was a burden which the wealthy, quite apart from the poor, did not bear. This was because of the manner in which the Empire used to collect the tax, which involved a contract and an auction. Thus when the annual date arrived, the door of the auction opened, and the master of the auction granted to the most acceptable candidate the right to collect the tax throughout the year. Then the tax collectors, or publicans, took something for themselves besides what they turned over to the contractor; and the contractor took something for himself besides what he turned over to the state treasury. In this way the amount collected would be more than twice the amount required.[39]

Because of this, tax collectors as a group were detested by the people. The Jews could not forgive those who so completely devoted themselves to serving foreign contractors, and who would pilfer money illegally from what the destitute had to sustain themselves.[40] They therefore disapproved when Christ used to speak to the tax collectors and enter their homes and listen as they would confide in him about their concerns.[41] However, as he listened to them, he would charge them to be trustworthy in their collection of the taxes. They would ask him:[42] "Teacher! What shall we do?" And he would say to them, "Do not take more than what has been allocated to you." And he would say to the soldiers who accompanied them, "Do not treat anyone unjustly and do not slander anyone, and be content with your fodder."[43] For the Empire used to send their soldiers to gather their food and the fodder for their mounts from the people![44]

So when the command concerning the general census was issued, the populace assumed that the Empire was not completely content with what it had collected. They believed that Rome intended to augment this with other taxes which it would exact from individuals separately, in addition to the excessive manner in which the taxes were being collected under the contract. The Zealots were thus provided with a motive to rebel. They defended their convictions even as they defended their livelihoods when they were ordered to return to register their names in the places where they were born or where they lived.[45]

* * *

There is no disagreement among historians, both Eastern and European, that the political situation was the worst it could be, especially in Palestine. Nevertheless, in spite of its excessive corruption, the political situation did not reach the scope of the social situation with regard to the despair and universal distress present among the people. The reader need only examine the Gospels, whatever he may believe about them from the religious point of view, to realize that they represent the hopeless and wretched conditions which prevailed among the villages and towns in the regions of Palestine. This applies especially to the region of Galilee which is mentioned repeatedly in the accounts. Whenever the Gospel writers record one of the journeys of Christ among the villages, there are reports about the feeble and the sick who venture to ask for healing after hopelessly trying every kind of medical treatment. Among these were the lame, the paralyzed, the insane, and those afflicted with the inability to speak or to hear or to see, or with arthritis. It is said about one of these that his body was inhabited by demons, or that a group of demons took turns inhabiting his body by night and by day.[46] Some of the sick were little children, some were youths, and others were adults of various ages. And this was in addition to the diseases of leprosy, hemorrhaging and epilepsy which were not associated with insanity.[47]

If these were the prominent cases, no doubt there were others with a lesser degree of severity and prominence. They indicate that physical and psychological disorders were rampant in that society, leaving it a nervous wreck subject to discontent and turmoil. Added to this fact is that the first century witnessed diverse groups of healers in Palestine. They treated the sick with spiritual remedies, believing that the power of faith and a pure lifestyle were necessary components in medical practice and treatment.[48] And when we say that the first century was a period which witnessed a nervous wreck, we are addressing our attention especially to a phenomenon which points to the psychological condition of that time in its totality. For no period had a greater need than that one for tranquillity and reliance on faith. And no period had a greater yearning than that one for the deliverance and purification which would come when souls would be refreshed by the guide who was expected to bring such deliverance and purification.

* * *

The time for the Messianic mission did not arrive until it was preceded by other missions which had prepared the way for it, and it was the objective of the Messianic mission to make use of the work of previous leaders. The most capable of these leaders was John the Purifier or John the Baptist, although he was not the only leader involved in mission and prophecy. John established a symbol for purification, namely, washing with water. His mission resulted in an all-out offensive against the seat of corruption in his time, i.e., the court of King Herod.[49]

This was the site where fornication and liaisons with women were allowed, irrespective of any law; where brothers and sons were killed; where worship and sanctity were profaned by the arrogance and boldness of their atrocities. The prophet's boldness in rooting out evil was equal to the wicked tyrant's boldness in his profanity and treachery. This messenger was predestined to complete his mission quickly as he pursued his unequivocal campaign. He left the arena as a martyr, but he left pulling behind him a corpse which bore no trace of life. So it was that the body of Herod was eaten by worms before it was even buried.[50] Yet Herod himself had characterized his era quite accurately when he granted the head of the prophet as a gift to a dancer who had expended her body in the dance.[51] Thus, the mission of "John the Purifier" must surely be considered as a transient one, or as one involving reconnaissance and preparation. It had sent out raids here and there; but only after it was finished did the primary battle begin, the one which would fill the entire arena. That was a battle which would not be concluded in one brief day.

Chapter 8

The Religious Life of the World in the First Century

At the time of Christ's birth, the Roman Empire had reached the limit of its extent.[1] It had brought the nations of all the inhabited world into its possession, except for the most remote parts of the East. Among its subjects were people who were diverse in race, language and creed. In Rome, Alexandria, Nablus[2] and Jerusalem, one could observe every form of worship professed by humanity from the borders of India to the shores of the Atlantic. There was considerable discussion among the people about various lords, religions, ideologies and creeds. These were the subject of studies which the intellectuals and philosophers exchanged among themselves, following the relocation of the schools of philosophy and science to Alexandria. Sages and scholars from every ideology and creed would meet in these schools. People were accustomed to contemplate on these matters from an international perspective, especially those who were given to study, meditation, and spiritual pursuits.

There is something even more significant than this international perspective which has influenced our study on the genius of Christ:[3] the first century witnessed numerous waves of religions that flowed in from the East, and that inundated the regions of the Roman Empire itself, including the greater capital area. This is contrary to the earlier assumption that creeds become predominant only through the predominance of political power.[4]

Thus the domination of the Roman Empire over the East was not a prelude to the domination of Roman religion, as has often been the case in many phases of history. Contrary to this, it was precisely the creeds of the East which became predominant over Rome and its citizens. Indeed, they traveled from the nations that were ruled to the ruling nation, and this later included Christianity. There was no exception to this principle; rather, each new application of it was more general and more extensive than every situation which preceded it.

There is nothing in this matter which is at variance with normal procedure, as would initially seem to be the case. For the spread of the creeds from the East to the West at that stage of history was the normal procedure. There is every reason to support this, and not a single good reason is lacking for its justification.

This adoption of the Eastern faiths was beneficial to both the emperors and their subjects at the same time. For the emperors had aspirations of divinity, and they heard that priests in the temples of the East had proclaimed that divinity resided in the bodies of kings, and that they brought up these kings in order to be worshiped. Also, it was still being proclaimed that Alexander was a son of the god Ammon, and this report was being passed on by those who were familiar with the life of that conqueror.[5] Some of these emperors used to imitate Alexander; they would strive after the same ambitions and they would conquer the same way he conquered. Such aspirations led to fierce dissension in the homeland of Christ when king Antiochus, the successor to Alexander, endeavored to claim divinity; he called himself "the Divine" or the one bearing the mark of divinity.[6]

Now the subjects of the Roman Empire were a combination of diverse peoples. This blending also applied to the armies which Rome dispatched to the East, and which it left there for some time. Furthermore, Rome intended to keep them there, since it was wary of discord among the troops whenever they stayed in the capital for too long a time. It was not characteristic of such a diverse group of people for them to be zealous about the religious observances of Rome, nor to raise objections concerning other forms of religious observances. Thus it was appropriate that they would copy from the East, as what had occurred in the age of Alexander — even to claim divinity for the emperors!

Since ancient times, the East has never ceased to hold a reputation among Westerners as the place of origin regarding heavenly mysteries. It has been said that the people of the East learned from their acquaintance with the heavens things which Western nations could not teach them, and that the priests of the East were magicians who made known the Divine Mystery and who penetrated into the innermost secrets of the various religions. The word "magic" has been attributed to the Zoroastrians, and the magic of Babylon has been proverbial in every language from ancient times to modern.[7] Also, the reckoning of time into weeks, by which one of the planets is thought to control each day, is an Eastern legacy deeply rooted in ancient times. The remnants of this system are still found in the European chronology employed from the frontiers of the north to those of the south.[8]

It is no wonder that the people were captivated by this magic, and that they condoned what they heard from those of the East concerning heaven and its secrets. As long as the land was within their power and they controlled it as they pleased, they could find priests and magicians who would acknowledge their sovereignty over it in the name of heaven!

As a result, several Eastern religions penetrated the spiritual world of that time: the cult of Mithra, the cult of Isis, and the cult of the Therapeutae. These came in the same way that the Greek cult of Orpheus had come from Asia Minor, and it also had recourse to the ancient East.

Vestiges of the cult of Mithra have been observed in the remotest regions of the western Roman Empire. They have been seen in the remains of the Roman wall in England, as well as in other places. This cult spread among the young men of the army because Mithra was a dual personality which united two popular attributes. One of these was the attribute of light, which disperses darkness, and of truth, which abolishes falsehood. The other was the attribute of the warrior, the Lord of Hosts. He is mentioned in the book of the Zoroastrians, known as the Avesta,[9] where it says that he drove his legions into victory, enabling the god of good, Ohrmazd, to overcome the god of evil, Ahriman. Mithra was also a popular god among people who were not soldiers, such as shepherds and those who worked at night. The shepherds and sailors worshiped him and were guided by his light in their activities of the night. They believed that he was born with a human body in an abandoned cave, similar to how poor people are born. For this reason they made use of caves as temples for him. Perhaps worshipers were attracted to this god because of the well-known yearning which people have to probe mysteries and to aspire to advance along the stages of knowledge about the unknown. For there were seven stages along which his worshipers were transported from one stage to another, with the help of the chosen masters. These worshipers were engaged in religious ceremonies for every occasion, worshiping either secretly or openly as a select group of companions. Some of them partook of bread and wine, and they revered sacred honey which they placed on their tongues as a symbol of the sweetness of faith.[10]

The Egyptian cult of Isis was bound up with the Persian cult of Mithra as together they invaded the land of the Romans and Greeks. Isis was called "Demeter" by the Greeks, and they ascribed to her the same attribute given by the Egyptians, i.e., the attribute of supreme motherhood, or of Mother Nature. Her worshipers regarded her as one with the moon, and thus they revered her as the goddess of the sea and of navigation. They would draw beautiful pictures of her which conveyed purity and compassion, and in her bosom would be a nursing infant whose face was radiant with light. These pictures symbolized motherhood, benevolence, and innocence. The priests of this cult in the West shaved their heads in imitation of the priests in Egypt. Among these priests were both male and female worshipers who designated Isis as the guardian of the home and family. Thus the cult of Isis spread among those Romans who were known for their family traditions and for honoring parental rights. And no doubt the secret ceremonies which accompanied the cult of Isis played a role in generating a desire among the people to adopt these ceremonies for themselves. This situation was like that regarding the cult of Mithra, whose secret ceremonies had a similar influence and a similar pattern of worship.[11]

There was also a sect originating in Egypt which was vigorous despite the small number of its members. This was the sect of the Therapeutae[12] mentioned by the Jewish philosopher of Alexandria, Philo.[13] He stated that the followers of this sect used to gather together on the Sabbath, and then afterwards they would disperse among the settlements for meditation, for philosophical studies, and for spiritual and physical exercise. Their name in Greek means "healers"[14] or "skillful devotees."[15] Most of their settlements were in the vicinity of Alexandria surrounding the ancient Mareotic Lake. Some historians believe that these Therapeutae were the mentors for the Jewish ascetics called the Essenes, whom we considered in our discussion on Jewish Sects.[16]

It has been observed that the Greek cult of Orpheus did not have the same level of circulation among the Romans as did the purely Eastern religions. It would seem that they considered the religious "mysteries" to be a prerogative of the ancient East, while they resorted to the Greeks in matters of philosophy, art and rhetoric. This was especially so after the cult of Orpheus developed into an Eastern religion which followed the practices of the East regarding asceticism and spiritual brotherhood. Originally, Greek Orphism had evolved along artistic lines. In the portrayal of Orpheus, it is said that whenever he played on a stringed instrument, the wild beasts, grazing animals and birds would approach him; they would forget their ravenousness and hearken to him, and this was how predatory animals became domesticated. The grazing animals became a symbol for the taming of people's hearts and the elimination of evil from the souls of the mighty. By the first century, the followers of the Orpheus cult professed in asceticism and renunciation. Eating meat was forbidden; they dressed in white clothes; and they would not taste wine except in their sacrificial ceremonies. They preserved in their legends the belief of the ancient Greeks about Orpheus the artist. They further claimed that he visited the world of the dead and returned from there, and they set aside certain times for mourning his death and for celebrating his resurrection.[17] There are similarities between the celebration of his resurrection and the celebration of the resurrection of Adonis, the god of Spring. It is often stated in books on comparative religion that the Egyptian god Aton, the Greek god Adonis, and the term "Adonai," meaning "master" or "lord" in Hebrew, are several names which go back to an ancient Egyptian source.[18]

* * *

It is clear that these sects were not universal religions, preaching to every nation about their rituals, whether manifest or hidden. For they carefully selected their members and new adherents, and they preserved their religious observances and symbols for their secret prayers. Rather, they were in essence more like confederations and alliances which draw together those who are occupied with a single goal or those who share the same disposition and sentiment. They were closer to professional sports teams which undertake to be selective in their tastes and to consolidate good relations among those who are similar and are like-minded.[19]

Those who sought out these sects were all young people who wanted to discover the truths about their lives which were unknown to them. They believed, or they thought it most likely, that these truths were among the secrets of knowledge and understanding, and that those who were wise and who had considerable experience could be their guides. These sects also had seekers among middle-aged and older people who had ceased to put confidence in the public religious ceremonies. They had abandoned these in order to go where they could search for the truth and could put their conscience at rest, where the surroundings would be familiar and their psychological and intellectual pursuits would find harmony. For some, these sects were not at all devotional or professional circles. For such people, these functioned as clubs in which principles were preserved from any confusion and any "alternative opinions,"[20] especially alternative opinions coming from others who spoke in an ignorant or trivial manner.

However, everything that can be said about the spread of these sects in the first century points to two significant conclusions. In the first place, it was an indication that people were searching for true conviction, and that those who were sincerely prepared to exercise faith had sensed the emptiness of the traditions and doctrines which surrounded them. Secondly, it was an indication of an international trend which began to penetrate parts of the inhabited world and to unite the people of diverse nations in a search for spiritual ideologies. This is because these secret sects were not restricted to any single nation, nor were they forbidden to anyone because of his race or origin. Thus anyone who opened himself emotionally to the beliefs and the social graces of these sects found that they welcomed him as a candidate who could move along their stages from the lowest to the highest.

The general populace, however, did not pay much attention to these exclusive sects which were restricted to those who sought them out and joined them. The masses persisted in continuing blindly with their customs and conventions. Nevertheless, there was still in these customs and conventions an international character which tended to eliminate distinctions among the followers of the various religions. It would bring them all together from time to time to celebrate the public feasts held for this or that god or goddess. Or, this character would often occur in the festivals of nature which were typically mixed in with religion as it had been practiced by the ancients. It was the policy of the Roman Empire to go along with this sentiment, and it even encouraged and fostered these feelings. For the golden rule among those Romans who were political leaders was that the people would not be concerned about who governed them as long as they could easily find food and entertainment. And one kind of entertainment which cost the Empire nothing was when the general masses were happy with their feasts and they could try to outdo one another with their festivals and birthdays and they could color them as they wished with a sacred quality. This indeed was safer than strife and discord and conflict.[21]

The sum of what can be said about the religious life of the inhabited world at that time is that it was a life of convention, i.e., a life of intense longing to believe in something. This conclusion derives from research and from evidence that there was a pride in conventional beliefs. It can also be said that this religious life proceeded along its course towards an "internationality" which was prevalent among the people and which did not single out any particular community according to the nature and origin of its creed. Even more important than the internationality of these sects and festive occasions was an internationality of language and culture, one which shattered the strongest barriers that had existed for about ten centuries. For the Jews had believed that Hebrew was the language of Yahweh by which he addressed the prophets and confided with the priests in the niches of the sanctuary. But it was not long before they acquiesced to using Aramaic when they offered their prayers and listened to the inspired writings, as well as to using the dialects of Syriac which were similar to Aramaic.[22] Moreover, a large number of the Jews had authorized the translation of the Hebrew Bible into Greek in the second century B.C.E.[23] This process continued without any restraint during the first century and afterwards. Thus it was Aramaic which was the language in which Jesus and the disciples preached the good news. And it was Greek which was the language of the Gospels. And it was Syriac which was the language of both the Hebrew Bible and the gospel after only one century had elapsed following Christ's birth.[24]

* * *

In connection with our discussion about the general state of religious affairs as the first century arrived, several phenomena have been recorded concerning the pagan creeds. The most important of these is that their condition was similar to a situation of liquidation prior to an announcement of bankruptcy. Thus the historian Suetonius reported that in 12 B.C.E.

Caesar Augustus collected almost two thousand sheets of prophecies and prayers written in Latin and Greek and ordered that they be burned in public. He preserved a few scraps that had been handed down, placed them in two gilded chests, and transferred them to the temple of the god Apollo.[25] This report provides a synopsis of our information about the pagan creeds in that generation.

Chapter 9

Intellectual Life in the First Century

The intellectual ideologies which are often the topic of discussion among the educated were widespread in the region of Galilee where Christ was born.[1] Westerners and Easterners had frequently mingled together there for several centuries before his birth. The most prevalent among these ideologies were Pythagoreanism, Epicureanism, and Stoicism. Quite apart from their reputation, these are the ones which interest us because they are the ideologies which had a bearing on the behavior and beliefs of the people. Two of these emerged among the Greeks at a time which for them was similar to the period in which Christ was born; these were Epicureanism and Stoicism. Despite their incompatibility, they both had reacted to a single situation which inundated Greece after its victory over the Persian Empire. This situation had to do with the luxury, arrogance, pleasure and oppression on the part of the masters, and the resentment towards this on the part of the slaves and the oppressed.

These three ideologies joined together in a single goal: the search for tranquillity and rest. However, Pythagoreanism had emerged before the time of luxury and domination, so it tended to be more spiritual and to exhibit a blending of beliefs from the various peoples of Greece, Egypt, Persia and India. All of them were closer to the East in origin, since they originated in Cyprus and Asia Minor.

The followers of Pythagoras were united in "a brotherhood" which included the use of religious ceremonies and prayers.[2] Some of these were reasonable, but others incorporated the kind of restrictions or prohibitions which were widespread among primitive tribes. Thus they considered it their duty to adhere to certain sacred customs, or to refrain from other customs. They believed that their leader Pythagoras was the son of the god Apollo, and that he never died but would appear after some time. This was because their beliefs were similar to those among the people of India regarding the transmigration of souls.[3] They believed that it was strange for the soul to be inside the body, that it sought for release, something which it could not experience except through the benefit of good deeds. They forbade the eating of animals, and in a similar way they forbade the eating of beans and recommended avoiding legumes altogether. Among their more remarkable prohibitions were these: they would not eat from a whole loaf of bread; they would not pick up anything that fell on the ground; they would not break blossoms off of trees; and they would not look in a mirror towards the light.[4] Some of them used to preach to animals, believing that they were addressing souls which were residing in them temporarily. For them, people were classified as being either human or half-way between human and divine, and Pythagoras was one of those in the latter group.

Pythagoras used to welcome both men and women into his brotherhood. He made it an obligation that they share the food and possessions which were acquired by the community. After his death, his followers believed that he continued to inspire them to discover further knowledge and teach them lessons of wisdom and proper morals. They also believed that for him life was a "spectacle," and that it would be the same for those who were like him. Thus, in the view of Pythagoras, the world was like the arena of the Olympic games. Those who entered the games with the purpose of winning were the most despicable. Those whose purpose was to compete were above these. And those whose purpose was to be spectators were the most superior of them all. Thus the philosophers, who visited the world in order to contemplate and observe, were more exalted than those who won or contended for the prizes of the arena.

The Pythagoreans considered philosophical ideas themselves to be a revelation from God. They derived the word "theory" from the name for God, *theos* in Greek. For them, all wisdom came from divine wisdom. The one who searched for it could obtain it through exercise and secret conversations, and through "the harmonization" between himself and the music of the universe. This was because for them, the entire universe was a system of numerical and musical relations, and the portrayal of its perfection was the number four; perhaps they thought this way because the universe was considered to unite the four elements by which all things were created.[5]

It has been said that the Pythagoreans had political intentions and that they used to conspire against the state in their secret gatherings. Pythagoras himself had lived in the sixth century B.C.E., and he traveled through every locality in the inhabited world. His sect, or brotherhood, continued to exist in every region, especially those in which Greeks lived who had adopted Eastern ways.

* * *

Epicureanism and Stoicism both appeared at the same time and then spread among the educated in all parts of the inhabited world. One might initially think that they contradicted each other, whereas actually they were quite similar; or, it is possible to say that they were about the same in practice according to their interpretation of life and proper behavior.

The philosophy of Epicurus arose during the third and fourth centuries B.C.E.[6] According to the best known account, he was born on the island of Samos which is near the coast of Asia Minor. He took refuge in Asia Minor with his family who had fled persecution, and he embarked on the study of philosophy when he was about fourteen. In the year 311 B.C.E., when he was about thirty, he opened his school in his famous garden in Athens.

When the philosophy of Epicurus is measured by his personal lifestyle, it is seen to advocate the austere life of hermits. This is because he spent most of his days living on bread and water or bread and cheese. However, his name has become associated with the notions of pleasure and desire, because he taught his disciples that the goal of life was happiness, and the greatest happiness can never arise from pain or remorse. For this reason, he avoided bestial desires, considering them to be of the sort which he called "agitated" happiness.[7] This was the happiness which is associated with effort and which arises from remorse and hardship. He classified happiness into two varieties: agitated happiness and stable or tranquil happiness. The best of these, as mentioned above, was the happiness of tranquillity and stability, and by this he meant the happiness of contemplation, repose, and contentment.

Epicurus welcomed into his school slaves and women who were dancers or who were otherwise employed. He saw no restriction in the search for happiness which was free of pain and remorse. He could not even see how the sage could imagine "the Good" when he eliminated from his consideration the joys of taste and sight and hearing. Anyone who renounced a joy which he could experience without pain or remorse was foolish, not wise.

Epicurus assailed the Greek religions, as well as other religions of his time, for being full of superstitions and lies. He taught his disciples that the gods existed, but they were distracted from the affairs of the world with their own well-being. Thus the world's affairs were not decreed by fate or destiny.[8] He made no distinction between gods and created beings, except in how sophisticated was their material makeup and how pure their composition. For they were all material, and nothing other than matter existed.

Accordingly, he welcomed every explanation which reduced the phenomena of the universe to natural causes, and he rejected every explanation which had recourse to the gods and the divine mysteries. He faced death itself with both happiness and pain, in accordance to his beliefs; although there was no joy in death, it was nevertheless a deliverance from the sufferings of life. For this reason, the ideology of Epicurus spread during those periods when there was uncertainty, weariness, and a lack of conviction and faith in providence. Those who accused the religions of falsehood preferred this ideology over that of Stoicism. This is because Epicureanism, in contrast to Stoicism, neither exempted its adherents from inconveniences, nor imposed an obligation on the mind and conscience which weighed them down. But in spite of this, Epicureanism united its precepts and injunctions into well-ordered principles; these resembled the religious invocations[9] which the novice learns by heart, observing them carefully with regard to his faith and worship.

* * *

If we wished to summarize Stoic teaching in only two words, these would be "self-control" and "restraint": self-control despite misfortune, and restraint from desire.[10] Stoicism taught that a person's well-being was dependent only on himself and his conscience. Thus the one who disciplined himself in the fight against pain and grief, and who repressed his desires and passion, would attain the limit of happiness which was destined for mere mortals. Stoics believed in predestination, and they were convinced that the entire universe was a well-ordered system which proceeded in accordance with the divine will. Through a knowledge of its mysteries and secrets, one could understand revelations, visions, omens, and the movements of the stars. A person would find that reason belonged with the gods, while the body belonged with dumb animals. It was his human virtue to submit to reason and to renounce the body; he would renounce his body by resisting its desires, and he would submit to reason by searching for knowledge. His entire well-being consisted of whatever happiness could be his from getting along without desires and from obtaining knowledge. Any happiness which was more than this was a delusion that could not be realized, or an intrusion that offered no benefit.

The first Stoics arose as materialists who believed that all existence came from a single source. However, they made gradual progress in spiritual beliefs; in the first century and subsequently, their successors ultimately arrived at belief in the freedom of the soul which was in opposition to matter. For the supreme god Zeus was incapable of making the body free from the bonds of matter, but he would provide us[11] with the opportunity to take on his divine soul. By his favor, we would become brothers with no distinction among them regarding nationality or race or language. Wherever they might go, they would be with God. They had no need for a temple or a place of worship; for sanctity existed within the reverent soul, not in a place of worship fabricated by the builder and the blacksmith.[12]

Among the prayers of the Stoics is the famous prayer which was passed down from their leader Cleanthes (310-230 B.C.E.).[13] In it he confided in Zeus, saying: "Guide me, oh Zeus, oh Fate. Lead me to where you want to send me. Help me, and I will follow you and not turn away or become afraid, even if doubt overcomes me and I flinch and hesitate. For I cannot run away nor escape from following you."[14]

The Stoic followed the way of Fate because for him it was "the Good"; it was not enough for Fate to be "the Necessity." The supreme god did not want evil, so he did not create it. The evils which were in the world were nothing but pre-determined contrasts which were required by the presence of the Good, and without which the Good could not be realized. Thus there would be no room for rest unless there were toil; no room for satisfaction unless there were hunger; and no room for mercy unless there were cruelty. And if cruelty was considered to be abhorrent, then the "mercy" which abandoned one to grief and sorrow could hardly be considered a divine virtue. Mercy was only a virtue when it was perceived, as a god was perceived, with respect to what it accomplished. For mercy rejected cruelty and did not yield to grief and sorrow, unless it were tricked into doing so. By such reasoning the sage included in his wisdom an antidote for every mystery and a remedy for every affliction.

Like Pythagoras, as the evidence seems to indicate, the Stoics borrowed from India the concept that the world passes away and returns in perpetual cycles for which no end is known. Some of them believed that the souls of the wise continued in every cycle until their termination. Eventually the burning of the everlasting fire would envelope them even as it would envelop the whole world. This was the fire which would purify everything that exists and liberate them from their crowded confinement. Thus they would return successively into existence after existence, world after world, resurrection after resurrection.[15]

The Stoic school was completely indebted to leaders with an Eastern background, especially the eminent personalities in this school, Zeno (340-270 B.C.E.) and Posidonius (135-51 B.C.E.). For they were all either Phoenicians or else Greeks who had adopted Eastern ways and who had lived for some time in Eastern countries. Following is a summary of the teachings of the greatest Stoic leader, Zeno,[16] as outlined in our book about God:[17]

"Zeno claimed that deity was 'material substance' *(sōma)* and that the entire universe was the structure which enclosed the substance of deity. This deity permeated the universe just as honey permeates the honeycombs of beehives. The 'Law' *(nomos),* which was synonymous to the expression 'Correct Reason' *(orthos logos)* or the 'Correct Word,' and the god Zeus were a single entity which watched over the destiny of each element of the universe. Zeno saw a divine character in the stars and the progression of the days. He believed [as we have already said] that the world would end in a conflagration, and that all the properties of whatever entities that might come into existence, along with their causes and their destinies, would be consumed by this fire. They would then reappear time after time through the activity and predestination of Reason. They were enclosed within an irrevocable fate and a firm ordinance, like a city guarded by the custodians of law and order.

"For Zeno, the ideas of God, Reason, Fate and Zeus were synonymous. All of these words, and other names like them, denoted a single Existence. This single Existence was solitary, without any companion. It willed to create the world; then the air came to exist, and the air became water. 'Created matter' *(logos spermatikos)* flowed within this water, just as matter produced by procreation flows within living beings. From this created matter emerged the basic principles, namely, fire, water, air and soil. All things then emerged, step by step, from these principles.

"Zeno defined Fate as that power which set primordial matter in motion. It was a rational power, because that which was characterized by reason was greater than that which was deprived of it; since there was nothing greater than the 'universe' *(kosmos),* it was therefore rational on account of its greatness.

"Zeno explained that the common people believed in numerous gods because they searched for God among the manifold expressions of nature. Thus the gods proliferated among the people as they wove legends around them by comparing them to ghosts. However, these comparisons were no more than figurative symbols which only pointed to actual truth."[18]

The last of the leading personalities among the Stoics who appeared before the first century was Posidonius,[19] whom we have already mentioned. He taught his disciples that the soul did not cease to exist along with the demise of the body. Rather, it ascended into heaven at a height corresponding to its ascent in knowledge and virtue. Thus there were some souls which fluttered close to the ground. But there were other souls which soared among the distant heavenly bodies, floating among them, taking pleasure in observing them and joyfully listening to their melodies until the Day of Resurrection.[20] This sage took an interest in India through his study of geography and astronomy, just as he took a similar interest in that country through his intellectual and religious studies. According to the author of *Stoics and Sceptics,* Posidonius determined that the distance between Cádiz and India was 70,000 stadia (a Greek unit of measurement which is equivalent to about 175 meters). It is said that Columbus utilized this estimate in his calculations when he headed for India by way of the Western sea.[21]

Historians of philosophy are in agreement concerning the magnitude of the influence which Stoic beliefs engendered in the Roman world, even to its most distant borders. The magnitude of this influence demonstrates the vastness of its reach, as its tenets extended to kings and slaves alike in about four centuries following the appearance of its first leader Zeno. Other leaders included the slave Epictetus (60-100 C.E.) and the great emperor Marcus Aurelius (161-180 C.E.).[22] Commanders and governors, who were among those who visited the East and lived there, boasted of belonging to this ideology.

As for Palestine in particular, where Christ was born, the ideologies of Stoicism and Epicureanism were about equally divided among the thinking of both religious and non-religious people there. These two ideologies had so penetrated the Jewish sects, they were like two forms of culture displayed by those who pretended to be knowledgeable and civilized. Thus, the Sadducees were favorably disposed to Epicureanism, while the Pharisees embraced Stoic wisdom despite their hatred of imitating foreigners. For the dominance of leading personalities among the Stoics who had an Eastern background had given the Stoic sect a nationalistic tinge, and the Pharisees did not desist from imitating this, in conformity with their inclination to take on new ideas.[23]

* * *

There is a particular event which happens to offer assistance in tracing the influence of the intellectual ideologies in the Jewish world. This was the fact that the first century produced the greatest of Jewish philosophers in ancient times, Philo Judaeus.[24] He was born in Alexandria in 30 B.C.E. and died in 50 C.E. He blended into his philosophy the various beliefs and philosophical ideologies of his time, drawing from every source, especially from the Greeks of Alexandria. He adopted the Stoic teaching about the "Word" *(logos)* from Heraclitus, who was the first to speak of it in ancient times.[25] Philo claimed that the Word was the agent of God in his relationship with this world.[26] He also adopted the interpretation of religious symbols found in the mystery religions such as the cult of Isis, and the cult of Osiris-Sarapis[27] which had been established at Alexandria and had branched out to Athens, Pompeii, Rome and some of the coastal cities of Asia. Then he applied this interpretation to the symbols found in the Torah, and he gave them a rational explanation which differed at many points from the traditional commentaries of the Torah.[28]

In his discussion on the creation of the world, Philo said that the style followed by Moses (peace be upon him) was different from the style of other lawgivers who simply compiled the regulations of their people, which concerned what was permitted and what was forbidden, without any independent action or revision. But it was also different from the style of those who delivered obscure laws which contained enigmas and augmentations. Philo presented the story of creation as a narrative which embraced the idea that the world is in conformity to the Law,[29] and the Law is in conformity to the world. He also stated that the man who observed this Law, as a virtuous citizen of the whole world, regulated his actions in harmony with the will of nature, which also regulated the whole world in harmony with its will.[30]

Philo was a Stoic who was on the brink of Epicureanism.[31] For this is how he explained the name of Isaac in his discussion on Abraham: "The meaning of Isaac in our language is 'laughing.' However, the laughter here is not that which comes from the happiness of the body; it is rather the happiness of virtuous knowledge, indeed it is joy. It has been reported to us that this joy is that which the sage Abraham[32] offered as a sacrifice to God. Thus he demonstrated through this symbol that joy is reliably linked to God alone. For people are subject to sorrow and fear which come from evils both present and anticipated. But there is no sorrow or fear in the nature of God."[33]

The teaching of Philo concerning prayer was that people should pray by giving thanks to God for whatever is in the entire universe, and for all created beings within it; and among these for all humans, men and women, Greeks and barbarians; and also among these for the personality of the one being prayed for,[34] including his body, spirit, speech, mind and senses. The prayer which follows this pattern is worthy of a response.[35]

For Philo, humanity was divided into three classes: the offspring of the earth, the offspring of the sky, and the offspring of God. The offspring of the earth were those who sought the pleasures of the body. The offspring of the sky were those who sought the pleasures of the mind. The offspring of God were those who renounced the world and who devoted themselves completely to a world beyond this world, one which was preserved from perishing and free of matter, where they would be in the company of the guides and messengers.[36]

Philo was not one of those who called people to live in isolated places as hermits. For him, it made no difference where someone lived. All good, wherever it may be, came only from God, and He was everywhere. So He guided wherever He willed those who aspired after the Spirit.[37]

In the same way, Philo did not consider the animals offered up as sacrifices to be of great importance. He referred to this in his discussion on special laws: "God does not rejoice over sacrificial animals, even if they number in the hundreds. For he is the owner of all things and the giver of all things to people, and these animals are among his gifts. It is sometimes more suitable to approach him with barley bread than to approach him with precious objects and treasures. Even the one who presents to God only himself brings along nothing but his own sincerity and pure intention.[38] For he is more honorable than the person who freely gives away his goods yet who speaks and acts in an evil manner."[39]

Philo was a universal figure who addressed humanity collectively. He used to say that Israel was called by this name only because he directed his attention to God; thus everyone who directed his attention to God was Israel.[40] But this universal vocation never turned Philo away from solidarity with his own people. And he never forgot in his deliberations that the children of Israel were the guides of the nations, and that they were the race most deserving of the admiration of all others. For the Athenians had rejected the rituals of the Lacedaemonians,[41] and the Lacedaemonians had rejected the rituals of the Athenians. The Egyptians were never known to have adopted the traditions of the Scythians, or the Scythians to have adopted the traditions of the Egyptians. And the people of Europe avoided the customs of the people of Asia, while the people of Asia avoided the customs of the people of Europe. But the seventh day in which the Jews rested was observed with reverence by all peoples. And every year the Day of Atonement was regarded as more holy than the sacred month observed by the Greeks. For that month was one in which they refrained from killing, but it was also one which incited the people to be excessive with their drinking and eating and their physical passions. What a difference this was from the season of fasting and despondency observed by the children of Israel![42]

Philo said this about his own people in his treatise on the life of Moses (peace be upon him). However, in his treatise on the Special Laws, he said that Israel existed among the nations like a prodigal orphan among strangers. No one ventured to help the Jews when the nations plotted and the peoples conspired. Their offense against these people was that they enjoined on themselves strict religious obligations. They were solemn in their way of life; its rigor weighed heavily on their disposition and imposed a loathsome burden on their spirits. "In spite of this, Moses said to us that the orphanhood of Israel attracted to itself the compassion of God, the director of the universe. Israel had a share in this universe, but it was set apart from the world in the same way that the first fruits are set apart as a gift to the Creator and the merciful Father."[43]

Such was the ultimate stage at which Philo arrived in his time. He is not considered to have been a leader in the Jewish religion who had many followers. But he is considered to have been an appropriate model of that religion, the kind of religion which was understood by the wise, informed and devout person at the beginning of the first century.

Part Three
Historical Factors Concerning Christ's Birth[1]

Chapter 10

The Land of Galilee

Christ was born in the land of Galilee[2] — or "Galilee of the nations,"[3] as the Jews used to call it. This was because it was a region which was open to all nations both Eastern and Western, and at no time had it been inhabited solely by Jews. The meaning of Galilee in Hebrew is "circle." By this they meant "enclosing," because it accommodated many who were not allowed to live in other towns of Palestine, especially the south of the country.[4]

Galilee was a part of the northern coastal regions which were known in ancient history by the name of "Canaan." Later the Greeks conferred on it the name "Phoenicia" because of the red color which could be seen, i.e., the color of the rocks and mountains.[5]

Canaan was distinguished in ancient times for its serviceable ports and for being situated along the commercial route which extended from the Mediterranean Sea to the Persian Gulf and the most distant parts of the East. Famous among these ports were Sidon, Tyre and Haifa.[6] Commerce between East and West was mostly concentrated on Sidon and Tyre, because in ancient times the southern coast lacked any serviceable ports. Furthermore, there were no roads behind the southern coast which were frequently used for commerce other than desert roads, and at that time those had little security and considerable inconvenience.

Because of this unique situation, from ancient times the land of Galilee was replete with travelers and residents from all the civilized nations of the East and West, and its ties with all human civilizations became firmly established. Various industries and skills, both practical and theoretical, were widespread throughout the land. This especially applied to those skills which were associated with navigation such as the art of building ships, the observation of the stars, and writing. Moreover, Phoenician merchants and sailors were the ones who spread the alphabet among the countries of the Mediterranean Sea, and from these countries it was carried to the rest of the European nations.

Part of the country of Galilee, or Canaan, was brought into the kingdom of David after it was founded. However, the relationship between Galilee and Judea was perpetually one of wariness and aversion, if not one of war and hostility. The effect of Jewish domination over the country of the Canaanites was that the Jews adopted certain aspects of Canaanite civilization while depending on the Canaanites for industry and commerce. It is mentioned in the Old Testament more than once that the Jews sought help from artisans and experts among the Canaanites in order to construct Jewish temples and palaces. In the Book of Kings, for example, Solomon sent a request to Hiram, king of the Canaanites, that he order wood to be cut for the building of the Temple. Solomon said to him, "You know that there is no one among us who knows how to cut wood like the Sidonians."[7] There is also a description of the craftsman whose father was from Tyre and whose mother was from the tribe of Naphtali, "and he was full of wisdom, understanding and knowledge of every kind of work with bronze."[8]

In Ezekiel chapter 27, it is said that the Canaanites had commercial dealings in wheat, honey, oil, balsam, sweets and other goods which could be transported among other nations.[9]

The Jews depended on the Canaanites in matters of culture and art in addition to their demands for commerce and industry. They copied from the Canaanites the art of writing, the meters used in poetry, and the hymns used in prayers. It happened more than once that they renounced the tenets of their religion and changed over to the beliefs of the Canaanites. The Old Testament indicates this in the book of Judges, where it says, "The children of Israel did evil in the eyes of the Lord; they worshiped the Baals and they renounced the god of their fathers who had brought them out of Egypt."[10] The Old Testament also indicates this in the book of First Kings, where the prophet Elijah said, "The children of Israel have renounced your covenant and destroyed your altars and killed your prophets."[11] Furthermore, it says, "I have preserved in Israel seven thousand people, all of whose knees have not bowed down to Baal and whose mouths have not kissed him."[12]

As the number of Jews who lived in the northern regions of Palestine such as Galilee and Samaria increased, their customs and traditions changed. The Judeans began to view them as outsiders[13] who had been cut off from their roots and who followed strange practices in their customs and morals. In fact, the people of Galilee especially became accustomed to speaking in Aramaic, the language spoken by the people of Syria proper, or in Greek, the language spoken by those who had come from the sea or from Asia Minor.[14] They took over many traditions from Persia, India and Iraq, because they encountered the people of these countries as they arrived on caravans from the East. Some historians think it is likely that the ancient Phoenicians originated entirely among tribes of the Persian Gulf which had left that area and had traveled by way of the caravans until they settled along the coast of the Mediterranean Sea; these then continued to maintain their connection to the Eastern seas.[15]

The hatred of the people of Judea towards those of their religion in the North reached a climax when John Hyrcanus, the Maccabean,[16] invaded the northern regions, among them the countries of Samaria and Galilee.[17] He then sent back some of the Jews in these places to the South, while he made those who lived in the North choose between leaving the country or accepting circumcision and the marks of Judaism. They preferred to remain rather than leave the country of their fathers and grandfathers, the country where these people had chosen to live a long time ago. So the Samaritans remained isolated in their traditions, while the people of Galilee remained suspect, regarded by the Jews with an attitude of uncertainty and perplexity.

There is agreement in what historians have said, and it is often repeated in historical accounts, that a large segment of the population of Galilee were Arabs[18] who spoke Aramaic. They pronounced Hebrew with a foreign accent which was evident to the people of the South, who would differentiate a speaker by this accent from only a few words which would escape from him by chance and without thought. This was how the disciples were recognized in the Temple, just as they were recognized in all of Palestine.[19]

One of the proverbs which made the rounds among those Jews who were fervent for their traditions and customs was this: "There is nothing good that comes from Galilee." In the Gospel of John, Nathaniel was amazed when his friend said to him, "We have found the one about whom Moses proclaimed," saying that he was from Nazareth in Galilee. Nathaniel then gave a curious answer: "Can anything good come from Nazareth?" (chapter 1).[20] Also in the Gospel of John there is the account about the men of the Temple, that they said sarcastically, "No prophet has ever arisen in Galilee" (chapter 7).[21]

The reason why the Judeans resented Galilee and its people comprised two factors: the religious tolerance and the lack of restraint among the Galileans.[22] For the Judeans rejected every form of tolerance, and they were inflexible regarding every kind of prohibition. However, this reason was precisely what made the land of Galilee a more fitting place of origin for the mission to humanity which the world was anticipating at that time. For it was not at all easy for this call for brotherhood to break forth among those nations which existed in an atmosphere of hardened inflexibility.

A few years after the birth of Christ, it so happened that Galilee moved outside the control of the king of Judea, immediately following the demise of Herod the Great. Along with the desert which bordered it, Galilee became part of the share which was designated to his son Herod Antipas. Christ (peace be upon him) was perhaps ten years old when the Romans had demolished the capital of this new ruler. A new capital, Tiberias, was built in the vicinity of Nazareth, where he (peace be upon him) grew up. No doubt he heard the news of this disaster when he was about ten, as well as the news of the rebellion which preceded it and which was the cause of the subsequent destruction.[23] For among the issues of politics and state, it was this problem of fanaticism, indeed the whole issue of religious tolerance, which had been the talk of his childhood and the first thing that had reached his ears.

When the new capital was named after the Roman emperor Tiberius, no doubt criticism was heard from dignitaries about that hypocritical flattery, and jokes were made prematurely by politicians and officials. So Christ realized that capitals are destroyed and built, that empires come and go,[24] that the oppressor flatters and the flatterer oppresses, and that the glory of hypocrisy was false and empty. Thus his innocent being drifted among other horizons, and his perceptive soul pictured the kingdom of heaven in another form, one which contrasted worldly kingdoms and which would continue to be different the older he grew.

Chapter 11

When Christ was Born [1]

The assumption of the Christian calendar is that Christ was born in the first year C.E., and the practice of European nations has followed this reckoning since 532 C.E. That was the year in which the monk Dionysius Exiguus (i.e., "the Small") called for the dating procedure to begin with the first year C.E. The reckoning which he calculated was considered valid, and so the practice has followed his computation until now.

This man was not small with regard to his religious position; rather, he applied the surname "the Small" to himself out of humility and contrition. He carried out his studies and revisions to the degree possible in his time, but he was not preserved from making an error in his computation by a few years.[2] Later, it was difficult to rectify this error because of its established position. It was decided to emend the error by adding four years to the old assessment which his companions had computed from the beginning of creation. According to how that assessment was computed, they considered Christ to have been born in the year 4004.[3]

The estimate that is predominantly maintained by historians, both religious and non-religious, is that the birth of Christ preceded the first year C.E. by a few years, and that the best assessment is that he was not born in the first year C.E.

According to the Gospel of Matthew, Christ (peace be upon him) was born before the death of Herod the Great; yet Herod died four years prior to the first year C.E.[4]

And in the Gospel of Luke, it is said that Christ undertook his mission in the fifteenth year of the rule of Caesar Tiberius, and that he was about thirty at that time.[5] Now Tiberius began to rule the Roman Empire in partnership with Caesar Augustus in the year 765 from the founding of the city of Rome. This means that Christ became thirty years old around the Roman year 779, and that he was born in the Roman year 749, i.e., before the first year C.E. by four years.

The Gospel of Luke also mentions that Caesar Augustus ordered the registration, i.e., the census, to be conducted in the entire inhabited world, and that this first registration occurred when Quirinius was governor over Syria. "So everyone went to be registered, each in his own town. And Joseph went up . . . from the town of Nazareth to Judea . . . to be registered with Mary, the woman to whom he was engaged; and she was pregnant. While there, her time arrived, and she gave birth to her first-born son."[6]

The registration meant here, it would seem, was the decree for the census referred to by the historian Josephus, who recorded this as though it occurred during the years 6 and 7 C.E.[7] It is not possible that this census occurred before that time, because the date when Quirinius began to rule is known, namely 6 C.E.. In that case, Christ would have been born in about 7 C.E., and his mission would have begun when he was twenty-three or twenty-four years old. This is an estimate which contradicts all others, and it also contradicts what is known from Jewish tradition. For the Jewish Levitical priest embarked upon his work only after reaching the age of thirty.[8] And the legal scholars[9] among them turned fifty before they would sit to offer interpretations or legal opinions in the most important matters of jurisprudence. Along these lines, they said that Christ had not yet turned fifty, yet he claimed to have seen Abraham and to have listened to him.[10] So if he had begun his mission before the age of thirty, they would naturally have been quite surprised to hear him speak before reaching the age of the Levitical priests.

The prevailing opinion among authoritative historians is that the census referred to above is the one mentioned by Tertullian, who said that it took place during the period of Saturninus, the governor of Syria until 7 B.C.E.[11] Thus, if this was the census which was meant, then Christ would have reached the age of seven in the first year C.E.

* * *

There are aspects which are connected[12] to the birth of Christ which we do not want to disregard. Among these is the connection with the star which is said to have been followed by the Zoroastrian priests[13] from the East, so that they would be guided by it to the place where Christ was born.

It is known that the experts of Phoenicia and Persia devoted themselves to the stars and to astrology, and that they were waiting at that time for a momentous event to occur in human history around the year of Christ's birth. They were likewise observing the stars from time to time in order to discover from their movements the glad tidings about that expected momentous event. Among the important celestial movements for the inhabitants of the East was the conjunction of Jupiter and Saturn. This was important both for those who lived by the sea, where the stars were observed for navigation and for ascertaining favorable omens, and for those in the interior of Persia, where the stars were observed for worship ceremonies and for deducing the divine will. It will suffice for us to indicate what remained of this custom in Phoenicia even after the time of al-Ma'arrī,[14] so that we may know the nature of the observations there as they existed in ancient times. For the blind al-Ma'arrī had been interested in these observations. Specifically, he said the following concerning the conjunction of Jupiter and Saturn in his *Al-Luzūmīyāt:*[15]

> The conjunction of Jupiter and Saturn was anticipated,
> So that eyes would wake from their slumber.
> How far has creation gone astray!
> Yet the sensible one realizes what has befallen it.
> And how often have the Bear and the Bull[16] looked down
> Upon tribes which ended up in their graves.
> The people pass away, generation after generation;
> But the stars are left behind, just as you see them!

Since this matter was not absent from the interest in celestial observations in Phoenicia up to the time of al-Ma'arrī, our investigation would lack integrity were we to disregard completely how these observations are connected to the birth of Christ, just because we dismiss astrology and the Zoroastrians' claim to it.

Now it is reasonable for us to deny that astrologers gained a knowledge of the Divine Mystery by observing the stars and the movements of celestial bodies. However, that does not make it necessary for us to disavow the appearance of the star which they observed, or to invalidate it as a sign along with the other signs, especially when this one agrees with all of those signs.

Frederic Farrar has mentioned in his book *The Life of Christ*[17] that the great astronomer Kepler had ascertained that the conjunction of Jupiter and Saturn would occur around the Roman year 747. In his description of this phenomenon, Farrar says,

> Now there is a conjunction of Jupiter and Saturn in the same trigon[18] about every twenty years, but in every 200 years they pass into another trigon, and are not conjoined in the same trigon again (after passing through the entire Zodiac) till after a lapse of 794 years, four months, and twelve days. By calculating backwards, Kepler discovered that the same conjunction of Jupiter and Saturn, in Pisces, had happened [no less than three times] in the year A.U.C. 747, and that the planet Mars had joined them in [the spring of] 748.[19]

It appears from this computation that the date of Christ's birth corresponds to the date which was derived in an approximate manner from the other estimates, and that he was born in about 5 or 6 B.C.E.[20]

We say once again that the proof of this observation does not necessitate that we place our faith in whatever knowledge of the Divine Mystery which the Zoroastrians might have gained from their surveillance of celestial bodies. What should be noted, and cannot be disregarded, is that those who wrote the history of Christ about two generations after his era passed on the report about this phenomenon. They believed it to be a sign pointing to a great event, for they connected it with the birth of the expected Messiah. Perhaps the Gospels were recorded at the same time when people were speaking of an astronomical "conjunction" of the kind that occurred during the rule of the emperor Hadrian. For a false Messiah had appeared at that time, one in whom Rabbi Akiba put his trust, hoping he would refute the claim of the Christians. Akiba called him "the son of the star" or "Bar Kokhba" in Hebrew, and he engraved a picture of a star on the coinage that he issued. This might well have prompted the Gospel writers to remember that rare astronomical phenomenon, and to refer to it some seventy years after the call of Christ.[21]

* * *

The most recent studies in the science of comparative religion carry the historian who writes with determination about the history of Christ into a complex field which is much more rigorous than that which deals with the year of Christ's birth. Indeed, the eighteenth century produced to the public a school of unrestricted skepticism concerning what could be determined from ancient knowledge and the developments of ongoing history. Thus, these writers doubted the existence of the prophets and emissaries,[22] and their doubt extended to almost every prophet and religious representative other than Muḥammad (peace be upon him). They had doubts about the Buddha as well as about Abraham, Moses and Jesus. This skepticism was applied to literature as well as to religion; they even doubted the identity of Homer and of Shakespeare. Some who acknowledged the more recent figures in history assumed that they actually existed, but that they did not produce what was attributed to them or write what was published in their names.

When Voltaire, the chief of skeptics, visited England, he found there the school of Bolingbroke which spoke with utter ease about their uncertainties concerning the existence of Christ.[23] And Napoleon asked the German scholar Wieland, "Do you believe that Christ was a historical person who existed just as they describe him?"[24] When the nineteenth century arrived, the domain of religious studies was inundated with books written by German, Danish, French and English authors in which they refuted the statements made by the historians, regarding it most likely that Christ was one of those personalities created by the imagination. It is impossible within the scope of this book for us to present their remarks on this subject, either in detail or in summary. A book similar in size to this one would be required in order to accommodate just the names of the authors (both men and women), the titles of the issues which they broach, and the gist of the evidence added to their elucidation of those issues.[25]

However, we are content to offer an outline of the two important foundations on which the school which doubts the existence of Christ is based. One of these is that Christ (peace be upon him) is never mentioned in the ancient historical works which present in detail the information of that period. The other is that the account about Christ written by the disciples had previously been narrated about other personalities of ancient times, some of whom were more likely mythical or hypothetical.

The historians who are singled out by name are Josephus, Tacitus and Suetonius. All of them are among those who chronicled the first century, yet it is said that they offer no confirmation of the existence of Christ when they write about his time.

Actually, copies of the history written by Josephus contain a brief reference to "Jesus the holy one." However, the historical critics insist that this is an addition to his text. They are convinced that it was added by someone among subsequent readers who were surprised at the lack of any reference in this history to the most significant event of that era. They would have felt justified in adding this reference, as though it were part of the text of Josephus, on the assumption that historical facts were entrusted to those who knew them, and they were not entrusted to the author alone regardless of whether or not he knew them. The critics also claim that it would not have been logical for this Jewish historian, who rejected Christianity, to write about the messenger of this religion with these words: "There lived at that time Jesus, that holy man[26] — if it is permissible to call him a man. For he performed evident miracles and taught the people; they received the truth and rejoiced in it. Many Jews and Greeks followed him. And he was the Messiah."[27]

The critics say that Josephus, who was a Jew and who died in his religion, did not write this nor did he believe in the faith of the Christians. If he had believed like they believed, then he would not have been content to record that great event in just three lines which occur incidentally and without any comment or elaboration.[28]

Among the theologians who have critiqued this comment is the Rev. Thomas Horne, author of *Introduction to the Critical Study and Knowledge of the Holy Scriptures.* In this book he was cognizant of the initial onslaught of doubts which were present in 1836.[29]

Horne mentions that this passage is found in all copies, both manuscript and printed, which are preserved in the Vatican library in Hebrew translation.[30] The passage itself is found in the Arabic copy which is preserved by the Maronites in Lebanon. Syrian, Greek and Egyptian writers of the fourth and fifth centuries were acquainted with this passage and quoted it. Also, Josephus referred to James as the bishop of Jerusalem in another passage, where he said, "Ananias convened the Jewish Sanhedrin and brought before it James the brother of Jesus who was called the Messiah, and others with him. Then he commanded that they be stoned as their punishment for disobeying the law."[31]

Horne further states that if Eusebius, the first of those who quoted the previously mentioned passage,[32] had recorded it as a forgery, there would have been no lack of critics among those who were acquainted with this work of Josephus who would have uncovered his ruse. Josephus' work enjoyed a respected position among the Romans which was long-standing, a position which allowed Josephus to obtain the honor of Roman citizenship. Moreover, it would have been most likely that the Jews would have counteracted anyone who interpolated this passage into their most famous history. They would have exposed him and refuted both him and the religion which he claimed.[33]

Horne then alludes to the doubts which surround this passage, since there is no mention of them in any known statement prior to Eusebius. He goes on to say that these doubts do not furnish any evidence for those who hold them, because Christian leaders had no need to cite the words of the historians; they were able to establish the mission of Christ from the prophecies contained in the books of the Hebrew Bible.[34]

Horne concludes his reply by directing the passage of Josephus towards a meaning which does not require the Jewish historian to be a believer in Christianity or in the mission of the expected Messiah. Perhaps he called him "the Messiah" by way of a report about his followers who were calling him a messiah, and who acknowledged him by his prevailing surname.[35]

As for the Roman historian Tacitus, who wrote his historical work around 115 C.E.,[36] the oldest evidence that he offers about Christ goes back only to 64 C.E. He did not mention him directly, but he referred to his name in the context of his discussion about the fire of Rome. There he says, "The Emperor Nero was disturbed because the people suspected him of burning the city. So he laid the accusation on the sect of commoners who are called Christians; they are related to Christ, whom Pontius Pilate had sentenced to death in the era of Caesar Tiberius."[37] The information on which Tacitus relied for his account of this ascription is not known at this time. But in any case, it was an account which was widespread among many people who had no personal experience with the era of Christ.

In a similar manner, Suetonius did not cite any direct report about Christ. However, in his history of Caesar Claudius he said, "He expelled from Rome the community of the Jews who were perpetually stirring up trouble at the instigation of *Chrestus*."[38] This was how he wrote the name in Latin, because he confused *"Chrestus,"* meaning "good,"[39] with *"Christus,"* meaning "Christ." Whatever source the historian may have used, there is nothing that can be inferred from his account, except that there were people in the Roman capital who were known by the name of Christians at the middle of the second century C.E.,[40] and that Suetonius considered their leader Chrestus to have personally instigated his followers at that date.

There were also writers and historians among the Jews who lived in the same period as Christ, such as the philosopher Philo who has previously been mentioned. Another was the historian Justus of Tiberias, who lived in Galilee in the period when Christ issued his call. He wrote a history of his people from the time of Moses to the end of the first century C.E. However, there is no reference found in this, either directly or indirectly, to the mission of Christ.[41]

And that, in short, is the evidence which exists, due to the lack of what contemporary historians said concerning the mission of Christ during the period in which it occurred.[42]

* * *

The other argument on which the school which doubts the existence of Christ is based has to do with the evidence concerning the similarity between the stories related about Christ and those related about the gods in the ancient Eastern religious traditions. This evidence depends on many details concerning accounts about the miracles and rites found in the ancient religions of Egypt, Babylonia, Persia, India and Canaan. Most of the critics who embrace this evidence are among the scholars of comparative religion who are acquainted with the religions of the East in their original languages. They consider it most likely that the accounts about Christ represent some of the remnants of religions which focused on the sun. This is indicated by the number "twelve" which refers to the signs of the zodiac as well as to the number of the disciples of Christ. It is also indicated in the celebration of the birth of Christ on the autumnal equinox as it was calculated in ancient times.[43] And it is indicated in the celebration of Sunday which the critics believe was in former times "the day of the sun," a connection which is acknowledged to this day in the languages of Europe.[44] All of this is in addition to the similarities which they find in the name of Christ's mother, in her giving birth to Christ in the manger, in Christ riding on "the donkey, the foal of a donkey,"[45] and in other rites and miracles.

The strange thing with regard to these scholars is that they do not bother to offer a reasonable explanation for the presence of so many Christians in the first century after only a single generation. For the explanations which they postulate are susceptible to numerous uncertainties, all of which are even stranger than what they say about the identity of the historical Christ. Their claim, that the antiquity of the stories about miracles and rites in other religions can explain the mission of Christ, quite apart from any herald or other pivotal person around whom that mission revolved, is not adequate. For Paul the apostle died about 67 C.E.,[46] and he had lived prior to his death for about thirty years, evangelizing in the name of Christ. Thus the era involving the history of the mission had not been long, and during that time nothing occurred which could explain how that mission could have originated from such miracles and rites. These had previously continued orally without interruption for hundreds of years, and this process had been more intense and widespread in ancient times than it had been later, after many years had passed.[47]

As for the silence about the mission of Christ among historians of that time, all that can be said with any certainty is that these historians did not grasp the significance of this mission, nor did they distinguish it from the sporadic movements which troubled the Jewish sects in general. This assertion is strengthened by the fact that this new sect is mentioned by a specific name only three times in all of the Gospels.[48] Thus the followers of Christ are mentioned by name as Christians in chapter 11 of the Acts of Paul the apostle,[49] where it is said that the disciples were called "Christians" for the first time in the city of Antioch.[50] Furthermore, we find in chapter 26 the words of King Agrippa,[51] in which he said in protest, "How easy it is for you to persuade me to become a Christian!"[52] And it says in chapter 4 of the letter of Peter, "If you are insulted because of the name of Christ, you are blessed. . . . If one of you should suffer, not because he is a murderer or a thief or an evildoer or involved in meddling, but he suffers because he is a Christian, he should not be ashamed."[53]

The sum of what can be inferred about this word in these three passages is that it was a reference of scorn and reproach spoken by the enemies of the Christians. Nor is it difficult to believe that any discussion about a sect which had no label was lost among the vast amount of historical material written about the people of that time. This would especially have been true if such a sect had not gained any significance as perceived by the historian of the most prominent events. So it was, among those historians, that they thought little of the circumstances of this sect, because in both religious and secular references it was an object of contempt. The Temple rejected it and the Roman government looked down on it. And it had never before happened that one of the sects of Palestine brought together the indignation of two powers, yet it was unknown by any label which might have been the focus of discussion!

* * *

It is clear to us that those in the eighteenth century who were caught up in the frenzy over the new science — the science of comparative religion — were driven to impose similarities and comparisons beyond what could be sustained. For we see today that these similarities are neither disproved nor confirmed, although perhaps in general they are closer to being confirmed than being disproved.

We see today that the followers of the various religions compete with one other. Every one attributes to his lord the miracles attributed to all the others. This is because each person believes in those miracles and does not doubt that they occurred, but he believes that only one lord is worthy of having performed them, so that is the one whom he chooses and whom he prefers over all the others.

We also see today, and in every era, that a person who is famous for a certain quality will be attributed with unusual and amazing phenomena associated with that quality. He then becomes an eminent personality representing that quality in all the stories told about it, so that they are ascribed to him. Thus, the person famous for his noble character is attributed with every noble deed, yet without support. And the person famous for his courage is mentioned whenever a particular unusual incident about courage is mentioned; then he is mentioned later as though he himself had been responsible for that unusual incident, or for one similar to it. He might even be attributed with a far greater incident to which attributes of this sort have been added.

We ought to mention here that Christianity existed before such rituals and traditions were associated with it, and that the first Christians avoided many of these which they rejected and restrained. Some of the early Christians prohibited the celebration of Christ's birthday on any day of the year; the most adamant of them was the great scholar Origen.[54] Three centuries had elapsed before any of the authorized churches celebrated Christmas on any date, but since then the churches have differed on this matter. Thus the Eastern church has celebrated Christ's birth on January 6, while the Western church has celebrated it on December 25. It is most likely that the Western church chose this date in order to dissuade Christians from participating in pagan gatherings which made use of that date as a festival to the sun. That festival included a proclamation of joyful celebration in the triumph of Light over Darkness, since the autumnal equinox was the time in which the nights began to shorten and the days began to lengthen.[55]

It is no secret that the apostle Paul was born in Tarsus and that this city was one of the centers for the cult of Mithra.[56] So it would not have been unusual for some of the terminology and customs of that cult to remain in the back of his mind, or for him to have accepted some of these as a means of facilitating his task of persuading the followers of Mithra to accept the new call. For it has always been a policy that when any religion issues its call, it tries to facilitate its acceptance whenever possible. This policy continued to be observed for several centuries, as can be seen in a letter of Gregory I (dated 601 C.E.) which was reported by the monk Bede in his history of the English church. He cites in this letter the counsel of the papal advisor Mellitus, who prohibited the destruction of the pagan temples.[57] Mellitus felt that these temples should be spared and be

> altered from the worshiping of devils into the service of the true God (that the people) may forsake their error of heart and be moved with more readiness to haunt their wonted places [to the knowledge and power of the true God].[58]

There is also no disagreement that the number "twelve" is found repeatedly in many religions. However, this repetition does not require that everything which is numbered in this way be a non-historical legend or myth. It would be proper for those who make such associations and comparisons to mention this fact specifically. For the historian who was most like them[59] was Suetonius, author of the history of "the Twelve Caesars," all of whom are "historical personalities."[60] And in the history of Islam, there is a similar classification in the school of Imāmī Shī'ites.[61] They confess a devotion to twelve Imāms who are known by name, and not one of them can be said to have been "a non-historical personality."

Nevertheless, the critics who have doubted the existence of Christ have likewise doubted the existence of Joshua son of Nūn. Their opinion about him is similar to their opinion about Christ, believing him to be one of the symbols of the religions which venerate the sun. This is because Joshua had set the sun in motion after having stopped it from moving.[62] These critics have not realized that the name of Joshua son of Nūn was found engraved on a stone at Numidia in North Africa. The Phoenicians had set up a colony there named "Qārah Ḥadāshah," later known as Carthage. On that stone, which was uncovered in 540 C.E., is a Phoenician inscription which states: "We left our homes in order to save ourselves from that highway robber Joshua son of Nūn."[63] Now those who wrote this statement about the Jewish prophet were not the kind which one would suspect of wanting to prove his existence or to deny any uncertainty about his life and history.

Those who make such associations and comparisons work hard to fish out similarities here and there, yet they never make the effort to accomplish what is primary in such effort and endeavor. That is, they never make use of their associations and comparisons to prove a single precedent which is compatible to what they claim for the rise of Christianity. For when has it happened in the history of the various religions that scattered fragments from certain rites and ceremonies pieced themselves together and emerged into the form of an independent ideology, without anyone knowing how this patchwork occurred, or how all of them became separated from their original religious traditions? Who would have wanted to issue such a call, or to gain benefit from doing so? Is there any witness to his existence among the historical sources which covered the current religious propagandists at the beginning of the first century? How did this momentous historical and religious factor emerge suddenly all at once before a single generation had elapsed? And why did this factor keep the sources of the original rites and ceremonies hidden, disclosing them only in relation to Christ?

The historians of religion should have used such associations and comparisons to carry out this test, rather than gathering all that material and analyzing the points of difference, just to wind up with some unique hypothesis.

* * *

The profession of historical criticism indicts itself with a profound failure whenever it is unable to rely on reported statements in order to establish "the personality of the speaker," or to verify his place in history. On the other hand, we have before us the words of Christ as they are related in the Gospels, and with regard to this they offer us quite a bit of information.

Whatever may be the last word about whether each Gospel was written independently or whether some of them were dependent on the others, they include distinct characteristics which could hardly have been intended by the Gospel writers. This is because we can only now understand these characteristics on the basis of our study of the development of Christ's mission.[64] They were never given a thought by those who related the events in the Gospels, whether as eye-witnesses or as transmitters.

For the Gospel accounts are in keeping with the logical development of the mission of Christ, from its beginning to its end. As this mission developed, it was logical for it to begin as a national, ethnic mission, yet end as a world-wide mission to all people; to begin with a reticent and conservative attitude, yet end with violence and conflict; to begin with little confidence in the personality of the herald, yet end with a confidence which was unlimited in the hearts of the followers and adherents of that mission. Thus the Gospels present the mission of Christ in such a way that the writers did not aim at accommodating the circumstances of its development, nor did they take into consideration the significance of those circumstances.

Perhaps this matter about the personality of the herald can be explained more clearly in that his sayings included criticism against all the schools of thought which were widespread in his time. These sayings indicate a single point of view which has never been found in any other personality. Thus the sayings of Christ criticized the Pharisees, but such criticism against them was not expressed from the standpoint of the Sadducees or the Samaritans. These sayings criticized the legalists, but such criticism against them was not expressed from the standpoint of those who were uninhibited and permissive. These sayings criticized the Essenes in their fanaticism, but they did not adhere to the views of the philosophers, or the Epicureans and Stoics. And they criticized the Samaritans, but they did not reject Samaria categorically, nor did they completely reject any other sect in a narrow-minded fashion. The sayings of Christ attested to the sayings of Moses, Abraham and the prophets, but they were not bound by every one of these sayings as if they had to imitate them, nor did they mimic those sayings like one who can only follow the leader.

If we were to combine the various aspects of this criticism into a single statement, it would be possible for us to attribute them all to a well-ordered point of view and a well-designed, personalized foundation, although there might be the exception where one ought to occur. This stands in contrast to the type of orderliness which brings forth a stream of activities in a mechanical and monotonous fashion. Such a method is not in keeping with the more vital and developed missions, especially those which take place in a period characterized by destruction and construction, by repetition and consolidation.[65]

These are the more "objective" characteristics which are the most important in explaining the personality of Christ. The most certain of these characteristics, after all of this, is that his mission came when it did in conformity with the demands of its time. It would have been strange for that period to be devoid of a messenger who could carry out that mission and who was worthy of being entrusted with it, rather than our thinking it strange that there should have existed such a messenger. And if, at a later time, an author had wished to create a messenger who was suited for the mission[66] to which he aspired, his imagination would have stopped short of the happy outcome which actually took place.

Chapter 12

A Descriptive Portrait of Christ

Among the oldest descriptive portraits which were preserved about Christ is one which circulated among Christians in the fourth century. Those who related it claimed that it came from the pen of Publius Lentulus, the friend of Pilate who was the governor of Galilee by the authority of the Roman Empire. He submitted this description to the Roman Council of Elders in the first century.[1] It reads as follows: "There has recently appeared a man having extraordinary power named Jesus,[2] and his disciples call him the Son of God. This man has a noble demeanor and a moderate stature. His face emanates with both compassion and dignity, so that whoever sees him loves him yet is afraid of him. His hair is like the color of wine, unkempt and rough, although next to his ears it is wavy and glistening. His forehead is smooth and delicate, and his face has no blemish, except that it is full with a rosy and vigorous complexion. His expression is completely sincere and compassionate. His mouth and nose are without fault, and his eyes are a sparkling blue. He inspires fear whenever he rebukes or reprehends others, but he is gentle and pleasant whenever he invites and teaches them. No one has ever seen him laugh, but many have seen him weep. He is tall and has handsome, sturdy hands. His speech is measured and composed, and he is not inclined to exaggerate. The gracefulness of his appearance surpasses what is observed in most men."

However, this account is dubious, as well as the historical process in which it was transmitted.[3] The same can be said for all such accounts which circulated among the people of that period and after. Some of them were unreasonable and it can only be assumed that they were contrived by the enemies of Christianity in early times. For example, some of these accounts said that Christ was stunted, hunchbacked and deformed.[4] Now the Mosaic law had stipulated that a priest should have a stable temperament and that his body should be free from defects.[5] No one could be ordained to religious service who was marred by some deficiency or deformity. So it would hardly be reasonable for someone to embark on a mission who was marred by being hunchbacked, deformed and stunted at the same time. It would also be unreasonable for there to be no statement attributed to either his opponents or his helpers which referred to such defects, either in the form of disapproval, or in the form of astonishment and of disguising such bodily defects by speaking only of his spiritual merits.

It is true that no one who portrayed the Hebrew prophets had ever designated conditions for prophecy which could be recognized, as were the conditions for the priesthood. However, the description of a prophet as someone who was deformed and hunchbacked could not have remained enveloped in secrecy as long as that prophet was being spoken about along with those who were truly deformed and afflicted — those whom he freed, who were driven to him in order to be cured from their own deformities and afflictions.

There is no reference to the features of Christ in the Gospels which is either stated explicitly or implied between the lines. However, it can be inferred from the statement of Nathaniel, when he saw Christ for the first time, that he had an impressive appearance and a royal demeanor. For Nathaniel said to him, "You are the Son of God; you are the king of Israel."[6] Christ would have wished to explain this statement as a greeting spoken in youthful enthusiasm in response to his own greeting. But in any case, it was a greeting which would not have been said to someone who was hunchbacked or had a detested deformity.

Nevertheless, we understand from the effect of Nathaniel's statement that Christ came across as being friendly; for when he spoke, he inspired confidence in his hearers. It was also said of him more than once that his words captivated them, because he "spoke with authority" and not the way in which the scribes and priests spoke.[7]

There is no doubt that Christ was articulate and quick-witted. He combined eloquence with the speed by which he would quote arguments from the Scriptures; he would utilize these to support his discussion at any given moment, whenever he was suddenly confronted with opposition or arrogance. He also had the ability to offer a balanced expression extemporaneously. For his exhortations were fashioned in forms of speech which, although not arranged poetically, were also not issued without any symmetry at all. It was his usual custom to speak in a rhythmical manner, to reiterate essential points, and to emphasize the tone of his message as he drew comparisons among its various parts.[8]

His taste for beauty was evident in his sensitivity, just as it was evident in his manner of expression and in his manner of meditation. His constant attention to flowers, vineyards and gardens, to which he frequently made comparisons in his parables, epitomized his natural taste for beauty and his admiration for the virtues of nature.[9] He often retired to meadows and gardens with his disciples. And he used a boat on the lake — Lake Tiberias[10] — as a pulpit from which he preached to his hearers on its grassy shore, as if his words affected even the swaying of the boat and the clapping of the billows and the fluttering of the breeze. The accounts indicate that he was not at home among the towns and cities, as he was in the open countryside. There he would pass the hours of the morning and the late afternoon, or the evenings of springtime, confiding secretly with the everlasting worlds as he sat upon the mountain peaks under the blue expanse.[11]

The Gospel accounts are in agreement that Christ made a tremendous impression on the souls of women. They followed him wherever he journeyed, and they listened to him in a loving and reverent manner. Now some prominent men have attracted the devotion of women as if such women were enchanted prisoners. Other prominent men have attracted the devotion of women because they struck the hearts of such women with the emotions of flesh and blood and with the inclinations of instinct and passion. However, the prominent man who draws the hearts of women to himself because he abundantly provides those hearts with tranquillity and grants them reassurance, who fills them completely with a pure and holy compassion and who gives them rest from the temptations brought on by weakness and trials — this man has a greater effect on the souls of such women than any other prominent man. Because of him they forget the body and they ascend in love to him beyond the realm of doubt.[12]

For this reason, we do not think it strange that the wife of Pilate is said to have cautioned her husband lest he harm that righteous man;[13] nor that the love for godliness triumphed over the love for the world in the souls of women who followed him and who renounced the adornment of life. And some of them were prosperous women whose lives had summoned them daily to obey some other cause.

* * *

Christ characterized himself as one who was "gentle and humble in heart."[14] He said that gentleness is the key to heaven; thus no one except those who are gentle may enter it.[15] Gentleness was embodied in many of his sayings and deeds, such as his compassion for those who fell into sin and failure. Such compassion realizes its objective when it comes from a messenger who himself is free of such sins and failures.[16]

Nevertheless, this gentle, compassionate messenger experienced indignation whenever gentleness and compassion had become exhausted. As he carried out his mission, his attitude was the same as that of all the messengers whenever the bonds of the spirit must rise above the bonds of flesh and blood, and the demands of Guidance[17] must precede the demands of fathers and mothers. "Who is my mother and who are my brothers? Whoever does the will of my Father in heaven is my brother and my sister and my mother." "Whoever is not with me is against me, and whoever does not gather with me scatters." "If anyone comes to me and does not hate his father, his mother, his wife, his children and his brothers, and even himself, he cannot be my disciple."[18]

These statements, and others similar to them, were some of the stringent conditions which Christ required of those who wanted to follow him. They were conditions which are inescapable in any death-defying mission which faces domination and tyranny. And whatever these statements incorporate by way of metaphors and allusions, their unambiguous message, which leaves no room for disagreement, is that the renunciation of ties to worldly gains and passions is the first rule of protocol by which soldiers are trained for every fierce battle. And if this applies to soldiers of war sent out to struggle against bureaucratic and political conquests, how much more does it apply to us as soldiers of war involved in spiritual conquests and the quest for perfection.

Christ (peace be upon him) commanded his followers to undertake perils along the way of truth and guidance. But he also established the extent of the risk they were to take: it was absolutely necessary to venture into death without any second thoughts.[19] The danger which faced the soul was to be avoided before any danger which faced the body, since the death of the body became insignificant when the death of the soul was taken into consideration. And if neither the body nor the soul were in danger, then there was no benefit in taking the risk. "So be innocent as doves and wise as serpents."[20]

* * *

It is reported in the Gospel of Mark that Christ escaped to the seaside when he learned that the Pharisees and Herodians were plotting against him in order to destroy him.[21] All of the Gospels show that he lamented his sorrow and distress when danger surrounded him, and that he called upon God to spare him from the cup from which he was about to drink. Thus he said to his disciples, "My soul is very sorrowful . . . remain here and keep vigil with me." Then he rebuked them when he saw them sleeping nearby while he endured the agony and anxiety which beset him. So he said to them, "Were you not able to keep vigil with me one hour?" Finally, since his destiny was decreed, he said to them, "Now sleep and take your rest!"[22]

Thus the venture into the struggle was not that he purge himself of his natural disposition in the face of apprehension and affliction. It was not forbidden for someone who had embarked into such a struggle to take precautions, or to have recourse to those whom he loved and to draw support from the affections of those who loved him. It was forbidden only for him to be afraid of danger to his body, when he should instead be afraid for his soul. Apart from this there was neither fear nor risk nor reproach.

To summarize briefly, it may be said that Christ was endowed with the temperament of those who, like him, were involved in the most significant missions, those who did not for a moment refrain from spiritual exercises. Even from the time they were young, these spiritual exercises made them susceptible to apprehension. It may be that an investigation into the depths of their hearts would show that they were cognizant of the extent to which they drew near to God or else withdrew from the way to Him. At one point they might be right next to the Light, and at another they might be kept away from it. At any point they would retreat into their innermost thoughts to consider the meaning of both the radiance and the hiddenness of the Light. Sometimes they would rejoice at finding signposts which guide the way; other times they would heap reproach upon themselves, accusing themselves of deviating from the way and digressing from the path. Such exercise, between this period of apprehension and that period of glad tidings, enabled him to grow and to prepare himself with perseverance and stability, equipping himself with assurance and faith.

No doubt it was these exercises that the writers of the Gospels had in mind concerning the period of temptation in the wilderness, where live the evil spirits.[23] Now the sinister suggestions of evil spirits there are precisely those which lead to apprehension; they cause one to wrestle with being enticed and seduced into yearning either to take unnecessary risks, or else to shrink back in fear. In such a place, one finds tranquillity for an hour, whereupon his tranquillity is tested by temptation the next hour. The temptation becomes loathsome to him because it leads him into doubt when he ought to be led into confidence. For God's mission is worthy of every sacrifice and deserving of every cost and every reward; but do you think, oh soul, that you are the one to choose God's mission? Or must you ask for proof? How do you think that you can ask for proof and also demonstrate true faith?

Christ triumphed over this ordeal, just as all the prophets who have been sent overcame similar ordeals following a period of apprehension, struggle and agonizing endurance. We can assume that after that trial, he dealt with apprehensions of this kind by surrendering to reality. He would try to ascertain events from the will of the Divine Mystery, whenever this will was concealed from him. Then he would allow events to proceed while he proceeded with them, anticipating whatever would be determined by destiny. In such situations, it would frighten him in the depths of his soul that he might ask for divine proof, because he did not want to put his God to the test. And it would frighten him that he might shrink back, knowing that his conscience would accuse him of doing so from fear of the outcome. Thus, in the final days of his mission, he endeavored to enter Jerusalem twice: on one occasion he entered it amidst welcome and acclaim; but on another occasion he entered it amidst warnings of danger, attempts to trap him, the betrayal of his companions and the conspiracy of his friends.[24]

These steps were steps of surrender. They incorporated a desire and a curiosity to know more, yet this was better than asking for proof, and better than drawing back whenever no proof was there. No one says in situations like these, "Let God do what He wills!" unless he allows his destiny to emerge within the course of events in which the will of God takes place.

In moments such as these, a man plunges completely into the depths of his conscience. In one such moment, those who observed Christ might have said, "He has lost touch with himself."[25] At another time, he might have been silent, giving no answer because he expected the answer from the Divine Mystery, which would be observed in what would soon take place.[26] Or, at another time, he might have embarked boldly, paying no attention to his welfare or to the outcome of the matter. Yet it was quite possible, when he reflected on one of the more decisive situations, that he would want to know its full outcome. But such an inquiry into the outcome would itself become the greatest problem. Would he then venture ahead only if the outcome were assured by way of a proof?

The activities of those entrusted with a message cannot be understood in their true sense unless we also understand a fundamental principle concerning the character of the messengers. This principle was that doubt was the greatest thing which they must fear, and that preserving their faith was the highest goal which they must seek. They often ventured into the most crucial matters, because surrendering to destiny was the nearest thing to faith, but to shrink back was either to doubt or to wait for proof. And sometimes, doubting was the same as waiting for proof.

It is frequently mentioned in the Gospel accounts that Christ offered supplications to God in the final days of his mission, in which he said, "O God, keep this cup from me! Yet may it be according to your will, and not according to my will."[27]

In this supplication was the key to every activity into which he later ventured, or rather, into which he ventured in similar situations.[28] For he did not avoid the cup according to his own will, but he left it to God to keep it from him, according to His will.[29] The only uncertainty in his noble heart was that he might want his own safety, and that he might take the path of withdrawal in order to avoid the cup. So let him be permitted to journey along a path other than the path of withdrawal, and let surrender be the path of faith.

Part Four
The Call

Chapter 13

The Call of Christ[1]

The entire history of the world's religions confirms a patent truth, and any doubt concerning it would render meaningless the writing of such history. What we mean by this patent truth is that certain universal conventions succeed one another in the greatest events of human history. For none of the stages of religion or of worldly matters would have occurred except that it was preceded by preliminaries which paved the way for its occurrence. Each stage took effect in the world in conformity to the factors which required it and called for it.

Christianity is no exception to this principle. Indeed, it is among the most powerful phenomena which support this principle and which follow this pattern. We shall see, after becoming familiar with the contents of the rest of this book, that the relationship between the two periods of time was never completely broken, and that the former period was leading gradually into the new period. And we shall see more than once in this book that the call of Christ[2] came when it did in accordance to the demands of its time.

Nothing could make this truth more obvious than a condensed representation of the entire period in a few words, in which we outline the prominent evils of that time, and are guided by these evils to their remedy — a remedy which was entrusted to correct doctrine. And what was the evil of that period which was so prominent in history? That evil whose description found agreement among the historians who were expecting a revolution, either by means of religion or by some other means?

There were two prominent evils belonging to that period. The first was that forms and conventions had become inflexible in both religion and society. The other was that relationships among nations and sects had deteriorated since they were compelled to live together in only one area in the inhabited world, especially in those regions which today we refer to as the Near East.

Forms and conventions had become inflexible, and external matters had prevailed over everything else. The people had rushed into a superficial life which was bereft of any substance. Thus, all that life meant for them was to follow the path of pomp and pageantry, of parties and tokens. Civilization had shifted from the inward to the outward, from the soul to the body, which is always the outcome of civilizations. They begin in the world of ideas and feelings. But later the edifice which they build becomes elaborate, leading to materialism and inflation. It loses the power of soul and conscience to the same extent that it acquires the external aspects of material and property.

Wealth and idleness accumulated on the one hand, while poverty and oppressive toil accumulated on the other. Thus masters became immersed in opulence, while slaves and bondsmen became immersed in wretchedness. And life became corrupt for both these groups.

The structure of society had also become inflexible, for it had developed into formalities and ceremonies which were devoid of meaning and purpose. Along with this, laws and regulations had become inflexible, for it was not uncommon for them to be engraved in stone. Nor was it uncommon for these laws to be controlled by a justice that was blind to impartiality; its scales were empty, so that the sides of the balance were equal because they were both empty!

Pagan beliefs had become inflexible in the Roman Empire, while beliefs about scripture had become inflexible among the Jews. For they would split hairs over two passages, and this would lead to a heated debate in which they would fight tooth and nail. Piety became merely knowing about texts and examining the ceremonial aspects of the law. The "external" aspects prevailed for those who clung to the texts and who administered them. For there was no disagreement among them regarding the pursuit of such external aspects, even though they disagreed over matters of literal meaning and interpretation.

Formalities and superficialities — these have no content, no substance.

Also, relationships had deteriorated between one nation and another, and between one sect and another. People had become insensitive to this deterioration, because those who put up with such conditions had to live within a single area of the world and be subject to a single government, from which there could be no possible means of liberation.

The evil of the world involved external matters of opulence and ideology. Beyond that, the internal aspect was nothing but air, and was devoid of any conscience. Surely any deliverance from this evil must come from an ideology which, if it believes in anything, believes in an unpretentious conscience; which, if it avoids anything, avoids external matters; and which, if it is weary of any disagreement, is weary of disagreements over texts and letters and those who split hairs regarding this interpretation and that analysis.

The basis of such an ideology must be that a man is considered lost if he were to obtain the whole world yet he forfeits himself;[3] that the kingdom of heaven is in the heart, not in palaces and thrones;[4] and that a man is to be judged by what is inside him and by what he thinks, not by what he eats or drinks or wears, or by the imposing temples and prayer niches which he builds.[5]

Was there any worse evil in the world than the bitter fighting which took place concerning external matters? Could there be any other deliverance from that evil? Was not Christianity precisely that ideology which was anticipated to call for such deliverance, and how could any other deliverance be possible?

Ambitions were completely different, whether among nations or sects or individuals. The entire age was characterized by fanaticism among those who ruled and those who were ruled, among those who governed and among those who were governed.

The Romans believed it was their right to be masters of the world, while the Israelites believed that their God had given them the right to be masters of the world. The Greeks, the Asians, and the Egyptians were each masters of their own nations, yet they all behaved like savages. Masters had no regard for their slaves as human beings, while slaves despised their masters as much as they despised death; they even preferred death rather than slavery which only brought them disgrace, suffering and hunger. The citizens of any given nation were divided into sects which propagated accusations, and hatred was pervasive.

It was to these people that the expected messenger of good news came. And if he said nothing else, he told them that God is the Lord of humanity,[6] and that he himself was the Son of Man;[7] that love is the best of virtues, and that the greatest love is love for one's enemies;[8] that generosity is giving to whoever asks from you, and that the greatest generosity is giving more than what is asked of you and to give without being asked;[9] that the kingdom of heaven is not inaugurated by riches;[10] that what belongs to Caesar is to be given to Caesar, and what belongs to God is to be given to God;[11] and that the kind of glory which people seek and fight about is not worth seeking, rather the glory which is worth seeking is not an issue for controversy.[12]

This messenger did not come as an unexpected intrusion. His own people had been promised that he would come at that time. And the people of other nations were expecting something which they did not really know; they knew only that their situation was unbearable and that it certainly required a change.

Acts of devotion became bankrupt. One of those who was worshiped — the Roman Caesar — decided to burn the books of religion and prophecy; nothing remained of them except those that were more like books of art that he placed in the temple of Apollo, the god of the arts.[13]

As for devotion which had not become bankrupt, whatever it had in reserve had been entirely postponed to a time that was anticipated. And these signs that the debt was being settled would be welcomed by those who believed them, yet anyone who denied them could not celebrate them. However, this was merely a disagreement concerning the signs, and whether or not they could be trusted, among those who saw and heard them.

So the call of Christ was in conformity with its time. It commenced at the appropriate season, arriving neither early nor late. There is thus sufficient evidence for its proper place in history. When the people had brought misfortune on themselves because they destroyed their internal affairs and built up their external affairs, there came to them a hope which promised to rectify that misfortune: a message of good news which was not concerned that external matters for the whole world were coming to ruin, as long as the inner conscience of humanity was preserved.

This was the call of Christ as it was directed by the Divine Mystery, and the world to which it was directed was looking forward to it. Had this call not been demanded by the world at that time, it would never have taken over that world within four centuries.

This call encountered the strongest opposition faced by any religion. It has not been sufficiently understood that it spread throughout the world in spite of such opposition, and without requiring anything from that world. Rather, the religion which people sought was one in which the reasons for accepting it were greater than the reasons for rejecting it. It was not a religion which people accepted in simple obedience and submission, as if it was sufficient without someone to call others to accept it. Indeed, there has never been a call which, as a matter of principle, had no need of people to do the calling.

So the messenger of brotherhood and peace set out to issue his call, knowing that this call was the most dangerous one ever. He knew that calling people to these things was much more dangerous than calling them to hatred and cruelty. This is because anyone who calls people to live in brotherhood calls them to root out all traces of hatred, and anyone who calls people to live in peace calls them to demolish the weapons of the mighty. Now rooting out all traces of hatred is no easy matter, and demolishing the weapons of the mighty is no work for a dreamer; for the path to these things is not one which people consent to and agree on.

Concerning this, Christ used to say, "I came to hurl fire upon the earth, and how good it would be if it were set ablaze." And he was asking his disciples and others who heard him, "Do you think that I came to bestow peace upon the earth?" Then he hastened to say, "Certainly not! Instead, there will be conflict and division. If there are five in the house, three of them will divide themselves against two, and two against three. The father will divide himself from his son, and the son from his father; the mother will divide herself from her daughter, and the daughter from her mother; and the mother-in-law will be divide herself from her daughter-in-law, and the daughter-in-law from her mother-in-law."[14]

There had been a saying similar to this spoken among the Israelites, as recorded by Micah: "No one among the people who is righteous; all of them lie in wait to shed blood and set up traps. . . . Do not trust a companion. Do not rely on a friend, and keep your words from her who lies on your breast. A son will despise his father; a daughter will rebel against her mother, and a daughter-in-law against her mother-in-law. A man's enemies will be those of his own household."[15]

In fact these sayings, and others similar to them, were a description of what actually took place — for it had never been prophesied that evil would lead to good, or that hatred would lead to brotherhood, or that war would attempt to gain peace. But the prophecy from this messenger proved true for his own people, because he set forth his call to brotherhood, and he included in that call "the birds of the air" which were a symbol of those who would come from all areas of the world.[16]

It was obvious that he would have influenced his people for good, if only they would have listened to him and followed him. But they refused the banquet to which they had been invited, while others attended it without an invitation, for they were more deserving of it.[17] Thus he told them the parable[18] of the wedding banquet, in which the one who issued the invitation sent his servant to request his guests to come. "Then one of them said, 'I have purchased a field, and I must go out to look at it.' And another said, 'I have purchased a pair of oxen, and I am leaving to try them out.' Then the master became angry and said to his servant, 'Go quickly to the roads and lanes of the city and bring me anyone you can see among the poor.' And the servant returned and said to the master, 'I have done what you ordered, and still there is plenty of room.' The master said, 'Then call in others from the byways and the street corners until my house is filled; for not one of those whom I invited, but who did not accept the invitation, shall taste my dinner.'"[19]

It is possible that countless things could be said when describing this general call, depending on the view which the reader takes concerning the sayings of Christ in the Gospels. For example, it is possible to say that this call was to go on for the time being, and that it would end just prior to the end of the whole world in the near future. Or it is possible to say that this call into a kingdom was to continue, and that no one knew when it would end.[20]

However, we are in absolute conformity with the essence of this call when we describe it as "a change of course," or the commencement of a new direction.[21] Nor was there any possibility of integrating the two courses or of vacillating between the two directions. For no one could serve two masters.[22] One had to choose either the direction of the spirit or the direction of the flesh; either the direction of God or the direction of "mammon,"[23] the god of material possessions and of wealth; either the temple of the conscience or a temple of stone and wood; either this or that.

The important thing was which course one chose, and whether he would stay with it to the end. All the particulars which followed this formed the steps which the traveler took along the way, whether long or short, swift or lingering, whenever he assumed his direction and turned his back to what was behind him. The decisive fork between the two directions was inevitable; the choice between the two masters was unavoidable!

Chapter 14

The Choice of Direction [1]

The situation, as we have presented it, consisted of a fork in the road. It was the traveler's responsibility to choose his course or direction. He had to carefully consider every aspect of that direction. Then either he accepted it, along with all its benefits and responsibilities, or else he rejected it, along with all its benefits and responsibilities. He had to put his whole heart into serving the Lord whom he worshiped, for he would not be able to worship two lords or to yield service and devotion to two masters.

Only in this manner could the call of Christ[2] be understood with clarity, or any ambiguity about it disappear. Even the contradictions and incompatibilities which would emerge would disappear, because they would be placed on the proper path when one's orientation was restored.[3]

For the people of that generation who devoted themselves with heart and soul to the sanctuary of "mammon,"[4] the true course was on the other side of that sanctuary. Those who worshiped "mammon" were immersed in their concerns about mere rubble; they wasted their time on nothing but satisfying their cravings and obtaining their food. It was up to the one who turned his back to that worldly direction to choose the new direction where no trace of that sanctuary could be found, nor any remnants of its pillars or its idols; where the only things he sought involved spirit and conscience; where he cast out everything regarding material possessions and mortal flesh.

Or, as the messenger of good news told them: "Life is more important than food, and the body is more important than clothes. . . . The lilies of the field flourish without working hard or spinning, yet Solomon in all his glory was not clothed like one of them. And if God clothes the grass, which today stands in the field and tomorrow is thrown in the oven, how much better will he clothe you — you who have so little faith."[5] "Yes; and if the nations of the world crave for food and drink and the anxieties of life, then you must seek what is more important and lasting. . . . Seek treasures which will not be depleted in heaven, where the thief will not get hold of them nor the moth wear them out."[6]

For anyone who had turned his back to the direction of "mammon," this was the direction in which he was to head. This was the ultimate goal of that direction, even if it did not comprise every step along the way.

It was in this regard that the hearer could understand the messenger of mercy when he said: "No one can be one of my disciples who is not able to hate his father and his mother and his wife and his children and his brothers, and even to hate himself. And no one can be one of my disciples who is not able to carry his cross and follow me in the way I must go."[7]

The one who said that is the same one who said: "Listen to me! Love your enemies.

Do good to those who hate you. Bless those who curse you. Call upon God for those who mistreat you.[8] If anyone strikes you on your right cheek, turn your left one to him. If anyone takes your cloak, give him your robe. If anyone takes something that you have, do not demand it back from him. You must do to other people whatever you want them to do to you. What credit do you get if you love those who love you? Even sinners love those who love them. . . . And what credit do you get if you lend to those who will pay back your loan? Even sinners lend to those who lend to them. Rather, you should love your enemies and do good; you must not expect any payment that is due to you."[9]

And the one who said that is the same one who said: "If your brother sins, admonish him. And if he repents, forgive him. If he sins against you seven times and turns to you in repentance seven times, accept his repentance."[10]

Each of these teachings contradicts the other: the compassion which embraces both enemies and loved ones contradicts the hate which includes those people who are most loved, i.e. fathers, mothers, children, and various close relatives. These two ideas contradict each other completely, except in one case: when a person turns his gaze toward another direction, another course, another ultimate goal different from the one to which he turned his back.

When the two roads separate, you are obligated to proceed on either one or the other. It is no fault of yours if you proceed on the road in which you guide your own steps, even if it means that you despise yourself and carry your cross and become cut off from your relatives.[11]

There is no one who refuses to love his relatives or to be loved by his relatives if they travel where he travels and if they stand with him for what he stands. In that case, no one needs to talk with him, and there is no reason to give him advice or to encourage him to make the better choice. However, he will need to be spoken to, and to listen to advice, when there are two roads which are incompatible and contradictory; he will need to be spoken to, and to listen to advice, at the point where these two roads meet, where you proceed on one road with God, or on the other with "mammon." At that fork, no contradiction exists among any of these pieces of advice or any of these lessons. All of them point to a single approach from the beginning of the road up to its goal. One must be converted to this ultimate goal if he wants to make his way toward it and embrace it passionately.

In one of the parables which incorporate the sayings of Christ, he made clear to them the entire situation: anyone who wants to build a high tower must take into account all the costs involved before setting up a single stone. "Which one of you who wishes to build a tower does not first sit down to calculate its cost, so that you know whether you have what is required in order to complete it?"[12] Such calculation of all the expenses must be done before laying the first stone for the foundation of the building. Otherwise, there will not be any stones or foundation or building. If anyone is not able to complete the building and he does not have the amount required, it is better that he relinquish that piece of ground, along with the stones and the building.

Thus, if anyone looks around at the earth and sees mountain trails which cut across each other and intersections which diverge from one another, let him lift his gaze from these trails, and let him look at the horizon on which the eyes of the travelers are fixed. There he will find his direction, for there the paths which had branched off meet together with it, and there the crooked trails become straight.

Those who listened to Christ, especially his disciples and followers, were amazed at him for two reasons: the way he welcomed little children, and the way he spoke to people who were rejected and degraded. Thus, he scolded them when he saw them sending the village children away from him, and he said: "Invite the children to come to me, and do not prevent them. For whoever does not approach the kingdom of God as a child will not enter it."[13]

Also, he said to people who were convinced that they were pious and who despised those who were notorious for their sins: "Two men went up to the Temple to pray, a Pharisee and a tax-collector. The Pharisee began to say in his prayer, 'Praise be to you, my God! I am not like the rest of those who seize wealth, who oppress others, and who commit adultery. I fast twice a day, and I give exactly one tenth of all that I acquire.' But the tax collector stood at a distance, not willing to raise his eyes toward heaven. He beat his breast and prayed in humility to God, 'Have mercy on me, my God, for I am a sinner.' Then they both went to their homes, one with his prayer answered, the other without receiving acceptance from God."[14]

Such parables recur elsewhere, and along with their recurrence is recorded the amazement of those who listened to him. Some believed in him and loved him, while others did not believe in him and were enraged by him. If those people who had been so amazed had only acknowledged his mission and accepted his direction, they would not have criticized him when he gazed into the distance, when he renounced his present so that he could extend his hope into the future. Instead, the day which he anticipated, when people would have child-like faith, would come in the future; and the one who was expected to change the current situation was not concerned about the present, except that it was coming to an end.

The sum of our discussion concerning this new call of Christ is that, like every new call, it seemed peculiar, contradicting its surroundings. But all its peculiarities and contradictions will be shaken off if we set our sights in the direction in which this call leads; for there the mountain trails come together, and the place to which people are drawn is pleasant.

Chapter 15

The Ordeals Incorporated in the Call[1]

The call of Christ was consummated by an ordeal which consisted of a brief period of time that lasted no more than three years.[2] But this was sufficient, because in fact there were two ordeals and two calls. They were carried out by two messengers who were different in nature and method: John the Baptist (i.e., John the Purifier) and Jesus the son of Mary.[3]

John the Baptist was an example of an austere hermit who did not show favors and who did not vacillate. Most of his preaching comprised pronouncements of warning rather than good news. He laid the ax on the root of the tree, and he did not care that with it he threw firewood into the furnace.[4]

His parents gave birth to him when they were very old, after they had given up all hope. They were both from the priestly family, i.e., the descendants of Aaron; their names were Zechariah and Elizabeth.

The story of this birth to aged parents is presented in the Gospel of Luke.[5] There it is mentioned that Zechariah had assumed certain religious responsibilities according to his tour of duty, and that he had been chosen by lot to enter the Temple and offer incense. He stayed for a long time in the sanctuary,[6] while the crowd of worshipers waited and wondered at his delay. Finally he returned to them quite unable to speak, and they realized that he had encountered a vision inside the sanctuary. Then he related[7] how he had seen an angel standing on the right side of the altar, and how this disturbed him and he trembled in fear. But the angel said to him, "Do not be afraid, Zechariah; God has answered your request. Your wife will give birth to a son, and you will name him John. You will be delighted with him, as will many people, for he will come from his mother's womb filled with the Holy Spirit.[8] He will bring the Israelites back to their God, and he will go forward in the spirit and power of Elijah."[9]

The story of Zechariah is also reported in *Sūrat Āl 'Imrān* of the Holy Qur'ān:

> Then Zachariah prayed unto his Lord and said: My Lord! Bestow upon me of Thy bounty goodly offspring. Lo! Thou art the Hearer of Prayer. And the angels called to him as he stood praying in the sanctuary: Allah giveth thee glad tidings of (a son whose name is John, (who cometh) to confirm a word from Allah, lordly, chaste, a Prophet of the righteous. He said: My Lord! How can I have a son when age hath overtaken me already and my wife is barren? (The angel) answered: So (it will be). Allah doeth what He will. He said: My Lord! Appoint a token for me. (The angel) said: The token unto thee (shall be) that thou shalt not speak unto mankind three days

> except by signs. Remember thy Lord much, and praise (Him) in the early hours of night and morning.[10]

And again it is reported in *Sūrat Maryam:*

> A mention of the mercy of thy Lord unto His servant Zachariah. When he cried unto his Lord a cry in secret, saying: My Lord! Lo! The bones of me wax feeble and my head is shining with grey hair, and I have never been unblest in prayer to Thee, my Lord. Lo! I fear my kinsfolk after me, since my wife is barren. Oh, give me from Thy presence a successor who shall inherit of me and inherit (also) of the house of Jacob. And make him, my Lord, acceptable (unto Thee). (It was said unto him): O Zachariah! Lo! We bring thee tidings of a son whose name is John; We have given the same name to none before (him). He said: My Lord! How can I have a son when my wife is barren and I have reached infirm old age? He said: So (it will be). Thy Lord saith: It is easy for Me, even as I created thee before, when thou wast naught. He said: My Lord! Appoint for me some token. He said: Thy token is that thou, with no bodily defect, shalt not speak unto mankind three nights. Then he came forth unto his people from the sanctuary, and signified to them: Glorify your Lord at break of day and fall of night. (And it was said unto his son): O John! Hold fast the Scripture. And We gave him wisdom when a child. And compassion from Our presence, and purity; and he was devout, and dutiful toward his parents. And he was not arrogant, rebellious. Peace on him the day he was born, and the day he dieth and the day he shall be raised alive![11]

The child grew up as one who was consecrated to a life of virginity; this is what the Holy Qur'ān means when it describes him as "chaste."[12] He was also learned with regard to the books of religion, having listened to his parents read them, and he would recite them during his times of solitude. He spent a great deal of time in seclusion which entailed night vigils and the ascetic way of life. When he appeared in public and issued his call, the people saw him dressed in a coarse robe made from animal hair, his waist wrapped in a leather belt. Although he fasted much of the time, he subsisted on locusts and wild honey.[13] He called out to the people in a strong and stern voice: "Repent and get ready!"[14] "The ax is laid at the root of the tree, and every tree that does not produce good fruit will be cut and thrown into the fire."[15] He was "the voice of someone who shouted in the desert," as was said by the ancient prophets.[16]

When John spoke, he had no apprehension about picking a fight with someone who was guilty of any sin or impurity. So with a strong, clear voice, he began to reprimand King Herod, because he had married his sister Herodias while her husband was still living. Even when the king had him arrested and brought before him, John did not keep quiet and would not stop accusing him and his sister, commanding the king to divorce her in order to escape

God's anger.

One evening, during one of the entertaining parties which Herod used to put on at his palace, his sister's daughter (Salome)[17] danced before him. He was so enraptured by this that he promised to give her what she asked, whatever it might be. So she asked for nothing less than the head of John on a platter. Because she was insistent, Herod granted her request, even though he was very reluctant to do so. He escaped the consequences of his action because John had spoken vehemently against the priests and legal scholars. Thus they acquiesced to Herod's crime without any criticism or objection.[18]

The priests and legal scholars had renounced the raving messenger long before he had renounced them. This is just what religious "professionals" usually do to preachers who are not affiliated with them and do not live among their company. So John would cry out to them, "You brood of vipers! Don't even think that you are descendants of Abraham. I tell you that God is able to bring from these stones children for Abraham."[19]

This was the most important theme which that raving messenger cried out. The people understood this to mean that salvation is an act of grace which God bestows upon whomever he wishes, and that he does not give preference to one race above all others. When Christians came and accepted his call,[20] he gave them a distinguishing mark: as he pronounced the name of God, he sprinkled them with water, anointing their heads.[21] Afterwards, they were included among those who had repented from their sins and who were seeking salvation, even if they were not members of the family of Jacob and Abraham.

This stern call did not take long before it clashed with blind passion and stubborn conceit. But it was not delivered in vain among the masses who were not deceived by the whims of the hierarchy. The name of John continued to be hallowed and loved among the people, while those who wanted to show off did not dare to speak against him. Later, the scribes and legal authorities came to Christ, wanting to corner him with questions and riddles. But he turned the tables on them and said, "First give me an answer to this: Did John's mission have a heavenly origin or a human origin?" And they could not answer him, because if they acknowledged John's mission they would have accused themselves, and if they denied his mission the people would have been furious with them. So they were completely dumbfounded.[22]

There is nothing more indicative of the important position which John held than the commendation made of him by the eminent historian Josephus. Although he was very careful not to anger people of opinion and authority, he said that John "was a devout man who counseled the Jews to treat each other with reverence and to fear God." Along with this testimony, the historian reiterates the testimony of John's fellow Jews, who testified in favor of John and against themselves.[23]

Thus the call issued by this stern messenger produced one of the two ordeals through which the call of salvation had to pass at that time. That stern messenger secluded himself from the world, knowing that the call of salvation would be lost if it were restricted only to one group of people, and that salvation was pledged to others who sought it and who were afraid that it might slip away from them, since they did not belong to that group.

* * *

Christ's disposition was different from that of John, the son of Zechariah. He did not live out in the wilderness, nor did he have an aversion to people. Rather, he would associate with the devout and sinners alike, and he used to attend banquets and weddings. He did not despise the friendly greeting which came from the heart, even if it had been given as an obligation or formality. Once he rebuked his disciples for their ascetic and frugal behavior. A woman had poured a flask of perfume on his head which had cost many denarii, and they regarded this as excessive behavior. They said, "Why this waste? It would have been better if this perfume had been sold and the money given to the poor." Then he said to them (peace be upon him), "Why do you trouble the woman? She has done a good deed to me. The poor will be with you tomorrow as well as today, but I will not be with you always."[24]

Such charity clashed with blind passion and stubborn conceit, just as the stern manner of John the Baptist had done. In both cases, Christ blamed the people of his time for such conflict when he said, "John came to you neither eating nor drinking, and they said that he was possessed by a demon. Then the Son of Man came eating and drinking, but they said that he was a glutton and a heavy drinker, and a friend of tax collectors and sinners."[25]

This mission was consummated by an ordeal, or rather, by two ordeals. There emerged from the two ordeals together an international community which appealed to anyone who would listen to it. But that community also renounced anyone who renounced its call, or rather, its two calls: the earnest call which was stern and disdainful, and the earnest call which was charitable and pleasant. If it had been the case that this call resided in only one group, and if that group had listened to the call, then it would have become isolated within that group and the rest of humanity would not have heard it.[26]

Chapter 16

The Law[1]

Anyone who reviews historically that particular era from whatever perspective of research — whether political, economic, social, religious or cultural — ends up with the same conclusion: that the victims of the extravagance and hypocrisy of that age, because of their large numbers and the harmful effects of this, had reached a point beyond which people can tolerate in a single period of time. Because that period faced such obstacles, it was not capable of moving into a new period without some kind of sudden development taking place; and that sudden development could be nothing less than total revolution.

The victims of the extravagance and hypocrisy of that age had reached the limit of what they could endure in a single period of time. It might be said that they were victims of hypocrisy in all its various social and psychological manifestations. For the extravagance of that age was nothing but a kind of social hypocrisy, since hypocrisy in all its expressions depends on pompous appearances. There is no difference between the soul's passion for pompous appearances which are empty and its passion for hypocrisy.

For an era such as this, the mission[2] of Christ was necessary.

However, it was not necessary that this mission enter the world with an increase of the law, or an increase in the application of the law. For there would be complete disaster in the application of the law if it were to follow the conventions of hypocrisy, and if duplicity were to triumph over truth and justice through such application.

Nevertheless, this mission was necessary for times such as that particular era, in order to give the world what it needed, and to bring deliverance for its victims. The greatest need, at a time when the inward aspects of convention and law were moth-eaten, was proper behavior toward others. And those who were victims of the hypocrisy of that age were the first to seize upon such proper behavior, for they sensed that this was the greatest need. The mission of Christ was compassionate and perceptive; it appealed to all the sensitivities of the people, especially the sensitivities of those who were victimized and oppressed.

Concerning such oppression, it was almost the case that anyone who was suspected of a crime would be oppressed, because crime existed entirely among those who ruled rather than those who were ruled. And when such oppression reaches epidemic proportions, those who are falsely accused are the first people in need of mercy and sympathy and deliverance. Such accused people were indeed the first ones to receive mercy and sympathy and deliverance, as they became enveloped by the new call, and by the messenger who preached the good news of salvation and redemption.

Blessed are those who mourn. Blessed are the poor. Blessed are those who hunger and thirst. Blessed are those who are driven away for the sake of righteousness. Blessed are the humble and the merciful.[3] "Come to me, all you who are weary and burdened. . . .

Take my yoke upon you and learn from me . . . and you will find rest for yourselves. For my yoke is easy and my burden is light."[4]

On the other hand, doom will come to those who are satisfied, not knowing that they are hungry; to those who are rich, not knowing that they are destitute; to those who are arrogant, not knowing that they are poor; to those who are proud, not knowing that they are broken.[5]

* * *

So the victims of the hypocrisy of that age responded to the cry of that eminent messenger in proportion to their yearning for consolation, and in proportion to the burdens they had to carry due to the blindness of the law and the pretense of piety. Perhaps it was more proper that the eminent messenger should expend his compassion on those victims of hypocrisy in proportion to their need of him and their awareness of the rest and mercy which he offered. So he taught that one's gratitude should be in proportion to the forgiveness received, and that one's hope for repentance should be in proportion to the generosity of the love conferred: "There were two debtors, one of whom owed five hundred denarii, and the other fifty. When neither of them had what they needed to pay off the debt, the one who thanked him the most profusely was the one who was forgiven of the larger debt."[6]

The most victimized of all people at that time were women; for women have always been the most victimized in any period when extravagance prevailed on the one hand, and the deprivation of rights prevailed on the other hand, and hypocrisy predominated in either case. The situation has been the same in every period similar to that one, that women would get caught up in distressing adversities of all kinds: the adversity of error, the adversity of destitution, the adversity of the disintegrated family, and the adversity of the confusion which destroys confidence. Yet what women have most needed in every age has been tranquillity.

When she had fallen prey to a curse for ages upon ages; when the adversities of that time especially had closed in upon her one after another — suddenly she perceived a tender cleansing which engulfed her frailty, restored her brokenness, wiped away the despair from the depths of her passion, and pervaded her soul with hope in God's mercy. This was a lesson of holy love which taught her something she could not have learned from the lessons of retribution found either in the law of the hypocrites or in the scales of justice.

So there emerged on the pages of time, in a particular moment of that confused age,[7] an elegant vignette — quite removed from the laws of the Temple or the laws of Rome — which continues to be prominent. It is at once a picture of forgiveness, appearing in the person of the eminent messenger, and also a picture of repentance, appearing in the person of an ostracized young woman who knelt at his feet, shed her tears upon them along with perfume, and wiped them with the tresses of her hair. His disciples and others around him were astonished; they wondered among themselves how he could claim to be a prophet yet be ignorant of her status as a sinful woman. So the master turned to them and said, "Have you[8] noticed this woman? When I entered your house, there was no water for my feet, but she has washed them with her tears and has wiped them with her hair. You did not present me with a kiss, but since I entered she has not ceased to kiss my feet. You did not anoint my head with oil, but she has anointed my feet with perfume. So the one who loves much will receive the greatest forgiveness of sins."[9]

It is no wonder that sincere repentance, and the mercy which is granted as a result, are the reasons why false law becomes bereft of its victims, and why fraudulent piety dreads losing its pride and arrogance. But woe to the one who preaches repentance and mercy, yet who does not consider that vengeance and retribution are already present.[10]

* * *

From the time that Christ first stepped into his mission of spreading the good news, he took it upon himself to keep his distance from the issue of "authority," and to forego entering its sphere of activity. He did not grapple with this issue, either to invalidate the existing authority or to salvage it; he did not try to substitute it or to claim its custody for himself. This is appropriate for any teacher who is able to follow such a path for the age in which he lives. As we have already mentioned, Christ grew up in a world which complained about the overabundance of laws and decrees and prohibitions, and of rulers and dictators. Whatever was lacking from Rome with all its laws was filled by the rituals of the Temple, along with its ceremonies and rules about what was permitted and what was forbidden. And whatever was lacking from Rome and the Temple was filled by the control of Herod, along with his sons and subordinates and followers. There was no need for any more rules along with the corruption of those who ruled.

Now if any of those rules might have been reformed, the value of that reform was not worth the effort for a certain powerless faction to wage a war against the empire of the Romans, and against the empire of the Temple, and against the Jewish district of Idumea which had supported both empires but worked for its own interests after theirs.[11] It is certain that the harm which ensued from that effort was more dangerous and burdensome than any good which resulted because of it — if indeed any good did result. That could only be attained by reforming people's hearts, by refining their moral behavior, and by teaching individuals such ethical standards as would guide those who followed them, where laws and ordinances only led them astray.[12]

By staying clear of any involvement with the issue of authority, Christ refrained from its sphere of activity. However, this issue would not leave him alone within his own sphere of activity. For no sooner had the crowds turned to him than the authorities — and above all the religious authorities — perceived the approaching danger from that popular propagandist. Indeed, any popular propagandist becomes dangerous to an authority which is traditional and inflexible.

These authorities entered his sphere of activity after he had left them to their own sphere of activity. Thus the clash which was inevitable came to pass: on one side, an authority whose hallmark was the excessiveness of accusations made, inconsistencies investigated, and penalties dispensed; on the other side, a call whose hallmark was the possibility of repentance for sinners and the promise of hope that they could be forgiven.

This pronouncement of forgiveness which comes from repentance was the greatest offense made by that newcomer who issued his call. For it was customary for the existing authority to point out sin and to mete out its punishment, and although this worked conveniently to their advantage, it was also the gateway to pride and arrogance.

So his enemies set out to drive him to the point where he had refused to be driven. And their greatest concern was to show evidence against him that he invalidated the law or that he hindered its implementation in a given case. They bent over backwards in their quest for problems and riddles which they could present to him. They hoped that in his response he might state his own legal opinion[13] in favor of something that would conflict, on the one hand, with the religious law or with the political ordinances, or something that would conflict, on the other hand, with the ethics of compassion and the commandments which required kindness and righteousness.

Once, someone from the crowd of those who heard him came up and said to him, "Teacher, order my brother to divide the inheritance with me." This man had assumed that Christ held the authority to make a pronouncement in this case because of the respect afforded to him by his disciples and by those who were listening. But Christ offered nothing more than this response: "Look, who appointed me to be a judge or an accountant over the two of you?"[14]

When he was in the Temple, they planned to force him into a situation whereby he must either pronounce a judgment or else reject the law. He was teaching the people when they stormed in with a woman whom they pushed into the middle of the group. They began shouting together, "Teacher, this woman was apprehended while committing adultery. Now Moses had charged us to stone any woman who commits adultery. So what do you have to say?"[15]

Indeed, what could he say? Why should they even ask for his permission, when they knew that he had no power to prevent them from taking her to be sentenced? Their trap was all too obvious; there was no way out of it, just as they had calculated and surmised. If he were to say, "Stone her," then he would be claiming for himself a sovereign right. And if he were to say, "Set her free," then he would be renouncing the law of Moses right there in the Temple. How could he escape this double-edged trap, even though it was one which was perfectly obvious?

They had anticipated every possibility, except that he might terminate this case by arriving at a solution whereby he would neither claim authority in the matter nor deny it. Nor would he allow the situation to lead him into flattery of their religious hypocrisy and vain piety. They kept waiting for him to respond, with no idea how he might get out of this dilemma which they thrust upon him. Meanwhile he listened to them while drawing on the ground with his finger, until they ended their clamor and questioning. Then he stood up and exposed their own hypocrisy, foiling their trap completely, saying, "Let him who is without sin among you proceed to throw a stone at her."[16]

He did not rescind the law of Moses; nor did he claim to uphold it; nor did he flatter them in their hypocrisy. Rather, he left them to figure out how to escape from their bewilderment and disgrace at his evading their trap!

Meanwhile, the poor woman was left standing alone in front of him. So he asked her (even though he knew the answer), "Where are your accusers? Has no one condemned you?" She replied, "No one, master." Then he sent her away, saying, "Neither do I condemn you. Go, and do not sin."[17]

Yes, he did not condemn her. Nor should it be held against him that he did not condemn her in this case, even though he stood as her judge. For a judge does not condemn a person without any accusation or witnesses or evidence!

Christ also dealt with the issues of marriage and divorce. At that time, it had reached the point where these matters were treated lightly, such that the family was split apart, and a wife was more deprived than a concubine would have been according to the custom of her people. Thus he said that a husband and wife are one flesh, and that no one should separate them when God has already joined them together.[18] He also said, "Whoever divorces his wife, except by reason of adultery, causes her to commit adultery. And whoever marries a divorced woman commits adultery."[19]

There were skirmishes of this kind between Christ and those who were long-winded, who treated knowledge as a profession and as an opportunity to ensnare him. Yet they always abandoned their attempt and went away dumbfounded, while he went away having given a better answer, or rather, a more noble answer.

It was not difficult for him to demolish whatever trap they laid for him in the area of politics. They hoped to hear from him some indication that one should pay taxes or else rebel against the Empire. So he demonstrated how they conducted business among themselves by using coins produced by Caesar, and how they amassed wealth and possessions through such coins. Then why should they not give to Caesar what belongs to Caesar, and to God what belongs to God?[20]

Nor was it difficult for him to silence the Sadducees and the Pharisees at the same time. The first group denied the resurrection, while the second group believed in the resurrection of both the body and the spirit. On one occasion, he was told that the law of Moses enjoined a man to bear children with the wife of his brother who had died, in order to preserve his brother's family. Then they asked him, "If a woman is married alternatively to seven brothers, which one of them will have her as his wife on the Day of Resurrection?" They imagined that he would not be able to respond to this question with an answer that would satisfy either the Sadducees or the Pharisees. Yet his answer left both groups dumbfounded, for he stated that those who live in the world to come will not intermarry as is done in this world, nor will they bear any offspring![21]

In fact, when the Gospels relate these debates, they tell us nothing but what we witness in similar cases today. In any teaching situation which is open to the public, teachers and preachers are confronted by long-winded people who pretend to be experts, and who try to render them ineffectual. This is true in any group, even if there are various intentions among the questioners, depending on the situation and the subject being taught.

It is also true that the ability of Christ to make a quick reply and to silence his opponents with his answers is yet another of the many indications which point to his "personality" in history, and to the consistency of his call. For this ability went beyond the capacity of his disciples and others who heard him to fully understand it. Although they later reported this ability, they did not comprehend the most important factors which gave rise to it within the policies of Christ's mission. For that mission undertook to avoid making new laws, and to avoid any opposition to existing legislation by invalidating the law or making a substitution for it. Its objective was always to refrain from claiming any authority which existed among the secular and religious authorities. It affirmed that the kingdom of Christ is not of this world, that it had nothing to do with other kingdoms in the form of empires and governments.

Christ spoke this way to the priests in the Temple, and he spoke this way to Pilate, the governor of the Romans.[22] His method of speaking followed a similar pattern in every situation and in every instance of his preaching. It was a method based on conventional ethics and the highest standards, not on literal interpretations and legal proceedings. And when, in reference to outright adultery, he spoke about adultery in relation to the eye, which should be plucked out whenever it looked at a woman lustfully; and when he spoke about the sin of the hand, which should be cut off whenever it fell into error; no one took these sayings to mean that he was making new laws. There was absolutely nothing in the way Christ conducted his mission which was imposed by a process of coercion.[23]

In spite of this, the narrators who passed on these accounts were predominated by those who considered Christ's method to be a legislation which was intended literally. There were few among such narrators who could make the distinction between a method based on a literal intention of the law, and a method based on human morals which rise to perfection upon perfection, and which penetrate into the meaning behind the literal words. This latter method depends on the conscience which calls the person to account; it does not depend on someone to judge whether his eye should be gouged or his heart should be examined in order to find traces of elements which may incite lust. If only the meanings of Christ's words had been fully understood by his hearers in the way that he meant them, the differences in understanding and interpretation which developed would not have occurred.

Chapter 17

The Law of Love

The inflexibility and hypocrisy of that age were both representative of the emphasis on external matters; for those who were inflexible concerned themselves only with words and texts. They fancied that these things were intended for their own sake. Words and texts became a preoccupation for them, such that they devoted all their efforts to interpret them, control them, and derive from them puzzles and riddles. It reached the point where they considered this to be a matter of skill and ingenuity, and they considered the making of regulations and penalties to be an opportunity for them as lawgivers, one which they could not allow to slip by. Otherwise, their skill and ingenuity would be discredited and they would be completely defeated before their antagonists, those who were intended to be subject to such regulations and penalties.

Among those who were inflexible were some who took pride in their knowledge of the legal texts. They would measure their knowledge by the extent to which they could create puzzles and obstacles out of the minute details of these texts; or the extent to which they could compare passages which preceded and which followed a given text, or passages which agreed and which disagreed with each other. This would happen for any "law" which might fall into the hands of those inflexible literalists. We are aware of similar people in Egypt who have written large tomes and who take pride in their ability to obstruct the process of revision, basing this on their need to write an additional text here or footnote there. They are quite versatile in squeezing out various renditions and digging up hidden treasures, thereby providing evidence of their vast knowledge and their superiority in the field of debate as they maneuver through all its twists and turns.

By the very nature of the case, those inflexible literalists did not take into consideration the human soul. Instead, all of their consideration was directed, on the one hand, to the written text, and on the other hand, to their claim to knowledge and proper exegesis. And the human soul became the prey which was guaranteed to be hunted down by the penalties which they enacted. It was guaranteed that all windows of escape would be closed by the knowledge which they flaunted. They used that knowledge of the mysteries and secrets of the law to take advantage of the surrounding world, so that it was beguiled into thinking that the poor soul was able to flee, that it would escape any punishment. Such was the failure of their laws and regulations; they failed to open their slaughterhouses and allow the sacrificial victims to be set free!

Thus the lawgiver who was skilled in the tradition of inflexibility was the most capable among his peers in spreading out the nets and hunting down the victims. And those who served the law had every bit of pride in supplying the quarry for it and in tightening the net around them. Their pride might well have swelled when they were in public; the people who were considered the most worthy of glorious accomplishments were those who were most capable of pronouncing others guilty.

This situation persisted until "righteousness" became a game in which they would display their skill with words, paralyzing those who were uneducated with their stratagems and legal opinions. It persisted until essence disappeared for the sake of transience; until centralities disappeared for the sake of trivialities; until righteousness and purity of conscience disappeared for the sake of words and texts; until realities disappeared for the sake of external matters and formalities.

And whenever moral qualities end up in external matters and formalities, truth and hypocrisy become equivalent. For the most which truth and hypocrisy can produce together is an external formality whose interior is empty. Then there is no difference in moral quality between the hypocrite and the honest person. And as long as this moral quality is inflexible, it will have no sympathy, no life, and no regard for the human soul which lies behind the texts and rules, the commands and prohibitions, and the penalties and stratagems.

Inflexibility and hypocrisy: both are representative of the emphasis on external matters. And the world of external matters is not the same as the world of the conscience.

These two worlds stood face to face when Christ set out to issue his call: a world entirely based on restrictions and formalities; and a world free from such restrictions and formalities, operating in the realm of the conscience.

In the fifth chapter of the Gospel of Matthew, it is reported that Christ said: "Do not think that I came to abolish the law or the prophets. I did not come to abolish them; rather, I came to fulfill them."[1]

But the Gospels also relate that Christ worked on the Sabbath day;[2] that he scoffed at the notion of certain forbidden things which could defile a person;[3] and that he addressed the people in a manner different from the way in which the law addressed them.[4]

So then, did Christ abolish what was said by those who preceded him? Or did he follow them in everything which they had endorsed? If you wish, you could say that he abolished everything. Or if you wish, you could say that he did not abolish anything in the least.

This is because Christ abolished the law of formalities and external matters, while he instituted the law of love, or the law of conscience. And the law of love allows no letter of the law of formalities and external matters to remain as it is. But it also does not abolish a single letter of the established law; rather, it goes beyond it.

We should offer here a correction to the concept of the law as it is usually understood. For the law means "the foundation" on which everything is based, and the law of religion consists of the eternal principles on which the human conscience is based, as long as the conscience exists. For the law will never cease to exist — as Christ had said — as long as earth and heaven exist.[5]

In fact, Christ fulfilled the established law, because he instituted the law of love; and the law of love goes beyond the established law. For that law had committed a person to carry out his duty. But love goes beyond duty; it does not wait to be commanded nor does it wait to be compensated.

Love does not settle accounts by referring to literal requirements and preconditions.

Love does not treat people on the basis of legal documents and witnesses. Rather, love does what is required of it, then it goes beyond that. It is happy to give without looking for compensation.

By this law — the law of love — Christ abolished every letter of the law of formalities and external matters.

By this law — the law of love — he removed from the law an edifice which rivaled heaven, and he established a foundation for the law which was firmly situated.

By this law — the law of love — he put an end to the law of arrogance and hypocrisy. He taught people that the divine commandments were not laid down so that they could show off, or bring lawsuits, or boast about themselves, or disgrace others by accusing and offending them. Rather, they were laid down so that they would judge themselves before judging others, and be favorably disposed toward people with mercy and forgiveness, not so that they would hunt down their mistakes and probe their shortcomings.

It is our belief that no factual evidence can substantiate the "personality" of Christ, as to his existence in history and his moral greatness, better than the commandments encompassed by this law, the law of love and conscience. For every word given in these commandments is one that should have been said; and every opportune remark that has been passed on is one that makes an impression on the mind, leaving one convinced that it could not have been fabricated.

The law of arrogance and hypocrisy compelled people to make use of religion as a means of expressing their superiority over others. But the law of love compelled one to say to those who felt superior to others, and who were devoted only to themselves, "Why do you notice the speck in your brother's eye, but you do not notice the beam in your own eye?!"[6]

The law by which people took pleasure in meting out punishment and in pursuing the faults of others compelled them to drive the sinful woman in public procession, and to rush to the place where she would be stoned, as if they were rushing to a wedding party. But the law of love compelled one to forbid that hypocritical crowd, to expose to them their hypocrisy, and to make them feel ashamed. Indeed, the crowd felt ashamed when it heard the master exclaim, "Let him who has never sinned among you throw a stone at her."[7]

The law of hypocrisy and arrogance compelled anyone who prayed to take pride in his prayer; it compelled anyone who fasted to indicate that he was fasting by assuming a demeanor suggesting gloom and discontent. But the law of love compelled one to forbid the people to pray and fast like the hypocrites, since they loved to pray standing in the synagogues and street corners. "And when you fast, do not look gloomy like the hypocrites. They alter their faces to make it look obvious to others that they are fasting. So they have already received their reward. But when you fast, each of you must anoint your head and wash your face. Your fasting will not be obvious to people, but it will be to your Father who looks at the heart."[8]

The law of hypocrisy and arrogance compelled anyone who gave alms to be proud of his gift, and to give it with a condescending attitude toward the poor. He would sound trumpets before him as he walked through the streets and markets, to announce that he was giving alms. But the law of love compelled those who gave alms to do so secretly, so that the left hand would not know what the right hand was doing.[9]

According to the law of arrogance, the proud person protected his piety so as to display it proudly toward wrongdoers; and he reproached the one who brought guidance and reform, because he sat with tax collectors and sinners. But according to the law of love and conscience, those who looked down on others in their piety were told what they ought to have been told: it is rather those who are sick who need a doctor, for love must be demonstrated in forgiveness.[10]

Thus, the seduction of external matters and formalities had reached its limit. It predominated everything from Temple to house, from office to market, from pulpit to table. Even a morsel of food could be permitted or forbidden only when invocations and incantations were recited over it, only when it was circumscribed by ceremonies and rituals, only when the priests could prescribe it from the regulations regarding sacrifices and feasts. It was appropriate that here the world of external matters and the world of the conscience collided. And for those who purified themselves by washing their hands and by offering recitations over morsels of food as well as the dishes on the table, it was appropriate that they were told these words: "Whatever enters the mouth does not defile one's conscience. Rather, defilement comes from the heart, where evil, falsehood, immorality and unbelief are found."[11]

* * *

The sum of what can be said is this: the concept of goodness was entirely based on the law of external matters and formalities, the law of arrogance and hypocrisy. It was also based on the problem of "official prerogative," which was monopolized by those who held it owing to ancestry and race, and was a matter which depended on issues of inheritance and legacy.

The benefit of "official prerogative" among the nations had been monopolized by Israel, since they were the descendants of Abraham. And the benefit of "official prerogative" among the Israelites had been monopolized by the descendants of Aaron and Levi, who claimed the priesthood by virtue of their lineage and heritage. And the benefit of religion and knowledge was monopolized as a profession by the scribes and the experts in the law, i.e., the legal scholars of that time. Indeed, it was almost the case that God's love toward his chosen nation was "a formal written contract" which guaranteed his preference for that nation. And if their deeds fell below the rest of the nations, "then it was not because you were the most numerous among the nations that the Lord stood by you and chose you; for you were less numerous than the rest of the nations. Rather, it was because he loved you and he kept the oath which he had pledged to your forefathers."[12]

So when the call of Christ advocated the law of love and conscience, its message was the same message which had been expressed in everything which the people had claimed for themselves, and in everything which they had appropriated and monopolized.[13]

Goodness was not a monopoly of lineage and ancestry. Rather, "the one who acts according to the will of God is my brother, my sister, and my mother."[14] Also, "many will come from the east and west, and they will recline with Abraham, Isaac and Jacob on the couches of the kingdom. But the children of the kingdom will be thrown outside into the darkness."[15]

Furthermore, mercy does not operate according to lineage or profession. This was a parable which Christ gave to them: "A man was attacked by thieves as he traveled. They stripped him and beat him, leaving him half-dead. A priest passed by, but he ignored the man and went on his way. Then came a Levite, who went on and paid no attention to him. But a Samaritan saw the man and had pity on him. He bandaged his wounds, placed him on his donkey, and brought him to an inn, where he entrusted the innkeeper to take care of him. When he left, he gave the innkeeper two denarii which he should spend to take care of the man; and whatever more he had to spend would be paid by the Samaritan when he returned." After Christ had given this parable to his disciples, he said to them, "Which of these three was most like a neighbor to that man who had been assaulted and wounded?" Of course no one could disagree about the answer, that the Samaritan, who was an outcast, was more like a neighbor to the man than were the descendants of Aaron and the Levites who were the most distinguished![16]

He began to confront the celebrated scholars who had strayed in the matters which they knew and upheld, matters concerning the riddles of jurisprudence and the enigmas of the law, in which they were specialists. So he said to them, "Religion consists of what you do, not what you teach."[17] He warned his followers and devotees about imitating their deeds or making similar claims. "For they tie up heavy loads and force people to carry them on their shoulders without lifting a finger to move them. Instead, they perform their deeds so that people will see them. They make their phylacteries wide, and they lengthen the tassels on their cloaks. They grab the most important couches at banquets and the principle seats in the synagogues. They aspire to be greeted in the markets and to have people call them 'Rabbi' wherever they go."[18]

He went on to shout at those hypocrites who had strayed, "You blind leaders! You settle accounts over a mere gnat,[19] yet you swallow a camel! . . . You cleanse the outside of your bowls and cups, but inside they are brimming with filth and debauchery. . . . Woe to you scribes and Pharisees, you hypocrites! You are like whitewashed tombs; on the outside is a beautiful coating, but inside are rotting bones."[20]

Once they tried to show him their superior knowledge by asking him questions about the mysteries found in the scriptures and the riddles found in the religious duties and commandments. So they asked him, "Which are the two greatest commandments in the law?" They figured that he would delve into minute details and take a long time investigating the mysteries and riddles. But he left aside the details and texts, and instead he answered them by consolidating all of religion and all the scriptures into just a few words: "You shall love your Lord with your whole heart, and from all of your soul and mind. And you shall love your neighbor as you love yourself."[21]

Among the excess baggage and paperwork which might burden the devout worshiper, these two commandments were all that were necessary. The result was not that he should invalidate the various religious obligations and regulations, or that he should consider permissible what was not permitted. Rather, he could hopefully be adamant concerning those commandments in which the legalists and literalists allowed themselves certain liberties. That is, a person should be adamant in calling his conscience to account, and in doing for the sake of love what he would not do for the sake of duty. The essence of all this is that virtue becomes something which inspires the soul and which calls the conscience to account. It goes far beyond anything which inspires established principles or which calls to account legal documents and stipulations. It goes far beyond efforts to evade the minute details of the law.

Surely the law of love and conscience was more intense and more strict than the law of external matters and formalities. For the conscience is first responsible for a person's intentions[22] and thoughts, and only then for his deeds and encounters. It calls the person to account when he faces misgivings and temptations, and it does not let him do what would be harmful or evil.

"It was said to the men of old, 'You shall not kill; and whoever kills shall be punished.' But I say to you that whoever is angry with his brother without reason commits a sin and is to be punished. . . . And if, while offering your sacrifice, you remember that your brother has a case against you, then leave your sacrifice in front of the altar, and go first and be reconciled with your brother."[23]

"It was said to the men of old, 'You shall not commit adultery.' But I say to you that whoever looks at a woman and lusts after her has already committed adultery with her in his heart. So if your right eye throws you into error, pluck it out and throw it away. It is better for you that one of your members perish than for your entire self to perish."[24]

"It was said to the men of old, 'You shall not break your oath. . . .' But I say to you, do not swear at all. . . . Let what you say be simply 'yes' or 'no'; anything more than this comes from the Devil."[25]

"You have heard that it was said, 'An eye for an eye and a tooth for a tooth.' But I say to you, do not confront evil with evil.[26] If anyone strikes you on your right cheek, turn the left one to him. . . . If anyone forces you to go one mile, go with him two miles."[27]

"You have heard that it was said, 'You shall love your neighbor and hate your enemy.' But I say unto you, love your enemies, bless those who curse you, do good to those who hate you, and pray on behalf of the one who wrongs you and drives you away, so that you may be sons of your Father who is in heaven. For he causes his sun to rise over those who are evil and those who are good, and he sends his rain to those who are righteous and to those who are sinners. What reward will you get if you love those who love you? Don't the tax collectors do the same? And what credit will you earn if you single out your brothers when you offer a greeting? Don't the tax collectors do the same?! But you must be devoted to perfection, for God is perfect, and he loves perfection."[28]

This was a law which destroyed every existing tradition, which devastated every external formality. Yet it did not destroy the original law nor devastate any of its principles. The duties prescribed by the original law may even have been increased by the new law without losing a single letter, since they were transferred from mere law books and outward appearances to a person's conscience and heart. For the person would then call himself to account rather than be satisfied with a system where the law never caught up with him or where justice never overtook him.

The clash between the two kinds of law was anticipated, as much as anything could have been. And the rivalry between them was one dictated by the law of love and conscience on the one hand, and by the law of external matters and formalities on the other hand. Every word spoken in that rivalry was witnessed by those who promoted hypocrisy and arrogance. Every response given was fully intentional in its goal, not randomly spoken by someone inappropriately. Thus we claim that there has never been any more reliable evidence confirming the historical personality of Christ and his well-organized call than the evidence of this rivalry. No one could have fabricated this clash between these two kinds of law, even if he had wanted to do so. For it was beyond the capacity of such a person to come up with the character of the two kinds of law, the law of love and conscience and the law of hypocrisy and arrogance, or to control the path they should pursue, or to dictate what should be their questions and replies.

The features of these two kinds of law were clear, and their goals were evident; the direction in which each was headed was well-known. If there were ever any confusion about the matter, there was nothing easier than for such confusion to be settled within the actual situations of those who held good intentions. In such situations could be found everything which concurred with the law of love and conscience and which contradicted the law of external matters and formalities. Also in such situations could be found everything which followed the way of external matters and formalities and which renounced the way of love and conscience. Confusion about anything which Christ meant would not last long except for those who worshiped mere words and texts. It was certainly neither fair nor agreeable to anyone's thinking that mere words and texts should pass judgment on a call which they despised, a call which was derived in every aspect from the goals of love and conscience. This was just as Christ had said, that he had placed new wine in an old wineskin, that he had sewn an unused piece of cloth on a worn cloak.[29]

Chapter 18

Ethical Living

The philosopher Origen maintains a noteworthy position in the history of philosophy and Christian religion. Many regard him to be the greatest of all religious thinkers who were prominent during the second and third centuries C.E. Even someone who would not regard him in quite this fashion would have no dispute in considering him to be among the three or four greatest thinkers of his time, including his former teachers.[1]

When he was young, Origen read the passage in which Christ said that some people are castrated by God, some are castrated by other people, and some castrate themselves for the cause of God.[2] He took the meaning of this saying literally, and he emasculated himself so that afterwards he could venture to teach women, believing that he had acted properly. But later he realized his mistake, and he departed from such a literal understanding of the sayings of Christ.[3]

Nevertheless, the fact that this story remained established in the biography of one of the most eminent personalities of that time completely overshadows the astonishing exploits encountered in many other stories which endured among the accounts of the Christian mission during its initial era. For a man would gouge his eye whenever he was aware that it looked at a woman lustfully; or he would totally disfigure his body whenever he was tempted by his passions, until he would be dripping with maggots while he was still alive. Given that there was a young man with the intelligence and keen discernment which Origen possessed, and who understood Christ's admonitions in this manner, it is no wonder that this understanding spread among a portion of the more simple folks who could not attain his level of discernment and expertise.[4]

But Origen himself had departed from his mistake after some time, as we have already mentioned. And there were others of his intellectual status, both before him and after him, who were confident that Christ had intended a figurative rather than literal meaning when he directed people to prevent the members of their bodies from becoming an aggravation. When he stated that someone's eye should be gouged, he meant nothing more than what we mean today when we say that someone's tongue should be cut when we want him to keep silent, or to be silenced. And when he talked about the discipline of the body, he meant nothing more than what we mean today when we talk about the discipline of sports or education. As Clement of Alexandria correctly remarked, when Christ stated that one should relinquish his possessions, he did not mean that we should reject them categorically in all situations. Indeed, alms-giving was not considered to be among the greatest virtues which Christ had directed.[5] Some time later, St. Augustine disavowed that religion imposed asceticism on everyone; he only condoned it for those who were able to bear it.[6]

Nevertheless, the disagreement over how to understand the commands of Christ continued even after Christian scholars had frequently interpreted them in this more figurative manner. This disagreement continues to exist in our own time, especially concerning those commands which deal with the renunciation of life. Not a few have interpreted them along the lines of Dr. Schweitzer. It is his opinion that Christ enjoined these commands on the people in connection to his belief that the hour was near, and that the world which they renounced would end within of a few years. Thus all of Christ's commands should be understood in the context of a journey in which the travelers made provisions for the world to come — provisions which were different from those which people stored up in this transient world.[7]

It is our belief that there is no room for disagreement concerning the commands of Christ as they were directed to his disciples and apostles, those who had devoted themselves to spreading the news about his call. For every such call, whether in Christ's time or in our own, whether involved in a religious struggle or a secular struggle, requires of its heralds the same kind of devotion and the same kind of detachment from other distractions. There is certainly no disagreement about the orderly conduct of modern military commando units. The first rule there is that the soldier who fights in the struggle must contemplate death before he contemplates life.[8]

On the other hand, it is different when these commands are directed, not to disciples and apostles, but to those who must live in the world and make their own living, those who must provide for their children and relatives. Did Christ demand that all of these withdraw from the world, renounce their lives, and become like the birds and plants, dependent for their food and clothes?[9]

I can say truthfully that I understand every one of Christ's commands, and that I find absolutely no difficulty in understanding them as long as two conditions are met: that we refuse to be inflexible in trying to interpret them literally, just as he (peace be upon him) refused to do so; and that we perceive that he (peace be upon him) said it all when he provided a summary of all his wisdom by saying, "People do not exist for the Sabbath, but the Sabbath for the people."[10]

Christ's concern in reforming the soul was to change motives, not quantities. His concern was to relocate ethics from one center to another. And since his goal was to relocate the center, distances and intervals no longer had any value.[11]

Outward displays had been the center around which revolved the lives of the nations and individuals of his time. Instead, it was necessary that one's innermost being become the center of life. The things of the world had been more important than the human soul. Instead, it was necessary for the human soul to become more important than things. It was necessary that gaining the human soul become one's most important achievement; for nothing would be held against the one who forfeited the world as long as he gained his soul.[12]

If the vanities of the world are the center of life, then it's all the same whether one has a lot or a little. The person who tries to get one dirham[13] is the same as the person who tries to get millions. For both of them, the focus is wrong and the effort is futile.

If lust is the center of life, then the person who lusts with his eye is the same as the person who stands and sits and stays awake and sleeps in pursuit of whatever gratifies and entices him. Both of them have plenty of time to be fully involved in such a center.

Instead, it is up to us to relocate our center, or to relocate our direction,[14] as we mentioned in a previous chapter. When this takes place, then everything is shifted, and the original core of every created being is changed.

If a person's goal in life is to obtain the human soul, to obtain this center, then the one who owns millions is as much an ascetic as the one who owns a small amount or the one who owns nothing at all.

If one's center is changed, then the distance of a few miles is the same as the distance of a few inches. And if this new center remains, then what is far becomes near and what is near becomes far.

This change of center is what Christ had in mind.

This change in center was necessary for that time. It is necessary for this time. It is necessary for every period whose bearings have gone astray. Thus the mission of Christ was a model for other missions; and it was not the last mission to appear among humankind.[15]

Therefore, we believe that Christ would have brought about another change of center if he had come again to the world a few generations later, and had seen the way people were engrossed in torturing their bodies, and in happily feeding their bodies to the maggots while they were still alive.[16]

However, there is no need for us to make assumptions, or to get involved in a matter which admits to disagreement. The fact is that Christ had changed the center the way he did in his time. He changed it when he allowed a woman to spend many denarii for perfume in order to anoint his feet.[17] And he changed it when he allowed himself to attend weddings, and when he told parables to his followers concerning the joys of life and the freedom to express every joy which comes from the heart, and which makes the body glad, and which does not grieve the spirit.[18]

The reforms made by the greatest calls ever issued were never concerned with quantities and distances. If you wear yourself out in order to store up a million, they did not say that you need only wear yourself out in order to store up ten thousand, without adding more. If you crave for everything which delights you all the time, they did not tell you to crave for them only a few days of the week, or crave for only some of them every day. If you keep yourself busy with enmity and hatred, they did not tell you to keep busy with them just a little, and not to make them your foremost and unceasing concern.

No, the reforms made by the greatest calls ever issued were never concerned with quantities and distances. On the contrary, they were always concerned with a center which should be relocated, or with motives which should be changed. After that, it was up to the people of the world to be aware of their situation regarding distances and quantities, so that whenever they went completely astray, they might return, or be returned, to the center from which they had gone astray, or else to a new center.

We do justice to ourselves, and not only to Christ, when we recognize that he knew what he was saying, when he said: "If anyone takes your cloak from you, give him your shirt along with your cloak."[19] Do you think that Christ did not realize what he was saying, that the very cloak and shirt which someone gives is the same cloak and shirt which another takes, indeed snatches away? Of course not. He certainly realized what he was saying, without any doubt at all.

Rather, what he meant was the human soul, not the cloak and shirt. He meant that the human soul is to be elevated above mere things. And he meant this to be one of his parables. This was surely a parable, just as surely as there were other parables!

Thus a person should give out of love and from his own free will. For when a person gives something under compulsion, or when he gives something that he doesn't worry about giving away, he loses what he gives while failing to lay hold of his soul.

This is not the case when someone gives simply because he wants to give. Indeed, he will gain what he gives without losing it. For the soul's prosperity is measured by what it gives; and the body's prosperity is measured by what it takes. And if someone is not concerned that he gives the whole world in order to gain his soul, it is certainly appropriate for him to gain his soul with a little giving.

Christ wanted people to serve one master, not to serve two masters.[20] This was all he wanted. Thus, if a person owns the possessions of the world, but he does not serve those possessions, it is not to be held against him. And if a person serves God while owning possessions, it is not to be held against him. And if a person endeavors to do anything else, he would not be able; even his greatest effort would be worthy of nothing more than to be acknowledged and paid.[21]

In our view, this prohibition against serving two masters determines very clearly the boundary between what is permitted and what is forbidden among the things which the world seeks with all their pleasures and frills. Thus, a person is not restricted from owning extensive possessions, as long as he does not serve those possessions or offer his soul as a sacrifice on their altar. But there is no deliverance for a person who owns even two dirhams, if he acquired them through serving the possessions of the world.

It would be appropriate for us to mention briefly that Christ did not intend to set up a society in place of another society.[22] Rather, he intended to refine human ethics, a process which would be maintained through the conscience of both the individual and the people as a whole. He set these ethical standards upon an unequivocal foundation through numerous commandments that betray no conflict among themselves.

Thus the body takes precedence over food and clothes. People take precedence over the Sabbath. It is more profitable to gain the soul than to gain the world. And the kingdom of the conscience, which lies in the depth of every heart, is more lasting than the kingdoms of this world.

Moreover, simplicity of faith is more virtuous than the pretense[23] of the scholars and custodians of religion who show off their skill. Were it not for such pretense, it would not be difficult for anyone to comprehend the commandments of Christ, along with other teachings which have followed the same pattern in every age. But those who persist in always showing off their skill work hard so that they will not understand, and they will not work hard even once in order to understand. It is people who act this way who always prevent all understanding from taking place, and who prevent all good deeds from being done, and who allow their concerns to turn their attention away from the inward aspects of the issues to the outward aspects. It was this pretense which interfered for those in the past who showed off their skill, keeping them from performing any deed according to any commandment. And none of them would listen to any prophet or sage.

Those who show off their skill are those who refuse to understand a saying such as this: "The early bird catches the worm." So we ask, is there anything in this saying that can be understood? Yes indeed. It contains advice for anyone who wishes to hear it and to act on it. But those who show off their skill are those who say in response to this counsel, "If the worm had not come earlier, the bird would not have eaten it."

Those who show off their skill say this because they do not want to act on that advice. Can you see that they have gained anything when they forfeited such action? Of course not. They would be correct in their ridicule if it were better for the worm to be late rather than early. But at the very least, these two situations are equivalent. In fact, if the worms are late they are more apt to be exposed to hundreds of beaks and hundreds of eyes, instead of just a single beak and a single eye!

In the same way, when Christ says, "If anyone demands your cloak from you, give him your shirt along with your cloak," those who show off their skill ask, "Why should the person who demands the cloak and shirt be entitled to own both of them, while the person who gives them is not entitled to keep either of them in his possession?"

So we ask, is there anything in Christ's saying that can be understood? Yes indeed. It contains something which is to be understood, and also something which can correct an understanding which has gone into error. But those who show off their skill do not want to understand it, nor to act on it. They only want to show off at the expense of understanding and action, in accordance with what they say. And even if this is not the case, then it does not escape them that there is something new in this situation: the one who gives is subjected to scrutiny as to how well he can be imitated in his good deed. There is no disagreement concerning the one who demands assistance, whether his deed should be considered a virtue. But the disagreement which requires a new understanding concerns the act of giving, whether it should be considered a virtue of generosity and unselfishness.

The world had been revolving around the center of greed, evil, hatred and hypocrisy. There is no doubt that it would have been better for it to revolve around a different center, and to be relocated to the center of contentment, good, love and sincerity. Then there would have been no argument about measuring distances and calculating quantities.

In any case, we would say that the mission of Christ was complete and sufficient, even though this relocation did not turn out to be temporary and did not have a limited scope. On the contrary, Christ's admonition simply added a new set of values for people to take into account. After that, it was up to those people to put them into practice as they were able. And it was up to the messengers[24] who came after that to bring about a renewal of this mission as they were able, whenever its path went astray, or whenever the conscience of the people needed a new center.

Chapter 19

The Kingdom of Heaven

> Lo! thou (O Muhammad) guidest not whom thou lovest, but Allah guideth whom He will. And He is best aware of those who walk aright. (*Sūrat al-Qaṣaṣ* 56)[1]

This noble verse serves as a reference point concerning the historical circumstances surrounding every call ever issued, and especially the greatest religious calls. For there is nothing which elicits more careful reflection than a comparison between what had been intended by those who issued the calls, and what was actually realized in the end quite apart from their intention, or even contrary to what they had intended. Thus, as time passed and as goals and objectives were met, it would become evident that the way in which the call itself proceeded was more correct than the way in which the caller was proceeding. It was as though the call and the caller together were a channel directed by the Everlasting Wisdom, such that neither those who called nor those who responded could discern where the call was being directed, or where they themselves were being directed.

So we ask: What if the people of Mecca had been more reasonable and had responded to Muḥammad's call? What if the Muslims never had to enter Mecca as victorious conquerors?

Certainly the emigration from Mecca to Medina was the most formative event in Islam; if that event had been eliminated from the history of Islam, that history would have been altered. Thus there is no benefit to that history, as we might think would be the case, if another event considered to be an obstacle had disappeared, even if it had been the greatest obstacle in the earliest period of Islam.

And what if the Israelites at the time of Christ had accepted and trusted him? What if they had opened the doors of the Temple for him and welcomed him in faith?

If this had been the case, the result would have been the addition of one more name to the list of prophets in the books of the Old Testament.[2] Israel would have continued to be secluded, and the world would have continued along its course. And Nazareth would have remained completely forgotten in history. At best it would have been remembered as one of those trivial little villages governed by almighty Rome, that city where the Caesars ruled as tyrants and made themselves into gods.

There can be no doubt that it was Israel whom Christ had intended to reach when he first issued his call. It was only natural for him to seek them out before some other group; for they were his closest relatives, they possessed the books which announced the good news of salvation, and they had been expecting the messenger-savior who was to come by means of the Divine Mystery.

Thus Christ had exhorted his disciples to have nothing to do with the other nations.[3] This was because the disciples belonged to a nation which was destined to be the first to hear the truth, ahead of all the other nations whose people had not been chosen.

When he sent forth the disciples to carry out the call, he prohibited them from entering Samaria.[4] And, speaking generally, he warned them about throwing pearls under the feet of swine.[5]

On one occasion, a Phoenician woman wanted him to treat her with the same respect that he extended to the Israelites. But instead of addressing her in a friendly manner, he chided her, because it was not right that bread belonging to the children of the house be taken from them and thrown to the dogs.[6]

As we have already mentioned, this preference for the Jews was only natural, inspired as it was by human nature and also by the Jewish scriptures and the studies that were made of them. Likewise, there was a profound wisdom inherent in this call, intended as it was for success. For if Christ had taken the same approach towards estranged[7] foreigners as he did towards his closest relatives, the relatives were apt to be driven away; at the same time, there was not the least bit of certainty that anyone would have drawn near to him from among the estranged foreigners, since they used to wage war against Christ and his people, and the two groups used to reciprocate in their mistrust of the other and, at times, in revenge.

Then what would have happened if, under the best circumstances and with the greatest facilitation, those who were called had responded to the call? What if they had responded without creating opposition, and without making martyrs of the Christians?!

If all of the Jews had responded to the call, then it would have entered the domain of "an ethnic clique."[8] Nothing would have changed anywhere as a result of that call, except in that limited domain.

And if the response had been only one group of Jews from among their various groups, the result would have been the addition of one more sect to the list of the Pharisees, Sadducees, Essenes and Zealots. In fact, it so happens that a group of Israelites had accepted Christianity, while remaining a Jewish sect. They were called "Ebionites", i.e., "the poor ones" or "the dervishes."[9] This sect faced adversity because it was on neither one side nor the other, and it completely dropped out of both Jewish and Christian history![10]

It also happened, in fact, that there was a Jewish-Christian church which emigrated from Jerusalem to the east side of the Jordan River. Thus the churches of Israel withdrew and resided in the east where it was forbidden for the rest of Israel to reside. This church continued for a long time, being neither distinctively Jewish nor distinctively Christian. So it faced the same adversity as did the Ebionites.[11]

* * *

We have already mentioned the parable which Christ told those who were called, but who failed to respond, i.e., the parable about the prince who prepared banquets.[12] He had sent for those who were the most distinguished and preferred among his relatives and friends, inviting them to rejoice with him and to share in his food and drink. But not one of them responded. Instead, they all excused themselves, giving reasons as to why they would be delayed until after the day of the banquet. At this, the prince swore that no one who had received an invitation would ever attend the banquet. Instead, he would by all means fill his banquet room with people, whether or not they were ready, including those crowded into alleys or abandoned in the road. He refused to leave a single place at the table without a guest present, and everyone who knocked at the door became an accepted and welcomed guest. In the same manner, those who were called to the banquet of heaven but who arrived late were to find it already full. They would be preceded by those who were more deserving, because those people longed for that which was considered detestable by the arrogant ones who had been called.

Christ was insistent in calling the Jews, but they were insistent in rejecting him. So he said to them: "The stone which the builders rejected has become the head of the corner. . . . The kingdom of God will be torn away from you and given to a nation which brings forth its fruit. . . . Whoever falls on that stone will be crushed by it, and when it falls on anyone, it will destroy him. . . ."[13] "In that place, people will weep and grind their teeth; in that place, many are called, but few are chosen."[14]

As the reality of this prophecy became more intense between Christ and those who were inflexible and bigoted, he preached less about how "the nation" of Israel was distinguished and set apart from the other nations. At the same time, he preached more about human ethics, whereby people could become worthy of the kingdom of heaven, one at a time, whatever might be the circumstances of the nation to which they belonged. Those who listened to him understood that this kingdom could rightfully be claimed by every human being who aspired to it.[15]

However, this phrase "the kingdom of heaven" is related in more than one fashion among the various Gospel accounts. Indeed, no single expression is used by all the Gospels to refer to it. Thus Mark and Luke refer to it as "the kingdom of God," while Matthew refers to it as "the kingdom of heaven." Occasionally, all the Gospels concur in referring to it as "the kingdom of the Son of Man."[16]

In the same manner, it would seem from some of Christ's sayings that the kingdom was about to arrive, that some who were alive and who heard him would not taste death before they would see the Son of Man coming in his kingdom (Matthew 16).[17]

In other sayings, it would seem that there was to be a great interval, and that he claimed people would go astray throughout its duration: "Let no one ever lead you astray. For many will come in my name, and many will be led astray by them. And you will hear of wars and reports about wars before that time will come. For nation will rise against nation, and kingdom against kingdom. There will be famines and epidemics and earthquakes in diverse places, and all of this will be signs of the sufferings to come. On that day, they will hand you over to be oppressed, and you will be killed, and all nations will hate you for my sake. . . . Then many false prophets will come and lead many astray. And for many, love will languish. But those who endure to the end will be saved. And this good news of the kingdom will be proclaimed throughout the world as a testimony to all the nations" (Matthew 24).[18]

And sometimes Christ spoke about the kingdom as if it were near, but that it would come suddenly at a time which no one knew: "Therefore, keep watch, because you do not know when your Lord will come. If the master of the house had known at what time of night the thief was coming, he would not have been robbed. In the same way, you must be ready, because the Son of Man will come at a time you do not expect."[19]

Among Christ's prophecies concerning this, he said that the Son of Man himself did not know the day nor the hour (Mark 13), and that the signs for this were imminent and would appear to that generation.[20]

Some passages indicate that the kingdom means the will of God, or what he commands and prescribes: "Seek first the kingdom of God and his righteousness" (Matthew 6).[21] And, "to you it has been given to know the kingdom of heaven" (Matthew 13).[22]

Sometimes the kingdom is applied to the mission which the disciples were to learn from Christ: "I confer on you a kingdom, just as my Father has conferred one on me."[23] And Luke says, "As Christ was going to Jerusalem, his disciples and followers were thinking that the kingdom of God was about to appear right away" (Luke 19).[24]

We have observed in several books and commentaries that these numerous descriptions of the kingdom were considered to be strange, that they provoked confusion among those of various opinions, and that, in the estimation of the commentators, they had appeared quite unexpectedly. In our opinion, it is instead more likely that these descriptions flowed naturally from the existing state of affairs.

Thus it is first of all necessary for us to consider that Christ definitely referred to the kingdom which every listener understood to be that world which was to come at the end of this present world. And since he referred to that kingdom, it was quite natural for his hearers to consult the prophecies which had established signs concerning this, and to consult the commentators and those who were anticipating this kingdom, who had associated those signs with the end of the fourth or the sixth millennium. But they disagreed as to whether the expected Messiah was to come and then later return, or whether this earthly world was to end when he came and he would not again return to this present, ordinary world![25]

It was quite natural for Christ to speak about the kingdom of heaven in this sense, and for those who heard him to consult those prophecies. There was nothing to be considered strange with regard to this. The only thing strange about what Christ said is that it included nothing about the Warner,[26] irrespective of whether he was to appear in that time or else later at a time when the prophecies were expecting the end, when everything concerning warning and good news and signs would be fulfilled.

But if we try to incorporate this meaning into the kingdom which Christ spoke about, we believe (and others should also consider) that this would be entering an area of ambiguity concerning the kingdom with its various meanings, and especially concerning the kingdom on which the mission of Christ stands. In fact, this would be true of all the missions.[27]

Now all of those missions, which came with prophets who called others to the world to come, dealt with a kingdom of contentment which would be fulfilled in heaven. But they also dealt with a kingdom for which the people had to work in this life. That is, each mission was one which the people heard in this world, and through it they could become worthy of the kingdom in the world to come.

It was this kind of kingdom — the kingdom of Christ's mission, or the kingdom of the Son of Man[28] — that definitely came to mind when he outlined its claims and commandments to his followers.

Of course, when we refer here to an ambiguity that occurred when Christ sometimes spoke about the kingdom of the Day of Judgment, we note that there was also ambiguity when he sometimes spoke about the kingdom before the Day of Judgment.

Nevertheless, the ambiguity concerning how we should understand the kingdom which centered around the mission of Christ — or the mission of the Son of Man — must be considered in relation, on the one hand, to how this mission developed according to its reception by those who heard it: whether the kingdom which was presented in Christ's call was one in which the Israelites received special preference, or perhaps was one from which they were excluded while it comprised instead all the nations.

On the other hand, this ambiguity must be considered in relation to the loftiness of that mission as it was perceived by those who heard it. Such ambiguity was inevitable when those people were being called by Christ to a much loftier mission than what they had expected or anticipated or were able to understand.

We can observe this enormous disparity that existed between Christ and his disciples and followers in those situations where it was especially prominent, where they constantly asked him questions which demonstrated their bewilderment. Thus Nicodemus, a member of the High Council,[29] did not understand what Christ meant concerning the kingdom, that a person was required to be born a second time and to enter the kingdom as a new person, just like a newborn baby enters this world.[30]

Likewise, after the call of Christ had reached its conclusion, the disciples persisted in thinking that the kingdom would come in the form of a state for the Israelites: "So they asked him, 'Lord, will you at this time restore Israel's sovereign power?'[31] Then he said to them, 'It is not for you to know the times and seasons which the Father has laid down by his authority. But you will receive power when the Holy Spirit has descended upon you; and you will be my witnesses in Jerusalem, and in all of Judea, and in Samaria, and to the most distant parts of the world.'"[32]

We reiterate again that this ambiguity which existed between what the speaker intended and what the hearers could grasp was completely natural. Yet it is this immense disparity which leads us to the proper understanding of the kingdom as Christ had it in mind. For the disciples did not have the capacity to create or formulate such a concept of the kingdom. The most for which they were capable was to remember the various descriptions of the kingdom which they heard, then to record and gather together those descriptions in the same way that someone gathers together expressions from a language which he hears but does not understand. If later it becomes possible for us to recast these expressions in a single form, using harmonious and intelligible terminology, this is a sign that the result is an authentic portrait, the description which had originally been intended.

The Gospels do indeed present a harmonious description of the kingdom in various passages: there is mention of a kingdom which is not of this world.[33] There is mention of a kingdom which exists in the conscience of man in every age; if one gains this kingdom then he has success, but if he forfeits this kingdom then the whole world is of no use to him.[34] There is mention of a kingdom which can be entered only with a pure, unblemished soul, like the soul of an innocent child.[35] There is mention of a kingdom which cannot be inaugurated by the sword, because whatever is taken by the sword will perish by the sword.[36] And on one occasion, "when the Pharisees asked him when the kingdom of God was coming, he answered them, 'It is not coming as something to be observed, nor will anyone say, "Here it is!" or "There it is!" Rather, it is now within you'" (Luke 17).[37]

Of course there are those who find these descriptions strange, and who see in them nothing but inconsistency and uncertainty! Then what do they make of this harmonized portrait? What kind of portrait do they expect if not this one, given the disparity in perception between the Teacher and the disciples, and given the fact that those who heard him thought of the kingdom only in relation to the Day of Judgment, and that sometimes Christ spoke of it along these lines? How can they expect to find anything other than this portrait, given the fact that it was absolutely necessary for the call to develop from a teaching addressed to a specific nation to one addressed to all nations?

The essential meaning of the kingdom can be found only after sifting through all the data. But the process of sifting is deficient if it is not carried out properly, and the one who is able to do this is at fault if he forgets that this process is necessary and that it is especially required in this case.

Suppose a man who does not know Chinese came and showed us a document with various strokes and figures; and suppose we had the ability to easily render these strokes and figures into words which form an intelligible sentence. Then the meaning of the original signs would be true according to the portrait we have conveyed. Such a portrait would then be more reliable than the product of a translator who can make additions or omissions, or bring about changes or substitutions, as he pleases.[38]

* * *

The call of Christ was transformed from one that was exclusive to one that was general. It was transformed from a call directed to one nation to a call directed to all the nations. It was a call directed to "man," understood either as an individual or as all people.

This transformation took place at a time when the world was ready, in the depths of its soul, for this new call. Yet it was no small matter for the world to fully understand its truth, or to fathom its depths.

The world of humanity was ready for that call to the same extent that it was in need of that call. It was not always necessary for the world to understand the call, in the same way that it needed that call or that it needed something like it.

We could say that world was like the ground which benefits from the rain because it is ready for it and thirsts for it. There is no place here for any talk about whether or not the ground "understands" the rain, or can "fathom its depths"!

It is true that in that world, human relationships had transcended the walls that had existed between nations and people. But those relationships existed in the regions of the earth and not in the recesses of the conscience. And perhaps people experienced from those relationships the harmful effects of hostility, hatred, racial hypocrisy and alienation from bigotry, before they could experience the advantages of unity or anticipate beyond this the realities of brotherhood and sincerity.

Furthermore, the walls which had existed between nations and people crumbled under the weight of human misery before they could crumble in the face of the call to brotherhood and sincerity. When this occurred, the world was in some sense united, encompassing all groups and races. But the only unity which they sensed among themselves came as a result of slavery and poverty. Such unity acted like a noose, comprising not only slavery *per se,* but also the slavery of dispossession and hopelessness.

The pagan world found it difficult to produce a messenger who would gather all people into one religion. For the history of paganism was not entrusted to bring forth messengers to the world, messengers who were filled with a spiritual enthusiasm which overflowed to those around them, as well as to those more distant. History has never known a pagan herald who was devoted solely to bearing the message of encouragement and of warning, who was unconcerned about death and undeterred by whatever obstacles he faced which might intimidate or threaten him. All that can be said about pagan religions is that whenever a nation which subscribed to them conquered other nations, it imposed submission to its gods in the same way that it imposed submission to its laws and regulations. The state would force the vanquished peoples to participate in acts of devotion which were associated with public rituals and official assemblies. After this, the state allowed them to worship whatever gods or idols they pleased.

Thus it was only those religions based on scriptures and on monotheism which were entrusted with that spiritual enthusiasm necessary for uniting the world of humanity under a single creed. And the messengers who came from these religions were only those who believed in a God who is greater than the world, greater than its empires, greater than everything that is.

By the wisdom of the Everlasting Wisdom, this messenger came for that era.

By the wisdom of the Everlasting Wisdom, this messenger was expelled by his people, and the call was not restricted to them. Then the world found in him what it most desired, just when it needed him. The call came as the greatest of signs, one which requires considerable reflection by scholars and historians. For it is more difficult and more extraordinary to explain the successful outcome of this call as a coincidence, than to explain it as something that was planned and ordained.

What was accomplished by this messenger was the opposite of what was accomplished by paganism with all its tyranny and power. For paganism was victorious only because it was the religion of the victorious Empire. But this mission — the mission of the kingdom of heaven — rose up in a small, lowly tribe which was sometimes ruled by the Western Roman Empire, and sometimes by the Eastern Roman Empire. Then after several generations, this mission overwhelmed the two empires and took control of its two capitals. Thus, the statement from Julian which has been handed down — whether or not he actually said it — can be considered true, that the "Galilean" triumphed by his heavenly kingdom over the kingdoms of the Caesars.[39] So the Caesars were added to the fringes of that kingdom, and by it they took what they wanted in the name of Caesar, and they took what they wanted in the name of God!"[40]

Part Five
The Tools of the Call

Chapter 20

The Ability of the Teacher

Whenever any of the great calls spread throughout the world, its very diffusion confirmed at least two things: that the world at that time was in need of such a call, and that the world was ready to listen to it. These two issues are different from each other, and they should not be considered as synonymous or equivalent. Rather, the world's need for the call could be compared to a disease, whereas its readiness to listen to that call would then be compared to an awareness of that disease, or a readiness to ask for treatment. It might be the case that both these factors occur at the same time. Or, the disease might occur without a simultaneous request for treatment, and such treatment would not be accepted even if it were set before the patient.

We have already summarized what has been written about the times which prepared the way for the call of Christ. In short, we know that the world in the first century was in need of that call, and also it was ready to listen to it. This is true whether we limit the discussion to the world of Israel or we speak generally in terms of the entire world.[1]

During that era, the world of Israel had been placing its faith in the expected Messiah and in his promised coming for quite some time. Meanwhile, the world in general had a "negative" faith, believing that paganism was bankrupt and that hope for one's soul could not be found. The common people were in misery and despair, while the privileged abandoned themselves either to pleasure or to mysticism.[2] Those among them who were more contemplative espoused Epicureanism or Stoicism, and those who were characterized by piety and the desire to seek out hidden things espoused one of the mystery religions, in which ritual and rite took the place of duty and devotion.

There were also many of the privileged class who were detached from Epicureanism, Stoicism and the mystery religions. Their condition was thus one in which they experienced the emptiness which occurs prior to being filled. It would be quite accurate to say that this emptiness could not overcome the resilience of the approaching ideology with the same kind of strength which was present in that ideology, and it might instead be open to accepting that ideology. In this case, their awareness of being empty would be one of the reasons why they would respond to and long for that ideology.

There is no doubt about the fact that the world in the first century was in need of that ideology, and that it was ready to listen to it. However, although the world was in need and was ready, it was not apt to gain that ideology casually and serenely; not without a struggle[3] by its messengers and heralds, and a high degree of capability among those messengers and heralds.

The world's need for the ideology, and its readiness to listen to it, were no substitute for the means by which that ideology could enjoy prosperity and success. Chief among those means was the ability of the one who called to win people over and to gain a hearing, and his ability to be victorious when opposing contentious and obstinate people.

Such ability was in abundance for the Teacher of Christianity. He was justly named "the Teacher," and he was called by this name in the various synagogues and meeting places; for his greatest task was that of teaching and of bringing about a vital spiritual revival by way of such teaching.

The Gospels often relate how Christ was called "Teacher." His disciples and opponents alike called him by this title, as well as others who heard him but who neither followed him nor disputed with him.

They called him by this title because when he spoke they realized his vast knowledge of the scriptures. It was only natural for him to quote them and to comment on them. There is sufficient evidence in the Gospels to firmly assert that he used to chant the Psalms and to memorize the books of Jeremiah, Isaiah and Ezekiel, quite apart from the five books which were attributed to Moses (peace be upon him), or quite apart from the various schools of thought as to how the commandments and regulations should be applied.

Some historians think it is likely that Christ knew Greek, and that the conversation which took place between him and Pilate was in that language. This is because Greek was widespread among the Galileans at that time. For there were many Jews living outside of Galilee who did not understand Hebrew and Aramaic and who needed the Greek translation of the scriptures; some of these used to make the pilgrimage to Jerusalem for the Jewish festivals. Also, some of the Galilean Jews used to travel to Alexandria and other regions where Greeks predominated, and while there they would communicate with their own people only in Greek. Thus it would not have been strange for Christ to know Greek, like many other Galileans who would have known it.[4]

However, what is certain is that he knew classical Hebrew, in which the books of Moses and the prophets were taught, and that he knew Aramaic and spoke it as eloquently as anyone.[5] What is also certain is that if he knew Greek, it was only for the purpose of addressing others, not for the purpose of study. For his sayings were devoid of any reference to a single source in the literature written in that language. Furthermore, the statements which are attributed to him in the Gospels (which were written in Greek) reveal their Aramaic origin, as is evident from their rhetorical structure, or from their grammatical style and rhythm of expression.[6]

On the other hand, he was not unique among the Jewish scholars of those days in his knowledge of the Jewish scriptures. There were in Jerusalem at that time perhaps hundreds of scribes and Pharisees who had memorized some of the same books which Christ had memorized; they were able to quote them and comment on them eloquently and spontaneously. Yet not a single one of them was as capable as the Teacher who dispersed spiritual life among people, and who transfused into their minds a tranquillity such as that which exists in the soul when its melodies are in harmony, melodies that had clashed before they were combined and fashioned together.

The language in which the call was initially conveyed was the language of the one who issued that call. It was a language without similarity and without rival in terms of its power and effect.

It was a language which was unique in the structure of its words and expressions; unique in its eloquence and the inflection of its concepts; unique in its character which was unlike any other mode of expression, whether oral or written. If this had not been the case, then his approach would not have been so popular among those who heard him, and he would not have won their hearts and minds so powerfully.

This language was structured in a mode somewhere between free prose and rhythmical poetry.[7] This mode was a distinctive form of art well suited for conventional instruction, or for motivating and stimulating the memory and imagination. It was arranged in a manner different from the system of versification into meters and measures[8] which we know in Arabic, for such a system was unknown in both Aramaic and Hebrew. Rather, this mode was more like the method of corresponding lines and repetitious rhyming[9] which an Arab listener would fully expect, although the rhyme itself did not recur in repeated phrases.[10]

The rhythmic style of Christ's speech was one in which his sayings were often repeated and confirmed. Its Arabic translation cannot do justice to this style, but with careful reflection it can be demonstrated to some extent. Here is one example:[11] "Ask, and you will receive. Seek, and you will find. Knock, and it will be opened to you. For the one who asks will receive; the one who seeks will find; and to the one who knocks the door will be opened. Which one of you, if his son asks him for bread, will give him a stone? Or if he asks for a fish, will give him a snake? Or if he asks for an egg, will give him a scorpion? So if you — you who are evil — give what is good to your sons, how much more will the Father who is in heaven give the Holy Spirit to the one who asks?"[12]

Here is another example: "As it was in the days of Noah, so will it be in the days of the Son of Man. They were eating and drinking, giving in marriage and getting married, until the day when he entered the ark, and the flood came and destroyed them all. In the same way, in the days of Lot they were eating and drinking, buying and selling, planting and building;[13] but on the day when Lot went out from Sodom, fire and brimstone rained from the sky[14] and destroyed them all. So will it be on the day when the Son of Man is revealed.[15] On that day, if someone is on the roof while his goods are in the house, let him not go down in order to take them. And if someone is in the field, let him not turn back; don't you remember Lot's wife? Whoever seeks to save his life will destroy it, and whoever destroys his life will preserve it. Listen to what I say to you: on that night two men will be in bed; one of them will be taken and his companion left behind. Two women will be grinding; one of them will be taken and the other left behind. Two men will be in the field; this one will be taken and that one will be left behind. . . . Wherever there is a carcass, there the vultures gather."[16]

A passage which exhibits a similar style as that found in the two previous examples is

Christ's warning to Jerusalem: "Oh Jerusalem, Jerusalem! You who kill the prophets and stone the messengers. How often have I wanted to gather your children together, as a hen gathers her chicks under her wings. But you would not have it. See, your house will be horribly devastated."[17]

And similar to this example is his warning to the daughters of Jerusalem: "Oh daughters of Jerusalem! Do not weep for me, but weep for yourselves and for your children. There will be days when they will say, 'Blessed are the barren, and the wombs which have not given birth, and the breasts which have not nursed.' There will be days when they will call on the mountains to fall on them, and the hills to cover them. If they do this when the plants are fresh and moist, what will they do when they are dry?"[18]

These examples give some indication of the manner in which Christ put words together, and the procedure by which he warned people and called their attention.

* * *

As for the manner in which he spoke figuratively, he was renowned for his method of using parables,[19] and these are found in all the various patterns which apply to parables. There was a pattern which took the form of an allegory, another pattern which took the form of a proverb, another which took the form of an analogy, and another which took the form of metaphors.[20] All of his parables were marked by his own unique character which was unparalleled and without equal among the prophets mentioned in the scriptures, even if they employed various kinds of parables like he did.[21]

An example of the kind of parable which takes the form of an *allegory* is the parable of the Sower and the Seed: "A sower went out to sow. As he went along, some of the seed fell on the path, and the birds of the sky came and ate it. Some fell on rocky ground where the soil was sparse, and it sprouted right away; but it did not take long for it to be scorched by the rising sun, and since it had no depth in the earth, it withered away. Some of the seed fell among the thorns, and the thorns grew up and choked it so that it did not bear any grain. But other seed fell on good soil, and it yielded grain which came up and grew, so that one plant produced thirtyfold, another sixtyfold, and another a hundredfold. He who has ears to hear, let him hear."[22]

Another example of this kind is the parable of the Wedding Girls:[23] "The kingdom of heaven can be compared to ten virgins who took their lamps and went out to meet the bridegroom: five of them were clever and five were careless.[24] The careless ones took their lamps but they did not take any oil as well, whereas the clever ones took their flasks of oil along with the lamps. As the arrival of the bridegroom was delayed, sleep overcame them all. Then a shout rose up at midnight: 'Look! The bridegroom is coming; go out to meet him.' So the careless ones tended their lamps which were going out, and they asked their companions for a little of their oil. But they replied: 'Perhaps there will not be enough for us all; go to where it is sold and buy some.' And as they were going, the bridegroom arrived, and those who were there and ready accompanied him to the wedding party. Then those who had been absent came, and the door was shut. They began to shout, 'Master, open the door for us; Master, open the door for us.' But he answered them, 'Who are you? I don't know you at all!'"[25]

Another example of the allegory pattern is this saying of Christ: "I am the bread of life. Whoever comes to me will not be hungry."[26]

Here are some examples of the kind of parable which takes the form of a *proverb:* "Do not throw pearls in front of swine."[27] "The measure you give will be the measure you get."[28] "Physician, heal yourself!"[29] "New wine in old wineskins."[30] "Do not let your left hand know what your right hand is doing."[31] "By their fruits you will know them."[32] "A prophet has no honor in his own country."[33]

Here is an example of the kind of parable which takes the form of an *analogy:* "If you love those who love you, what credit is that to you? Isn't that the way the tax collectors behave?"[34]

Another example of this kind of parable is when he rebuked those who disapproved of his association with sinners: "Those who are healthy have no need of a doctor; rather, it is those who are sick who need doctors."[35] And another example: "If the light within you is darkness, how great is the darkness!"[36]

An example of the kind of parable which takes the form of *metaphors* is his address to his disciples: "You are the salt of the earth. But if the salt becomes spoiled, how shall it be made salty?[37] It is no longer useful except to be thrown on the ground and be trampled. You are the light of the world. Nothing hides a city which is standing on top of a mountain. A lamp is not lit to be placed under a bowl, but to be set up on a stand, giving light to everyone in the house."[38]

Here is another example of this kind: "Do not accumulate treasures for yourselves on earth, where they can be spoiled by moths and rust, and where thieves can break in and steal them. Rather, accumulate treasures for yourselves in heaven, where there are no moths or rust or robbers. Where the treasure is, there is the heart."[39]

It is also related that Christ, in all his parables, loved to make comparisons concerning his opponents. This was so that he could clarify what he meant and illustrate what lay behind the comparison with regard to their distinctive characteristics. "They see the speck in the eyes of others, yet they don't see the board in their own eyes."[40] "They settle accounts over a mere gnat, yet they swallow a camel."[41] "On the outside are whitewashed walls, yet on the inside are rotting bones."[42] "A rich man can enter the door of heaven no more than a thick rope can enter the eye of the tailor's needle."[43]

On most occasions, these parables came to mind spontaneously, either as a response to a question, or a comment on an incidental event, or a word of rebuke to an arrogant person. The perceptive Teacher rarely elaborated on a parable following the occasion which inspired it. Because of this, some modern interpreters think it is most likely that those parables which appear in succession in the Gospels, but which have different objectives, originated with Christ in more than one context or situation. And they say that the Sermon on the Mount[44] — which of all the speeches of Christ is the most replete with various objectives and themes — is a combination of miscellaneous sayings which were grouped according to the themes that arose from their original settings.

Whenever Christ was alone in meditation, and several of the lessons he wanted to teach would simmer within his soul, his thoughts would organize themselves in a naturally inspired manner. Then, when the circumstances were different, this natural manner would quickly come to his aid, and his words would flow in their usual way and in simple fashion. People might well have assumed that his words had been prepared ahead of time since they were organized rather than haphazard, when in fact there had been no prior preparation. The most that can be suggested concerning any preparation is that the thoughts which he generously shared were always thought out at the time, and that he became accustomed to such thinking in comparable situations. Then the pattern of his expressions was molded in the depths of his disposition without any intention or constraint on his part.

Such patterns become a familiar habit for those who are accustomed to thinking as they express themselves, and who are accustomed to a sense of affection present between themselves and the crowds. I have heard speakers bestow their most profound rhetorical masterpieces which were improvised on a moment's notice; yet the occasion overflowed with mutual affection and an enthusiasm which emanated from speaker and listeners alike. Although they improvised, such speakers were the first to imagine that they were listening to familiar words. They would almost ask themselves where on earth they had heard them previously. But in reality they had transferred the words from their subconscious mind to their conscious mind, so that they were just as amazed at what they were saying as were their listeners. In reality as well, when the people listened to these words, they found them both strange and simple at the same time: strange because they were gripped by those words even though they could not comprehend them, and simple because they acted on them by virtue of the speaker's eloquence despite the obstacle of their comprehension.

* * *

Was there anyone like Christ who had been raised since childhood reciting the books of the prophets, whose hearing and speech never ceased to echo the chanting of the psalms and the refrains of the proverbs? His upright disposition was inspired, so that there was nothing more natural for him than to break forth in words that would revive you as soon as you heard him proclaiming the very first pages, words that came from the depths of his heart and the abundance of his spontaneity. It was this spontaneity which Christ had in mind when he charged his disciples to rely on nature, and to leave behind any anxiety about making their speech elegant and exquisite before being called upon to give an account of what they were saying.[45]

It is possible that in the time of Christ, people who used to listen to sermons had heard the various patterns of parables many times. It is possible that they used to hear them over and over whenever they entered a synagogue or listened to speakers in other places. Critics of Hebrew and Aramaic rhetoric trace these rhetorical forms back to ancient times which had preceded the birth of Christ by hundreds of years; they say that the use of parables did not originate with Christ, nor did their patterns which took the form of allegories or proverbs or metaphors or the logic of analogy.[46] However, the absolute truth of the matter is that in the time of Christ, those people had never known such magnanimity as that which pervaded their souls when they inclined their ears and hearts to that beloved Teacher, the one who entrusted them with wonders and secrets which were familiar yet alive. They felt these wonders and secrets deep within themselves, as realities from which they would never be separated for an instant. They were lavished with the abundance of his radiant presence and were overpowered by his kindly affection and unsullied compassion.

Sometimes, the manner in which Christ spoke was frightening or intimidating, and it would seem to someone listening to that teaching that he was being alienated from its source whenever he heard it. But other times, that manner was attractive and conciliatory, and it would seem to someone listening that with every word an obstacle was removed or a gap closed, and that any estrangement between speaker and listener was eliminated. This manner in which that beloved Teacher spoke was one which was able to reconcile those who listened through tender instruction, so that whoever understood was brought near, and whoever did not understand was not left far away. We can imagine those simple folks drawing near to listen, confined in the darkness of their ignorance, quite unaware of what they would hear. Then their minds were opened, and the images within were brought into conformity, while the contrasting disparities became clear. Little by little, the darkness faded away, and little by little, light entered in. Slowly they were overcome with the sensation felt by a blind person who regains his sight, astounded at being able to see for the first time; or the sensation felt by one who is up before dawn until daybreak. They found a gentle and compassionate guidance, one which drew near to them without causing them hardship and without overwhelming them.

We can imagine those simple folks drawing near to their Teacher in understanding and knowledge, drawing near to him in love and affection.

Because of this, we can imagine the priority of the messenger in proclaiming his message.[47] For surely there is no message without a messenger; there is no way to establish Christianity apart from a Christ. The origin of that spiritual message must also be its essence and core, the fundamental basis of its power and effect. Whatever particulars go beyond the original messenger are but offshoots and additions.

The heart of Christ's message was in its messenger Christ: a man who guided others while holding no influence over them other than one of affection and inspiration and the revealing of hearts and minds. If the priority of the message had not been in its messenger, then John the Baptist would have taken precedence regarding that message, for he would have issued its call and presented its witness. However, this was a call which anticipated its own caller, and that was Christ. It was not enough that the whole world was in need of a call which it demanded. The world's need also required someone capable of issuing that call, someone suitable for carrying it out; for those who are in need cannot on their own lay hold of that which they need.

Chapter 21

The Fidelity of the Disciples

For any call in which there are disciples, the first priority concerning them is that they become those who call. That is, they are to share with the teacher the task of spreading the call.

However, the first priority concerning the disciples called by Christ was that they become those who respond. For there were no other leaders who were called to their ranks. They were indeed the very first group to respond, after which other groups like them were to follow. Yet none of them had been leaders, nor had they been led by others; and by accepting the call, all of them became equal.

The priority for the disciples in Christianity was that they should be the first to accept the call of Christ. Here, it is necessary that we distinguish between the character of those who accept and the character of those who work.

The disciples were linked to Christ as the small community[1] which he established. In the same manner, that community grew larger with time; a large community developed which emulated the small community in its response to the call. The disciples were the initial group, to be followed by others like them. They were the first company in a single army; yet they were not the kind of army which carried out its mission by confronting another army, forcing it to concede and join with them.

At the beginning of the mission, the disciples formed the model for what the Christian community should be like. The Christian community continued for several generations without diverging from that model with respect to its formation and style. Accordingly, we would say that when the disciples issued their call, they did not impose their system of belief on others; rather, they and all those who followed them were simply responding to the call, one battalion after another, one squadron after another.

Whenever a call is issued, there are both those who lead and those who are led. However, the disciples who responded to the call of Christ did not lead others. Rather, they were the initial group from the ranks that followed and succeeded one another. There was no difference in makeup between those who were first and those who were last.

There is nothing from the early history of the disciples to indicate that they were distinguished by any mark of leadership. Rather, they all came from the same environment. Perhaps they all shared a common ancestry or came from neighboring homes.[2] It was as if the lot had fallen upon that group from among everyone else who were in the exact same situation. And afterwards, they were privileged to be taught and trained by Christ himself.

Christ used to observe some of them, and he would say to them, "Follow me"; then they would follow him.[3] They did not seem to be superior to others, as if they had any intellectual or psychological advantage. The only advantage they had was what the Master was able to see within them, that they were people who would listen attentively and follow after him.

There was nothing obvious to indicate that they had a better grasp of things than anyone else. If the lot had fallen on twelve others, they would have been just as capable of learning from Christ and just as ready to accept his call. For there is no doubt that their qualifications were quite average, the same as for any group of that number and coming from that environment. No one among them was a prominent personality, as would be the case for any other group at first sight. It could not be said of any of them that he was one in a hundred or one in a thousand, never to appear again; or that any of them would have learned things which others would not have learned had they been disciples of that capable teacher. Rather, the most that could be said was that he was a recruit, just like other recruits. Moreover, the credit had to go to his leader for whatever success was achieved in training and instructing him.

Thus, they were those who were chosen, as it is mentioned in the Gospels. However, there is no evidence that it was an unusual or difficult choice for the wise and judicious leader. Perhaps the biggest factor in choosing them is that they had already known each other and were in harmony with one another.[4] It was certainly better for them to come together this way than to come together independently from alienated environments. For those who are in harmony are better suited to be companions than those who are alienated.

We believe that the comparison to military recruitment here is apt to bring home the meaning of this concept, since we see this as one of the most important aspects enabling us to understand that call and the reasons why it spread.

And so the recruits were enlisted. Everyone met the same conditions for recruitment. But as they stood before the Master, he set aside one band of men who were, in his judgment, akin to each other, even though all the others were generally equal to them as to the conditions for recruitment.

They would have represented only the darkest disposition of humanity, had it not been for that heavenly breath[5] which the spirit of the capable teacher breathed into them.

He knew their shortcomings. And because of their faithfulness and fidelity, they did not deceive themselves concerning those shortcomings.

When he spoke to them, they would not understand him and they would ask him for more clarification. When they were possessed with doubts, he sensed this within them, and they would not deny it. Sometimes they would speak first, initially expressing doubts. Then they would ask him to increase their faith, and he would do so, teaching them how to be on their guard concerning doubts like those.

He fully realized that they were not an unshakable mountain; that their determination would wane; and that as they encountered all the hardships that lay ahead, they would some day face some terrifying experience when the soul's frailty would overtake them.

He had told them that they would forsake him.[6] When he had asked them to stay awake with him, they slept.[7] More than once he had rebuked them because they would argue about who was the greatest;[8] or because they felt that their reward for their faith was slow in coming;[9] or because they discriminated between people and espoused a law other than the law of love and forgiveness — even after he had preached to them and reminded them how they should act.[10]

Yet he certainly expected no more from them than what he could observe. Nor did he fail to recognize how their initial deficiencies would turn out in the end. He knew what would be demanded of them, yet he perceived that they would be up to the task; he knew that they would become a model for others who would continue to follow their example. The people of this vast world have never been required to reach a level of faith beyond one of fidelity and happily being ready to reform their shortcomings. The disciples reached that level on the day when Christ commissioned them to journey throughout God's world and make themselves an example which could be emulated by those who would be saved.[11]

It was not his intention that after their preparation they would become infallible, as if they had no fault or defect. Instead, he intended that they should set a good example, gathering around themselves those who would behave in the same manner and who would head in the same direction.[12] So they took on only as much as they could handle, and perhaps those who were to follow in their footsteps would be able to do even more.

* * *

Some passages in the Gospels give the distinct impression that Christ progressed far along in his mission without telling his disciples that he was the expected Messiah.[13] As his reputation spread among the villages, people would ask among themselves, "Who is he?" Some of them would say that he was John the Baptist risen from the dead, others that he was Elijah, and others that he was a prophet who had been sent.[14] But Christ did not tell the disciples that he was the Messiah. Instead, it was only after his reputation had spread and people were inquiring about him that he asked them, "And who do you say that I am?" Peter answered him, "You are the Messiah." Then Christ reprimanded him and charged them not to mention this to anyone. This is how the Gospel of Mark reports this incident.[15]

However, the Gospel of Matthew relates that Peter said, "'You are the Messiah, the Son of the living God.' Jesus[16] then answered, 'Blessed are you, Simon son of Jonah. This has not been revealed to you by anything created from flesh and blood, but by my Father who is in heaven. And I say to you that you are Peter,[17] and upon this rock I will build my church, and the gates of hell will have no power against it. I will give you the keys of heaven; whatever you bind on earth will be bound in heaven, and whatever you set free on earth will be set free in heaven.' Then he charged his disciples not to tell anyone that he, Jesus, was the Messiah."[18]

The account of this incident in the Gospel of Luke is closer to that found in the Gospel of Mark: "While he was praying alone, and the disciples were with him, he asked them, 'What do the crowds say about me?' They answered, 'They say that you are John the Baptist, and others say Elijah, and others say that one of the ancient prophets has risen.' Then he asked them, 'And who do you say that I am?' And Peter said, 'The Messiah of God.' Then he reprimanded them and charged them not to tell this to anyone."[19]

The account in John is fairly close to the portrayal which we have presented. Christ noticed the people moving away from him, "and many of his disciples drew back and would not go along with him. So he said to the twelve, 'Could it be that you also wish to go?' Simon Peter answered, 'Lord, where would we go? You have the words of eternal life. We have believed and come to know that you are the Messiah, the Son of the Living God.' Then he answered them, 'Did not I choose you . . . and one of you is a demon?'"[20]

There were many "disciples," as they were being called, and Christ gave them these words as mentioned in the Gospel of John: "Jesus said to the Jews who had believed in him, 'If you persevere in my words, you are truly my disciples. You will know the truth, and the truth will set you free.' Then they answered him, 'We are the descendants of Abraham and are not slaves to anyone. So how can you say, "You will become free"?' He said, 'I tell you the truth, everyone who is involved in sin is a slave to sin. The slave does not remain in the house forever; but the son remains in it forever. So if the Son makes you free, you will be free indeed. I know that you are descendants of Abraham. But you want to kill me because my words find no place among you. I speak of what I have seen with my Father, and you know what you have seen with your father.'[21] They answered him, 'Our father is Abraham.' He said, 'If he were your father, you would do the deeds he has done. But now you seek my death, though I am a man who has told you the truth which I heard from God. This is not what Abraham did; you do the deeds of your father.' So they said to him, 'We were not born through fornication; we have one Father, and he is God.' He said, 'If God were your Father, you would love me, because I have come from God and I came to you. I did not come of my own accord, but it was he who sent me. . . . You are from one father, and he is the devil. . . .'[22]

"The Jews answered him, 'Are we not right when we say that you are a Samaritan and have a demon?'" And when he said to them, "Whoever keeps my words will not see death," they answered back saying, "Now it is clear to us that you have a demon. Abraham died, yet you say, 'If anyone keeps my words, he will not taste death.' Who do you claim to be? Do you think you are greater than our father Abraham who died?"[23]

The lesson from this passage is that Christ progressed in his mission for some time without mentioning to his disciples that he was the promised Messiah; and that he used to teach some of those who sought to be his disciples that they could not comprehend what he was saying. They could not differentiate between the language which they perceived with their senses and the spiritual or figurative language by which Christ spoke. One day, he was concerned that his chosen disciples might be driven away from him, just as those who had wanted to be considered his disciples had been driven away. These would-be disciples alleged that they were just like him,[24] but he rejected their claim and told them, "People are judged to be children of God by their works, but it is clear from your works that you are children of the devil!"

Christ realized[25] that he would not remain for long with those who sought to be his disciples to the end, and that he could not continue with them until their knowledge and faith led them to that perfect goal above all other goals. Sometimes they were weak; other times they just could not understand. Yet if such people remained steadfast with him, if they had a fairly accurate belief about him and if they anticipated that their hope of salvation would be fulfilled in what he taught, then in spite of their weakness they were better than those who failed to understand and who were arrogant and who conspired to do away with him.

* * *

It is well known that the disciples were a band of fishermen who fished in the Sea of Galilee.[26] People who hear that this was their occupation assume that they belonged to a working class of tradesmen who were illiterate. But this is a rash assumption built on faulty reasoning. In fact, they could read and write; they were often found in the synagogues listening to the sermons and participating in the prayers; and they could consult what was said by the prophets. It is true that they had not attained the knowledge of the legal scholars of their time. This was just as well, for if they had come from that group, they would have been overcome with jealousy and would have confronted the call with resistance and arrogance. On the other hand, they were not at the point of being simple folks who were illiterate and uneducated.[27]

Indeed, one of the disciples was what we might call today a secretary for accounts or a revenue collection official; this was Matthew the tax collector. It was he who wrote the Gospel which is known by his name, and his ability to write it "in the Greek language, as is most likely" was one found only among the well-educated.[28] Another disciple was John, to whom the Fourth Gospel is attributed. He was a cousin of Christ, through either the sister or a brother of Christ's mother.[29] He had a successful business in commercial fishing along with his brother James, as can be inferred from the Gospel of Mark where it says, "They left their father in the boat with the hired servants, and they followed Christ."[30]

Also among the disciples were James, the relative of Christ; and John, or "the son of thunder" as Christ called him, due to the vehemence by which he pronounced judgment and the severity by which he reproached others.[31] Also among them was Peter, a man who spoke boldly and with strong determination. It can be inferred from some passages in the Gospels that he was accustomed to carrying a weapon.[32] All of the disciples were ready to be involved in the call, arguing and debating and preaching among the people. Most of them faced death because of their work in propagating the call, and they were not concerned about being opposed by those who held power and authority.[33]

The call of Christ also attracted to itself, both at the time he lived and afterwards, several well-educated scholars such as Nicodemus, the member of the High Council,[34] and Luke, the physician and friend of Paul the Apostle.[35] Also among these was the Apostle Paul himself, an expert in religious jurisprudence and a scholar of history.[36] Most of these well-educated people were favorably disposed toward the call out of sympathy for the disciples in their efforts to stand up to the tyranny of oppressive domination. For they despised the system of doctrine and tradition in which the disciples had no part, and they could not ignore the role of their spiritual enthusiasm in completely demolishing that system.[37]

* * *

Among our contemporaries are those who like to think of Christ as a man who called for political anarchy and who was detached from the prevailing system. They say this because of the severity with which he assailed the law as well as those who were inflexible concerning it and who hypocritically claimed to follow it. These contemporaries fail to realize that it was the law, having been corrupted by those inflexible hypocrites, which had actually created anarchy in another form. Anyone who might discredit and assail a law such as that would not have been numbered among anarchists and enemies of the system.

Furthermore, the evidence against the folly of this assumption is demonstrated in the way Christ organized his disciples and disciplined them to accept obedience and self-denial. He divided the various activities among the members of his small community — the community of the disciples. Thus, one of them became the treasurer, another supervised the requirements of the group, and another served as shepherd of the flock whenever the Master was absent. The entire community was only a small band which did not exceed twenty followers, including the disciples and others on the periphery.[38]

There is another matter which I should include in this discussion on how Christ organized his disciples. Initially, he chose twelve disciples. But later he chose seventy and charged them to go forth two by two in every direction, proclaiming the call. When they returned from their journey, he took them towards a mountain, so that he could hear their reports and review their activities, and he gave them further instruction and advice.[39]

He turned every occasion which was related to his mission into an opportunity for teaching his chosen disciples. He was always warning them against that deadly temptation which shatters the organization of any group, the temptation to compete with each other for leadership. He taught them that whoever would be first among them must be the first to serve the others.[40] He also gave them a parable which is unique in religious history, so that whenever they remembered it they might keep themselves from coveting leadership: he gathered them all together so that he himself could wash their feet. At first, some of them shrank back; but then they relented and acquiesced when they realized the lesson which he intended by this example. Then those who shrank back at first said that they wished he would order them to submit to his washing their hands and heads as well.[41]

He focused all his effort in getting them accustomed to the concept of self-denial, the greatest of virtues among everyday activities. He taught them that when they work, they should not expect any reward for what they do. He allowed them to accept the hospitality of any home which they might enter in order to announce the call to the family living there. But he told them, "Do not take along any bag or satchel or sandals. . . . Give greetings to any home which you enter. . . . And if the people of any city which you enter do not welcome you, leave that city and shake off the dust from your feet as you go."[42]

He often charged them to strive for simplicity in what they do and say. So he commanded them not to be preoccupied with anxiety about how and when they should speak, because they would be inspired at the time about what they should say. It would not be they who speak, but the Spirit of their Father speaking through them.[43]

He did not hide from them the fact that they would experience adversity from others; they had to be "wise as serpents and innocent as doves."[44] But if the situation were to become quite serious, they should have no fear of anyone who could destroy the body, although they should certainly fear anyone who could destroy the spirit.[45]

There was an emphasis on love as that spiritual army was being trained, and the result was something which cannot be produced from an emphasis on harsh austerity, as when soldiers are trained for combat. As they went forth, they worked, knowing that if they were to falter in achieving their task faithfully, they would be diminished in their own eyes as well as before God. And nothing is more harsh to one's soul than this sense of lowliness.

It was not long until the proper time for them to work arrived.[46] So the disciples were scattered across the earth, traveling in every direction and making long journeys to every inhabited area. Among them were those who went as far as the islands of East India, such as the Apostle Thomas. Others went as far as Scythia and Asia Minor, such as the Apostle Andrew. Another worked by himself in the regions of Europe and sent his companions to North Africa. The call also encompassed Egypt and the regions of Arabia and Iraq, not to mention Palestine.[47]

However, they were not as concerned about preaching to the Jews as they were about preaching to the "Gentiles" living in Galilee and Asia Minor and Alexandria.[48] They profited from the fact that they were preceded by the Jewish sects and by those who adhered to the mystery religions, for these paved the way and set the stage for their mission. They operated in the same manner as did the Essenes and Zealots, going out two by two and setting up small groups of believers in each locality. Then they stayed in contact with those groups through correspondence and visitation. It can be correctly said here that the new call benefited from calls which had been issued previously in the period preceding the first century. Certainly the greatest success achieved by the disciples was seen in Asia Minor and Alexandria, where the system of small groups and itinerant preachers had been known previously.

Likewise, the way in which the "world situation" at that time influenced the spread of the new call can be seen in a marvelous phenomenon which repeated itself in every area: the throngs to whom the new religion was proclaimed were quick to accept it and eager to aid and support its progress. Thus, the only danger those messengers experienced came from the prevailing "authorities" whenever the worship of Caesar clashed with the worship of God.[49]

On one occasion, the person who was the most enthusiastic for his religion resorted to accommodating his behavior, hoping that this would gain some believers who would otherwise renounce the call were they to be confronted directly without discretion. When Peter was in Antioch, he accommodated to the conservatives and would not associate with the Gentiles whenever he noticed that members from "the party of James" were around. Then the Apostle Paul rebuked him publicly, warning him against allowing his behavior to become inconsistent with the call for the sake of pleasing others.[50]

Even Paul himself tried to identify with others through a degree of accommodation. As he said in the book of First Corinthians, "I have made myself a slave to all people, so that I might win most of them. To the Jew I became as a Jew, that I might win the Jews. To the legalists I became as a legalist, and to others, as one without any law. . . . I have become all things to all people, so that perhaps I may rescue some from any condition."[51]

Consequently, there can be no doubt that people who had converted to Christianity from paganism intermingled with the earliest Christians, and those people brought with them certain pagan customs and rituals. For a while, the first Christians completely overlooked this situation, thinking that perhaps the newcomers, after renouncing their paganism, would correct their ways as they followed the path of the new religion.[52]

One of the novel characteristics of the twentieth century is the ease by which critics raise suspicions whenever they examine ancient historical records. They find accounts which they cannot fathom and features which they themselves did not witness, and so they cannot accept them as reasonable. One of the accusations they make is that the apostles were lying when they testified to some of the amazing events which they saw, or which they passed on and related. But we believe that authentic history rejects this, because such an accusation is more difficult to substantiate than the claim that those heralds were free of any intent to lie or invent stories.

There is every bit of difference between the behavior of the believer who has no concern about death as he affirms his faith, and the behavior of the impostor who is lying, and who knows that he is lying and calling people to believe his lies. Such a person does not risk death for the sake of an innovative creed, for he would be the first to know of its dishonesty and deception. It is out of the question that intentional liars would be among those who defy death in order to propagate their religion, as did the apostles of Christianity. If the credible historian is one who accepts the most reliable of two statements, then the most reliable statement is that the apostles did not lie concerning what they related and what they claimed to have seen or to have heard from someone who saw it. No one has ever disagreed with the fact that a person believes what he sees whenever he believes it in the depths of his heart, especially when that person leads thousands more to believe that truth, and none of those who speak of it or hear it say that it had to be impossible.

Those of our time who claim to be careful investigators tell us to insist that a man of the first century should have accused another man of lying for no reason, even though he trusted that man and would never have suspected him of producing inventions or fabrications. As an example of this kind of accusation without reason, it is said that the people of that era should have hastened to call someone a liar whenever they heard him relate a story that included miracles. Yet that would have been exactly like someone of our time calling another man a liar just because he heard him talking about some astronomical or industrial phenomenon which was really not strange at all. Such an accusation would be even more unreasonable if the speaker had no history of lying intentionally or of fabricating stories.

It is utter nonsense to say that any particular religion must have been based only on signs and wonders. Belief in such signs and wonders by itself would have been something that required the greatest faith. Besides, there has never been a religious call which was lacking in talk concerning signs and wonders, both those which were considered reasonable and those which were not. Instead, people welcomed the apostles of Christianity with an overwhelming response never before seen, because they came with destitute and longing souls. They looked around and saw folks who were just like themselves, yet who could believe without being concerned what would befall them and without worrying about where they were headed. We must pay attention to what they said and believe with their kind of faith. For if Christ (peace be upon him) had not been confident that people would respond to their message, he would not have charged his disciples to go wherever they would be heard, and to shake the dust from their feet whenever a country treated them with rejection and antagonism.[53]

Part Six
The Gospels

Chapter 22

The Gospels [1]

The word "Gospel" comes from a Greek word which means "good news."[2] Christians in the first century were already circulating numerous versions[3] of the Gospels. Later, the Church Fathers authorized four of those versions by casting lots (i.e., by a majority vote), namely, the Gospels of Mark, Matthew, Luke and John. These were included in the New Testament, along with a number of documents in which the teachings of the apostles were recorded.[4]

The prevailing view among the authoritative historians who deliberate these matters is that all of the Gospels are dependent on an Aramaic version which is now lost. They designate this version by the letter "Q" which is an abbreviation of the word "Quelle," meaning "source." Other historians refer to it as the "Logia," meaning "sayings." By this they have in mind the oral sayings of Christ which were heard and were later put in writing, in what most of them believe to have been Aramaic. They go on to explain the agreement among some passages in Matthew and Luke as due to the mutual dependence of these two Gospels on that lost version.[5]

In any case, the Gospels as they now exist were all written in "common" or "Koinē" Greek.[6] It can be observed even in translation that the Greek of the Gospels is dependent on an Aramaic manner of expression, and that it preserves some of the rhetorical structure, synonymous concepts, and terminology of Aramaic.[7] Scholars are agreed that these Gospels do not comprise everything which was uttered by Christ. For example, the Acts of the Apostles, which is also included in the New Testament, contains a saying which is attributed to Christ but is not found in the Gospels: "Remember the words of Christ, 'It is more blessed to give than to receive.'"[8] The unauthorized Gospels also contain sayings of this type, as do some papyrus fragments discovered in Egypt which go back to the middle of the second century, and whose manner of expression is not like that of the Gospels.[9]

Scholars are also agreed that two of the Gospels were written by Christians who had never met with Christ and had never heard him speak. One of these is the version written by Mark. It is said that he wrote down what he heard from the Apostle Peter, without putting it in chronological order and without intending that it to be brought together into a book. He wrote his Gospel in Rome after the Apostle Peter was killed, and there were no other disciples with him at that time. Estimates as to its date of writing vary between the years 67 and 70.[10]

The other of these two Gospels is the version written by Luke, the companion of the Apostle Paul, who wrote down what he heard from him. It is possible that he added to this a segment from the version which has been lost, then also a segment from the Gospel of Mark after he had examined it. Most likely it was written in the year 80.[11]

The Gospel of John was the last Gospel to be written and revised. Most critics agree that its author was John the disciple of Christ. Others believe that its author was a different person named John who was from Ephesus and who had not seen Christ. This latter view is held because John the disciple of Christ was responsible for the Book of Revelation which was composed, according to the most reliable accounts, in the year 96; the assumption here is that the same author could not write at the same time two books with such a disparity of method and content between them.[12]

A different view regarding the date is held by Fr. Ferrar Fenton, who translated the Gospel of John in the "Oxford Edition" of the Bible. He conjectures that it was the earliest of the four Gospels, and that John wrote it first in Hebrew between the years 30 and 40, and later he translated it into Greek.[13] However, the fact that this Gospel was written quite late is demonstrated by the way it presents certain matters in detail which had been given only general treatment in the other Gospels, and from the way it added philosophical expressions and expounded doctrines which had been passed on from the Apostle Paul. Thus, this Gospel is considered to have been written no earlier than the year 96.

With respect to the order in which the Gospels were written, historians think it is most likely that Mark was the earliest Gospel; after that followed Matthew, and then Luke. These three Gospels have become commonly known as the "Synoptic Gospels,"[14] since it is possible to make comparisons among them regarding various accounts and directives, in spite of their differences regarding the order of events. One should keep in mind here that the Gospels were originally written in an unbroken fashion, without divisions and without places where one unit ended and another was joined. They were not divided into chapters until the thirteenth century C.E.[15]

* * *

It is incorrect to dismiss all the Gospels as a reliable basis for determining the history of Christ, just because they were not recorded right away but were written after a long time and in a distant place from the words of Christ. Nor should they be dismissed because originally there was only one source, but numerous people were involved in passing on and transcribing the accounts about Christ. Nor should they be dismissed because the Gospels report certain events which are not mentioned by any of the historians of that time, such as when the tombs were split open and the dead that were inside rose and walked among the people, as well as other extraordinary and frightening incidents.[16]

On the other hand, it is correct to accept the Gospels as the sole basis for writing that history, since they contain sayings which are appropriate and are difficult to claim as fabrications. Where there are areas of disagreement among the Gospels, these are shown to be plausible by carefully investigating the reasons for their existence, and by recognizing the relationship between these disagreements and what gave rise to them. It is more difficult to reject these disagreements out of hand, than to accept them after looking into the reasons for this or that discrepancy.

For example, it is clear that the Gospel of Matthew was addressed to Jews, and that Matthew attempted to dispel their aversion towards the new call. He constructed the wording of his Gospel in a manner which was appropriate for the church in Jerusalem in the middle of the first century C.E.[17]

On the other hand, it is clear that the Gospel of Mark was addressed to the "Gentiles"; he had no reservations about citing accounts involving divinity which had prevented the "conservatives" among the Jews from belief in the divinity of Christ.[18]

The Gospel of Luke was written by a doctor who presented his work to a high-ranking nobleman. The accounts and directives in this Gospel are reported from the human perspective. Luke kept in mind the culture of this nobleman to whom he dedicated his version, and of those like him from the upper class.[19]

The Gospel of John is predominated by philosophical concepts, beginning with a discourse about the "Word" or "Logos." In it he portrayed the divine incarnation in a manner which was familiar to the Greeks, as well as to those who participated in their gatherings and followed the same customs.[20]

Regardless of whether these Gospels derive from a single source or from more than one, we ought to keep in mind that they formed the basis on which people depended who lived closest to the time of Christ. And after almost two thousand years, we ourselves do not have a more worthy basis on which to depend.

We have relied on the Gospels in order to study the life of the Messenger and to comprehend fully the stages of his mission and their surrounding circumstances — and we have not found any more trustworthy source than these. However, as we have examined them we have pursued a method different from that followed by those who emphasize the historicity of events and reports. We have not examined the Gospels with respect to the historical events they relate, nor with respect to the purposes which were intended by those who wrote them and who passed them on. Rather, as we have compiled the various events and reports, we have inquired concerning what lies behind these which would elucidate the personality of the Messenger. And for the purpose of our examination, the unusual events were as useful as the familiar, and the intentional and unintentional goals of the writers were equally important to us.

Is there, then, a "uniform personality" behind these accounts which is intelligible? If characteristics are found in them which indicate such a uniform personality, that is sufficient for our purpose without any further need for those events and reports. We must understand here that the contradictions which surface from our examination might well offer reasons for affirming the reliability of the Gospels, rather than reasons for skepticism and denial. Thus, the end result for us is to make this personality itself a gauge by which we measure every event, every report, and every word which has been related. And wherever one approach coincides with the other, it is merely something of interest.

As an example concerning the difference between our method and that followed by the historians who only consider events for their own sake, we feel obligated to search for peculiarities in the Gospel records, even if they do not present themselves to us immediately. For if that history were devoid of peculiarities, that in itself would be peculiar. To demand that something be certain, or nearly so, is what is unconventional. Just because a particular nation believes in peculiarities and has no doubt about their existence, must its history be devoid of them?

* * *

At this point we would like to explain our position concerning extraordinary events and miracles wherever they are found in the history of the world's religions. Our approach here is to raise a question: Is this miracle necessary in order to explain a particular issue? If the issue can easily be explained without the miracle, there is no need for us to argue whether or not the miracle is possible. The explanation which is accepted by everyone is sufficient; there is no longer the need for an explanation which compels us to investigate its possibility and to investigate the sincerity of those who reported it.

Nevertheless, our own opinion regarding the possibility of miracles is the same opinion that we have regarding the possibility of all causes: our reasoning is limited if we account for events only on the basis of their causes. Nor is it reasonable to say that so-called "natural causes" are the only factors sufficient for bringing things into existence. Nothing is more true concerning this than what was said by al-Ghazālī (God have mercy on him), that causes and effects take place together. The relationship between them is no greater than the relationship between companionship and mutual agreement whenever they occur.[21] Otherwise, it would be necessary for matter to be divided into thousands of constituents, each of them autonomous with regard to its qualities, its effects, and its relationship with other constituents. Al-Ghazālī does not say that this is anything remotely reasonable. Thus, if our reasoning does not always make use of natural causes for making explanations, then it goes beyond proper bounds when it is quick to deny miracles and to insist that they are impossible.[22]

So when we discuss miracles, we should do so in the same manner by which we discuss causes: Are they necessary in order to explain this issue? Just as we say, "Is this cause necessary?" so we must also say, "Is this miracle necessary for a proper understanding and explanation?" By this balance must events be weighed; by this balance must the history of the world's religions (and any other subject as well) be studied.

We have not dealt with the miracles which are mentioned in the Gospels because we find that our explanation of events moves along quite well without them. Indeed, there is no evidence in the Gospels which indicates that the miracles surrounding Jesus' birth prompted anyone to believe Christ's message after he set out issuing his call.[23] Often we read in the Gospels that miracles did not persuade those who were arrogant, and that "the evil generation seeks a sign, but none will be given to it."[24] Sometimes people rejected his miracles even when they were amazed at what they saw; instead they claimed that these were due to the work of Satan.[25] In fact, Christ's activity in performing miracles was, according to the priests, one of the reasons why they wanted to act quickly to seize him.[26]

In any case, we can truly say that the greatest miracle of Christ is what took place in history; a miracle which has endured for all of time, which did not come to an end even when the miracle itself ended in the first century. It is the miracle about a man who grew up in the house of a carpenter in an obscure village among a vanquished people; by a single word he conquered nations which the Roman Empire had forfeited, taking less time to accomplish this than it took for that tyrant to annex a single province; and though that province might submit for a while before revolting and throwing off its yoke, it was never so submissive as were those who surrendered to that word with heart and soul.[27]

Chapter 23

The Results of Gospel Research [1]

Interpreters of the Gospels have labored with exhausting precision in order to arrange the events of the life of Christ (peace be upon him) to the degree that these can be derived from the Gospels. However, they have not reached a consensus as to the proper arrangement because the course of events varies among the four Gospels. In some cases, the writers recorded certain accounts as they heard them on sporadic occasions and according to what seemed appropriate, rather than recording them in the chronological sequence by which the events actually occurred. As a result, the order of events as they are written in the Gospels does not always agree with the order in which they took place.[2]

Nevertheless, it is evident from the life of Christ as it is presented in the Gospels that certain events were preliminary, while other events resulted from those preliminaries. If we further regard other events in this manner, some as the result of others according to a plausible assessment of the evidence, it is then possible to consider the following life of Christ to be quite likely in its broadest outlines. After establishing these outlines in a sound fashion, there is no harm done if the actual circumstances turn out to have been different for events which could be assigned to any period without changing either the narrative as a whole or the essence of any topic within it.

The turning point in the life of Christ was his encounter with John the Baptist. Prior to that meeting, we find nothing mentioned in the Gospels about the early life of Christ (peace be upon him) except for two events: first, the journey to Egypt when he was an infant, and second, the journey to Jerusalem when he was twelve years old.[3]

The first event is recounted in the Gospel of Matthew, where it says: "The angel of the Lord appeared to Joseph in a dream and said, 'Get up and take the child and his mother, and flee to Egypt. . . . For Herod is determined to search for the boy and destroy him.' So he got up and took the child and his mother at night, and he went off to Egypt. And he remained there until the death of Herod." The account goes on to say, "Then Herod killed all the boys who were in Bethlehem and its surrounding areas who were two years old and under."[4]

The account of this massacre is mentioned only in the Gospel of Matthew.[5] The reason why the family was in Bethlehem is now unknown, since they were actually from Nazareth. Although the Gospel of Luke states that every family had to travel to its birthplace because of the census, it has been determined that this actually took place in the year 6 C.E. This census was the cause of a violent rebellion during the time of Quirinius, governor of Syria.[6]

It is the Gospel of Luke which elaborates on what is portrayed concerning the childhood of Christ. It relates the accounts of his circumcision, his naming, and his journey to Jerusalem. "After eight days, when it was time to circumcise the boy, he was named Jesus. . . ." When the time of purification ended according to the Law of Moses, "they brought him up to Jerusalem to present him to the Lord. . . and to offer as a sacrifice a pair of doves or two young pigeons." This was the offering which was accepted from those who were poor.[7]

The Gospel of Luke also says:

> His parents used to go to Jerusalem every year for the feast of the Passover, and when he was twelve years old, they went up to Jerusalem as was the custom regarding the feast. When Joseph and his mother returned, the boy remained in Jerusalem without their knowledge. They had assumed he was among the company of travelers, and after going a day's journey, they looked for him among their relatives and friends. And when they did not find him, they returned to Jerusalem to look for him. After three days, they found him in the Temple sitting among the teachers, listening to them and asking them questions; and all who heard him were amazed at his understanding and his answers. And when they saw him they were astonished, and his mother said to him, 'My son, why have you treated us so? . . .' He said to them, 'Why have you been looking for me? Did you not know that I must be about my Father's business?' And they did not understand the words which he spoke to them. Then he went down with them and came to Nazareth, and was obedient to them. . . . And he increased in wisdom and in stature, and in favor with God and with people.[8]

Beyond this, the Gospel of Luke mentions nothing about the early life of the boy, until he became thirty years old,[9] when John appeared with "a baptism of repentance for the forgiveness of sins."[10] "At that time, Jesus came from Galilee to the Jordan River, to be baptized by him," as stated in the Gospel of Matthew. "Then John prevented him, saying, 'I need to be baptized by you, and do you come to me?' Jesus answered, 'You shall allow this now, for in this way it is appropriate for us to fulfill all righteousness.' So he allowed it for him. And when Jesus was baptized, immediately he went up from the water, and behold, heaven was opened to him, and he saw the Spirit of God descending like a dove and coming upon him. And a voice from heaven said, 'This is my beloved Son.'"[11]

In a Gospel which is not included among the four authorized Gospels, i.e., the Gospel of the Hebrews, there is an account concerning this period in the life of Christ (peace be upon him). It runs as follows: "His mother and brothers said to him, 'John the Baptist continues to baptize for the forgiveness of sins. Let us go to him so that he may baptize us.' Then he said to them, 'What sin have I committed, that I should go to him to be baptized? Unless my sin should be what I have just said.'"[12]

Nothing is said in the Gospels or any other source about the education of Christ during his childhood, either before he was twelve or after. But in accordance with the system of instruction at that time, he would have begun his studies in a school-room adjacent to the synagogue. As in every large village, the synagogue would have been supervised by a *"ḥazzān"* or *"khazzān,"* meaning a storekeeper or guard. It was rare for any pupil who studied in the school-room to get hold of a handwritten copy of the scriptures, other than the copy belonging to the synagogue which was intended for public reading during the prayers; this copy was also utilized for teaching young students, and everyone relied on it for committing the scriptures to memory.[13]

In those days, every Jewish family used to hope that it would bring forth the anticipated Messiah. On the basis of this expectation, they would name their child "Jesus," i.e., "Joshua,"[14] because this name was composed of two words which together mean "the pursuit of Yahweh," or "the help of Yahweh," or "the salvation of Yahweh." Such a child was then given an education which was strictly religious. It would not be difficult, then, to offer an explanation as to why the family of Christ traveled to Bethlehem: they would have anticipated a miracle there, since Bethlehem was mentioned in some of the prophetic Scriptures as the birthplace of the promised Messiah, because it was the homeland of David.[15]

It is not unlikely that by the time the blessed child was twelve, he had a complete grasp of all the lessons which young boys learned in the village schools. Thus, as he listened to the new ideas given by the Temple priests and experts of the Law, his soul longed to comprehend them fully; he simply forgot his family and the time when they should return to their village, as he was carried away by the lessons taught by the experts of the Law and the priests.[16]

It is probable that Christ already had a strong relationship with John the Baptist, and that John had seen him and was aware of his graciousness and sanctity of life before he met him at the Jordan River after embarking on his mission of baptism.[17] By its very nature, that mission was one of preparation and facilitation.

It was only natural, when that young man of thirty came to be baptized, that the words of John should reverberate within his vigilant soul. There was nothing more likely than that those words should impress a soul like his. They would have confirmed his hope, consolidated his conviction, and prompted him to reflect on the purpose for which he was created, and to reflect on what he anticipated and what was anticipated for him concerning his preaching about the salvation and judgment which everyone was talking about everywhere.[18]

* * *

One result of that prophetic greeting from John was his seclusion in the wilderness. It was the kind of seclusion in which one must face temptation, submit to testing, raise questions within himself, and make sure of his calling. Every prophet must undergo such a period of seclusion before he can carry out his orders, even before he can know for certain what it is God has ordered him to do.

As the basis for the portrayal of this Temptation, we will use the account from the Gospel of Matthew, which runs as follows: "After he (peace be upon him)[19] fasted in the wilderness forty days and forty nights, he finally became hungry. Then the tempter came to him and said to him, 'If you are the Son of God, tell these stones to become bread.' But he answered, 'It is written, "Man shall not live by bread alone, but by every word which proceeds from the mouth of God."' Then the devil took him to the holy city and stood him on the wing of the Temple, and he said to him, 'If you are the Son of God, throw yourself from up here. For you have been promised that "he will charge his angels concerning you to carry you on their hands, and you will not strike your foot against a stone."' Jesus answered, 'It is also written, "Do not tempt the Lord your God."' Then the devil took him to a high mountain, and he showed him all the kingdoms of the world and their glory, and he said to him, 'I will give all of these to you if you will worship me.' Jesus said, 'Get away from me, Satan! It is written, "You shall worship the Lord your God and serve him alone."'"[20]

The Gospel of Matthew goes on to say, "When Jesus heard that John had been handed over to Herod, he went away to Galilee; he left Nazareth and lived in Capernaum." And he began his mission, calling for repentance, "for the kingdom of heaven is near."[21]

As we stated previously, the turning point in the life of Christ was his encounter with John the Baptist. Prior to that meeting, the life of that young believer involved preparation, willingness and expectation. After that meeting, his life involved spiritual exercise, testing and determination. The words of the prophet of judgment brought him back to his innermost thoughts; he probed their depths, examined their endurance, and asked both them and the Divine Mystery to guide him to the true nature of his mission and the source of his assignment.

But in the experience of the Temptation, evil suggestions enticed him to demand a sign, to handle the evidence. All temptations of this kind, portrayed in their simplicity in the Gospel narratives, revolved around the mystery of the Messianic mission as it was enveloped in the proclamations and promises of the ancient books. Were not the people expecting a Messiah who would cause goodness to spread and end the arduous search for daily food, who would bring a time when bread would be so plentiful that people would throw it away like the stones of the road? Was it not promised that the Messiah would come on the clouds, carried on the wings of the angels? Was it not promised that he would rule the world with crown and scepter? All of these are genuine temptations which assault the conscience of anyone engaged in a messianic mission. They leave him standing on the pinnacle of faith and on the brink of hell at the same moment. On the one side, he is enticed by a mission which focuses on the body, on authority, and on making deals in order to gain proofs and signs. On the other side, he is restrained by a mission which focuses on the spirit, on holiness, and on a conviction which does not make deals in order to gain a proof.[22]

Were the words of John the first avenue of prophetic inspiration to Christ concerning his mission? It is abundantly clear that as soon as these vivid words reached his ears, they opened in his serene soul a door of contemplation and inquiry.[23] The period of seclusion in the wilderness which took place immediately afterwards was thus one of solitude: for drawing out the truth from the depths of his conscience; for seeking assistance as he fasted and kept vigil while communing with the Divine Mystery; and for resolving with absolute determination — and without a trace of ambivalence or reluctance — to undertake the decisive step purposed by God.

The most valuable information which helps in determining the progression of faith in the soul of that great messenger is, for us, this report concerning his temptation when he was alone in the wilderness. This report explains for us the situation of Christ before he undertook any decisive step. Or we could say that it explains the progress of his faith by way of the causes at work in his unblemished conscience.

For whenever Christ undertook any decisive matter, he pondered the situation for quite some time. He continued to ponder it, to deliberate and examine the matter from every angle, until it came to his mind that his work should be deferred while he waited for a sign by which he could make sure that it was according to God's will. At that moment he would quickly and resolutely repudiate such an idea; for the worker who suspends his work while he waits for a sign demonstrates a weak faith. But if anyone looks after his own soul properly, such that his faith, though as tiny as a mustard seed, can move a mountain from its place and pull out trees by their roots,[24] his faith will not be dependent on a sign which he has to see before he carries out his work and devotes himself to his goal. This is especially the case when he recognizes that the sign would only cause him to expect from it a safeguard from danger and a guarantee of security, something which it could not offer. It is thus better to face danger than to remain uncertain; anything is safer than depending on a security which in fact is not available without the guarantee of evidence.

Whenever Christ found himself at this dividing line, after thinking through and deliberating the matter, the proper course of action was for him to make the best of events as they were, and to seek inspiration from the Divine Mystery about how to move forward. So let him accomplish what he might otherwise avoid, without imposing as a condition his own protection. And let God accomplish what he wills. What happens after all of that is but the will of God.

* * *

So Christ left his isolation and entered into his mission, without telling anyone that it was messianic in nature. Instead, he kept silent on that issue until word got around about his call. Eventually he gained more than eighty disciples who shared in spreading the news about this mission and who drew guidance from his inspirational preaching.[25]

At first, his mission in Galilee was characterized by a distinctively ethnic tone as a mission to Israel. The most intense aspiration of Christ (peace be upon him) was to refrain from stirring up the people against the ruling authorities, and from stirring up the ruling authorities against him. He opted for segregation and prudence as much as he could, until Destiny was fulfilled[26] and the time drew near for him to proceed to the next step. His first step had been a shift from the isolation of the wilderness to the call to the Israelites; the next step was the call to humanity in general. It involved making the best of events and seeking inspiration from the Divine Mystery in a domain which was broader and more lasting. He took this step in accordance with a particular feature which had been established deep within his conscience.[27] He was guided to this by the inspiration of God, and nothing remained except for the events of Destiny to sustain it according to its will.

This feature which had been established deep within the conscience of Christ (peace be upon him) frequently took the form of various illustrations by which he described himself. Thus, he was "the light of the world," "the bread of life," and "the true vine";[28] and he was "the Son of God" and "the Son of Man."[29]

The concept of God as Father had already appeared in numerous passages in the Old Testament.[30] Thus in the book of Genesis, the angels are described as the sons of God: "And the sons of God saw that the daughters of men were beautiful, and they took some of them as wives" (Genesis 6).[31]

According to the words of Moses (peace be upon him), all the Israelites are sons of God, as when he said to Pharaoh, "Let my son go."[32] This phrase, with the same meaning, appears in other books such as the book of Deuteronomy, where it is said, "you are the sons of God" (Deuteronomy 14), and where all the people are referred to as his sons and daughters (Deuteronomy 32).[33] More than once this same phrase appears in the Psalms, where it is said, "Offer to the Lord, Oh sons of God . . ." (29), and "Who is like the Lord among the sons of God?" (89).[34] The same phrase also occurs in the book of Hosea, where the people are addressed with the words, "You are the sons of the living God."[35]

In the New Testament, God is addressed as Father in the prayer which begins by calling upon God, "Our Father who is in heaven";[36] also, in the passage where Christ said to his disciples, "You have one Father, who is in heaven";[37] also, in the passage where he speaks about spiritual birth and physical birth, such that everyone who is born of the Spirit is a son of God.[38]

The phrase "the Son of Man" also appears in the Old Testament in both Aramaic and Hebrew. In Aramaic, it is *"bār nāshā"* from *bār,* meaning "son," and *nāsh* meaning "man." In Hebrew, it is *"ibn ādam."* In both languages, the term is applied to man *per se,* or to man as a particular kind of living creature in comparison to others.[39]

This phrase appears ninety times in the book of Ezekiel, where the prophet is addressed by "Yahweh" as "son of man."[40] It also appears once in the book of Daniel, where Gabriel addresses the prophet as "son of man" (chapter 8).[41] Also in the same book, this phrase occurs in Aramaic in the passage where Daniel speaks about creatures in the form of beasts; there he prophecies about a messenger who comes in the form of a man, someone whom the prophet saw, during night visions, "on the clouds, like a son of man" coming with authority which will never pass away.[42]

In the books of the New Testament, there are passages in which this phrase has the simple meaning of "man." Among them is Christ's saying in the Gospel of Matthew: "Every sin and blasphemy will be forgiven for people, [. . . .] And whoever says a word against the Son of Man will be forgiven; but whoever speaks against the Holy Spirit will not be forgiven, either in this world or in the world to come" (chapter 12).[43]

Sometimes the phrase is used as a synonym for the first person pronoun "I" when Christ spoke about himself. Thus we read in Luke 12, "Every one who acknowledges me before others, the Son of Man will acknowledge before the angels of God." But in Matthew 10 we read, "Every one who acknowledges me before others, I will also acknowledge before my Father who is in heaven."[44] And Matthew 16 says, "When Jesus came into the district of Caesarea Philippi, he asked his disciples, 'Who do people say that I, the Son of Man, am?'"; while Mark 8 reads, "Jesus went on with his disciples to the villages of Caesarea Philippi, and on the way he asked his disciples, 'Who do people say that I am?'"[45]

Thus, in some of the Gospels this phrase is a synonym or substitute for the first person pronoun when the Master spoke about himself.[46] And it should be observed here that the disciples recognized its usage in this connection; yet they themselves never called Christ by the title "the Son of Man."

Other times, this phrase carries a meaning similar to that found in the prophecy of Daniel. For example, "Just as the weeds are gathered and burned with fire, so it will be at the end of the world. The Son of Man will send his angels, and they will gather out of his kingdom all causes of sin and all evildoers" (Matthew 13). Like the passage in Daniel, this is a reference to the Day of Judgment, and its wording in Aramaic is the same for both passages.[47]

These are the names by which Christ was called, both during the first phase of his call, and at the end of it. During his call he was also sometimes called "the Good Teacher," at which he said, "Why do you call me good? No one is good except God alone."[48] And at the end of his call he asked his disciples concerning what the people were saying about him; and when Peter said to him, "You are the Messiah, the Son of God," Christ blessed him, then ordered them to keep silent about this.

There is no need for us to mention that people understood these titles at that time as they would have been understood in the usual sense by those who read the Scriptures. Christ gave no command to his disciples that they were to understand those titles in some other way, whenever they remembered him as "the Son of God" or "the Son of Man."

* * *

If matters had proceeded along the same course which the call had properly followed in Galilee in accordance with Christ's mission, then that mission would have continued in this way for years, without getting embroiled in a serious conflict with the community of priests in Jerusalem. As it was, events fulfilled their destiny in the year now considered to be 30 C.E.[49] The time for the feast of Passover drew near, when Jewish families followed the custom of visiting Jerusalem. Among them was Christ's own family: his mother, his brothers and his relatives.

Christ (peace be upon him) used to go along with his family to these rituals, and there was certainly no harm in that. He did not try to restrain the people from observing their traditions, when, as was customary, they would celebrate and enjoy meeting together to wish one another well. On the other hand, he rejected whatever was in those traditions that would impede their conscience or make them proud with false piety and blatant hypocrisy. Aside from this, he would participate with his family in the national festivities, going with them to the Temple. He would instruct them to purchase the sacrifice and even to pay the tax which was imposed on every person among the Israelites.[50]

He had visited Jerusalem in previous years; nowhere is it mentioned that he stayed away during any of the years when he was proclaiming his message in Galilee. He would go to Jerusalem with his few companions and return to Galilee, without attracting any attention from the custodians of the Temple and other religious authorities there, and without the two sides getting embroiled in controversy.[51]

But what would happen when he traveled to Jerusalem this year? His journey to the capital with his companions would be different from the way it had been in previous years.

At that time there were thousands of people living throughout Galilee. We have already estimated that there were some eighty followers of Christ who were considered disciples; the followers of Christ[52] who were not among them might have reached ten times that number or even more. How could those hundreds of followers have gone with their Teacher to Jerusalem secretly, stealing into the city without disclosing their allegiance to the Teacher who made the pilgrimage with them? Why should there have been any stealth or secrecy?

Here was one of those situations to which we referred, which required seeking inspiration from the Divine Mystery and making the best of events as they were. Would he go to Jerusalem, along with hundreds of disciples and followers, disavowing his mission and wary of proclaiming it because of this crowd which could hardly be concealed or disguised?

And what would have been the effect of such concealment and disguise on the hearts of those who had put their faith in that spiritual mission, except to diminish the mission of Christ? Would any of them have believed that Christ's spiritual mission could spread throughout the world in a concealed and disguised manner for any reason at all, let alone the one that first comes to mind, that Christ was wary and cautious?

It was necessary for Christ to go to Jerusalem, and it was necessary for him to go openly; the necessity in either case could not be avoided. In due time, events would reveal the sign indicating the divine purpose concerning this journey.

We may assume that at the end of his mission, Christ followed the same course which he had followed previously: that of making the best of events as they were. Thus it is especially indicative of his approach that Christ (peace be upon him), on the night when he would bid farewell to his disciples, spent the night in prayer and confiding with his Lord, saying, "Let this cup pass from me, oh Father! Yet may it be according to your will, not according to my will." Then he woke his sleeping disciples, and he said to them, "Watch and pray that you may not enter into temptation; the spirit indeed is willing, but the flesh is weak."[53]

He had already prepared himself to confront his enemies, since it was inevitable that they would confront him. He had prepared his disciples to remain firm, and he set about to rejuvenate their minds, so that they could endure the trial which they were about to undergo. He dismissed from their minds any thought of an initial assault which would result in immediate victory over that group of worldly priests; for this was the time to accommodate to the worst which was to come. Yet they should not despair if weakness should overwhelm them and they desert him. They should not resign themselves to the assumption that such behavior invariably meant the battle was lost, that they were soundly defeated. For such weakness would be something predestined, and would definitely soon be followed by victory.[54]

The Gospels report that Christ (peace be upon him) rode into Jerusalem on the back of a donkey, in accordance with some prophecies concerning the manner in which the promised Messiah was to come. The people carried palm branches before him and spread their cloaks under the animal's feet. They were shouting an exclamation of victory; it was one which the Jews used to memorize from childhood, and they used to sing it during festive times of pageants and celebrations in memory of David, and of the glory which would be reclaimed at the end of time.[55]

The commands of Christ indicate that while he remained in Jerusalem, he respected the position of the priests and legal scholars, and he did not trouble them regarding their desire to retain the rights and claims of their position. He said in one of his commands, while addressing the crowds and disciples, "The scribes and Pharisees sit on Moses' seat; so observe and practice whatever they tell you to observe. But do not do what they do, for they preach but they do not practice."[56]

Nor can a single word be found in the Gospel accounts in which Christ changed what he had prescribed for himself according to his well-known maxim concerning what belongs to Caesar and what belongs to God.[57] Everything he said in Jerusalem reiterated what he had stated previously when he proclaimed the kingdom and called people to embrace it. He declared that he was not of this world, that he had nothing to do with the authority invested in crowns and thrones.[58]

* * *

Nevertheless, from the first moment he entered Jerusalem, he became aware of situations in which his enemies were setting traps for him at every step. He knew, from the questions which they showered on him, that they were plotting to destroy him, since their questions were all heading towards the same goal: to lure him into saying something which endorsed disobedience and rebellion against the state, or something which convicted him of "apostasy"[59] and violation of the law. All of his answers were ones they had heard before in similar situations when they tried to constrain or embarrass him. He responded with expertise and in keeping with his goal and his mission, and he put to shame those who tried to embarrass him by exposing what they concealed behind the veil of hypocrisy. It is quite possible that he had heard details of the intricate plot from some leaders of the Temple, since one of them — Nicodemus — had been visiting him at night, and perhaps there were many others as well.[60]

But the inevitable occurred, what could not but transpire at such a festival between those who were enraged against the new call and those who were devoted to its propagation and enthusiastic for its leader. Christ became embroiled in a moral battle with the delegates from the Temple, and it was not long before this turned into a physical battle. He (peace be upon him) overturned the tables used by the money-changers and by those who sold animals for the sacrifices. And he shouted at them and at the Temple delegates, reminding them that they were in the house of God; but they had transformed it from a place of prayer and sanctity into a den of robbers.[61]

From all appearances, this was the decisive encounter. Perhaps Christ endeavored to resolve the situation one way or another. As it was, the Temple delegates became absolutely furious, and they used the pretext of averting a riot as an excuse for taking immediate action.[62] The manner in which that action unfolded has been related in several accounts which go their separate ways.

Here the role of history ends, and the role of faith begins.[63] History provides nothing definite in any of the accounts as to what took place following this event in the Temple, and what might have provoked the Temple priests to violence and spite.

Concerning the arrest of Christ, anyone following the events as they are recorded cannot determine who carried out the arrest and who served as their guide. Also, was Christ indeed someone who was well-known after visiting the Temple, or was he some unknown person who needed to be pointed out by a guide?[64]

Concerning his trial, it is said that he was sentenced at night, and that his sentence was issued on the same day. However, the system of justice promoted by the Jewish law was in opposition to this: it prohibited conducting a trial at night; in cases involving capital punishment, it rescinded any sentence which had been issued in a single session in one day; also in such cases, the sentence was not carried out unless it had been issued unanimously.[65]

And concerning the execution, it is said this took place in spite of the declaration by the Roman governor that he was absolved of his sentence.[66] Furthermore, the Gospel of John says he was handed over to be executed at about the sixth hour, while the Gospel of Mark says that "it was the third hour when they crucified him."[67]

Prof. Richard Husband, in his book *The Prosecution of Christ,* has investigated the dates for the Passover festival during the five years[68] from 27 to 33 C.E. He demonstrates that Passover occurred on Thursday in the year 30, and on Friday in the year 33. Now according to the accounts in the Gospels, the trial and crucifixion took place on a Friday, and the observance of the Passover meal took place on a Thursday, which coincided with April 6 in the year 30. On the other hand, for years other than 30 and 33, the Passover festival occurred on some other day of the week: Wednesday in the year 27, Monday in the year 28, Sunday in the year 29, Tuesday in the year 31, and Monday in the year 32.[69]

One of the accounts concerning the day of execution states that there was an earthquake in which some tombs broke open; then saints came out from these open tombs and went walking among the people.[70]

It is further related in the Gospel accounts that the tomb of Christ was opened on the following day, and there was no body found inside.[71] Christ is said to have appeared to his disciples several times. On one occasion, he asked them why they should believe him to be a ghost; "touch me and see, for a spirit does not have flesh and bones. . . . And he asked them, 'Do you have anything here to eat?' So they gave him a piece of broiled fish and a little honey, which he took and ate" (Luke 24).[72]

This topic has already been dealt with by a large number of authorities from the field of theology. Among them are Rev. Cheyne, the Evangelical; Prof. Henrik Poulus, professor of Eastern Languages at the University of Jina; Dr. Weigall, a specialist on archaeological studies in Egypt and the Near East; Dr. Hugo Toll of Sweden; as well as other scholars of religion and historical studies. They have concluded that the aspect of history should be separated from the aspect of belief with regard to the accounts which cover this phase of the Gospel record.[73]

There is, however, an account of a historical nature which would be improper to neglect, since it deserves particular attention. A tomb is reportedly located in the capital of Kashmir, on the street named "Khān Yār," which the people there call "the Tomb of the Prophet" or "the Tomb of Jesus." It is also mentioned in the history of al-A'ẓamī, written two hundred years ago, that this was the tomb of a prophet named "Yūz Āṣaf";[74] a tradition among the people of Kashmir, passed down by their ancestors, says that he arrived in that land two thousand years ago. Furthermore, in his translation of the Holy Qur'ān, Maulvi Muḥammad 'Alī refers to a book called *"Ikmāl al-Dīn"* which has been preserved for a thousand years; he states that the name "Yūz Āṣaf" is mentioned there, and that it says he was a traveler who journeyed through many countries. 'Alī goes on to refer to another book by "Barlaam and Josaphet" which mentions on page 111 that Yūz Āṣaf preached "good news," and that the people of Kashmir have memorized one of the parables which he taught which is similar to Christ's parable about the Sower and the Seed.

These remarks are set forth by Maulvi Muḥammad 'Alī in his comments on the noble verse,

> And We made the son of Mary and his mother a portent, and We gave them refuge on a height, a place of flocks and water-springs. (*Sūrat al-Mu'minīn* 50).[75]

Similar remarks are presented in his comments on the saying of God (be He exalted),

> I am gathering thee and causing thee to ascend unto Me. (*Sūrat Āl 'Imrān* 55)[76]

and on other verses from the Qur'ān which deal with the life of Jesus the son of Mary (peace be upon him).

* * *

In conclusion, this book has been confined to one objective, that of elucidating the genius of Christ[77] in a contemporary fashion. We now understand his genius, just as we did when we studied the genius of other leading personalities with respect to each one's destiny and to his innermost aspirations.[78] Throughout all of history, few of them matched the eminent genius which Christ exhibited. And still there is room for others to offer their own presentations and illuminations from various points of view. But if Destiny has allowed us to succeed in adding something to the sacred reservoir, that is enough for us. Nor was there any need within these pages for us to stir up controversy in matters which were not connected with the purpose which we intended and for which we limited the scope of this book.

As we stated previously, we have not been able to resolve with certainty how the life of Christ ended from the historical point of view. But we have been able to resolve with certainty that it ended in its appointed time at the moment conferred to us by history. That moment witnessed the last generation in which religious fanaticism monopolized the guidance and mercy of God for a single race among the children of Adam and Eve. It also witnessed the first generation in which the call to divine guidance became universal, a guidance which embraced anyone within humanity who would be guided. Within forty years, the religion of fanatical self-centeredness collapsed, as did the Temple in which it took refuge and sought renewal.[79] But a living call arose for the human conscience, one which extended its light as the sun extends its light to everyone who watches for it and anticipates it. Thus there was a certain wisdom in the inspiration by which the Herald, whenever he referred to himself, used the title "the Son of Man."[80]

Epilogue

If Christ Were to Return [1]

In a novel by the great Russian author Dostoyevsky, one of the heroes imagines that Christ returned to earth for a brief visit, and that he came to Seville at the time when "the Inquisition" was in full force. He preached to the people and he performed miracles; the weak, the sick and the grieving came to him, kissing his feet and asking him to grant them relief and mercy.[2]

He continued to move among the people, imparting his love and compassion, while they presented him with their grievances and apprehensions. Then suddenly, the chief administrator of the Inquisition — the Grand Inquisitor — passed by. For a moment, he closely watched the Master and the people all around him; then he motioned to the guards and ordered them to arrest him. They placed him where the prisoners were kept, and he waited there until his interrogation.

When evening came, the Grand Inquisitor went to the cell, and he spoke to the noble messenger. "I know who you are; you have not escaped my attention. And that is the reason I have put you in prison. Why did you come here? Why do you hinder us, throwing hurdles and obstacles in our path?"

Then the Grand Inquisitor continued: "You have constrained the people to do what is beyond their ability; you have constrained them with freedom of conscience. You have constrained them with the burden of using their own judgment, with having to distinguish good from evil by themselves. You have constrained them to travel the most difficult path, and they could not bear it; their efforts to do what you required of them failed miserably. But *we* knew the disease they suffered; we released them from their constraint and brought them back to rules and rituals. Do you return to us now in order to take from us our method, and to speak to them once again of free will and freedom of conscience?

"Nothing is more oppressive for people than the burden of freedom. But they are never more fortunate than when they are relieved of that burden, when they are guided in submission to the one who stripped them of that freedom, when they are simultaneously led to believe that he is the one who released them and who authorized what they should believe and what they should do. Then why do you once again oblige these people to open their eyes, to long for knowledge, and to choose for themselves what they want — when they don't even know what they want?

"Long ago you granted us absolute authority. You have no right to take it back now, and we are determined not to forfeit it. So leave these people to us, and go back from where you came. If not, then tomorrow we will hand you over to them and we will give you into their power. We will call you to account for your signs, and denounce you for your miracles. You will surely see these people, who today were kissing your feet, coming tomorrow to us and pleading with us to deliver them from you and to condemn you like all the other victims of torture and burning."

Ivan Karamazov, the hero of the novel in which this imaginative rendezvous and dialogue take place, remarked, "Christ did not say a word, nor did he counter his threats and animosity by scowling or turning aside. Instead, he came up to the Grand Inquisitor (who was a very old man of ninety), kissed his lips and went out into the darkness of the city, never to be found again."

In summary, what was envisioned by this great author, comprised within a long speech filled with life's wisdom, was the way in which perceptive people view life from the other extreme, the view that contrasts Christian wisdom, i.e., the wisdom of the noble messenger. We believe that the imaginative tale within this remarkable passage is not far from the truth, and we would not consider what the Grand Inquisitor said to be that farfetched, when he warned the noble messenger that he would hand him over to those who would rage against him and would pour out on him their condemnation and fury, after they had surrounded him and kissed his feet and implored him for help. Yes, the imaginative tale in this remarkable passage is not far from the truth; it would have been the most natural thing for those people to carry out such a deed and to follow the Grand Inquisitor in his revenge against the noble messenger.

And it would most likely be the case, if Christ were to return to earth, that he would renounce many things which are being done today in his name. He would find scribes and Pharisees among his followers, and he would reproach them for their hypocrisy. He would teach them once again that the Sabbath exists for people, not people for the Sabbath;[3] that the important thing is what is in the conscience, not what is spoken or what is evident on someone's face;[4] that the inspiration which is full of life lies in people, not in books and texts.[5]

It would most likely be the case that he would reproach people for the same things which he criticized nineteen hundred years ago. He would find the people of today to be the same as they were before with regard to their evil behavior and their enmity, their hypocrisy and their dissension, their departure from essential matters and their emphasis on trivialities, their superior piety whenever they are pious and their persistence in unbelief and hostility whenever they are unbelieving and hostile. It would again be like putting new wine in an old wineskin.[6]

This would most likely be the case if Christ were to return.

And if an imaginative tale such as this should run through our minds, we would most likely want to repeat what was said by Abū al-'Alā' [al-Ma'arrī]:

> There is no benefit in exerting oneself;
> Diligence can never make itself indispensable.[7]

Then why are the reformers miserable, and why do the martyrs perish? Why do prophets come and go? Why do religions disagree and their adherents quarrel over their virtues? Why all this? Why should messenger after messenger come to them? And why do they continue to have followers, some who are faithful, others who are not? These messengers came and they went back:

> They departed, but our distress remains;
> Still we languish in our disease.[8]

If this can be claimed, then it asserts virtually the same truth as was stated in the form of that imaginative tale.

However, the greatest truth by which all truths are measured is that the truth cannot be seen from merely one perspective. This especially applies to the truth which has remained throughout the stages of human existence, and which will remain forever in the future of humanity.

This truth is that freedom of conscience is not a limited quest, as if someone could journey in its pursuit, then when he arrives he could give up his quest and forgo any further effort. Rather, freedom of conscience is an endless struggle[9] and a painstaking task, in which one can make progress only step by step, one level at a time. If ever he could relinquish this struggle, it would only be to gaze beyond it and find there its resumption. If at any stage he could be rid of evil, it would only be to encounter it again and continue his struggle against it, with never a moment of peace.

We can be guided to a proper analysis of this problem by considering certain issues of concern to us which are tangible. This is the better procedure, since we can discern these more easily than our hidden concerns which contend with the conscience. These hidden concerns force the conscience to work, perhaps only once when the conscience can see where it is going, but many times when the conscience looks out and can see only clouds and darkness.

Thus, no one would say that the effort involved in teaching others is in vain, even if they observed a five-year-old child studying a book, then they saw him again at ten studying the same book, and again at twenty and at thirty; even if throughout that person's life he could neither dispense with knowledge nor eradicate his ignorance at all.

Nor would anyone say that the effort involved in providing medical treatment is in vain, even if they found that people were getting sick despite their knowledge of bacteria and their expertise in medicine, and despite the many places for medical and preventive care.

No one would say that a goal is futile just because the path to its accomplishment is long, or because it is immediately followed by another goal before the first one is ever met.

We do not say things like this concerning tangible matters which we can see and handle. Should we then talk this way about a goal such as freedom of conscience, a goal which has always been and will always be the most profound mystery of human life?

The lesson here is not about the reality of evil; rather, the lesson is how we can perceive it, how we can fight against it, how we can be on our guard concerning it.

If two people fall into evil, the one who was happy to get into that situation does not ask for anything more, while the one who was forced into that situation is regretful about it. The one who is aware of his predicament is not like the one who is oblivious to his. Or perhaps the latter person is deceived into thinking that he is somewhere between being aware of his predicament and being oblivious to it, that he neither intended it nor was forced into it.

On the one hand, people are not wild animals, since each one has a conscience. On the other hand, a person's conscience must be judged by the values it forms and the ideals it embodies, by the demands it makes and whether or not it acquires them. And as long as the reformers and messengers teach values which people treasure and promote ideals which people strive to reach, they are effective and their work is necessary. Such work will surely bear fruit, even though evil persists and the number of crimes and misdeeds does not diminish in any measurable way.

If we should ever speak of a person in our time who seeks what is good but does not attain it, then we should certainly say as well that he is better than the person who does not seek what is good or is even aware of it, who behaves with apathy and ignorance just like a wild animal.

As for the world's religions, they are beneficial to the extent that they entrust values and incentives to the soul; they help people to the degree that they add their share concerning freedom of conscience, or the freedom to distinguish what is good and what is shameful. The religions have done a great deal and they have the capacity to do much more. But they can never relieve a person of the struggle which his conscience must undertake.

In times past, ignorant people used to look forward to a period of a thousand years, a time when good would prevail, evil would end, suffering would cease and everyone everywhere would be happy. Those who are "enlightened" say that such people were ignorant.

But the enlightened people are actually more ignorant when they believe that none of the religions are working effectively, that they are utterly useless since the world is still full of evil and injustice and unbelief.

Is there any difference between those who are enlightened, who expect religion to achieve perfection in this world, and those who were ignorant, who expected absolute bliss in the "millennium" which was promised for the end of time and would come only after centuries or even hundreds of centuries should pass? Perhaps the ignorant people assessed the situation more appropriately; those who are enlightened have thought carefully, and still they expect a "millennium," whereas those who were ignorant cannot be blamed for having such an expectation without really thinking about it!

If Christ were to return today, he would find many things to do, and he would have to resume the work he had done before. He would do many things among his followers, among those who carry out deeds in his name and who go around repeating his commands. But at least a world in which people can be guided in many areas is better than a world where there is no room for those who guide and no struggle with the conscience.

Yet if Christ were to return to the world, he would not complete his mission of goodness and guidance. The next stage in achieving these things belongs to the conscience, and its work is never completed. Indeed, the goal of any mission which comes to an end is that the conscience should take over.

People of modern times must realize (if they have not realized already) that a person's convictions do not come from without, as if by adopting them he could please the one who appealed to him or show him special favors. On the contrary, a person's convictions are his conscience and the guardian of his inner life. If it becomes necessary for him to restore his conscience, he does so in the same way he restores his body by going to a doctor. He does not show special favors to the doctor, nor does he contemplate treating himself so as to please him.

A person's convictions are thus his own affair; they are a matter for the prophets only insofar as the person first accepts them as his responsibility. It is up to him, whenever he provides for his own restoration, to treat his convictions as a part of himself, indeed, the very guardian of his soul. He should not treat them as mere commodities which he can return to their owner and no longer be concerned about them. For there will never come a time when a person can no longer be concerned about his convictions.

SECTION THREE

APPENDIXES

A. The Various Editions of 'Abqarīyat al-Masīḥ

Al-'Aqqād wrote the content of *'Abqarīyat al-Masīḥ* during the year 1952, as he himself later noted.[1] It was published in January 1953 as part of a popular *Kitāb al-Yawm* [Book of the Day] series.[2] This original edition (referred to here as "ed. 1") was divided into four Parts, and further divided into several chapters, some of which were untitled. It did not include a Table of Contents, but the following outline represents the manner in which the book was arranged. (For chapters which were untitled, or whose titles were later changed, the title of the same chapter in the current edition is given at the right.)

Part One: The Messiah in History	
[no separate title]	[= The Blessed Tree]
[no separate title]	[= The Messiah]
Prophecy Among the Israelites	
Jewish Sects in the First Century	
Political and Social Life in the First Century	
The Religious Life of the World in the First Century	
Intellectual Life in the First Century	
Galilee of the Nations	[= The Land of Galilee]
The Date of Christ's Birth	[= When Christ was Born]
A Descriptive Portrait of Christ	
Part Two: The Call	
[no separate title]	[= The Call of Christ]
The Choice of Direction	
The Ordeals Incorporated in the Call	
The Law	
The Law of Love	
Ethical Living	
The Kingdom of Heaven	
Part Three: The Tools of the Call	
The Ability of the Teacher	
The Fidelity of the Disciples	
The Gospels	
Part Four: Conclusion	
[no separate title]	[= The Results of Gospel Research]
The End after Every Conclusion	[= If Christ Were to Return]

In 1958, al-'Aqqād produced a revised edition of this book (referred to here as "ed. 2"). The title was changed and a subtitle added: *Ḥayāt al-Masīḥ: Fī al-Tārīkh wa-Kushūf al-'Aṣr al-Ḥadīth* [The Life of Christ: In History and the Discoveries of the Modern Age].[3]

However, as discussed in the Introduction (pp. 45-46), the change of title was probably the decision of the editors rather than the author. Al-'Aqqād's revision consisted of adding a Preface and three new chapters at the beginning of the book. The rest of his work was left essentially intact, although the format was somewhat altered. The original Part One was divided into two Parts, and titles were given to all Parts and chapters. However, in two cases, the Part title and the title of the initial chapter of that Part are the same. Also, a few chapter titles were abbreviated. Finally, a Table of Contents was provided; following is a translation.

- Preface
- Part One: The Discoveries of Wadi Qumran
  - In Wadi Qumran
  - Evaluations on the Philosophy of History
  - Response and Critique
- Part Two: The Messiah in History
  - The Blessed Tree
  - The Messiah
  - Prophecy Among the Israelites
  - Jewish Sects in the First Century
  - Political and Social Life [abbreviated from ed. 1]
  - Religious Life [abbreviated from ed. 1]
  - Intellectual Life [abbreviated from ed. 1]
- Part Three: Historical Factors Concerning Christ's Birth
  - The Land of Galilee
  - When Christ was Born
  - A Descriptive Portrait of Christ
- Part Four: The Call
  - The Call [= The Call of Christ]
  - The Choice of Direction
  - The Ordeals Incorporated in the Call
  - The Law
  - The Law of Love
  - Ethical Living
  - The Kingdom of Heaven
- Part Five: The Tools of the Call
  - The Ability of the Teacher
  - The Fidelity of the Disciples
- Part Six: The Gospels
  - The Gospels
  - The Results of Gospel Research
- Epilogue: If Christ Were to Return

A few of the changes regarding the titles for the Parts and chapters in ed. 2 should be noted:

1. Part Three is the result of a two-fold division of the original Part One, as noted above; the Ar. title of Part Three is *Tārīkh al-Mīlād.* Literally, this means "The History of Christ's Birth," although *Tārīkh* can also be translated as "Date." In ed. 1, this was the title of what is now chapter 11. In the outline for ed. 1 above, that title is translated as "The Date of Christ's Birth," since that chapter begins with a discussion about the date when Jesus was born (although it later moves on to other topics). However, this same translation would not be appropriate as the title for Part Three in ed. 2 (and later, in ed. 3), since the three chapters incorporated in Part Three deal with much more than simply the date of Jesus' birth. The title given ("Historical Factors Concerning Christ's Birth") is a rather loose translation of *Tārīkh al-Mīlād,* but it is one that tries to incorporate the various subjects covered in Part Three.

2. The chapter that had originally been entitled *Tārīkh al-Mīlād* was thus given a new title for ed. 2: *Matā Wulida al-Masīḥ.* The first word *matā* [when] could be understood as an interrogative particle, leading to the translation "When was Christ Born?" Indeed, a question mark appears at the end of this title in some printings of ed. 2. However, it is best to read *matā* as an adverb of time, and to translate the title as a statement ("When Christ was Born") for three reasons: (a) the original title was a statement; (b) the chapter deals with much more than an answer to the question about the date of Jesus' birth; and (c) the title does not include a question mark in ed. 3.

3. Another title change occurs in Part Three: "Galilee of the Nations" *(Jalīl al-Umam)* in ed. 1 becomes "The Land of Galilee" *(Arḍ al-Jalīl)* in ed. 2. The reason for the change can only be surmised. Both phrases occur in the very first sentence of that chapter, and al-'Aqqād goes on to discuss the international character of Galilee. Perhaps he (or the editors of ed. 2) felt that the original title, if read before its explanation, would be confusing.

Several printings of ed. 2 were made, some by other publishers. Noteworthy among these is the one that was published in Beirut;[4] the original title was utilized, but appended to this (rather inappropriately) was the subtitle of the second edition produced in Cairo. The Beirut edition also contained a Foreword by Munīf Luṭfī, presumably a Lebanese. This basically consisted of a brief synopsis of the book with appreciative comments.

The book was published in Cairo again in 1996, more than thirty years after al-'Aqqād's death.[5] Although the title of the Cairo second edition was retained, a significant number of editorial revisions were made, so that it is referred to here as the third edition (or "ed. 3"). It conforms to the organization of ed. 2 to a great extent. However, the following changes were made with regard to the placement and names of the Parts and chapters:

1. "The Blessed Tree" (which in ed. 1 was the first chapter of Part One, and in ed. 2 was the first chapter of Part Two) was relocated to appear immediately after the Preface, prior to the beginning of Part One. In this way, it stands as a Prologue, which, given its character as such, serves the intention that al-'Aqqād apparently had in mind from the beginning.

2. The titles of the three abbreviated chapters in Part Two were restored to their original full titles.

3. The titles of the two initial chapters of Parts Four and Six were changed slightly in an apparent attempt to differentiate the chapter title from the Part title. Thus, the title of Part Four remained as "The Call," while its first chapter was entitled "The Call of Christ." The change for Part Six, however, was quite inappropriate; the first chapter was renamed "The Gospel" *(Al-Injīl)* rather than "The Gospels" *(Al-Anājīl)*, while the Part title retained the plural form. Since this chapter is a discussion of the issues surrounding the authorship and content of the four NT Gospels, the original plural form of its title should have been retained, while making some other slight alteration in either of the two titles. In order to avoid confusion without departing significantly from ed. 3, the titles for both the Part and the chapter are translated simply "The Gospels" as in ed. 2.

4. The Epilogue, "If Christ Were to Return," follows Part Six in a distinct manner, rather than being incorporated in Part Six as seems to be the case in ed. 2.

Thus (as can be seen from the Table of Contents for the translation), ed. 3 begins with the Preface and the Prologue, continues with six numbered and titled Parts, each comprising two to seven chapters, and concludes with the Epilogue. It should be noted that in none of the editions are the chapters themselves given numbers; these have been added in the translation for the sake of convenience.

The text of the book, as well as its organization, exhibits a significant number of variations among the three editions. Ed. 1 contains numerous instances of illegible printing. While the print quality improved with each new edition, the process of transcription for subsequent editions was not carefully followed. Thus, ed. 2 embodies a very large number of typographical errors. The editors of ed. 3 apparently recognized this problem, so that the text of ed. 3 more closely follows that of ed. 1 (except, of course, for the new material of ed. 2). In fact, the title page of ed. 3 states that it is the "Expanded and Corrected Edition" *(ṭab'ah muzayyadah wa-muṣaḥḥaḥah)*. This claim is certainly open to question. In the first place, nothing significant has been added to the text, unless the "expansion" refers to the material that had been added to ed. 1. More importantly, ed. 3 is replete with typographical errors of its own, including several instances of haplography (where several words are omitted accidentally, usually because of the similarity of adjacent words). Still, the errors in ed. 3 are fewer than in ed. 2.

Thus, in order to determine al-'Aqqād's original text as closely as possible, it has been necessary to conduct a process of "textual criticism," i.e., a thorough comparison between the three editions. The translation basically follows the text of ed. 3; this edition has the advantage of currently being in print and available from the publisher in Cairo. In a number of cases, however, the translation follows eds. 1 and/or 2 over against a different and usually inferior reading in ed. 3. Where haplography has occurred, the missing material has been incorporated into the translation from the previous editions. The few cases of dittography (where one or more words are accidentally added) have been removed. Where other differences in wording occur, the principle followed throughout has been to determine what was most likely the reading intended by al-'Aqqād, while remaining aware of how the alternate reading(s) might have arisen. In the dissertation of which the present book is a revision, all departures from the text of ed. 3 in the translation are indicated by the use of brackets, while footnotes provide the Arabic text of the reading adopted.[6] However, these features are quite numerous, rather technical, and tend to disrupt the flow of the passage; thus, for the current revision, it was decided to exclude most of the brackets and notes related to variations among the editions, while leaving intact the translation of the emended text.

Ed. 3 also exhibits a few changes in the text that are clearly due to deliberate editorial revision. An example of an alteration which can be regarded as appropriate are the half-dozen words that were added for clarification near the end of the Preface; these deal with the positive reception of the first edition of the book (see p. 69). Other changes are more questionable, particularly with regard to the title of the book. There are several instances in ed. 3, especially in the material that had been added for ed. 2 (the Preface and ch. 1 - 3), where the editors have sought to eliminate any reference to the fact that the original title of the book was *'Abqarīyat al-Masīḥ*. In ch. 1 (p. 73), al-'Aqqād refers to "my book concerning 'the genius of Christ'"; in ed. 3, this phrase is replaced by "this book of mine." In ch. 2 (p. 79), he discusses his awareness of a particular dispute "when we first wrote *The Genius of Christ";* the title is given as "*The Life of Christ"* in ed. 3. A similar exchange of phrases is found twice more in ch. 2 (both on p. 80), and again in ch. 8 (p. 115). Finally, in ch. 3 (p. 86), al-'Aqqād makes a reference to the new, revised edition of the book, adding the words "with the title *The Life of Christ*," obviously pointing to the change in title that had taken place; in ed. 3, these words are deleted, giving the appearance that the title of the book had always been "*The Life of Christ*."[7] These changes, of course, had not been made by al-'Aqqād himself. In fact, al-'Aqqād's references in ch. 1 - 3 to the book by its original title, despite that title's change for ed. 2, probably indicates his preference for the original version of the title. In any case, whereas the editors of ed. 2 seem to have concerned themselves only with the change in title itself, and not with the internal references to that title, the editors of ed. 3 sought to make the change consistent throughout the work.

These examples of revision may well represent an effort by the editors of ed. 3 to bring the book into greater conformity to an Islamic orientation, at least in appearance. As mentioned in the Introduction (pp. 45-46), the change in title for ed. 2 may have been due to pressure from conservative Muslims. The likelihood increases that this continued to be the case for ed. 3, when certain other editorial changes are observed which bear a distinctly "Islamic" character. Most evident in this regard is the manner in which quotations from the Qur'ān are presented. In previous editions, these are incorporated within the main body of the text and placed in normal typeset; in ed. 3, the quotations are set apart and reprinted directly from an authorized text of the Qur'ān, complete with vocalization and versification. Verses which are quoted only partially by al-'Aqqād are reproduced in full in ed. 3. Furthermore, the *"basmallah"* (the standard Muslim preface) has been added in ed. 3 at the head of the Prologue ("The Blessed Tree"), which begins with a full page of Qur'ānic quotations. Other changes unique to ed. 3 are perhaps more subtle, yet they provide further evidence for an editorial partiality. For example, the "lying spirit," said in the Bible to have been sent by God, was apparently deemed inappropriate and the verse was re-worded (ch. 5, p. 93); and al-'Aqqād's reference to the Jews as an "ethnic clique" has become "an ethnic fanaticism" in ed. 3 (ch. 19, p. 186). In these minor cases, the translation follows the original wording as represented in eds. 1 and 2, while a note is provided to indicate the change in ed. 3.

B. Remarks Concerning the English Translation

The English translation of *'Abqarīyat al-Masīḥ* seeks to be fairly literal while also sufficiently readable. Al-'Aqqād's Arabic prose, however, is frequently ambiguous. Points of uncertainty are often clarified in the translation, but when the meaning was especially difficult to ascertain, the ambiguity has been preserved. At times, words or phrases which are not part of the original text are supplied when something more is required for a reasonably accurate understanding.[1] It has also been necessary to add considerably more punctuation, since Arabic writing typically uses very little; but where parentheses or quotation marks appear, these are usually found in the original text as well.

Many of the chapters of the Arabic text, especially the longer ones, are divided by means of section breaks — centered lines consisting of three asterisks (* * *). Only a few such breaks are found in ed. 1, and the same is the case for ed. 3, which usually follows the text of ed. 1. They appear much more frequently in ed. 2, perhaps added by the editor, since they are often found at locations which are hardly suitable. A more practical approach was taken for the translation, which utilizes section breaks at points that are especially appropriate. Most of the breaks found in ed. 3 are included, while a few others have been added.

As noted in the Introduction (p. 50), al-'Aqqād incorporated into *'Abqarīyat al-Masīḥ* numerous quotations from the Arabic Bible (the Van Dyck version, or VD). He also translated into Arabic several passages from modern English works which he presents as quotations. Furthermore, there are a few citations from Greek and Latin classical sources, and presumably he rendered these into Arabic from standard English translations of these works, or from translations found in English secondary sources. Yet his "quotations" from all of these sources are often incomplete, imprecise or simply a paraphrase. In order to preserve al-'Aqqād's style and approach, these are almost always translated directly from his Arabic rendition rather than taken from the source itself, and thus even long quotations form part of the main text of the translation. In rare instances where al-'Aqqād has very accurately reproduced or translated such material, the citation is taken from the original source and rendered here as a block quotation. In any case, the degree of al-'Aqqād's accuracy is often noted along with the source of his quotation. Block quotations are also used for passages from the Qur'ān (following the translation by Pickthall), which are always quoted precisely by al-'Aqqād.

The many quotations or allusions from the Bible are often discussed in the notes (where the reference is also given), particularly where the wording or meaning of the biblical text differs from al-'Aqqād's rendition. At times this discussion includes matters pertaining to the original biblical language(s) in question. At other times, al-'Aqqād himself refers to a Hebrew, Aramaic or Greek term. Throughout the process of translation and analysis, the standard critical editions of the Hebrew Bible, the Septuagint, and the Greek NT have been utilized.[2] Various standard lexicons, grammars, and commentaries were consulted as well, and a reference to these is often provided in the notes.

A few important terms which are frequently employed by al-'Aqqād, and their English translation, deserve comment. One such word is *al-masīḥ,* used by both Christians and Muslims in reference to Christ. As noted in the Introduction (p. 49), al-'Aqqād almost invariably employs this title rather than the name "Jesus." Where the reference to Jesus is clear, *al-masīḥ* is translated as "Christ." In these cases, al-'Aqqād usually prefaces the word with *al-sayyid,* a title of respect; as this is almost impossible to translate in an unobtrusive fashion, it is here left untranslated. However, *al-masīḥ* can also be rendered as "the Messiah," i.e., the expected figure of Jewish hope who was, or is, yet to come. It is simply the case that the title "Christ" tends to refer specifically to the person whom Christians, as well as Muslims, believe to have fulfilled that role. Thus, wherever al-'Aqqād uses the term in the context of Jewish messianic hope without a specific reference to Jesus, it is translated as "the Messiah."[3]

It should be noted that al-'Aqqād only occasionally uses the Muslim salutation *'alayhi al-salām* ("peace be upon him") when referring to Christ or others recognized as prophets in Islam. That being the case, the phrase is left fully translated wherever it appears, but placed in parentheses (which are not in the Arabic text).

Two related but significant terms frequently appear with regard to the mission of the prophets in general and of Christ in particular. The noun *da'wah* comes from the root *da'ā,* meaning "to call" or "to invite"; in most cases here, *da'wah* refers to the "call" issued or proclaimed by Christ and is translated by that word. In other cases it is better rendered as "invitation" or "mission." The active participle *dā'in* is usually given as "herald" rather than the more stilted "caller." The comparable noun *risālah* (from the root *arsala,* "to send") is usually translated as "mission" and sometimes as "message." Occasionally the related verbal forms occur in conjunction with these words. Often a note is provided to alert the reader that these terms are used in the Arabic text.

The word *al-tawrāt* literally means "the Torah." Islam recognizes the Tawrat to be the scripture revealed to the prophet Moses. As in Judaism, the word can refer to the Jewish law in general, or to the Pentateuch (incorporating the books of Genesis, Exodus, Leviticus, Numbers, and Deuteronomy). But the Arabic term can also be applied to the entire Hebrew scriptures.[4] Al-'Aqqād evidently has this latter sense in mind most of the time; thus, *al-tawrāt* is usually translated as "the Hebrew Bible."

Finally, al-'Aqqād makes frequent use of the word *al-ghayb* (lit. "absence" or "hidden") as an indication of the mystery of divine reality, and thus as a cryptic reference to God. (See the Introduction, p. 31 concerning its use in his Islamic works in general, and p. 58 regarding its appearance in *'Abqarīyat al-Masīḥ).* It is usually translated here as "the Divine Mystery."

C. The Bible in Arabic

Arabic translations of the Bible seem first to have appeared soon after the rise of Islam, since there is no evidence of pre-Islamic Arabic versions. The oldest extant manuscript which bears a date was written in 867 C.E., while printed Arabic Bibles were first produced in 1590.[1] The most commonly used version among Arab Christians today is referred to as the Van Dyck version (abbreviated here as VD).[2] This had its genesis in Beirut, under the auspices of the American Board of Commissioners for Foreign Missions. In 1847 the Board appointed Eli Smith to produce a new Arabic Bible translated directly from the original languages. With the help of educated Arab assistants, Smith completed drafts of the New Testament and most of the Old Testament prior to his death in 1857. The Board then charged Cornelius Van Dyck, a medical doctor and master of the Arabic language, with revising and completing the translation. The New Testament was first printed in 1862, and the Old Testament three years later. Several revisions were later made, the most recent in 1916.[3]

Although Smith had utilized various contemporary editions of the Greek text for the New Testament, the Board determined that only the so-called "Textus Receptus," i.e., the source of the English Authorized Version, should be followed by Van Dyck. As a result of this policy, his revision of Smith's draft of the NT was essentially a new translation.[4] The style of the Arabic was intended to reflect the original — clear and simple in the narrative and didactic portions, more poetic for the Psalms, etc. Although Van Dyck employed a Muslim *shaykh* to assist him in his work, he is said to have intentionally avoided Qur'ānic expressions, a decision which was to remain controversial. While some missionary colleagues reportedly encouraged a Qur'ānic style, this was rejected by all the Arab Christian scholars.[5] Such an approach has led to the criticism that this version has thus never been accepted by Muslim Arab readers.[6]

In recent years, several modern Arabic translations of the Bible have appeared. The most important of these are the Jesuit version, the Arabic version of the "Living Bible," and the Arabic version of the "Good News Bible."[7] Reference to these versions is occasionally made in the notes to the translation, for comparative purposes.

D. Al-'Aqqād's Personal Library[1]

By the time of his death in 1964, al-'Aqqād had gained a reputation for having amassed what was probably the largest personal library in Egypt at that time. He stored this in his home located in the *Miṣr Jadīdah* district of Cairo. Family members living in the same house today relate that all eight rooms and two hallways were stacked floor to ceiling with his books. They have preserved a notice from one of the local newspapers, written shortly after his death, which reports that the number of volumes he owned exceeded ten thousand. A large portion of these were in English, and it can be assumed that several of them constituted the primary sources for al-'Aqqād in his writing of *'Abqarīyat al-Masīḥ*.

Family members also say that it was al-'Aqqād's wish for his library to be made available to the Egyptian people following his death. They therefore donated his books to *Al-Maktabah al-Qawmīyah al-Miṣrīyah* [the National Library of Egypt], which is today called *Al-Hay'ah al-Miṣrīyah al-'Āmmah lil-Kutub* [The Public Board of Egypt for Books], but which continues to be known popularly as *Dār al-Kutub* [The House of Books]. It was their understanding that al-'Aqqād's library would be displayed openly for public use.

Nevertheless, these books were instead locked away for years in *Dār al-Kutub*. After many pleas by al-'Aqqād's family, they were finally exhibited in 1984; but poor security soon led to the theft of several works and the closure of the exhibition. Since that time, the books have again been kept packed in cartons and stored in the basement of *Dār al-Kutub*, where they remain unavailable to the public. Officials at *Dār al-Kutub* have claimed that the books will eventually be placed in a permanent display. But at the present time, it is impossible to make an examination of them in order to try to determine what might have been some of al-'Aqqād's sources.

However, al-'Aqqād frequently visited his home town of Aswan, where he kept a few of his books in his family's house there. Upon his death, family members donated these books to the town council, and they continue to be exhibited in Aswan in a small museum built in his honor called *Maktabat al-'Aqqād*. The display incorporates perhaps three hundred books, most of which are in English. These are mainly semi-scholarly paperbacks, with a large number from the "Pelican" series of Penguin Books. Several titles deal with ancient and classical history, and a few works cover themes in comparative religion and Christianity. Included in the latter are copies of *The City of God* and *The Confessions* of St. Augustine.

Within this Aswan collection, there is only one book which is mentioned directly by al-'Aqqād in *'Abqarīyat al-Masīḥ*, i.e., *King Jesus* by Robert Graves.[2] However, a few other titles deserve to be noted because of the pertinence of their themes to al-'Aqqād's book on Christ. While he may not have utilized them directly in his writing, it is quite likely that these works helped form his overall perspective on the relevant issues.

For example, *The Hero in History* by Sidney Hook[3] may well have influenced al-'Aqqād's approach in his biographies. The thrust of Hook's work is that the true hero is an "event-making" person rather than one who is merely eventful in himself; thus there are actually far fewer heroes than is commonly held, a view which al-'Aqqād would undoubtedly espouse.

Three books were found which deal with the Dead Sea Scrolls. Two of these are of a much more popular nature, but the work by John Allegro is a judicious contribution to the Pelican series.[4] It covers most of the details which are dealt with by al-'Aqqād in ch. 1. While Allegro's bibliography is sizable, it is somewhat less than the "fifteen large pages" referred to in *'Abqarīyat al-Masīḥ* on p. 73. Assuming that al-'Aqqād also owned the work by Millar Burrows (to which this statement probably refers), one can only surmise that it can be found among the cartons containing the bulk of his library at *Dār al-Kutub.*

Finally, the Aswan collection also contains two significant biographies of Jesus. The Pelican contribution by Cecil Cadoux[5] is a sober historical approach. Cadoux argues in a moderately orthodox vein, against both the fundamentalists' claim that Jesus' knowledge was infallible as well as the liberals' insistence that nothing historically accurate can be known about Jesus. He completely discredits the "Christ-myth" theory, that Jesus never lived at all[6] — an important issue for al-'Aqqād.[7] After summarizing the sources for Jesus apart from the Gospels, Cadoux states "this does not, of course, guarantee the accuracy of everything recorded in the Gospels: but it does justify the presumption that at least their main outlines are true."[8]

The other Jesus biography is a rather small book by R. J. Campbell.[9] Despite its size, there is a fairly long discussion concerning the Gospels as reasonably credible sources. Unlike Cadoux, Campbell accepts the reliability of the Gospel of John, although he states that it "is more of a spiritual treatise than a biography."[10] Of particular note is his argument that the message of Christ spread primarily due to the remarkable change that occurred among the first disciples following the crucifixion;[11] this parallels al-'Aqqād's own argument concerning the disciples' willingness to risk death for the sake of their message.[12]

In conclusion, the search for the sources that were directly utilized by al-'Aqqād in writing *'Abqarīyat al-Masīḥ* remains inhibited. Of course, he made truncated references to several works, and fortunately most of these have been traceable. But there were undoubtedly numerous others from which he drew many of his arguments, and these are presumably included among the thousands of books in his personal library which remain inaccessible. While there is no evidence that any of the titles found in the small Aswan collection were used as firsthand sources (with the exception of Graves' book), the works noted above at least give some indication of the types of books which al-'Aqqād purchased and read, and which helped to formulate his unique perspective on the life and mission of Christ.

Notes

Introduction
Jesus and the Gospels in Arab-Islamic Thought

[1] Several presentations of the Qur'ānic data concerning Jesus are available, mostly by non-Muslims who discuss the material fairly but usually in relation to the perspective presented by the Gospels. The most thorough in this regard is Geoffrey Parrinder, *Jesus in the Qur'ān* (London: Sheldon Press, 1965); see also the extensive discussions in Kenneth Cragg, *Jesus and the Muslim: An Exploration* (London: George Allen & Unwin, 1985), 17-40; Maurice Borrmans, *Jésus et les musulmans d'aujourd'hui,* Collection "Jésus et Jésus-Christ", ed. Joseph Doré, no. 69 (Paris: Desclée, 1996), 19-54; and Olaf H. Schumann, *Der Christus der Muslime: Christologische Aspekte in der arabish-islamischen Literatur,* 2d ed., Kölner Veröffentlichungen zur Religionsgeschichte, ed. Michael Klöcker and Udo Tworuschka, no. 13 (Cologne and Vienna: Böhlau Verlag, 1988), 13-31. Useful summaries are found in Hugh Goddard, *Muslim Perceptions of Christianity,* CSIC Studies on Islam and Christianity (London: Grey Seal, 1996), 1-4; David A. Kerr, "Christology in Christian-Muslim Dialogue," in *Christology in Dialogue,* ed. Robert F. Berkey and Sarah A. Edwards (Cleveland: Pilgrim Press, 1993), 201-203; Oddbjørn Leirvik, *Images of Jesus Christ in Islam: Introduction, Survey of Research, Issues of Dialogue,* Studia Missionalia Upsaliensia LXXVI (Uppsala: Swedish Institute of Missionary Research, 1999), 23-27; and Neal Robinson, *Christ in Islam and Christianity* (Albany: State University of New York Press, 1991), 3-7. Dispassionate presentations in English by Muslim authors are rare, although the chapter "Jesus in the Qur'an" in Muhammad Ata ur-Rahim, *Jesus: Prophet of Islam* (Alexandra, Singapore: Omar Brothers, 1978), 206-220, is remarkably objective despite the polemical nature of the book as a whole. Perhaps the most helpful summary written by a Muslim is Isḥaq Mūsā al-Ḥusaynī, "Christ in the Qur'ān and in Modern Arabic Literature," *The Muslim World* 50 (1960): 298-99.

[2] All references and quotations from the Qur'ān are taken from *The Meaning of the Glorious Koran,* trans. Mohammed Marmaduke Pickthall (New York: Mentor, 1930).

[3] Goddard, *Perceptions,* 2; William Montgomery Watt, *Muslim-Christian Encounters: Perceptions and Misperceptions* (London: Routledge, 1991), 22.

[4] See Willem A. Bijlefeld, "Other Faith Images of Jesus: Some Muslim Contributions to the Christological Discussion," in *Christological Perspectives: Essays in Honor of Harvey K. McArthur,* ed. Robert F. Berkey and Sarah A. Edwards (New York: Pilgrim Press, 1982), 204-205; al-Ḥusaynī, 299.

[5] See especially William Montgomery Watt, "The Christianity Criticized in the Qur'ān," *The Muslim World* 57 (1967): 197-201; also Goddard, *Perceptions,* 11-14, and Parrinder, 133-35.

[6] Bijlefeld, "Other Faith Images," 204.

[7] Goddard, *Perceptions,* 1; Kerr, "Christology," 202.

[8] David A. Kerr, "The Problem of Christianity in Muslim Perspective: Implications for Christian Mission," *International Bulletin of Missionary Research* 5 (1981): 154. The Muslim colleague who formulated the outline is not named.

[9] See especially Goddard, *Perceptions,* 7-11; also Parrinder, 142-46.

[10] For the classical period, the most extensive surveys (though still very partial) are Robinson,

Christ in Islam, 78-190 (which focuses primarily on *tafsīr* literature); and Jean-Marie Gaudeul, *Encounters and Clashes: Islam and Christianity in History* (Rome: Pontificio Istituto di Studi Arabi e Islamici, 1990), 1:21-241 (which focuses primarily on apologetic material). Other valuable overviews are Georges C. Anawati, "Polémique, apologie et dialogue islamo-chrétiens: Positions classiques médiévales et positions contemporaines," *Euntes Docete* (Rome) 22 (1969): 380-415; Cragg, *Jesus and the Muslim*, 41-51; Goddard, *Perceptions*, 17-38; and Leirvik, *Images*, 42-121.

[11] A helpful overview of *ḥadīth* material about Jesus is given in Leirvik, *Images*, 42-52. A brief collection of passages appears in Ata ur-Rahim, 221-29. Several accounts dealing with the ascetic dimension of Jesus' teaching are in Alfred Guillaume, *The Traditions of Islam: An Introduction to the Study of the Hadith Literature* (Oxford: Clarendon Press, 1924), 147-49.

[12] Further background on each of these commentators and their works, as well as others of importance from the classical period, can be found in Jane Dammen McAuliffe, *Qur'ānic Christians: An Analysis of Classical and Modern Exegesis* (Cambridge: Cambridge University Press, 1991), 37-78; short summaries are also given by Robinson, *Christ in Islam*, 70-74; and Mahmoud Ayoub, *The Qur'an and Its Interpreters*, vol. 1 (Albany: State University of New York Press, 1984), 3-5.

[13] See Mahmoud Ayoub, "Jesus the Son of God: A Study of the Terms *Ibn* and *Walad* in the Qur'an and *Tafsīr* Tradition," in *Christian-Muslim Encounters*, ed. Yvonne Yazbeck Haddad and Wadi Zaidan Haddad (Gainsville, FL: University of Florida Press, 1995), 66-78.

[14] Robinson, *Christ in Islam*, 153. As an example of the overlap among various literary genres, Muslim apologetic writers took up this same theme; see David Thomas, "The Miracles of Jesus in Early Islamic Polemic," *Journal of Semitic Studies* 39 (1994): 221-43.

[15] Neal Robinson, "Creating Birds from Clay: A Miracle of Jesus in the Qur'ān and in Classical Muslim Exegesis," *The Muslim World* 79 (1989): 7-13.

[16] Robinson, *Christ in Islam*, 117-26; Mahmoud Ayoub, "Towards an Islamic Christology, II: The Death of Jesus, Reality or Delusion (A Study of the Death of Jesus in Tafsir Literature," *The Muslim World* 70 (1980): 106-109.

[17] Ayoub, "The Death of Jesus," 94-102; Robinson, *Christ in Islam*, 127-41.

[18] This summary stems from a personal study, in which I analyzed fifty-four *aḥādīth* found among the six "canonical" *ḥadīth* collections as well as two of their important predecessors (Abū Dāwūd al-Ṭayālisī and Aḥmad ibn Ḥanbal).

[19] E.g., 4:159 and 43:61. See Robinson, *Christ in Islam*, 78-105.

[20] The references to al-'Aqqād's comments in the Translation are as follows: the term "Son of God," pp. 222-23; the miracles of Jesus, pp. 214-15; the crucifixion, p. 226; and the return of Christ, pp. 230, 232).

[21] Cragg, *Jesus and the Muslim*, 50-51; Goddard, *Perceptions*, 19-20; Leirvik, *Images*, 67; and Robinson, *Christ in Islam*, 44. A complete translation of this account can be found in Dwight M. Donaldson, "Al-Ya'qūbī's Chapter about Jesus Christ," in *The MacDonald Presentation Volume*, ed. William G. Shellabear et al. (Princeton: Princeton University Press, 1933), 90-105. Goddard (19) and Donaldson (89) state that al-Ya'qūbī was a Shī'ī; but it may simply be the case that (as a Sunnī) he included a considerable amount of material derived from the descendants of 'Alī (so Hugh Kennedy, *The Prophet and the Age of the Caliphates: The Islamic Near East from the Sixth to the Eleventh Century*, A History of the Near East, ed. P. M. Holt [London: Longman, 1986], 361).

[22] Goddard, *Perceptions*, 18-19, 37; Leirvik, *Images*, 67-68 ; Robinson, *Christ in Islam*, 44-45;

and Watt, *Encounters*, 44-48..

23 See Suleiman A. Mourad, "A Twelfth-Century Muslim Biography of Jesus," *Islam and Christian-Muslim Relations* 7 (1996): 39-45; this is summarized in Leirvik, *Images*, 68-69.

24 Jane Dammen McAuliffe, "The Qur'ānic Context of Muslim Biblical Scholarship," *Islam and Christian-Muslim Relations* 7 (1996): 144-48; Watt, *Encounters*, 30-33; and especially Jean-Marie Gaudeul and Robert Casper, "Textes de la tradition musulmane concernant le taḥrīf (falsification) des écritures," *Islamochristiana* 6 (1980): 61-104. This charge is also present in the *tafsīr* literature, as detailed by Ignazio de Matteo, "*Taḥrīf* or the Alteration of the Bible According to the Moslems," abbr. and trans. M. H. Ananikian, *The Moslem World* 14 (1924): 61-84.

25 Anawati, "Polémique," 394-95; Gaudeul, 1:39-41; and Leirvik, *Images*, 109-110. Most likely, 'Alī al-Ṭabarī was also the author of the work entitled *Kitāb al-Dīn wa-al-Dawlah* [The Book of Religion and Empire]; this sought to prove that Muḥammad was foretold in the Bible (Anawati, "Polémique," 392-94; Gaudeul, 1:41-44; and Robinson, *Christ in Islam*, 47-48).

26 Anawati, "Polémique," 396-99; Gaudeul, 1:45-48; Goddard, *Perceptions*, 32-33; and Robinson, *Christ in Islam*, 46. Excerpts from this tract are translated in Charles Pellat, *The Life and Works of Jahiz: Translations of Selected Texts*, trans. D. M. Hawke, The Islamic World Series, ed. G. E. von Grunebaum (Berkeley: University of California Press, 1969), 86-91.

27 Goddard, *Perceptions*, 26-28; Robinson, *Christ in Islam*, 47; and especially the two definitive articles by S. M. Stern, "Quotations from Apocryphal Gospels in 'Abd al-Jabbār," *Journal of Theological Studies* n.s. 18 (1967): 34-57, and "'Abd al-Jabbār's Account of How Christ's Religion was Falsified by the Adoption of Roman Customs," *Journal of Theological Studies* n.s. 19 (1968): 128-85.

28 Anawati, "Polémique," 400-401, 407-411; Gaudeul, 1:87-94, 170-72; Gaudeul and Casper, 78-89; Goddard, *Perceptions*, 35-37; Leirvik, *Images*, 113-16; and Robinson, *Christ in Islam*, 46-47. But see especially on Ibn Taymīyah the translation and thorough introduction to his work in Thomas F. Michel, ed. and trans., *A Muslim Theologian's Response to Christianity: Ibn Taymiyya's Al-Jawab al-Sahih*, (Delmar, NY: Caravan Books, 1984), in particular pp. 112-27.

29 Anawati, "Polémique," 401-405; Cragg, *Jesus and the Muslim*, 46-49; Gaudeul, 1:95-99; Goddard, *Perceptions*, 28-30; and Robinson, *Christ in Islam*, 48, 59.

30 See especially Mahmoud Ayoub, "Towards an Islamic Christology: An Image of Jesus in Early Shī'ī Muslim Literature," *The Muslim World* 66 (1976): 163-88; also Ayoub, "The Death of Jesus," 102-103; Leirvik, *Images*, 76-79; and Robinson, *Christ in Islam*, 167-77.

31 Goddard, *Perceptions*, 20-23; Leirvik, *Images*, 79-80; and Robinson, *Christ in Islam*, 55-57. A translation of the complete text of the relevant section is given in Lootfy Levonian, "The Ikhwān al-Ṣafā' and Christ," *The Moslem World* 35 (1945): 27-31.

32 Cragg, *Jesus and the Muslim*, 59-63; Goddard, *Perceptions*, 23-24; Leirvik, *Images*, 81-101; Robinson, *Christ in Islam*, 57-58, 178-90; and Annemarie Schimmel, "Jesus and Mary as Poetical Images in Rūmī's Verse," in *Christian-Muslim Encounters*, ed. Yvonne Yazbeck Haddad and Wadi Zaidan Haddad (Gainsville, FL: University of Florida Press, 1995), 145-49.

33 Only a few general surveys of modern Arabic literature concerning Christianity have been produced. Arthur Jeffery briefly covers a number of works found in Cairo in the early twentieth century, all of which he found to be polemical in nature ("A Collection of Anti-Christian Books and Pamphlets Found in Actual Use among the Mohammedans of Cairo," *The Moslem World* 15 [1925]: 26-37). Kenneth E. Nolin provides an annotated list of a dozen books written in the mid-twentieth century, appended to a review of another book ("Truth: Christian-Muslim," *The Muslim World* 55 [1965]: 243-45). Brief descriptions of several works are found in Anawati, "Polé-

mique," 419-48, and in Hugh Goddard, "An Annotated Bibliography of Works about Christianity by Egyptian Muslim Authors (1940-1980)," *The Muslim World* 80 (1990): 252-76. More substantive surveys, including reviews of several individual works, are found in Borrmans, 55-215; Goddard, *Perceptions*, 39-166; and Leirvik, *Images*, 140-47, 168-73, 176-207.

[34] Nikki R. Keddie, *An Islamic Response to Imperialism: Political and Religious Writings of Sayyid Jamāl al-Dīn "al-Afghānī"* (Berkeley: University of California Press, 1968), 128. The title of the tract (originally written in Persian) is given as "Commentary on the Commentator," and is a criticism against the contemporary Indian Muslim reformer Sayyid Aḥmad Khan (d. 1898). On al-Afghānī, see also Goddard, *Perceptions*, 40-43. The primary work about Khan is Christian W. Troll, *Sayyid Ahmad Khan: A Reinterpretation of Muslim Theology* (New Delhi: Vikas Publishing House, 1978); see also Goddard, *Perceptions*, 51-55.

[35] Gaudeul, 1:266. See also Goddard, *Perceptions*, 45-46. *Risālat al-Tawḥīd* has been published on numerous occasions, e.g., Cairo: Dār al-Rashād al-Ḥadīthah, n.d. It was translated by Isḥāq Musa'ad and Kenneth Cragg with the title *The Theology of Unity* (London: George Allen & Unwin, 1966).

[36] *Al-Islām wa-al-Naṣrānīyah* has also been printed many times; the edition used here is Cairo: Maktabat wa-Maṭba'at Muḥammad 'Alī Ṣabīḥ, n.d. See the summary and analysis of this book by Mahmoud Ayoub, "Islam and Christianity: A Study of Muhammad Abduh's View of the Two Religions," *Humaniora Islamica* 2 (1974): 121-37. A shorter version is also given in Ayoub's "Muslim Views of Christianity: Some Modern Examples" *Islamochristiana* 10 (1984): 51-54.

[37] 'Abduh, *Al-Islām wa-al-Naṣrānīyah*, 23, 24-25, and 27, respectively. The Gospel passages referred to are, respectively, Mt. 18:18, 6:34, and 10:34.

[38] Ibid., 44. See Ayoub, "Islam and Christianity," 131.

[39] Ayoub, "Islam and Christianity," 123.

[40] *Al-Islām wa-al-Naṣrānīyah*, 28; this statement is typical of this section of the book.

[41] [Commentary of the Judicious Qur'ān], 12 vols. (Cairo: Dār al-Manār, [1910]).

[42] See J. Jomier, *Le commentaire coranique du Manar: Tendances modernes de l'exégèse coranique en Égypte*, Islam d'hier et d'aujourd'hui, no. 11 (Paris: G.-P. Maisonneuve, 1954), 50-52; Borrmans, 80-90; Leirvik, *Images*, 140-43; and McAuliffe, *Qur'ānic Christians*, 78-85.

[43] Jomier, *Le commentaire*, 301.

[44] *Tafsīr al-Qur'ān*, 3:345.

[45] Ibid., 2:160. A more complete text of these passages by 'Abduh, along with an English translation, is given in Gaudeul, 2:278-80, 298-99. See also the discussion in Borrmans, 85-86.

[46] For summaries of Riḍā's views of Jesus and the Gospels in *Tafsīr al-Qur'ān*, see Jomier, *Le commentaire*, 306-314; Borrmans, 80-88; McAuliffe, *Qur'ānic Christians*, 172-73, 183-84; and Ayoub, "The Death of Jesus," 113-15.

[47] (Cairo: Dār al-Manār, [1928]). An overview of this book is given by Ayoub, "Muslim Views," 54-60.

[48] Riḍā, 4.

[49] Ibid., 35. These passages are quoted more extensively (the Arabic text plus an English translation) in Gaudeul, 2:302-303.

[50] Lonsdale Ragg and Laura Ragg, *The Gospel of Barnabas, edited and translated from the Italian MS. in the Imperial Library at Vienna* (Oxford: The Clarendon Press, 1907). A current edition (New Delhi: Idara Isha'at-e-diniyat, n.d.) is typical of Muslim versions in omitting Ragg's critical introduction. Thorough evaluations are made by Jan Slomp in two articles, "The Gospel in Dispute: A Critical Evaluation of the First French Translation with the Italian Text and Introduc-

tion of the So-called Gospel of Barnabas," *Islamochristiana* 4 (1978): 67-111, and "The 'Gospel of Barnabas' in Recent Research," *Islamochristiana* 23 (1997): 81-109; and by David Sox, *The Gospel of Barnabas*, (London: George Allen & Unwin, 1984). Also valuable is Leirvik, *Images*, 127-39.

[51] Gaudeul, 1:268; Goddard, *Perceptions*, 57-58; Leirvik, *Images*, 133; Slomp, "The Gospel in Dispute," 71; Sox, 10.

[52] Anawati, "Polémique," 426-31; Gaudeul, 1:268.

[53] (Cairo: Dār al-Fikr al-'Arabī, [1942]). See the reviews in Ayoub, "Muslim Views," 61-69; and Goddard, *Perceptions*, 59-67.

[54] *Iẓhār al-Ḥaqq* was produced in 1864 by an Indian Muslim, Raḥmatullāh al-Hindi al-Kairānawī (d. 1891), and was based on his debate in 1854 with the German missionary Carl Pfänder. The debate was organized in response to the Pfänder's celebrated work *Mīzān al-Ḥaqq* [The Balance of Truth], in which he attacked the Qur'ān, Muḥammad, and Islam. See Anawati, "Polémique," 420-22; Gaudeul, 1:259-61; Goddard, *Perceptions*, 47-51; and Leirvik, 124.

[55] Goddard, *Perceptions*, 67.

[56] (Cairo: Dār Miṣr lil-Ṭabā'ah, [1951]). This book has been reviewed in a number of places; see especially Cragg, *Jesus and the Muslim*, 54-56; Goddard, *Perceptions*, 118-20; and J. Jomier, "Quatre ouvrages en arabe sur le Christ," *Mélanges de l'institute dominicain d'études orientales du Caire* (MIDEO, Cairo) 5 (1958): 378-85.

[57] Jomier, "Quatre ouvrages," 379.

[58] Al-Saḥḥār, 300.

[59] (Cairo: Maktabat al-Nahḍah al-Miṣrīyah, [1954]). An English translation was made by Kenneth Cragg and published as *City of Wrong: A Friday in Jerusalem* (Amsterdam: Djambatan, 1959).

[60] Foremost among them was Cragg, who added a seventeen-page Introduction to his translation, and who also wrote an extensive review (under the name of 'Abd al-Tafāhum): "'City of Wrong': A Muslim Studies the Cross, I & II," *The Muslim World* 46 (1956): 132-43, 225-36). See also the chapter devoted to Ḥusayn in Cragg's *The Pen and the Faith: Eight Modern Muslim Writers and the Qur'ān* (London: George Allen & Unwin, 1985), 126-44. Among the numerous other reviews and references to this work, see especially Goddard, *Perceptions*, 96-118 (covering other works of Ḥusayn as well); Leirvik, *Images*, 176-80, 202-203; and the review by Wilfred Cantwell Smith in *The Muslim World* 51 (1961): 134-37.

[61] See Smith's review, 137. Along these lines, Goddard overstates his case in claiming that "*Qarya Ẓālima* is the most important book on Christian themes produced in Egypt since 1950" (*Perceptions*, 118).

[62] (Cairo: Maktabat al-Nahḍah al-Miṣrīyah, [1972]). The passage under consideration appears on pp. 104-108; see Gaudeul, 2:304-307 for a reproduction of the Arabic text and an English translation. Cragg (*Pen*, 133) offers a short discussion of this book, whose title is one of the names for the Qur'ān among Muslims. Surprisingly, Goddard does not refer to this book in his otherwise extensive review of Ḥusayn's works in *Perceptions*.

[63] 2d ed. (Cairo: al-Dār al-Qawmīyah lil-Ṭibā'ah wa-al-Nashr, [1966]). See Cragg, *Jesus and the Muslim*, 56; Goddard, *Perceptions*, 121-23; Leirvik, *Images*, 189-92, 201-202; Schumann, *Der Christus*, 132-46; and the review of the first edition by Kenneth E. Nolin in *The Muslim World* 53 (1963): 252-54.

[64] 'Uthmān, 26-27.

[65] Goddard, *Perspectives*, 123.

[66] (Cairo: Dār al-Kutub al-Ḥadīthah, 1958). For reviews, see Cragg, *Jesus and the Muslim*, 52, 57; Goddard, *Perceptions*, 156-58; Jomier, "Quatre ouvrages," 371-78; and Leirvik, *Images*, 195-200, 204-207. There is a particularly interesting detail concerning this book: on p. 2, Khālid mentions five sources to which he had referred; in addition to the Qur'ān, the Bible, the *ḥadīth* literature, and Will Durant's *The Story of Civilization*, he lists *The Son of Man* by Emil Ludwig — the very book which al-'Aqqād had criticized in a series of articles some thirty years earlier (see p. 52).

[67] (Cairo: Dār al-Karnak, [1963]); 2d ed. published as *Dīn Allāh Wāḥid: 'Alā Alsinat Jamī' al-Rusul* [The Religion of God is One: On the Tongues of All the Messengers] (Cairo: 'Alam al-Kutub, [1970]). See Goddard, *Perceptions*, 158-63, for a review.

[68] (Cairo: Maṭba'at al-Kīlānī, 1971). Among the references cited which survey the literature of this period, only Borrmans, 192, and Goddard, "Bibliography," 259, have brief references to this book.

[69] Fahmī, especially 33. Borrmans, however, makes the assumption that the author is a Shī'ī (Borrmans, 192).

[70] Fahmī, 88-89.

[71] See Goddard, *Perceptions*, 123-33, 140, 165-66; and Leirvik, *Images*, 180-82, 192-94. See also the chapter entitled "Themes Related to Christianity and Judaism in Modern Egyptian Drama and Fiction," in Pierre Cachia, *An Overview of Modern Arabic Literature*, Islamic Surveys, ed. C. Hillenbrand (Edinburgh: Edinburgh University Press, 1990), 137-51.

[72] See Borrmans, 192-206; and Leirvik, 168-73. Borrmans also presents a survey of contemporary Islamic educational manuals, but he concludes that they regrettably contain very little material on Jesus (Borrmans, 71).

[73] (Cairo: Al-Sharikah al-Miṣrīyah lil-Tibā'ah, 1963); 2d ed. (Cairo: Maktabat 'Alā' al-Dīn, 1972). Nolin reviews the first edition in "Truth: Christian-Muslim," 237-43.

[74] See ch. 12, pp. 148-49; ch. 23, p. 224.

[75] (Cairo: Dār al-Kutub al-Ḥadīthah, 1966). See the review by Kenneth E. Nolin in *The Muslim World* 59 (1969): 74-79.

[76] 'Abd al-Karīm al-Khaṭīb, "Christ in the Qur'ān, the Taurāt, and the Injīl: A Continuing Dialogue," trans. and ed. Kenneth E. Nolin, *The Muslim World* 61 (1971): 90-101.

[77] *Muqāranat al-Adyān* [The Religions in Comparison], vol. 2, *Al-Masīḥīyah* [Christianity] (Cairo: Maktabat al-Nahḍah al-Miṣrīyah, 1961). See Ayoub, "Muslim Views," 61-69.

[78] 2d ed. (Cairo: Maktabat Wahbah, 1988). The author also wrote an English edition, in which he spells his name Ahmed Abdel-Wahab Ali: *The Christ as Seen in the Sources of the Christian Beliefs*, 2d ed. (Cairo: Wahba Book Shop, 1985).

[79] Ed. John Hick (London: SCM, 1977).

[80] Goddard, *Perceptions*, 94.

[81] It should be noted that the survey here reviews only a few works about Jesus written by *Arab*-Muslim authors. There is also a significant amount of literature which deserves consideration written by non-Arab Muslims (especially those originating in India, Pakistan and Iran). Many such works offer a positive approach to the study of Jesus. For overviews, see Leirvik, *Images*, 147-59, 163-68; Hugh Goddard, "Modern Pakistani and Indian Muslim Perceptions of Christianity," *Islam and Christian-Muslim Relations* 5 (1994): 165-88; and (for Persian and Urdu poets only) Asghar Ali Engineer, "Ḥaḍrat 'Īsā, Holy Qur'ān and Muslim Thinkers and Writers," *Journées Romaines* (Rome) 18 (1991): 18-22.

[82] This statement, of course, does not apply in all cases. An important example of one who

demonstrated little appreciation for Christian views and who clung to a traditional Islamic orientation, despite considerable dialogue with Western Christians, is Ismāʻīl al-Farūqī (d. 1986). See my own survey of his writing in "Isma'il al-Faruqi on Muslim-Christian Dialogue: An Analysis from a Christian Perspective," *Islam and Christian-Muslim Relations* 4 (1993): 268-82.

[83] The names of these three scholars are each spelled in the Anglicized manner which they have customarily used in their writings.

[84] *Revue de l'Occident musulman et de la Méditerranée* 5 (1968): 79-94. An English translation appears as "Christ According to the Qur'an" in *Encounter: Documents for Muslim-Christian Understanding* (Rome) 69 (November, 1980): 1-17. Brief overviews of this article are given in Bijlefeld, "Other Faith Images," 209-210; and Kerr, "Christology," 207-209.

[85] Merad, 88. The translation is from *Encounter*, 11.

[86] The article, which appears in *International Review of Mission* 65 (1976): 216-25, was originally an address given to a group of Christians in Cairo in 1974. The unpublished address, delivered in Boston in 1978, is summarized in Bijlefeld, "Other Faith Images," 206-208; and in Goddard, *Perceptions*, 137-38 (who also discusses other works of al-Nowaihi).

[87] Al-Nowaihi, 1978 address, as quoted in Bijlefeld, "Other Faith Images," 207.

[88] Ayoub, "An Image of Jesus," 187.

[89] Ayoub, "The Death of Jesus," 94.

[90] "The Miracle of Jesus: Muslim Reflections on the Divine Word" in *Christology in Dialogue*, ed. Robert F. Berkey and Sarah A. Edwards (Cleveland: Pilgrim Press, 1993), 222, 226.

[91] Ayoub, "The Death of Jesus," 117.

Introduction
Al-ʻAqqād in His Context

[1] See M. E. Yapp, *The Making of the Modern Near East: 1792-1923*, A History of the Near East, ed. P. M. Holt (London: Longman, 1987), 50-51; and Nadav Safran, *Egypt in Search of Political Community: An Analysis of the Intellectual and Political Evolution of Egypt, 1804-1952*, Harvard Middle Eastern Studies, no. 5 (Cambridge: Harvard University Press, 1961), 26-27.

[2] Yapp, *The Making*, 145-57; Safran, 27-37; Afaf Lutfi al-Sayyid Marsot, *A Short History of Modern Egypt* (Cambridge: Cambridge University Press, 1985), 51-70; and Charles D. Smith, *Islam and the Search for Social Order in Modern Egypt: A Biography of Muhammad Husayn Haykal*, SUNY Series in Middle Eastern Studies, ed. Shahrough Akhavi (Albany: State University of New York Press, 1983), 10-11.

[3] Yapp, *The Making*, 216-17; Smith, *Islam and the Search*, 12-14; and Albert Hourani, *Arabic Thought in the Liberal Age: 1798-1939* (Cambridge: Cambridge University Press, 1983), 69-83.

[4] Yapp, *The Making*, 214-32; al-Sayyid Marsot, 70-78; and Safran, 38-50.

[5] Hourani, 103-29; Keddie, 3-97; Smith, *Islam and the Search*, 15-18; and Yapp, *The Making*, 218-19.

[6] Hourani, 130-60; Safran, 62-75; and Smith, *Islam and the Search*, 18-22. The most extensive study of ʻAbduh remains that of Charles D. Adams, *Islam and Modernism in Egypt: A Study of the Modern Reform Movement Inaugurated by Muḥammad ʻAbduh*, The American University at Cairo Oriental Studies (London: Oxford University Press, 1933), 18-176.

[7] Yapp, *The Making*, 235-39; al-Sayyid Marsot, 78-79; and Safran, 85-97.

[8] Yapp, *The Making*, 340-45; M. E. Yapp, *The Near East Since the First World War*, A History of the Near East, ed. P. M. Holt (London: Longman, 1991), 51-68, 211-20; al-Sayyid Marsot, 79-122; and Safran, 101-107.

[9] Hourani, 222-244; and Safran, 75-84.

[10] Yapp, *The Near East*, 64-66; and Safran, 231-44. For further details, see the extensive study by Richard P. Mitchell, *The Society of the Muslim Brothers* (New York: Oxford University Press, 1969), especially 1-79.

[11] Safran, 125-37; and Cachia, *Overview*, especially 1-28. Ḥusayn, Haykal and al-Ḥakīm have each been the focus of biographical studies: Pierre Cachia, *Ṭāhā Ḥusayn: His Place in the Egyptian Literary Renaissance* (London: Luzac, 1956); Smith, *Islam and the Search;* and Richard Long, *Tawfīq al-Ḥakīm: Playwright of Egypt* (London: Ithaca Press, 1979). Also valuable despite being dated is the survey by Hamilton A. R. Gibb, "Studies in Contemporary Arabic Literature, III: Egyptian Modernists," *Bulletin of the School of Oriental Studies, London Institute* 5 (1928-30): 445-66; this is reprinted in Gibb's *Studies on the Civilization of Islam*, ed. Stanford J. Shaw and William R. Polk, Beacon Books on World Affairs, ed. William R. Polk (Boston: Beacon Press, 1962), 268-86, 309-314.

[12] Cachia, *Overview*, 205-206.

[13] Haykal made this statement on several occasions: in the introduction to his biography, and especially in separate articles. See Smith, *Islam and the Search*, 113-18; and Antonie Wessels, *A Modern Arabic Biography of Muḥammad: A Critical Study of Muḥammad Ḥusayn Haykal's Hayāt Muhammad* (Leiden: E. J. Brill, 1972), 44. This theme of countering the attacks of Western and missionary criticism against Islam is explored in detail for Ḥusayn, Haykal and al-'Aqqād in Zahia Ragheb Dajani, *Egypt and the Crisis of Islam*, American University Studies, series 9, vol. 56 (New York: Peter Lang, 1990); see the summary argument on vii-ix.

Haykal began writing his biography of Muḥammad in 1932 as a series of articles; these were published in book form as *Ḥayāt Muḥammad* in Cairo in 1935, and subsequently underwent several editions (Smith, *Islam and the Search*, 113). A 1968 edition was published in Cairo by Maktabat al-Nahḍah al-Miṣrīyah. The work was translated into English from the "8th edition" by Ismā'īl Rāgī A. al-Fārūqī as *The Life of Muḥammad* (n.p.: North American Trust Publications, 1976).

[14] See Cachia, *Ṭāhā Ḥusayn*, 59-61, for a summary of this incident.

[15] Safran, 140; Charles D. Smith, "The 'Crisis of Orientation': The Shift of Egyptian Intellectuals to Islamic Subjects in the 1930's" *International Journal of Middle East Studies* 4 (1973): 383-84; and Cachia, *Overview*, 206-207.

[16] In Cachia's Bibliography of modern Arabic works that have been translated into West European languages, there are eight entries for Ṭāhā Ḥusayn and twenty-one for Tawfīq al-Ḥakīm (Cachia, *Overview*, 224, 227). As for Muḥammad Ḥusayn Haykal, his biography of Muḥammad is apparently the only work to have been translated (see above, note 13).

[17] The two complete books of al-'Aqqād thus far translated into Western languages are: *Athar al-'Arab fī al-Ḥaḍārah al-Ūrubbīyah,* 2d ed. (Cairo: Dār Nahḍat Miṣr, n.d. [1st ed. published in 1946], translated by Ismail Cashmiry and Muhammad al-Hadi as *The Arab's Impact on European Civilisation*, 2d ed., rev. Shawki Sukkary (Cairo: Supreme Council for Islamic Affairs, n.d.); and al-'Aqqād's only novel, *Sārah* (Cairo: Dār Nahḍat Miṣr, [1960]), translated by Moustafa Badawi as *Sara* (Cairo: General Egyptian Book Organization, 1978). In addition, five of his poems appear in Arthur J. Arberry, *Modern Arabic Poetry: An Anthology with English Verse Translation*, Cambridge Oriental Series, no. 1 (Cambridge: Cambridge University Press, 1950), 41-45. Occasion-

ally, al-'Aqqād wrote an article for a Cairo periodical in English. One of these, "Salient Characteristics of Arabic Literature" (*Arab Observer*, 9 November 1964: 48-49), was slightly adapted and reprinted in a New York magazine as "Unique Legacy of a Flexible Language," (*The Arab World* 12 [October - November 1966]: 26-27). It would seem that this is the extent of al-'Aqqād's vast number of works which has reached the West.

[18] Cf. the biographies of Ḥusayn, Haykal and al-Ḥakīm, by Cachia, Charles Smith and Long, respectively, mentioned above (note 11).

[19] Louis Awad, *The Literature of Ideas in Egypt, Part I: Selection, Translation, and Introduction*, vol. 3 in *Arabic Writing Today*, Studies in Near Eastern Culture and Society, no. 6 (Atlanta: Scholars Press, 1986), 166-71.

[20] Safran, 135-37; M. M. Badawi, *A Critical Introduction to Modern Arabic Poetry* (Cambridge: Cambridge University Press, 1975), 86; and EI^2, s.v. "al-'Aḳḳād, 'Abbās Maḥmūd" [Supplement, 57-58], written by R. Allen.

[21] Xiaorong Gu, "Resources, Choice, and Power: A Contemporary Study in Social Change and Ideological Transformation of Germany (1848-1914), Italy (1861-1963), and Egypt (1919-1983)" (Ph.D. diss., Temple University, 1988), 178-89; and Badie K. Nijim, "'Abbās Maḥmūd al-'Aqqād: A Modern Muslim Apologist" (M.A. thesis, Hartford Seminary, 1970), 1-17.

[22] Ḥamdī al-Sakkūt, *'Abbās Maḥmūd al-'Aqqād*, A'lām al-Adab al-Mu'āṣir fī Miṣr [Leaders of Contemporary Literature in Egypt], no. 5, (Cairo: Dār al-Kitāb al-Miṣrī, 1983), 2:799-846.

[23] *Anā* (Cairo: Dār Nahḍat Miṣr, [1964]); *Ḥayāt Qalam* (Cairo: Dār Nahḍat Miṣr, [1964]).

[24] Ṭāhir al-Ṭanāḥī, Foreword to *Anā*, 4.

[25] 5th ed. (Cairo: Dār al-Ma'ārif, 1988), 9-51.

[26] *Anā*, 35.

[27] Ḍayf, 15.

[28] *Anā*, 53.

[29] Wajdī (d. 1954) went on to become editor of *Majallat al-Azhar* from 1933-52, through which he was an ardent apologist for Islam with a distinctly modernist outlook. See Hourani, 162, and the extensive study in Wilfred Cantwell Smith, *Islam in Modern History* (Princeton: Princeton University Press, 1957), 122-56.

[30] (Cairo: Maṭba'at al-Hilāl, [1911]). Although most scholars believe this to have been published in 1912, al-Sakkūt has traced a reference to its actual publication in the previous year (1:175).

[31] For more details on the "Dīwān School," see Badawi, *Poetry*, 84-92; A. M. K. al-Zubaidi, "The Dīwān School," *Journal of Arabic Literature* 1 (1970): 36-48; and Cachia, *Overview*, 90-91.

[32] Safran, 136.

[33] Dajani, 29.

[34] EI^2, Supplement, s.v. "al-Aḳḳād" (p. 58).

[35] Al-Sayyid Marsot, 99; Nijim, 9.

[36] Safran, 136-37.

[37] "Contemporary Egyptian Authors," *The Muslim World* 45 (1955): 32-36.

[38] Nijim, 6-11.

[39] Al-Sakkūt, 1:175-576, 2:577-771.

[40] *Al-Majmū'ah al-Kāmilah li-Mu'allifāt al-Ustādh 'Abbās Maḥmūd al-'Aqqād* [The Complete Works of al-'Aqqād] (Beirut: Dār al-Kitāb al-Lubnānī, 1974-84).

[41] 'Abd al-Sattār 'Abd al-Ḥaqq al-Ḥalwajī, *'Abbās Maḥmūd al-'Aqqād: Nashrat Bibliyūjrāfīyah bi-Āthārihi al-Fikrīyah* [A Small Bibliography of His Scholarly Works] (Cairo: Maṭba'at Dār al-

Kutub, 1964).

[42] A list of al-'Aqqād's biographies is also given in Jābir Qumayḥah, *Manhaj al-'Aqqād fī al-Tarājim al-Adabīyah* [Al-'Aqqād's Method in his Biographical Studies] (Cairo: Maktabat al-Nahḍah al-Miṣrīyah, 1980), 101-103. Otherwise, this book is not very helpful.

[43] *Falsafat al-Ghazālī* [The Philosophy of al-Ghazālī], Maṭbū'āt al-Idārah al-'Āmmah lil-Thaqāfah al-Islāmīyah bi-al-Azhar [Publications of the General Office of Islamic Culture at al-Azhar (University)] (Cairo: Maṭba'at al-Azhar, 1960). Al-'Aqqad claimed that al-Ghazālī had the greatest mind of all people in the pre-modern period (*Anā,* 84).

[44] *'Abqarī al-Iṣlāḥ wa-al-Ta'līm: al-Ustādh al-Imām Muḥammad 'Abduh* [The Genius of Reform and Education] (Cairo: Dār Nahḍat Miṣr, [1963]).

[45] Badawi, *Poetry,* 109-14.

[46] This is the primary theme in *Athar al-'Arab.*

[47] Schoonover, "Contemporary," 33.

[48] For a thorough analysis of al-'Aqqād's perspective on literature, see David Semah, *Four Egyptian Literary Critics,* Studies in Arabic Literature: Supplements to the Journal of Arabic Literature, ed. M. M. Badawi, P. Cachia, M. C. Lyons and J. N. Mattock, vol. 3 (Leiden: E. J. Brill, 1974), 3-65.

[49] Gibb, "Contemporary Arabic Literature," 462.

[50] Safran, 157; Ibrahim Ibrahim, "Aḥmad Amīn and 'Abbās Maḥmūd al-'Aqqād Between *al-Qadīm* and *al-Jadīd:* European Challenge and Islamic Response," in *Arab Civilization: Challenges and Responses: Studies in Honor of Constantine K. Zurayk,* ed. Ibrahim M. Oweiss (Albany: State University of New York Press, 1988), 220-22.

[51] Safran, 157-58; EI^2, Supplement, s.v. "al-Aḳḳād" (p. 58). See especially the discussion of al-'Aqqād's view of women, as evident in his novel *Sārah,* in Hilary Kilpatrick, *The Modern Egyptian Novel: A Study in Social Criticism,* St. Anthony's Middle East Monographs, no. 1 (London: Ithaca Press, 1974), 30-35.

[52] These works have been gathered in a separate seven-volume collection entitled *Mawsū'at 'Abbās Maḥmūd al-'Aqqād al-Islāmīyah* [The Islamic Encyclopedia of al-'Aqqād] (Beirut: al-Maktabah al-'Aṣrīyah, n.d.). The characterization of al-'Aqqād as "A Modern Muslim Apologist" is the subtitle of Nijim's thesis, which surveys the religious concepts present in many of these works.

[53] (Cairo: Dār Nahḍat Miṣr, [1961]). See Ḍayf, 78, and the fine overview of this book in Ibrahim, 223-26.

[54] This is the main thesis of al-'Aqqād's book *Al-Dīmūqrāṭīyah fī al-Islām* [Democracy in Islam] (Cairo: Dār Nahḍat Miṣr, [1952]). However, see the analysis of this work by Safran (215-26), who criticizes a number of historical inaccuracies and logical inconsistencies.

[55] EI^2, s.v. *"al-Ghayb."* See 'Abd al-Ḥayy Diyāb, *Al-'Aqqād wa-Taṭawwuruhu al-Fikrī* [Al-'Aqqād and His Intellectual Development], Salsalat al-Kutub al-Ḥadīthah [Modern Books Series], no. 28 (Cairo: Al-Mu'assasah al-'Āmmah lil-Ṣaḥāfah wa-al-Ṭibā'ah, 1969), 213-17; and Muḥammad Ṭāhir al-Jabalāwī, *Min Dhikrīyāt fī Ṣuḥbat al-'Aqqād* [From the Memories of My Friendship with al-'Aqqād], 2d ed. (Maktabat al-Anjalū al-Miṣrīyah, 1967), 74-75.

[56] 'Uthmān Amīn, *Naẓarāt fī Fikr al-'Aqqād* [Reflections on the Thought of al-'Aqqād] (Cairo: Al-Maktabah al-Thaqāfīyah, 1966), 13-18. This entire book focuses, somewhat monotonously, on this single theme in al-'Aqqād.

[57] (Cairo: Dār Nahḍat Miṣr, [1947]).

[58] *Allāh,* 137. See also the discussion in Nijim, 55.

[59] (Cairo: Dār Nahḍat Miṣr, [1953]).

[60] (Cairo: Dār Nahḍat Miṣr, [1955]).

[61] This theme is the focus of Rotraud Wielandt's chapter "'Abbās Maḥmūd al-'Aqqād (1889-1964): Nutzen und Nachteil religionsgeschichtlicher Studien für den Glauben," in her *Offenbarung und Geschichte im Denken moderner Muslime*, Akademie der Wissenschaften und der Literatur, die orientalische Kommission, vol. 25 (Wiesbaden: Franz Steiner, 1971), 102-109, 113.

[62] (Cairo: Dār Nahḍat Miṣr, [1957]), and (Cairo: Dār al-Rashād al-Ḥadīthah, [1963]).

[63] Ḍayf, 79.

[64] *Mā Yuqāl*, 63-68, 113-17, and 145-49 respectively. See also Nijim, 129-35; and Dajani, 30-31.

[65] *'Abqarīyat Muḥammad* [The Genius of Muḥammad] (Cairo: Dār Nahḍat Miṣr, [1942]); *'Abqarīyat al-Ṣiddīq* [The Genius of Abū Bakr] (Cairo: Dār al-Ma'ārif, [1943]); *'Abqarīyat 'Umar* [The Genius of 'Umar] (Cairo: Dār Nahḍat Miṣr, [1942]); *'Abqarīyat al-Imām: 'Alī ibn Abī Ṭālib* [The Genius of the Imām] (Cairo: Dār Nahḍat Miṣr, [1943]); *Dhū al-Nūrayn: 'Uthmān ibn 'Affān* [The Possessor of the Two Lights] (Cairo: Dār Nahḍat Miṣr, [1954]).

[66] Details for the last three works (which are referred to elsewhere) are as follows: *'Abqarīyat Khālid* [The Genius of Khālid] (Cairo: Dār Nahḍat Miṣr, [1945]); *Fāṭimah al-Zahrā' wa-al-Fāṭimīyūn* [Fāṭimah "the Shining One" and the Fāṭimids] (Cairo: Dār Nahḍat Miṣr, [1954]); and *Mu'āwiyah ibn Abī Sufyān fī al-Mīzān* [Mu'āwiyah ibn Abī Sufyān in the Balance] (Cairo: Dār Nahḍat Miṣr, [1956]). For the others (none of which include "*'Abqarīyah*" in the title), see al-Sakkūt, 1:181-82.

[67] *Al-'Abqarīyāt al-Islāmīyah* [The Islamic "Genius" Series] (Beirut: Dār al-Ādāb, 1966); and *Islāmīyāt* [Islamic Studies] (Cairo: Dār al-Ma'ārif, 1969).

[68] *Anā*, 82-83.

[69] *'Abqarīyat Muḥammad*, 3-6.

[70] The edition used here is edited and introduced by Carl Niemeyer (Lincoln, NE: University of Nebraska Press, 1966). The chapter on Muḥammad covers pp. 42-77. See the Introduction, xii-xvi, on the circumstances surrounding the original lectures and the subsequent popularity of the book.

[71] See the discussion in Chris R. Vanden Bossche, *Carlyle and the Search for Authority*, Studies in Victorian Life and Literature (Columbus: Ohio State University Press, 1991), 97-102.

[72] W. Montgomery Watt, "Carlyle on Muḥammad," *The Hibbert Journal* 53 (1954-55): 253. See also Norman Daniel, *Islam and the West: The Making of an Image*, 2d ed. (Oxford: Oneworld Publications, 1993), 313.

[73] Carlyle, 57; italics his.

[74] Ibid., 64, 65; italics his. See Watt, "Carlyle," 253; Daniel, 313-14.

[75] *'Abqarīyat Muḥammad*, 26-54.

[76] *'Abqarīyat Muḥammad*, 6.

[77] Safran (212-13) is especially critical of al-'Aqqād's exoneration of Muḥammad's use of force, claiming that he has relinquished historical integrity and adapted his judgment to suit the occasion. While there is some truth to this accusation at several points, it is overly stated.

[78] M. M. Badawi, *Modern Arabic Literature and the West* (London: Ithaca Press, 1985), 55; see also Wessels, 18-19.

[79] Nijim (138).

[80] *Mu'āwiyah*, 13.

[81] The first edition was published in 1932, the second in 1960. See al-Sakkūt, 1:178).

[82] See note 44 above.

[83] The criticism itself actually appears near the end of the Preface in *'Abqarīyat al-Ṣiddīq* (7-8), but al-'Aqqād's prior remarks are clearly made in light of that.

[84] Ibid., 3. This phrase is difficult to translate. It could literally be rendered "a psychological picture," but the term *nafsī* is best understood in al-'Aqqād's writings in reference to a person's soul or essential being.

[85] Ibid., 4, 8.

[86] 'Aṭā' Kafāfī, *Al-Naz'ah al-Nafsīyah fī Manhaj al-'Aqqād al-Naqdī* [The Psychological Trend in al-'Aqqād's Critical Method] (Cairo: Hajr lil-Ṭabā'ah, 1987), 116, 121.

[87] Ḍayf, 86.

[88] Abdel-Fattah el-Didi, *Jesus und der moderne Islam*, Arabische Kulture, no. 1 ([Bonn]: n.p., [1956]), 6-7.

[89] Muḥammad Khalīfah al-Tūnisī, "Al-'Aqqād: Muḥāmī al-'Uẓamā'" [Advocate for the Eminent Personalities], in *Al-'Aqqād: Darāsah wa Taḥīyah* [A Study and a Tribute], ed. Muḥammad Khalīfah al-Tūnisī (Cairo: Maktabat al-Anjilū al-Miṣrīyah, n.d.), 181.

[90] "Da'wan fī al-Mīzān" [An Allegation in the Balance]," in *Yawmīyāt 1* [A Daily Chronicle, Part 1] (Cairo: Dār Nahḍat Miṣr, [1963]), 368-69. According to the book, this was originally an article which appeared in *Al-Akhbār,* 5 December 1962.

[91] Nijim, 120-23.

[92] Ibid., 126-27.

[93] Kermit Schoonover, "A Survey of the Best Modern Arabic Books" *The Muslim World* 42 (1952): 48-49, 54.

Introduction
An Assessment of *The Genius of Christ*

[1] "The Blessed Tree" (Ar. *al-Shajarah al-Mubārakah)* had appeared at the beginning of the book in ed. 1. In ed. 2, it followed the first three chapters (as well as the Preface) which had been added by al-'Aqqād. It was moved to its present location for ed. 3, an editorial decision which can be considered appropriate. (See Appendix A).

[2] The Qur'ān is quoted in *'Abqarīyat al-Masīḥ* in only three other places: pp. 161-62, 185, and 227. Muḥammad is directly mentioned again only at the beginning of ch. 19 (p. 185).

[3] E.g., *Allāh*, 109-112; *Maṭla' al-Nūr*, 38-40; and "The Seal of the Prophets," *Majallat al-Azhar* 32 (October 1960): English section, 8.

[4] A year after the publication of ed. 2, al-'Aqqād returned to the subject of the Dead Sea Scrolls in a brief article: "Al-Sayyid al-Masīḥ fī Kunūz Wādī al-Qumrān" [Christ among the Treasures of Wadi Qumran], *Al-Hilāl* 67 (December 1959): 8-13. Although this is a completely new analysis, the content is much the same as in ch. 1 of the book, including his conclusion. Indeed, the title of the article is somewhat misleading, since he affirms that the Essene sect of Qumran had no direct bearing on Jesus or Christianity, but was merely preparatory for the mission of Christ (11-13).

[5] "Nazirites" are to be distinguished from the "Nazarenes." The latter was a term originally applied by Jews to Christians, although it was later applied by Christians to a sectarian group among them. See ch. 6, p. 105, n. 69.

[6] Some of the material in ch. 8 reflects themes which al-'Aqqād had presented in his book *Allāh*, especially the chapters there on the religions of Egypt, Persia and Greece.

[7] Al-'Aqqād had previously covered the material of ch. 9, with greater detail, in his book *Allāh*, in the chapter entitled "Philosophy" (concerning the Greek philosophical systems), and in the chapter entitled "Judaism After Philosophy" (concerning Philo).

[8] See ch. 7, p. 108; and ch. 11, pp. 133-34.

[9] Kenneth Cragg, "'The Genius of Christ' — A Muslim Estimate," review of *'Abqarīyat al-Masīḥ*, by 'Abbās Maḥmūd al-'Aqqād, in *The East and West Review* 20 (1954): 88; Kermit Schoonover, "Some Observations on Modern Arabic Literature," *The Muslim World* 44 (1954): 20.

[10] Nijim, 127.

[11] Butrus 'Abd al-Malik, review of *'Abqarīyat al-Masīḥ* [The Genius of Christ], by 'Abbās Maḥmūd al-'Aqqād, in *The Muslim World* 43 (1953): 218-19. See ch. 2, p. 80, n. 16.

[12] Awad, 169.

[13] *Fuṣūl min al-Naqd 'ind al-'Aqqād* [Passages from the Critical Writings of al-'Aqqād] (Cairo: Maktabat al-Khānijī bi-Miṣr, n.d.), 283-84, n. 1. See p. 52 concerning Ludwig's book, al-'Aqqād's articles, and the possibility that this work influenced *'Abqarīyat al-Masīḥ*.

[14] Engineer, 23-24.

[15] *Ḥayāt-e-Masīḥ: Shakhsyat, Kirdār, 'Aẓmat: Tārīkh awd Jadīd 'Aṣrī Iktashāfāt kī Āynī May* [The Life of Christ: His Personality, Character and Greatness: In the Light of History and Modern Discoveries], trans. Minhāj el-Dīn Iṣlāḥī [from the 2d Cairo edition] (Lahore: Pakistan Cooperative Publishers, 1965).

[16] This remark is mentioned in passing by Jan Slomp in his review of *Der Christus der Muslime: Christologische Aspekte in der arabish-islamischen Literatur* (1st ed.) by Olaf H. Schumann, in *Al-Mushir* (Rawalpindi) 19 (1977): 89.

[17] 'Abd al-Malik, 218.

[18] Cragg, Review, 88, 96.

[19] E.g., "City of Wrong," 132-33; "Jesus in Contemporary Islam," *The Listener* 63 (25 February 1960): 347; *The Call of the Minaret*, 2d ed. (London: Collins, 1985), 226-27; and *Jesus and the Muslim*, 53-54.

[20] Leirvik, 185-89.

[21] Goddard, *Perceptions*, 120-21. Goddard's presentation is rather brief in comparison to the attention he gives to other works, especially those of Muḥammad Kāmil Ḥusayn.

[22] Nabih Amin Faris, "The Muslim Thinker and His Christian Relations," *The Muslim World* 47 (1957): 70; al-Ḥusaynī, 301-302; Kerr, "Christology," 203-204; Nolin, "Truth," 243; Schoonover, "Contemporary," 36; and J. Dudley Woodberry, "The Muslim Understanding of Jesus," *Word & World: Theology for Christian Ministry* 16 (1996): 177-78.

[23] Hisham Safwat Kamel, "Christ in Contemporary Arabic Literature" (D.Missiology diss., Fuller Theological Seminary, 1990), 79-122.

[24] "Le Christ et l'Islam contemporain," in *Mediterranée, carrefour des religions*, Recherches et débats du centre catholique des intellectuels français, n.s. no. 28 (September 1959), (Paris: Librairie Arthème Fayard, 1959), 31-52.

[25] Ibid., 36.

[26] "Des écrivains musulmans d'aujourd'hui nous parlent du Christ," *Cahiers religieux d'Afrique du Nord* (Algiers) 10 (January-March 1959): 28-31, 34-36. The other two works considered here are Ḥusayn's *Qaryah Ẓālimah* and Khālid's *Ma'an 'alā al-Ṭarīq*.

[27] "Deux livres récents sur le Christ." *La revue du Caire* 35 (August 1955): 163-71.

[28] "Polémique," 446-47; "La personne du Christ d'après deux livres récents d'auteurs musulmans," in *ATTI: dell'VIII Congresso Internazionale di Storia delle Religioni (Roma 17-23 Aprile*

1955) [ATTI: The Eighth International Congress for the History of Religions (Rome, April 17-23, 1955)], (Florence: G. C. Sansoni, 1956) 443-44.

[29] EI², s.v. *"Īsā"* (4:85).

[30] "Quatre ouvrages," 368-69.

[31] Gaudeul, 1:273.

[32] Pontificio Istituto di Studi Arabi, "Christ Seen by Contemporary Muslim Writers," translated by Penelope Johnstone. *Encounter: Documents for Muslim-Christian Understanding* (Rome) 87 (August, 1982): 3-5, 12-13.

[33] Borrmans, 164-68.

[34] Ibid., 168.

[35] El-Didi, 18.

[36] Wielandt, 109-113.

[37] Ibid., 112.

[38] Schumann, *Der Christus,* 111-31. Schumann had previously written a similar assessment of the book in his English article "Present-day Muslim Writers on Christ," *Al-Mushir* (Rawalpindi) 19 (1977): 32-36.

[39] Schumann, *Der Christus,* 126-29; "Present-day," 35-36.

[40] Gibb, "Contemporary Arabic Literature," 462. The more complete, block quotation appears on p. 30.

[41] E.g., he includes himself as a subject of Zeus when discussing Stoicism (ch. 9, p. 124), and he numbers himself among the "soldiers of war involved in spiritual conquests" (ch. 12, p. 147).

[42] Ayoub, "Islam and Christianity," 122.

[43] E.g., *marīj* ("confused"), p. 166; and *mawtūr* ("estranged"), p. 186.

[44] E.g., *manẓūr / mandhūr,* p. 105, n. 66; *al-duwal tadūlu,* p. 131, n. 24; *qirān / qarīnah,* p. 134, n. 12; and perhaps *ta'malu / tu'allimu,* p. 175, n.17.

[45] E.g., *mutarawman* ("Romanized"), p. 109; *aghyār* ("alternatives"), p. 118; and *mathnawīyah* ("second thoughts" in its context), p. 147.

[46] Page references to all quotations from the Qur'ān in *'Abqarīyat al-Masīḥ* are as follows: p. 71 on "The Blessed Tree"; pp. 161-62, on John the Baptist; p. 185, on the Meccans' rejection; and p. 227, on the end of Jesus' life.

[47] In other works where al-'Aqqād deals with the Jewish or Christian perspective of a particular issue, he also incorporates references to the Bible; e.g., *Allāh,* 74-79, 103-105; *Ibrāhīm,* 13-49; *Iblīs* [Satan] (Cairo: Dār Nahḍat Miṣr, [1958]), 89-102; *Juḥā: al-Ḍāḥik al-Muḍḥik* [Juḥā: the Laugher and the Jester] (Cairo: Dār Nahḍat Miṣr, [1956]), 74-78.

[48] See Appendix C.

[49] Cragg, Review, 89.

[50] An observation also made by 'Abd al-Malik, 219.

[51] For further information about the Revised Standard Version, see ch. 2, p. 79, n. 2.

[52] Page references for these are as follows: al-Ghazālī, p. 214; al-Jāḥiẓ, p. 87; al-Ma'arrī, pp. 134, 230-31.

[53] However, the identity of this work can be ascertained from his description as that of Millar Burrows; see ch. 1, p. 73, n. 2.

[54] This tendency among many of al-'Aqqād's works was noted on p. 34.

[55] *The Quest of the Historical Jesus: A Critical Study of Its Progress from Reimarus to Wrede,* trans. W. Montgomery, 3d ed. (London: Adam & Charles Black, 1954). The German original was first published in 1906 and went through several minor revisions. The English translation of the first

edition appeared in 1910 and has remained unchanged, except for the addition of Schweitzer's new Introduction in the third edition. For overviews of Schweitzer and his book, see DJG, s.v. "Historical Jesus, Quest of" (331-32); and Stephen Neill and Tom Wright, *The Interpretation of the New Testament: 1861-1986,* 2d ed. (Oxford: Oxford University Press, 1988), 205-215.

[56] See ch. 18, p. 180, n. 7.

[57] *The Son of Man: The Story of Jesus,* trans. Eden and Cedar Paul (New York: Boni & Liveright, 1928). This book prompted sharply mixed reactions by reviewers. One described it as "one of the most beautiful, reverent and appreciative of all the lives of Jesus" (Winfred Ernest Garrison, "A Human Jesus," review of *The Son of Man: The Story of Jesus,* by Emil Ludwig, in *The Christian Century* 45 [1928]: 906), while another castigated it as a "worse than worthless piece of 'psychological analysis'" (Review of *The Son of Man,* by Emil Ludwig, *The New Statesman* 31 [June 2, 1928]: 262).

[58] Al-'Aqqād's articles concerning Ludwig's book began with a general essay entitled "Siyar al-'Uẓamā'" [The Biographies of Great Personalities], *Al-Balāgh al-Usbū'ī* 90 (1 August 1928): 12-13. They continued with a five-article series under the general title "Tārīkh al-Masīḥ li-Amīl Ludfig" [The History of Christ according to Emil Ludwig], *Al-Balāgh al-Usbū'ī* 93 (31 August 1928): 12-14; 94 (7 September 1928): 12-13; 95 (14 September 1928): 12-13, 20; 96 (16 January 1929): 12-13; and 97 (23 January 1929): 12-13. (The four-month gap between numbers 95 and 96 was due to a temporary suspension of publication). The articles were reprinted in al-'Aqqād's book *Sā'āt bayn al-Kutub: Al-Juz' al-Thānī* [Hours among the Books: Part Two] (Cairo: Maktabat al-Nahḍah al-Miṣrīyah, 1945), 142-79. All references here are to page numbers in the book rather than to the original articles. Al-'Aqqād quoted a passage from his second article in *Allāh,* 105-106. In addition, a brief excerpt from the fifth article is reproduced in al-Tūnisī, *Fuṣūl,* 283, where al-Tūnisī also draws a comparison between Ludwig's *Son of Man* and al-'Aqqād's *'Abqarīyat al-Masīḥ,* as was noted above (n. 13).

[59] *Sā'āt bayn al-Kutub,* 174, 165.

[60] Ibid., 149-50.

[61] Schoonover states that in *'Abqarīyat al-Masīḥ,* al-'Aqqād was "emulating Emil Ludwig" ("Contemporary," 36); Goddard suggests that the book was the result of "the considerable influence upon him of the *Life of Jesus [sic]* by the German scholar Emil Ludwig" (*Perceptions,* 120), and this claim is echoed by Borrmans (164).

[62] (Paris: Michel Lévy Frères, 1863); English edition: *The Life of Jesus,* Everyman's Library, ed. Ernest Rhys, no. 805 (London: J. M. Dent & Sons, 1927). (References here are made to the English edition.) This work cost Renan his academic post, but it instantly became popular. It went through eight printings in the first three months and was quickly translated into several languages. Schweitzer himself made a penetrating study of Renan's work in his *Quest* (180-92; see Neill and Wright, 207-208). Helpful modern overviews are found in Colin Brown, *Jesus in European Protestant Thought: 1778-1860,* Studies in Historical Theology 1, ed. David C. Steinmetz (Durham, NC: Labyrinth Press, 1985), 233-38; and Richard M. Chadbourne, *Ernest Renan,* Twayne's World Authors Series, ed. Sylvia E. Bowman, no. 34 (New York: Twayne Publishers, 1968), 65-68.

[63] Brown, *Jesus,* 236.

[64] *Sā'āt bayn al-Kutub,* 150.

[65] Ibid.

[66] The only reviewer to suggest a parallel (much less an influence) between the respective works of Renan and al-'Aqqād is el-Didi; he observes that for both authors, the real miracle of Jesus was that he transformed the world (11).

[67] Renan (English edition), 42, 47, 62.

[68] Ibid., 69, 70.

[69] Ibid., 136-41.

[70] Chadbourne, 66.

[71] *Sā'āt bayn al-Kutub,* 164.

[72] Nijim, 81 n. 3; see also Wielandt, 106-107.

[73] A fine overview of this is given in DJG, s.v. "Historical Jesus, Quest of." The name for this phenomenon comes from the English title of Schweitzer's book, which remains an excellent source for the period of the Quest up to 1910. A second wave of interest which took place during the 1950's is reviewed in James M. Robinson, *A New Quest of the Historical Jesus,* Studies in Biblical Theology, no. 25 (London: SCM Press, 1959). A so-called "Third Quest" has been in process since around 1980, including the infamous "Jesus Seminar"; this is well documented in Ben Witherington III, *The Jesus Quest: The Third Search for the Jew of Nazareth* (Downers Grove, IL: InterVarsity Press, 1995).

[74] "Injīl Barnābā," *Al-Akhbār* 2277 (26 October 1959): 10; reprinted in *Al-Sharq wa-al-Gharb — Orient & Occident* 56 (December 1959): 384-86. This was translated into English by Kenneth Cragg, who also added his own comments, in "The Gospel of Barnabas," *The News Bulletin of the Near East Council of Churches* (Eastertide 1961): 9-12.

[75] Ibid. (English edition), p. 11.

[76] The traditional Christian belief about the birthplace of Jesus is based on the so-called Infancy Narratives of Matthew and Luke (i.e., the first two chapters of each Gospel). Both narratives state unequivocally that Jesus was born in Bethlehem, and that he later moved with Mary and Joseph to Nazareth (Mt. 2:1, 22-23; Lk. 2:1-7, 39). However, there are a number of problems with this claim. On the one hand, there are difficulties in reconciling the reasons given in the two Gospels as to why Jesus was born in Bethlehem. The apparent assumption in Matthew is that Mary and Joseph originated from there; following their escape to Egypt, they intended to return to Judea, but out of fear they went instead to Galilee and settled there. In Luke, Mary and Joseph originally lived in Nazareth; they traveled to Bethlehem only because of the Roman census, and returned to Nazareth following the birth of Jesus and his presentation in the Temple. Furthermore, the rest of the NT is silent regarding the birthplace of Jesus. In many passages, the clear assumption is that he originated in Nazareth. See, e.g., Mk. 6:1-3, where the inhabitants of Nazareth are offended at Jesus' teaching, since they know him so well as a simple carpenter from a local family; they seem completely ignorant that he might have been born somewhere else.

For these reasons, many biblical scholars have concluded that the birth in Bethlehem is not historical but was a later Christian invention. In this case, however, there are problems in explaining why such an invention might have been felt necessary. See the thorough discussions in Raymond E. Brown, *The Birth of the Messiah: A Commentary on the Infancy Narratives in Matthew and Luke,* 2d ed., The Anchor Reference Library, ed. David Noel Freedman (New York: Doubleday, 1993), 513-16; and John P. Meier, *A Marginal Jew: Rethinking the Historical Jesus,* The Anchor Reference Library, ed. David Noel Freedman (New York: Doubleday, 1991-94), 1:214-16. On the questions surrounding the historicity of the census under Quirinius, see ch. 11, pp. 133-34, nn. 7, 11.

[77] Ayoub, "Muslim Views," 62. Ayoub goes on to examine this approach in the works of Abū Zahrah and Shalabī.

[78] After utilizing some 350 pages in a detailed analysis of the accounts of Jesus' miracles in the Gospels, Meier concludes, "any historian who seeks to portray the historical Jesus without giving due weight to his fame as a miracle-worker is not delineating this strange and complex Jew, but rather a

domesticated Jesus reminiscent of the bland moralist created by Thomas Jefferson" (2:970).

[79] See ch. 23, p. 227, n. 73 regarding al-'Aqqād's reference in his Ludwig articles to the views of Arthur Weigall regarding Jesus' crucifixion.

[80] *Sā'āt bayn al-Kutub,* 167-72.

[81] According to Notovitch, Jesus spent the entire period, from age fourteen to the beginning of his Palestinian ministry, wandering among the regions of India, Tibet and Persia. He was welcomed by the people there and learned many things, such as healing and exorcism, from Hindu, Buddhist, Jain and Zoroastrian monks. The story of Notovitch's own travels and "discovery" of the ancient texts describing these matters is equally imaginative. He published his book in 1894, entitled *La vie inconnue de Jésus-Christ* (Paris: M. Paul Ollendorf), and this was translated the following year as *The Unknown Life of Jesus Christ* by Violet Crispe (London: Hutchinson). It caused an immediate sensation, but its fraudulent character was soon demonstrated. Accounts of Notovitch, his story about Jesus, and rejections of his claims are given in Per Beskow, *Strange Tales about Jesus: A Survey of Unfamiliar Gospels* (Philadelphia: Fortress Press, 1983), 58-65; and Günter Grönbold, *Jesus in Indien: Das Ende einer Legende* (Munich: Kösel, 1985), 13-33.

[82] Wielandt, 105. This discussion appears in Wielandt's review of al-'Aqqād's book *Allāh,* but it is evident that she has the same perspective for al-'Aqqād's other Islamic works, including *'Abqarīyat al-Masīḥ.*

[83] Most of these themes are present in other works of al-'Aqqād where he deals with the message of Jesus to a lesser extent, e.g., *Allāh,* 103-105; *Ḥaqā'iq al-Islām,* 105-106; and *Maṭla' al-Nūr,* 36-37. In *Iblīs,* he states that the Kingdom of God which rules in the spiritual realm is greater than the power of Satan in the earthly realm (116-17). In *Mā Yuqāl,* there is a chapter entitled "The Message of Christ" *(Risālat al-Sayyid al-Masīḥ),* but this is a misnomer; the first section (118-22) discusses the history of Christianity after Jesus, and the chapter goes on to cover completely different issues.

[84] *Allāh,* 103, 109.

[85] Schumann, *Der Christus,* 128.

[86] See Adams, 166-67.

[87] Leirvik, in noting the many reference to "conscience" in the writings of al-'Aqqād, Khālid, and Muḥammad Kāmil Ḥusayn, suggests that this concept could serve as a significant point of dialogue among Muslims and Christians, as well as those of other religions (189, 251-53).

[88] Al-'Aqqād reiterated this theme, and made a similar criticism, some years later in a review of the book *Jesus of Nazareth: The Hidden Years,* written by the Jewish author Robert Aron (trans. Frances Frenaye [New York: William Morrow, 1961]). The bulk of this work is an attempt to grasp Jesus' thoroughly Jewish upbringing, but Aron also claims that Jesus' message was for the Jews only. Al-'Aqqād states in response that Jewish rejection of the call opened the door for that call to go into the whole world. Again, he refers to the parable of the Great Banquet. ("Ba'that al-Masīḥ fī Banī Isrā'īl" [The Mission of Christ among the Israelites], *Minbar al-Islām* 19 [May 1962]: 22-23).

[89] Cragg, Review, 94.

[90] See ch. 20, p. 193, n. 1. In the second edition, al-'Aqqād returns to this disease-medicine comparison specifically with regard to the Essenes. Although he states that they were "prepared" for the call of Christ, he does not there elaborate on the distinction between "need" and "readiness." See ch. 1, p. 76, n. 29.

This theme of the world's readiness for the call of Christ had already been presented by al-'Aqqād in his 1928-29 Ludwig articles, although the disease-medicine comparison is not mentioned there *(Sā'āt bayn al-Kutub,* 177-78). It is also interesting to note that this same comparison appears in a work written two years after *'Abqarīyat al-Masīḥ* concerning the world's need for the message of

Muḥammad *(Maṭla' al-Nūr,* 3).

[91] See Henry Chadwick, *The Early Church,* The Penguin History of the Church, ed. Owen Chadwick, vol. 1 (London: Penguin Books, 1967), 15-18.

[92] Ibid., 23-26.

[93] This perspective of Paul is found in other writings of al-'Aqqād as well. He states in *Allāh,* without passing judgment, that Paul "blended" *(imtazaja)* philosophy with religion in order to help explain the latter (118). Similar views are expressed in *Iblīs,* 100-101; and *Ḥaqā'iq al-Islām,* 46.

[94] *Tafkīr,* 131; *Maṭla' al-Nūr,* 39; *Allāh,* 119.

[95] Faris, 70.

[96] See my own survey and analysis of this subject in "The Qur'ān as Sacred Scripture: An Assessment of Contemporary Christian Perspectives," *The Muslim World* 83:2 (April, 1993): 142-64.

Preface

[1] This Preface, along with the three chapters which form Part One (ch. 1, 2 and 3), were added by al-'Aqqād in ed. 2 (1958). Ed. 1 (1953) began directly with "The Blessed Tree," followed by "The Messiah" (ch. 4).

[2] Al-'Aqqād also wrote studies of Abraham (*Ibrāhīm,* 1953) and Muḥammad (*'Abqarīyat Muḥammad,* 1942); his desire to publish a similar book about Moses, however, never did materialize. See the Introduction, p. 32.

[3] In this and the following two paragraphs, al-'Aqqād summarizes a topic he had discussed in detail in "Mudun al-Qawāfil" [The Trading Towns], a chapter of his book *Ibrāhīm* (pp. 131-44). This book had also been published in 1953, but after *'Abqarīyat al-Masīḥ.* His claim that prophets came only from the Semitic race reflects a concept found in the Qur'ān. The references there to the term "prophet" (Ar. *nabī),* and to the names of specific prophets, indicate that prophets prior to Muḥammad appeared only among Abraham and his descendants, i.e., within the communities of the "People of the Book" *(ahl al-kitāb),* meaning the Jews and Christians. See EI^2, s.v. *"nabī "*; and Willem A. Bijlefeld, "A Prophet and More than a Prophet? Some Observations on the Qur'ānic Use of the Terms 'Prophet' and 'Apostle,'" *The Muslim World* 59 (1969): 17, 25.

[4] Yathrib was the name of Medina prior to the *Hijrah* (Muḥammad's emigration to there from Mecca).

[5] A town in the Hejaz region of Arabia, where the prophet Shu'ayb lived and proclaimed God's message, according to the Qur'ān, e.g., 7:85 (EI^2, s.v. *"Madyan Shu'ayb").*

[6] The phrase following the dash (up to the note number) is an editorial addition in ed. 3. See Appendix A, p. 241.

[7] This is undoubtedly a reference to the numerous studies which appeared during this period on the newly discovered Dead Sea Scrolls. See ch. 1.

Prologue
The Blessed Tree

[1] Ed. 1 of *'Abqarīyat al-Masīḥ* began with this Prologue. In ed. 2, it formed the initial chapter

of Part Two (i.e., it followed the new material added for ed. 2, retaining its position just prior to "The Messiah"). It was relocated to its present position by the editors of ed. 3. See Appendix A for further details.

[2] This standard Muslim preface, known as the *"basmallah,"* is not original to the book, but was added in ed. 3 by the editors. See Appendix A, pp. 241-42.

[3] Qur'ān 24:35. All quotations from the Qur'ān are reproduced from Pickthall's translation.

[4] Qur'ān 6:141, but the verse is numbered 142 in Pickthall. Al-'Aqqād had ended this quotation with the word *ḥaṣādihi* [the harvest day], as seen in eds. 1 and 2. The remainder of the verse has been added in ed. 3.

[5] Qur'ān 16:10-11. Al-'Aqqād had ended this quotation with the word *wa-al-zaytūn* [and the olive], as seen in eds. 1 and 2. The remainder of v. 11 has been added in ed. 3.

[6] Qur'ān 95:1-3.

[7] Qur'ān 80:24-30.

[8] Al-'Aqqād's remarks in the Prologue accurately reflect both the nature of the olive tree (including its remarkable longevity) and the variety of its uses in the ancient world (see ABD, s.v. "Flora" 2:807-808). The high regard in which the olive tree has been held among the Arabs is reflected in the passages quoted from the Qur'ān; see the comments in *The Holy Qur'ān: Text, Translation and Commentary*, ed. 'Abdullah Yūsuf 'Alī, 2d ed. (Brentwood, MD: Amana Corporation, 1989), p. 847 n. 2880 and p. 877 n. 3000-3002.

[9] I.e., about thirty feet (nine meters).

[10] Ar. *musūḥ al-ihāb;* the phrase could also refer to the tanning of hides.

[11] In the text, "splints for broken bones" (Ar. *jabā'ir al-'iẓām)* follows the list of items obtained from the "juice" of the olive tree, and following this phrase is a comma. The translation here assumes that the comma has been misplaced in the printing and that the phrase naturally belongs with what follows, i.e. the list of items obtained from the "wood" of the tree.

[12] Ar. *mashaṭahā,* from the same root as "Christ" (*al-Masīḥ,* "the Anointed One").

[13] Ar. *al-rasūl al-amīn,* i.e., the Prophet Muḥammad (see EI^2, s.v. *"amīn").* Al-'Aqqād means that the mission of Christ was not a limited one for the Jews only (a theme he later develops); it even had bearing on the mission of Muḥammad.

Chapter 1
In Wadi Qumran

[1] "Qumran" is, first of all, the name given to a wadi which ends at the northwest area of the Dead Sea. It was near the mouth of this wadi, beginning in 1947, that most of the so-called Dead Sea Scrolls have been found. The scholarly consensus continues to be that these documents constitute the library of the Essene community which inhabited the settlement on the north bank of the wadi known as Khirbet Qumran, from the mid-second century B.C.E. to 68 C.E. See ABD, s.v. "Qumran, Khirbet," on the archaeology of the settlement ruins. For a review of the discovery, content and importance of the scrolls, see ABD, s.v. "Dead Sea Scrolls." A more thorough study of the various historical and critical questions surrounding these scrolls is Hershel Shanks, ed., *Understanding the Dead Sea Scrolls: A Reader from the Biblical Archaeology Review* (New York: Random House, 1992). Many of the scrolls had until recently been inaccessible to scholars (see the story in Shanks, xv-xxxviii). An excellent translation of virtually all the documents and fragments is Geza Vermes,

The Complete Dead Sea Scrolls in English (London: Allen Lane, The Penguin Press, 1997).

[2] Al-'Aqqād's reference here is undoubtedly to the bibliography appearing at the end of Millar Burrows, *The Dead Sea Scrolls* (New York: Viking Press, 1955), which covers a little more than fifteen pages. This scholarly yet popular work, written by one who was involved with the scrolls from the beginning, was probably al-'Aqqād's primary source for this chapter. Interestingly, Burrows later published *More Light on the Dead Sea Scrolls: New Scrolls and New Interpretations, with Translations of Important Recent Discoveries* (New York: Viking Press, 1958), with a bibliography of mostly additional material covering twelve pages.

It cannot be determined whether or not al-'Aqqād might have owned either of these books personally; but other works on the Dead Sea Scrolls have been located in the Aswan portion of his personal library. See Appendix D for details.

[3] A reference, of course, to the establishment of the State of Israel in 1948 and the conflicts surrounding that event. See Harry Thomas Frank, "Discovering the Scrolls," in Shanks, 3-19, for the story of how the discovery, verification, and handling of the first scrolls became embroiled in the circumstances of the time.

[4] Ar. *kitābī 'an "'abqarīyat al-masīḥ"* according to ed. 2. Ed. 3 reads *kitābī hādhā,* "this book of mine." See Appendix A (p. 241) concerning the editorial changes which have taken place in ed. 3 with respect to the title of the book. The year 1952 was when al-'Aqqād actually wrote the book; it was published in January 1953 (see Appendix A, p. 237).

[5] See below, in the next section of this chapter, for al-'Aqqād's more detailed discussion of the contents of the scrolls.

[6] I.e., the re-publication of this book.

[7] I.e., the books of Genesis, Exodus, Leviticus, Numbers and Deuteronomy, which are together known as the Pentateuch. Included in the Dead Sea Scrolls are manuscripts of all the books of the OT except the book of Esther. In every case, they are much older than all previously known manuscripts (ABD, s.v. "Dead Sea Scrolls" 2:89).

[8] As mentioned in the Preface (n. 2), al-'Aqqād never did publish a book about Moses, although this remained a desire for the remainder of his life.

[9] This was discussed in more detail by al-'Aqqād in his Preface; see n. 3 there for the reference to his book *Ibrāhīm.*

[10] Al-'Aqqād deals with the latter two issues, to some extent, in ch. 2 and 3.

[11] The Isaiah Scroll (1QIsa[a]) was one of the first manuscripts to be discovered at Qumran, and the first to be identified. It contains a nearly complete text of the biblical book of Isaiah. Also found at Qumran were eighteen other portions of Isaiah; one (1QIsa[b]) preserves the text partially, while the others are very fragmentary. Although these precede all previously known manuscripts by a millennium, the text presented in them is remarkably close to the MT (generally regarded as the standard text of the Hebrew Bible). (See ABD, s.v. "Isaiah Scroll, The").

[12] The Commentary on Habakkuk (1QpHab) is well-preserved, but contains an exposition of only two of the three chapters of this book of prophecy (Vermes, *Complete*, 478). Only tiny fragments of the Commentary on Micah (1Q14) were found, which elucidate vv. 5-6 of ch. 1 (ibid., 472). Portions and fragments of commentaries on other prophetic books were also found, and together they indicate that biblical prophecy, for the Qumran community, was removed from its historical context and applied only to "the last generation" (ABD, s.v. "Dead Sea Scrolls 2:90).

[13] This major text is known as the War Scroll or War Rule (1QM). It is presented as a manual of military warfare, focusing on the eschatological battles against the Gentiles. But it would also seem to symbolize the eternal struggle between representatives of good and evil, and the continual

dependence of the "Sons of Light" on divine and angelic assistance. (See ABD, s.v. "War Rule"; Vermes, *Complete*, 161-83).

[14] Although many liturgical texts have been discovered at Qumran, al-'Aqqād probably refers here to the longest such manuscript, called the Thanksgiving Hymns (1QH); this was also the first work of its kind to be discovered there. It consists of about twenty-five hymns, which in format and style are similar to the biblical Psalms. The emphasis is on thanksgiving for salvation and knowledge. (See ABD, s.v. "Thanksgiving Hymns"; Vermes, *Complete*, 243-300).

[15] This reference to an Aramaic work almost certainly refers to one of the earliest scrolls discovered and published, the so-called Genesis Apocryphon (1QapGen). The very partially preserved text recasts the events of the biblical Genesis, in some cases adding greater detail and explanation. (See ABD, s.v. "Genesis Apocryphon"; Vermes, *Complete*, 448-59).

[16] Al-'Aqqād's wording here would seem to refer to the "Apocrypha," i.e. the assortment of Jewish writings from the third century B.C.E. to the first century C.E., which were not a part of the Hebrew canon but which have been accepted as canonical by the Roman Catholic Church and/or certain Orthodox churches. In many Bible translations (including some editions of the RSV), they are grouped together into a separate category at the end of the Old Testament. However, among the Dead Sea Scrolls, only fragments from the Apocryphal books of Tobit and Ecclesiasticus have been identified. Al-'Aqqād probably intends to include other works from the so-called "Pseudepigrapha" (i.e., other Jewish religious writings from the same period which have not attained any canonical status). Within this group, fragments from the books of Jubilees, Enoch, the Testament of Levi and others have been found at Qumran (Vermes, *Complete*, 11).

[17] This "book about proper behavior" undoubtedly refers to the Community Rule (1QS), also known as the Manual of Discipline, again one of the first scrolls to be discovered and published. This document provides one of the best insights into the beliefs, practices and organization of the Qumran community. It includes regulations concerning admission to the group, communal property, strict discipline even in minor matters, and excommunication of apostates. It thus contributes key evidence leading to the probable identification of the group as an Essene community. (See ABD, s.v. "Community, Rule of the [1QS]"; Vermes, *Complete*, 97-117).

[18] Al-'Aqqād is quite correct in noting the extensive scholarly research on the scrolls which had already been produced at that time. As might be expected, there was indeed considerable disagreement (as there continues to be) regarding detailed wording of the texts, which ones should be considered within orthodox Judaism rather than sectarian, and various interpretations of the texts. However, there has developed a wide consensus, as al-'Aqqād himself observes below, that the Qumran community was a group of Essenes. See the arguments advanced in Emil Schürer, *The History of the Jewish People in the Age of Jesus Christ (175 B.C. - A.D. 135)*, rev. and ed. Geza Vermes and Fergus Millar, 2d ed. (Edinburgh: T. & T. Clark, 1973-87), 2:583-85. Even this conclusion, however, is disputed: see "The Sadducean Origins of the Dead Sea Scroll Sect" by Lawrence H. Schiffman in Shanks, 35-49, and the strong rebuttal in favor of an Essene identification by James C. VanderKam, "The People of the Dead Sea Scrolls: Essenes or Sadducees?" in Shanks, 50-62.

[19] Al-'Aqqād elaborates on this matter at the end of the chapter. See the notes there.

[20] Ar. *al-asīnīyīn*. Al-'Aqqād had already discussed the Essenes, from the references to them in the works of Josephus and Philo, in ch. 6 (pp. 98-100).

[21] These quotations are from ch. 6, pp. 99-100.

[22] Ar. *al-mutanaṭṭisīn*. On the meaning of this word and the nature of this group, see al-'Aqqād's brief discussion in ch. 8 (p. 117).

[23] Ar. *al-āsīn aw al-asinīyīn.* See ch. 6, p. 98, n. 21.

[24] Ar. *al-mutanaṭṭisīn.*

[25] Interestingly, al-'Aqqād does not raise the question here of whether John the Baptist or even Jesus had at one time been Essenes — an issue that had already been deliberated when he wrote this chapter (see Burrows, *The Dead Sea Scrolls,* 328-30). That Jesus was an Essene is generally not held, and al-'Aqqād later rejected this suggestion in his article *"Al-Sayyid al-Masīḥ"* (11-12). However, there is some consensus that John the Baptist may well have originally been a member of an Essene community such as at Qumran. See James C. VanderKam, "The Dead Sea Scrolls and Christianity" in Shanks, 188-90, and Otto Betz, "Was John the Baptist an Essene?" in the same book, 205-214, for careful considerations of this view. Both authors conclude that John probably spent his early life in the Qumran community, but that he would have left it in order to carry on his own public ministry.

[26] See al-'Aqqād's discussion of Jewish Sects in ch. 6.

[27] Ar. *al-rāshidīn.* In Islam this word is used to refer to the four Caliphs who immediately succeeded the prophet Muḥammad.

[28] Al-'Aqqād's negative assessment of the Qumran community, which is stronger than his earlier comments about the Essenes, is perhaps prompted by the puritanical character and eschatological orientation of the group as portrayed in the scrolls — a portrayal which is somewhat different from the descriptions of the Essenes in Josephus and Philo (ABD, s.v. "Dead Sea Scrolls" 2:99). Nevertheless, this assessment is the result of his own interpretation, one that is necessary for his central thesis concerning the need for the mission of Christ.

[29] Al-'Aqqād's statement that the Essene sect "was prepared" *(tumahhad)* for Christ's mission, and his comparison of this to the need for medical treatment, is reminiscent of his earlier discussion of the world's "readiness" *(isti'dād)* for the new call. See ch. 20, p. 193, and n. 1 there; also the Introduction, p. 60, n. 89.

[30] Al-'Aqqād was not swayed by the more extravagant claims of some early publications about the scrolls, which alleged direct references in some manuscripts to Jesus or John the Baptist. His view reflected that of Burrows, whose widely used book he apparently consulted (see above, n. 2): "There is no danger . . . that our understanding of the New Testament will be so revolutionized by the Dead Sea Scrolls as to require a revision of any basic article of Christian faith" (*The Dead Sea Scrolls,* 327). As scholarly research on the scrolls has continued, it is this view that has generally been maintained. Although the scrolls provide a wealth of background information along with numerous parallels between the community of Qumran on the one hand, and the ministry of Jesus and life of the early Christian community on the other, there is little if anything of direct borrowing (ABD, s.v. "Dead Sea Scrolls" 2:100; VanderKam, "The Dead Sea Scrolls and Christianity," in Shanks, 185 and 201).

[31] In fact, the Dead Sea Scrolls indicate that the messianic expectations of the Qumran community incorporated two distinct personages, the "messiah of Aaron" (fulfilling a priestly role) and the "messiah of Israel" (fulfilling a leadership role). Their purpose is not fully clear, but no text points to a salvific role in the Christian sense (ABD, s.v. "Dead Sea Scrolls" 2:99; Schürer, 2:550-54; and VanderKam, "The Dead Sea Scrolls and Christianity," in Shanks, 196).

Chapter 2
Evaluations on the Philosophy of History

[1] Ar. *tafsīrāt min falsafat al-tārīkh.* This title apparently refers to al-ʻAqqād's own interpretation and conclusions regarding the books discussed in this chapter, which he here includes within the broad category of "the Philosophy of History."

[2] A reference to the Revised Standard Version of the Bible (RSV), which had recently been published in its entirety. Studies of the purpose, process and style of the RSV include F. F. Bruce, *History of the Bible in English: From the Earliest Versions,* 3rd ed. (formerly *The English Bible)* (New York: Oxford University Press, 1978), 186-203; E. H. Robertson, *The New Translations of the Bible,* Studies in Ministry and Worship, ed. G. W. H. Lampe and David M. Paton (Naperville, IL: Alec R. Allenson, 1959), 144-54; and, more briefly, ABD, s.v. "Versions, English (American)" (6:835-36). The NT had been published in 1946 (New York: Thomas Nelson and Sons), and the revision of the whole Bible (OT and NT, with a few changes) appeared in 1952 (produced by several publishers; Bruce, *History,* 201). Al-ʻAqqād had probably made reference to this version when writing the first edition of this book (see the Introduction, p. 50).

The publication of the RSV, particularly the OT, generated widespread and intense criticism from conservative Christian circles in the United States. Especially at issue were several OT passages in which "messianic" prophecies were alleged to have been diminished. The most frequent example cited was Isa. 7:14, the passage discussed by al-ʻAqqād below. (See Bruce, *History,* 196-98; Robertson, 146-47).

[3] Ar. *wa-kidnā naḥṣir,* lit. "we almost restrained. . .", as if al-ʻAqqād himself were to play a role in diffusing the debate. As the rest of this discussion indicates, he was in fact merely an observer.

[4] See ch. 1 (p. 74, n. 11) concerning the Isaiah Scroll (1QIsa[a]).

[5] Ar. *al-tarjamah al-mutadāwalah.* Al-ʻAqqād probably refers here to the immensely popular Authorized Version (AV, also known as the King James Version) of the Bible, first published in 1611. However, it could refer to one of the "official," but not well received, revisions of the AV: the Revised Version of completed in 1885 (Oxford and Cambridge: Oxford University Press, Cambridge University Press, 1881, 1885), or the American Standard Version of 1901 (New York: Thomas Nelson & Sons, 1901). On the process of this revision, see Bruce, *History,* 135-52.

[6] Al-ʻAqqād expresses here his belief that the Dead Sea Scrolls were not consulted for the RSV translation of Isaiah, but he is mistaken. Although other biblical texts from Wadi Qumran were not yet available, the publication of the Isaiah Scroll (1QIsa[a]) led to thirteen instances where the Qumran reading was preferred over that found in the MT (Bruce, *History,* 193). In fact, the revision committee included Millar Burrows (ibid.), whose book on the Dead Sea Scrolls had apparently been utilized by al-ʻAqqād (see ch. 1, p. 73, n. 2). Al-ʻAqqād implies here that the text of the Isaiah Scroll should have influenced the RSV translation of Isa. 7:14 and settled the debate concerning this verse in favor of the traditional reading of "virgin." In fact, the Hebrew text there is the same as in the MT, so that the revised translation was based on other factors (see n. 8 below).

[7] Isa. 7:14. Al-ʻAqqād's Arabic translation follows the VD closely, although not exactly. In any case, he retains the term *al-ʻadhrā',* meaning "virgin."

[8] The controversy surrounding Isa. 7:14 focuses on its supposed prediction of the Virgin Birth of Christ, based on its quotation in support of this belief in Mt. 1:23. At issue is the translation of the Heb. word *ʻalmāh* (incorrectly rendered here in Arabic by al-ʻAqqād as *ʻalāmah),* which in the AV had been translated as "virgin." Although it is possible for this word to carry such a restricted

sense, it primarily refers to a young woman of marriageable age, without any reference to her sexual experience. In fact, this word is used in Pr. 30:19 in the context of sexual love. Had the writer of Isa. 7:14 intended to refer to the woman as a virgin, a more common term explicitly meaning this was available *(bᵉtûlāh)*. Furthermore, the context of the passage, which is a prophecy directed to the unbelieving King Ahaz of Judah ca. 734 B.C.E., requires the hearers to expect a fulfillment shortly thereafter; and the lack of any notion of a "virgin birth" in ancient Hebrew religion strongly suggests they would expect this to occur within the normal course of events. The "sign," then, refers to a woman who is, or will shortly become, pregnant (the Heb. construction is not precise as to tense), presumably through valid sexual relations within marriage. The identity of the woman is not clear, but she could be the wife of King Ahaz. The force of the sign lay not with the birth of the child, but with his name and the events which would follow his birth. Subsequent Jewish interpretation supports this conclusion, making no use of this passage in Jewish messianic prophecy.

However, the Heb. word *'almāh* was rendered into Gk. in the LXX as *parthenos,* which almost always indicates a virgin in the strict sense. (Al-'Aqqād refers to this word in both Roman and Arabic transliteration, imprecisely in each case: "Parenthos" and *bārānthūs* respectively). This highly unusual translation is made more perplexing by the fact that three other ancient Gk. translations of this passage use *neanis* ("girl," "young woman"). The best explanation is that the LXX translators understood the woman to be a virgin at the time of the prophecy, but that she would soon be married and become pregnant in typical fashion. This interpretation is strengthened by the fact that the verb "will become pregnant" is explicitly rendered in Gk. in the future tense.

Centuries later, as Matthew sought to explain how Mary gave birth to Jesus as a virgin, and to provide theological validity for this unique event, he found a ready proof-text in the LXX version of Isa. 7:14. Although his interpretation departed significantly from a historical understanding of the Heb., and even LXX, text, his method was one which he and other NT writers often employed rather freely, and which readers of that time would readily accept. For a thorough presentation of the above discussion, including references to lexicons, commentaries, translations, etc., see Robert G. Bratcher, "A Study of Isaiah 7:14: Its Meaning and Use in the Masoretic Text, the Septuagint and the Gospel of Matthew," *The Bible Translator* 9, no. 3 (July 1958): 97-126. Also valuable is the discussion in Brown, *Birth,* 143-53.

Christian translators of Isa. 7:14 naturally sought to harmonize the verse with Mt. 1:23, despite the imprecision of the Heb. word *'almāh.* The word "virgin" is found in virtually all the major early English translations, including the AV. The Revised Version and the American Standard Version both retained "virgin," but placed as a marginal reading the word "maiden." The first English translation to read "young woman" in the main text was the little-known "Baptist Bible" of 1912 (*The Holy Bible containing the Old and New Testaments: An Improved Edition* [Philadelphia: American Baptist Publication Society, 1912]). Some other English translations of the early twentieth century followed suit, but no wide disapproval was voiced until the appearance of this rendition in the RSV OT in 1952. Despite the inclusion of "virgin" as an alternative reading in a footnote, and the retention of "virgin" in the text of Mt. 1:23, the departure from the text of the AV in Isa. 7:14 was regarded as expressing a lack of belief among the translators in the Virgin Birth of Christ. (See Bratcher, 104; Bruce, *History,* 198-99; Robertson, 146-47).

As mentioned in the previous note, the word *al-'adhrā'* in VD also clearly means "virgin." This has been followed in all the modern Ar. translations, except that the Good News Arabic Version supplies a footnote stating that the word could mean the young woman who was married to the king.

[9] Ar. *batūlah.* Al-'Aqqād uses this word, and its cognate *batūl* ("Virgin"), in the rest of this

paragraph, even though the Arabic of Isa. 7:14 (which he quoted above) has *'adhrā'* ("virgin"; the cognate for "virginity" is *'udhrah).* While the terms are somewhat synonymous, *batūl* has been a traditional epithet in Islamic devotion applied to Mary as well as to Fāṭimah (Jane I. Smith and Yvonne Y. Haddad, "The Virgin Mary in Islamic Tradition," *The Muslim World* 79 (1989): 180). It is interesting in this regard that al-'Aqqād had previously mentioned the two women in the same sentence in his book *Fāṭimah,* where he referred to Fāṭimah as *al-batūl* but to Mary as *al-'adhrā'* (p. 46).

The word *al-batūl* is also the special term applied to the Virgin Mary in Arabic Orthodox and Roman Catholic churches, whereas Arabic Protestant churches prefer *al-'adhrā'.* This reflects the differing perspectives of Mary among these Christian groups, discussed in the following note. Since the Coptic Orthodox Church holds the most prominent place in Egyptian Christian society, both historically and numerically, it may also be that al-'Aqqād chose the word which would be most appreciated by the majority of his Christian compatriots. Nevertheless, as his discussion below indicates, he was careful not to take sides on the doctrinal issues involved.

[10] Al-'Aqqād has confused the more recent debate over the RSV reading of Isa. 7:14 (and with it, the accusation that some deny the Virgin Birth of Christ entirely) with the long-standing controversy concerning the Perpetual Virginity of Mary. The first of the "schools of thought" (Ar. *al-madhāhib)* described here represents the traditional position of the Orthodox and Roman Catholic churches (see the *New Catholic Encyclopedia,* ed. William J. McDonald [New York: McGraw-Hill, 1967], s.v. "Virgin Birth" [14:695-96]). The belief that Mary continued to retain her virginity is also a feature of Muslim tradition about her (Smith and Haddad, 175). Protestant churches, on the other hand, generally hold to the second position, that Mary gave birth to Jesus as a virgin but later bore other children naturally. (The historical development of the doctrine of Perpetual Virginity is traced in Raymond E. Brown et al., eds., *Mary in the New Testament: A Collaborative Assessment by Protestant and Roman Catholic Scholars* [Philadelphia: Fortress Press, 1978; New York: Paulist Press, 1978], 273-75).

The third group mentioned by al-'Aqqād would logically be those who deny the Virgin Birth altogether; yet he has instead referred to those who favor the RSV reading of "young woman" in Isa. 7:14, as if this automatically placed them in the more liberal camp. (This is the clearest indication that he has sided with the conservative Christian opponents to the RSV on this issue). In fact, as discussed in the n. 8 above, fidelity to the Hebrew wording and historical context of Isa. 7:14 in no way implies this; interpreters who favor the RSV wording can be found in either of the two "schools of thought" which hold to the Virgin Birth.

[11] Several passages in the NT (representing all four Gospels, Acts and Paul) make reference to the "brothers" (and sometimes "sisters") of Jesus, e.g. Mk. 3:31-32 (= Mt. 12:46 = Lk. 8:19-20). In every instance the Gk. word is *adelphos,* which normally denotes a blood brother of the same parents. However, it is also used in the NT for "step-brother" (Mk. 6:17-18 and parallels), and to describe relationships outside the family. In the LXX, *adelphos* can also mean "cousin" or "relative," but this reflects the original Heb. word *'āḥ* which can carry this sense along with "(blood) brother." It is possible that the "brothers" of Jesus could be understood in this broader sense, perhaps indicating Aramaic usage (which was the same as Heb.), but exegetically, there are no strong reasons to reject the usual meaning.

Beginning in the second century C.E., three views developed in the church: (a) the "brothers" (and "sister") were blood siblings of Jesus, born to Mary and Joseph after his birth; (b) they were step-brothers and sisters, the children of Joseph by a previous marriage; (c) they were cousins, children of a sister of Mary. Of course, the latter two interpretations (which al-'Aqqād has amalgamated into one) parallel the doctrine of the Perpetual Virginity of Mary, and Christian scholarly views continue to be held along confessional lines. (See ABD, s.v. "Jesus, Brothers and Sisters of"; Brown et al., 52-58, 65-72, 166-70, etc.). The conclusion in Brown et al., which is an ecumenical work, is that "it cannot be said that the NT identifies them *without doubt* as blood brothers and sisters and hence the children of Mary," and that "the solution favored by scholars will in part depend on the authority they allot to later church insights" (72).

[12] Ar. *'Abqarīyat al-Masīḥ* according to ed. 2. Ed. 3 has *Ḥayāt al-Masīḥ*. A similar exchange of titles occurs twice more in this chapter. See Appendix A (p. 241) concerning the editorial changes made in ed. 3.

[13] Al-'Aqqād had discussed various historical factors surrounding Christ's birth in ch. 11 (pp. 133-35). It is evident that he accepts the Virgin Birth in connection with the biblical data which he presents, although he nowhere states his views on the matter.

[14] Ar. *"akhī al-rabb"* and *"Jayms"*, respectively.

[15] Ar. *"Jayms qarīb al-masīḥ."* Al-'Aqqād had referred to a disciple named James in this manner in ch. 21 (p. 205). There, he evidently means the James who is described in the NT as the "brother" of Jesus, although some confusion is apparent in his discussion of various disciples who have the names James and John; see ch. 21, p. 205, n. 31 (especially item 2).

In Gal. 1:19, Paul states that he "saw none of the other apostles except James the Lord's brother" (Gk. *adelphos).* VD reads the last part as *illā Ya'qūb akhā al-rabb.* This person's precise identification and relationship to Jesus is naturally connected to the matter concerning the "brothers" of Christ which al-'Aqqād previously discussed in this chapter (see n. 11 above, and also ABD, s.v. "James, Brother of Jesus"). His use of *qarīb* rather than *akh* was probably meant to appeal to Coptic Orthodox sensitivities, which would have predominated among his Christian readers. (See n. 9 above on his similar use of *batūlah).* Presumably, the "critics" mentioned in the next sentence were Protestant Christians who take the NT phrase more literally.

Al-'Aqqād's choice of *al-masīḥ* in place of *al-rabb* (as in VD) is consistent with most of his references to Jesus throughout the book, and follows Islamic sensitivities regarding these terms (in Islam, *al-rabb* may be used only in reference to God, EI^2, s.v. *"rabb").* His reason for writing "James" as a transliteration from English, rather than using his Arabic name *Ya'qūb,* is less clear; but see the following note.

[16] Here, al-'Aqqād is dealing with a criticism which is related to, yet different from, the one mentioned at the beginning of the paragraph. There, the issue was the relationship of James to Jesus, whereas here it concerns the manner in which he renders the name for James in Arabic. Almost certainly al-'Aqqād is responding here to the review of *'Abqarīyat al-Masīḥ* (ed. 1) by Butrus 'Abd al-Malik: "Some of the proper names appear in Western transliterated form, like *Jayms* (for James) where it might have been expected that the author would know that the Arabic equivalent was *Ya'qūb"* (219). 'Abd al-Malik's reference was to al-'Aqqād's use of this term in ch. 21, p. 205. However, the real issue is far more complex than 'Abd al-Malik indicates, since on the same page al-'Aqqād had referred to James the brother of John by the name *Ya'qūb,* and since he demonstrates there some confusion regarding various disciples named James and John. Here, al-'Aqqād states that the criticism is minor. However, he has also added a footnote in ed. 2, at the point where the name *Jayms* appears, in which he tries to explain its use. Unfortunately, his "explanation" only adds to the confusion of his presentation. For a full discussion, see ch. 21, p. 205, n. 31 (especially items 5 and 6).

[17] That is, if he had wished, al-'Aqqād could have produced his second edition earlier than he did, including in it a discussion of the debate over the virginity of Mary. This was especially true

since further study of the Dead Sea Scrolls (which was the main reason for the delay of the second edition) offered no resolution to that debate.

[18] Al-'Aqqād seems to be responding to anticipated criticism that his second edition has not been revised in light of the many books about Jesus that appeared since his first edition. Perhaps they would think that his response to the new RSV translation of the OT (which he had set aside because it was caught up in an issue for which he had little sympathy) would be transferred to those other books. Al-'Aqqād insists this is not the case: he has in fact reviewed many of these books, but he found that they did not change his earlier views.

[19] Al-'Aqqād provides two footnotes which give approximate English renditions of the titles and authors. The full references are: Rupert Furneaux, *The Other Side of the Story: The Strange Story of Christianity, the Dark Spot of History* (London: Cassell, 1953); and Robert Graves and Joshua Podro, *The Nazarene Gospel Restored* (Garden City, N.Y.: Doubleday, [1953]; London: Cassell, [1953]).

[20] Al-'Aqqād's critical remarks nevertheless point fairly accurately to the methodology employed by the authors of these two books. Writing in a more popular as well as polemical vein, they represent the radical end of the spectrum of discussion on the life of Jesus. Both books completely reject the traditional reading of the Gospels and assume that the Gospel writers had distorted the historical events and sayings of Jesus for the sake of later church doctrine.

Furneaux in particular states that the Jesus of the Gospels "is the creation of a later period which conceived him in its own image" (6). He relies instead on scattered non-Christian references which he claims are quite antithetical to the Gospels and which establish that Jesus was "an agitator and a fomenter of rebellion, whose followers exercised considerable influence in the revolt of the Jews against the Roman Empire" (27).

Graves and Podro view Jesus more as a devout ethicist with an apocalyptic bent, working fully within the Pharisaic Judaism of the first century (Garden City ed., p. vi). His immediate followers formed a sect of Judaism, while Paul and his Gentile converts produced a radically different Jesus in the NT Gospels. The "genuine" Christians were ostracized, forming the Nazarene and Ebionite sects of the second century which were branded as heretical by the "Orthodox" church (p. x; see ODCC, s.v. "Ebionites" and "Nazarene [3]" on these groups. Also, al-'Aqqād refers to the Ebionites in ch. 19, p. 186; see n. 10). The book by Graves and Podro is essentially a cut-and-paste re-writing of the Gospels based on their thesis, using Jewish and non-canonical Christian sources as well. See the review by H. John McLachlan (in *The Hibbert Journal* 52 [April 1954]: 315-18), who concludes that it is based on "conjecture" which is "altogether beyond permissible bounds" (318).

[21] Robert Graves, *King Jesus* (New York: Noonday Press [Farrar, Straus, Giroux], 1946; London: Cassell, 1946). (Al-'Aqqād translates the title as *'Īsā al-Malak,* using the Islamic name for Jesus). Graves refers to his approach in this novel, in characteristically enigmatic fashion, as "the analeptic method — the intuitive recovery of forgotten events by a deliberate suspension of time" (New York ed., 421; London ed., 353). See the review by W. E. Garrison ("Branch from 'The Golden Bough,'" in *The Christian Century* 63 [October 2, 1946]: 1184-85), who states that "Graves treats the mass of data with which he buttresses and embellishes his hypothesis as though all parts of it were of equal credibility, though much of it has no sound historical evidence" (1184). Nevertheless, this book has achieved a measure of popularity: a fourteenth printing of the New York edition was issued in 1996.

Of all the sources referred to by al-'Aqqād in *'Abqarīyat al-Masīḥ,* this particular book was the only title found in the small portion of his personal library which is on display in Aswan. For details, see Appendix D.

[22] Graves, *King Jesus* (New York ed., 203-18; London ed., 175-93). According to the novel, the group's members were Essenes. Their leader, the former High Priest Simon, had arranged for Jesus' birth as a king through the secret marriage of Mary with Antipater, the estranged son of Herod the Great. She was then passed off as Joseph's wife so that Jesus' true lineage would remain secret until the appropriate time (New York ed., 60-66, 78-82, 127-32; London ed., 53-59, 68-79, 110-15).

[23] Ibid., New York ed., 228-31, 259-60; London ed., 196-201, 230-31.

[24] Ar. *al-da'wah.* This word is used for the early Christian mission throughout the remainder of this chapter.

[25] The discussion from here to the end of this chapter is al-'Aqqād's summary of a thesis held by the authors previously mentioned (after dismissing what he considers to be the more extravagant assertions) concerning the mission of the early church. Although al-'Aqqād has concentrated thus far on the novel about Jesus by Graves, this thesis is not presented there. Rather, he is drawing primarily from the introductory chapters of Graves and Podro, (*The Nazarene Gospel Restored,* Garden City ed., 3-42, and especially 19-21 and 35-36), and, to a lesser extent, from Furneaux (29-57). It is important here to note that while al-'Aqqād is reporting what might be considered the more plausible aspects of these authors' views, they do not represent his own perspective, as is clear from his critique in the following chapter.

[26] Ar. *Jayms ay (Ya'qūb) al-musammā bi-akhī al-rabb.* Al-'Aqqād means that *al-rabb,* as a reference to Jesus, is the usage of the NT; it is not his own preference. See n. 15 above.

[27] This thesis concerning early Jewish Christianity, thus far, has been promoted, in various degrees, by numerous authors. A thorough analysis of the issues, sources, and modern literature on the subject is provided by James D. G. Dunn, *Unity and Diversity in the New Testament: An Inquiry into the Character of Earliest Christianity,* 2nd ed. (London: SCM Press, 1990; Philadelphia: Trinity Press International, 1990), 235-66. Dunn's own conclusions represent a mediating position: among the several diverse streams of early Christian expression, one could certainly be labeled as "Jewish" in the sense that it saw itself fully within the bounds of first-century Judaism, over against the Gentile churches established by Paul and the other Hellenistic Jews (237-39). While this Jewish stream appeared in many forms, three general traits distinguished early Jewish Christianity, as evidenced in the NT: an adherence to Jewish law, the exaltation of James and denigration of Paul, and adoptionist tendencies with regard to the person of Jesus (i.e., that Jesus was naturally born of Mary and Joseph and became God's Son at a later time; 248-60). Undoubtedly, the Ebionites and other early sects were later developments of this stream (239-45). Yet Dunn also sees earliest Jewish Christianity as fluid and developing, so that it could accommodate towards Hellenistic Christianity in each of these areas: Jewish law was reinterpreted by Jesus' ethic of love; the mission to the Gentiles could nevertheless be embraced; and, most significantly, Jesus was recognized to be "the Son of God" in a manner which Ebionism could never accept (261-66).

Although most of the views held by Graves, Podro and Furneaux concerning early Jewish Christianity, as summarized by al-'Aqqād, fall within this mediating position, some assertions remain problematic. For example, it is maintained that the missionary activity of the contingent associated with Paul (what Dunn refers to as Hellenistic Christianity) was not prominent until after the fall of Jerusalem in 70 C.E. But historically, this mission was well in place long before this date. Nor were the Jewish and Hellenistic expressions of early Christianity mutually exclusive, as implied here. Rather, as Dunn insists, early Christianity was sufficiently flexible so as to allow numerous perspectives to co-exist throughout the period, while there was also a fundamental basis for unity. Finally, this basis for unity was precisely the person of Christ; though many Christologies can be located in the NT, the unifying factor was the conviction that Jesus of Nazareth, crucified and buried, is now the risen Lord (Dunn, 227). Even Jewish Christianity could hold some sense of the "divine characteristic" of Jesus which these authors claim was absent.

It is significant that much of this thesis coming from Western authors has also been advocated by Muslim writers wishing to demonstrate that the historical Jesus fits more closely to the Islamic conception of him, and that the early church (especially Paul) transformed him into a divine being while groups such as the Ebionites preserved the authentic Christ. Probably the best representative of this argument from the classical period is 'Abd al-Jabbār, and in the modern period, this theme has been championed by Ismā'īl al-Farūqī (see the references to these figures in the Introduction, p. 8, and p. 18, n. 82 respectively). Furthermore, some contemporary Christian theologians, notably Hans Küng and Wilfred Cantwell Smith, have argued that Islam may well serve as a kind of corrective towards a more pristine Jewish perspective of Jesus (see Kerr, "Christology," 213-14).

Nevertheless, al-'Aqqād does not follow this line of thought. He acknowledges the Jewish context of Jesus, but for him this context becomes less significant in view of the rejection of his message by the Jews and its acceptance by the Gentiles. As the disciples carried the Gentile mission forward, they preserved this message faithfully. It was only later that the church went astray by trying to join religion to politics and philosophy (see ch. 3 and the Introduction, pp. 61-62).

[28] I.e. (according to the view being summarized by al-'Aqqād), the Gospels preserved the original, Jewish focus of Jesus and his mission at a time when the Gentile mission was heading in a different direction by introducing divine attributes to Jesus.

[29] Ar. *wa-ta'allamūhu.* VD has *wa-f'alūhu,* "practice." Otherwise, the quotations in this paragraph follow VD almost exactly.

[30] The biblical quotations in this paragraph are all from the Gospel of Matthew: 23:2-3; 5:17-18; 10:5-6; and 15:24, respectively.

[31] The views presented in this final paragraph represent a natural continuity in the overall thesis of these authors (there is no break from the previous paragraph in the Arabic text). However, the positions expressed, concerning the purpose of the Gospels, Jesus' relationship to the Pharisees and the Jewish law, and the nature of his mission, all move into areas of speculation which is beyond what is held by most scholars. They are also in contradiction to al-'Aqqād's own views, as related in the following chapter and elsewhere in this book.

In the first place, the claim that the Gospels preserve and promote early Jewish Christianity over against its Hellenistic counterpart cannot be maintained without a radical revision of their contents. It is true that Matthew has long been recognized as the most "Jewish" of the four Gospels: the author clearly seeks to demonstrate that Jesus' life and ministry fulfilled OT prophecy, and that Jesus "did not undermine the righteousness of Judaism, but, on the contrary, enhanced and completed it, and that to belong to Christ is truly to belong to Israel" (C. F. D. Moule, *The Birth of the New Testament,* 3rd ed., Black's New Testament Commentaries, ed. Henry Chadwick [London: Adam & Charles Black, 1981], 93). The four passages from Matthew quoted here (none of which has any close parallels among the other Gospels) represent this perspective. But in other passages, Matthew is quite antagonistic to Judaism, especially Jewish religious leaders. These contradictions in Matthew are best explained by assuming that part of his purpose was to provide a manual for a Christian community, made up primarily of Jews but also including Gentiles, which found it necessary to defend its self-understanding as the true Israel, and its mission to the Gentiles, against the hostility of traditional Judaism (Moule, 124-28; see also Donald A. Hagner, *Mat-*

thew, Word Biblical Commentary, ed. David A. Hubbard and Glenn W. Barker, [Dallas: Word Books, 1993], 33A: lxv-lxxi.

Thus, Jesus' relationship to the Pharisees as presented in Matthew is quite varied. Graves and Podro, as al-'Aqqād insinuates, label Jesus "an apocalyptic Pharisee whose message was neither unorthodox nor original" (*The Nazarene Gospel Restored,* Garden City ed., 14). Although the range of scholarly opinion concerning Jesus' interaction with the Pharisees is quite broad, such a close identification between them is not generally made by most scholars. The debate rests on many factors, but a key one is whether or not the Gospel accounts of Jesus' confrontation with the Pharisees can be regarded as historically reliable, since these often conflict with the picture of the Pharisees presented in other sources (ABD, s.v. "Pharisees"). So one scholar states that "our discussions of the sinners, the law, purity and legalism all point towards finding little contact, either hostile or cordial, between Jesus and the Pharisees. . . . Thus I find no substantial conflict between Jesus and the Pharisees" (E. P. Sanders, *Jesus and Judaism* [Philadelphia: Fortress Press, 1985], 219). Yet another claims, "The constant references in the Gospels to strife between the Pharisees and scribes on the one hand, and Jesus on the other, leaves no doubt that such strife, even if the Gospels exaggerated it, had genuinely existed" (Michael Grant, *Jesus: An Historian's Review of the Gospels* [New York: Charles Scribners' Sons, 1977], 117). In any case, Matthew presents a distinct confrontation; the positive statement concerning the Pharisees in 23:2 immediately gives way to some of the most sustained and severe criticism from Jesus toward the Pharisees found anywhere in the Gospels. Passages from this chapter are quoted by al-'Aqqād in ch. 17 (p. 175) as examples of Jesus' criticism against "the celebrated scholars who had strayed."

In a similar manner, the passage emphasizing Jesus' commitment to the Jewish law (Mt. 5:17-18) must be read in the context of the rest of Matthew ch. 5. Jesus' loyalty to the law may be comparable to that of the Pharisees, but his *interpretation* of the law is contrasted sharply with theirs. Jesus is presented by Matthew as the one with the authority to provide, not a new meaning to the law, but the originally intended meaning to that law (see Hagner, 33A:103-104; and Gerard S. Sloyan, *Is Christ the End of the Law?,* Biblical Perspectives on Current Issues, ed. Howard Clark Kee [Philadelphia: Westminster Press, 1978], 50-54).

The last two quotations (Mt. 10:5-6, 15:24) are used to support the assumption of these authors that Jesus intended his mission, and that of his disciples, to be restricted to Jews. Yet Matthew also includes statements in support of the mission to the Gentiles (e.g. 21:43, 24:14, and especially 28:19). The best explanation is one that recognizes a variety of concerns among Matthew's readers. Like the other Gospels, it cannot be denied that Matthew supports the Gentile mission; but he also included a word for Jewish Christians concerned for their non-Christian compatriots, that the gospel was being offered equally to them. If the statements do go back to Jesus (and this best explains their presence in the text), it must be concluded that Jesus himself regarded his mission (and that of the disciples during his ministry) to be restricted to Israel only temporarily. His ultimate vision was one in which the Gentiles would also be incorporated into his community of salvation (Hagner, 33A:270-71; see also the thorough and still important monograph by Joachim Jeremias, *Jesus' Promise to the Nations* [Philadelphia: Fortress Press, 1967], especially the conclusion on p. 71. Al-'Aqqād's view is much closer to this, as is apparent in the following chapter and in ch. 19. Indeed, his argument moves to the other extreme, that a full-fledged Gentile mission was present within Jesus' own ministry.

Chapter 3
Response and Critique

[1] This chapter must be read as a continuation of the last section of the previous chapter. There, al-'Aqqād discussed some recently published books concerning Jesus in which he believed the authors had made unwarranted conclusions.

[2] Ar. *al-da'wah.* This term is translated as "mission" through the middle of the next paragraph.

[3] In rejecting this thesis from the more liberal element of Western discussion on the life of Jesus and the early Christian mission, al-'Aqqād places himself alongside of mainstream and even conservative Christian scholarship. His reference here to the "characteristics" (Ar. *ṣifāt)* which early Christian missionaries preached as belonging to Jesus is particularly interesting. In the previous chapter, he had used the same term in reference to a messenger-savior anticipated by the Gentiles, in the phrase "divine characteristics" (Ar. *ṣifāt ilāhīyah,* p. 83. Thus, al-'Aqqād almost seems to admit that the early church was correct in regarding Jesus to be in some sense "the Son of God." But that is certainly more than he means to say here, as evidenced by the rest of the book and his other writings.

[4] Ar. *al-da'wah.* The word for "mission" in the rest of this paragraph is *al-risālah.*

[5] Al-'Aqqād reiterates a thesis which had been the main theme of ch. 19 (pp. 185-87). Both there and here, he overstates the data found in the Gospels. They record that Jesus' activity among Gentiles was extremely limited, and that such contact as he had with non-Jewish individuals usually came about from their initiative rather than his. It cannot be said that Jesus renounced his mission to Israel in favor of the Gentiles. Rather, the Gospels indicate that Jesus created the vision and laid the foundation for incorporating Gentiles into the Kingdom. The book of Acts describes how the early church, as well, never renounced its mission activity among Jews. Although in certain cases Paul is said to have turned away from unresponsive Jews in order to take his message to Gentiles (e.g. Acts 13:46, 18:6), his theology and practice always incorporated both groups. (See the Introduction, pp. 42-43 and 59, and ch. 19, p. 187, n. 15).

[6] This paragraph reflects many of the themes which al-'Aqqād had presented in ch. 21. In addition, here he may well have had in mind a passage such as 1 Ths. 2:1-5 or 2 Cor. 4:2, in which Paul renounced deception as a means of evangelism, but rather accepted suffering as part of his missionary calling.

[7] Al-'Aqqād is undoubtedly referring to the discussion of various world religions in his book *Allāh;* the presentation of Hinduism is on pp. 44-51. Brahma is one of three important gods in Hinduism, regarded as the creator of the universe (ER, s.v. "Brahmā").

[8] I.e., no single person, Muslim or otherwise, would be considered capable of writing objectively about *all* the world religions.

[9] Ar. *al-khulafā' al-rāshidīn,* lit. "the rightly-guided caliphs," the usual epithet for these four men. The reference is to al-'Aqqād's separate studies of Abū Bakr, 'Umar, 'Uthmān and 'Alī which formed part of his *'Abqarīyah* series (see the Introduction, pp. 33-34). Shī'ites hold the highest regard, after Muḥammad, for 'Alī. Al-'Aqqād's book about him is somewhat mixed: he praises 'Alī and his family for their virtues, excusing him of practically any fault; yet he concedes that politically 'Alī was hopelessly incompetent (see Nijim, 138-39, 146). But probably the most controversial matter concerned the acquisition of leadership following Muḥammad's death. Shī'ites generally claim that Muḥammad had appointed 'Alī as his immediate successor (EI^2, s.v. "'Alī b. Abī Ṭālib" [1:381-82]). Sunnis, along with virtually all non-partisan historians, recognize

that Muḥammad made no statement as to who would take over the leadership of the community, and that there was confusion on this matter among the Muslims on the day of his death. The emergence of Abū Bakr as the first Caliph was the result of a consensus, in line with Arab tradition, that his standing and personality made him the most suitable choice (see M. A. Shaban, *Islamic History: A New Interpretation* [Cambridge: Cambridge University Press, 1971-76], 1:16-19). On the one hand, al-'Aqqād relates the uncertainty that followed Muḥammad's death in *'Abqarīyat al-Ṣiddīq* (18-34); on the other hand, he asserts in *'Abqarīyat 'Umar* that Muḥammad had actually appointed Abū Bakr to succeed him, and that he knew by a dream that 'Umar would follow Abū Bakr as leader (130-32; see also Nijim, p. 52, n. 1). In either case, Shī 'ites would naturally have faulted al-'Aqqād.

[10] A reference to his book *Mu'āwiyah.* As governor of Syria, Mu'āwiyah had opposed 'Alī 's authority as the fourth Caliph. In the confrontation that followed, he emerged as the leader of the Sunnī Muslim community, establishing the Umayyad dynasty. He was a decisive and shrewd leader, yet he knew when to be forbearing to his enemies (Shaban, 1:73-80). As noted in the Introduction (p. 34), al-'Aqqād's book is more reserved in its assessment of Mu'āwiyah than is the case with his other studies of early Islamic figures.

[11] The words "with the title *The Life of Christ*" are present in ed. 2 but have been deleted by the editors in ed. 3. The fact that the original title had been changed for ed. 2, and that the new title was reinforced through editorial changes in ed. 3, may give some indication as to the nature of the criticism regarding the first edition. See the Introduction, p. 45-46, and Appendix A, pp. 241-42.

Chapter 4
The Messiah

[1] In fact, messianic movements among American Indian tribes are not original to their religions, but have arisen primarily as a result of contact with Westerners. In North America, this has been true primarily among the Plains Indians, the best example being the Ghost Dance movement of 1890 (Sam D. Gill, *Native American Religions: An Introduction* [Belmont, CA: Wadsworth, 1982], 164-67). In South America, a similar reactionary movement had occurred among the Andean Indians in the sixteenth century (ER, s.v. "South American Indians: Indians of the Andes," [13:471]). For a thorough phenomenonological study of reactionary messianic movements among aboriginal peoples, see Bryan R. Wilson, *Magic and the Millennium: A Sociological Study of Religious Movements of Protest among Tribal and Third-World Peoples* (New York: Harper & Row, 1973).

[2] Al-'Aqqād here provides a footnote (in Arabic) indicating that this quotation is from Jack Finegan, *Light from the Ancient East,* p. 79. The title of Finegan's book is actually *Light from the Ancient Past* (Princeton: Princeton University Press, 1946; an expanded second edition was published in 1959). It is possible that al-'Aqqād confused the title with a work by Adolf Deissmann, *Light from the Ancient East* (London: Hodder and Stoughton, 1927). Finegan in turn acquired this quotation from James Henry Breasted, *The Dawn of Conscience* (New York: Charles Scribner's Sons, 1933), 198. Al-'Aqqād's Arabic translation is fairly exact, although partial. The quotation rendered here follows Finegan (and Breasted), with ellipses to indicate omissions by al-'Aqqād.

Ipuwer was an Egyptian sage who lived, perhaps, during the period between the Old and Middle Kingdoms (2300-2050 B.C.E.). He is unknown apart from the single oracle from which this quotation is taken. The full text in English, with introduction, is given in James B. Pritchard, ed., *Ancient Near Eastern Texts Relating to the Old Testament,* 3d ed. (Princeton: Princeton University Press, 1969), 441-44, and the definitive study is Alan H. Gardiner, *The Admonitions of an Egyptian Sage* (Leipzig: J. C. Hinrichs, 1909). The oracle comprises Ipuwer's complaint against the Pharaoh for allowing a breakdown in the social and economic structure. While both Breasted and Finegan interpret this particular passage in a messianic manner, such a conclusion is open to question. Gardiner (79-80) offers a convincing argument that the reference is not to a future coming ruler, but is an idealized picture of how the Pharaoh should have acted.

[3] Marduk, originally an obscure god of the Sumerian pantheon, eventually became the chief deity in twelfth-century B.C.E. Babylon. There is no evidence for al-ʻAqqād's claim that the Babylonians believed Marduk would return in a messianic sense. One text from the period has been thought to refer to Marduk's past death and resurrection, but this interpretation is today considered untenable. See "Marduk" in ER, s.v. "Marduk"; and Helmer Ringgren, *Religions of the Ancient Near East,* trans. John Sturdy (Philadelphia: Westminster, 1973), 85-87.

[4] Ar. *al-majūs,* which can also be translated as "the Mazdeans" or "the Magi."

[5] The belief did indeed develop in Zoroastrianism that a series of three saviors would appear every thousand years. However, these saviors were to be conceived from the miraculously preserved seed of Zarathushtra, rather than a re-appearance of the prophet himself. See ER, s.v. "Zoroastrianism" (15:586); Mary Boyce, *Zoroastrians: Their Religious Beliefs and Practices* (London: Routledge & Kegan Paul, 1979), 42, 74-75.

[6] ʻAmr al-Jāḥiẓ (d. 255/869) was a popular prose writer during the middle ʻAbbāsid period, known for his anecdotal style and his extreme ugliness. In his numerous works he supported the ʻAbbāsid dynasty, Muʻtazilite theology, and social etiquette. His treatise against Christians was noted in the Introduction (p. 8). For a general discussion, see EI^2, s.v. "al-Djāḥiẓ"; or Marshall G.S. Hodgson, *The Venture of Islam: Conscience and History in a World Civilization* (Chicago: University of Chicago Press, 1974), 1:466-68. A more thorough overview is in Pellat, 3-27.

[7] Al-Naẓẓām (d. between 220/835 and 230/845) was a theologian of the Muʻtazilite school and also a respected poet. However, his theology was elaborate and speculative; even his pupil al-Jāḥiẓ, who greatly admired him, rejected his more eccentric claims (EI^2, s.v. "al-Naẓẓām").

[8] The source for this quotation among al-Jāḥiẓʻ many works has not been identified. However, a similar statement concerning al-Naẓẓām is attributed to al-Jāḥiẓ in one of the standard modern Arabic biographical dictionaries, Khayr al-Dīn al-Ziriklī, *Al-Aʻlām: Qāmūs Tarājim lil-Ashhar al-Rijāl wa-al-Nisāʼ min al-ʻArab wa-al-Mustaʻribīn wa-al-Mustashriqīn* [The Eminent Ones: A Biographical Dictionary of the Best Known Men and Women among the Arabs, as well as Arabists and Orientalists], 3d ed. (Beirut: Dār al-ʻIlm lil-Malāyīn, 1979), 1:43.

[9] The Talmud refers to either of the two encyclopedic collections of Jewish law and theology which served to define post-biblical, or "rabbinic," Judaism (ABD, s.v. "Talmud"). It is composed of the Mishnah (the third-century C.E. collection of rabbinic legal traditions) and the Gemara (subsequent rabbinic commentary on the Mishnah) (ABD, s.v. "Mishnah" and "Gemara"). Haggadah refers to a variety of rabbinic literature, including narrative, anecdotal and homiletical material (ABD, s.v. "Haggadah").

Al-ʻAqqād's presentation in the remainder of this chapter reflects a somewhat traditional Christian understanding which assumes that the Old Testament spoke directly of a futuristic "Messiah," and which presupposes among the Jewish people of Jesus' day a universal expectation of a messianic king who would overthrow the Romans and establish a time of peace and prosperity. More recent scholarship has shown that this concept was much more vague and complex. Old Testament references to a "Messiah" were always applied to a political or religious leader of that time who was considered to be appointed by God. Although references to "Messiah" in other early Jewish literature often point to a future ideal king similar to David, there was actually a wide variety of interpretations among different Jewish groups concerning the Messiah. Rabbinic sources, such as those mentioned by al-'Aqqād here, are late and offer nothing definitive concerning messianic expectations prior to 70 C.E. See ABD, s.v. "Messiah"; EJ, s.v. "Messiah"; and, for extensive treatments: Schürer, 2:488-554; and James H. Charlesworth, ed., *The Messiah: Developments in Earliest Judaism and Christianity* (Minneapolis: Fortress Press, 1992), especially the chapter "The Concepts of *Māšîaḥ* and Messianism in Early Judaism" by S. Talmon, 79-115.

[10] Ar. *al-masḥ,* from the same root as *al-masīḥ,* meaning "the Anointed One," "the Messiah," or "Christ." In Hebrew, the Messiah, *māšîaḥ,* also means "the Anointed One." The title "Christ" comes from the Greek equivalent, *christos.*

[11] Gen. 28:18-19. It should be noted, however, that the specific word for "anoint" is not present in the biblical text here (in Hebrew or Arabic).

[12] Ex. 30:22-30. Al-'Aqqād is very selective in his quotation of this passage, such that his rendition is unclear. The portions appearing in brackets have been added from the biblical text. The words within the middle set of brackets, however, are present in ed. 1 and 2, but are missing in ed. 3; this is apparently a case of haplography.

[13] 1 Chron. 16:22.

[14] Isa. 45:1. The ascription of this term to a Gentile king who had never acknowledged the God of Israel is certainly unusual; nevertheless, it is a recognition of the pivotal role played by Cyrus in Israel's history of salvation. In any case, Cyrus is merely the agent; it is God who is seen to bring about this accomplishment. (John L. McKenzie, *Second Isaiah: Introduction, Translation, and Notes,* The Anchor Bible, ed. William Foxwell Albright and David Noel Freedman, vol. 20 (Garden City, NY: Doubleday, 1968), 76-78.

[15] Hab. 3:13. Al-'Aqqād assumes here that the parallelism of "people" and "anointed" indicates identification. (The same feature is present in Ps. 28:8, which he evidently had in mind in his reference to the Psalms.) However, the nature of Hebrew poetry does not require a complete identification of parallel lines, and in fact this is usually not the case. It is better to understand the "anointed one" as the Israelite king who also stands as the representative of his people. In other passages of the Psalms where the "anointed one" appears, the reference is clearly to the king, e.g. Ps. 2:2, 20:6. See Ralph L. Smith, *Micah-Malachi,* Word Biblical Commentary, ed. David A. Hubbard and Glenn W. Barker, vol. 32 (Waco, TX: Word Books, 1984), 116; and ABD, s.v. "Parallelism."

[16] This statement is incorrect. In Jewish post-biblical literature, the Messiah is sometimes referred to as a descendent of Joseph, or that he was prefigured in the person of Moses; but neither of these figures are ever identified as a Messiah (Raphael Patai, *The Messiah Texts* [Detroit: Wayne State University Press, 1979], 165-67).

[17] Isa. 53:3. This passage makes no mention of a "Messiah"; rather it is a poem which speaks of the "Servant" of Yahweh who suffers on behalf of his people. There is no indication as to the identity of the Servant, but he was probably understood to be a contemporary historical person. The application of this passage to Jesus was an early Christian development which is already present in the NT. (McKenzie, 132-36).

[18] Zech. 9:9. This passage as well does not mention a "Messiah"; however, the figure depicted is a coming, victorious king, and the tone of the passage is clearly eschatological. The fact that the

king comes riding on a donkey is indicative of his humble advent, without the need for a show of military force. Jesus may well have modeled his "Triumphal Entry" into Jerusalem on these words; in any case, the early church believed that this passage was fulfilled in that event, as evidenced in Mt. 21:5 and Jn. 12:14-15. (Smith, *Micah-Malachi,* 255-56).

[19] Al-'Aqqād renders the name of Elijah first as *Īlīyā,* according to the Arabic Bible, then, in parentheses, as *Ilyās,* according to the Qur'ān.

Actually, only one passage predicts the coming of Elijah, namely Mal. 4:5-6, where it says simply that he will precede the "day of the Lord." It was later Jewish thought which claimed that Elijah would appear before the Messiah (Smith, *Micah-Malachi,* 342). However, Elijah was also seen as figurative of the Messiah as such (Charlesworth, 368). According to Matthew, Jesus applied the name of Elijah to John the Baptist rather than to himself (Mt. 11:13-14).

[20] Although Roman rule in Syria (which incorporated Palestine) officially began in 65 B.C.E., Palestine itself, along with the rival factions of the Hasmonean dynasty, was not subdued until the invasion of Pompey in 63 B.C.E. (Schürer, 1:236-41).

[21] The implication of this paragraph is that both concepts concerning the Messiah (i.e., the Messiah as King and the Messiah as Guide) were present among the Jews when Jesus embarked on his mission. As noted above, the actual situation seems to have been more complicated.

Chapter 5
Prophecy Among the Israelites

[1] Ar. *khitām al-nubū'āt,* lit., "the seal of the prophecies." This statement could strictly apply only to Judaism, Christianity and Islam, each of which has generally rejected prophecy or prophets bringing divine revelation subsequent to its own. Al-'Aqqād's terminology, however, is distinctly Islamic, since Muḥammad is said to have been "the seal of the prophets" (*khātam al-nabīyīn,* Qur'ān 33:40).

[2] Al-'Aqqād speaks here as a Muslim addressing his co-religionists. He had remarked previously that prophets had appeared only within the Semitic race (Preface, p. 69), and this reflects the concept of the prophet in the Qur'ān (see n. 3 to the Preface). Here, it should be observed that the Qur'ān identifies a number prophets by name, and most of these names are important figures of the OT. However, only a few of these are designated as prophets in the OT; and, more importantly, the vast majority of people designated as "prophets" in the OT are not mentioned in the Qur'ān (see EI[2], s.v. *"nabī";* and Bijlefeld, "A Prophet," 16-17). Thus, Muslims would consider the appearance of a true prophet to have been a rare phenomenon; they would find the frequent reference in the OT to various figures as "prophets" as rather strange, even inappropriate.

[3] 1 Kg. 22:6. The example which al-'Aqqād chooses here is questionable. As he observes later in this chapter, the four hundred "prophets" turn out to have been inspired by a "lying spirit" sent by God to deceive King Ahab (vv. 19-23).

[4] Ar. *'ulamā' ummatī ka-'anbiyā' bani Isrā'īl.* This *Ḥadīth* is not found among any of the six canonical collections, and thus is not considered strong. Among several non-canonical collections of *aḥādīth,* it is included in Jamāl al-Dīn 'Abd al-Raḥmān al-Suyūṭī, *Al-Durar al-Muntathirah fī al-Aḥādīth al-Mushtahirah* [Scattered Pearls among Famous Ḥadīth Traditions], ed. Muḥammad ibn Luṭfī al-Ṣibāgh (Riyad: 'Imādat Shu'ūn al-Maktabāt — Jāmi'at al-Malak Sa'ūd, 1983), p. 148 (no. 294). It is interesting to note the al-'Aqqād places the name "Muḥammad," along with the saluta-

tion, in parentheses after "the Prophet"; probably he felt the need to be specific in light of his discussion of the many prophets.

[5] Ar. *al-'ālim al-faqīh.* As technical terms in Islam, there is some overlap in the connotation of these words. The term *'ālim* (pl. *'ulamā',* from the verb *'alima,* "to know") is the more general of the two, indicating a recognized scholar (and usually teacher) of theology and law. The *faqīh* is the more specialized expert in *fiqh,* i.e., religious jurisprudence. (EI[1], s.v. *"'ulamā'";* and EI[2], s.v. *"faḳīh").*

As Munīf Luṭfī observes in his *Taqdīm* (Foreword) to the Beirut edition of ed. 2 (p. 4), al-'Aqqād is saying here that the majority of those called "prophets" in Israel had a more limited role than did the great prophets such as Abraham and Moses. The task of the larger group was to confirm, interpret and apply what had already been given. However, this distinction between two types of prophet is not represented in the OT. No specific conditions were required of a prophet except that he speak forth "the Word of the Lord" which came upon him. Numerous prophets thus arose, and there was a need (as al-'Aqqād notes) to distinguish genuine prophets from "false prophets." But there was otherwise no hierarchy among them. The only discernible distinction was a gradual evolution towards more professional and literary prophets. For a more thorough discussion, see ABD, s.v. "Prophecy (Preexilic Hebrew)" and "Prophecy (Postexilic Hebrew)"; and the general discussions in Klaus Koch, *The Prophets,* 2 vols. (Philadelphia: Fortress Press, 1982-84).

[6] Dt. 18:21-22. Al-'Aqqād places most of his reference to Dt. 18 in quotation marks. However the first portion is actually a loose paraphrase, although the second portion (rendered here as a quotation) follows VD for the most part. It is especially noteworthy that he refers to "prophets" like Moses when the biblical text has "prophet" in the singular. This passage has been interpreted by Muslims throughout the history of Christian-Muslim relations to be a prediction of the Prophet Muḥammad. On this see Watt, *Encounters,* 33.

[7] Dt. 13:1-3. The quotation marks are absent in the text, perhaps because al-'Aqqād has rearranged and abbreviated the biblical passage to some extent. However, much of the wording follows VD.

[8] Jer. 20:7-9. The phrase "you have persuaded me" is *aqna'tanī* here and also in VD. The Hebrew *pittīthanī* can also mean "deceive," as rendered in the RSV, and this is preferable. The passage thus portrays Jeremiah's bitter complaint to God because of the people's rejection of his message (J. A. Thompson, *The Book of Jeremiah,* The New International Commentary on the Old Testament, ed. R. K. Harrison [Grand Rapids, MI: William B. Eerdmans, 1980], 456-59). The Ar. wording somewhat diminishes the intensity of emotion present here; nevertheless, al-'Aqqād is undoubtedly attracted to the passage, since he will later portray Jesus as a prophet who faced a similar inner struggle.

[9] Jer. 23:15-16. The phrase "they nullify your work" is *yubaṭṭilūn 'amalakum,* as compared with the more stilted wording of VD, *yaj'alūnakum bāṭilan* ("they make you ineffective"). RSV has "filling you with vain hopes," which is preferable. The MT is problematic here, and the LXX may well preserve the better text (Thompson, *Jeremiah,* 496).

[10] 1 Kg. 22:23-24. Micaiah is not to be confused with the prophet Micah or the OT book attributed to him. The Arabic name for both is *Mīkhā.* Al-'Aqqād's previous reference in this chapter to the four hundred prophets is from the same passage.

The words "lying spirit" (Ar. *rūḥ kadhib)* are found in eds. 1 and 2, as well as VD. Ed. 3 has *al-rūḥ ka-dhālika,* which significantly alters the meaning of the sentence to read, "Behold, the Lord has likewise put the Spirit in the mouths of all these your prophets." The editors of ed. 3 apparently viewed the wording of this verse, which is accurately quoted by al-'Aqqād, as inappropriate. Indeed, the notion that God would provide inspiration which was intentionally deceptive is a concept difficult to appreciate, perhaps especially among Muslims.

[11] Dan. 10:3-5.

[12] This passage is actually found in ch. 10, vv. 5-6. In the biblical context, these words are spoken by the prophet Samuel to Saul, whom he had just anointed as king.

[13] 2 Kg. 3:14-15.

[14] Ezk. 1:1. Al-'Aqqād seems to have mistakenly omitted "the heavens," which is in the biblical text.

[15] Abimelech, according to Gen. 20, was the pagan king of Gerar who took Abraham's wife Sarah, believing her to be his sister. God warned him in a dream that he would die if he did not return her to Abraham. Balaam, according to Num. 22-24, was the pagan prophet whom the Moabite king Balaak summoned to pronounce a curse on the Israelites as they were preparing to enter Canaan. Instead, God inspired him to proclaim several blessings on the people.

[16] This reference does not clearly illustrate either of the situations in this paragraph. In Isa. 7:10-13, King Ahaz rather is given permission by God to ask for a sign. But the king refuses, claiming that he does not want to put God to the test. He is then reprimanded by the prophet Isaiah who states that it is his refusal which in fact tries the patience of God.

[17] Ar. *bid'ah,* the Islamic term for a practice or belief not established by the Qur'ān or the Sunnah, and hence often to be rejected (EI[2], s.v. *"bid'a").*

[18] Al-'Aqqād here speaks against the belief, somewhat prevalent among Muslims, that a true prophet could not be killed. Perhaps he had in mind the prophets Yaḥyā (John the Baptist) and his father Zakarīyā (Zechariah), both of whom are praised in the Qur'ān; yet according to Muslim tradition they were killed after Yaḥyā had denounced King Herod. See EI[1], s.v. "Yaḥyā" and "Zakārīyā" [*sic*].

[19] Al-'Aqqād seems not to be aware here of developments in the history of ancient Israel. Prophetic activity reached a climax of sorts among the literary prophets before, during and shortly after the Babylonian Exile; but then it began to wane. By the second century B.C.E., it was claimed that prophets no longer existed, and that none would come until the dawn of the eschatological future (see 1 Maccabees 9:27; Koch, 2:188). By the time of Christ, there may have been a general hope for a fresh "Word of the Lord," but there was no consensus as to how this would be mediated.

Chapter 6
Jewish Sects in the First Century

[1] Al-'Aqqād discusses the historicity of Jesus more thoroughly in ch. 11 (pp. 135-43; see the related notes there). Here, he argues that the existence of various sects in Judaism prove that Christ also existed, since his message met their needs. This argument can hardly be considered a strong one.

[2] E.g., 2 Sam. 8:17, 15:24; 1 Kg. 1:32-34. The general accuracy of al-'Aqqād's remarks about the Sadducees can be seen against modern discussions such as in ABD, s.v. "Sadducees"; and Schürer, 2:404-14; exceptions in matters of detail are noted. Although the Sadducees were closely connected with the Temple priesthood, it should not be construed that all Sadducees were

priests, nor all priests Sadducees (Schürer, 2:404-405).

[3] The Sadducees' complete rejection of oral tradition is firmly documented. However, the idea that they also rejected the writings of the Prophets is found only in the Church Fathers and has no factual basis. "A real rejection of the Prophets is unthinkable, but it is quite possible that the Sadducees considered only the Pentateuch as canonical in the strict sense of the word" (Schürer, 2: 408-409).

[4] Any association of the Sadducees with Epicurean philosophy is doubtful. See al-'Aqqād's comment regarding this in ch. 9 (p. 126), and n. 23 there.

[5] The Gospels and Acts refer to both Annas and Caiaphas as "High Priest" at the time of Jesus' ministry and shortly thereafter. The term in the Arabic Bible (both VD and modern versions) is *ra'īs al-kahinah.* (Al-'Aqqād refers to them here as "the leading priests," Ar. *kibār al-kahinah).* In fact, only Caiaphas was High Priest at that time; Annas had been High Priest between 6 and 15 C.E. Nevertheless, Annas continued to hold considerable influence following his tenure and into the period of Caiaphas. The NT references to Annas as High Priest, though technically incorrect, are probably best understood as an indication of his superior status among the ruling priests. (See ABD, s.v. "Annas" and "Caiaphas.") For the important roles of Annas and Caiaphas in the trial against Jesus according to the Gospels, see Mt. 26:3, 57-66, and Jn. 11:49-50, 18:12-14, 19-24.

The name Annas, here rendered as *Ḥanānīyā,* should be *Ḥannān* as it is found in the Arabic Bible (e.g., Lk. 3:2, Jn. 18:13). Al-'Aqqād seems to have confused this name with that of another later high priest, Ananias, who figures in the narrative about Paul (Acts 23:1-5, 24:1).

[6] There is considerable discussion among modern scholars concerning the nature and role of the Pharisees, but al-'Aqqād's remarks generally represent the consensus of opinion. However, his presentation is rather weak in highlighting the hallmarks of this group (in contrast to the Sadducees), i.e., their commitment to oral tradition and to ritual purity. See ABD, s.v. "Pharisees"; and Schürer, 2:388-403.

[7] Lev. 20:26.

[8] This discussion on the origin of the Pharisees' name is probably accurate, but the details can only be surmised from the data (Schürer, 2:396-98). The Hebrew word *pārūš* (the basis for the name "Pharisees") and the Arabic word *farz,* both having to do with "separation," can be considered reasonably equivalent within the Semitic family of languages.

[9] Ar. *thawratuhum al-ūlā.* Al-'Aqqād implies that the two incidents related in this paragraph apply only to the Pharisees; in fact, the records concerning them refer to pious Jews in general (see the following notes).

[10] Antiochus IV Epiphanes (d. 164 B.C.E.) was the Selucid ruler who sought to wipe out Jewish religion in Palestine and to Hellenize the region completely. Accounts of his devastation of Jerusalem and the Temple, and of the resistance of the Jews which led to their slaughter, are given in Josephus and the Apocryphal books of 1 and 2 Maccabees (Schürer, 1:151-54). The detail that he had swine offered on the altar of the Temple is related by Josephus *Jewish War* 1.1.2 (Loeb 2:3-4).

[11] Al-'Aqqād has paraphrased this incident (including the dialogue) as it is related in Josephus *Antiquities* 18.8.2-3 (Loeb 9:154-61). The Emperor Caligula (37-41 C.E.) had ordered Publius Petronius (governor of Syria 39-42 C.E.) to set up a statue of himself in the Temple in Jerusalem. Petronius tried to convince the Jews to acquiesce to Roman authority, but to no avail. As Petronius delayed carrying out the order, the crisis was defused, in part by King Agrippa's intercession before Caligula, and ultimately by Caligula's death. (Schürer, 1:394-96).

[12] The accuracy of this sentence is uncertain. The Pharisees were leaders in the worship and activities of the synagogue, but they were not entirely antithetical to the Temple (Schürer, 2:402).

[13] Ar. *ashadd min al-mutashaddadīn.* The exact meaning of this sentence is unclear, but probably the "conservatives" refer to the Sadducees.

[14] Ar. *qiyās,* the term used in Islamic jurisprudence for the principle by which regulations found in the Qur'ān and Sunnah are applied in a corresponding fashion to situations not explicitly covered in the two primary sources (EI², s.v. *"ḳiyās,"* 5:239).

[15] Ex. 21:24, Lev. 24:20, and Dt. 19:21.

[16] In fact, there does not seem to be any clear "Pharisaic" version of messianic hope prior to 70 B.C.E. As noted in ch. 4, n. 9, later Rabbinic ideas cannot necessarily be read back into the earlier part of the first century.

[17] Hillel and Shammai were prominent Jewish teachers among the Pharisees who lived during the late first century B.C.E. and the early first century C.E. The debates concerning the Jewish law which took place between them and their followers comprise the major part of the "oral law" that was later to define rabbinic Judaism. As al-'Aqqād notes, Hillel and his school were generally more liberal in their outlook, while Shammai and his school were more conservative. It was the school of Hillel which eventually gained prominence. For overviews, see EJ, s.v. "Hillel (the Elder)"; "Shammai"; and "Bet Hillel and Bet Shammai."

[18] This statement was the first in a series of phrases in which Hillel taught against the urge to accumulate. Most likely he means here that the person who allows himself to become obese will only produce more worms as his body rots in the grave. However, the Heb. word *basar,* like the Ar. *laḥm* used here, can mean "meat" as well as "flesh"; thus the first part of the statement could refer to a person's lust for meat. See Yitzhak Buxbaum, *The Life and Teachings of Hillel* (Northvale, NJ: Jason Aronson, 1994), 237-38.

[19] This is undoubtedly the most famous teaching of Hillel; however, he was probably repeating a common phrase which was already found in the book of Tobit 4:15. This in turn was the negative rewording of the command "you shall love your neighbor as yourself" (Lev. 19:18). Perhaps more important than the teaching itself was the manner in which he is said to have presented it: a Gentile asked that he be taught the entire law while he stood on one foot, and this was Hillel's response. Since this person would have been only beginning a study of the Torah, the negative dimension of this statement might then be considered as an initial step before the more difficult positive dimension could be followed. (EJ, s.v. "Hillel [the Elder] [12:484]; Buxbaum, 95-102).

[20] The historians consulted by al-'Aqqād have made a claim which cannot be supported and is unlikely. See al-'Aqqād's discussion of Jesus' education in ch. 23 (pp. 218-19), and n. 13 there.

[21] Ar. *al-āsīn aw al-asīniyīn.* Al-'Aqqād had used the former term for the Essenes at the beginning of this chapter, but the latter one is the more proper Ar. form. See his subsequent discussion on the etymology of the name.

[22] The most important classical sources on the Essenes are: Josephus *Jewish War* 2.8.2-13 (Loeb 2:366-85); Josephus *Antiquities* 18.1.5 (Loeb 9:14-21); Philo *Every Good Man is Free* 12-13 (Loeb 9:52-63); and Philo *Hypothetica* 11.1-18 (Loeb 9:436-43). A full compilation of classical sources (including a few minor references from other than Josephus and Philo) is presented in Geza Vermes and Martin D. Goodman, eds., *The Essenes According to the Classical Sources* (Sheffield: JSOT Press, 1989); see especially the fine summary of the data on pp. 2-6. Other excellent discussions are in ABD, s.v. "Essenes"; and Schürer, 2:555-74. Al-'Aqqād is clearly intrigued with this sect, and his presentation is generally well done.

[23] *āsī* in Arabic is the active participle of the verb *asā,* meaning to dress or treat a wound. The equivalent Aramaic word is *'asī '.*

[24] This statement concerning the relationship between Aramaic and Arabic is questionable. The

modern consensus is that Arabic formed one of two branches of the Central group of Semitic languages. The other branch, known as Syro-Palestinian or Northwest Semitic, comprised several languages including Aramaic, Hebrew, Phoenician and Ugaritic. The affinity which Arabic shares with Aramaic is best seen as one that it shares with the entire Syro-Palestinian branch. See ABD, s.v. "Languages (Introductory)," especially the chart on 4:157.

[25] Ar. *awrād* (sg. *wird*). This is a technical term in Islam, referring to a designated time of private prayer in addition to the five prescribed prayers, and also to the formulas recited on such an occasion. (EI[1], s.v. *"wird"*).

[26] Al-'Aqqād is correct that several theories have been advanced as to the etymology of the name "Essenes." The most common finds it to be a derivation of the Syriac word *ḥase'* meaning "pious." However, Vermes presents a strong case for the Essenes as "healers," similar to al-'Aqqād's remarks here. For a full overview, see "The Etymology of 'Essenes'" in Geza Vermes, *Post-Biblical Jewish Studies,* Studies in Judaism in Late Antiquity, ed. Jacob Neusner, vol. 8 (Leiden: E. J. Brill, 1975), 8-29.

[27] The claim that the Essenes borrowed from Pythagorean philosophy is quite conjectural. It was advanced by A. Dupont-Sommer, e.g., in his *The Jewish Sect of Qumran and the Essenes: New Studies on the Dead Sea Scrolls,* trans. R. D. Barnett (London: Vallentine, Mitchell & Co., 1954), 132 and elsewhere; but it is not held by most scholars. Aside from a few parallels between Pythagorean and Essene practice, the only substantial basis for this claim is a single statement by Josephus, that the Essenes were "a group which follows a way of life taught to the Greeks by Pythagoras" (*Antiquities* 15.10.4 [Loeb 8:178-79]). However, Josephus probably meant only to draw certain comparisons between the two groups rather than point to any direct influence of one on the other (see Schürer, 2:589-91 and the footnote in Loeb on 8:179). Al-'Aqqād discusses the Pythagoreans in more detail in ch. 9 (pp. 121-22); see the notes there.

Scholars today regard the origin of the Essenes to be either Palestine itself (Frank Moore Cross, "The Historical Context of the Scrolls," in Shanks, 20-32), or Babylonia (Hershel Shanks, "Essene Origins — Palestine or Babylonia?" in Shanks, 79-84).

[28] In fact, there is little evidence from Josephus and Philo indicating the nature of any messianic beliefs among the Essenes. Evidence from the Dead Sea Scrolls, however, points to a belief in both a kingly Messiah and a priestly Messiah in the Qumran community. See al-'Aqqād's comment at the end of ch. 1 (p. 77), and n. 31 there.

[29] Amos 5:21-24.

[30] Ar. *al-ghulāt,* sg. *ghālin* [extremist, fanatic]. The more proper Arabic word is *ghayūr* [jealous, zealous], a term applied to one of Jesus' disciples named Simon (Lk. 6:15). The Hebrew and Aramaic terms refer to "zeal" or "jealousy" (i.e., for the Law of God; Schürer, 1:382 n. 128, 2: 604).

[31] Overviews on the Zealots are given in ABD, s.v. "Zealots"; and Schürer, 1:381-82, 2:599-606. Terminology for the various Jewish rebel groups during the first century is problematic. The designation "Zealots" is sometimes applied to all such groups, beginning with Judas and his band. But their name more properly belongs to the later rebels in the Jewish War of 66-74 C.E. The followers of Judas were also called the "Sicarii." Although Judas himself was from the region of Galilee (the designation "Judas the Galilean" is found in Acts 5:37 as well as Josephus), the use of the name "Galileans" for his or any other rebel group is a misreading of Josephus (see ABD, s.v. "Galileans" [2:877]). As for the origin of the "Zealots," al-'Aqqād is quite mistaken in pointing to the Essenes. The group under Judas was an offshoot of the Pharisees (Schürer, 1:382); during the War, they were made up from various segments of society.

[32] The rebellion against the census of Quirinius actually took place in 6 or 7 C.E. (not B.C.E.), and is considered to be the commencement of the rebel activity of this period. The philosophical basis for Judas' revolt, as summarized by al-'Aqqād, is noted in Josephus *Antiquities* 18.1.1 (Loeb 9:4-7). Al-'Aqqād discusses the factors which led to this event in more detail in ch. 7 (pp. 110-112; see the notes there). He mentions the census again in ch. 11 (pp. 133-34) in relation to the birth of Jesus; there he states the date correctly.

[33] Here, al-'Aqqād apparently has in mind the incident related in Josephus *Antiquities* 17.6.2-3 (Loeb 8:438-47) and *Jewish War* 1.33.2-4 (Loeb 2:306-311). These passages report that Herod the Great had erected an eagle (the symbol of Rome) over the main gate of the Temple. Shortly before his death (4 B.C.E.), two leading Jews incited a large group of young men to join them in tearing it down. Their speech to the crowd was more of an encouragement to martyrdom than a threat to compliance. Josephus describes the two leaders as interpreters of the Jewish law who were held in esteem; Schürer takes this to mean "rabbis" (1:325). In any case, since this event took place well before the census, al-'Aqqād's designation of the two men as "Zealots" is definitely anachronistic. In fact, it would seem here that he considers this incident to be part of the revolt over the census; in the Ar. text there is no break or punctuation between the two accounts. However, he refers to the same incident in his discussion of Herod the Great, whom he knows to have died prior to the birth of Jesus (ch. 7, p. 109).

[34] The only mention of the death of this Judas (presumably when his revolt was crushed) is in Acts 5:37. Nothing is said there about his relatives.

[35] This is a fair assessment of Roman policy towards the Jews of Palestine (see Schürer, 1:356-57, 379-81).

[36] Al-'Aqqād has clearly confused the Assyrian conquest of the northern kingdom of Israel or Samaria (722 B.C.E.) with the Babylonian conquest of the southern kingdom of Judah (586 B.C.E.). According to 2 Kg. 17, Shalmaneser, the king of Assyria, deported the Israelites to his own country and repopulated Samaria with captives from other lands; a later king sent back a priest to teach them the religion of their land, but the result was a syncretistic system of worship.

However, according to an Assyrian inscription, relatively few Israelites were actually deported (see Pritchard, 284-85). The Samaritans themselves insisted they were direct descendants of the northern tribes of Ephraim and Manasseh, but undoubtedly considerable intermarriage occurred between the remaining Jews and the immigrant Gentiles. From all that can be determined about the Samaritan religion, it was essentially identical to Jewish monotheism. The primary differences were their adherence to Mount Gerizim as the only true holy site (their temple was built there sometime during the intertestamental period), and their rejection of all but the Pentateuch as valid scripture. Josephus included them within the wider population of Jews.

Nevertheless, the Jews who later returned from the Babylonian Exile refused to acknowledge the Samaritans or their religion as properly Jewish. Antagonism between the two groups was exacerbated when the Jewish Maccabean leader John Hyrcanus destroyed the Samaritan temple in 128 B.C.E. Later, the Romans managed to keep hostilities to a minimum. Despite many setbacks, the Samaritans have continued to exist as a separate entity, and today they number a few hundred. For details, see ABD, s.v. "Samaritans"; Schürer, 2:16-20.

[37] This, properly, is a reference to the Jews of the Babylonian Exile.

[38] See Ezr. 4:1-3.

[39] This statement is incorrect. The Samaritan temple was never rebuilt following its destruction by Hyrcanus; rather, the Roman Emperor Hadrian built a temple to Zeus on the same site at Mt. Gerizim in the second century C.E. This was converted to a church in the fifth century and was

destroyed by the Arab invasion of the seventh century. (ABD, s.v. "Gerizim, Mount").

[40] The chief city of Samaria, Shechem, was actually destroyed by the forces of John Hyrcanus in 107 B.C.E. The area lay devastated until the Emperor Hadrian built the city of Neapolis in 72 C.E., about a mile west of the ruins of Shechem. This was later called Nablus by the Arabs. (ABD, s.v. "Shechem (place)" [5:1185]; Schürer, 1:520-21).

[41] Al-'Aqqād's discussion in these two paragraphs concerning the influence which the Samaritans had on the messianic expectations of the Jews is quite conjectural. Although the concept among the Samaritans of a coming Messiah was somewhat similar to that found among the Jews (from what can be ascertained), there is no reason to suppose that the beliefs of either group had any bearing on the other (ABD s.v. "Samaritans" [5:946]; Schürer, 2:513).

[42] Josephus mentions in his autobiography that he lived with the desert hermit Bannus (who is otherwise unknown) for three years until the age of nineteen (*Life* 2 [Loeb 1:4-7]). However, he states in the same passage that he spent an equal amount of time learning about the Pharisees, the Sadducees and the Essenes, also completing this study at the age of nineteen. It is unclear whether the discrepancy is a problem of text or interpretation. (ABD, s.v. "Josephus" [3:982]). Al-'Aqqād's comments about Bannus are a paraphrase of Josephus' remarks.

[43] Ar. *Yaḥyā al-Mughtasil.* "Yaḥyā" is the Islamic name for the prophet John the Baptist. Muslim tradition does not provide a title following his name as does Christianity. It seems that al-'Aqqād wished to supply one, using a form of the verb *ghasala* [to wash] as an indication of John's role as one who baptized. But curiously, he chose a reflexive form of the verb, as if John's baptism were a ritual of self-cleansing. The assumption here, however, is that al-'Aqqād intended this word to parallel the Christian term "the Baptist," and so the translation "the Purifier" has been chosen.

[44] Ar. *Yūḥannā al-Ma'madān,* in agreement with the terminology of the Arabic Bible and of Arabic Christian usage. Al-'Aqqād devotes most of ch. 15 to the life and ministry of John.

[45] Biblical passages such as Ex. 33:7-14 seem to indicate that the earliest sanctuary among the Jews in the wilderness was a simple tent pitched outside the camp, called "the tent of meeting" (*khaymat al-ijtimā'* in the Ar. versions). However, the bulk of chapters 25-40 describe the construction within the camp of an elaborate Tabernacle (Ar. *al-maskan*), for which the term "tent of meeting" is also used. As al-'Aqqād indicates, this is said to have been a wooden frame covered with heavy curtains which could be disassembled and transported along with its furnishings. For details on the Tabernacle's history and construction, see ABD, s.v. "Tabernacle." While it is said that God appeared to Moses in the tent of meeting and to the High Priest in the Tabernacle, there is no indication that "prophets" in general received such visitations inside these structures.

[46] These figures are mentioned in 1 Chr. 22:14 as the amount which David had set aside for the construction of the Temple which his son Solomon was to supervise. David is also said to have made significant personal contributions (1 Chr. 29:3-4). It is estimated that in OT times a talent was equivalent to about 66 lbs. or 30 kg.; this was considered to be the load which a man could carry (ABD, s.v. "Weights and Measures" [6:905]).

[47] According to the financial sections of June 1952 editions of *Al-Aḥrām* and *The New York Times,* at the time al-'Aqqād wrote the Egyptian pound was worth about 0.19 pounds sterling, and the pound sterling was worth about 2.80 U.S. dollars. The equivalent to al-'Aqqād's half billion Egyptian pounds is thus about 95 million pounds sterling, or 266 million U.S. dollars.

Given that the figures in 1 Chr. calculate to about 3300 tons of gold and 3,300,000 tons of silver, al-'Aqqād's figure is but a fraction of the value of this incredible amount. It can only be assumed that the numbers are vastly exaggerated in the biblical text. Sara Japhet suggests that this hyperbole was intentional, in order to create "an impression of the grandeur and exaltation of the house of God, beyond the power of humans to conceive" (*I & II Chronicles: A Commentary,* Old Testament Library [London: SCM Press, 1993], 400).

[48] Cyrus' edict giving permission for the Jews to build the Temple was actually issued in 538 B.C.E. Two versions of the proclamation, each with its own details, are recorded in the book of Ezra, one in Hebrew (1:2-4; a shortened form is in 2 Chr. 36:23) and one in Aramaic (6:3-5). (A Greek rendition in the Apocryphal book 1 Esdras 2:3-7 is a translation of the Hebrew version). Ezr. 3:8 states that construction began "in the second year of their coming to the house of God in Jerusalem" (RSV); this is usually assumed to mean 536 B.C.E., but this verse could be interpreted such that a later date is preferable. See H. G. M. Williamson, *Ezra, Nehemiah,* Word Biblical Commentary, ed. David A. Hubbard and Glenn W. Barker, vol. 16 (Waco, TX: Word Books, 1985), 8, 47.

[49] Details concerning the Jewish Temple at the time of Jesus can be found in many sources, e.g. ABD, s.v. "Temple, Jerusalem." References in Schürer are thorough but scattered. A fine systematic presentation is in S. Safrai and M. Stern, *The Jewish People of the First Century: Historical Geography, Political History, Social, Cultural and Religious Life and Institutions,* Section 1 in Compendia Rerum Iudaicarum ad Novum Testamentum (Philadelphia: Fortress Press, 1974-76), 2:865-907. Most of al-'Aqqād's comments here are accurate.

[50] Al-'Aqqād's low assessment of the Temple's influence in the first century is one aspect of his discussion that cannot be substantiated. Despite the rise of other facets of religious life such as the synagogue, the Temple retained a central role in the lives of most Jews. It was regarded as the dwelling-place of Israel's God and thus it was believed that it would exist eternally. The psychological impact of the Temple's destruction in 70 C.E. was at least as great as any other aspect of the devastation which occurred at that time. See Safrai and Stern, 2:904-906.

[51] Al-'Aqqād has chosen distinctly Islamic terminology to describe this aspect of the priestly/ Levitical duties: Ar. *imāmat al-ṣalāt wa-al-iftā' fī masā'il al-fiqh.*

[52] This is inaccurate; marriage and burial rites were local, community events, although records of such were kept in the Temple (Safrai and Stern, 2:752-60, 773-87).

[53] Zerubbabel's name more precisely means "seed of Babylon." He was a descendant of David and governor of postexilic Judah during the restoration of the Temple. Ezr. 2:1-2 seems to indicate that he led the first group of exiled Jews back to Palestine following the edict of Cyrus. However, this would equate him with Sheshbazzar (Ezr. 1:11), an identification which other passages seem to deny. Ezr. ch. 2 may be a composite sketch of those who returned in various stages. (ABD, s.v. "Zerubbabel").

The figures recorded for the numbers of priests from each of four clans who returned from the Exile are identical in Ezr. 2:36-39 and Neh. 7:39-42, producing a sum of 4289 priests. The total is one less in 1 Esdras 5:24-25.

[54] Josephus reports that there were 20,000 priests living in Judea. Their participation in the Temple ceremonies was according to division and lot, and many were never chosen. However, priests lived throughout Palestine and were often involved in other occupations as well. (Safrai and Stern, 2:580-96; Schürer, 2:238-74).

[55] Ar. *fuqahā' al-dīn.* The Scribes were the specialists of the Jewish law who studied it and interpreted it for the people. A Scribe was highly respected and was usually addressed as "Rabbi," meaning "my lord." Although most Scribes were also Pharisees, this was not universally the case; some were found among the Sadducees. (Schürer, 2:322-36). See n. 3 above concerning al-'Aqqād's statement on p. 95 that the Sadducees' acknowledged only the Pentateuch.

[56] Much remains obscure about the history and nature of the "Great Sanhedrin" in Jerusalem; al-'Aqqād's comments reflect what can be determined fairly accurately. The number twenty-three, however, did not apply to the Great Sanhedrin but to the number of members of the various smaller Sanhedrins which were set up in other towns around Palestine. The Great Sanhedrin was directed by the High Priest and dominated by members of the priesthood and the Sadducees, but most likely Pharisees were also included. For details, see ABD, s.v. "Sanhedrin"; Schürer, 2:200-226.

[57] Num. 11:16-17.

[58] This statement is actually based on a very uncertain passage in the Talmud. Other evidence is divided as to whether the Sanhedrin could execute a capital sentence on its own, and the matter continues to be debated. See Schürer, 2:221-23.

[59] Since the attitude of the Sanhedrin regarding the people and regarding the ministry of Jesus can only be surmised from the NT and other sources, this paragraph must be considered conjectural. However, given the aristocratic position of the Sanhedrin's members and its probable ties to local Roman authority, al-'Aqqād's remarks here may well represent the actual situation.

[60] Ar. *al-nadhrīyīn aw al-mandhūrīn.* These are derivatives of the verb *nadhara,* meaning "to make a vow" or "to consecrate." The term in the Arabic Bible is *nadhīr* which is taken from the Heb. *nāzîr.* However, the Ar. word *nadhīr* more properly means "warner" (from the fourth form of this verb, i.e., *anthara,* meaning "to warn"), and it is frequently so used in the Qur'ān, e.g. 35:42. This is probably why al-'Aqqād uses *nadhrī* rather than *nadhīr* to indicate the Nazirite. Nevertheless, he makes use of the concept of warning in his discussion below.

Virtually the only biblical source concerning the status and requirements of the Nazirite is Num. 6:1-21. Al-'Aqqād's discussion reflects this passage fairly accurately. Several other sources give evidence to its ongoing practice, and it receives considerable discussion in the Mishnah and Talmud; but there is no indication as to popularity of the Nazirite vocation among the people. (See EJ, s.v. "Nazirite").

[61] Ar. *al-jihād fī sabīl al-dīn.*

[62] Ar. *yundhiru,* from the fourth form of the verb *nadhara.*

[63] While al-'Aqqād's discussion of the Arabic word *nadhīr* is acceptable, his suggestion about the Hebrew word *nāzîr* is not plausible, since that does not carry the sense of warning others, but only of one who is consecrated to God (Francis Brown, S. R. Driver, and Charles A. Briggs, *A Hebrew and English Lexicon of the Old Testament.* [Oxford: Clarendon Press, 1907], 634).

[64] Amos 2:11-12. The words "from among you" *(min baynakum)* is an obvious misreading or mistranscription by al-'Aqqād of the Arabic biblical text, which has "from your sons" *(min banīkum).* The final words, *an yadda'ū al-nubū'ah,* are a less than satisfactory paraphrase of VD, which reads *qā'ilīn lā tatanabba'ū,* "and you charged the prophets saying, 'Do not prophesy!'"

[65] There is no evidence concerning the number of people who might have become Nazirites at the time of Christ. The lack of such evidence would seem to indicate that only a few had chosen this path in life.

The various chronological schemes concerning the coming of the Messiah, the Resurrection, etc., which had existed among the Jews at that time were extremely complex. They were generally based on the prophecy concerning the seventy weeks in Dan. 9:24-27, but there were many different systems of calculation and many variations within each system. The belief in the Messiah's appearance four thousand years after the creation of the world was one of the most common, as evidenced by the pseudepigraphical work *The Assumption of Moses* (composed about the time of Jesus' birth). Among the later rabbis, this period was generally believed to be six thousand years, corresponding to the six days of creation in accordance with Ps. 90:4, as mentioned here by al-'Aqqād. (See Roger T. Beckwith, *Calendar and Chronology, Jewish and Christian: Biblical, Intertestamental and Patristic Studies,* Arbeiten zur Geschichte des antiken Jundentums und des Urchristentums, no. 33 [Leiden: E. J. Brill, 1996], 217-75, and especially 264-66; and Schürer, 2:523-24).

[66] Al-'Aqqād is here making a play on two words which sound very similar: *manẓūran,* meaning "anticipated," and *mandhūran,* meaning "consecrated." The Nazirites *(al-nadhīrūn)* are thus "those who are anticipating" *(nāẓirūn)* the Messiah.

[67] It would seem that al-'Aqqād is making a veiled reference here to Jesus as a Nazarite. But from the remarks which follow, this is not clear.

[68] See above (n. 43) concerning al-'Aqqād's designation of John as *al-Mughtasil,* here translated as "the Purifier." Whether or not John the Baptist was considered to be a Nazirite continues to be debated among scholars. In favor of this claim is R. Brown (*Birth,* 273-74); but Meier fails to see sufficient historical evidence for its support (2:48-49, 90 n. 138).

[69] The Heb. for "Nazirite" is *nāzîr;* "Nazarene" in Heb. is *nāṣrî* (or incorrectly *nōṣrî)* from *nāṣrat,* "Nazareth," although neither term is found in the OT (see Reuben Alcalay, *The Complete English-Hebrew Dictionary* [Tel Aviv: Massadah, 1962], 2438, and Ernest Klein, *A Comprehensive Etymological Dictionary of the Hebrew Language for Readers of English* [New York: Macmillan, 1987], 424). The similarity is also present between the Gk. terms found in the NT: *nazeiraios* for "Nazirite," and both *nazōraios* and *nazarēnos* for "Nazarene."

Clearly, Jesus' social behavior did not qualify him as a Nazirite in the strict sense of the word. However, it could be that his followers preferred to view him in this fashion. Most important here is Matthew's enigmatic quotation of a supposed OT text in Mt. 2:23: "He shall be call a Nazarene." This is quite likely a play on words, in which Matthew simultaneously identifies Jesus' home town as Nazareth, and also his consecration as a Nazirite. See Brown, *Birth,* 223-25; and W. D. Davies and Dale C. Allison, Jr., *A Critical and Exegetical Commentary on the Gospel According to Saint Matthew,* The International Critical Commentary on the Holy Scriptures of the Old and New Testaments, ed. J. A. Emerton, C. E. B. Cranfield, and G. N. Stanton (Edinburgh: T & T Clark, 1988-97), 1:275-77.

The term "Nazarenes" was also applied to the early Christians by their Jewish opponents, according to Acts 24:5. This designation was apparently based on the name Nazareth. "Nazarenes" continued to be used for Christians, in writings by both Jewish Christians and Jewish antagonists. However, among Gentile followers of Jesus, the term "Christians" was preferred. By the fourth century, Christian writers completely disowned this title. In 375, the bishop Epiphanius applied it instead to a Jewish-Christian group which he considered heretical. See ABD, s.v. "Nazarenes."

[70] Nazareth was indeed a very obscure village. It is never mentioned in the OT, Josephus, Philo, or any other early Jewish literature. Nevertheless, archaeology indicates that it has been inhabited since the seventh century B.C.E. That the adult Jesus came from Nazareth is beyond dispute. (Meier, 1:229, 268, 300 n. 77).

[71] Ar. *al-ṭalī'ah. Nadhīrah* technically means "a votive offering." In fact, the etymology for "Nazareth" is rather uncertain (ABD, s.v. "Nazareth"). Al-'Aqqād's argument here is convoluted and quite speculative.

[72] Mt. Hermon (Ar. *jabal al-shaykh* [mountain of the old man]) is the highest peak of the Anti-Lebanon range. Mt. Carmel is a mountain range on the Mediterranean coast, due west of Nazareth. "Ibn 'Āmir" is a correction of the text (all editions), which has *Ibn 'Amīr.* Ibn 'Āmir (d. 118/736) was one of the *tābi'ūn* (the generation which followed that of the Companions of the

Prophet Muḥammad). He was a *qāḍī* of Damascus and is associated with one of the seven official "readings" of the Qur'ān. (EI^2, s.v. "Ibn 'Āmir"). According to a native Palestinian acquaintance, the area of land bearing the name of Ibn 'Āmir lies a few miles south-west of Nazareth.

[73] Ar. *al-mandhūrīn* and *al-nadhīrah,* respectively.

Chapter 7
Political and Social Life in the First Century

[1] This revolt, also called "the War of the Gladiators," broke out in Italy in 73 B.C.E. Spartacus, a Thracian, led a small group of gladiator slaves who seized Mt. Vesuvius. Roman efforts to quell the uprising initially ended in failure, and the rebels grew in number and took control over the entire south of Italy. The following year, the rebellion lost momentum, and Spartacus and his troops were crushed by Crassus in 71. Pompey actually arrived late on the scene from his successful campaigns in Spain. Although his task was merely to subjugate the remaining fugitives, he sought to take equal credit with Crassus for the victory. For an overview, see S. A. Cook, F. E. Adcock, and M. P. Charlesworth, *The Cambridge Ancient History,* vol. 9, *The Roman Republic: 133-44 B.C.* (Cambridge: Cambridge University Press, 1932), 329-32; and for a more detailed presentation, see Keith R. Bradley, *Slavery and Rebellion in the Roman World, 140 B.C.-70 B.C.* (Bloomington and Indianapolis: Indiana University Press, 1989), 83-101.

[2] Al-'Aqqād's remarks in this sentence are problematic. The reference to a three-year rebellion should more properly be two years in the case of Spartacus and his followers. The reference to seventy thousand participants more properly belongs to the uprising in Sicily mentioned in the next paragraph; see the following note.

[3] This uprising is known as the First Servile War. The slave Eunus was known as a wonder-worker and claimed to foretell the future by means of visions from the gods. The year when the uprising began is actually unknown; sometime between 141 and 135 B.C.E. is most likely. The year when it ended, however, is known to be 132 B.C.E. Al-'Aqqād's estimate of a ten-year rebellion is thus probably too long. In one key battle during this period, the number of rebels was estimated by Livy at 70,000; thus, al-'Aqqād's reference to this figure in the previous paragraph probably belongs here. See Cook, Adcock and Charlesworth, 9:11-16; Bradley, 46-65.

[4] This was the uprising in 132 B.C.E. led by Aristonicus. Apparently of royal blood, he stood to inherit the rule of Pergamum. When it passed instead into Roman hands, he sided with the slaves in rebellion. Under the influence of the Stoic philosopher Blossius of Cumae, Aristonicus attempted to establish a socialist society. This was named and patterned after the utopian "Sun-State," envisioned by Iambulus of the third century B.C.E., which would be without class distinction and was based on a unity of concord and love. See Cook, Adcock and Charlesworth, 9:103-104; and William Tarn, *Hellenistic Civilisation,* 3rd ed. rev. by William Tarn and G. T. Griffith (London: Edward Arnold, 1952), 40-41, 122, 125.

[5] In fact, the "Sun-State" did not last long. After only limited success with his policies, Aristonicus surrendered to Roman forces two years after the initial uprising. (Cook, Adcock and Charlesworth, 9:104-105).

[6] The precise manner in which the first revolt in Sicily ended is not clear. Bradley gives a report that twenty thousand slaves died at this time (61), whereas Cook, Adcock and Charlesworth believe that there was no large-scale massacre and instead the slaves were returned to their owners

(9:15-16). In any case, al-'Aqqād undoubtedly meant to refer instead to the tragic end of the rebellion in Italy under Spartacus, in which six thousand slaves were crucified by Crassus along the Appian Way (Cook, Adcock and Charlesworth, 9:332; Bradley, 98).

[7] Details of this are in Cook, Adcock and Charlesworth, 9:55-60.

[8] Al-'Aqqād has mistakenly identified the person here as Julius (Ar. *yūliyūs)* Philippus, a Roman emperor of the third century C.E. (OCD, s.v. "Philippus [1]"). The name should be Lucius Marcius Philippus, a tribune who was later to have an influential career (ibid., s.v. "Philippus [4]"). The purpose of his law can in fact only be conjectured, since it was withdrawn before voting took place. See Cook, Adcock and Charlesworth, 9:164.

[9] Cicero *De Officiis* 2.21.73 (Loeb 21:248-49).

[10] The Roman territory of Carthage had been partitioned into several (probably six) administrative districts. These were placed under the oversight of local Carthaginians, whose rule was harsh and unpopular. See J. D. Fage, ed., *The Cambridge History of Africa*, vol. 2, *From c. 500 BC to AD 1050* (Cambridge: Cambridge University Press, 1978), 129-31.

[11] Ar. *al-ḥawārī*. This is the Qur'ānic term for a disciple of Jesus, whereas the Arabic Biblical words are *tilmīdh* [disciple] and *rasūl* [apostle].

[12] Mt. 8:20 = Lk. 9:58. As written, al-'Aqqād's statement is inaccurate. Although the birth of Jesus occurred during the reign of Augustus (27 B.C.E. - 14 C.E.), he conducted his ministry during the reign of Tiberius (14-37 C.E.).

This is the first instance in the book where the phrase "the Son of Man" appears. Al-'Aqqād recognizes that Jesus used it in reference to himself. See his discussion of the term in ch. 23, pp. 222-23; see n. 39 there and also ch. 19, p. 189, n. 28 concerning his understanding of this phrase.

[13] The Imperial Cult began when Julius Caesar was deified at his death, and it was developed under Augustus. It was a means by which Rome and its Emperor could be honored while Roman culture could be spread throughout the provinces. Strictly speaking, Augustus was deified only at his own death; but the divine honors bestowed on him during his life set a precedent for future Roman policy. (S. A. Cook, F. E. Adcock, and M. P. Charlesworth, *The Cambridge Ancient History*, vol. 10, *The Augustan Empire: 44 B.C.-A.D. 70* [Cambridge: Cambridge University Press, 1934], 481-89).

[14] Trajan was Emperor 98-117 C.E. His administration was strict and progressive, but reasonably humane; he expanded various frontiers of the Empire. He was succeeded by the more cultured Hadrian (117-138 C.E.), who consolidated the frontiers and reorganized the army. (OCD, s.v. "Trajan" and "Hadrian").

[15] Mt. 16:26 = Mk. 8:36 = Lk. 9:25.

[16] Ar. *al-Furs*. This term is primarily used of the Persians, but it can also refer to the Parthians. They were of nomadic origin and closely related to the Persians, ruling over the general territory of Persia from 248 B.C.E. - 38 C.E. (OCD, s.v. "Parthia"; and Cook, Adcock and Charlesworth, 9:574-613).

[17] Al-'Aqqād's figure of twenty years should more accurately read twenty-six. Following the Roman conquest of Syria and Palestine in 63 B.C.E., Pompey established uneasy relations with the Parthians. He had in mind to invade that Eastern empire, but he regarded this as too hazardous. The attempt was then made by Crassus in 53 B.C.E., but he was badly defeated and killed. The civil war (beginning 49 B.C.E.), which thrust Julius Caesar into absolute power, distracted the Romans from their concerns with Parthia. Meanwhile, Crassus' lieutenant Cassius held a firm control over Syria and Palestine. During that time, Jewish support for a Parthian takeover was actually much stronger than support for Rome. See Cook, Adcock and Charlesworth, 9:602-12;

Michael Grant, *The Jews in the Roman World* (New York: Charles Scribners' Sons, 1973), 58.

[18] Caesar had granted control of Palestine to the Idumeans Antipater and his sons. The Parthians then invaded Syria and Palestine in 40 B.C.E. and installed Antigonus as ruler in Jerusalem, a change which most Jews welcomed. Meanwhile, Herod, son of Antipater (later known as Herod the Great), gained imperial backing and the title of "king" in order to drive out the Parthians from the area once and for all, achieving final victory in 37 B.C.E. (See Cook, Adcock and Charlesworth, 10:47-50, 316-21; Grant, *The Jews,* 64-66).

[19] John Hyrcanus II had been High Priest almost continuously since 76 B.C.E., and he had consistently supported the Romans (Schürer, 1:267-80). The gruesome manner in which Hyrcanus was mutilated by Antigonus is related by Josephus *Jewish War* 1.13.9 (Loeb 2:124-27).

[20] This was in accordance with the regulations regarding priests set out in Lev. 21:16-23.

[21] A reference to Herod the Great, who ruled as Governor of Galilee (47-37 B.C.E.) and then over all of Palestine as King of the Jews (37-4 B.C.E.). His tribe had converted to Judaism during the second century B.C.E. His complex rule was characterized by self-advancement and unswerving loyalty to Rome; he sought to appease the Jews while also eliminating any trace of resistance. For details, see ABD, s.v. "Herod the Great"; Schürer, 1:287-329; and Grant, *The Jews,* 66-82. Al-'Aqqād provides a good, though brief, summary.

[22] Al-'Aqqād means here that Christ was born in Galilee itself, and not just the region as a whole. This would be in accordance with his statements to this effect later on p. 109, at the beginning of ch. 9 (p. 121), and especially at the beginning of ch. 10 (p. 129). However, other statements in this book show that he is quite inconsistent as to the birthplace of Jesus. See the discussion in the Introduction, pp. 55-56.

[23] Ar. *"al-mutarawmanīn."* This would be the second form passive participle of an assumed quadraliteral verb *(rawmana),* based on the term for the Romans, *al-Rūm.* Al-'Aqqād is fond of using innovative terminology, as evidenced elsewhere in this book.

[24] This is the same incident referred to by al-'Aqqād in ch. 6 (p. 100), concerning the two "Zealots" who pulled down the emblem of the eagle over the Temple gate. The details given here are included in the accounts of Josephus mentioned in ch. 6, n. 33. As noted there, the designation of the men as "Zealots" is anachronistic.

[25] This incident occurred a short time after that mentioned in the first part of the paragraph. It is reported by Josephus, who later stated that Herod's sister Salome did not carry out his order, but upon Herod's death allowed the men to go free (*Antiquities* 17.6.5, 17.8.2 [Loeb 8:450-55, 460-61] and *Jewish War* 1.33.6-8 [Loeb 2:312-17]; see also Schürer, 1:325-26).

[26] See n. 22 above.

[27] Ar. *al-ḥawārī* (see n. 11 above, concerning Matthew). In fact, Luke, who was a Gentile and a companion of Paul, was not among the initial followers of Jesus, nor was he considered to be one of the apostles.

[28] Lk. 19:12, 14. Despite al-'Aqqād's disclaimer, his quotation of these verses follows VD fairly closely, on a par with his other quotations from the Bible. He is not explicit as to the purpose of this quotation, but probably he wants to illustrate the efforts by all three sons (but especially Archelaus) to gain the entire kingdom of their father by traveling to Rome and arguing their cases before the Emperor Augustus. A delegation of Jews also went to Rome, pleading with the Emperor that none of them should rule. Augustus' decision was that the kingdom should be divided between the three sons, in accordance with Herod's last will. (Schürer, 1:330-35; Grant, *The Jews,* 83-86).

It can only be surmised whether this incident was intentionally in the background of Jesus' parable. In favor of this view is John Nolland, *Luke,* Word Biblical Commentary, ed. David A. Hubbard and Glenn W. Barker (Dallas: Word Books, 1989-93), 35C:914; against this is Joseph A. Fitzmyer, *The Gospel According to Luke,* The Anchor Bible, ed. William Foxwell Albright and David Noel Freedman (Garden City, NY: Doubleday, 1981-85), 28A:1234. In any case, it is interesting to note that the parallel to this parable in Mt. 25:14-30, which differs from Luke in several details, omits entirely this reference to the purpose of the man's journey and the hard feelings of his people towards him.

[29] Augustus' decision to partition the land among the three sons seems to have been mostly an attempt to achieve equity among all parties (Schürer, 1:333).

[30] See ch. 11.

[31] The reference here is to the revolt by Judas the Galilean and his band, precipitated by the census of Quirinius in 6 C.E., to which al-'Aqqād had referred in ch. 6 (p. 100; see n. 32 there). Here, it seems that al-'Aqqād has misunderstood the remarks by Josephus concerning the bloodshed which ensued because of the activities of Judas and others like him (*Antiquities* 18.1.1 [Loeb 9:4-9]); the passage there develops imperceptibly into a general statement covering the period from the census through the Jewish War of 66-74 C.E. The initial rebellion was actually put down fairly quickly; opposition to the census was abandoned due to the persuasion of the High Priest, and the census was allowed to proceed. However, resentment smoldered; Judas and others continued to incite occasional uprisings. (Schürer, 1:381-82; and Grant, *The Jews,* 89-91).

[32] Josephus mentions that Quirinius was sent by the Emperor (Augustus) to become the governor of Syria, and that he "also visited Judea, which had been annexed to Syria, in order to make an assessment (i.e., a census for the purpose of taxation, Gk. *apotimēsomenos)* of the property of the Jews and to liquidate the estate of Archelaus" (*Antiquities* 18.1.1 [Loeb 9:4-5]). He goes on to discuss the revolt against the census by Judas and his band, including their reasons for opposing it. Al-'Aqqād's presentation in the next several paragraphs incorporates this material while expanding on it considerably. However, his comments reflect the situation fairly accurately (see Grant, *The Jews,* 88-91; and Schürer, 1:381).

[33] Ar. *musaḥā',* pl. of *masīḥ,* [messiah, Christ].

[34] Ar. *mu'āmalah.* In fact, this word does not properly refer to a coin but to an activity involving business transaction. Al-'Aqqād has reproduced the word found in VD (Mt. 22:19), but VD has not accurately translated the Gk. word *nomisma* (used in the NT only here; the parallels in Mk. 12:15 and Lk. 20:24 use the word for "denarius"). Matthew's term refers specifically to the coin required by the state for payment of the tax. The modern Arabic translations more correctly have either *'umlah* [currency] or *naqd* [coin].

[35] This is a paraphrase of Mt. 22:16-21 = Mk. 13-17 = Lk. 20:20-25; in each of the parallel passages, the incident takes place during the week prior to the crucifixion. Al-'Aqqād's version follows the text of Matthew in VD fairly closely. There are two important differences, however. In the biblical text, those who question Jesus are disciples of the Pharisees who go *"with" (ma')* the Herodians rather "from" *(min)* them. Also, the biblical text prefaces their initial statement with *na'lamu,* "we know that. . . ." The "Herodians," as their name implies, supported Roman rule, but they are an otherwise unknown group. Presumably they were normally in opposition to the Pharisees. Here, they are shown to join forces in an attempt to trap Jesus: if he simply answered "yes," he would set himself against the nationalistic aspirations of the people; but if he answered "no," he would open himself to the charge of treason. His reply not only turns the tables on his opponents, but also conveys the essence of his teaching about God. (See Davies and Allison, 3:210-20; and Hagner, 33B: 633-37). Al-'Aqqād is clearly impressed with this saying of Je-

sus; he refers to it again in on pp. 153, 169 and 225.

36 In addition to the tithe, which covered the personal income of the priests, all male Jews age twenty and over were required to pay the "half-shekel tax"; this was utilized to defray the expenses of the sacrifices and other Temple activities (Schürer, 2:270-72).

37 Here, al-'Aqqād retains the biblical term for "his disciples," *talāmīdhihi.*

38 This is a paraphrase of Mt. 17:24-27, in which the portion involving the dialogue follows VD almost exactly. The incident is recorded only in Matthew. Al-'Aqqād makes no mention, however, of how Jesus told Simon Peter to pay the Temple tax, i.e., through a miracle in which Peter was to catch a fish and find a coin which would pay the tax for Jesus and Peter (and not, as al-'Aqqād indicates, for any other disciples as well). His silence on this matter is in keeping with his avoidance of any discussion of the miracles of Jesus (see the Introduction, pp. 44, 56).

39 Methods of tax collection varied from time to time and from place to place. Al-'Aqqād's description here is probably fairly accurate of what occurred in Palestine at the time of Christ (Schürer 1:372-76). That taxes were a burden on the poor is well attested (Safrai and Stern, 1:259-60, 332).

40 Jewish literature of that time abounds with denunciation against tax collectors (or "publicans") and their unjust practices. Frequently they were employed from among their own people. (ABD, s.v. "Tax Collector"; and Schürer, 1:376).

41 Jesus' association with tax collectors, and the Jewish response to that, is frequently mentioned in the Gospels (especially Luke); the disciple Matthew is also said to have been a tax collector. See Mt. 9:9-11 = Mk. 2:13-16 = Lk. 5:27-30; Lk. 15:1-2; and Lk. 19:1-10.

42 The dialogue which follows reproduces almost exactly Lk. 3:12-14, where the "teacher" in the conversation is not Jesus, but John the Baptist! No such remarks are recorded of Jesus.

43 "Fodder" (Ar. *'alā'if)* is the word found in VD; since the Greek word behind it, *opsōnion,* clearly means "wages," it might be assumed that the Bible translators had this meaning in mind, although another word would certainly have been more appropriate. Al-'Aqqād, however, takes the word literally, as seen in the following sentence, and so this is reflected in the translation.

44 Al-'Aqqād's final statement is probably accurate for Roman (Gentile) soldiers; but the soldiers who came to John the Baptist would have been Jews, either mercenaries or those in the service of Herod (Fitzmyer, 28:470; Nolland, 35A:150).

45 A Roman census would require people to return to the location of their residence, but it did not, as far as is known, require people to migrate to their birthplace or ancestral home. Nevertheless, it is possible that the Romans adapted to Jewish customs in this regard. (Schürer 1:411-13; and Brown, *Birth,* 549).

46 This evidently refers to the "Gadarene Demoniac" (Mk. 5:1-20, Lk. 8:26-39; there are two such men in Mt. 8:28-34). While the accounts refer to a multitude of demons named "Legion," there is no indication that these inhabited the man (or men) in an alternating manner.

47 It is striking that al-'Aqqād refers to the various types of illness and demon-possession which are so prominent in the Gospels, while barely hinting at Jesus' involvement with these through his miracles of healing and exorcism. This again is in keeping with his view concerning the miracles of Jesus in general (see n. 38 above). For an overview of the nature and purpose of Jesus' healing miracles, see DJG, s.v. "Healing."

48 A general statement such as this can be surmised from the Jewish literature from this period. See ABD, s.v. "Medicine and Healing" (4:661).

49 This was Herod Antipas, son of Herod the Great, who was Tetrarch of Galilee and Perea from 4 B.C.E. to 39 C.E. He was therefore the ruler in Galilee during the ministries of John the

Baptist and Jesus. Al-'Aqqād's remarks about the Herodian household is in keeping with what is known from Josephus and the NT. (ABD, s.v. "Herod Antipas").

[50] Al-'Aqqād has here confused Herod Antipas, who actually died in exile, with his nephew Herod Agrippa I, who ruled over the northern territories 37-44 C.E. and over all of Palestine from 41 C.E. Agrippa died quickly in 44 C.E. at Caesarea. The two accounts of his death are fairly similar. According to Acts 12:19b-23, God struck him down because of his pride, and he was eaten by worms and died. According to Josephus (*Antiquities* 19.8.2 [Loeb 9:376-83]), he acquired severe stomach pains and died five days later. (For more details, see ABD, s.v. "Agrippa [person (1)]").

[51] Al-'Aqqād describes this incident in more detail in ch. 15 (p. 163). See the notes there.

Chapter 8
The Religious Life of the World in the First Century

[1] Basically this is an accurate statement, although some additional territory was later acquired along a few frontiers, e.g., Britain (ABD, s.v. "Roman Empire," 5:803-804).

[2] Al-'Aqqād has mistakenly included Nablus as a prominent city at the time of Jesus' birth. "Nablus" is the Arabic name for Neapolis, a city founded only in 72 C.E. See al-'Aqqād's reference to Nablus in his discussion about the Samaritans in ch. 6 (p. 101), and n. 40 there.

[3] Ar. *'abqarīyat al-Masīḥ* according to ed. 1 and the Beirut printing of ed. 2. The Cairo printing of ed. 2 and ed. 3 have *ḥayāt al-Masīḥ*. See Appendix A (p. 241) concerning the editorial changes that have taken place regarding the title of the book.

[4] Al-'Aqqād's main point about the movement of Eastern religious ideas to the West in Hellenistic times is generally recognized. The Western versions of Eastern cults are sometimes referred to as "mystery religions" because of the secret ceremonies in which adherents sometimes participated. General overviews are covered in ABD, s.v. "Mystery Religions"; and ER, s.v. "Hellenistic Religions." Concerning the prominence of Alexandria in this regard (mentioned in the previous paragraph), see ER 6:252.

[5] Ammon (or "Amon" or "Amun") was an imperial deity of Egypt who became very popular in Greece due to the oracle in his temple at the North African oasis of Siwa (OCD, s.v. "Ammon"). A summary of the legend that he fathered Alexander the Great is given in ER, s.v. "Hellenistic Religions," 6:255.

[6] "Antiochus" was the name taken by over a dozen kings of the Seleucid dynasty, one of the four political entities which took over the empire of Alexander the Great. Several of these kings took on a second name indicating their claim to divinity: Antiochus II Theos ("god") (261-246 B.C.E.); Antiochus IV Epiphanes ("manifest" [as a god]) (175-164 B.C.E.); and Antiochus VI Epiphanes Dionysus ("the manifest Dionysus") (145-142 B.C.E.). (ABD, s.v. "Antiochus").

[7] The Gk. word *mageia* is derived from the Persian word *magush,* i.e., the astrology, divination, etc., practiced among the Zoroastrians (ER, s.v. "Magic: Magic in Greco-Roman Antiquity" [14: 93]).

[8] In fact, the Zoroastrians adopted the week from the Jews, using it as a fourth part of the lunar month. Yet the week was not nearly as important as the month. They named individual days of the month, not the week; and these were named after divine beings, not planets (Boyce, 71). The practice of naming the days of the week after planets was a Roman custom which developed

shortly before the Christian era; it was taken over into Christian usage in the late third century (ODCC, s.v. "Week").

9 "Avesta" is the name given to the totality of Zoroastrian scriptures. These were originally transmitted orally and portions were first written down in the sixth century C.E. Only a fraction of these, almost entirely liturgical in nature, survive as a sacred book by this title. It is written in an ancient Eastern Iranian dialect which has no surviving literary parallels, but its explanation was passed on in Pahlavi religious literature. See Boyce, 3, 134-36; and R. C. Zaehner, *The Dawn and Twilight of Zoroastrianism* (New York: G. P. Putnam's Sons, 1961), 24-27.

10 Mithra was one of three important gods of Zoroastrianism. His name means "covenant" and apparently he was originally associated with oath-making. But he developed primarily into the god associated with both light and war, as al-'Aqqād notes. The other two prominent gods were Ohrmazd (or Ahura Mazdā) who was the supreme god, and Ahriman (or Angra Mainyu); these represented the eternal dualistic struggle between good and evil. (ER, s.v. "Mithra" and "Ahura Mazdā and Angra Mainyu"; and Boyce, 8-10, 20-21).

The cult of Mithra was one of the most prominent of the mystery religions throughout the Roman Empire. Al-'Aqqād's remarks about its popularity among various levels of society and the seven stages of spiritual progression are accurate. However, he seems to assume that it was prominent at time of Christ, when in fact the earliest attestation to its presence in Rome is about 80 C.E. The older view is that its arrival in the West came gradually, but some believe that it was brought by a particular religious propagandist and then spread quickly. (See ABD, s.v. "Mithras, Mithraism" and "Mystery Religions" [4:943-44]). In any case, al-'Aqqād later draws a connection between the cult of Mithra and the teaching of the apostle Paul (ch. 11, p. 140).

11 The close link which al-'Aqqād implies between the cults of Mithra and Isis actually concerned only their similar religious practices and their widespread circulation in the Western world. The cult of Isis had gained a foothold much earlier, by the third century B.C.E. It's point of origin was also, of course, completely different. In Egypt, Isis' principle role was twofold: she was the devoted wife of the god Osirus, and the queen of the dead. The Greeks transformed her into a goddess in her own right, where she assumed the roles of supreme mother and goddess of navigation. Demeter had already been revered by the Greeks as the goddess of fertility and motherhood. Thus, while the two had originally developed separate traditions, they became equated in later times in the Greek-speaking world. (See ER, s.v. "Isis" and "Demeter and Persephone"; Siegfried Morenz, *Egyptian Religion,* trans. Ann E. Keep [Ithaca, NY: Cornell University Press, 1973], 248-50, 263; and Walter Burkert, *Greek Religion: Archaic and Classical,* trans. John Raffan [Cambridge, MA: Harvard University Press, 1985], 159-61).

12 Ar. *al-mutanaṭṭisīn,* lit. "those who are skillful," or "those who examine carefully." Here, al-'Aqqād also gives the English word "Therapeuts" to indicate that he is using the Arabic word as a technical term for this group. However, in scholarly discussions in English the Latin plural is preferred.

13 Philo wrote an entire treatise on this Jewish ascetic group entitled *On the Contemplative Life* (Loeb 9:112-69). This is the only ancient source concerning this group. For summaries, see Vermes and Goodman, 15-16, and Schürer, 2:591-97.

14 Ar. *al-asāt,* pl. of *al-āsī,* the active participle of *asā,* "to nurse," "to treat" (a wound). Al-'Aqqād had previously used this word in connection with the Essenes in ch. 6 (pp. 98-99).

15 Ar. *al-mutanaṭṭisīn,* here used in a descriptive manner. The Greek name of the group was *therapeutai,* pl. of *therapeutēs,* "one who serves." The verbal root *therapeuō,* "to serve," can refer to service rendered to fellow humans, thus "to provide for" or "to treat medically"; or it can refer

to service rendered to the gods, thus "to worship" (Henry George Liddell and Robert Scott, *A Greek-English Lexicon,* revised and augmented by Henry Stuart Jones and Roderick McKenzie, 9th ed. with a Supplement, ed. E. A. Barber (1968) (Oxford: Clarendon Press, 1940), 792-93.

[16] See ch. 6 (pp. 98-100). A summary of the major points of comparison and contrast between the Therapeutae and the Essenes is presented in Vermes and Goodman, 16-17. A close relationship is apparent, particularly if the name "Essenes" is derived from "healers" as was the name "Therapeutae." Yet the two groups cannot be completely identified. Unlike the "historians" mentioned by al-'Aqqād, Vermes and Goodman conclude that the Therapeutae were probably an Egyptian off-shoot of the Palestinian Essenes (17; a similar conclusion is reached in Schürer, 2:597). Furthermore, Vermes elsewhere interprets Philo as making a distinction between the two groups at the beginning of his treatise, implying that the Therapeutae were more "contemplative" than the Essenes who pursued an "active life" (Vermes, *Post-Biblical,* 34-35).

[17] Orphism dates from the sixth century B.C.E. in Greece, and had a long and complex history. Its general characteristics are reflected well in al-'Aqqād's comments. Direct influence from the East is uncertain, although one Hellenistic document bears distinct Indian traits (Burkert, 298). The uncompromising prohibition against killing, whether for food or for sacrifice, was the key that led adherents of Orphism into an ascetic lifestyle. (ER, s.v. "Orpheus; ABD, s.v. "Orphism"; and Burkert, 296-99).

[18] The common linguistic relationship between these various names for deity is generally recognized (OCD, s.v. "Adonis"; and Burkert, 176-77). However, the original source has been debated. While some have suggested an Egyptian derivation, more likely it stems from a proto-Semitic origin (*Theological Dictionary of the Old Testament,* ed. G. Johannes Botterweck, Helmer Ringgren and Heinz-Josef Fabry, trans. John T. Willis, et al. [Grand Rapids, MI: Wm. B. Eerdmans, 1974-], s.v. *"'ādhôn, 'ᵃdhōnāi"* [1:59-60]).

[19] Al-'Aqqād's comments here are on the right track. "A popular feature of the religious life of this age was the great vitality of the associations or clubs formed by the adherents of the various cults" (ER, s.v. "Hellenistic Religions" [6:253]).

[20] Ar. *al-aghyār.* This invented word, which al-'Aqqād places in quotation marks, is a pl. noun based on the preposition *ghayr,* [other than].

[21] This perspective is fairly accurate. "The Roman government was in practice tolerant of any cult provided that it did not encourage sedition or weaken morality" (Chadwick, 25).

[22] Syriac is actually a dialect of late Aramaic (ABD, s.v. "Languages [Aramaic]" [4:175]).

[23] This is undoubtedly a reference to the Septuagint (LXX). According to the purported "Letter of Aristeas," this translation was made in the third century B.C.E. by seventy-two scholars, who miraculously completed their work in seventy-two days. The actual circumstances surrounding the origin of the LXX are debated. Most, however, accept that the Pentateuch was indeed translated in the third century B.C.E. in Alexandria, while the remainder of the books were completed over the course of the next two centuries. (ABD, s.v. "Septuagint" and "Versions, Ancient [Greek]").

[24] There is little dispute among scholars that Jesus and the disciples spoke Aramaic or that the Gospels were written in Greek. However, al-'Aqqād's final statement here is problematic. Portions of the oldest Syriac translation of the OT (the Peshitta) may date from the first to second centuries C.E., but it was probably not completed until the third century. The oldest Syriac translation of the NT (Tatian's "Diatessaron" or Harmony of the Gospels) dates from the latter half second century. (ABD, s.v. "Versions, Ancient [Syriac]"). Al-'Aqqād's date of 100 C.E. is thus too early. Furthermore, he implies that the Syriac translations superseded the original Hebrew and

Greek versions, when in fact these continued to be utilized while the Syriac versions remained restricted to a small linguistic community.

[25] Suetonius *Augustus* 31.1 (Loeb 1:171). Suetonius actually states that Augustus burned "more than two thousand" such writings.

Chapter 9
Intellectual Life in the First Century

[1] On the claim that Jesus was born in Galilee, see al-'Aqqād's similar remark in ch. 7, p. 109, and n. 22 there. Concerning the assertion that Greek philosophy was "widespread" in Galilee, see al-'Aqqād's discussion later in this chapter (p. 126) and n. 23 there.

[2] Brief overviews of Pythagorean beliefs and practices are found in OCD, s.v. "Pythagoras (1)"; and ABD, s.v. "Pythagoreanism." Further details are presented in Émil Bréhier, *The History of Philosophy,* vol. 1, *The Hellenic Age,* trans. Joseph Thomas (Chicago: University of Chicago Press, 1963), 44-48, 67-68; and Émil Bréhier, *The History of Philosophy,* vol. 2, *The Hellenistic and Roman Age,* trans. Wade Baskin (Chicago: University of Chicago Press, 1965), 171-72. (Subsequent references to Bréhier are noted simply by volume number). Classical Pythagoreanism flourished in the sixth and fifth centuries B.C.E. but then went into decline. Its revival, beginning with the first century B.C.E., is known as "Neo-Pythagoreanism." While there is certainly a continuity between the two periods, it is sometimes difficult to know whether certain features are to be assigned to one period or the other, or to both. In any case, al-'Aqqād has accurately and aptly described the main characteristics here. (He had previously claimed that the Essenes had borrowed from the Pythagoreans, in ch. 6 [p. 99]; as noted there [n. 27], this is unlikely).

[3] Some ancient sources held that the doctrine of the transmigration of souls was original to Pythagoras. In fact, this idea was commonly believed among many primitive peoples. (Bréhier, 1: 45).

[4] Many of these prohibitions were not intended to carry moral significance, but to distinguish members of the sect from other people (ibid.).

[5] Al-'Aqqād is not quite correct in this sentence. In Pythagoreanism, various numbers represent different aspects of the universe; the number "four" actually represented "justice." If any number had been considered the number of perfection, it would have been "ten" (the sum of the first four numbers), by which members of the sect took an oath. Furthermore, the complex number symbolism of Pythagoras should be distinguished from other Greek ideas regarding the basic elements of the universe. (Bréhier, 1:47, 67).

[6] Sources on Epicureanism include OCD, s.v. "Epicurus"; ABD, s.v. "Epicureanism"; and Bréhier, 2:69-94, 139-43. Again, al-'Aqqād has summarized well the main facets of this philosophy. The criticism that Epicurus' outlook was hedonistic originated in his own lifetime and has continued ever since.

[7] Ar. *al-surūr "al-mutaḥarrik".* It would be more proper to say that Epicurus believed that such bestial desires did not cause any pleasure at all; these were classified among those causes which disturbed the soul and brought it fear. (Bréhier, 2:71).

[8] Epicurus believed that one of the causes of the soul's disturbance is the concern about the gods' involvement in the world (Bréhier, 2:87-88).

[9] Ar. *awrād* (sg. *wird).* On this term, see ch. 6 (p. 99), n. 25.

[10] Stoicism is summarized in OCD, s.v. "Stoa"; and ABD, s.v. "Stoics, Stoicism"; it is well covered in Bréhier, 2:23-65. Al-'Aqqād's presentation is, again, generally accurate, including his discussion of the various early Stoic leaders.

[11] Al-'Aqqād here writes in the first person plural, and also in the following sentence.

[12] Al-'Aqqād's remarks correctly point to the monotheistic nature of the Stoic concept of deity, approaching that of the Semitic religions. But, as he mentions later, there is also a pantheistic element to this concept. See Bréhier, 2:35, 52 for further details.

[13] Cleanthes was a disciple of Zeno (the founder of Stoicism) and was his successor as head of the Stoic School. The dates for his birth vary widely: OCD (s.v. "Cleanthes") has 331-232 B.C.E., as do both sources mentioned in the next note; Bréhier, (2:28) has 264-232 B.C.E.

[14] Al-'Aqqād clearly has in mind the famous "Hymn to Zeus" by Cleanthes; only fragments survive of his other works (Michael Grant, *Greek and Latin Authors: 800 B.C. - A.D. 1000* [New York: H. W. Wilson, 1980], 103). However, al-'Aqqād's quotation is at best an extremely loose paraphrase. While divine guidance is mentioned in the hymn, it is guidance not for the speaker but for the "world" (Gk. *kosmos).* Although the speaker displays utmost reverence for the power and generosity of Zeus, the notion of following him without fear can only be surmised. The Greek text, along with a translation and commentary, are given in E. H. Blakeney, trans., *The Hymn of Cleanthes,* Texts for Students no. 26 (London: SPCK, 1921).

[15] Al-'Aqqād's use of the word "resurrection" (Ar. *qiyāmah)* in this context is unfortunate. In Christianity and Islam it is a term for the bodily resurrection at the end of time, but this is a concept foreign to Eastern religions and Greek philosophy alike. The word appears again on p. 125; see n. 20 below.

[16] Zeno (who was probably a Phoenician by race) was the founder of the Stoic school who formulated its basic ideas. Again, the dates for his life are uncertain. OCD (s.v. "Zeno [2]) has 335-263 B.C.E.; Bréhier (2:28) has 322-264 B.C.E.

[17] The quotation presented in the next few paragraphs is a nearly exact reproduction from the chapter "Philosophy" in al-'Aqqād's earlier book *Allāh,* pp. 90-91. The paragraphs in the translation are divided as they are in *Allāh,* although they are combined in a single long paragraph in *'Abqarīyat al-Masīḥ* (all editions). The Greek words given in parentheses appear in English type in the text of both works. The phrase "as we have already said," appearing mid-way through the first paragraph, is an addition by al-'Aqqād in *'Abqarīyat al-Masīḥ.*

[18] The portion which al-'Aqqād has quoted from his book *Allāh* ends here.

[19] The dates which al-'Aqqād gives above for Posidonius, 135-51 B.C.E., are in agreement with modern estimates. He was apparently an extremely versatile and influential philosopher, historian and scientist. Unfortunately, his numerous works are preserved only in quotations made by later writers. (OCD, s.v. "Posidonius [2]"; and Bréhier, 2:133-39).

[20] Here, al-'Aqqād has evidently summarized a discussion on Posidonius about the soul found in the book which he mentions later in this paragraph, i.e., Edwyn Bevan, *Stoics and Sceptics: Four Lectures Delivered in Oxford during Hilary Term 1913 for the Common University Fund* (Oxford: Clarendon Press, 1913), 107-12. However, al-'Aqqād is quite mistaken in his reference to "the Day of Resurrection" (Ar. *yawm al-qiyāmah),* as if Posidonius were referring to the bodily resurrection known in Christianity and Islam. (See n.15 above on this term). Bevan, in his explanation of Posidonius' view of the souls among the heavenly spheres, states that such souls would remain there "till the next world-conflagration" (110).

[21] Here is an example of the occasional imprecision in al-'Aqqād's use of sources. The book to which he refers, giving the title in English (but without further information), is clearly that by Ed-

wyn Bevan mentioned in the previous note, which contains a full chapter on Posidonius. (An inter-library search has led to no other book by this title, nor any subsequent edition of this book). Yet this matter of Posidonius' calculation of the distance between Cádiz (a major seaport in southwest Spain) and India is not mentioned there. Whereas he most likely used Bevan as his source for the first part of this paragraph, he must have gained this information from some other source.

According to the historian-geographer Strabo (ca. 64 B.C.E. - 21 C.E.), Posidonius indeed determined that 70,000 stadia was "the length of the inhabited world," defined elsewhere by Strabo as the distance from the extremities of Spain to the extremities of India (*The Geography of Strabo* 2.3.6 [Loeb 1:392-93]). Posidonius displayed a keen interest in scientific matters; he had estimated the circumference of the earth and proposed the dependence of the tides at Cádiz on the revolution of the moon (see F. H. Sandbach, *The Stoics* [New York: W. W. Norton, 1975], 131-35).

[22] Epictetus (d. ca. 135 C.E.) was a slave who, after being set free, taught Stoic philosophy, seeking to popularize it among the humble masses (OCD, s.v. "Epictetus [2]"; Bréhier, 2:159-60). Marcus Aurelius (the dates given by al-'Aqqād are for his rule as Emperor) found solace in the Stoic teaching on the link between the individual and the universe as he faced discouragement from political and military concerns (OCD, s.v. "Aurelius [1]"; Bréhier, 2:160-62).

[23] There is no question that Greek philosophical ideas made an impact on some Jews living outside of Palestine. Philo of Alexandria (whom al-'Aqqād discusses next) is the primary example, and other Jewish literature of this period demonstrates this as well (e.g., the Apocryphal work entitled "The Wisdom of Solomon"). However, the extent of this influence is difficult to assess and would appear to have been modest; whatever inspiration was provided was in the area of ethics but not theology. (See Schürer, 3:567-68).

In Palestine, the various schools of Greek philosophy would have been represented among Gentiles. But al-'Aqqād has definitely overstated the influence of these schools among Jews there. Apparently he has exaggerated certain statements made by Josephus concerning the relationship between some of the Jewish sects and various Greek philosophical schools. Al-'Aqqād's comparison between the Essenes and the Pythagoreans was noted in ch. 6 (see n. 2 above). Josephus also likens the Pharisees to the Stoics (*Life* 3 [Loeb 1:6-7]), and elsewhere he implies a similarity between the Sadducees and the Epicureans. However, his purpose in this seems merely to present the Jewish sects in a manner that would be intelligible to Greek readers rather than to claim any direct connection. See the footnotes in the Loeb edition of Josephus in 8:179 and 9:10.

[24] A fine introduction to the life, works and significance of this important figure is in ABD, s.v. "Philo of Alexandria." A more extensive survey is Samuel Sandmel, *Philo of Alexandria: An Introduction* (Oxford: Oxford University Press, 1979). The dates for his birth and death are very uncertain; most scholars accept 50 C.E. as the approximate date of death, but 20 B.C.E. is a more likely figure for his date of birth rather than 30 as given by al-'Aqqād. His family was quite wealthy and active in politics. The Jewish community of Alexandria was the largest outside of Palestine. Philo, like many other Jews there, was in regular contact and dialogue with the various philosophical schools which flourished in Alexandria. As a biblical exegete, he borrowed many Greek philosophical ideas, especially from the Stoics. Yet Philo was extremely loyal to his own religious heritage, and this always superseded any outside influence; al-'Aqqād has minimized this fact in his presentation here.

[25] Heraclitus flourished ca. 500 B.C.E. His philosophical approach was somewhat obscure with many opposites held in tension. For him, all the elements in the universe are in a state of flux, yet they fall under an all-embracing governing principle which he called the *logos;* from this divine

Word were derived all human laws. (OCD, s.v. "Heraclitus"; and Grant, *Greek and Latin Authors,* 191-92).

[26] This is an apt, albeit brief description of Philo's understanding of the *"logos"* as the point of intersection between the transcendent God and the intelligible world. The background of this concept is partly Stoic philosophy; but equally important is the Wisdom literature of Philo's Jewish heritage. (Sandmel, 94-99).

[27] Osiris was the Egyptian god who was identified with the dead Pharaoh, and thus he was the god of the underworld. Sarapis was a Hellenistic god who combined the traits of many others, especially Osiris. (Morenz, 267-68). The Egyptian goddess Isis was discussed by al-'Aqqād in ch. 8 (p. 117; see n. 11 there).

[28] There is no question that Philo's allegorical method in explaining Scripture went far beyond what is found in traditional Rabbinic exegesis. But the claim that this method was dependent on the mystery religions for its content as well as its terminology cannot be substantiated (Sandmel, 23-25, 140-47). Such a view was championed by Erwin R. Goodenough, especially in his *By Light, Light: The Mystic Gospel of Hellenistic Judaism* (New Haven: Yale University Press, 1935); this may well have been al-'Aqqād's source here.

[29] Ar. *al-niẓām (aw al-sharī'ah).* The Greek term used by Philo is *nomos,* the usual word for "law."

[30] Philo *On the Creation* 1.1-3 (Loeb 1:6-7). Al-'Aqqād has summarized this treatise well; see Sandmel 52-55.

[31] This unusual statement is quite exaggerated. Philo embraced and utilized certain Stoic ideas, but it would be wrong to classify him as an outright Stoic. (See Sandmel, 23-28, and concerning the Stoic concepts in *On the Creation* and *On Abraham,* 53-54, 59). Any direct links between Philo and Epicureanism are much more tenuous.

[32] The name "Abraham" is not in Philo's text at this point, but he is evidently the one being referred to here.

[33] Paraphrased (despite the quotation marks) from Philo *On Abraham* 36.201-202 (Loeb 6:98-99). On the allegorical identification in Philo of Isaac with "joy," see Sandmel, 86.

[34] Ar. *al-muṣallā,* read as a passive participle in agreement with Philo, rather than as an active participle *(al-muṣallī,* [the one who prays]).

[35] Philo *On the Special Laws I* 38.210-11 (Loeb 7:218-21). Philo commended prayer as superior even to ritual sacrifice (Sandmel, 115). See al-'Aqqād's quotation below concerning animal sacrifices.

[36] Philo *On the Giants* 13.60-61 (Loeb 2:474-75). Al-'Aqqād's final remark about the "guides and messengers" is his addition.

[37] This paragraph does not seem to have a specific source, but it reflects Philo's thought in general; this despite his glowing report about the Therapeutae (see ch. 8, p. 117, n. 13; Sandmel, 113).

[38] Ar. *al-nīyah.* This is a technical term in Islam, where it is legally required to express one's intention to perform a ritual immediately before its fulfillment (EI^2., *"niyya").* The word does not appear in Philo's discussion, but the concept is clearly present.

[39] This is a rather free paraphrase (despite the quotation marks) of Philo *On the Special Laws I* 50.271-72 (Loeb 7:256-57).

[40] This statement does not seem to have a specific source but reflects Philo's thought in general. See Sandmel 59, 87-88.

[41] Lacedaemon was the official name for Sparta (OCD, s.v. "Sparta").

[42] The second half of this paragraph incorporates selections from Philo *On the Life of Moses* 2.4.19, 21, 23-24 (Loeb 6:458-61). Al-'Aqqād's remark about the Greeks refraining from killing in their "holy month" is his addition, but it is an accurate reflection of current practice (see Loeb 6:460-61, note b).

[43] Philo *On the Special Laws IV* 34.179-80 (Loeb 8:118-21). The quotation marks are missing in ed. 3 but present in eds. 1 and 2. The portion which they comprise is translated fairly accurately by al-'Aqqād.

Chapter 10
The Land of Galilee

[1] Ar. *Tārīkh al-Mīlād.* In ed. 1, this was the title of what is now ch. 11. See Appendix A on the differences with respect to the titles of the Parts and chapters among the various editions of the book, as well as the translation of this particular phrase.

[2] Al-'Aqqād here reiterates unambiguously his previous statements regarding Jesus' birth in Galilee. Presumably, he means that Jesus was born in Nazareth, the Galilean town in which he was raised, rather than in Bethlehem of Judea according to the "Infancy Narratives" of Matthew and Luke. However, he is inconsistent on this matter elsewhere in this book. For a full discussion, see the Introduction, pp. 55-56, and n. 76 there.

[3] Ar. *Jalīl al-Umam;* the second word could also be translated as "Gentiles." This designation derives from Isa. 9:1 (MT 8:23), where the Hebrew phrase *g^elîl haggôyîm* can likewise be rendered "Galilee of the nations" or "Gentiles." Whichever translation is adopted, the essence of this phrase is the focus of this chapter. Indeed, its title in ed. 1 was "Galilee of the Nations" and was changed, for some reason, in ed. 2 (see Appendix A). Al-'Aqqād's remarks in this chapter reflect some common assumptions about the character of Galilee; these are considered below in the light of modern scholarly research, such as found in ABD, s.v. "Galileans" and "Galilee"; Schürer; and in the major work of Seán Freyne, *Galilee from Alexander the Great to Hadrian, 323 B.C.E. to 135 C.E.: A Study of Second Temple Judaism,* University of Notre Dame Center for the Study of Judaism and Christianity in Antiquity, no. 5 (Wilmington, DE: Michael Glazier, Notre Dame: University of Notre Dame Press, 1980).

[4] More likely, the name points to the experience of the early Israelites who felt themselves surrounded by other peoples. Alternatively, the name could have a geographical connotation, referring to the central highlands surrounded by plains. (Freyne, 3, 15-16).

[5] "Phoenicia" in Greek means "dark red"; however, the name actually derives from the dyes of this color which were produced in this region. Furthermore, the area of Phoenicia was mostly north of Palestine along the Mediterranean coast; only the southern portion of Phoenicia overlapped the western region of Galilee. (ABD, s.v. "Phoenicia, History of" [5:349]).

[6] In fact, Haifa, situated at the foot of Mount Carmel, is only a modern seaport which did not exist in biblical times. Al-'Aqqād most likely had in mind the seaport of Acco, about fourteen miles north along the coast. This city was in decline until the Ptolemies renamed it Ptolemais and upgraded it (Freyne, 30).

[7] 1 Kg. 5:6. Eds. 2 and 3 improperly place a footnote here indicating that this reference is from "the seventh chapter in First Kings." This note belongs instead to the following quotation, and indeed it is properly placed there in ed. 1.

Al-'Aqqād is not quite accurate regarding the position of Hiram as "king of the Canaanites." In pre-exilic times, the Canaanites consisted of several ethnic groups and city-states without a central authority. According to 1 Kg. 5:1 and elsewhere, Hiram was the king of Tyre.

[8] 1 Kg. 7:14. In the biblical text, the craftsman's name is given as Hiram, but he is clearly not to be identified with the king of Tyre. The parallel text in 2 Chr. 2:13 gives his name as Huram-abi. The word for "bronze" is *nuḥās,* lit. "copper," but it can also be used of the copper-tin alloy used at that time, as is the case in the biblical text.

[9] Ezk. 27:17.

[10] Judg. 2:11-12.

[11] 1 Kg. 19:10, 14.

[12] 1 Kg. 19:18. The phrase just prior to this quotation, "it says," could be translated as "he said"; but in that case, one would assume from al-'Aqqād's text that the speaker was Elijah, when in fact at this point in the biblical text it is God who is speaking.

[13] Ar. *al-khawārij,* which could also be translated as "dissenters." This is also the Arabic term for the Khārijites, who formed the earliest sect in Islam and who opposed both 'Alī and Mu'āwiyah regarding the arbitration following the Battle of Ṣiffīn (EI², s.v. "Khāridjites").

[14] Aramaic was in fact the primary language of the entire Near East from about 600 B.C.E. Greek, in its Koine dialect, had spread throughout the region conquered by Alexander the Great and became the principal language of commerce. (ABD, s.v. "Languages" [4:173, 197]). Thus, Jews throughout Palestine conversed mainly in Aramaic and would have been familiar with Greek to some extent (Schürer, 2:20-28, 74-80).

[15] The only basis for such a view is the claim by Herodotus that the Phoenicians migrated from the Persian Gulf 2300 years before his time (OCD, s.v. "Phoenicians").

[16] "Maccabeus" or "Maccabee" was the nickname given to Judas son of Mattathias, and subsequently to members of his family (the Hasmoneans) and other heroes who led the Jewish revolt against the Seleucids in the second century B.C.E. Its derivation is uncertain, but many believe it is derived from a word meaning "hammer." (ABD, s.v. "Maccabeus").

[17] The previous paragraph is apparently meant to serve as a transition between the Israel of Elijah on the one hand, and the conquests of the Hasmoneans on the other; but it does not do justice to the centuries of history which elapsed between them. No mention is made of the Assyrian conquest of the northern kingdom of Israel and the repopulation of Samaria; nor of the subsequent domination of this region by the respective empires of Babylonia, Persia and Alexander; nor of the instability it endured during the struggles between the Ptolemies and Seleucids. Instead, Samaria and Galilee are treated by al-'Aqqād as if they share a common situation at the time of the Hasmoneans. In fact, the two areas must be considered separately.

Following the Assyrian invasion of Israel, Samaria experienced the deportation of some Jews and the immigration of some Gentiles, so that a mixed population ensued. No such policy is known to have been carried out in Galilee. However, scholars disagree as to whether the people of Galilee in the subsequent centuries were almost exclusively Gentile (so Schürer) or whether they were predominantly Jews loyal to Jerusalem (so Freyne). The sources on Galilee during this period are extremely scanty. Much hinges on one's interpretation of a passage in Josephus which tells of Galilee's incorporation into the Hasmonean kingdom in 105-104 B.C.E., which occurred under Aristobulus I (and not, as al-'Aqqād states, under his father Hyrcanus I). Josephus mentions that some of the population were brought into "the bond of circumcision" at that time. Schürer takes this to mean that the Gentiles who would have predominated in Galilee were "Judaized" under Aristobulus; Freyne interprets this Judaizing activity to a Gentile group on the fringes of Galilee, while the Galileans themselves (mostly Jews) would have welcomed the change. In any case, both scholars agree that by the time of Christ, the population of Galilee was mostly Jewish even though a significant number of Gentiles also lived there. The Galilean Jews kept their distance from their Gentile neighbors; although there were some differences in customs and dialects between Galilee and Judea which led to some racial discrimination, Galilean Jews were considered by the Jews of Judea as fully within the fold of Judaism — unlike the Samaritans. See Schürer, 1:142, 217-18, 2:1-14; Freyne, 25-44, 291-93.

[18] This is a remarkable claim which al-'Aqqād has obviously derived from a source unknown to us. It is possible that Arabs were a part of the cosmopolitan non-Jewish population in Galilee, or even that Jewish Arabs resided there. But there is no evidence to support such a claim, and they certainly could not have formed a major group. There is a single reference in the NT to Jewish "Arabs" in Acts 2:11; however, these people are clearly not from Galilee. Along with the other Jewish groups mentioned, they represent the geographical diversity of Diaspora Judaism. Jews had come to Jerusalem for the Feast of Pentecost "from every nation under heaven" (v. 5). In Greco-Roman usage, "Arabia" usually referred to the kingdom of the Nabateans, which was at the height of its power at that time. See F. F. Bruce, *The Acts of the Apostles: The Greek Text with Introduction and Commentary,* 3d ed. (Grand Rapids, MI: William B. Eerdmans, 1990), 116-18.

It is more likely that al-'Aqqād is using the term "Arab" with a broader connotation equivalent to "Semitic"; this perspective can be observed in some of his other works (Nijim, 57-58; Wielandt, 107). As noted in the Introduction (p. 60), he apparently wishes to minimize the Jewish background to Jesus, at least in the ethnic sense.

Al-'Aqqād's perspective is reminiscent of another, more recent, Arab Muslim who wrote about Christianity. Ismā'īl al-Farūqī promoted the concept of "Arab consciousness" as the true foundation of the three monotheistic religions, using the term "Arab" as synonymous with "Semitic." Yet, he claimed, only the Arabs kept this consciousness pure, while it became corrupted among the Jews and Christians. Although Jesus was a Jew, he stood fully within this Arab consciousness. (See Ford, "Isma'il al-Faruqi," 270-71).

[19] E.g., see Mt. 26:73, where Peter, standing in the courtyard of the High Priest and having denied that he knew Jesus, was nevertheless suspect because of his (Galilean) accent.

[20] Jn. 1:45-46. The existence of a "proverb" concerning all of Galilee, as alleged by al-'Aqqād, is not substantiated. Nathaniel's rhetorical question cannot be considered as such, since Nathaniel himself was from Cana of Galilee; at best, it might have been a local proverb reflecting animosity between the two towns (Raymond E. Brown, *The Gospel According to John: Introduction, Translation, and Notes,* The Anchor Bible, ed. William Foxwell Albright and David Noel Freedman [Garden City, NY: Doubleday, 1966-70], 29:83).

[21] Jn. 7:52. This statement made by the Temple leaders, as reported by John (according to most mss.), is not quite accurate; the prophet Jonah was from Gath Hepher, in Galilee (2 Kg. 14:25). It is possible, however, that the original statement in John should read, "*the* Prophet does not come from Galilee," referring to the expected Messiah (the addition of the Gk. article *ho* is found in two early papyri; see Brown, *John,* 29:325; and Bruce M. Metzger, *A Textual Commentary on the Greek New Testament* [London: United Bible Societies, 1971], 219).

[22] This perspective is no longer considered to reflect the actual situation. As noted above, "the Galileans were not made to feel [as] outsiders in the Jerusalem cult, as were the Samaritans. . . . The Jerusalem temple remained the focus of the Galileans' loyalty to the end" (Freyne, 291-92).

[23] Again, al-'Aqqād is correct on some facts and in error on others. The implication is that Jesus would have been ten years old when both the old capital was destroyed and the new one built.

In fact Sepphoris, the northern headquarters for Herod the Great and situated only four miles north of Nazareth, was destroyed by the Romans in 4 B.C.E., shortly after the death of Herod. The cause was indeed a rebellion, led by Judas the son of Hezekiah, who took advantage of the disturbances following Herod's death. However, Antipas, the son of Herod who gained control of Galilee, rebuilt Sepphoris and made it his capital for some time. It was not until 20 C.E. that Antipas built Tiberias, fifteen miles north-west of Nazareth on the shore of the Sea of Galilee, to replace Sepphoris as the capital. See ABD, s.v. "Sepphoris" and "Tiberias (place)"; and Schürer, 1:332, 342-43.

[24] Ar. *al-duwal tadūlu* (lit. "the empires alternate"); a play on words belonging to the same root.

Chapter 11
When Christ was Born

[1] Ar. *Matā Wulida al-Masīḥ.* This phrase could be rendered as a question, "When was Christ Born?"; however, the translation adopted is preferable. For a full discussion, see Appendix A.

[2] Dionysius Exiguus was a Scythian monk who lived in Rome ca. 500-550 C.E. Very little is known about his life. He was indeed the man responsible for introducing the system of dating from the year of Jesus' birth. However, he wrongly assumed that this was equivalent to the year 754 of the Roman calendar (A.U.C.). Later, it was demonstrated that Jesus' birth must have occurred some years earlier. (ODCC, s.v. "Dionysius (7) Exiguus"; Brown, *Birth,* 167; and Jack Finegan, *Handbook of Biblical Chronology: Principles of Time Reckoning in the Ancient World and Problems of Chronology in the Bible* [Princeton: Princeton University Press, 1964], 132-33).

[3] The last part of this paragraph seems to be a confused amalgamation of Dionysius' error, ancient Jewish reckoning of time, and the introduction of the year "4004 B.C." for the creation of the world. The latter proposal was not made until about 1700, and was based on calculations made by James Ussher (d. 1656), Archbishop of Armagh (ODCC, s.v. "Ussher, James").

[4] See Mt. 2:1-19.

[5] Lk. 3:1, 23.

[6] Lk. 2:1-7. In this chapter, al-'Aqqād seems to accept that Jesus was born in Judea, in contrast to his earlier statements that he was born in Galilee. But note that in his quotation from Luke, he has omitted the phrase "to the city of David, which is called Bethlehem" (which follows "Judea" in the biblical text). Here his concern is the date of Jesus' birth, and not the place. His inconsistency on the latter issue is discussed in the Introduction, pp. 55-56, and n. 76 there.

[7] Undoubtedly the passage in question here is Josephus *Antiquities* 18.1.1 (Loeb 9:2-5). Al-'Aqqād previously referred to this census in relation to the revolt that ensued, led by Judas the Galilean, and in relation to the problems associated with taxation among the Jews (ch. 6, p. 100; ch. 7, p. 110). Here, the census is discussed in relation to the date of Jesus' birth and the veracity of the passage in Lk. 2. Although Josephus does not mention a time reference in this passage, the dates when Quirinius was governor of Syria are well established (6-9 C.E.), and no other census in Palestine is known prior to that time. Al-'Aqqād notes the problem fairly accurately, although his proposed solution is not generally held. The details of this issue, and the solutions that have been advanced, are thoroughly discussed in Brown, *Birth,* 547-56, and in Schürer, 1:399-427. The conclusion for both authors, to which most scholarly opinion agrees, is that Luke's reference contains

some kind of historical inaccuracy (Brown, *Birth,* 554-55; Schürer, 1:426-27).

[8] This statement is problematic. In the first place, al-'Aqqād has juxtaposed two distinct offices of the Temple hierarchy, the priests (who performed the sacrificial offerings) and the more inferior Levites (who carried out the general maintenance of the Temple); he has simply listed the two terms without a conjunction (Ar. *al-kāhin al-lāwī).* There is no biblical regulation concerning the age when priests could be admitted to office; Rabbinic tradition set it at twenty years old. Several OT passages state the youngest age allowed for Levites, but this varies considerably: thirty (e.g., Num. 4:3); twenty-five (Num. 8:23); or twenty (e.g., Ezr. 3:8); (see Schürer, 2:243). Thus, the verse in Lk. 3:23, giving Jesus' approximate age at thirty, has nothing to do with the age of admission into a religious office. "The most that can be suggested is that such an age denotes an adequate measure of maturity" (Nolland, 35A:171).

[9] Ar. *al-aḥbār al-mujtahidūn.* The second word can mean "diligent," but it also refers to those (in Islam) who formulated independent legal decisions based on the four roots *(uṣūl)* of the law.

Al-'Aqqād's claim that fifty was the required age for such scholars cannot be attested. The only requirements for admission to the Sanhedrin were a legitimate Jewish lineage and recognized scholarly capability (Schürer, 2:211).

[10] A reference to the dispute in Jn. 8:56-57, where, however, there is no mention of Jesus having "listened to" Abraham. The statement that Jesus had not yet turned fifty was merely to say that he had not yet reached the age of retirement (as it was considered to be at that time; George R. Beasley-Murray, *John,* Word Biblical Commentary, ed. David A. Hubbard and Glenn W. Barker, vol. 36 [Waco, TX: Word Books, 1987], 139). As the context indicates, Jesus' remarks in this passage, as represented in John, amount to a claim of divinity; the Jews recognize this as such and accuse him of blasphemy (ibid., 139-40; Brown, *John,* 29:367).

[11] Tertullian *Adversus Marcionem* 4.19.10 (Oxford Early Christian Texts, ed. and trans. Ernest Evans [Oxford: Clarendon Press, 1972], 2:262-63). Saturninus' period as governor in Syria is actually considered to be ca. 9-6 B.C.E. (OCD, s.v. "Saturninus [2]").

It is true that some have appealed to Tertullian's reference, claiming that a textual corruption must have occurred in Lk 2:2 so that "Saturninus" should be read in place of "Quirinius." However, this is difficult to support. In the first place, there is absolutely no ms. evidence for such a reading. Furthermore, the passage in Tertullian is a reference to censuses (pl.) in general under Saturninus; it does not deal specifically with the birth of Jesus. There is no other reference in antiquity to a census under Saturninus. See Brown, *Birth,* 553-54.

[12] Ar. *wa-min al-qarā'in.* In a play on words, al-'Aqqād regards the "conjunction" *(qirān)* of Jupiter and Saturn to be an important "connection" *(qarīnah,* pl. *qarā'in)* to his discussion about Jesus' birth. Both words are from the same root, *qarana* [to connect, join].

[13] Ar. *kuhhān al-majūs. kuhhān* can also be translated as "diviners," while *al-majūs* can be translated as "the Mazdeans" or "the Magi."

Al-'Aqqād's discussion in the following paragraph is a plausible interpretation of the account in Mt. 2:1-12, concerning the visit to Bethlehem of the Magi (assuming that account to be historically reliable). However, there are other possibilities. The origin of the Magi could have been Persia, but Babylon or Arabia are also to be considered. The "star" might refer to a supernova or a comet rather than a planetary conjunction. For an outline of these views, see Brown, *Birth,* 167-73.

[14] Abū al-'Alā' al-Ma'arrī (d. 449/1058) was a well-known Arab poet during the late 'Abbāsid period. He was blind and lived a rather ascetic life, but he was beloved and had many students. His poetry is acknowledged to be both brilliant and aesthetic. For a full overview, see EI^2, s.v. "al-

Ma'arrī"; or for a shorter discussion, Hodgson, 2:164-65. Al-'Aqqād, as a poet himself, was very fond of al-Ma'arrī; he referred to him frequently in his writings, and he had previously written a book about him: *Raj'at Abū al-'Alā'* [The Return of Abū al-'Alā'] (Cairo: Dār Nahḍat Miṣr, [1939]).

[15] The title *Al-Luzūmīyāt* refers to the poems contained in al-Ma'arrī's second collection of poetry, called *Luzūm Mā Lā Yalzam* [The Necessity of What is Not Necessary], named for its self-imposed metrical and rhyming patterns (EI², s.v. "*Luzūm Mā Lā Yalzam*"). The most accessible printed edition is *Luzūm Mā Lā Yalzam — al-Luzūmīyāt,* 2 vols. (Beirut: Dār Ṣādir and Dār Bayrūt, 1961). The quotation here incorporates the first lines of a poem entitled "Al-Barīyah fī Ḍalāl" [Creation Gone Astray], in 2:622-25. R. K. Lacey refers to these lines as one piece of evidence for al-Ma'arrī's unorthodox belief in the eternity of the stars, and indeed, of the entire universe ("An 11th Century Muslim's Syncretistic Perspective of Cosmology: Abū al-'Alā' al-Ma'arrī's Philosophical-Poetic Reflections in *Luzūm Mā Lā Yalzam* on the Make-up and Dynamics of the Universe," *The Muslim World* 85 [1995]: 128).

[16] "The Bear and the Bull" are the constellations Ursa Minor and Pleiades. Al-'Aqqād does not provide the short vowels which indicate the parts of speech, but in the printed edition of al-Ma'arrī's poem, these constellations are the subject of the verb.

[17] Al-'Aqqād here provides a footnote (in Arabic) as follows: "Section One, page 31, second edition by Cassell Press." The book *The Life of Christ,* by Frederic W. Farrar, seems to have been published in several places, including New York (H. M. Caldwell, 1874). However, it is not divided into sections, and the discussion and quotation to which al-'Aqqād refers is found in Chapter Three, on pp. 43-44. A "Popular Edition" (without footnotes or Appendix) was printed in London by Cassell in 1892, but the divisions and text remained unchanged. There the quotation appears on p. 14. It is possible that al-'Aqqād used a copy printed by Cassell which had a slightly different arrangement and pagination.

[18] I.e., a triangle of three stars, referred to previously by Farrar as part of the constellation Pisces. Al-'Aqqād translates this term with the word for "triangle," *al-muthallath.*

[19] Since al-'Aqqād's Arabic translation of this quotation from Farrar (1874 ed., pp. 43-44) is fairly accurate, the English text is here taken directly from Farrar's book and is arranged as a block quotation. However, al-'Aqqād omits two short phrases, here placed in brackets.

[20] This date agrees with the consensus of most scholars (Brown, *Birth,* 166-67, 205).

[21] The reference here is to the unsuccessful Jewish revolt in Palestine against Rome which occurred in 132-135 C.E. This is known as the Bar Kokhba Revolt or the Second Jewish Revolt, the first one being the Jewish War of 66-70 C.E. Apparently al-'Aqqād has confused the two events, since he assumes that the Bar Kokhba Revolt took place at about the same time that the Gospel of Matthew was written.

The second revolt was led by Simon bar Kosiba, an inspirational and forceful leader. He was considered to be the Messiah by the influential Rabbi Akiba ben Joseph, and probably he based this on the prophecy of Num. 24:17, "a star [Heb. *kôkāb*] shall come forth out of Jacob." Simon was thus known as "the Son of the Star" (*bar kôkbā'* in Aramaic, rather than the "Hebrew" of al-'Aqqād). Coins were indeed issued bearing this name and emblem. See ABD, s.v. "Bar Kokhba"; Grant, *The Jews,* 242-57; and Schürer, 1:542-52. Farrar also makes a brief reference to this revolt, but without making any connection between it and the writing of Matthew's Gospel (1847 ed., p. 42).

[22] Ar. *mursalīn,* which is closely related to *rusul* [messengers, apostles].

[23] Voltaire visited England during the years 1726-28 and met often with Lord Bolingbroke

(Theodore Besterman, *Voltaire,* 2d ed. [Chicago: University of Chicago Press, 1976], 117-30). Bolingbroke's actual influence on Voltaire, however, was minimal. In any case, neither of them denied the historicity of Christ; rather they attacked the church's belief about him. Voltaire was far more scathing in this respect than was Bolingbroke (Norman L. Torrey, *Voltaire and the English Deists* [Oxford: Marston Press, 1963], 150-51).

[24] Napoleon's conversation with the German poet Christoph Wieland, at Weimar in 1808, is related in several biographies of Napoleon. However, the matter of the existence of Christ has been found only in the work by Emil Ludwig (*Napoleon,* trans. Eden and Cedar Paul [New York: Liveright, 1926], 320-22), and undoubtedly this was al-'Aqqād's source. There, Napoleon is reported to have stated, "It remains an open question whether Christ ever lived"; Wieland replied that it would be just as absurd to doubt the existence of Julius Caesar, or even of Napoleon himself, at which Napoleon congratulated Wieland. Thus, even if Ludwig's story is accurate, it's support for al-'Aqqād's claim is rather weak.

[25] One would wish that al-'Aqqād had provided some further information, at least mentioning a few of the writers or the arguments to which he refers here. Certainly his references above to Voltaire and Napoleon provide little evidence for his concern. His reference prior to that, and also below (pp. 138 and 139), to "the science of comparative religion" seems to indicate that those who advocated this approach were the primary culprits. Yet he has misunderstood their intentions. It was the aim of Max Müller and others to demonstrate, by a comparison of the world's religions, that the large number of similarities these displayed pointed to the existence of a "Natural Religion" which served as the basis for them all. Meanwhile, the proponents of a Darwinian approach to religion viewed Christianity as the product of an evolutionary process. (For a historical overview, see Eric J. Sharpe, *Comparative Religion: A History,* 2d. ed. [La Salle, IL: Open Court, 1986], 27-71). As noted in the Introduction (p. 54), the question of whether or not Jesus actually existed was not seriously raised in this discipline. It was generally accepted that he existed, but that he was merely one of many human and circumstantial factors in the stream of religious reality. For them, Jesus had a role to play for the genesis of Christianity; but this was not a divine role, and it was quickly superseded by the impact of other religious traditions. Al-'Aqqād has transferred this denial of Jesus' lasting influence to a denial of his existence, and this theme forms the background for the remainder of this chapter.

[26] Ar. *dhālika al-insān al-qadīs,* whereas the text in Josephus reads "a wise man" (Gk. *sophos anēr).*

[27] Josephus *Antiquities* 18.3.3 (Loeb 9:49-51). Al-'Aqqād's translation is fairly accurate, but it is incomplete. The passage in Josephus goes on to relate that Pilate condemned Jesus to be crucified, but that he appeared alive on the third day in fulfillment of prophecy, and that the Christians continued into his time. It is hardly surprising that al-'Aqqād, who does not accept Jesus' death and resurrection as reported in the Gospels, omits that portion.

[28] This paragraph is a paraphrase of the critics' argument as presented in the book to which al-'Aqqād refers in the following paragraph, i.e. Thomas Hartwell Horne, *An Introduction to the Critical Study and Knowledge of the Holy Scriptures,* rev. from the 7th London ed. (Philadelphia: Desilver, Thomas & Co., 1836), 1:463. Al-'Aqqād's reference to the passage in Josephus as consisting of only "three lines," while true of the portion which he renders in Arabic, is somewhat of an exaggeration with regard to the original text. Horne says more accurately that it is "one short paragraph."

[29] Here al-'Aqqād provides a footnote giving the title of this work in English (minus the initial article). First published in 1818, it went through several increasingly expanded editions. From al-

'Aqqād's reference to the year 1836, it can be assumed that he utilized the edition published that year (see the preceding note). Al-'Aqqād's argument concerning the passage in Josephus draws from Horne's discussion in 1:463-64.

[30] Al-'Aqqād's wording in the last part of this sentence is not clear. In any case, Horne's original reads as follows: "It is found in all the copies of Josephus' works, which are now extant, whether printed or manuscript; in a Hebrew translation preserved in the Vatican Library, . . ." (Horne, 1:463).

[31] Josephus *Antiquities* 20.9.1 (Loeb 10:106-109). Al-'Aqqād's translation is sufficiently accurate, even if not precise.

[32] Eusebius *Ecclesiastical History* 1.11.7-8 (Loeb 1:82-83).

[33] This paragraph is a summary and paraphrase of Horne's remarks on 1:463.

[34] Horne, 1:463-64.

[35] Ibid., p. 464. Both Horne and al-'Aqqād argue for the authenticity of this passage *in toto,* over against those who deny it completely. Modern scholars, however, generally regard the core of this passage to be genuine while believing certain phrases to have been added by Christian editors. See Meier, 1:56-69; and F. F. Bruce, *Jesus and Christian Origins Outside the New Testament* (Grand Rapids, MI: William B. Eerdmans, 1974), 32-41.

[36] The reference here is to the *Annals* of Tacitus, which was written between 115 and 117 C.E. (and which is the source of al-'Aqqād's quotation), and not to the *Histories* which were composed earlier. (See the "Introduction" for Tacitus in Loeb 3:232-34).

[37] A paraphrase of a portion of Tacitus *Annals* 15.44 (Loeb 5:282-83). The passage goes on to accuse Christians of all kinds of evil practices. Given this anti-Christian tone, the passage could hardly have been a Christian fabrication, and scholars accept it as genuine. This also happens to be the only non-Jewish and non-Christian reference to Pilate. As al-'Aqqād notes, Tacitus gives no indication of the source of his information. (Meier, 1:89-91; Bruce, *Jesus,* 21-23).

[38] Suetonius *Claudius* 25.4 (Loeb 2:52-53). Acts 18:2 also mentions an expulsion of Jews from Rome by Claudius; this is almost certainly a reference to the same event (Bruce, *Acts,* 390).

[39] Ar. *al-ṭayyib. Chrestus* is the Latinized form of the Gk. *chrēstos,* meaning "good" in either a moral sense [kind, friendly] or in a practical sense [useful] (Liddell and Scott, 2007). It was a popular name for slaves at that time, and there are good arguments in support of al-'Aqqād's claim that Suetonius (or perhaps his source) confused this name with *Christus,* the Latin form of "Christ." In any case, as al-'Aqqād also notes, there is no direct reference here to the fact of Jesus' historical existence. (Meier, 91-92, 102 n. 16; Bruce, *Jesus,* 20-21).

[40] Al-'Aqqād must surely have intended to write "the middle of the first century C.E.," since the dates of Claudius' rule were 41-54 C.E. (OCD, s.v. "Claudius [1]).

[41] The life and works of Justus of Tiberias are known only through Josephus, who states that he was active during the Jewish War of 66-70 C.E. Josephus gives no indication whether Justus had made any reference to Jesus. His history ends with the death of Agrippa II, which one ancient source places at 100 C.E.; however, that date is considered unreliable and Agrippa's death occurred more likely in 92 or 93 C.E. (Schürer, 1:34-35, 481).

[42] This statement is on target. There are other early reports concerning Christianity in general which mention Jesus as its founder, but these are considered to be too broad to serve as independent historical witnesses to Jesus. They include the Letter of Pliny the Younger (proconsul in Bithynia 111-113 C.E.); a satire by Lucian of Samosata (d. ca. 200 C.E.); and a few polemical references in early Rabbinical literature. See Meier, 1:92-98; and Bruce, *Jesus,* 23-29, 54-65.

[43] Al-'Aqqād should have said that advocates of the science of comparative religion have asso-

ciated Christmas and the winter solstice, not the autumnal equinox. See his further discussion of this issue below, p. 140, and n. 55 there.

[44] Al-'Aqqād points to European languages regarding the word "Sunday," since the Ar. word for that day *(yaum al-aḥad,* lit., "the first day") makes no reference to the sun *(al-shams).*

[45] A reference to Zech. 9:9 (which al-'Aqqād quoted previously in ch. 4, p. 88), and to its fulfillment by Christ in his entrance into Jerusalem according to Mt. 21:4-5 and Jn. 12:14-15.

[46] The date of Paul's death, which is not mentioned in the NT, is not known and is difficult to determine. Christian tradition indicates that he was executed by Nero in 64 C.E. But there are many other factors involved in assessing the data, including the date and authenticity of the Pauline writings in the NT. For an overview, see F. F. Bruce, *Paul: Apostle of the Heart Set Free* (Grand Rapids, MI: William B. Eerdmans, 1977), 441-55.

[47] The point of al-'Aqqād's argument in the final sentence is not clear.

[48] From the discussion that follows, al-'Aqqād means here the entire NT rather than just the four Gospels.

[49] While the proper title of the book is "the Acts of the Apostles," indicating a more general perspective, it is true that Paul figures far more prominently than any of the other early Christian leaders.

[50] Acts 11:26. From the evidence of these passages, the name "Christians" seems to have been coined by those who were antagonistic towards the new movement rather than by its adherents. "Christian" does not appear as a self-designation until the second century C.E. (Bruce, *Acts,* 274-75).

[51] A reference to Herod Agrippa II, great-grandson of Herod the Great; he ruled over various northern regions of Palestine from ca. 49 to his death, ca. 93. Chapter 26 of Acts presents Paul's legal defense before him (in 59 C.E.) (ABD, s.v. "Agrippa [2]").

[52] Acts 26:28. The exact meaning of al-'Aqqād's wording is somewhat obscure: *ahwan bimā tuqni'unī bihi an aṣīra masīḥīyan,* lit. "It is easier in what you persuade me that I become a Christian." This follows VD only partially, which has *biqalīlin tuqni'unī an aṣīra masīḥīyan* ("With so little do you persuade me to become a Christian!"), and which is in agreement with RSV and the Gk. text.

[53] 1 Pet. 4:14-16. As is the case with the two other references in the NT to the word "Christian," the name "appears to reflect the viewpoint of Jewish and pagan outsiders toward those who followed and worshiped Jesus" (J. Ramsey Michaels, *1 Peter,* Word Biblical Commentary, ed. David A. Hubbard and Glenn W. Barker, vol. 49 [Waco, TX: Word Books, 1988], 268).

Although al-'Aqqād correctly points out the three references to the word "Christian(s)" in the NT, he does not mention other designations such as "the Way" (Acts 9:2, 24:14) and "the sect of the Nazarenes" (Acts 24:5). Nevertheless, his point that such names appear infrequently bears some validity, since the NT evidence indicates that the earliest (Jewish) Christians considered themselves within the framework of first-century Judaism.

[54] Origen of Alexandria (d. ca. 254) was a very important, and sometimes controversial, theologian and Biblical scholar of the early church. He led a rather ascetic life, and this aspect is mentioned by al-'Aqqād in ch. 18 (p. 179). A reference to his view concerning the celebration of Jesus' birth has not been located, but his objection to this would fit well with his opposition to pagan tradition and his dependence on the Bible for church practice. For overviews, see ODCC, s.v. "Origen"; Chadwick, 100-113.

[55] Al-'Aqqād presents here the most common argument for how the celebration of Jesus' birth was set on the 25th of December; the argument is primarily drawn from the "history of religions"

approach which he has been discussing. However, he mistakenly presents Christmas as being associated with the autumnal equinox *[al-i'tidāl al-kharīfī]* rather than the winter solstice *[al-inqilāb al-shatwī]*. The Roman "festival to the sun" which he mentions had been established on 25 December by the Emperor Aurelian in 274 C.E.; and it is known that after 312 C.E., when Christianity was granted protection under the Emperor Constantine, there was a clear association between the celebration of Christmas and that festival. However, it is also possible that Christians had already been celebrating Jesus' birth on 25 December prior to these events. For a full discussion of this issue, see Thomas J. Talley, *The Origins of the Liturgical Year*, 2d ed. (Collegeville, MN: Liturgical Press, 1991), 85-103.

[56] Tarsus, the birthplace of Paul, was a major city of Asia Minor. According to Strabo, it surpassed even Athens and Alexandria as a center for culture and learning, including philosophy; but other sources are less flattering (ABD, s.v. "Tarsus"). In any case, there is no evidence for the presence of Mithraism there at the time of Paul. As noted in ch. 8 (p. 117, n. 10), it is questionable whether the cult of Mithra had arrived in the Roman world prior to 80 C.E.

However, al-'Aqqād has probably made this claim based on the source which he identifies later in the same paragraph, i.e., Walter Woodburn Hyde, *Paganism to Christianity in the Roman Empire* (Philadelphia: University of Pennsylvania Press, 1946), 68-69. Hyde claims that "it would seem only natural that Paul, reared in Tarsus, a Mithraic center, should have been influenced by Mithraic ideas" (68).

[57] Gregory I, also known as Gregory the Great (d. 604) was Pope from 590 to his death. He was the fourth and last of the "Doctors" of the Latin Church (ODCC, s.v. "Gregory I"). St. Bede "the Venerable" (d. 735) was a biblical scholar and historian of the church in England up to his time (ODCC, s.v. "Bede"). St. Mellitus (d. 624) was sent to England by Gregory in 601 to be a missionary bishop; he became Archbishop of Canterbury in 619 (ODCC, s.v. "Mellitus").

[58] Al-'Aqqād here provides a footnote in Arabic and English indicating the source of this quotation as "Paganism into *[sic]* Christianity in the Roman Empire by Hyde" (see n. 56). The quotation is from p. 69 of Hyde's work. Since al-'Aqqād's Arabic translation is fairly accurate, the passage is here taken directly from Hyde's quotation of Bede. Unfortunately, however, al-'Aqqād cut the quotation short, leaving it difficult to interpret; the missing words have been provided in brackets for the sake of clarity.

In addition to al-'Aqqād's statement about Paul above, his comments in general concerning the relationship between the pagan religions of that time and Christianity has clearly been influenced by Hyde's book.

[59] Ar. *aqrab al-mu'arrikhīn ilayhim,* lit. "the nearest of the historians to them." It is not exactly clear what al-'Aqqād means by this phrase, but perhaps he is referring to the dearth of critical analysis found in the works of Suetonius. See OCD, s.v. "Suetonius (2)."

[60] *The Lives of the Caesars,* written by Suetonius in the early second century, comprises biographies of the twelve emperors from Julius to Domitian (ibid.).

[61] This is the main branch of Shī'ī Islam, also called "Ithnā 'Asharīyah" or "Twelver" Shī'ism. This is in distinction of other branches such as the Ismā'īlī branch (which recognizes only the first seven Imams) and the Zaydī branch (which recognizes only the first five Imams). (EI^2, s.v. *"Imāma"*[3:1166-67] and *"Ithnā 'Asharīyah").*

[62] See Josh. 10:12-14.

[63] Al-'Aqqād here provides a footnote indicating his source for this quotation as "Chamber's papers, volume 3, part 4." The reference in full is William Chambers and Robert Chambers, *Carthage and the Carthaginians,* no. 20 in *Chambers's Papers for the People,* vol. 3-4 (Edinburgh:

William and Robert Chambers, 1850), p. 1. (Paper no. 20 appears fourth in vol. 3, which is bound with vol. 4; each paper is independently paginated). There the quotation reads "We have fled from the robber Joshua, the son of Nun." The paper claims that this inscription "was discovered in Numidia A.D. 540" but it does not give a source; it goes on to accept its authenticity.

In fact, the only basis for the existence of such an inscription is a statement by the sixth-century Greek historian Procopius. He claimed that in Numidia "are two columns made of white stone near by the great spring, having Phoenician letters cut in them which say in the Phoenician tongue: 'We are they who fled from before the face of Joshua, the robber, the son of Nun'" (Procopius *History of the Wars* 4.10.22 [Loeb 2:288-89]). The genuineness of such an inscription was refuted by Heinrich Ewald in his *The History of Israel,* vol. 2, *History of Moses and the Theocracy,* 3d ed. (London: Longmans, Green, 1876), 229-30. Modern scholars simply ignore it as unsubstantiated.

[64] Or, "call" (Ar. *da'wah),* and so until the end of this chapter. Concerning the nature of the Gospels as documents and their possible interdependence, see al-'Aqqād's remarks in ch. 22 (pp. 211-12).

[65] The intention of this paragraph is not entirely clear, but al-'Aqqād seems to be underscoring the character of Jesus' mission as one that was uniform yet not mechanistic. In the last phrase, he seems to be describing the ambivalence and uncertainty of life under the domination of Rome.

[66] Here, the Ar. term for "mission" is *risālah,* from the same root as *rasūl* ("messenger").

Chapter 12
A Descriptive Portrait of Christ

[1] The "Letter of Lentulus" is a Latin text which actually originated in the thirteenth century. It states that Publius Lentulus, an official in Judea at the time of Christ (but in fact unknown in history), observed Jesus and sent his description to the Roman Senate. See the discussions and English translations in J. K. Elliot, *The Apocryphal New Testament: A Collection of Apocryphal Christian Literature in an English Translation* (Oxford: Clarendon Press, 1993), 542-43; and Edgar J. Goodspeed, *Modern Apocrypha* (Boston: Beacon Press, 1956), 88-91. There is a similar, shorter discussion of this letter, along with a translation, in Farrar's *Life of Christ* (1874 ed., p. 694). This is the book which al-'Aqqād had used regarding the star of the Magi (ch. 11, p. 135; see n. 17 there), and he may well have used this as his source here. However, it is not clear how al-'Aqqād thought that Lentulus was allegedly Pilate's friend, or that this description circulated among Christians in the fourth century. His translation from English, though neither complete nor always precise, is reasonably close.

[2] Here, al-'Aqqād uses the Christian Arabic name for Jesus, *Yasū'.*

[3] Although al-'Aqqād doubts the validity of this document, he still seems to favor its circulation in the fourth century according to his initial remarks.

[4] If this statement is accurate, one would expect to find such claims among Jewish polemic or rabbinic literature dating from the first few centuries C.E. However, an extensive search has failed to locate any such examples.

[5] See Lev. ch. 21.

[6] Jn. 1:49. Al-'Aqqād's comment which follows seeks to minimize the high christological claim which is intended by the Gospel writer. If Nathaniel spoke in this manner, he probably used

both phrases as messianic titles; John, however, saw much more being expressed in Nathaniel's witness about Jesus (Brown, *John,* 29:87-88).

[7] This is a reference to statements made in each of the Synoptic Gospels concerning the popular response to Jesus' ministry (Mt. 7:28-29 = Mk. 1:22 = Lk. 4:32; there is also an allusion to Jesus' authoritative teaching in Jn. 7:46). Mark and Luke record their comments in connection with Jesus' ministry in Capernaum, while Matthew places his statement at the end of the Sermon on the Mount. Although Matthew and Mark (only) refer to the people's comparison of Jesus' teaching to that of the scribes, there is no mention of a comparison to the teaching of the priests.

[8] The style of Jesus' teaching is a subject which al-'Aqqād develops further in ch. 20 (pp. 195-96); see the notes there.

[9] It may be argued on the basis of the Gospels that Jesus had a penchant for nature. He included aspects of nature in his sayings, e.g., his reference to "the birds of the air" and "the lilies of the field" (Mt. 6:25-30 = Lk. 12:22-28); and his retirement to the garden of Gethsemane was a matter of personal "custom" (Lk. 22:39, cf. Mt. 26:36 = Mk. 14:32, Jn. 18:1). However, al-'Aqqād's romantic perspective in this paragraph is probably a reflection of Renan's book about Jesus, which is replete with similar language (see the Introduction, p. 53).

[10] Although this body of water in northern Palestine is called "the Sea of Tiberias" in Jn. 6:1 and 21:1 (after the city which was built on its western shore by Herod Antipas), it is more commonly referred to as "the Sea of Galilee" in the Gospels.

[11] Several passages in the Gospels indicate that Jesus often spent time alone at prayer, especially during the night or early morning: Mk. 1:35 = Lk. 4:42; Mt. 14:23 = Mk. 6:46; Lk. 6:12.

[12] See, e.g., Lk. 8:2-3, where several women are mentioned who accompany Jesus and the twelve disciples in his itinerant ministry, and who provide for their needs from their own means. This must be viewed as "a recollection about Jesus which differed radically from the usual understanding of women's role in contemporary Judaism" (Fitzmyer, 28:696). However, al-'Aqqād's portrayal of these women as anxious and gullible coincides with his rather low view of women in general (see the Introduction, p. 30).

[13] The incident of Pilate's wife is recorded briefly only in Mt. 27:19, where it is stated that she made her request on the basis of a dream she had just experienced. There is no indication that she knew Jesus personally. The brevity with which she is presented was later expanded by church tradition, which made her into a noble woman and a saint (Raymond E. Brown, *The Death of the Messiah: From Gethsemane to the Grave: A Commentary on the Passion Narratives in the Four Gospels,* The Anchor Reference Library, ed. David Noel Freedman [New York: Doubleday, 1994], 1:803-804).

[14] Mt. 11:29.

[15] This comment is most likely a reference to the "Beatitudes" of Mt. 5:3-12, particularly vv. 3 and 5. Also applicable would be the saying about receiving the kingdom of God like a child in order to enter it (Mt. 18:3 = Mk. 10:15 = Lk. 18:17).

[16] Muslims generally believe that the prophets were without sin, at least in their role as prophets. One of the signs which was considered necessary, in order for genuine prophecy to take place, was *'iṣmah* [moral infallibility] on the part of the spokesman (EI^2, s.v. *"nubuwwa"* [8:94]). It is, of course, a tenet of Christian belief that Jesus was without sin (see 2 Cor. 5:21, Heb. 4:15, 1 Pet. 2:21-22).

[17] Ar. *al-hidāyah,* i.e., guidance from God.

[18] Mt. 12:48, 50 = Mk. 3:33, 35; Mt. 12:30 = Lk. 11:22; and Lk. 14:26, respectively. In the last quotation, the biblical text adds "and his sisters" after "brothers." There is a parallel to that

passage in Mt. 10:37, but Jesus' words are presented there in milder terms. The saying that one must "hate" one's family members in order to be Jesus' disciple is also found twice in the non-canonical *Gospel of Thomas.* Most commentators regard the harsh wording of Luke (and/or Thomas) to be original. Understood as hyperbole, the saying nevertheless requires Jesus' followers to renounce family ties when necessary. (Fitzmyer, 28A:1060-63; Nolland, 35B:762).

[19] "Second thoughts" is presumably the sense of al-'Aqqād's invented word *mathnawīyah,* found in eds. 1 and 2. It is probably intended as a derivation of *thānawī,* "secondary." The innovative nature of the word perhaps explains the typographical error in ed. 3, where the text has *mathwīyah,* a meaningless word.

[20] Since the verb is in the imperative, this statement would seem to be a quotation of Mt. 10:16. However, no quotation marks are present here, and the two parts of the saying have been reversed. The same verse is quoted more accurately, however, in ch. 21, p. 207).

Al-'Aqqād's prior remarks in this paragraph, concerning the dangers to the body and to the soul, echo Mt. 10:28. The entire chapter in Matthew portrays Jesus sending out the twelve disciples on a mission, and warning them of the dangers they will face.

[21] Mk. 3:6-7 records the plot of the Pharisees and Herodians, followed by Jesus' withdrawal to the sea. The parallel of Mt. 12:14-15 makes a definite connection between the two events: "Jesus, aware of this [plot], withdrew from there" (v. 15). However, there is no explicit connection in Mark. In fact, the paragraph beginning with v. 7 structurally serves as an introduction to what follows rather than a sequel to what preceded it (C. S. Mann, *Mark: A New Translation with Introduction and Commentary,* The Anchor Bible, ed. William Foxwell Albright and David Noel Freedman, vol. 27 [Garden City, NY: Doubleday, 1986], 245).

[22] The reference in the second half of this paragraph is to Jesus' prayer of anguish in the Garden of Gethsemane at night, just prior to his arrest. This incident is recorded in all three Synoptic Gospels (Mt. 26:36-46 = Mk. 14:32-42 = Lk. 22:39-46). The "cup" was a common Semitic symbol for intense suffering; to drink the cup was to undergo a terrible fate. In the context of the Gospels, this cup clearly refers to the suffering which Jesus was about to encounter in his arrest, trial and crucifixion (Brown, *Death,* 168-70).

Al-'Aqqād's quotations are from Matthew's account. (The final quotation can be rendered from the Gk. as either a command or a question, "Are you still sleeping and taking your rest?" Whereas RSV presents it as a question, VD translates it as a command, as does al-'Aqqād here.) Mark's version is almost identical to Matthew's, but there the words "with me" are absent in both of the verses quoted by al-'Aqqād. Luke's rendition covers other aspects of this incident and does not record most of the details to which al-'Aqqād refers.

It is not clear whether al-'Aqqād intends to include John in his reference to "all the Gospels." Although John does not record the event of Jesus' prayer in Gethsemane, he does mention in 12:27 a prayer of Jesus to his Father concerning his troubled soul and his acceptance of the events which were soon to take place; and in 18:11, as Jesus is arrested, he states, "Shall I not drink the cup which the Father has given me?" The first passage gives the distinct impression of serving as a Johannine parallel to the prayer in Gethsemane (Brown, *John,* 29:475; *and* Beasley-Murray, 207).

In any case, it is especially noteworthy that al-'Aqqād makes no attempt to identify the meaning of the "cup" or the "destiny" to which he refers. As the subsequent paragraphs indicate, his focus is on the "struggle" *(jihād)* of the soul of Jesus.

[23] Ar. *al-shayāṭīn,* the pl. of *shayṭān* [devil, Satan]. The Temptation of Jesus is mentioned only briefly in Mk. 1:12-13, but it is given detailed expansion in Mt. 4:1-11 and Lk. 4:1-13 (John omits it altogether). In all three accounts, there is only one tempter: "Satan" in Mark, "the devil" in

Matthew and Luke. Al-'Aqqād covers this event in more detail in ch. 23 (pp. 219-21).

[24] The reference to the first entry of Jesus into Jerusalem is clearly to the "Triumphal Entry" on what is traditionally called Palm Sunday (Mt. 21:1-9 = Mk. 11:1-10 = Lk. 19:28-40 = Jn. 12:12-19). The Gospels record that during the following week, Jesus spent the nights outside of Jerusalem in Bethany; from there he entered the city each day, where the controversy with the Jewish authorities grew more and more intense. Al-'Aqqād's "second" entry of Jesus is probably an amalgamation of these subsequent trips into the city. In any case, he briefly describes the Triumphal Entry in ch. 23 (p. 225).

[25] Ar. *innahu ghā'ib 'an nafsihi.* Possibly al-'Aqqād had in mind here a passage such as Mk. 3:20-22 or Jn. 10:20, where Jesus' opponents accuse him of being "beside himself" and possessed with a demon.

[26] It is quite possible that al-'Aqqād had in mind here the periods of Jesus' silence during his trial, either before the Sanhedrin (Mt. 26:63 = Mk. 14:61), or before Pilate (Mt. 27:14 = Mk. 15:5), or before Herod (Lk. 23:9). Although al-'Aqqād later states his reservations about the historicity of that event (ch. 23, p. 226), elsewhere he refers to Jesus' appearance before Pilate as if it had actually taken place (ch. 16, p. 170; see n. 22 there).

[27] This was the prayer of Jesus in the Garden of Gethsemane according to the Synoptic Gospels (Mt. 26:39 = Mk. 14:36 = Lk. 22:42; see n. 22 above). The wording is slightly different in each account, but al-'Aqqād follows none of them; the most significant difference is that in each of the Gospel accounts Jesus addresses God as "Father." However, al-'Aqqād quotes the prayer again in ch. 23 (p. 224), where he includes the address of "Father."

[28] Al-'Aqqād corrects himself here. He knows that Jesus prayed this at the end of his mission; yet he sees it as representative of Jesus' approach throughout that mission.

[29] The implication here, and elsewhere in the book, is that God *did* take away the "cup." This is a position argued more forcefully by Manṣūr Ḥusayn 'Abd al-'Azīz, whose book on Jesus was published ten years after al-'Aqqād's (see the Introduction, p. 18). For further analysis on the significance of al-'Aqqād remarks here, see the Introduction, p. 64-65.

Chapter 13
The Call of Christ

[1] Ar. *Da'wat al-Masīḥīyah,* lit., "The Call of Christianity." This title in fact appears only in ed. 3. In ed. 1, there was no title for this chapter, but the title of the part which began with this chapter was simply *Al-Da'wah,* "The Call." In ed. 2, the title *Al-Da'wah* was given to both the part as well as to this chapter. Apparently the editors of ed. 3, in an effort to avoid repetition of the same title for both the part and the chapter, made a slight change in the title for the chapter. (See Appendix A, especially p. 240).

It is true that al-'Aqqād begins this chapter by referring not to Christ but to Christianity (second paragraph). Yet it becomes quite evident that he considers the message of Christianity to be one that continues (or at least ought to continue) the message of its founder. Since the focus of the chapter (as well as the book) is on Christ far more than his followers, the translation for the chapter title reflects this.

The first word of the title, *al-da'wah,* could be translated as "mission"; but the emphasis of this word as it is used in this section of the book is on the message of Jesus by which he "called" others to a new way of life.

[2] Ar. *al-da'wah al-masīḥīyah,* lit. either "the Messianic call" or "the Christian call"; yet the context, as well as the subsequent discussion, clearly refers to the message of Jesus himself. This phrase is slightly different from the title of the chapter in ed. 3, where the article is missing from the word *al-da'wah* (see the previous note).

[3] Al-'Aqqād clearly implies in this paragraph that the appropriate remedy for the evils of society at that time would necessarily be similar to what in fact came in the mission of Jesus. This first statement is an obvious allusion to the saying of Jesus found in Mt. 16:26 = Mk. 8:36 = Lk. 9:25.

[4] The use of the phrase "kingdom of heaven" would imply that this statement is meant to be another allusion to a saying of Jesus. Yet no such saying is recorded in the Gospels. The closest is in Lk. 17:21, to which al-'Aqqād refers in ch. 19 (p. 190; see n. 37 there).

[5] Again, this statement does not correspond directly with any of Jesus' sayings as recorded in the Gospels. However, parts of the statement have allusions to his teaching about anxiety (Mt. 6:25-34 = Lk. 12:23-32), and to his discussion concerning what defiles a person (Mt. 15:11-20 = Mk. 7:14-23).

[6] Perhaps al-'Aqqād is thinking here of the first half of "the Great Commandment," concerning love for God: Mt. 22:37 = Mk. 12:29-30 = Lk. 10:26.

[7] Al-'Aqqād elaborates on this claim in ch. 23 (pp. 222-23). See n. 39 there, and also ch. 19, n. 28, for his understanding of the phrase "the Son of Man."

[8] Included here would be the second half of "the Great Commandment," love for one's neighbor: Mt. 22:39 = Mk. 12:31 = Lk. 10:27. More specifically, however, the reference to love for one's enemies is to Mt. 5:43-48 = Lk. 6:27-36.

[9] Mt. 5:40-42 = Lk. 6:29-30.

[10] Probably this is an allusion to Mk. 10:23 (= Mt. 19:23 = Lk. 18:24): "How hard it will be for those who have riches to enter the kingdom of God!"

[11] Mt. 22:21 = Mk. 12:17 = Lk. 20:25. This is a favorite passage for al-'Aqqād. See ch. 7, pp. 110-11, n. 35.

[12] This seems to be a general statement rather than an allusion to any specific passage.

[13] A reference to the incident, previously mentioned by al-'Aqqād (ch. 8, pp. 119-20), when Augustus publicly burned a large quantity of religious works.

[14] Lk. 12:49; Lk. 12:51-53 = Mt. 10:34-36. The passage in Matthew is shorter and somewhat different; al-'Aqqād follows the version in Luke, although he omits v. 50 and his wording is not precisely that of VD.

[15] Mic. 7:2, 5-6. This passage thus forms the OT basis for Jesus' saying quoted in the previous paragraph. The last phrase, which is omitted by Luke, is included in Matthew's version.

[16] Al-'Aqqād seems to mean here that Jesus' call to brotherhood led to a split among the Jews regarding him, because of his inclusion of the Gentiles. The phrase "the birds of the air" is a reference to the parable of the Mustard Seed in Mt. 13:31-32 = Mk. 4:30-32 = Lk. 13:18-19. There, Jesus compares the kingdom of God to a tiny mustard seed, which when planted produces a large shrub in whose branches "the birds of the air" make nests. The idea that these birds must have represented the Gentiles was put forward by T. W. Manson, *The Teaching of Jesus* (Cambridge: Cambridge University Press, 1937), 133 n. 1, and possibly this is al-'Aqqād's source here. Modern commentators are a bit more skeptical (Davies and Allison, 2:420; Mann, 272; Fitzmyer, 28A:1017).

[17] The words "invited" and "invitation" in this paragraph, which are the more appropriate trans-

lations concerning a banquet, are from the same verbal root as "call" *(dā'ā).*

18 Ar. *al-mathal,* "metaphor," "example" or "proverb." This word, found frequently in the Gospels for Jesus' parables, is the standard term used in VD. Al-'Aqqād uses it here for the first time.

19 Lk. 14:16-24. Al-'Aqqād has abbreviated certain details, e.g., the second man had actually purchased five pair of oxen, and there is a third man who declined the invitation because he had just been married. (A similar parable is found in Mt. 22:1-10, but it differs from Luke's version in several important respects).

Al-'Aqqād understands this parable to point to a rejection of Jesus' call by the Jewish community at large, and the shift of his message to the Gentiles instead; see his reference to this same parable in ch. 19 (pp. 186-87). Yet Luke is careful to demonstrate that although the Jewish religious leaders refused to respond to Jesus, many Jews from the lower segments of society did indeed accept his invitation (those from the roads and lanes of the city). It was only after they had come in that the invitation was extended to the Gentiles (those from the byways and street corners which would have been situated outside of the city). (Fitzmyer, 28A:1053-54; and Nolland, 35B:759).

20 Al-'Aqqād is not clear in this paragraph, but perhaps he is referring to the discussion about whether Jesus expected the imminent coming of the kingdom and end of the world (as expressed by Albert Schweitzer), or whether he preached the reality of the present kingdom which would continue indefinitely (as expressed by C. H. Dodd; see ABD, s.v. "Eschatology [Early Christian], [2:599-600]). In any case, his point seems to be that whatever view one might hold, Jesus' message experienced a transferal from the Jews who rejected it to the Gentiles who accepted it.

21 Ar. *qiblah.* This is the first appearance of this term. See the note to the title of the next chapter.

22 An obvious allusion to the saying of Jesus in Mt. 6:24 = Lk. 16:13.

23 Here al-'Aqqād includes a footnote, translated as follows: "An Aramaic word which stands for worldly ambitions and carnal desires. It is now used in European languages to refer to the god of material possessions and of wealth." In fact, the Aramaic word *māmônā'* (transliterated in Gk. as *mamōnas)* refers to actual property or wealth, not the desire for such; in itself, the word had no pejorative connotation (ABD, s.v. "Mammon"; Davies and Allison, 1:643).

Chapter 14
The Choice of Direction

1 Ar. *Ikhtiyār al-Qiblah. "qiblah"* is a distinctly Islamic term, meaning the direction towards which Muslims face when at prayer. Originally the orientation of the *qiblah* was Jerusalem, but this was changed to the *ka'bah* in Mecca by Muḥammad, about a year and a half after the *hijrah* to Medina. This is said to be in response to revelation, i.e., Qur'ān 2:142-44; the reasons for the change vary in Muslim tradition, but it was evidently connected to Muḥammad's deteriorating relations with the Jews of Medina. (EI^2, s.v. *"ḳibla"* [5:82]). Al-'Aqqād's discussion of a "change" in one's *qiblah* in response to the message of Christ may well be an allusion to the original change of *qiblah* for Muslim prayer. He first used this term at the end of the previous chapter (p. 155). In this chapter, the word "direction" is almost always a translation of *qiblah.*

2 Ar. *al-da'wah al-masīḥīyah.* On this phrase, see ch. 13, p. 151, n. 2.

3 The contradictions mentioned here undoubtedly refer to the sayings of Jesus which al-'Aqqād later discusses in this chapter concerning the requirement to "hate" one's own family while also to

"love" one's enemies.

[4] On the meaning of "mammon," see ch. 13, p. 155, n. 23.

[5] Lk. 12:23, 27-28 = Mt. 6:25, 28-30.

[6] This quotation is somewhat equivalent to a combination of Lk. 12:29-30 and 12:33 (= Mt. 6:31-32 and Mt. 6:20). However, al-'Aqqād omits two sayings which are significant components of these passages: "Instead, seek [first] his kingdom [and his righteousness], and [all] these things shall be yours as well" (Lk. 12:31; = Mt. 6:33, for which the additions there are noted here in brackets); and "For where your treasure is, there will your heart be also" (Lk. 12:34 = Mt. 6:21).

[7] Lk. 14:26-27; although al-'Aqqād does not follow VD exactly, he retains the use of the word *yubghiḍu,* "hates"; the parallel in Mt. 10:37-38 is not so strong. He had previously quoted Lk. 14:26 in ch. 12 (p. 147; see n. 18 there). On the phrase "carry his cross," see n. 11 below.

[8] Ar. *ud'ū li-man yusī'ūna ilaykum.* Al-'Aqqād's use of the verb *dā'ā* (although with a different connotation in this context) forms an interesting departure from VD, which has *ṣallū* [pray for] in both the Luke and Matthew versions.

[9] Lk. 6:27-32, 34-35a. The parallel in Mt. 5:39-47 (along with 7:12) is arranged differently. Al-'Aqqād uses the version in Luke, following VD somewhat closely, although occasionally his wording reflects instead that found in Matthew.

[10] Lk. 17:3-4. An expanded version is in Mt. 18:15-22.

[11] There is a degree of irony in the fact that al-'Aqqād includes the element of carrying one's cross (also mentioned above in his quotation of Lk. 14:27), even though he does not accept the historicity of Jesus' own crucifixion.

[12] Lk. 14:28. The rest of the parable, which is reflected in al-'Aqqād's subsequent comments, runs as follows: "Otherwise, when he has laid a foundation, and is not able to finish, all who see it begin to mock him, saying, 'This man began to build, and was not able to finish.'" (vv. 29-30, RSV).

[13] Mt. 19:14 = Mk. 10:14 = Lk. 18:16. Again, al-'Aqqād's wording only approximates that of VD, but here he is careful to retain the opening command from the verb *dā'ā.*

[14] Lk. 18:10-14. Al-'Aqqād's brief introduction to this parable is taken directly from v. 9. Two departures from the biblical text can be noted: (1) the parable actually has the Pharisee claiming to fast twice a week, rather than twice a day; (2) the final comment made by Jesus in v. 14 is omitted: "for every one who exalts himself will be humbled, but he who humbles himself will be exalted" (RSV).

Chapter 15
The Ordeals Incorporated in the Call

[1] Ar. *Tajārib al-Da'wah,* lit. "The Trials (or Temptations) of the Call."

[2] The duration of Jesus' public ministry is not easy to ascertain from the Gospels. The Synoptics record a visit by Jesus to Jerusalem for the Passover feast only at the end of his ministry; this would seem to imply that it lasted a year or less, but it is possible that previous visits are simply not mentioned. Proponents of a three-year ministry base their arguments on the references to several visits to Jerusalem in the Gospel of John; but these references can be variously interpreted and may serve as a theological framework rather than a historical one. For a summary of the data and viewpoints, see ABD, s.v. "Chronology" (1:1014-15); and Meier, 1:403-406. Meier's conclu-

sion is that Jesus' ministry most likely lasted "two years plus a month or two" (1:406).

[3] Al-'Aqqād's blending of Christian and Muslim variations on these names is interesting. He gives the Christian version of John first, then places the Islamic version (along with his own form for "Baptist") in parentheses, Ar. *Yūḥannā al-Ma'madān (Yaḥyā al-Mughtasil);* (see ch. 6, p. 102, nn. 43-44 on al-'Aqqād's use of these terms). He then gives only the Islamic version for Jesus, *'Īsā ibn Maryam.* References to John by name in the rest of this chapter follow the Christian version.

[4] An allusion to Mt. 3:10 = Lk. 3:9. However, in the biblical text, the verbs are in the passive voice; the subject of the action is presumed to be God, since the reference is clearly to the final judgment (Davies and Allison, 1:309; and Meier 2:29-30). Al-'Aqqād quotes this passage more carefully on p. 162, with the verbs properly in the passive voice.

[5] Lk. 1:5-22. Although most of this paragraph is not in quotation marks and al-'Aqqād has made some rearrangement, he has borrowed much of the wording and style from the account given in VD.

[6] Ar. *miḥrāb,* i.e., the recess in one of the walls of a mosque which indicates the *qiblah,* or direction of prayer. This is the word which appears in the Qur'ānic version of the story, presented below. In Luke's version, VD has simply "the Temple" (*al-haykal,* v. 21).

[7] Ar. *rawā;* or the verb could be read in the passive voice as *ruwiya* [it was related]. In any case, it could be understood here either that Zechariah communicated his vision without actually talking, or that he told his story later when he was able to speak.

[8] Ar. *al-rūḥ al-qudus.* This is the standard Christian Arabic term for the Holy Spirit and is the phrase which appears in Lk. 1:15. The same phrase appears in the Qur'ān three times in connection with the birth of Jesus, where God states that he has "strengthened" or "confirmed" (Ar. *ayyada)* Jesus with the Holy Spirit (e.g., 2:87). Muslim commentators agree that this spirit is the angel Gabriel; his holiness speaks either of his purity or of the blessing he brings (Ayoub, *Qur'an,* 1:124-25). Jesus himself is also spoken of in the Qur'ān as "a spirit from [God]"; (see the presentation of the data, along with a discussion, in Parrinder, 48-51). The Christian concept of the Holy Spirit as the third "person" of the Trinity is, of course, rejected by Muslims. It is noteworthy that al-'Aqqād allows the term to stand here, and elsewhere in the book, without further comment; this is another indication of his effort to avoid issues of controversy between Muslims and Christians.

[9] Al-'Aqqād gives first the Christian version of this name, *Īlīyā,* and then the Muslim version, *Ilyās,* in parentheses. This biblical prophet is also mentioned in the Qur'ān and in later Muslim tradition (EI^2, s.v. "Ilyās").

In the full account given by Luke, the vision of the angel (who is identified as Gabriel) and his conversation with Zechariah is presented prior to Zechariah's departure from the Temple. More important, however, is the manner in which al-'Aqqād deals with Zechariah's inability to speak; he gives the impression that Zechariah was startled into silence by the wonder of the vision. In fact, Luke states that this was imposed on Zechariah as a punishment when he demonstrated a lack of faith. After coming out, he made signs to the people, and he remained unable to speak until after the baby was born (Lk. 1:23, 62-64). Most likely al-'Aqqād omits this detail because of its variance with the Qur'ānic account given below (see the second paragraph of the following note).

[10] Qur'ān 3:38-41. The translation of this quotation follows eds. 1 and 2. In ed. 3, a very strange printing error appears at this point. The quotation from the Qur'ān (which in ed. 3 has been reproduced directly from an authorized text) has v. 41 through the word "mankind" *(al-nās),* which comes at the end of a line. The next line inexplicably continues, not with the rest of v. 41, but with the words of a verse from Sūrat al-Mu'minīn, so that the entire quotation ends with as

follows: "And We made the son of Mary and his mother a portent, and We gave them refuge on a height, a place of flocks and water-springs" (23:50).

In this passage (and also the one following), Zechariah's inability to speak is said to be a "token" *(āyah)* from God; he was to communicate via "signs" (*ramz,* given in the sg. accusative) for three days. The assumption is that he regained his ability to speak after that period of time. The exact reason for Zechariah's inability to speak is not clear, and commentators differed on this point. Al-Ṭabarī believed that Zechariah was punished for doubting God's power, but most commentators rejected that view, claiming that this "token" was a miracle which confirmed his faith or which allowed him to spend time in meditation (see Mahmoud M. Ayoub, *The Qur'an and Its Interpreters,* vol. 2, *The House of 'Imran* [Albany: State University of New York Press, 1992], 115-22).

[11] Qur'ān 19:1-15. This sūrah actually begins with five *muqaṭṭa'āt* [abbreviated letters]. In the book, these are present only in ed. 3.

[12] Ar. *ḥaṣūr,* so used in the first passage from the Qur'ān quoted above (3:39). The root *ḥaṣara* means "to surround" or "limit." This particular derivative is found only in classical Arabic. It refers primarily to "one who has no sexual intercourse with women, . . . though able to have it, . . . abstaining from them from a motive of chastity, and for the sake of shunning worldly pleasures"; however, it could also mean "castrated" (E. W. Lane, *Arabic-English Lexicon* [Cambridge, England: Islamic Texts Society, 1984], 1:583). Commentators on this verse in the Qur'ān demonstrated various views. Al-Ṭabarī favored the belief that John was made incapable of sexual intercourse. Most others rejected this, saying that John was simply protected from involvement in sexual impropriety. Ibn Kathīr went as far as saying that John was probably married and produced children in a legitimate manner. (See Ayoub, *Qur'an,* 2:109-112).

[13] These details of John's character and behavior seem to be drawn primarily from the Gospel accounts (e.g., Mt. 3:4 = Mk. 1:6). The passage in Josephus noted below is too general. However, the reference to his learning from books and from his parents, which is not found in the biblical data, may be an allusion to a passage in the Qur'ān, i.e., 19:12-14.

[14] Although these few words summarize John's preaching according to the Gospels, they are not found as such among the various reports of what he said. However, they are comparable to the outline of Jesus' early preaching: "The time is fulfilled, and the kingdom of God is at hand; repent, and believe in the gospel" (Mk. 1:15, RSV; cf. Mt. 4:17).

[15] Mt. 3:10 = Lk. 3:9. Note that al-'Aqqād alluded to this verse at the beginning of the chapter, there making John himself the subject of the cutting. Curiously, although he here follows the wording of VD more closely, he refers to the "head" of the tree *(ra's al-shajarah)* rather than the "root" *(aṣl)* as used not only in VD, but also in his allusion above. Although *ra's* is not equivalent to *aṣl* (it ought to refer rather to a tree's branches), it is difficult to imagine that he means anything other than the "root"; and so it has been translated here.

[16] Mt. 3:3 = Lk. 3:4, quoting Isa. 40:3.

[17] Al-'Aqqād's spelling of Salome's name *(Salāmah)* is not precise. Thus, the editors of ed. 3 have added a footnote here: *"al-mashhūrah bi-ism Sālawmī"* ("Better known as Salome"; the note is not found in eds. 1 and 2). This name is not mentioned in the Bible, but it is given by Josephus in his discussion of the Herodian dynasty (*Antiquities* 18.5.4 [Loeb 9:92-93]).

[18] The "Herod" mentioned in these two paragraphs is Herod Antipas, son of Herod the Great; al-'Aqqād had referred to him at the end of ch. 7 (p. 113), mentioning his reputation for corruption and his murder of John the Baptist. The material here concerning John's rebuke of Herod and his subsequent death are drawn from Mk. 6:17-29; a less detailed version is in Mt. 14:3-12. (Jose-

phus also mentions John's arrest and death under Herod [*Antiquities* 18.5.2. (Loeb 9:80-85)], but none of the details given here are found there).

Al-'Aqqād's version contains a few errors and a number of differences from the biblical account. Concerning Herodias, Mark and Matthew mention only that she had been the wife of Herod's brother Philip. According to Josephus, Herodias was actually the niece of Herod Antipas; she had been married to Philip, by whom she gave birth to Salome, but she divorced him to marry Herod (ABD, s.v. "Herodias"). Mark and Matthew say nothing about frequent parties staged by Herod, only that this one was in honor of his birthday. It was Herodias who prompted her daughter to ask for John's head; Herod acquiesced in order to save face in front of his guests, rather than due to Salome's persistence. Finally, al-'Aqqād's reference to the lack of condemnation from Jewish religious leaders is his own addition, although this can appropriately be surmised.

[19] Mt. 3:7-9 = Lk. 3:7-8. As the next paragraph demonstrates, al-'Aqqād interprets this passage to mean that John envisioned the inclusion of the Gentiles in God's kingdom, an interpretation which is central to his overall thesis. This is probably reading more into the passage than is warranted. Although Matthew and Luke may have taken John's words in this fashion, John himself probably meant no more than to denounce Jewish reliance on ethnic identity as a protection against God's wrath (Hagner, 33A:50; Fitzmyer, 28:468).

[20] Al-'Aqqād's reference to "Christians" *(al-masīḥīyīn)* coming to John the Baptist is, of course, anachronistic.

[21] More likely, the form of John's baptism involved the immersion of the candidate's body (Meier, 2:93 n. 152).

[22] Mt. 21:23-27 = Mk. 11:27-33 = Lk. 20:1-8. According to the Gospels, this confrontation took place in the Temple precincts during the week prior to the crucifixion. The question initially posed by the religious leaders to Jesus was, "By what authority are you doing these things, or who gave you this authority to do them?" (Mk. 11:28, RSV). When they would not give an answer to Jesus' question, he in turn refused to answer theirs.

[23] Al-'Aqqād's statement about Josephus' approach in his writings, which are essentially apologetic in nature, is fairly accurate. His works were partly addressed to fellow Jews, in which he sought to defend his shift of allegiance to Rome during the Jewish War, and partly addressed to Romans in which he sought to justify Jewish religion and culture (ABD, s.v. "Josephus" [3:982]).

The quotation about John the Baptist is from his *Antiquities* 18.5.2 (Loeb 9:80-81). Josephus adds there that many Jews responded well to John and accepted his baptism as a sign of consecration to God; al-'Aqqād's claim that the Jews thus testified "against themselves" is rather strong.

[24] From Mt. 26:6-13 = Mk. 14:3-9 = Jn. 12:1-8. Al-'Aqqād follows the version in Matthew and Mark (which are very close) with the exclusion of a few details: the setting in the home of "Simon the leper"; the assumed cost of the perfume at more than three hundred denarii; and, significantly, Jesus' comment that her action was in preparation for his burial. The parallel in John provides other details, e.g., that the woman was Mary, the sister of Lazarus and Martha. There is a similar incident recorded in Luke 7:36-50, which al-'Aqqād discusses in ch. 16 (p. 166-67); see n. 9 there regarding its possible relationship with these passages.

[25] Mt. 11:18-19a = Lk. 7:33-34. Al-'Aqqād has followed the text of VD very closely. However, and not surprisingly, he has omitted the word *khamr* [wine], which in VD follows *shirrīb* [heavy drinker], thereby diminishing the accusation against Jesus and making it more compatible with Islamic stipulations.

[26] In this final sentence, al-'Aqqād claims that if the Jews had responded to Jesus' call, then it would not have spread among the Gentiles as well. This claim will become the primary theme of

ch. 19.

Chapter 16
The Law

[1] Ar. *Al-Sharī'ah.* Although this word especially refers to the authoritative system of law in Islam, it is also used in the generic sense of "law."

[2] Ar. *al-risālah,* and also for the next two paragraphs.

[3] These sentences are taken from the so-called "Beatitudes" of Jesus found in Mt. 5:3-12 = Lk. 6:20-23. Al-'Aqqād has not used quotation marks here, and in fact his rendition is very partial. The wording follows the version in Matthew (vv. 4, 3, 6, 10, 5 and 7, in that order), and none of the statements includes the subsequent characteristic promise (e.g., after "Blessed are those who mourn," Matthew has "for they shall be comforted"). Al-'Aqqād has also shortened two of the statements: Matthew has "the poor *in spirit*" and "those who hunger and thirst *for righteousness.*" The result is that al-'Aqqād renders Matthew's somewhat spiritual emphasis as more materialistic, thus making it similar to the version found in Luke. In fact, most commentators believe that Luke's version is the more original (Davies and Allison, 1:442-43, 451; Hagner, 33A:90-93).

[4] Mt. 11:28-30. Although the quotation is not complete, it follows the text of VD almost exactly.

[5] An allusion to the "Woes" which follow Luke's version of the Beatitudes (Lk. 6:24-26).

[6] A synopsis of the parable found in Lk. 7:41-43. The setting which forms the context for this parable, though not mentioned here, is discussed by al-'Aqqād a few paragraphs later.

[7] Ar. *dhālika al-'aṣr al-marīj.* The adjective is a classical Arabic word, echoing a similar situation expressed in the Qur'ān, 50:5. See Lane, 2:2704.

[8] The pronoun here, and for the rest of the quotation, is singular. See the following note.

[9] From Lk. 7:36-47. Some interpreters have proposed that this passage refers to the same incident as the one found in Mt. 26:6-13 and parallels, which was discussed by al-'Aqqād in ch. 15 (p. 164). However, the large number of differences and apparent contradictions make this claim disputed. (For details, see Nolland, 35A:351-52; and Fitzmyer, 28:685-86).

Al-'Aqqād's presentation of the Lukan text is not precise. In the biblical account, there is no mention of disciples or bystanders. There Jesus interacts only with his host, Simon the Pharisee, and it is he who questions within himself whether Jesus, in allowing the woman to touch him, is indeed a prophet. Also in Luke, Jesus' response to Simon begins with the parable of the two debtors referred to by al-'Aqqād above.

An additional element missing in al-'Aqqād's rendition is the conclusion of the incident as presented by Luke, in which (for the first time) others are mentioned as present: "And [Jesus] said to her, 'Your sins are forgiven.' Then those who were at table with him began to say among themselves, 'Who is this, who even forgives sins?' And he said to the woman, 'Your faith has saved you; go in peace'" (vv. 48-50, RSV). Luke does not imply here that forgiveness comes from Jesus rather than from God, but that the forgiveness which comes from God comes through Jesus as God's authorized agent (Nolland, 35A:359; and Fitzmyer, 28:629). Al-'Aqqād seeks to portray Jesus as a prophet who pronounced divine forgiveness for those who repented, and he recognizes that this pronouncement caused considerable offense (see p. 168). However, the indication here that Jesus invoked for himself the divine prerogative of dispensing such forgiveness would go beyond what he, as a Muslim, could admit.

[10] Lit., "And woe to the one who opens a door for repentance and mercy, yet he does not care about the doors which have been opened for vengeance and punishment." This paragraph seems to be referring to the idea that anyone who offers forgiveness based on repentance, such as Jesus did, should be aware of the stiff opposition that will follow.

[11] The incident referred to here is probably the uprising by Judas the Galilean and his band in response to the census of Quirinius in 6 C.E.; al-'Aqqād had discussed this in ch. 6 (p. 100) and ch. 7 (pp. 110-12). The reference to Idumea, the region to the south of Judea, is probably an allusion to the family of Herod the Great, which originated from there.

[12] The theme of this sentence is the focus of ch. 17.

[13] The phrase "he might state his own legal opinion" represents a single Arabic verb, *aftā*. It is the terminology used in Islamic jurisprudence for the formal pronouncement of a legal opinion, i.e., a *fatwā* (from the same root). A person who declares a *fatwā* (i.e., a *muftī)* is not the same as a judge, but is simply someone authorized to render opinions for how the law *(al-sharī'ah)* should be interpreted and applied in a given situation. (See EI^2, s.v. *"Fatwā").*

[14] From Lk. 12:13-14. The word for "judge", both here and in VD, is *qāḍin*. However, the word translated here as "accountant" is *ḥasīb,* whereas VD has *muqassim,* "divider." In modern Arabic, *ḥasīb* means "respected" or "noble," but in classical times its primary meaning was "reckoner" or "taker of accounts" (Lane, 1:567). Perhaps al-'Aqqād's word choice was meant to reflect the Islamic title of *muḥtasib,* an official responsible for enforcing proper behavior within the Muslim community. (See EI^2, s.v. *"Ḥisba"* [3:487]).

This particular passage does not serve al-'Aqqād's purpose here, since the man who makes a request is not attempting to trap him nor is he portrayed as a religious leader. He was simply a man from the crowd who had wrong assumptions about Jesus' mission.

[15] Jn. 8:2-5. Al-'Aqqād is oblivious to the major textual problem regarding the passage in 7:53-8:11, probably because it is present, without comment, in VD. Many early and varied mss. omit this passage altogether, while a few others include it in another location; undoubtedly, it is not original to the Gospel of John. (For details, see Metzger, *Textual Commentary,* 219-22; and Brown, *John,* 29:335-36). RSV places the entire passage 7:53 - 8:11 in a footnote.

Al-'Aqqād's discussion in the subsequent paragraphs continues the story, but only after an analysis of the nature of the question and the motives at work among the religious leaders as well as for Jesus. In general, his comments are on target (see Brown, *John,* 29:337; and Beasley-Murray, 146).

[16] Jn. 8:7. This variation on the text of VD does not quite capture the force of the original statement. Al-'Aqqād has *fal-yataqaddamu wal-yarmihā bi-ḥajar,* whereas VD reads *fal-yarmihā awwalan bi-ḥajar,* "let him be the first to throw a stone at her." It is of course the latter which more accurately translates the Gk. text.

Despite his relatively lengthy analysis of this incident, al-'Aqqād does not venture to suggest what Jesus may have been drawing, or writing, on the ground. This has puzzled commentators throughout the centuries, with no consensus of opinion (Brown, *John,* 29:333-34; Beasley-Murray, 146).

[17] Jn. 8:9-11.

[18] Mt. 19:5-6 = Mk. 10:7-9. The first half of the statement is Jesus' quotation of Gen. 2:24; the second half is his elaboration on that concept.

[19] Mt. 5:32. Al-'Aqqād follows the VD text of this verse very closely, even though there are a number of variations on these statements found in the following, somewhat parallel, passages: Mt.

19:9; Mk. 10:11-12; and Lk. 16:18. According to Mt. 19:3, 7 = Mk. 10:2, 4, the teaching of Jesus on this subject in those passages was a response to the questioning of some Pharisees, although it is not stated that they intended it to be a trap.

[20] A reference to the incident presented in Mt. 22:15-22 and parallels, previously mentioned by al-'Aqqād in ch. 7 (pp. 110-11; see n. 35 there) and ch. 13 (p. 169). Here, he presents Jesus' statement as a question.

[21] This is taken from the incident recorded in Mt. 22:23-33 = Mk. 12:18-27 = Lk. 20:27-40; in all three Gospels, this immediately follows the previously mentioned incident concerning taxes, and both events occur during the week prior to the crucifixion. In the biblical text, it is only the Sadducees who come to Jesus with their query and who are addressed by him in his response. As al-'Aqqād observed in his discussion of Jewish sects, the Pharisees believed in the final resurrection whereas the Sadducees did not (ch. 6, pp. 96, 97).

[22] Ar. *ḥākim al-Rūmān.* This title is imprecise; it should read either "the governor of the Romans in that region" or simply "the Roman governor."

The statement (in the last sentence of the previous paragraph) that Jesus' kingdom "is not of this world" does not occur in Jesus' conversations in the Temple precincts, but al-'Aqqād is probably speaking in a general manner in the first half of this sentence. However, this statement is found in Jn. 18:36, where Jesus speaks before Pilate during his trial.

[23] This reference to Jesus' sayings is to Mt. 5:27-30 (a partial parallel is in Mk. 9:43, 47). Al-'Aqqād quotes the first part of this passage in ch. 17 (p. 176); but it is ch. 18 where he discusses the figurative manner by which injunctions such as these are to be followed.

Chapter 17
The Law of Love

[1] Mt. 5:17. Al-'Aqqād follows the wording of VD almost perfectly here. The precise meaning of "fulfill" in the biblical text is difficult to determine, and numerous proposals have been advanced. It is best interpreted in the wider context of this chapter, such that "fulfill" means to "'bring to its intended meaning' — that is, to present a definitive interpretation of the law, something now possible because of the presence of the Messiah and his kingdom" (Hagner, 33A:106; see also Davies and Allison, 484-87).

[2] See, e.g., Mt. 12:1-8 = Mk. 2:23-28 = Lk. 6:1-5.

[3] An allusion to Mt. 15:17-20 = Mk. 7:18-23, which al-'Aqqād also mentions on p. 174.

[4] This is perhaps an allusion to Mt. 7:28-29 = Mk. 1:22 = Lk. 4:32, where the people are said to be astonished at Jesus' teaching because it conveyed more authority than the teaching of the scribes.

[5] An apparent reference to Mt. 5:18: "For truly, I say to you, till heaven and earth pass away, not an iota, not a dot, will pass from the law until all is accomplished" (RSV; = Lk. 16:17). There is also a similar saying concerning "my words" rather than "the law" in Mt. 24:35 = Mk. 13:31 = Lk. 21:33.

[6] Mt. 7:3 = Lk. 6:41.

[7] This paragraph refers to the incident recorded in Jn. 8:2-11, which al-'Aqqād discussed at length in ch. 16 (pp. 168-69).

[8] This paragraph is drawn from sayings of Jesus found in Mt. 6:5, 16-18.

[9] This paragraph is drawn from sayings of Jesus found in Mt. 6:2-4.

[10] This paragraph is drawn from Mt. 9:9-13 = Mk. 2:13-17 = Lk. 5:27-32.

[11] A summary and adaptation of Jesus' words presented in Mt. 15:17-20 = Mk. 7:18-23.

[12] Dt. 7:7-8.

[13] I.e., the divine love which the Jews had claimed only for themselves was now being proclaimed for all people in the message of Christ.

[14] Mt. 12:50 = Mk. 3:35 = Lk. 8:21.

[15] Mt. 8:11-12 (= Lk. 13:28-29). This passage speaks of the eschatological banquet which was envisioned by Jews and in which they assumed only they would participate. Most commentators understand that those who "come from the east and west" refer to Gentiles (so Hagner, 33A:205; and Fitzmyer, 28A:1023). But others think that they refer instead to Jews of the Diaspora who would respond to the message of Jesus (so Davies and Allison, 2:27-28; and Nolland, 35B:735).

[16] An adaptation of the parable of "The Good Samaritan" in Lk. 10:29-37. In the biblical version, Jesus told the parable to an expert in the law who had questioned him concerning the meaning of the commandment to love one's neighbor (referred to by al-'Aqqād below).

[17] Ar. *"inna al-dīn bi-mā ta'malu lā bi-mā tu'allimu."* Although this saying is given in quotation marks, it is not present in the Gospels. The vocalization of the last word is thus in question; it is possible to read it as *ta'lamu* [you know]. In favor of this is that a play on words would be more obvious, due to the greater similarity of *ta'lamu* [you do] with *ta'malu.* However, the context argues strongly for the translation given. The quotations which follow in this paragraph and the next are all from Mt. 23, where Jesus criticizes the practice of the scribes and Pharisees. Thus, this statement is almost certainly an allusion to the beginning of that chapter: "The scribes and the Pharisees sit on Moses' seat; so practice and observe whatever they tell you, but not what they do; for they preach, but they do not practice" (Mt. 23:2-3, RSV). One could still argue for a play on words between the two verbs.

[18] Mt. 23:4-7. A phylactery was small box strapped to one's forehead or arm, containing a written passage of scripture; the wearing of phylacteries was a literal observance of the injunction to "bind [God's commandments] as a sign upon your hands, and they shall be as frontlets between your eyes" (Dt. 11:18, RSV; see also Ex. 13:9, Dt. 6:8). Tassels were placed at the four corners of a garment in compliance with Num. 15:37-39 and Dt. 22:12; they were to serve as reminders of God's commandments. Enlarging these tokens drew attention to one's piety (Hagner, 33B:660).

The Ar. for "Rabbi" is simply *sayyidī* [my master] (here and in VD). But the Gk. word behind it is *rhabbi,* which was "an honorary title for outstanding teachers of the law" (Walter Bauer, *A Greek-English Lexicon of the New Testament and Other Early Christian Literature,* trans. and ed. William F. Arndt and F. Wilbur Gingrich, 2d ed. revised and augmented by F. Wilbur Gingrich and Frederick W. Danker [Chicago: University of Chicago Press, 1979], 733). This in turn was a transliteration of the Aramaic *rabbî,* meaning "my master."

[19] Ar. *alladhīna yuḥāsibūna 'alā al-ba'ūḍah.* VD reads *alladhīna yuṣaffūna 'an al-ba'ūḍah,* "who strain out a gnat." Al-'Aqqād apparently misunderstood this difficult saying as rendered in VD, since the verb *ṣaffā,* when followed by *ḥisāb,* means "to settle an account." The Gk. word *diulidzō* clearly means "strain out" as translated in RSV. The saying refers to the Pharisees' practice of filtering their wine through a cloth so as not to swallow a gnat, the smallest of animals considered "unclean." The saying continues with the hyperbole of swallowing a camel as a reference to spiritual poverty. (Davies and Allison, 3:295-96).

[20] Mt. 23:24, 25, 27.

[21] A summary of Mt. 22:34-40 = Mk. 12:28-31 = Lk. 10:25-28; in all three accounts, the ques-

tion is posed by a single legal expert. According to Matthew and Mark, the question was simply "Which is the greatest commandment?" rather than the two greatest. Luke's portrayal is somewhat different, where the initial question is "What shall I do to inherit eternal life?"; when Jesus responds with his own question, "What is written in the law?" the man replies with these two commandments and receives Jesus' approval. Then follows another question from the man, "And who is my neighbor?" which leads to Jesus' parable of "the Good Samaritan," related by al-'Aqqād above.

[22] Ar. *nīyāt* (sg. *nīyah).* On the significance of this word as a technical term in Islam, see ch. 9, p. 127, n. 38.

[23] Mt. 5:21-24. Several important mss. of the Gk. text do not have "without reason" (Gk. *eikē,* Ar. *bāṭilan* here and in VD), and the word was most likely added by copyists to lessen the intensity of the statement (Metzger, *Textual Commentary,* 13).

[24] Mt. 5:27-29.

[25] Mt. 5:33-37. The Gk. word behind "Devil" *(ponēros)* can be rendered either as "evil" or "the evil one."

[26] Ar. *lā tuqābilū al-sharr bi-al-sharr.* VD has simply *lā tuqābilū al-sharr,* which in the context would be better translated "Do not resist one who is evil" (so RSV; the Gk. word *ponēros,* like *sharr,* can mean either "evil" or "evil one," [see n. 25]). Al-'Aqqād has obviously amalgamated this verse with a similar statement in Rom. 12:17, which reads "Repay no one evil for evil" (RSV), and in VD *lā tujāzū aḥad 'an sharr bi-sharr.*

[27] Mt. 5:38, 39 (= Lk. 6:29), 41.

[28] Mt. 5:43-48 (= Lk. 6:27-28, 32-33, 36). Al-'Aqqād has followed the VD text of Matthew closely; this includes v. 44, much of which is not present in the best Gk. mss., but was added later by scribes who drew somewhat from the parallel passage in Luke. (RSV has the additional words in a footnote). Also, the more reliable Gk. mss. read "Gentiles" in place of the second instance of "tax collectors"; al-'Aqqād has followed VD there as well. (Metzger, *Textual Commentary,* 14). However, al-'Aqqād has somewhat altered the text of v. 48, and the final phrase of his quotation ("and he loves perfection") is completely his own.

[29] From Mt. 9:14-17 = Mk. 2:21-22 = Lk. 5:36-38. The metaphors, which are here reversed and abbreviated, indeed seem to have expressed Jesus' evaluation of his own ministry. The sayings go on to indicate the result of such actions, which would have been well understood in the first-century culture of Palestine: the fermenting activity of new wine would burst old wineskins which no longer had the capacity to expand; an unused piece of cloth would shrink and tear the old garment onto which it was sewn. (Hagner, 33A:244; Mann, 235; and Fitzmyer, 28:600-601).

Al-'Aqqād had previously avoided referring directly to a text which indicated that Jesus drank wine (see ch. 15, p. 164, n. 25). Here, the simple comparison of Jesus' ministry to "new wine" would perhaps not be quite so offensive to his Muslim readers.

Chapter 18
Ethical Living

[1] See ch. 11, p. 140, n. 54 on al-'Aqqād's previous reference to Origen (d. ca. 254).

[2] A reference to Mt. 19:12. Here, the first phrase, lit. "that God castrates some people" *(anna unāsan yakhṣīhum allah)* is not as crude in the biblical text: "there are eunuchs who have been so

from birth" (RSV); *li-annahu yūjadu khiṣyān wulidū hākadhā min buṭūn ummahātihim* (VD). The third phrase is also less harsh in the biblical text: "there are eunuchs who have made themselves eunuchs for the sake of the kingdom of heaven" (RSV).

The context of this saying is Jesus' teaching about divorce, in which he states that "whoever divorces his wife, except for unchastity, and marries another, commits adultery" (Mt. 19:9; the parallels to this verse in Mk. 10:11 and Lk. 16:18 are even stronger, with no exception clause). Only Matthew continues the passage with the disciples' recognition of the radical nature of this teaching: "If such is the case of a man with his wife, it is not expedient to marry" (v. 10), to which Jesus responds that not everyone can accept this teaching, but "only those to whom it is given" (v. 11). The first two examples of literal castration are meant to contrast the metaphorical nature of the third example, which points to a renunciation of marriage for the sake of God's kingdom. There have been a few cases in history when self-castration has been taken literally; "happily, a figurative interpretation has been dominant in Christian exegesis" (Davies and Allison, 3:23; see also Hagner, 33B:550-51).

[3] Information on Origen comes primarily from the fourth-century church historian Eusebius, who held him in high regard. His is the only report on Origen's alleged self-emasculation (*Ecclesiastical History* 6.8 [Loeb 2:28-31]), one that al-'Aqqād summarizes accurately. While such an act could well be historical (though it was somewhat extreme for that early period), its accuracy must be questioned in light of Origen's later exposition of Mt. 19:12. There "he strongly deplored any literal interpretation of the words" (Chadwick, 109). The theory of biblical interpretation developed by Origen held that most passages accommodate two, three, or even four levels of meaning. While this usually included a literal sense, he came to view Mt. 19:12 as a rare exception (ibid., 107-108).

[4] Although persecution pressured many in early Christianity to adopt an ascetic lifestyle, examples of extreme behavior such as al-'Aqqād mentions are difficult to document and seem to have been rare exceptions. In particular, self-castration was discouraged and finally condemned at the Council of Nicea in 325. (See DCE, s.v. "Asceticism").

[5] Clement of Alexandria (d. ca. 215; not to be confused with the earlier Clement of Rome) was an important figure in the early history of Alexandrian theology. He headed the so-called Catechetical School of Alexandria, where Origen studied and succeeded him as leader. (ODCC, s.v. "Clement of Alexandria"). The reference here is to a relatively minor work by Clement entitled *The Rich Man's Salvation.* This is a fascinating exposition of Mk. 10:17-31 (= Mt. 19:16-30 = Lk. 18:18-30), the account of the rich man who came to Jesus asking what he should do to gain eternal life. The essence of al-'Aqqād's brief statement is incorporated especially in chapters 11-15 (Loeb pp. 290-301), where Clement states that possessions which are serviceable should not be renounced, but only those which inhibit godly character; what is most important is the rooting out of the deadly passions of the soul.

[6] Augustine (d. 430) was bishop of Hippo in North Africa, and one of the most influential personalities for the theology of the western church. Attracted to Christianity through his study of Neoplatonism, he became a stalwart defender of the faith against a variety of heresies. His "Confessions" and "City of God" are among the classics of western literature. (ODCC, s.v. "Augustine, St., of Hippo"). Al-'Aqqād's reference here is a general statement of Augustine's moderate perspective of asceticism. For him, virginity was preferable, but marriage still good; the gospel did not forbid earthly wealth, only its use for evil. (See Eugène Portalié, *A Guide to the Thought of Saint Augustine,* trans. Ralph J. Bastian, Library of Living Catholic Thought [Chicago: Henry Regnery, 1960], 285).

[7] Albert Schweitzer (d. 1965) was a prominent German theologian and missionary whose seminal work *The Quest of the Historical Jesus* is noted in the Introduction (p. 52, n. 55; p. 54, n. 73). Al-'Aqqād has summarized fairly well Schweitzer's concept of Jesus' ethical teaching, which was closely connected to his view that Jesus mistakenly believed the end of the world was near. According to Schweitzer, Jesus preached an "interim ethic" which was to apply until that end had arrived. Unfortunately, al-'Aqqād does not follow through on how Schweitzer applied this ethic, which he seemed to view as relevant for Jesus only in the context of his own day. In fact, he saw an essential core to Jesus' teaching, a "religion of love," which could form the basis for ethical living in all times. It called simultaneously for renunciation and affirmation of the world, a concept which Schweitzer himself lived out when he abandoned his distinguished academic career for medical service in Africa. Al-'Aqqād's subsequent discussion here may well have been influenced by Schweitzer's views in this area. For a summary of Schweitzer's perspective on ethics, see DCE, s.v. "Schweitzer, Albert."

[8] The word *jihād* or a cognate appears three times in this paragraph. The role of the disciples in propagating the message of Jesus is developed by al-'Aqqād in ch. 21.

[9] An allusion to Jesus' teaching about anxiety in Mt. 6:25-30 = Lk. 12:22-28.

[10] Or, "People do not belong to the Sabbath, but the Sabbath belongs to the people" (Ar. *laysa al-insān lil-sabt, wa-innamā al-sabt lil-insān).* The reference is to Mk. 2:27 (no parallels), where VD is more specific: *al-sabt innamā ju'ila li-ajli al-insān lā al-insān li-ajli al-sabt* ("The Sabbath was made for people, not people for the Sabbath"). Al-'Aqqād does not elaborate on how this saying fits in with his discussion. He is probably interpreting Jesus' words concerning the Sabbath laws as representative of all types of regulations; people should not follow such rules thoughtlessly, but should seek to grasp the intention that lies behind them and their purpose in serving humanity.

[11] The significance of the various abstract terms here becomes apparent in subsequent paragraphs. The word "center" (Ar. *miḥwār)* could also be translated as "axis" or "pivot," and so throughout this chapter.

[12] An allusion to Jesus' teaching about the value of one's soul (or life) in the context of true discipleship: Mt. 16:26 = Mk. 8:36 = Lk. 9:25; cf. Jn. 12:25.

[13] The dirham was the basic unit of currency in the Arab world from the seventh to the thirteenth centuries (EI^2, s.v. "Dirham"). It is also found in a few modern Arab countries. Perhaps al-'Aqqād, in using this term rather than a unit of Egyptian currency, was trying to address a wider Arab constituency.

[14] Ar. *al-qiblah,* the key term of ch. 14.

[15] Undoubtedly al-'Aqqād has in mind here primarily the mission of Muḥammad.

[16] Al-'Aqqād censures the extreme forms of Christian asceticism which he mentioned at the beginning of this chapter as an unfortunate deviation from what Christ intended. He does not dwell on this issue here, but in the Epilogue he considers how Jesus would respond to Christian practices if he were to "come again to the world."

[17] This could be a reference to the incident in Mt. 26:6-13 and parallels, which al-'Aqqād had discussed in ch. 15 (p. 164), especially since he mentions here the "many denarii" spent on the perfume. On the other hand, it could be a reference to the similar incident in Lk. 7:36-47, which al-'Aqqād had discussed in ch. 16 (pp. 166-67), since he mentions the woman anointing Jesus' "feet" rather than his head (as in the passage in Mt. and Mk.). There are many similarities, as well as important differences, between the various accounts which appear in all four Gospels, and the debate as to whether or not they all refer to the same incident was noted previously (ch. 16, n. 9).

In fact, the account in Jn. 12:1-8, which is generally thought to be closest to Mt. and Mk., also refers to Jesus' feet rather than his head. It is little wonder that al-'Aqqād seems to have amalgamated his two previous portrayals in his brief reference here.

[18] Only one instance where Jesus attended a wedding is recorded in the Gospels, i.e., Jn. 2:1-11; this was in Cana of Galilee, where it is said that he performed his first miracle, that of changing the water into wine. The parables that al-'Aqqād has in mind here are probably the related parables of the Lost Sheep, the Lost Coin and the Prodigal Son (Lk. 15:1-32). In each case, the person who had experienced the loss, when it was found, gave a party for friends and neighbors.

[19] Mt. 5:40 = Lk. 6:29. Al-'Aqqād had referred to this saying briefly in ch. 14 (p. 158). The wording in each reference is different, and both differ from either of the versions in VD.

[20] An allusion to Mt. 6:24 = Lk. 16:13. The verb "serve" (Ar. *ya'budu)* could also be translated as "worship," and so throughout this paragraph and the next.

[21] This last statement may be an allusion to the parable of the "Unworthy Servants" in Lk. 17:7-10.

[22] Ar. *mujtama'.* That is, Christ would not create another exclusive society to replace the Jews; since his message was universal, he made no distinction among his followers.

[23] Ar. *ḥadhlaqah,* a word which appears frequently in the remainder of this chapter; it entails a display of one's presumed knowledge and skill.

[24] Or, "apostles" (Ar. *al-rusul).* It is unclear whether al-'Aqqād means here the disciples of Jesus, to whom he referred using this term on p. 180; or messengers in the strict Islamic sense, those (especially Muḥammad) who embark on the "other missions" mentioned on p. 181.

Chapter 19
The Kingdom of Heaven

[1] Qur'ān 28:56. Muslim tradition holds that this verse was revealed to Muḥammad when his beloved uncle, Abū Ṭālib, lay dying. Muḥammad, anxious because Abū Ṭālib held onto the pagan faith of his fathers, tried to persuade his uncle to profess Islam. The verse was meant to encourage Muḥammad concerning the sovereignty of God. The standard classical work containing this report is Abū al-Ḥasan 'Alī ibn Aḥmad al-Wāḥidī, *Asbāb Nuzūl al-Qur'ān* [Occasions for the Revelation of the Qur'ān]; see the edition by Kamāl Basyūnī Zaghlūl (Beirut: Dār al-Kutub al-'Alamīyah, 1991), 347-48. See also the edition of the Qur'ān by Yūsuf 'Alī, p. 976, n. 3388.

The significance of the verse for al-'Aqqād is that Abū Ṭālib's rejection of Islam exemplified the refusal of the Meccans in general to accept the message of Muḥammad. Had they done so, there would have been no need for Muḥammad and his followers to emigrate to Medina, and this would have changed the whole course of Islamic history. Yet that refusal was precisely within the providential wisdom of God regarding the progress of Muḥammad's call.

[2] I.e., Jesus would have remained a prophet only to the Jews.

[3] This is apparently the meaning of a rather ambiguous phrase which is rendered by al-'Aqqād as a question asked by Jesus: *mā-dhā taraktum lil-umam?,* lit. "What did you leave for the nations?" The question as it stands does not appear in the Gospels, and al-'Aqqād probably intends it to summarize Jesus' instructions to the disciples, especially in Matthew, that they should go only among the people of Israel.

[4] A reference to the commissioning of the twelve disciples, and particularly to the restrictions

set forth in Matthew's version; the full citation is even stronger: "Go nowhere among the Gentiles, and enter no town of the Samaritans, but go rather to the lost sheep of the house of Israel" (Mt. 10:5-6). This passage was cited in ch. 2 (p. 83) as an example which other writers quoted in order to demonstrate Jesus' exclusive mission to Israel. Al-'Aqqād's argument is that Jesus followed this method only initially; later, as the Jews rejected his message, he rejected this exclusive approach.

[5] From Mt. 7:6. Al-'Aqqād is probably correct that in this passage, Jesus speaks "generally"; i.e., the "swine" (like the "dogs" also in this verse) do not necessarily represent the Gentiles, but anyone who rejects the kingdom. (See Hagner, 33A:171-72; and Davies and Allison, 1:674-77).

[6] From the incident recorded in Mt. 15:21-28 = Mk. 7:24-30. Al-'Aqqād has omitted several details. The woman, a Gentile, begged Jesus to cast out a demon from her daughter. Jesus ignored her, claiming that he was sent "only to the lost sheep of the house of Israel" (Mt. 15:24). When she persisted in her request, he addressed her with the statement that it was not right to throw the children's bread to the dogs. She then responded with a remarkable statement of faith and humility: "Yes, Lord; yet even the dogs under the table eat the children's crumbs" (Mk. 7:28); whereupon Jesus commended her and sent her away, saying her daughter was healed. Here, the "children" refer the Israelites, while the "dogs" refer to the Gentiles (Davies and Allison, 2:553; Hagner, 33B:442; and Mann, 321).

[7] Ar. *al-mawtūrīn.* This is the pl. of a classical word meaning "one who has his relation slain, and so is separated from him, and rendered solitary" (Lane, 2:2919). It is from the root *watara,* which today means either "to string (a bow)" or "to harm (someone)," but which originally meant "to make (something or someone) one" (ibid., 2:2917).

[8] Ar. *"al-'uṣbah al-'unṣurīyah"* according to eds. 1 and 2. Ed. 3 has a slight change, *"al-'aṣabīyah al-'unṣurīyah,"* which renders a stronger meaning: "ethnic (or racial) partisanship" or even "fanaticism." This may indicate a subtle editorial bias in ed. 3; see Appendix A, p. 242.

[9] Ar. *darāwīsh,* sg. *darwīsh.* The term refers broadly to members of a Ṣūfī order, but more narrowly to those dedicated to a life of poverty (EI^2, s.v. *"darwīsh").* Al-'Aqqād's application of this term to the Ebionites is his own.

[10] The Ebionites were an early Jewish-Christian sect later regarded as heretical by both Christian and Jewish writers. Their name in Hebrew is *'ebyônîm,* meaning "the poor." Little information is known about them and comes only from secondary sources. Their origins and relationship to Jewish-Christian groups in the NT can only be surmised. They reportedly observed some form of the Jewish law and regarded Jesus as having been born naturally. They indeed disappeared from history after the fourth century. (ABD, s.v. "Ebionites"; see also the references to early Jewish Christianity and the Ebionites in ch. 2, nn. 27 and 31).

[11] Early Christian historians report that the Christians who were living in Jerusalem at the time of the Jewish War fled the city in 70 C.E. just prior to the siege of the city, and went to Pella on the east side of the Jordan River. However, the same sources report that they returned to Jerusalem after the war, although some scholars dispute this. In any case, virtually nothing more is heard about the Jerusalem Christians. (ABD, s.v. "Jewish-Christian Relations 70-170 C.E." [3:835]).

[12] Al-'Aqqād quoted this parable (from Lk. 14:16-24) in ch. 13 (pp. 154-44); see n. 19 there. The parable actually indicates that the Gentiles are included only after there is a response to the invitation from among the Jewish masses. Here, al-'Aqqād refers to the host as a "prince" *(amīr),* whereas he is simply a "man" in Luke's text but a "king" in Matthew's somewhat different version (Mt. 22:2).

[13] Mt. 21:42-44. The first sentence (v. 42) is a quotation from Ps. 118:22; there, the "stone" represents Israel who had been rejected by the nations, but here, Jesus applies the metaphor to himself. The second sentence (v. 43) is the key for al-'Aqqād; for him, the "you" represents all the Jews and the "nation" represents the Gentiles. In this context, however, Jesus is speaking to the Jewish *leaders* who reject him. Although the word "nation" (Gk. *ethnos)* of itself might allude to the "Gentiles" (Gk. *ethnoi,* the pl. of *ethnos),* more likely Matthew has in mind the "church" (cf. Mt. 16:18) which is composed of believing Jews and Gentiles (see Davies and Allison, 3:184-90; and Hagner, 33B:622-23) . The third sentence (v. 44) is absent from many important mss. and was probably later derived from Lk. 20:18 (Metzger, *Textual Commentary,* 58; and Davies and Allison, 3:186, n. 65).

[14] Mt. 22:13-14; these vv. conclude Matthew's version of the parable of the Great Banquet, referred to above.

[15] The argument of this paragraph is fundamental to the chapter. Yet al-'Aqqād has read too much of a mission to the Gentiles into Jesus' own ministry. Nor is there any evidence for a progression from an exclusive to a more general "call," as al-'Aqqād indicates. The Gospels portray Jesus' ministry as one that was essentially and consistently directed to his own people. On the other hand, the Gentiles are part of the picture: a few individuals approach him and receive the same blessings; a mission that includes the Gentiles is envisioned for his disciples subsequent to his own mission; and especially prominent is the inclusion of the Gentiles in the eschatological kingdom. Yet the inclusion of the Gentiles is much less explicit in Jesus' mission than al-'Aqqād indicates. (See DJG, s.v. "Gentiles").

Al-'Aqqād's discussion seems to combine all these elements into the immediate message of Jesus. He also recognizes that the disciples will carry on this mission beyond the borders of Israel itself (ch. 21). However, he also incorporates into the present ministry of Jesus eschatological aspects of his message which clearly belong to the future. Al-'Aqqād reiterated his views in the second edition of his book; see his discussion in ch. 3, p. 85, n. 5.

[16] The two forms "kingdom of God" and "kingdom of heaven" must be seen as equivalent. Mark, Luke and John use the former construction exclusively, while Matthew generally has "kingdom of heaven." However, "the kingdom of God" is also found in Matthew on five occasions, including Mt. 21:43 to which al-'Aqqād referred above. (DJG, s.v. "Kingdom of God/Heaven [426]). Nowhere does the phrase "the kingdom of the Son of Man" appear. The closest to this would be Mt. 16:28 which has "the Son of Man coming in his kingdom." This is al-'Aqqād's own phrase in which he seeks to describe the relationship between "the kingdom of heaven" and "the Son of Man," as he understands it. Concerning this, see n. 28 below.

[17] Mt. 16:28 = Mk. 9:1 = Lk. 9:27.

[18] Mt. 24:4-14 = Mk. 13:5-13 = Lk. 21:8-18.

[19] Mt. 24:42-44, with partial parallels in Mk. 13:35 and Lk. 12:39-40.

[20] From Mt. 24:33-36 = Mk. 13:29-32 = Lk. 21:31-32. The phrase "the Son of Man" does not appear in the biblical text. Mark and the most reliable mss. of Matthew have simply "the Son"; Luke and other mss. of Matthew have no reference to the Son at all (Metzger, *Textual Commentary,* 62).

[21] Mt. 6:33 (= Lk. 12:31).

[22] Mt. 13:11 = Mk. 4:11 = Lk. 8:10. Al-'Aqqād has quoted the verse in Matthew (VD) exactly, except for one crucial word; the biblical text actually reads "the *secrets* (Ar. *asrār)* of the kingdom of heaven." In this way he applies the passage in an entirely inappropriate manner. The biblical context is the privilege given to the disciples by which they might understand his parables.

Al-'Aqqād seems to make it mean that they should know the commands of the kingdom, and thus, of God.

[23] Lk. 22:29. The context of this saying, which is present only in Luke, is the Last Supper just prior to Jesus' arrest.

[24] Lk. 19:11.

[25] See al-'Aqqād's previous discussion in ch. 6 on the variety of Jewish chronological schemes concerning the coming of the Messiah (p. 105, n. 65).

[26] Ar. *hādhā al-nadhīr.* It is not at all clear who is in view here. In the Qur'ān, *nadhīr* is used of the prophets in general and of Muḥammad in particular (EI², s.v. *"nadhīr"),* and it is possible that this is a reference to the coming Prophet of Islam. In ch. 23 (p. 220), al-'Aqqād refers to John the Baptist as "the prophet of judgment" *(al-nabī al-nadhīr),* but it is unlikely that John is meant here since the time reference indicates the future (whether near or distant). In light of the context, it is probably best to understand al-'Aqqād's "Warner" as the future messianic figure of Jewish prophecy who was to come at the end of the world. Al-'Aqqād seems to believe that Jesus was not specific about who that figure would be, although from the perspective of the Gospels it is quite apparent that the coming Son of Man who would usher in that kingdom would be Jesus himself. See also n. 28 below.

[27] Although al-'Aqqād acknowledges that Jesus spoke about the future aspect of the kingdom, he quickly chooses to set it aside, claiming that the subject is too "ambiguous." It is evident, however, that he regards this future dimension as extraneous to his focus on the relevance of Jesus' message (and thus of the kingdom) to the present. Al-'Aqqād thereby omits one of the most important facets of Jesus' teaching from this book. For modern scholars, "it is clear that this future, transcendent salvation was an essential part of Jesus' proclamation of the kingdom" (Meier, 2: 350).

[28] Jesus' use of the phrase "the Son of Man" is a prominent feature of the Gospels. It is only in ch. 23 (pp. 222-23) that al-'Aqqād discusses the meaning of this phrase, and thus its significance in this chapter is not immediately clear. The phrase has also appeared in previous chapters, twice in quotations from the Gospels (pp. 108, 164), and once where al-'Aqqād remarks briefly that Jesus referred to himself as the Son of Man (p. 153). He will elaborate on this latter claim in ch. 23.

When comparing al-'Aqqād's discussion here and in ch. 23, two things become clear: (1) He recognizes that Jesus often used this phrase as a self-designation, in accordance to its Aramaic background. Thus the phrase is closely associated with the present mission of Jesus. (2) He also recognizes that Jesus referred to "the Son of Man" as someone who was to come in the future, reminiscent of the eschatological figure of Dan. 7. Several of his quotations from the Gospels include "the Son of Man" in this sense. However, al-'Aqqād does not indicate that Jesus was talking about himself in such passages; he leaves the matter open, seeming to imply that the future Son of Man might well be someone else. (For a reference to the scholarly debates on all of this, see the nn. 39-42 in ch. 23).

In this chapter, al-'Aqqād relates "the Son of Man" to the kingdom of God. It is clear that he understands "the kingdom of the Son of Man" to be equivalent only to the *present* aspect of the kingdom. This is in conformity with his view that the future aspect of the kingdom, including the "Son of Man" who is central to it, is not important in understanding the mission of Jesus and its relevance for the present.

[29] Ar. *al-majma' al-a'lā,* i.e., the Sanhedrin; this religious assembly was discussed by al-'Aqqād in ch. 6 (pp. 103-104). Nicodemus appears in the NT only in the Gospel of John, and there only in three places. In Jn. 3:1-15, he came to Jesus with questions, but was chided for failing to

understand the meaning of being "born again" in order to enter the kingdom of God, as al-'Aqqād observes here. In 7:50-52, he objected to the Sanhedrin's condemnation of Jesus without a fair hearing. In 19:39-42, he accompanied Joseph of Arimathea in the burial of Jesus. Most interpreters assume that he was a historical individual, and that he was probably a secret but committed disciple of Jesus (ABD, s.v. "Nicodemus"). Al-'Aqqād refers to him again on pp. 205 and 225.

[30] Al-'Aqqād has summarized the early part of the discussion between Nicodemus and Jesus in Jn. 3. There is an interesting observation, however: his statement that a person was to "be born a second time" *(yūladu wilādah thāniyah)* most closely reflects the English of RSV rather than the Arabic of VD in v. 3. RSV reads "unless one is born *anew*," whereas as VD reads *in kāna aḥad lā yūladu min fawq* ("unless one is born *from above"*). The difference reflects the ambiguity of the Gk. word *anōthen,* which can have either meaning. In fact, later editions of RSV supply a footnote at "anew" indicating an alternate translation of "from above," while the modern Arabic versions all reflect the original RSV reading rather than following that of VD. Most likely John intends the double meaning of the word "as part of the technique of misunderstanding"; Nicodemus assumes Jesus means "again," whereas the meaning for Jesus is primarily "from above" (Brown, *John,* 29: 130-31).

[31] Ar. *al-mulk,* both here and in VD; this is from the same root as "kingdom" *(al-malakūt).*

[32] Acts 1:6-8. Here al-'Aqqād has quoted VD almost exactly. Yet it is surprising that he utilizes this passage at all. In the first place, the setting for this incident (what al-'Aqqād vaguely refers to as the "conclusion" *[khitām]* of Christ's call) is, in Acts, forty days *after* the resurrection of Jesus, which he does not consider historical. The passage also mentions "the Father" and "the Holy Spirit," expressions which primarily belong to Christian terminology.

[33] Jn. 18:36. Al-'Aqqād alluded to this statement in ch. 16 (p. 170), where he also observed that Jesus spoke in this manner at his trial before Pilate.

[34] An allusion to Mt. 16:26 = Mk. 8:36 = Lk. 9:25. Al-'Aqqād's comment, that this implies a kingdom which exists in the conscience, is his own elaboration.

[35] An allusion to Mk. 10:15 = Lk. 18:17, and Mt. 18:3.

[36] An apparent reference to Mt. 26:52: "All who take the sword will perish by the sword." The meaning has been somewhat altered by al-'Aqqād, since there is no direct reference to the kingdom in this saying. The context of this verse is the arrest of Jesus in the Garden of Gethsemane.

[37] Lk. 17:20-21. Al-'Aqqād quotes VD very closely here. In both cases, the word for "within you" is *dākhilakum* (the "you" is pl.). However, RSV states that the kingdom of God is "in the midst of you," with a footnote indicating an alternate translation of "within." Indeed, there is some uncertainty regarding the precise translation of the final Greek phrase *entos humōn estin.* The preposition is rare and difficult to determine with a plural object. The translation "within you" has been the traditional rendition (e.g., AV); it could also be translated as "within your grasp." However, most modern commentators prefer "within your midst" or "among you," meaning that the kingdom was present in the person of Jesus among his hearers. In fact, while the Gospels depict the kingdom of God as a spiritual reality (cf. Jn. 18:36), it is never claimed to be merely internal. (See Fitzmyer, 28A:1160-62; and Nolland, 35B:853-54). Here, the translation "within you" reflects the intent of al-'Aqqād.

[38] Al-'Aqqād is thus critical of those who, in his view, try to interpret the kingdom of God without taking into account all the data, and who present an interpretation which is not faithful to the meaning (in all its shades) of the original concept. Yet the same accusation could be made against al-'Aqqād himself, since his focus is only on the present aspect of the kingdom without a balanced view of the future aspect as presented in the Gospels.

[39] Flavius Claudius Julianus (d. 363), also known as "Julian the Apostate," was Roman Emperor from 361 to his death. He was a nephew of the Emperor Constantine, who had promoted toleration of Christianity in the Empire and who later professed Christian faith. Julian, however, adhered to Greek philosophy; as Emperor, he sought to minimize Christianity (short of outright persecution) and promote paganism. (ODCC, s.v. "Julian the Apostate" and "Constantine the Great"). This statement mentioned by al-'Aqqād is attributed to Julian in extant copies of the Church history by Theodoret (d. ca. 466), Bishop of Cyrrhus (in Syria). At the moment of his death, Julian is said to have exclaimed, "You have won, O Galilean!" (Theodoret *Ecclesiastical History* 3.25; in *A Select Library of Nicene and Post-Nicene Fathers of the Christian Church,* Second Series, trans. and ed. Philip Schaff and Henry Wace [Grand Rapids, MI: Wm. B. Eerdmans, 1953], 3:106; however, the chapter reference there is mistakenly given as 20). Most scholars reject the passage as a much later embellishment to Theodoret; nevertheless, "it accurately represents the restoration of official Christianity that followed" Julian's death (Grant, *Greek and Latin Authors,* 241).

[40] This final sentence seems to be a criticism of the way in which secular power was joined to the church in the subsequent history of Christianity.

Chapter 20
The Ability of the Teacher

[1] There is some inconsistency in al-'Aqqād's discussion here. In the first paragraph, where he compares the situation of the world to a disease, he clearly differentiates between the *need (ḥājah)* that a disease or patient has for medicine, and the *readiness (isti'dād)* to ask for treatment. This differentiation, in conjunction with his emphasis in ch. 19 on the shift of Jesus' mission from the Jews to the Gentiles, would indicate that the Jews are like the patient who refuses treatment despite his need, while the Gentiles are like the patient who recognizes his need and displays a readiness to respond. Yet in the second paragraph, al-'Aqqād places Jews and Gentiles in the same camp; both groups were in need *and* were ready to respond. Perhaps this is a recognition that the features of Jesus' ministry, as described in the current chapter, were displayed primarily among a Jewish audience. This inconsistency seems to demonstrate that al-'Aqqād's thesis of a clear Jewish-Gentile shift was not completely established even in his own mind. See the Introduction, p. 60, n. 90; see also al-'Aqqād's similar comparison with regard to the Essenes in ch. 1, p. 76, and n. 29 there.

[2] Lit., "Ṣūfism" (Ar. *taṣawwuf*).

[3] Ar. *jihād.*

[4] Al-'Aqqād's arguments here and in the next paragraph, concerning the use of Greek among Jews in general and by Jesus in particular, are reasonable. Jesus probably possessed a very rudimentary knowledge of Greek, enough to do business in the market; but most likely, this was the extent of his knowledge in that language. It is very unlikely that he taught in Greek. (For a fine discussion, see Meier, 1:258-62). Jesus might have conversed with Pilate in Greek, but it is equally conceivable that Pilate insisted on using Latin along with an interpreter (ibid., 1:294-95, n. 41).

[5] Jesus' knowledge of biblical Hebrew is not as "certain" as al-'Aqqād believes, but most likely this was the case. As for Aramaic, it is well recognized that this was the standard language for ordinary Palestinian Jews. (Ibid., 1:262-64).

[6] An Aramaic substratum to many of Jesus' sayings in the Gospels has long been recognized (ibid., 1:265-66).

[7] Ar. *bayn al-nathr al-mursal wa-al-shi'r al-manẓūm.* This paragraph contains several technical terms dealing with Arabic poetry which are rather difficult to render comprehensively. The translation here seeks to provide the gist of the argument using general terms, while footnotes make reference to the more precise meanings. Basically, Arabic poetry consists of *meter,* in which words are arranged in various patterns according to the length of their syllables, and *rhyme,* in which the final consonant or syllable is the same for each line in a verse, and also usually in the entire poem. (For an overview of the rules of Arabic poetry, see J. A. Haywood and H. M. Nahmad, *A New Arabic Grammar of the Written Language* [London: Lund Humphries, 1965], 455-61; for a detailed presentation, see W. Wright, *A Grammar of the Arabic Language,* revised by W. Robertson Smith and M. J. de Goeje, 3d ed. [Cambridge: Cambridge University Press, 1955], 2:351-90.)

As mentioned in the Introduction (p. 29), al-'Aqqād was himself an accomplished poet. In this paragraph, he states that Jesus' mode of expression in his teaching bore some resemblance to Arabic rhyming patterns, although rhyming itself did not occur; nor did it exhibit any metrical arrangement such as found in Arabic poetry.

[8] Ar. *naẓm al-a'āriḍ wa-al-taf'īlāt.* Although the sg. form of the latter two terms could both refer to the process of analyzing the metrical units of a verse of poetry (Lane, 2:2010, 2420), in the pl. they indicate certain kinds of the metrical units themselves (Hans Wehr, *A Dictionary of Modern Written Arabic,* ed. J Milton Cowan [Ithaca, NY: Cornell University Press, 1966], 604, 721).

[9] Ar. *al-fawāṣil al-mutaqābilah wa-al-taṣrī'āt al-muraddadah.* The sg. *fāṣilah* refers to the group of words which occurs at the end of a verse of rhymed prose, or a verse of the Qur'ān (Lane, 2: 2407). The verb *ṣarra'a* (of which *taṣrī'āt* is the pl. verbal noun) indicates making the first and last hemistiches (half-verses), or the final portions of these, rhyme with each other (ibid., 2:1678).

[10] Al-'Aqqād has accurately described Jesus' semi-poetic mode of teaching, which was clearly in Aramaic. The classic but still relevant study of his teaching style is Joachim Jeremias, *New Testament Theology: The Proclamation of Jesus,* trans. John Bowden (New York: Charles Scribner's Sons, 1971), 8-37; his discussion of antithetic parallelism and rhythm are on pp. 14-27.

[11] In al-'Aqqād's text, each of the sentences in the following quotation forms a separate, short paragraph, as an attempt to demonstrate the style of the original sayings. The same is true for the next three paragraphs.

[12] Mt. 7:7-11 = Lk. 11:9-13. Al-'Aqqād has produced a conflation of the two versions: only Matthew has the sentence concerning bread, and only Luke has the sentence concerning an egg. Curiously, at the end of the quotation he has chosen to use the phrase "the Holy Spirit" according to Luke, rather than "good things" (VD *khayrāt)* according to Matthew.

[13] The word "buying" *(yashtarūna)* has been added in the translation, taken from VD; presumably al-'Aqqād omitted this inadvertently, since its presence highlights the balanced structure he seeks to portray.

[14] Or, "from heaven" *(min al-samā'),* i.e., from God.

[15] Ar. *yuẓhar,* following VD, which correctly translates the passive form of the Gk. word *apokaluptō.* The word here could also be vocalized as *yaẓhar,* "appears."

[16] Lk. 17:26-37. (The parallel in Mt. 24:17-18, 28, and 37-41 is shorter and arranged differently).

[17] Mt. 23:37-38 = Lk. 13:34-35.

[18] Lk. 23:28-31. This prophecy of Jerusalem's destruction appears only in Luke; there, it is proclaimed by Jesus as he is being led out of the city to be crucified.

[19] Ar. *al-amthāl* (sg. *mathal).* This is the standard term in VD for Jesus' parables. The Ar. word used generally can also refer to other forms of figurative speech, such as metaphors, similes, proverbs, etc. (see the following note).

[20] Al-'Aqqād employs four terms to represent the four types of parables which he discusses. While the translation provided may not always be precise, each one seeks to capture in a single English word what al-'Aqqād tries to express in a single Arabic word, based on the term itself and also the examples which he provides. Following are the four terms (English translation and Arabic original) which he uses:

"allegory" = *ramz,* lit. "symbol." Normally, "allegory" is expressed by the phrase *qiṣṣah ramzīyah.*

"proverb" = *ḥikmah,* lit. "wisdom," but it can also mean "maxim" or "proverb." The usual word for "proverb" is *mathal,* but this is also the word for "parable," and al-'Aqqād wishes to distinguish these terms.

"analogy" = *qiyās,* lit. "measurement," but it can also refer to a comparison made by analogy.

"metaphors" = *tashbīhāt,* lit. "comparisons." This word can refer to any form of comparison such as an allegory or simile; however, the examples listed by al-'Aqqād contain metaphors.

Such a systematic presentation almost certainly indicates that al-'Aqqād utilized some kind of source here. However, this kind of scheme is problematic. In the first place, there is disagreement as to what should be included as "parables" from among the wide range of Jesus' sayings. The English word is normally restricted to a short narrative which conveys a secondary meaning; but the Greek word *parabolē* (as well as the Hebrew word behind it, *māšal)* can incorporate proverbs, riddles and simple comparisons as well. Furthermore, the designation of various types of parables and the lines of distinction between them cannot be made firm; indeed, there is a degree of overlap in al-'Aqqād's own terminology and examples. The main concern for modern interpreters (an issue which al-'Aqqād does not address) is the proper interpretation of Jesus' parables, in particular to what degree the different features of the parable are meant to be considered metaphorical. See DJG, s.v. "parable"; and ABD, s.v. "parable."

[21] The OT abounds with parables in the broad sense of the word, especially the Wisdom and prophetic literature. Among these are a few of the narrative type normally associated with the English word "parable," e.g., the story of the ewe lamb told to King David by Nathan (2 Sam. 12: 1-4), and the song of the vineyard in Isa. 5:1-7.

[22] Mt. 13:3-9 = Mk. 4:3-9 = Lk. 8:5-8. Al-'Aqqād's rendition is closest to Mark's version, which is the longest of the three. In all three Gospels, this parable is immediately followed by an explanation of why Jesus spoke in parables: "To you it has been given the know the secrets of the kingdom of heaven, but to them it has not been given" (Mt. 13:11 = Mk. 4:11 = Lk. 8:10; al-'Aqqād quoted this verse out of context in ch. 19, p. 188). Immediately following that, in all three Gospels, is Jesus' explanation of this particular parable: the seed is the teaching about God and his kingdom, and the different kinds of ground represent different types of people, only some of whom accept the word faithfully and produce good works (Mt. 13:18-23 = Mk. 4:13-20 = Lk. 8: 11-15).

[23] Ar. *fatayāt al-'urs.* This is usually referred to in English as the "Parable of the Ten Virgins."

[24] Ar. *khams minhunna faṭināt wa-khams ghāfilāt.* Although al-'Aqqād has followed VD somewhat closely for this parable, he has slightly changed the description of the two groups of girls: VD reads *ḥakīmāt* [wise] and *jāhilāt* [foolish] respectively. (In RSV the terms are reversed, in accordance with the best Gk. mss.).

[25] Mt. 25:1-12. Al-'Aqqād has omitted v. 13, in which Jesus mentions the point of the parable:

"Watch therefore, for you know neither the day nor the hour." The eschatological reference of the verse probably explains its omission here.

[26] Jn. 6:35. Most interpreters would not call this an allegory, since there is no story line.

[27] Mt. 7:6. Only part of the saying is quoted here; the full saying is: "Do not give dogs what is holy; and do not throw your pearls before swine, lest they trample them under foot and turn to attack you." Al-'Aqqād had referred to this saying in ch. 19 (p. 186); see n. 5 there.

[28] Mt. 7:2 = Mk. 4:24 = Lk. 6:38. The context of this saying in the biblical text is important for its understanding. Interestingly, this is not the same in each case. For Matthew and Luke, the context is one of judging others: one will be judged in the same way that he renders judgment. The context in Mark, however, concerns the interpretation of parables, and the meaning of the saying there is uncertain. Probably it refers to the profit gained when one pays attention to Jesus' teaching (Mann, 268).

[29] Lk. 4:23. According to the passage, this saying is not original to Jesus; he refers to it as a well-known "proverb" (or "parable," *mathal* in VD; the Gk. word *parabolē* can also be translated either way). This proverb has a number of parallels in other ancient literature, Greek as well as Jewish (Fitzmyer, 28:535). Again, the lack of context for the quotation here is unfortunate; the meaning in the biblical passage is given in the next sentence: "What we have heard you did at Capernaum, do here also in your own country" (RSV).

[30] Mt. 9:17 = Mk. 2:22 = Lk. 5:37. Al-'Aqqād does not supply the verb which is present in all three instances of the biblical text; the full sentence is "No one puts new wine into old wineskins." He alluded to this verse at the end of ch. 17 (p. 177; see n. 29 there concerning the context of this saying).

[31] Mt. 6:3. The biblical context for this saying concerns the giving of alms.

[32] Mt. 7:16. The biblical context is one of warning against false prophets; they will be recognized by the evil works they do. (Lk. 6:44 is similar: "Each tree is known by its own fruit.")

[33] Mt. 13:57 = Mk. 6:4 = Lk. 4:24 = Jn. 4:44. The wording is different in each Gospel; al-'Aqqād's rendition is in fact closest to that found in John, where it is mentioned parenthetically as an indirect quotation of Jesus in reference to the whole of Galilee. In the Synoptic Gospels, the context is Jesus' rejection at Nazareth; in Luke, this saying quickly follows "Physician, heal yourself!" There are parallels to this proverb in ancient Greek literature (Davies and Allison, 2:459-60).

[34] Mt. 5:46 = Lk. 6:32. The wording is slightly different in each instance; al-'Aqqād has drawn from both to render his own version.

[35] Mt. 9:12 = Mk. 2:17 = Lk. 5:31.

[36] Mt. 6:23. This is a rare instance where al-'Aqqād has quoted VD exactly.

[37] Salt served many beneficial functions in ancient times, including preservation, fertilization, as well as seasoning. Probably no one function is meant to be identified here; the service which the disciples render to the world is vital whatever its nature. It is difficult to explain how salt might become spoiled or lose its saltiness, given its chemical stability. Most likely, this is simply an example of hyperbole. (See Davies and Allison, 1:472-73; and Hagner, 33A:99).

[38] Mt. 5:13-15. (There are approximate parallel passages in Mark and Luke, but these are disjointed and worded rather differently.)

[39] Mt. 6:19-21 (= Lk. 12:33-34).

[40] Al-'Aqqād has adapted Mt. 7:3 = Lk. 6:41. There (in both Gospels), this statement does not concern Jesus' opponents, but it is directed to his disciples as part of his teaching about judging others.

[41] Mt. 23:24. Al-'Aqqād had previously quoted this verse in ch. 17 (p. 175). See n. 19 there concerning his misreading of VD, and the meaning of this saying.

[42] An adaptation of Mt. 23:27. Al-'Aqqād also quoted this verse in ch. 17 (p. 175), where he followed VD more closely.

[43] Mt. 19:24 = Mk. 10:25 = Lk. 18:25. Once again, the biblical context here does not involve Jesus dealing with his opponents. Rather, the saying was made to the disciples following the incident in which a rich man asked Jesus what he should do to gain eternal life, but he was not willing to follow Jesus' requirement of selling his possessions.

Al-'Aqqād has significantly altered the wording of this saying, which reads: "It is easier for a camel to go through the eye of a needle than for a rich man to enter the kingdom of God" (RSV; the wording is virtually identical in all three Gospels). It is especially interesting that he should substitute the phrase "a thick rope" *(ḥabl ghalīẓ)* for "a camel" *(jamal).* One possibility is that he misread the word *jamal* in VD, since it bears some resemblance to *ḥabl.* More likely he used a translation or commentary which relied on a few unimportant Gk. mss. which have *kamilos* [rope or ship's cable] instead of *kamēlos* [camel]. In any case, the change serves to diminish the extreme hyperbole of the original saying, which is meant to be taken literally, indicating the impossibility of the act (Davies and Allison, 3:51-52; and Fitzmyer, 28A:1204). (It might be observed here that the saying of a camel going through a needle's eye is also found in the Qur'ān, 7:40).

[44] Ar. *al-khuṭbah 'alā al-jabal.* The "Sermon on the Mount" is the name given to the long discourse of Jesus presented in Matthew, chapters five through seven. Al-'Aqqād uses the Islamic word for "sermon"; Christian Arabs refer to this discourse as *al-wa'ẓ 'alā al-jabal.*

[45] This is probably a reference to Mt. 10:19-20 = Mk. 13:11 = Lk. 12:11-12 (see also Lk. 21:14-15). The passage in Mark reads: "And when they bring you to trial and deliver you up, do not be anxious beforehand what you are to say; but say whatever is given you in that hour, for it is not you who speak, but the Holy Spirit" (RSV). Al-'Aqqād refers to this passage more directly in ch. 21 (p. 206).

[46] Of course, this statement is true; the use of proverbs and stories to illustrate truth goes back to very ancient times. For the variety of uses for "parables" in Greco-Roman literature, see ABD, s.v. "Parable" (5:146).

[47] Or, "in carrying out his mission" (Ar. *fī al-risālah).* The word *risālah* is normally translated as "mission," but for the remainder of this chapter it is rendered as "message" because of its relationship with "messenger" *(rasūl).*

Chapter 21
The Fidelity of the Disciples

[1] Ar. *ummah.* This word has several levels of meaning. In general, it can be translated as "nation" or "people." In the Qur'ān, it refers to an ethnic or religious group which has received a messenger and which will stand in judgment. More specifically, it applies to the community established by Muḥammad in Medina, which then grew to incorporate all Muslims whatever their ethnic identification (EI^2, s.v. *"umma").* Undoubtedly al-'Aqqād sees a parallel between the *ummah* of Jesus and the subsequent *ummah* of Muḥammad.

[2] The twelve disciples that were specifically chosen by Jesus were apparently all Galileans, with the probable exception of Judas Iscariot; his name most likely indicates that he came from

the town of Kerioth in Judea (DJG, s.v. "Disciples" and "Judas Iscariot"). It might be noted that never once does al-'Aqqād refer to the betrayal of Judas.

[3] E.g., Mt. 4:19-22 = Mk. 1:17-20; Mt. 9:9 = Mk. 2:14 = Lk. 5:27-28.

[4] Any "harmony" among the twelve disciples cannot be taken as a blanket statement, as evidenced by the Gospels. As al-'Aqqād himself later observes (p. 202), they argued among themselves about which of them was the greatest. Other passages suggest occasional animosity among the group; e.g., when James and John requested Jesus to grant them places of honor in the coming kingdom, the others became indignant (Mt. 20:24 = Mk. 10:41).

[5] Ar. *tilka al-nafḥah al-'ulwīyah.* This statement is reminiscent of the incident in Jn. 20:22, where the resurrected Jesus breathes on the disciples and says "Receive the Holy Spirit." But that passage exhibits a high Christological emphasis (Brown, *John,* 29A:1037), which is certainly not intended by al-'Aqqād if he does indeed allude to that verse. Undoubtedly he means nothing more than that Jesus was the means by which the disciples experienced divine renewal.

[6] Mt. 26:31 = Mk. 14:27; Jn. 16:32. In these passages, Jesus predicts the desertion of the disciples, which took place at the time of his arrest.

[7] This is a reference to Jesus' period of prayer in Gethsemane, just prior to his arrest (Mt. 26: 36-46 = Mk. 14:32-42 = Lk. 22:39-46). Al-'Aqqād had referred to this incident, including the behavior of the disciples, in ch. 12 (p. 148).

[8] Lk. 9:46, 22:24.

[9] Perhaps this is an allusion to Peter's statement, "Lo, we have left everything and followed you" in Mt. 19:27 = Mk. 10:28 = Lk. 18:28.

[10] E.g., once when a Samaritan village rejected Jesus, James and John asked, "Lord, do you want us to bid fire come down from heaven and consume them?"; but Jesus rebuked them (Lk. 9:52-56).

[11] According to Matthew and Luke, Jesus commissioned his disciples following his resurrection (Mt. 28:18-20, Lk. 24: 46-49, Acts 1:8). Nothing is mentioned about the disciples' level of maturity at that time. In fact, Luke (in his Gospel and in Acts) states that they will only be able to carry out that commission after they are empowered by the Holy Spirit.

[12] Ar. *al-qiblah,* the key word in ch. 14.

[13] In the early part of Mark especially, Jesus exhibits a desire to keep his identity as Messiah from becoming public knowledge. (This is known among scholars as the "Messianic Secret"). There seems also to be some reluctance on his part to discuss the matter with his disciples, until he elicits Peter's confession at Caesarea Philippi. (See DJG, s.v. "Mark, Gospel of" [523-24]).

[14] These sentences actually figure into the text of the first three passages which al-'Aqqād goes on to mention (i.e., from Mark, Matthew and Luke; they do not appear in John). When Jesus asked his disciples, "Who do people say that I am?" they responded by quoting these various opinions about him (Mt. 16:13-14 = Mk. 8:27-28 = Lk. 9:18-19).

[15] Mk. 8:29-30.

[16] Here al-'Aqqād employs the Christian Arabic term *Yasū'* in reference to Jesus. He repeats this usage in subsequent cases where he quotes more or less directly from the Gospels.

[17] Al-'Aqqād has provided a footnote at this point, translated as follows:

> The Aramaic word here is *"Ṣafā"* [or, this word can be vocalized as *"ṣafan";* see the comments at the end of this note], meaning "stone" [Ar. *ḥajar*], just as in Arabic; and "Peter" is the translation of the Greek word.

Through this statement (which is all too brief and not entirely satisfactory), al-'Aqqād tries to explain an important feature of this passage. There is a play on words in the Gk. text ("you are *Pet-*

ros, and upon this *petra* . . .") which is not evident in translation, either in English ("Peter" / "rock") or in Ar. (*"Buṭros" / "ṣakhrah"* both in VD and in al-'Aqqād's quotation). Behind both Gk. words lies (evidently) the Aramaic word *kephā',* meaning "rock" or "stone." Despite many attempts to circumvent the obvious meaning of this word play, it must be recognized that Matthew clearly quotes Jesus as stating that Peter will become some kind of foundation for the "church." (Davies and Allison, 2:626-27; see the following note).

Al-'Aqqād refers to the Aramaic word for "Peter" rather than the Gk. word, but he does not present it in Ar. transliteration. Rather, he uses the Ar. name *Ṣafā* which appears in a number of other NT passages in VD, as a name for Peter (e.g. 1 Cor. 1:12). The Gk. text of those passages reads *Kēphās,* which is simply a transliteration of the Aramaic word. VD's choice of *Ṣafā* was probably influenced by the English form of the Gk. word, "Cephas," found in AV (and followed by RSV). It is also possible that the translators of VD recognized this name's near equivalence with the Ar. word *ṣafan,* meaning "rock" or "stone," although technically this word is a collective noun. In any case, the modern Ar. translations do not follow VD in those passages and instead have either *Kayfā* or simply *Buṭros.*

Since al-'Aqqād places the unvocalized word *ṣfā* in quotation marks, he most likely intends the *alif* to be read as a long vowel, indicating the name *Ṣafā.* Since he also notes that the word can mean "stone" (*ḥajar,* also a collective noun), he indicates that the same letters can be read with *tanwīn* as *ṣafan,* and in this way he points out the meaning which lies behind the word.

[18] Mt. 16:16-20. This passage is replete with exegetical difficulties. Among the questions it raises are: How much of this is original to Jesus and how much was later church interpretation? In what sense did Peter understand Jesus to be "the Son of the living God"? What did Jesus mean by designating Peter as the rock on which he would build his church? What kind of "church" was envisioned? What was the nature of Peter's authority to "bind" and "loose"? The scope of the issues involved is indicated in the extensive analysis of this passage by Davies and Allison, which covers forty-two pages, plus nearly five pages of bibliography (2:602-652).

Most of these issues would be particularly problematic for Muslim readers. Yet al-'Aqqād includes the quotation (along with their parallels) without any further comment here. (He does, however, deal with the title "Son of God" in ch. 23, p. 222). His reference to these passages is simply meant to indicate that it was not until this incident that Jesus expressed himself, by way of Peter's confession, as the Messiah. The question then becomes, why did al-'Aqqād go to the trouble of including all four versions? Perhaps he meant to demonstrate the reality of variations among the Gospels, along with the complexities which surface from this fact; perhaps his lack of comment (which might well have been mostly critical) was out of deference to Christian sensitivities. But this can only be conjectured.

[19] Lk. 9:18-21.

[20] Jn. 6:66-70. Al-'Aqqād has followed VD, including the phrase "the Son of the Living God." However, there are several variations of this phrase among the Gk. mss.; RSV has "that you are the Holy One of God," following the most reliable Gk. mss. (Metzger, *Textual Commentary,* 215). The biblical passage continues with v. 71, which explains the last statement as a reference to Judas Iscariot, who was to betray Jesus. Although this passage is not a direct parallel to the three Synoptic accounts of Peter's confession, the many points of comparison make it a "Johannine" version of that event (Brown, *John,* 29:301-302).

[21] Al-'Aqqād has written *ta'lamūna* [you (pl.) know] instead of *ta'malūna* [you (pl.) do] as found in VD. This is obviously a misreading, especially since the rest of this sentence (which is v. 38 of the passage) quotes VD exactly, and the entire paragraph follows VD very closely.

However, the second half of the sentence in VD, like AV, differs from RSV which reads "and you do what you have heard [rather than "seen"] from your father." This again reflects variations among the Gk. mss.; the original reading is uncertain (Metzger, *Textual Commentary*, 225).

[22] The adjective *wāḥid* [one] is present in ed. 3, but it does not appear in eds. 1 and 2, nor in VD. Its addition by the editors of ed. 3 was probably meant to clarify the difficulty of the indefinite noun *āb* [father].

[23] Jn. 8:31-44, 48-53. Again, this passage contains several distinctly "Christian" features on which al-'Aqqād is silent. However, it is not surprising that he omits the final portion of this passage (vv. 54-59), in which Jesus dramatically responds to the question of his identity; he invokes the divine name ("I Am") for himself, and the Jews recognize this claim as blasphemy (see Brown, *John*, 29:367).

[24] I.e., they claimed that they obeyed the laws of God, and that God was their Father.

[25] Ar. *'alama;* or, possibly this should be read *'allama,* [taught].

[26] Al-'Aqqād makes this statement categorically, even though his first example (Matthew) is an exception. In fact, only a few disciples are directly said to have been fishermen, and others very likely were not (DJG, s.v. "Disciples").

[27] Al-'Aqqād's comments about the disciples' education may or may not be accurate. There is little direct knowledge about Jewish education in Palestine in the period before 70 C.E., and it is debated how much can be read back into that time from what is known of Judaism in the second and third centuries. See al-'Aqqād's discussion of Jesus' education in ch. 23 (pp. 218-19), and n. 13 there.

[28] Matthew is said to have been a tax collector when Jesus called him (Mt. 9:9; the parallels in Mk. 2:14 and Lk. 5:27-28 indicate that he was also known as Levi). Early church tradition is unanimous that "the Gospel of Matthew" was written by Matthew, one of the twelve disciples. Many modern scholars have disputed this view for various reasons, but their arguments are by no means conclusive. Early church tradition is also in agreement that Matthew wrote in Hebrew or Aramaic, and that his Gospel was later translated (i.e., into Greek). This is based on the earliest statement about this Gospel by Papias (d. ca. 130), as recorded in Eusebius *The Ecclesiastical History* 3.39.16 (Loeb 1:296-97): "Matthew collected the oracles in the Hebrew language, and each interpreted them as best he could." However, this statement is better understood as indicating the *style* rather than the *language* of authorship, the "interpretation" being one of explanation rather than translation. The Gk. text of this Gospel bears no evidence of having been translated from a Semitic language, and it was almost certainly originally composed in Greek. See DJG, s.v. "Matthew, Gospel of" (527-28), and "Disciples" (180) for further details.

Al-'Aqqād has clearly used a secondary source here, since the statement "in the Greek language, as is most likely" is placed in quotation marks in all editions. However, he provides no indication as to the source of this quotation. He discusses the purpose of Matthew's Gospel in ch. 22 (p. 213; see n. 17 there).

[29] It has been proposed that Jesus and the disciple John were cousins, both their mothers being sisters. The sole basis for this claim is a comparison of texts concerning the women who were present at Jesus' crucifixion. Matthew states that they included John's mother (Mt. 27:56), and she might well be the "Salome" also mentioned by Mark as being nearby (Mk. 15:40). According to the Gospel of John, those standing by included the sister of Jesus' mother (Jn. 19:25), and it has been suggested that she is the same woman as Salome and John's mother. But this identification is dubious at best. (Brown, *Death*, 2:1013-17). The possibility of a relationship through a brother of Jesus' mother (one of the suggestions by al-'Aqqād) has no basis whatsoever. Concerning John

as the author of the Fourth Gospel, see al-'Aqqād's discussion of this in ch. 22 (p. 212) and n. 12 there.

[30] Mk. 1:20 = Mt. 4:22 = Lk. 5:11. Only Mark mentions the "hired servants," an indication that their business was reasonably prosperous (DJG, s.v. "Disciples" [179]).

[31] There are several problematic and interrelated issues concerning this sentence:

(1) The reference here to a James and a John, apparently different from the brothers John and James just mentioned, is confusing. This is particularly so when it is clear from the descriptions given that the John in both paragraphs is the same person mentioned as a disciple in the Gospels. (Only one of the Twelve was named John.) This error on al-'Aqqād's part might lead one to assume that the James mentioned here should be the brother of John, especially since here he is said to be a relative *(qarīb)* of Jesus, which could be understood to mean that he was a maternal cousin as had been claimed for John. However, despite the error regarding John, al-'Aqqād evidently meant to refer to a different disciple named James.

(2) There was one other disciple named James among the Twelve, i.e., "the son of Alphaeus" (e.g. Mk. 3:18). Nothing further is known about him, and he can hardly be the person al-'Aqqād has in mind here. Rather, he evidently means the James who in the NT is said to be a "brother" of Jesus (e.g. Mk. 6:3, Gal. 1:19) and an early leader of the church in Jerusalem (e.g. Gal. 2:9, Acts 15:13); he is also thought to be the author of the Epistle of James. However, this James was not one of the Twelve as al-'Aqqād would have us believe. It appears from the NT that this James became a disciple only after the resurrection of Jesus. (See ABD, s.v. "James, Brother of Jesus" and "James, Epistle of"). There is no indication here why al-'Aqqād refers to him as "the relative of Christ" rather than his brother, but it is clear that this became a point of criticism among the readers of this book; see al-'Aqqād's discussion of this issue in ch. 2 (p. 80) and n. 15 there.

(3) One reason for differentiating the James mentioned here is that only John is said by al-'Aqqād to have been called by Jesus "the son of thunder." This term is found only in Mark's list of the Twelve disciples, which includes "James the son of Zebedee and John the brother of James, whom he surnamed Boanerges, that is, sons of thunder" (Mk. 3:17, RSV). No reason is given in the NT as to why Jesus designated them this way, but the scanty evidence as to the brothers' character makes al-'Aqqād's statement the most plausible (see, e.g., Mk. 9:38-41, Lk. 9:51-54; DJG, s.v. "Disciples" [179]).

(4) Related to the previous item is a slight but significant textual variation among the editions of this book. The conjunction preceding the quotation mark which begins the phrase "the son of thunder" is *aw-* [or] in ed. 2; but in the eds. 1 and 3, it is *wa-* [and], which would designate "the son of thunder" as a person, otherwise not named here, distinct from John. The reading in ed. 2 must surely be considered al-'Aqqād's correction of an original error which has unfortunately been transferred to ed. 3.

(5) The other reason for differentiating the James mentioned here from the one in the previous paragraph is that al-'Aqqād has used a different spelling in each case. In the first instance, he writes *Ya'qūb,* which is the standard Arabic version for the name "James" throughout VD (as well as for the name "Jacob" which is its OT equivalent). But here, al-'Aqqād has written *Jayms,* a direct transliteration of the English spelling. The use of this term was obviously another point of criticism, to which al-'Aqqād also refers in ch. 2 (p. 80; see n. 16 there).

(6) Finally, an explanation as to why al-'Aqqād used the term *Jayms* is given in a rather puzzling footnote which he appended to that word in ed. 2; (it is missing, however, in ed. 3, following ed. 1). In translation it reads as follows (the terms for "James" are left in their original Arabic spelling):

> Certain reference works mention that *"Jayms"* is a Greek misspelling [or, "distortion," Ar. *taṣḥīf]* of the word *Ya'qūb.* However, the name *Ya'qūb* appears in the Greek translations. Thus, we should most likely understand that when the Greek translator heard the name *Jayms* pronounced by Aramaic speakers, he did not change it.

This statement is not at all clear. The "Greek translations" are presumably those of the OT. But al-'Aqqād writes as if the English version of "James" was originally Gk., and that it was so written because the Aramaic name sounded like that! The source(s) he used for this argument cannot be determined. In any case, there was no misspelling or distortion involved in the transformation of the name from Heb. (and Aramaic) to Gk. The Gk. word in the NT for "James" is *Iakōbos;* this is simply a more natural Gk. form of the name *Iakōb* (for "Jacob"), which in turn was a direct transliteration from the Heb. word *Ya'ᵃqōb* (Bauer, 367).

[32] The Gospels present Peter as the recognized spokesman for the twelve disciples. His strong temperament often caused him trouble, but he proved to be an able leader of the early church. (DJG, s.v. "Disciples" [179]). The only reference to Peter carrying a weapon is in Jn. 18:10, where he tries to prevent the arrest of Jesus by striking the slave of the High Priest with a sword. (The three Synoptic Gospels also relate this incident, but they do not identify Peter by name). Al-'Aqqād's claim that Peter was thereby "accustomed to carrying a weapon" is reading more into that text than necessary.

[33] Many of the twelve disciples appear in the book of Acts as faithful witnesses to Jesus (especially to his death and resurrection). The martyrdom of only one of them is reported there (James, the brother of John, in 12:2). Judas Iscariot committed suicide according to apparently conflicting reports (Mt. 27:3-10 and Acts 1:18-19). The NT is silent as to the fate of the rest, but early church tradition states that most of them became martyrs as they carried out their missionary tasks. (DJG, s.v. "Disciples" [179-81]).

[34] Nicodemus was mentioned by al-'Aqqād in ch. 19 (p. 189; see n. 29 there).

[35] There are a few references in the Pauline letters to Luke as a physician and as Paul's "fellow worker": Phile. 24; Col. 4:14; 2 Tim. 4:11.

[36] Al-'Aqqād refers to Paul in the Christian manner, as "the Apostle" *(al-rasūl).* In Acts and in his letters, Paul makes occasional references to his strict Jewish education, claiming also to have been a Pharisee. In this regard, al-'Aqqād's statement that he was "an expert in religious jurisprudence" *(ustādh fī fiqh al-dīn)* is fairly accurate. However, "a scholar of history" seems inappropriate, although this could be a reference to Paul's use of OT historical material in his letters, e.g., accounts concerning Abraham and Moses. Most important here is that al-'Aqqād makes no adverse statement about Paul, either in this book or elsewhere, whereas Muslim critics often blame him for changing the message of Jesus.

[37] Al-'Aqqād's claim that later disciples such as Paul "despised" and "demolished" the Judaism in which Christianity was born is much too strong. In addition, as noted elsewhere, a large contingent of early Jewish Christians continued to operate within the framework of the Jewish religious system, hardly perceiving it to be "oppressive."

[38] It is mentioned in Jn. 12:4-6 and 13:29 that Judas was the group's treasurer. Presumably, al-'Aqqād means Peter as the "shepherd" who led when Jesus was absent, but there is no direct reference to this. Lk. 8:3 states that a small number of women followed Jesus as disciples and provided for the needs of the group. Otherwise, al-'Aqqād's remarks about the disciples' organization are only conjectural. Nowhere is the number twenty given as a number of disciples. It would seem that often there were many more.

[39] The choice of twelve primary disciples by Jesus is recorded in Mt. 10:1-4 = Mk. 3:13-19 = Lk. 6:12-16; these are later sent on a mission of preaching and healing. Only Luke records a subsequent commissioning of seventy disciples (Lk. 10:1-12, 17-20). The Gk. mss. differ on whether the number is seventy or seventy-two, the choice between these being fairly balanced. Also, most mss. read that these are seventy (-two) "others," presumably differentiating them from the twelve; but again, this is not clear. (See Fitzmyer, 28A: 845-56; and Nolland, 35B:549-50). Al-'Aqqād's other comments here reflect accurately the passage in Luke, except that there is no mention of Jesus taking them to a mountain.

[40] Mk. 9:35; and Mt. 20:26-27 = Mk. 10:43-44 = Lk. 22:26.

[41] Jn. 13:1-16. Only Peter is said to have initially resisted Jesus' action, and then to request that Jesus wash his hands and head (vv. 6-9). The setting for this incident is the Last Supper, just prior to Jesus' arrest.

[42] Mt. 10:10-14 = Mk. 6:8-11 = Lk. 9:3-5, when Jesus sent the Twelve on a preaching mission. He gave similar instructions when he sent the Seventy (Lk. 10:4-11). The act of shaking (or wiping) the dust from their feet would have been a public demonstration that they had no fellowship with and no responsibility for those who rejected the message (Davies and Allison, 2:178).

[43] Mt. 10:19-20 = Mk. 13:11 = Lk. 12:11-12, concerning how the disciples were to behave when brought to trial. (There is an allusion to this passage in ch. 20, p. 198). Although these words are written in the third person pl., al-'Aqqād has actually placed them in quotation marks.

[44] Mt. 10:16. Although al-'Aqqād has not used quotation marks here, these words are taken verbatim from VD. He had quoted the same verse in ch. 12 (p. 147), but there he had reversed the two parts of the saying.

[45] Mt. 10:28 (= Lk. 12:4-5). Al-'Aqqād has altered the wording of this verse in such a way that part of the original meaning is lost. He has used the general relative pronoun *man* [anyone who, i.e., sg. or pl.] in both halves of the sentence, whereas VD (reflecting the Gk.) uses the more specific relative pronouns *alladhīna* [those who] and *alladhī* [the one who] respectively. Furthermore, the full ending of the verse in VD reads: *alladhī yaqdiru an yuhlika al-nafs wa-al-jasad kilayhimā fī jahannam,* "the one who is able to destroy both the soul and the body in hell." Most interpreters understand this to be a reference to God who executes judgment (Davies and Allison, 2:206-207; and Hagner, 33A:286).

[46] Al-'Aqqād's direct transition from the disciples' training by Christ to their ministry in the world should be noted. "Thus the author's treatment of the first disciples and their relation with the Teacher merges imperceptibly into an outline of the progress of the apostolic Church throughout the world of its time" (Cragg, Review, 91). This kind of shift is inconceivable in the NT, where the disciples are able to carry out their mission only after witnessing the death and resurrection of Jesus, and after being empowered by the Holy Spirit.

[47] Al-'Aqqād's remarks here, concerning the travels of some of the disciples, are drawn from Christian tradition, although the basis for some of his comments is uncertain. According to the Gnostic "Acts of Thomas," that disciple brought the gospel to India; (al-'Aqqād's reference to "islands" is puzzling). The Syrian Christians of Malabar strongly affirm this. However, Eusebius reports that Thomas went to Parthia. Eusebius also reports that Andrew went to Scythia. According to Acts, Asia Minor and Europe were first evangelized by Paul; but how North Africa was evangelized is completely unknown. Eusebius reports that Mark went to Egypt, and this also continues as a strong tradition in the Coptic Orthodox Church. It is unknown how Christianity was spread in the Arab regions. (ODCC, s.v. "Thomas, St."; "Andrew, St."; "Africa"; and "Coptic Church").

[48] This claim is an important part of al-'Aqqād's thesis, but it does not match the earliest phase of the disciples' mission as presented in Acts. There, it took a number of years, plus persecution from the Jews, plus a divine vision to Peter to convince them to share the word among Gentiles. Even Paul, "the Apostle to the Gentiles" (Rom. 11:13), made it his custom to preach in the synagogue first whenever he entered a new city, according to Acts (e.g., 17:2). Al-'Aqqād's remarks in the rest of this paragraph are also conjectural.

[49] Again, this statement does not match the picture presented in Acts regarding the earliest phase of Christian mission; in most cases, opposition to the disciples' message came from the Jews.

[50] This incident is recorded by Paul in Gal. 2:11-14.

[51] 1 Cor. 9:19-22. The last phrase in al-'Aqqād's quotation reads *li-'allā astakhliṣ min kulli ḥāl qawman.* Al-'Aqqād has made here some subtle changes. Probably this is to smooth over an apparent difficulty in the biblical text which reads: "that I might by all means save some" (VD, *li-ukhalliṣ 'alā kulli ḥāl qawman).* In the NT, the subject of the verb "save" (Gk. *sōzō),* when dealing with eternal judgment, is almost always God, and only rarely does it involve people who are mediators of salvation (Bauer, 798). Al-'Aqqād was probably uncomfortable with the idea that Paul assigned such a role to himself.

[52] Al-'Aqqād's assertion of widespread syncretism in the earliest phase of the spread of Christianity is distorted. Paul's letters are replete with ethical injunctions for Gentile Christians which required them to refrain from pagan ways. Al-'Aqqād seems to want to claim an early basis for a subsequent blending of Christian and pagan practice.

[53] On the symbolism of shaking the dust from one's feet, see p. 206, n. 42 above.

Chapter 22
The Gospels

[1] Ar. *Al-Anājīl* according to eds. 1 and 2. Ed. 3 has the sg. *Al-Injīl.* Apparently the editors of ed. 3 changed the title of the chapter to the sg., while leaving the title of the Part in the pl., in an attempt to avoid exact repetition. The result is unfortunate, however, because al-'Aqqād's original pl. form reflects the content of this ch. far better than does the sg. form. For further details, see Appendix A, p. 240, item 3.

[2] Al-'Aqqād is correct as far as he goes; the Gk. word for "Gospel" (or "gospel") is *euangelion,* from the words *eu* [good] and *angellō* [to announce]. Unfortunately, al-'Aqqād does not discuss the original, non-technical meaning of this word. It appears several times in the Synoptic Gospels with reference to the "good news" (or "gospel") announced by Jesus (DJG, s.v. "Gospel [Good News]"). The technical application of the word as "Gospel," in reference to a document which elucidates both the "gospel" Jesus preached and the "gospel" about him, probably originated in the second century C.E. The present superscriptions to the four canonical Gospels were not a part of the original mss. (ABD, s.v. "Gospel, Genre").

[3] Ar. *nusakh* (sg. *nuskhah).* This word technically means "copies." However, al-'Aqqād's use of the same word in the following sentence, as well as in subsequent paragraphs, indicates that he does *not* have in mind numerous manuscripts copied from a common original document. Rather, he is referring to different original renditions of a common subject matter. In addition to the four

canonical Gospels, these versions included several other early accounts which are today called "Apocryphal Gospels." Most of these bear little resemblance to the genre of the four canonical Gospels, and few, if any, can be dated to the first century as al-'Aqqād supposes. (One important exception might be the "Gospel of Thomas," a document from Gnostic circles which may well preserve a few authentic sayings of Jesus not found in the canonical Gospels). See DJG, s.v. "Gospels (Apocryphal)"; and Wilhelm Schneelmelcher, ed., *New Testament Apocrypha,* English translation ed. R. McL. Wilson, 2d ed. (Cambridge, England: James Clarke, 1991-92), 1:77-87.

[4] Al-'Aqqād does not do justice to the complex process in which the NT writings came to be recognized as scripture and incorporated into a "canon" (i.e., an authoritative list of scriptural books). In addition to the articles on "Canon" in ABD and DJG, a fine presentation is given in Bruce M. Metzger, *The Canon of the New Testament: Its Origin, Development, and Significance* (Oxford: Clarendon Press, 1987); see especially his Introduction, pp. 1-8. Non-Christians often fail to appreciate that while the writings themselves were not officially recognized for many decades, they were nevertheless each widely accepted as an authoritative witness to the life and teaching of Jesus and his apostles. As such, they were generally given the same status as the Jewish scriptures. At official church councils, their recognition was much more by consensus than by the "majority vote" claimed by al-'Aqqād. The earliest reference to the institutional approval of the canon by means of a distinct process of voting is to the Council of Trent in 1546 (ibid., 246).

[5] Al-'Aqqād shows some awareness here of the so-called "Synoptic Problem," i.e., the attempt to explain the frequent similarities (in the order, content and/or wording of individual units) between the three Synoptic Gospels (Mt., Mk. and Lk.). Many issues concerning this matter continue to be debated; but the most commonly accepted explanation is the "two-source (or two-document) hypothesis." Briefly, this states that Mk. was the first of the three Gospels to be written, and that it was independently used as a source in the composition of Mt. and Lk. In addition, Mt. and Lk. each used another source as well, usually considered to be a document which is now lost. This source has been named "Quelle" (German for "source"), and usually abbreviated as "Q." Passages in Mt. and Lk. which agree with each other but which are not found in Mk. are usually attributed to Q. For overviews, see the articles on "Synoptic Problem" and "Q" in ABD and DJG.

It is clear, however, that al-'Aqqād is confused about some of the details of this matter. His most glaring error is the claim that "all" the Gospels are dependent on Q when in fact this is said only for Mt. and Lk. (indeed, his concluding statement admits this). His use of the term "Logia" as equivalent for Q is also incorrect; the "Logia" (a pl. Gk. word meaning "sayings") refer simply to the sayings of Jesus, only some of which would have been incorporated into Q (ABD, s.v. "Logia"). Furthermore, it is debated whether the language of Q was Aramaic or Gk., if indeed Q was even a written document. Finally, al-'Aqqād's transliteration into Arabic seems rather peculiar; he uses the letter *kāf* for "Q" rather than *qāf,* and he renders "Quelle" as *kwīl.*

[6] Al-'Aqqād's translation of "Koinē" (which he gives in plain Roman letters) as "common" (Ar. *'āmmah)* is correct. As the empire of Alexander expanded, Koinē Greek spread throughout the Near East and served as a common form of communication, especially for commerce. (ABD, s.v. "Languages [Greek]").

[7] By "translation," al-'Aqqād seems to mean that the Aramaic features of NT Gk. can be observed, even when that Gk. text is translated into English or Arabic.

[8] Acts 20:35.

[9] The "Gospel of Thomas" is the most widely recognized apocryphal work which may comprise authentic sayings of Jesus; it exists in its entirety only in a Coptic translation from Gk. (ABD, s.v.

"Thomas, Gospel of"). The "papyrus fragments" mentioned by al-'Aqqād probably refer to the four fragmentary Gk. texts discovered at Oxyrhynchus in Egypt (1897-1905); three of these are now recognized to derive from a Gk. version of the Gospel of Thomas (ABD, s.v. "Sayings of Jesus, Oxyrhynchus").

[10] This is a good summary of early Christian tradition about the Gospel of Mark. His association with Peter is fairly strong, and he is usually identified as the John Mark who traveled with Paul and Barnabas on their first missionary journey, and later with Barnabas alone (Acts 13:5, 13; 15:36-39). There is no indication that this Mark knew Jesus; some have proposed that the "young man" who was nearly apprehended at Jesus' arrest (Mk. 14:51-52) was Mark himself, but this is quite speculative (Brown, *Death,* 1:299). In fact, however, the Gospel of Mark is anonymous, and the author's identity cannot be determined from internal evidence. The date of composition is equally difficult; this involves many factors, including the solution to the Synoptic Problem and possible references in the Gospel to the destruction of the Temple. 70 C.E. or shortly before is usually accepted. (See the articles "Mark, Gospel of" in ABD and DJG).

[11] Questions regarding the Gospel of Luke must be considered in conjunction with the book of Acts, as these two were almost certainly two parts of a single work (a point which al-'Aqqād does not mention). The attribution of this work to Luke is based partly on Christian tradition and partly on internal indicators in Acts; but in the end, these books also remain anonymous. A date of 80 C.E. for composition is reasonable. Al-'Aqqād's claim that he depended on Paul for the writing of the Gospel is hardly likely; indeed, Luke's prologue to the Gospel (1:1-4) indicates that he sought for reports from eyewitnesses of Jesus' ministry, something which would not have applied to Paul. Evidently, however, Luke considered the Gospel of Mark, and Q, to qualify as such. (See DJG, s.v. "Luke, Gospel of"; and ABD, s.v. "Luke-Acts, Book of").

[12] The authorship of the Gospel of John, and its relationship to the disciple John, is a very complex issue with numerous proposed solutions. Few modern scholars hold that the apostle John alone was responsible for the Gospel in its present state, but most believe that he stands as the authority behind the material on which it draws. There is also evidence within the Gospel that the original version was edited at least once. The date of composition is equally difficult, but most place it late in the first century. See DJG, s.v. "John, Gospel of" (368-71); and Brown, *John,* 29:lxxxviii-cii. The difference in style which al-'Aqqād notes between the Gospel of John and the book of Revelation has long been recognized. The author of Revelation identifies himself as "John" (1:9), but his precise identity is disputed. The book is usually dated near the end of the first century. (ABD, s.v. "Revelation, Book of").

[13] Al-'Aqqād's reference is to an independent and somewhat idiosyncratic translation of the Bible by Ferrar Fenton, a British businessman. After publishing his rendition of Paul's epistles, he produced the whole NT in translation in 1895, followed by the complete Bible in 1903. The edition referred to here is the fourth (*The Holy Bible in Modern English,* trans. Ferrar Fenton, 4th ed. (London: S. W. Partridge, 1909; New York: Oxford Press, 1909). This version earned a degree of popularity and continued to be reprinted into the 1940's (see Bruce, *History,* 160-61).

Fenton took the unusual step of placing the Gospel of John first in the NT, immediately followed by the First Epistle of John; (thereafter, the NT books follow the usual order). His reasoning is briefly stated in introductory notes to these two books (pp. 1, 29). He claims that a "Jerusalem edition" of the Gospel was written in Hebrew shortly after the crucifixion, and that John translated this Gospel into Greek about 90 C.E. The Epistle of John was then appended to this "Ephesian edition." Fenton does not mention specific dates for the earlier edition, nor for any of the other Gospels; al-'Aqqād's reference of "between the years 30 and 40" is evidently his assumption based on Fenton's remarks.

[14] Ar. *anājīl al-muqābalah,* lit. "the Gospels of the comparison." Al-'Aqqād clearly means to provide a technical term; however, the proper Arabic expression in the field of biblical studies is *al-anājīl al-mutashābihah* [parallel, corresponding] (Richard W. Thomas, *A Workbook of Religion: English-Arabic* [Arabic title: *Dalīl al-Muṣṭalaḥāt al-Dīnīyah: Inklīzī-'Arabī]* [Beirut: Rābiṭat al-Maṭbū'āt al-Masīḥīyah al-'Arabīyah, 1969], 39).

[15] Al-'Aqqād mentions this fact presumably because certain units which in one Gospel appear in a single chapter might span two chapters in another Gospel. The man credited with introducing chapter divisions into the books of the Bible is Stephen Langton (d. 1228), who became Archbishop of Canterbury in 1207. Prior to this, he taught at the University of Paris, where it seems that he developed the use of chapter divisions as an aid to teaching. In any case, the method became standard in Paris and then everywhere else. See ODCC, s.v. "Langton, Stephen"; and for further details on this process, Beryl Smalley, *The Study of the Bible in the Middle Ages,* 3d ed. (Oxford: Basil Blackwell, 1983), 221-24.

[16] The incident concerning the tombs is recorded in Mt. 27:52-53 as one of the events which occurred at the time of Jesus' crucifixion and resurrection. Al-'Aqqād mentions this report again in ch. 23 (p. 226), where he includes it among those events that cannot be verified historically; see n. 70 there.

[17] Al-'Aqqād had referred to Matthew the disciple as the author of the Gospel of Matthew in ch. 21 (p. 205; see n. 28 there). On the purpose of Mt., see ch. 2, n. 31. The issue of where that Gospel was directed is more conjectural.

[18] The intended audience of Mk. is not easy to ascertain. The supposition that his readers were mostly Gentiles stem's from the frequent explanation of Jewish customs and Aramaic expressions (DJG, s.v. "Mark, Gospel of" [515]). Whether Mk. places a greater emphasis on the "divinity" of Jesus than does Mt. is open to interpretation. It is interesting that al-'Aqqād admits to this feature in Mk. while arguing for the authenticity of the Gospels as a whole.

[19] The designated recipient of the Gospel of Luke and of Acts was a nobleman named Theophilus (Lk. 1:3, Acts 1:1). Yet the effort expended in this project indicates a wider audience. Many indicators such as language and style support al-'Aqqād's idea that Lk. anticipated his readers to be educated. (DJG, s.v. "Luke, Gospel of" [498]). However, al-'Aqqād's statement that Lk. writes "from the human perspective" *(min al-wujhah al-insānīyah)* is unclear.

[20] Al-'Aqqād has overstated the philosophical orientation of the Gospel of John. It is true that the concept of the *logos* was popular in Stoic thought, yet John's usage is in many ways different. Rather than direct influence, one should talk in terms of a common general background. As Brown concludes, "There is no real reason to suppose that the Gospel [of John] was influenced by any more Greek philosophy than what was already present in the general thought and speech of Palestine" (Brown, *John,* 29:lvii).

[21] I.e., companionship cannot occur without mutual agreement, and vice versa.

[22] Abū Ḥāmid Muḥammad al-Ghazālī (d. 505/1111) was one of Islam's most renowned intellectuals, at once a philosopher, theologian, jurist and mystic. He gave up an illustrious academic career and, experiencing a crisis of faith, embarked on an eleven-year spiritual and physical pilgrimage. He returned to teaching and to Ṣūfism, hoping to help bring about religious revival. (EI², s.v. "al-Ghazālī, Abū Ḥāmid"; and Hodgson, 2:180-92). See the Introduction (p. 9) concerning the references in his works to Jesus.

It is not clear from al-'Aqqād's argument whether he has drawn from al-Ghazālī's thought in general or from one of his many works. In any case, no direct source has been located. However, the theme of cause and effect seems to have been a popular one for al-Ghazālī. It is present, e.g., in his *Tahāfut al-Falāsifah* [The Inconsistency of the Philosophers], a work which undercuts philosophy as a means for arriving at truth (EI², 2:1040). There, he lists several examples of causes and effects which of necessity must occur together, such as fire and burning, father and son. In any case, God is the ultimate Cause (see the edition edited by Sulaymān Dunyā, 4th ed. Dhakhā'ir al-'Arab [Arab Treasures], no. 15, [Cairo: Dār al-Ma'ārif, n.d.], 242, 249).

As mentioned in the Introduction (p. 29, n. 43), al-'Aqqād greatly admired al-Ghazālī and wrote a small book about him, *Falsafat al-Ghazālī.* An argument concerning miracles, similar to the one here, appears there (pp. 7-8).

[23] Al-'Aqqād refers here to the "miracles" of Christ's birth in the plural. Aside from the Virgin Birth itself, events described in the Gospels concerning the birth of Jesus which might be deemed miracles would include the angelic visits to Mary, Joseph and the shepherds, and the "star" which led the Magi to Bethlehem. Possibly al-'Aqqād also had in mind the miracle related in the Qur'ān in which Jesus speaks while in the cradle (3:46, 19:29-34). In any case, there is no evidence in the Gospels that people during Jesus' ministry were even aware of such miracles.

[24] Mt. 12:39 = Mt. 16:4 = Mk. 8:12 = Lk. 11:29.

[25] A reference to the allegations of the scribes and Pharisees when Jesus was casting out a demon (Mt. 12:22-30 = Mk. 3:22-27 = Lk. 11:14-23; see also Mt. 9:32-34).

[26] A reference to the plot by the Jewish Council (Sanhedrin) to put Jesus to death (Jn. 11:47-53). They were afraid that Jesus' miracles would cause a commotion among the people, and that the Roman authorities would intervene in a destructive manner.

[27] Al-'Aqqād had made a similar claim about Muḥammad: "He is the miracle which is above all miracles" (*'Abqarīyat Muḥammad,* 17). Al-'Aqqād's assertion about Jesus finds resonance in a similar view expressed by a contemporary Muslim: "The miracle of Jesus, like the miracle of the Qur'an, is not a once-only event, but an everlasting source of blessing, guidance, and salvation" (Ayoub, "Miracle," 227).

Chapter 23
The Results of Gospel Research

[1] Ar. *Shurrāḥ al-Anājīl,* lit., "The Interpreters of the Gospels," based on the opening words of the first sentence. However, the contents of the chapter deal far more with the results of their research than with the interpreters themselves.

[2] Almost all modern scholars agree to some extent with this perspective of the Gospels. Each is carefully arranged to meet the author's purpose, while also not oblivious to chronology. See Meier, 1:408-409, 2:237.

[3] Al-'Aqqād does not include here the birth of Jesus itself, presumably because he had dealt with issues concerning the birth at the beginning of ch. 11 (although there the discussion is limited).

[4] Mt. 2:13-16. In this chapter, al-'Aqqād closely follows the wording of VD for his biblical quotations.

[5] There is no direct historical evidence to support this account of Herod's slaughter of the infants. Differing perspectives on this observation can be taken. On the one hand, its historical possibility cannot be ruled out, especially since it would have been in keeping with the character of

Herod. On the other hand, the theological motifs which pervade the infancy narrative, particularly the connection with Moses, suggest that it was composed as an interpretive tale. (See Davies and Allison, 1:265; and Brown, *Birth,* 225-29).

[6] Al-'Aqqād here seems puzzled about the family's presence in Bethlehem, but he later offers an explanation as to why this was so (p. 219). See n. 15 below concerning his view of Jesus' birthplace. He has mentioned the census of Quirinius several times: ch. 6 (p. 100) and ch. 7 (pp. 110-12), in connection with the revolt by Judas the Galilean; and ch. 11 (pp. 133-34) in reference to the passage in Lk. 2:2.

[7] Lk. 2:21-24. Luke has conflated two separate requirements of the Jewish law related to birth: the ritual presentation of the child to God (in the case of a first-born son), and the purification ceremony for the mother (required for the birth of any child). The sacrifice of two doves or young pigeons was in relation to the latter rite, and was an acceptable offering according to Lev. 12:8. There, the sacrifice called for a year-old lamb, but the mother could offer the two birds "if she cannot afford a lamb." Luke's reference would thus seem to imply that Mary and Joseph were poor (so Fitzmyer, 28:426); however, it is "not certain that the alternative [of the lamb] offered in Leviticus was still an active custom in Jesus' time" (Brown, *Birth,* 448, n. 12).

[8] Lk. 2:41-52. The translation here is given as a block quotation since al-'Aqqād has copied VD almost exactly. The only exception is in the line, "He [Jesus] said to them" (i.e., to Mary and Joseph), where al-'Aqqād has "He said to *her.*" See al-'Aqqād's interpretation of this passage on p. 219, and n. 16 below.

[9] Al-'Aqqād's assumption that Jesus was thirty years old at the beginning of his ministry is derived from Lk. 3:23: "Jesus, when he began his ministry, was about [Gk. *hōsei*] thirty years of age." This is the only biblical reference to the age of the adult Jesus. Luke's statement is clearly an approximation and should not be pressed (Fitzmyer, 28:499).

[10] Lk. 3:3 = Mk. 1:4.

[11] Mt. 3:13-17; cf. Mk. 1:9-11, Lk. 3:21-22, Jn. 1:29-34. Here, al-'Aqqād allows this text to stand without offering any comment on the identity of the "Holy Spirit" or the meaning of this event for Jesus. However, he later refers to "the words of John" which encouraged Jesus (p. 219; see n. 18 below). See the ch. 15, n. 8 for a brief comparison between the Christian and Qur'ānic views of the Holy Spirit.

[12] This account actually comes from an Apocryphal Gospel today designated as "The Gospel of the Nazareans" (or, "Nazaraeans"). This is to be distinguished from another, similar work called "The Gospel of the Hebrews." The confusion evident in al-'Aqqād's reference is undoubtedly due to the fact that the fourth-century biblical scholar Jerome referred to both of these documents as "The Gospel of the Hebrews." "The Gospel of the Nazareans" was an early Jewish-Christian Gospel written in Aramaic, dating from the first half of the second century. Only fragments survive as quotations in various early church fathers, especially Jerome. (Schneemelcher, 1:134-65).

The verse quoted by al-'Aqqād is related by Jerome in his *Adversus Pelagius* 3.2, and is translated in Schneemelcher, 1:160, as "fragment no. 2." Al-'Aqqād's rendition is very close. The account was likely created by Christians in order to deal with the "problem" of Jesus' baptism by John, since it was a baptism of repentance. Jerome's quotation does not indicate whether or not Jesus was indeed baptized by John. The verse does not deny that event, only that it's purpose was not because Jesus was a sinner.

Aside from al-'Aqqād's quotation from the "Letter of Lentulus" at the beginning of ch. 12, this is the only instance where he quotes from apocryphal material. Probably he approves of its content, since the sinlessness of Jesus is an important doctrine for Muslims as well as for Christians.

[13] Al-'Aqqād's comments here, and in ch. 21 (p. 205) concerning the disciples' education, reflect the traditional view that the training of Jewish boys to read the Torah (and perhaps to write Hebrew) was widespread in Palestine at that time. See, e.g., Schürer, 2:418-20; and Safrai and Stern, 2:945-50. However, this view is based primarily on what is known about Jewish education in the second and third centuries C.E., and it is not certain that this information reflects the situation in Palestine prior to 70 C.E. See the extensive discussion on this issue in Meier, 1:271-78. Meier concludes, however, that Jesus himself was probably literate, but this is based more on later tradition about him in the Gospels than on external evidence about education in general.

On the other hand, al-'Aqqād's earlier claim in ch. 6 that it was the Pharisees who had taught Jesus (p. 98) is hardly likely. In the first place, there is no indication that he had studied further under a noted scholar in some urban center such as Jerusalem. Indeed, one passage in particular mitigates against this: "The Jews marveled at [his teaching], saying, 'How is it that this man has learning, when he has never studied?'" (Jn. 7:15, RSV). The context portrays Jesus adeptly arguing with the Jewish authorities, yet without the benefit of a formal education which they likely possessed. (Meier, 1:269, 278). Secondly, his frequent disputes with the Pharisees concerning the hallmark of their group — their acceptance of the detailed requirements of the oral law — make such a claim improbable.

Al-'Aqqād's reference here to the terms *ḥazzān* and *khazzān* is meant to indicate the Heb. word *ḥazzān.* (The two forms reflect alternative ways in Ar. to denote the Heb. letter *ḥêt).* This man was an officer of the synagogue who carried out a number of duties including, on occasion, the education of boys (Schürer, 2:438; Safrai and Stern, 2:936).

[14] Ar. *Yasū' aw Yahawshu'.* The first term is the Ar. Christian name for Jesus. The second term, which al-'Aqqād places in quotation marks, is meant to indicate the Heb. form of Joshua, i.e., *Yehôšûa',* which originally would have had the meanings indicated by al-'Aqqād. (The name for Joshua in the Ar. Bible is *Yašū').* In Jesus' day, the name *Yehôšûa'* had been shortened to *Yēšûa'* or, less formally, *Yēšû.* (Meier, 1:205-206; 231, n. 1). This name was very common among Jews in Palestine at that time. (Josephus refers to some twenty different people by the name Jesus). An additional term of reference was customary, such as "Jesus of Nazareth." However, there is absolutely no indication that this particular name carried messianic overtones; it was simply one among several names which were frequently chosen from great heroes of the past. (Ibid., 1:206-208).

[15] This "explanation," that Mary and Joseph went to Bethlehem so that Jesus could be born there in fulfillment of prophecy, answers al-'Aqqād's earlier question as to why the family had been in Bethlehem and escaped from there to Egypt, "since they were actually from Nazareth" (p. 217). Here, the clear implication is that Jesus was indeed born in Bethlehem rather than Nazareth. Al-'Aqqād had previously stated that Jesus was born in Galilee, but he later implied that he was born in Judea. His inconsistency regarding Jesus' birthplace is discussed in the Introduction (pp. 55-56).

Al-'Aqqād's explanation also counters both that given by Matthew (where both Mary and Joseph seem to have originated from Bethlehem) and Luke (where they travel to Bethlehem from Nazareth because of the Roman census). However, the Jewish belief that the Messiah was to be born in Bethlehem is reflected in Mt. 2:4-8, where the Magi are told by Herod to search for the Messiah in Bethlehem, after the Jewish scholars inform him that this was the predicted birthplace according to Mic. 5:2. Jn. 7:41-42 also reflects this belief. It is probably true that such an expectation existed at that time, but it would have been only one among other expectations. Though it is found in later Jewish writings, it is not attested in any other contemporary literature. (See Brown,

Birth, 511-12). Thus it is quite unlikely that such an expectation would of itself lead a couple to travel to Bethlehem specifically to give birth there.

[16] Although al-'Aqqād's explanation (as to why the twelve-year-old Jesus remained in Jerusalem) may seem plausible, it is difficult to deduce this from the text in Lk. 2:41-52 (which he quoted on p. 218). There, Jesus' action of remaining behind in Jerusalem seems to have been intentional, since he regarded his service to God, as his "Father," to be more important than his relationship to his natural family. (Brown, *Birth,* 490).

[17] Al-'Aqqād does not elaborate on the nature of the prior "strong relationship" (Ar. *ṣilah wathīqah)* between Jesus and John. The data on this is very scanty. Lk. 1:36 states that their mothers were relatives (although the degree of kinship is not indicated), and this would point to some kind of blood relationship between the two men. Two other passages may indicate some kind of prior relationship: John's rather vague reference to "he who is coming after me" (Mt. 3:11 = Mk. 1:7 = Lk. 3:16 = Jn. 1:27); and John's apparent recognition of Jesus' piety when Jesus came to him for baptism (Mt. 3:14, quoted by al-'Aqqād on p. 218). According to Jn. 1:33, John the Baptist declared "I myself did not know him"; however, this phrase could be interpreted to mean simply that John had not recognized Jesus as the one who was to come (Brown, *John,* 29:65).

[18] This paragraph clearly implies that John himself spoke words of encouragement to Jesus when the latter came to John for baptism. Yet the only conversation between the two men recorded in the Gospels is the passage in Mt. 3:14-15 which al-'Aqqād quoted on p. 218. John's words hardly seem to fit al-'Aqqād's remarks here. More likely, al-'Aqqād is thinking of the "voice from heaven [saying], 'This is my beloved Son,'" which forms the conclusion of his quotation above. Of course, the biblical text assumes that these words came directly from God. Al-'Aqqād's reluctance to acknowledge this source is understandable given their christological character. Yet he recognizes that such an event would have made a dramatic impact on Jesus' sense of vocation.

[19] Al-'Aqqād includes the Muslim salutation in the quotation. It is, of course, not present in the text of VD.

[20] Mt. 4:2-10. The order of events and much of the wording follows VD fairly closely, but al-'Aqqād has departed from it in a number of details. This account is also related in Lk. 4:1-13, where the second and third temptations are reversed. Mk. 1:12-13 mentions the incident only briefly, and it does not appear in the Gospel of John at all.

The narrative portrays the importance of the written scriptures for Jesus. He quotes three passages, all from Deuteronomy (8:3, 6:16, and 6:13), and even the devil is said to quote a passage (Ps. 91:11-12).

[21] Mt. 4:12-13, 17. The parts in quotation marks follow VD; the rest is a summary statement.

[22] The three rhetorical questions in this paragraph parallel the three temptations of Jesus; al-'Aqqād states that each was a genuine temptation, enticing Christ to take on the role of Messiah in a tangible, powerful way. Here, al-'Aqqād has perceptively interpreted the essential meaning of the Temptation as recorded in Matthew and Luke. Whether or not this particular event is historical (by its nature, this cannot be ascertained scientifically), the Gospels have presented both the reality and intensity of Jesus' struggle to remain true to his mission as he saw it. (See Meier, 2: 271-72, n. 1; Hagner, 33A:69-70; and Fitzmyer, 28:509-510).

[23] The implication here is that Jesus had already been experiencing the inward call to mission, and that John's words both confirmed that call and stimulated him to reflect on it further.

[24] A reference to Jesus' words about faith in Mt. 17:20 and Lk. 17:6.

[25] A figure of "more than eighty" disciples is not found anywhere in the Gospels. Probably al-

'Aqqād combined the original twelve disciples plus the seventy later sent out on a mission; he had mentioned both these groups in ch. 21 (p. 206).

[26] Lit., "until the book reached its appointed time" (Ar. *ḥattā balagha al-kitāb ajalahu),* a distinctly Islamic phrase.

[27] By "feature" (Ar. *al-ṣifah),* al-'Aqqād seems to be referring to Jesus' realization that his mission would eventually take on a universal nature. He had elaborated on this theme in ch. 19.

[28] These three self-descriptive metaphors are among the several so-called "I am" sayings of Jesus found only in the Gospel of John: 8:12 and 9:5; 6:35, 48; and 15:1 respectively. For John, they are meant to describe who Jesus is in relation to his ministry and the people for whom he has come. They are implicitly universal in scope, as al-'Aqqād wishes to emphasize here. However, their main purpose in the context of Johannine christology is to focus on the person of Jesus, and in particular to give some indication of his relationship to the Father by means of invoking the divine name "I AM." (See Brown, *John,* 29:534-37). This christological understanding can hardly be in view for al-'Aqqād.

[29] Ar. *ibn Allāh wa-ibn al-insān.* Nowhere in the Gospels is Jesus said to have referred to himself directly as "the Son of God." However, Mt. 27:43 has his opponents stating that he made this claim: "for he said, 'I am the Son of God.'" Probably this refers to the trial, where the High Priest asked, "Tell us if you are the Christ, the Son of God"; Jesus' answer, "You have said so," is taken for blasphemy (Mt. 26:63-65; Davies and Allison, 3:527-34, 620). Throughout the Gospels, Jesus is recognized as the Son of God by demons, disciples, and the voice from heaven (e.g., Mt. 8:29, Mt. 14:33, Mt. 3:17, and parallels). Jesus frequently refers to God as his "Father" and to himself as "the Son."

Naturally, there is considerable debate among scholars concerning the historicity of these references, and, for any that are deemed historical, the nature of the relationship implied by Jesus and/or the Gospel writers. (For an overview of the issues, see DJG, s.v. "Son of God"). Taken at face value, the Gospels point to a relationship between Jesus and God which was based both on intimacy and on obedience. Although his disciples are also brought into a relationship with God as Father, the relationship which Jesus experienced is nevertheless portrayed as unique. There is no direct implication in the Synoptics as to a pre-existent, ontological relationship, but this forms a significant part of the christology of John's Gospel.

There is also debate about the background to this title. It sometimes occurs in the OT with regard to angels, the people of Israel, or the king. There is, however, no clear reference to the Messiah being designated "the Son of God" in either the OT or other early Jewish literature. Some have therefore claimed that the early church utilized the Hellenistic concept of the "divine man" for interpreting Jesus; but there are significant differences between the Hellenistic and NT perspectives which make this problematic. (See DJG, s.v. "Divine Man/*theios anēr").*

In any case, al-'Aqqād approaches the issue in a rather straightforward manner. He simply observes the way in which "son of God" is used in a general sense, in both the OT and the Gospels. He makes no further comment, but clearly his assumption is that when the phrase is ascribed to Jesus, it should mean no more than that he was a member of common humanity.

On the title "the Son of Man," see n. 39 below.

[30] Lit., "the books of the Prophets" *(kutub al-anbiyā').* However, only the last reference is from one of the Prophetic books, the rest coming from the Pentateuch or Psalms. The quotations given do not follow VD closely; some depart from it significantly. This would indicate that al-'Aqqād has probably taken this argument from a secondary source in English, and has translated passages directly from that work.

[31] Gen. 6:2. In fact, it is not indicated whether these "sons of God" are to be understood as heavenly or human beings. The former is most likely, since they are clearly contrasted with "the daughters of men." As "sons," these beings are considered by the writer simply "as belonging to the world" of God (Gerhard von Rad, *Genesis: A Commentary,* trans. John H. Marks, 2d ed., Old Testament Library [Philadelphia: Westminster Press, 1961], 114).

[32] Ex. 4:23. The immediate context is needed here: "And the Lord said to Moses, '. . . You shall say to Pharaoh, "Thus says the Lord, 'Israel is my first-born son, and I say to you, "Let my son go that he may serve me"'"'" (vv. 21-23, RSV). Thus, the Israelites are here referred to as God's "son" in a collective sense.

[33] Dt. 14:1, 32:19.

[34] Ps. 29:1, 89:6. In both cases, RSV translates the phrase as "the heavenly beings," adding a footnote as to the literal translation "sons of gods." Most commentators agree that this is the proper designation here (A. A. Anderson, *The Book of Psalms,* The New Century Bible, ed. Ronald E. Clements and Matthew Black, [Grand Rapids, MI: Wm. B. Eerdmans, 1972; London: Marshall, Morgan & Scott, 1972], 1:234, 2:635).

[35] Hos. 1:10; the phrase is applied there prophetically to the Israelites.

[36] Mt. 6:9, which begins what is known as "the Lord's prayer" (vv. 9-13). The parallel in Lk. 11:2-4 is considerably shorter; there it starts, in the most reliable mss., simply with "Father" (Metzger, *Textual Commentary,* 154). However, Lk. 11:2 in VD (following AV) includes the full address as given in Matthew.

[37] Mt. 23:9.

[38] The concept of spiritual birth, as contrasted with physical birth, is found almost exclusively in the Gospel of John and the epistle of 1 John. Nowhere is it stated directly that in spiritual birth God is the person's "Father," although this is clearly implied. The passage closest in language to the statement by al-'Aqqād is Jn. 1:12-13; this is not presented as the words of Jesus, but is a summary of what it means to have faith in Christ: those who receive him "become children of God" and are "born, not of blood nor of the will of the flesh nor of the will of man, but of God." (Similar language is found throughout 1 John, e.g. 3:9-10.) The closest passage which is presented as the words of Jesus is in his dialogue with Nicodemus, Jn. 3:3-8; but there, although the phrase "born of the Spirit" is repeated, there is no mention of God as "Father" or the believer as "son."

[39] Al-'Aqqād's Arabic transliteration of the Hebrew and Aramaic forms of "the Son of Man" are reasonably close. More precisely, the Hebrew form is *ben 'ādām* and the Aramaic *bar 'enāš.*

This phrase, particularly as it appears in the Gospels, has been the subject of considerable debate among biblical scholars, as can be seen in the articles "Son of Man" in ABD and DJG. Partly at issue is to what extent Jesus himself used this phrase, as well as what he might have meant by it. This is complicated by the variety of contexts in which the phrase appears, both in early Jewish literature and in the Gospels. Most scholars accept that Jesus used the phrase as a form of self-designation in reference to his ministry, as maintained by al-'Aqqād. What is debated is whether this was a simple reference to his humanity expressed in Semitic fashion, or a claim to an eschatological messianic title drawn from Dan. 7:13, or both simultaneously. One's conclusion here is tied to one's interpretation of the phrase in the eschatological sayings of Jesus. What is clear, at least, is that the Gospel writers assume that the Son of Man who comes in power is identical with the risen and exalted Jesus.

Thus, al-'Aqqād follows many scholars in attempting to separate the eschatological "Son of Man" sayings from Jesus' use of the term in self-designation. His approach here is connected with his earlier discussion about the kingdom of heaven in ch. 19; see n. 28 there.

40 More precisely, Ezekiel is addressed by this term ninety-three times. Interpreters disagree whether the designation is one of honor (Ezekiel being singled out from others), or whether he is depicted as an ordinary human being who is nevertheless called to prophesy by the God of heaven. (ABD, s.v. "Son of Man" [6:137]). The latter view is more commendable (William H. Brownlee, *Ezekiel 1-19,* Word Biblical Commentary, ed. David A. Hubbard and Glenn W. Barker, vol. 28 [Waco, TX: Word Books, 1986], 25-26).

41 Dan. 8:17. This occurs in the Hebrew portion of the book. The phrase should be interpreted here in the same manner as in Ezekiel (John E. Goldingay, *Daniel,* Word Biblical Commentary, ed. David A. Hubbard and Glenn W. Barker, vol. 30 [Dallas: Word Books, 1989], 214).

42 Dan. 7:13. In this passage, the phrase appears in Aramaic, since the entire section of Daniel from 2:4 to end of ch. 7 is in that language. This verse and its context presents innumerable interpretive difficulties. The consensus is that the figure depicted, though in appearance human, is a heavenly being; he represents Israel who, though lowly and suffering, would be exalted over all other nations. The passage was to take on many forms of messianic interpretation in various Jewish and Christian circles. (ABD, s.v. "Son of Man" [6:137-38]).

43 Mt. 12:31-32. Al-'Aqqād has quoted the text of VD exactly, except for an ellipsis from v. 31 which he does not indicate ("but the blasphemy of the Holy Spirit will not be forgiven," RSV). However, he has badly confused the issue regarding an already complicated text. He clearly means to supply an example of a text in which the phrase "son of man" signifies "man" in the generic sense, but this passage is not the right one. The one he should have used is the parallel passage in Mk. 3:28-29, which reads, ". . . all sins will be forgiven the sons of men, and whatever blasphemies they utter; but whoever blasphemes against the Holy Spirit never has forgiveness, but is guilty of an eternal sin" (RSV). Matthew's text, which has simply "men" (or, "people," Ar. *al-nās),* also includes "the Son of Man" as a self-reference to Jesus, and so is an example best suited for the next paragraph.

Al-'Aqqād may have been confused, however, by the reading of Mk. 3:28 in VD, which has *banī al-bashar* [the sons of mankind] rather than *banī al-nās.* This translation was apparently an attempt to distinguish that term from "the Son of Man," despite the direct plural readings in AV ("the sons of men") and the Gk. text *(tois huiois tōn anthrōpōn).* The modern Ar. translations follow VD here, with either *banī al-bashar* or simply *al-nās.*

44 Lk. 12:8, Mt. 10:32. Al-'Aqqād is not concerned that these passages are eschatological in nature.

45 Mt. 16:13, Mk. 8:27. Al-'Aqqād has reproduced the text of VD exactly for both passages, despite the rather cumbersome ending in Matthew which has both the personal pronoun as well as the phrase "the Son of Man" (Ar. *man yaqūlu al-nās innī anā ibn al-insān).* VD followed AV, which in turn translated Gk. mss. which included both of these in some fashion or another. RSV uses the most reliable mss. and reads simply, ". . . that the Son of Man is?" In Mark, the ending of 8:27 in VD is *man yaqūlu al-nās innī anā,* and the parallel passage in Lk. 9:18 follows suit.

46 Al-'Aqqād should rather have said, "sometimes in the Gospels," since "the Son of Man" is found in all four Gospels as a self-designation of Jesus.

47 Mt. 13:40-41. Apparently al-'Aqqād has momentarily forgotten that the Gospel of Matthew was written in Greek. The Aramaic wording which underlies the phrase in Mt. can only be presumed.

Al-'Aqqād mentions this future aspect briefly, and he is careful to avoid any indication that Jesus was referring to himself in this saying. He clearly wishes to separate the "Son of Man" who figures in the eschatological passages from the "Son of Man" who carries out his mission. This is because only the latter aspect is important for his thesis. Thus, the implication is that the future Son of Man may be some other figure. (See ch. 19, n. 28).

[48] Mk. 10:17-18 = Lk. 18:18-19. The repetitive use of the word "call" in the translation here reflects its multiple usage in al-'Aqqād's text (both verbal and nominal forms).

[49] See al-'Aqqād's discussion concerning which year the ministry of Christ ended later in this chapter (p. 226), and n. 69 below.

[50] Much of this paragraph is speculative. On the one hand, the Gospels indicate that Jesus' family customarily attended the Jewish feasts in Jerusalem, and presumably Jesus accompanied them as long as he lived at his home in Nazareth. Lk. 2:41-42 states that this was the case concerning the Passover feast during Jesus' childhood; also in Jn. 7:10, the brothers of Jesus plan to attend the Feast of Tabernacles. But beyond this, the details mentioned by al-'Aqqād here are completely conjectural.

[51] Only the Gospel of John indicates that the adult Jesus had previously visited Jerusalem for various feasts, including Passover. However, John also relates that these visits often involved controversy with the Jewish authorities. According to Jn. 2:13-21, on Jesus' Passover visit at the beginning of his ministry, his "cleansing" of the Temple led to a disparaging response from the Jews.

[52] Lit., "Christians" (Ar. *masīḥīyīn).* Al-'Aqqād uses this term here (twice) for the larger number of Jesus' followers who had a status less than that of full disciples. The figure of "eighty" was mentioned previously on p. 221; see n. 25 there.

[53] Mt. 26:39, 41 = Mk. 14:36, 38 = Lk. 22:42, 46. According to the Gospels, the setting for this prayer was the Garden of Gethsemane outside of Jerusalem; it followed the "Last Supper" with the disciples, and it was here that Jesus was arrested. Al-'Aqqād referred to this occasion in ch. 12, where he also quoted Jesus' prayer as representative of his approach throughout his mission (pp. 148-49; see nn. 22, 27-29 there).

[54] This paragraph, coming as it does immediately after al-'Aqqād's reference to Jesus' prayer in Gethsemane, is remarkably reminiscent of the arrest of Jesus which, according to the Gospels, occurred also in Gethsemene immediately following Jesus' experience of intense prayer (Mt. 26:47-56 = Mk. 14:43-52 = Lk. 22:47-53 = Jn. 18:2-12). There are several points of contact between al-'Aqqād's comments and these passages: Christ's firm resolution to face his enemies is evidenced in his determined submission to the band which came to seize him; his rejection of any opposition is demonstrated by his rebuke to Peter for attacking one of them with a sword; the possibility of the disciples' weakness became a reality when they forsook him and fled. Even the concept that this would have been predestined is realized in Jesus' words, "But all this has taken place, that the scriptures of the prophets might be fulfilled" (Mt. 26:56). That Jesus' life should end in apparent defeat, yet one which God would turn into victory, is, for Christians, the heart of the gospel.

But al-'Aqqād cannot take himself that far. Instead, the subsequent paragraphs indicate that the confrontation to which he refers here does not take place in the arrest in Gethsemane, but in events which occurred in Jerusalem itself earlier in the week. He will follow those events up to the "cleansing of the Temple," but will admit to nothing historical beyond that, including the arrest and, of course, the crucifixion. For further reflection on this passage in the context of the entire book, see the Introduction, pp. 64-65.

[55] This is the so-called "Triumphal Entry" which is celebrated by Christians on Palm Sunday; it's description appears in all four Gospels: Mt. 21:1-9 = Mk. 11:1-10 = Lk. 19:28-40 = Jn. 12:12-19. All four accounts report that Jesus rode on a young donkey along the final approach to Jerusalem, and that crowds met him carrying branches and shouting acclamations. Other details vary among the Gospels: Mt. and Jn. include a quotation of Zech. 9:9 as a prediction of this event (it is

the only OT passage which speaks of a coming king riding on a donkey); Mt. (only) mentions that the colt's mother was included in the procession; all three Synoptics (but not Jn.) refer to the garments spread on the road, but only Jn. states that the branches used by the crowd were from palm trees. The precise wording of the crowd's acclamation is also different in each account, but each of the following is included in more than one Gospel: the shout of "Hosanna! [lit., "Save us!", a shout of praise] Blessed is he who comes in the name of the Lord!" (a quotation of Ps. 118:25-26; Mt., Mk., Jn.); a reference to the recipient of the praise as "the king" (Lk., Jn.; cf. Mk. which has "kingdom"); and a reference to David as ancestor (Mt., Mk.).

56 Mt. 23:2-3. This saying stands in contrast to the generally negative attitude in Matthew towards the Jewish religious leaders, e.g., Jesus' warning to "beware of the leaven [i.e., teaching] of the Pharisees and Sadducees" (Mt. 16:11-12). The saying here might be intended as hyperbole (so Davies and Allison, 3:270), or it might be a genuinely positive recognition of the Pharisees effort at teaching the law of Moses (so Hagner, 33B:659). In any case, it is followed by a long list of condemnations by Jesus against their practice, many of which al-'Aqqād had noted in ch. 17 (p. 175). His statement here that Jesus was conciliatory towards the religious leaders contradicts his claim there that "he began to confront the celebrated scholars who had strayed . . ." Here, it seems that al-'Aqqād wishes to attribute the impending crisis solely to the Jewish leaders, and to disavow any possibility that Jesus himself may have contributed to the tensions that were mounting.

57 I.e., Jesus did not change the way he operated: he allowed the government its power but demanded that God be given primary loyalty. The reference is to Mt. 22:21 = Mk. 12:17 = Lk. 20: 25; al-'Aqqād previously referred to this passage on several occasions; see especially ch. 7, p. 110-11, n. 35.

58 An allusion to Jn. 18: 36, where Jesus tells Pilate during his interrogation, "My kingship is not of this world."

59 Ar. *al-kufr,* placed in quotation marks by al-'Aqqād. This is the special word in Islam denoting rejection of belief in the one true God and in the message of Islam (EI^2, s.v. *"kāfir").*

60 Al-'Aqqād previously mentioned Nicodemus in ch. 19 (p. 189, see n. 29 there) and ch. 21 (p. 205), where he observed that Nicodemus was a member of the Sanhedrin and a "disciple." Here, there is no substance for the suggestion that Nicodemus warned Jesus of the council's plot. His visit to Jesus by night (Jn. 3:1-15) is recorded as having occurred early in Jesus ministry. The incident in Jn. 7:50-52, where Nicodemus protests against the Sanhedrin's condemnation of Jesus, is understood to have occurred some time before Jesus' final week in Jerusalem.

61 This incident, referred to as the "Cleansing of the Temple," is related in Mk. 11:15-17, and more briefly in Mt. 21:12-13 and Lk. 19:45-46. It took place at the beginning of the week (Sunday, according to Mt. and Lk., Monday according to Mk.). The Gospel of John records a very similar incident, but which is situated at the beginning of Jesus' ministry (Jn. 2:13-17). Most interpreters regard this as the same event, transferred by John to the beginning of his account for theological reasons (Brown, *John,* 29:117-18).

62 Ar. *al-'amal al-'ājil.* Al-'Aqqād does not indicate his own view as to what this action of the Jewish authorities might have been. Perhaps he has in mind some kind of attempted arrest, from which Jesus would have escaped. In any case, this is as far as he is willing to go in dependence on the Gospels for a historical account of the end of Jesus' mission.

Mk. 11:18 states that it was this incident which provoked the Jewish authorities to seek the death of Jesus. Yet the Gospels agree that they took no definitive action for several days. Although they were afraid of Jesus stirring up the people, they were more afraid that a worse situation might develop if they were to arrest him publicly (Mt. 21:46 = Mk. 12:12 = Lk. 20:19).

Meanwhile, Jesus continued to teach in the Temple while the tension between him and the authorities deepened. In fact, many of the incidents and quotations utilized by al-'Aqqād come from that period.

[63] Ar. *wa-hunā yantahī dawr al-tārīkh wa-yabda'u dawr al-'aqīdah.* It is this section in general, and this line in particular, which is a focal point of concern (and sometimes disappointment) for several who have reviewed or referred to this book from a Christian perspective: 'Abd al-Malik, 218; Anawati, "La personne du Christ," 444, and "Polémique," 447; Borrmans, 167; Cragg, *Jesus and the Muslim,* 54, and Review, 91, 96; Farès, 45-46; Goddard, "An Annotated Bibliography," 257; and Teissier, 30, 35.

[64] See n. 54 for the Gospel accounts of the arrest of Jesus. Al-'Aqqād's skepticism concerning who arrested Jesus, and the identity and purpose of the guide, bear little justification. It is true that some uncertainty exists as to who comprised the crowd which came to arrest Jesus, since various terms are used, and only John mentions Roman soldiers; but all accounts include the "chief priests," either as part of the crowd or as those who sent the crowd (Mt. 26:47, Mk. 14:43, Lk. 22:52, Jn. 18:3). There is no question that it was Judas, one of Jesus' disciples, who served as the guide; (he is named at the beginning of each account). One might raise the question as to why the crowd needed a guide when they should have been able to recognize Jesus. Yet they are presented as hostile participants who may not have had much contact with him previously. Furthermore, it is night and he is surrounded by disciples, making quick identification difficult. (See Brown, *Death,* 1:246-52).

[65] The issues raised by al-'Aqqād concerning Jesus' trial by the Jewish leaders would seem to be more serious than those concerning his arrest. The objections he raises all stem from requirements of Rabbinic law as found in the Mishnah. Yet this was an early third-century document; although it certainly preserved regulations that went back many years, there is no clear indication that these regulations were in effect prior to 70 C.E. These objections also assume that the Pharisees dominated the Sanhedrin, which is unlikely. On the other hand, there would have been pressure on the Jewish leaders to conduct their business quickly due to the oncoming feast. The data is discussed in detail in Brown, *Death,* 1:357-63.

[66] Again, al-'Aqqād's argument is weak. The Gospels portray Pilate as one who vacillated in his response to Jesus' arrest by the Jewish leaders. He was convinced of his innocence and wished to release him, yet he gave in to the pressure of the crowds and the possibility of earning disfavor with the Emperor. While he sought to absolve *himself* of any guilt, he was clearly a participant in it. (See Brown, *Death,* 1:851, 854).

[67] Jn. 19:14, 16; Mk. 15:25. According to John, then, the crucifixion took place at noon; according to Mark, it occurred at 9:00 AM. Many attempts have been made to harmonize these two time references, usually by proposing differing schemes for keeping time (one Roman and one Jewish). Brown regards the possibility of two schemes as highly unlikely, saying that the two accounts cannot be reconciled; at least one must be considered a theological or liturgical statement. (Brown, *Death,* 2:958-60).

[68] As the subsequent discussion indicates, al-'Aqqād should have written here "seven years," i.e. the years between and inclusive of 27 to 33 C.E.

[69] The reference here is to Richard Wellington Husband, *The Prosecution of Jesus: Its Date, History and Legality* (Princeton: Princeton University Press, 1916), in his chapter "The Date of the Trial," 44-47. There are several points discussed by Husband which al-'Aqqād has not made clear in his summary. First, the years 27 - 33 are the only ones considered because of other information which narrows the time span when the end of Jesus' ministry most likely occurred. The calcula-

tions are based on the manner in which the Jews determined the date of Passover according to their lunar calendar. However, the Gospels disagree as to the day when Passover was celebrated during Passion Week: for the Synoptic Gospels, it was Thursday evening, but for the Gospel of John it was Friday evening (p. 40). It is for this reason that the years 30 and 33 are the only ones seriously considered. Husband continues with an extensive argument in favor of the year 33 (pp. 48-69); but he admits that "the year 30 is almost universally thought to have been that in which the death of Jesus happened" (p. 47).

Al-'Aqqād stated his acceptance of 30 C.E. as the year when Jesus' ministry ended (p. 223 above). Of course, this date is based partly on events which he does not accept as historical, i.e., the trial and crucifixion. He has, however, claimed that Jesus went to Jerusalem to celebrate the Passover, and he seems to acknowledge that *something* occurred on Friday which brought Jesus' ministry to an end, so that he would have celebrated Passover on Thursday evening.

Modern scholars have worked out similar calculations with similar results. Both Brown and Meier propose that either 30 C.E. or 33 C.E. was the year of Jesus' death; Brown remains indecisive between the two options, while Meier favors the earlier date (Brown, *Death,* 2:1373-76; Meier, 1:401-402).

[70] This unusual event is recorded only in Mt. 27:52-53. The historical questions that surround this account are complicated by the claim that the tombs were split open on the day of crucifixion, but the bodies were not raised until "after his resurrection." After a thorough analysis, Brown concludes that these verses must be read for their "theological interpretation of the import of the death of Jesus, an interpretation in the language and imagery of apocalyptic" (*Death,* 2:1133). Al-'Aqqād probably includes this brief reference precisely because of its problematic historicity. He has also mentioned it briefly in ch. 22 (p. 212).

[71] Al-'Aqqād is careless in stating that Jesus' resurrection is reported to have occurred on "the following day," which would have been Saturday. The NT is unanimous that this took place on Sunday, the third day (counting Friday).

[72] Lk. 24:36-43.

[73] The reference to "Cheyne" is most likely to the Old Testament scholar T. K. Cheyne, although if this is the case, the title "Evangelical" is best regarded as misapplied. Al-'Aqqād may well have used Cheyne's *Encyclopaedia Biblica* (ed. with J. Sutherland Black [New York: Macmillan, 1903]). In the article on Jesus there, the passion narrative is considered to be "not pure truth, but truth mixed with doubtful legend" (2:2452).

The reference to "Weigall" can be determined on the basis of a similar and longer reference in al-'Aqqād's 1928-29 articles (which were written in response to Emil Ludwig's book on Jesus; see the Introduction, p. 52). There, he discusses briefly how Ludwig, and also Renan, believed that Jesus actually died on the cross, although neither accepts the historicity of the resurrection. Al-'Aqqād instead prefers the argument by Weigall, and he mentions the title of the book in question; the full reference is Arthur Weigall, *The Paganism in Our Christianity* (New York: G. P. Putnam's Sons, 1928). Claiming that "we especially depend on this book," al-'Aqqād presents Weigall's view that Jesus was only close to death when his friends took him down and placed him in the tomb; he later revived and went to inform his disciples that he was alive; thus the disciples did not see a spirit but the real, living Jesus (*Sā'āt bayn al-Kutub,* 164-65). Weigall's full argument is given in his book on pp. 97-101. The book as a whole deals with his claim that pagan religious beliefs and practices heavily influenced Christianity; in the case of the crucifixion, the influence came from pagan rituals of human sacrifice (88).

Efforts to trace the references to "Henrik Poulus" (or possibly "Boulus") and "Hugo Toll" (or possibly "Tool") have not met with success.

[74] The name is rendered here according to how it appears in the source given in the following note. Al-'Aqqād has written it in Arabic as *'Ūs Āṣāf* here and elsewhere in this paragraph.

[75] Qur'ān 23:50. Al-'Aqqād has summarized here a long footnote found at this verse in *The Holy Qur'ān: Containing the Arabic Text with English Translation and Commentary,* 2d ed., trans. and ed. Maulvi Muhammad Alī (Lahore: Ahmadiyya Anjuman-i-Ishāat-i-Islam, 1920), 686-87. (This note also appears in a slightly abbreviated form in *Translation of the Holy Quran (without Arabic Text): With Short Notes and Introduction,* trans. and ed. Muhammad Ali [Lahore: Ahmadiyya Anjuman-i-Ishāat-i-Islam, 1928], 348-49; however, the details referred to by al-'Aqqād indicate that he used the Arabic-English version).

Muḥammad 'Alī (d. 1951) was the leader of the Lahore branch of the Aḥmadīyah sect of Islam. (This group is generally considered to be more orthodox than the Qadiyan branch. "Maulvi" is an honorific title which is sometimes rendered in English as Maulana). 'Alī's comments, and al-'Aqqād's summary, represent the somewhat unique Aḥmadīyah belief that Jesus was nailed to the cross but did not die there; rather he is said to have resuscitated from his wounds and escaped from Palestine, traveling to Kashmir. There he preached to the so-called "lost tribes" of Israel, died at the age of 120 and was buried. The details of this teaching were spelled out by the founder of the sect, Ghulam Aḥmad (d. 1908), in his book *Masīh Hindustān Mēn,* which has been translated from the Urdu as *Jesus in India: Being an Account of Jesus' Escape from Death on the Cross and of His Journey to India* (London: The London Mosque, 1978). On the Aḥmadīyah sect, see EI^2, s.v. "Aḥmadiyya"; ER, s.v. "Aḥmadīyah"; and the detailed account of Spencer Lavan, *The Ahmadiyah Movement: A History and Perspective* (Delhi: Manohar Book Service, 1974); further details on Muḥammad 'Alī are found in Lavan, 98-109.

The tradition of Jesus' death and burial in India is analyzed in Paul C. Pappas, *Jesus' Tomb in India: The Debate on His Death and Resurrection* (Berkeley, CA: Asian Humanities Press, 1991). Each of the various sources concerning Yūz Āṣaf mentioned by 'Alī are discussed by Pappas: the history of Kwaja Muḥammad A'ẓam (i.e., al-A'ẓamī, p. 92); the *Ikmāl al-Dīn* (or *Kamal-ud-Din* as Pappas has it) which was written by the Arab historian Sa'īd al-Ṣādiq (d. 962; p. 82); and "Barlaam and Joasaph" (as Pappas has it), a medieval popular story of the Greek Christian church with an origin in India (p. 90). Pappas goes on to reject the claim that Yūz Āṣaf was Jesus, although he believes that he was a historical figure; "he most likely was a Jewish Essene whose teachings resembled those of Jesus" (117). The tradition is also discussed and rejected by Grönbold, who treats Yūz Āṣaf as legendary (43-55).

Al-'Aqqād's partiality for the Aḥmadīyah view concerning the end of Jesus' life focuses here only on the connection with India, rather than the crucifixion itself. However, he had also stated his preference for a theory of the crucifixion, similar to the Aḥmadīyah view, in his Ludwig articles; see his reference to Weigall's book in n. 73 above.

[76] Qur'ān 3:55. Only part of this verse (in which Jesus is being addressed) is quoted here. 'Alī translates the phrase "I am gathering thee" *(innī mutawaffīka)* as "I will cause you to die," and he discusses his rendition in a footnote (p. 159-60, v. 54 in his text). Muslim commentators have offered a variety of interpretations for this phrase. Most agree that the verb generally means "to cause to die"; however, most also prefer to understand a meaning here whereby God "receives" Jesus into heaven, in accordance with the traditions about Jesus. (See Ayoub, *Qur'an,* 2:169-83).

In mentioning "other verses from the Qur'ān" where 'Alī discusses this subject, al-'Aqqād probably has in mind especially his long footnotes at 4:157-59, where he summarizes the Aḥmadīyah view of Jesus on the cross (pp. 241-44).

[77] Ar. *al-'abqarīyah al-masīḥīyah.*

[78] See the Introduction (pp. 32-35) concerning al-'Aqqād's *'Abqarīyah* series which deals with Muḥammad and other major figures of early Islam. However, he is probably referring here as well to his many other biographical studies of historical and contemporary leaders.

[79] A reference to the fall of Jerusalem to the Romans in 70 C.E.

[80] Al-'Aqqād apparently means here that Jesus' self-designation as "the Son of Man" indicated his universal appeal to all people.

Epilogue
If Christ Were to Return

[1] Ar. *Fī al-Khitām: Law 'Āda al-Masīḥ.* This is the title given in ed. 2, and retained in ed. 3. In ed. 1, the title of this chapter was *Al-Ghāyah ba'da Kulli Khitām,* [The End after Every Conclusion]. Although the revised title is used in the translation, it should be observed that the original title especially indicates the chapter's role as something of a postscript. See Appendix A regarding the changes among the various editions of *'Abqarīyat al-Masīḥ.*

In 1955, al-'Aqqād published an article entitled "Law 'Āda Muḥammad" [If Muḥammad Were to Return] in *Al-Hilāl* 63 (January 1955): 16-20. There, he follows a theme similar to the thesis of this chapter for the Prophet of Islam. He also mentions briefly in that article what would happen if Christ were to return. This article seems to have prompted the same newspaper to reprint the final chapter of this book a couple years later, as a separate unit, with the title "Law 'Āda al-Sayyid al-Masīḥ" (*Al-Hilāl* 65 [December 1957]: 14-19). Both articles were also reprinted in *Ḥayāt Qalam,* 197-201 (on Muḥammad) and 201-206 (on Christ). Finally, "Law 'Āda al-Sayyid al-Masīḥ" was again reprinted in honor of the Western Christmas celebration in *Al-Akhbār* 4832 (25 December 1967): 5, although a few paragraphs were omitted.

[2] The reference is to Fyodor Dostoyevsky's *The Brothers Karamazov.* Al-'Aqqād probably used the English translation by Constance Garnett (London: Heinemann, 1912); a recent translation is by David McDuff, Penguin Classics (London: Penguin Books, 1993), from which page references here are taken. Dostoyevsky (1821-81) was a Russian journalist and novelist. His works explore the human consciousness of salvation as God's gift to a weak humanity; the human response, however, is based on irrational emotions rather than reason. (ODCC, s.v. "Dostoievsky").

The "Inquisition" mentioned here is the so-called "Spanish Inquisition" of the Roman church, begun in the late fifteenth century and not completely abolished until the early nineteenth century. It was initially conducted against converts from Judaism and Islam, but later against Protestants. It was directed by a High Council led by the "Grand Inquisitor." (ODCC, s.v. "Inquisition").

The scene described by al-'Aqqād is in the chapter from *The Brothers Karamazov* entitled "The Grand Inquisitor" (283-304). There, Ivan Karamazov relates to his brother Alyosha the tale he has conceived concerning a return by Christ to earth — not the final return in power and glory, but a quiet and simple visit to sixteenth-century Seville (in southern Spain) during the Inquisition. Al-'Aqqād's summary of the story and the long dialogue within it is fairly accurate. However, his reference here to Jesus' "preaching" is somewhat misleading; in the tale, Jesus spoke few words, and simply walked among the people, blessing and healing them (286).

[3] Mk. 2:27. Al-'Aqqād had quoted this verse in ch. 18 (p. 180), regarding it as a worthy summary of the wisdom of Jesus which emphasizes the intent of the law.

4 This statement is a general reference to such teachings of Jesus as Mk. 7:14-23 (defilement and purity come from the heart, not from food or rituals), and Mt. 6:5-18 (prayer and fasting must be done in secret, not to show off in front of others).

5 This is al-'Aqqād's interpretive understanding of the way in which Jesus focused on the internal aspects of the Jewish Law over against the more literal approach prevalent among the religious authorities (e.g., Mt. 5:17-48).

6 Mt. 9:17 = Mk. 2:22 = Lk. 5:37-38. See al-'Aqqād's previous reference to this passage at the end of ch. 17 (p. 177), and n. 29 there.

7 A primary source for this line from al-Ma'arrī has not been located. However, the poem in which it is found is quoted and discussed in 'Adullah al-Ṭayib, *Al-Murshid ilā Fahm Ash'ār al-'Arab wa-Ṣanā'atihā* [Guide to Understanding the Poetry of the Arabs and its Production], 4th ed. (Khartoum: Maṭba'at Jāmi'at al-Kharṭūm, 1991), 1:265-67. Al-'Aqqād's quotation is line six of the poem. However, he has made a slight change at the beginning. He quotes the first phrase as *ta'b ghayr nāfi'*, whereas the initial word should be *asf* [regret, sorrow] as quoted by al-Ṭayib. Al-Ma'arrī original wording would lead to the translation: "There is no benefit in feeling sorry."

Al-'Aqqād had previously referred to al-Ma'arrī and quoted from his poetry in ch. 11 (p. 134); see n. 14 there on al-Ma'arrī and al-'Aqqād's high regard of his work.

8 This quotation from al-Ma'arrī is line eight in a poem entitled "'Ālam al-Sū'" [The World of Iniquity], included in his *Luzūm Mā Lā Yalzam,* 1:50. (On this work, see ch. 11, p. 134, n. 15).

9 Ar. *jihād.* This word and its cognates appear several times throughout the remainder of this chapter.

Appendix A
The Various Editions of *'Abqarīyat al-Masīḥ*

1 See ch. 1, p. 73. This reference has apparently led to the mistaken belief among some reviewers that 1952 was the year of publication.

2 Cairo: Maṭba'at Dār Akhbar al-Yawm, [1953]. See al-Sakkūt, 1:185; Cragg, Review, 88.

3 Cairo: Dār al-Hilāl, [1958].

4 *'Abqarīyat al-Masīḥ: Fī al-Tārīkh wa-Kushūf al-'Aṣr al-Ḥadīth* [The Genius of Christ: In History and the Discoveries of the Modern Age], with a Foreword by Munīf Luṭfī (Beirut: Al-Maktabah al-'Aṣrīyah, n.d.). This Beirut edition, although having different pagination, is virtually identical to ed. 2 with regard to the text.

5 *Ḥayāt al-Masīḥ: Fī al-Tārīkh wa-Kushūf al-'Aṣr al-Ḥadīth* [The Life of Christ: In History and the Discoveries of the Modern Age] (Cairo: Dār Nahḍat Miṣr, 1996).

6 F. Peter Ford, Jr., "A Modern Muslim Assessment of Jesus: A Translation and Analysis of 'Abbās Maḥmūd al-'Aqqād's *The Genius of Christ,*" 2 vols. (Ph.D. diss., Temple University, 1998), 184-85.

7 There is, however, a single instance where a reference to ed. 1 as "*The Genius of Christ*" has been left unaltered by the editors of ed. 3 (ch. 1, p. 75); one can only assume that this was an oversight on their part.

Appendix B
Remarks Concerning the English Translation

[1] In the dissertation of which the present book is a revision, most words or phrases which are supplied in the translation, but which are not part of the original Arabic text, are enclosed in brackets. Ford, "Modern," 187-88.

[2] *Biblia Hebraica Stuttgartensia*, ed. K. Elliger and W. Rudolph (Stuttgart: Deutsche Bibelstiftung, 1967-1977); *Septuaginta*, ed. Alfred Rahlfs (Stuttgart: Württembergische Bibelanstalt, 1979); *The Greek New Testament*, ed. Barbara Aland, Kurt Aland, Johannes Karavidopoulos, Carlo M. Martini, and Bruce M. Metzger, 4th ed. (Stuttgart: Deutsche Bibelgesellschaft and United Bible Societies, 1993). In the case of the Gospels, the use of a synopsis (which arranges parallel accounts in vertical columns for comparison) is virtually essential; the standard work offering both the Greek text and an English translation is *Synopsis of the Four Gospels: Greek-English Edition of the Synopsis Quattuor Evangeliorum with the Text of the Revised Standard Version*, ed. Kurt Aland (N.p.: United Bible Societies, 1946, 1964).

[3] See al-'Aqqād's discussion of this term in ch. 4 (pp. 87-88), and n. 10 there.

[4] EI^1, s.v. *"Tawrāt."*

Appendix C
The Bible in Arabic

[1] For surveys of the history of Arabic Bible translation, see Bruce M. Metzger, *The Early Versions of the New Testament: Their Origin, Transmission and Limitations* (Oxford: Clarendon Press, 1977), 257-68; and 'Abd al-Masīḥ Isṭafānūs, *Taqdīm al-Kitāb al-Muqaddas li-Qāri' al-'Arabī: Tārīkhuhu, Ṣiḥḥatuhu, Tarjamātuhu, Dirāsatuhu* [Introduction to the Holy Bible: Its History, Veracity, Translation and Study] (N.p.: Dār al-Kitāb al-Muqaddas fī al-Sharq al-Awsaṭ, 1994), 61-86.

[2] *Al-Kitāb al-Muqaddas* [The Holy Bible (the Van Dyck Arabic version)] (N.p.: Dār al-Kitāb al-Muqaddas fī al-'Ālim al-'Arabī, n.d.).

[3] Isṭafānūs, 79-81. In English, a fair and well-researched account of the development of VD is in Issa A. Saliba, "The Bible in Arabic: The 19th-Century Protestant Translation," *The Muslim World* 65 (1975): 254-63. An eye-witness report, informative though sentimental, is by Henry Harris Jessup, *Fifty-Three Years in Syria*, (New York: Revell, 1910), 1:66-78. A shorter sketch is in A. B. Tibawi, *American Interests in Syria, 1800-1901: A Study of Educational, Literary and Religious Work* (Oxford: Clarendon, 1966), 121-23, 138-39.

[4] Saliba, 259, 261.

[5] Jessup, 75.

[6] Tibawi, 139.

[7] *Al-Kitāb al-Muqaddas* [The Holy Bible (the Jesuit Arabic version)] (Beirut: Dār al-Mashriq, 1986); *Al-Kitāb al-Muqaddas — Kitāb al-Ḥayat: Tarjamah Tafsīrīyah* [The Holy Bible — The Book of Life: An Explanatory Translation] (N.p.: L[iving] B[ibles] I[nternational], 1988); *Al-Kitāb al-Muqaddas* [The Holy Bible (Good News Arabic version)] (Beirut: Bible Society in Lebanon, 1993, 1995). For a brief history of these, see Isṭafānūs, 84-86.

Appendix D
Al-'Aqqād's Personal Library

[1] The contents of Appendix D are based on a personal visit to Egypt in September, 1997, which included the sites of al-'Aqqād's homes in Aswan and Cairo. I am especially grateful to members of al-'Aqqād's family for providing certain details.

[2] See ch. 2, p. 82 for al-'Aqqād's remarks about this book.

[3] Sidney Hook, *The Hero in History: A Study in Limitation and Possibility* (London: Secker & Warburg, 1945).

[4] John M. Allegro, *The Dead Sea Scrolls*, Pelican Books (Harmondsworth, England: Penguin Books, 1956).

[5] Cecil John Cadoux, *The Life of Jesus*, Pelican Books (West Drayton, England: Penguin Books, 1948).

[6] Ibid., 10.

[7] See al-'Aqqād's remarks against this claim (that Jesus never existed) in ch. 11, pp. 135-43.

[8] Cadoux, 12.

[9] R. J. Campbell, *The Life of Christ*, Benn's Sixpenny Library, no. 128 (London: Ernest Benn, 1927).

[10] Ibid., 29.

[11] Ibid., 18-19.

[12] See ch. 21, pp. 208-209.

References Cited

The Bible — Texts and Translations

Biblia Hebraica Stuttgartensia. Edited by K. Elliger and W. Rudolph. Stuttgart: Deutsche Bibelstiftung, 1967-1977.

The Greek New Testament. Edited by Barbara Aland, Kurt Aland, Johannes Karavidopoulos, Carlo M. Martini, and Bruce M. Metzger. 4th ed. Stuttgart: Deutsche Bibelgesellschaft and United Bible Societies, 1993.

The Holy Bible. [American Standard Version]. New York: Thomas Nelson & Sons, 1901.

The Holy Bible. [Authorized (King James) Version]. 1611.

The Holy Bible. Revised Standard Version. Division of Christian Education of the National Council of Churches of Christ in the U.S.A. 1946, 1952.

The Holy Bible. [Revised Version]. Oxford and Cambridge: Oxford University Press, Cambridge University Press, 1881, 1885.

The Holy Bible containing the Old and New Testaments: An Improved Edition. Philadelphia: American Baptist Publication Society, 1912.

The Holy Bible in Modern English. Translated by Ferrar Fenton. 4th ed. London: S. W. Partridge, 1909. New York: Oxford Press, 1909.

Al-Kitāb al-Muqaddas. [Good News Arabic version]. Beirut: Bible Society in Lebanon, 1993, 1995.

Al-Kitāb al-Muqaddas. [Jesuit Arabic version]. Beirut: Dār al-Mashriq, 1986.

Al-Kitāb al-Muqaddas. [Van Dyck Arabic version]. N.p.: Dār al-Kitāb al-Muqaddas fī al-'Ālim al-'Arabī, n.d.

Al-Kitāb al-Muqaddas — Kitāb al-Ḥayat: Tarjamah Tafsīrīyah [The Book of Life: An Explanatory Translation]. N.p.: L[iving] B[ibles] I[nternational], 1988.

Septuaginta. Edited by Alfred Rahlfs. Stuttgart: Württembergische Bibelanstalt, 1979.

Synopsis of the Four Gospels: Greek-English Edition of the Synopsis Quattuor Evangeliorum with the Text of the Revised Standard Version. Edited by Kurt Aland. N.p.: United Bible Societies, 1946, 1964.

The Qur'ān — Texts and Translations

The Holy Qur'ān: Containing the Arabic Text with English Translation and Commentary. 2d ed. Translated and edited by Maulvi Muhammad Alī. Lahore: Ahmadiyya Anjuman-i-Ishāat-i-Islam, 1920.

The Holy Qur'ān: Text, Translation and Commentary. Edited by 'Abdullah Yūsuf 'Alī. 2d ed. Brentwood, MD: Amana Corporation, 1989.

The Meaning of the Glorious Koran. Translated by Mohammed Marmaduke Pickthall.

New York: Mentor, 1930.
Translation of the Holy Quran (without Arabic Text): With Short Notes and Introduction. Translated and edited by Muhammad Ali. Lahore: Ahmadiyya Anjuman-i-Ishāat-i-Islam, 1928.

Classical Works — Greek and Latin

Cicero. *De Officiis.* With English translation by Walter Miller. Loeb Classical Library, vol. 21. Cambridge: Harvard University Press, 1913.

Cleanthes. *The Hymn of Cleanthes.* Translated by E. H. Blakeney, with Introduction and Notes. Texts for Students, no. 26. London: SPCK, 1921.

Clement of Alexandria. With English translation by G. W. Butterworth. Loeb Classical Library. Cambridge: Harvard University Press, 1982.

Eusebius. *The Ecclesiastical History.* With English translation by K. Lake, J. E. L. Oulton, and H. J. Lawlor. Loeb Classical Library. 2 vols. Cambridge: Harvard University Press, 1926, 1932.

Josephus. With English translation by H. St. J. Thackeray, R. Marcus, A. Wikgren, and L. H. Feldman. Loeb Classical Library. 10 vols. Cambridge: Harvard University Press, 1926-65.

Philo. With English translation by F. H. Colson, G. H. Whitaker, and Ralph Marcus. Loeb Classical Library. 12 vols. Cambridge: Harvard University Press, 1929-53.

Procopius. With English translation by H. B. Dewing. Loeb Classical Library. 7 vols. Cambridge: Harvard University Press, 1914-40.

Strabo. *The Geography of Strabo.* With English translation by Horace Leonard Jones. Loeb Classical Library. 8 vols. Cambridge: Harvard University Press, 1917-32.

Suetonius. With English translation by J. C. Rolfe. Loeb Classical Library. 2 vols. Cambridge: Harvard University Press, 1913-14.

Tacitus. With English translation by M. Hutton, et al. 5 vols. Loeb Classical Library. Cambridge: Harvard University Press, 1914-37.

Tertullian. *Adversus Marcionem.* Edited and translated by Ernest Evans. Oxford Early Christian Texts, ed. Henry Chadwick. 2 vols. Oxford: Clarendon Press, 1972.

Theodoret. *The Ecclesiastical History.* In vol. 3 of *A Select Library of Nicene and Post-Nicene Fathers of the Christian Church.* Second Series. Translated and edited by Philip Schaff and Henry Wace. Grand Rapids, MI: Wm. B. Eerdmans, 1953.

Classical Works — Arabic

al-Ghazālī, Abū Ḥāmid Muḥammad. *Tahāfut al-Falāsifah* [The Inconsistency of the Philosophers]. Edited by Sulaymān Dunyā. 4th ed. Dhakhā'ir al-'Arab [Arab Treasures], no. 15. Cairo: Dār al-Ma'ārif, n.d.

al-Ma'arrī, Abū al-'Alā'. *Luzūm Mā Lā Yalzam — al-Luzūmīyāt* [The Necessity of What is Not Necessary]. 2 vols. Beirut: Dār Ṣādir and Dār Bayrūt, 1961.
al-Suyūṭī, Jamāl al-Dīn 'Abd al-Raḥmān. *Al-Durar al-Muntathirah fī al-Aḥādīth al-Mushtahirah* [Scattered Pearls among Famous Ḥadīth Traditions]. Edited by Muḥammad ibn Luṭfī al-Ṣibāgh. Riyad: 'Imādat Shu'ūn al-Maktabāt — Jāmi'at al-Malak Sa'ūd, 1983.
al-Wāḥidī, Abū al-Ḥasan 'Alī ibn Aḥmad. *Asbāb Nuzūl al-Qur'ān* [Occasions for the Revelation of the Qur'ān]. Edited by Kamāl Basyūnī Zaghlūl. Beirut: Dār al-Kutub al-'Alamīyah, 1991.

Works by 'Abbās Maḥmūd al-'Aqqād — Articles

"Ba'that al-Masīḥ fī Banī Isrā'īl" [The Mission of Christ among the Israelites]. *Minbar al-Islām* 19 (May 1962): 21-23.
"Injīl Barnābā." *Al-Akhbār* 2277 (26 October 1959): 10. Reprinted in *Al-Sharq wa-al-Gharb — Orient & Occident* 56 (December 1959): 384-86. English edition: "The Gospel of Barnabas." Translated by A. Kenneth Cragg. *The News Bulletin of the Near East Council of Churches* (Eastertide 1961): 9-12.
"Law 'Āda Muḥammad" [If Muḥammad Were to Return]. *Al-Hilāl* 63 (January 1955): 16-20.
"Law 'Āda al-Sayyid al-Masīḥ" [If Christ Were to Return]. *Al-Hilāl* 65 (December 1957): 14-19. Reprinted in *Al-Akhbār* 4832 (25 December 1967): 5.
"Salient Characteristics of Arabic Literature." *Arab Observer* (Cairo), 9 November 1964: 48-49.
"Al-Sayyid al-Masīḥ fī Kunūz Wādī al-Qumrān" [Christ among the Treasures of Wadi Qumran]. *Al-Hilāl* 67 (December 1959): 8-13.
"The Seal of the Prophets." *Majallat al-Azhar* 32 (October 1960): English section, 5-9.
"Siyar al-'Uẓamā'" [The Biographies of Great Personalities]. *Al-Balāgh al-Usbū'ī* 90 (1 August 1928): 12-13.
"Tārīkh al-Masīḥ li-Amīl Ludfig" [The History of Christ according to Emil Ludwig]. *Al-Balāgh al-Usbū'ī* 93 (31 August 1928): 12-14; 94 (7 September 1928): 12-13; 95 (14 September 1928): 12-13, 20; 96 (16 January 1929): 12-13; and 97 (23 January 1929): 12-13.
"Unique Legacy of a Flexible Language." *The Arab World* (New York), 12 (October - November 1966): 26-27.

Works by 'Abbās Maḥmūd al-'Aqqād — Individual Books

Note: Al-'Aqqād's books have been printed by various publishers over the years. Many are currently in print, some by more than one publisher. The pagination often varies in each case, and occasionally a title has been abbreviated in subsequent printings. The publisher cited here (and in the endnotes, along with page references) is for the book which I was able to obtain, most often through the purchase of a currently printed edition. However, the date given in all cases is the original date of publication. Where this is not provided in the book, it is given according to the dates presented in al-Sakkūt, 1:175-98 (see below, under "Other Modern Works — Arabic"), and placed in brackets. Also, the original full title (including subtitle, if any) is given here.

'Abqarī al-Iṣlāḥ wa-al-Ta'līm: al-Ustādh al-Imām Muḥammad 'Abduh [The Genius of Reform and Education]. Cairo: Dār Nahḍat Miṣr, [1963].

'Abqarīyat al-Imām: 'Alī ibn Abī Ṭālib [The Genius of the Imām]. Cairo: Dār Nahḍat Miṣr, [1943].

'Abqarīyat Khālid [The Genius of Khālid]. Cairo: Dār Nahḍat Miṣr, [1945].

'Abqarīyat al-Masīḥ [The Genius of Christ]. Cairo: Maṭba'at Dār Akhbār al-Yawm, [1953]. 2d ed. published as *Ḥayāt al-Masīḥ: Fī al-Tārīkh wa-Kushūf al-'Aṣr al-Ḥadīth* [The Life of Christ: In History and the Discoveries of the Modern Age]. Cairo: Dār al-Hilāl, [1958]. 2d ed. published as *'Abqarīyat al-Masīḥ: Fī al-Tārīkh wa-Kushūf al-'Aṣr al-Ḥadīth.* With a Foreword by Munīf Luṭfī. Beirut: Al-Maktabah al-'Aṣrīyah, n.d. 3d ed. published as *Ḥayāt al-Masīḥ: Fī al-Tārīkh wa-Kushūf al-'Aṣr al-Ḥadīth.* Cairo: Dār Nahḍat Miṣr, 1996. Urdu edition: *Ḥayāt-e-Masīḥ: Shakhsyat, Kirdār, 'Aẓmat: Tārīkh awd Jadīd 'Aṣrī Iktashāfāt kī Āynī May* [The Life of Christ: His Personality, Character and Greatness: In the Light of History and Modern Discoveries]. Translated by Minhāj el-Dīn Iṣlāḥī [from the 2d Cairo edition]. Lahore: Pakistan Cooperative Publishers, 1965.

'Abqarīyat Muḥammad [The Genius of Muḥammad]. Cairo: Dār Nahḍat Miṣr, [1942].

'Abqarīyat al-Ṣiddīq [The Genius of Abū Bakr]. Cairo: Dār al-Ma'ārif, [1943].

'Abqarīyat 'Umar [The Genius of 'Umar]. Cairo: Dār Nahḍat Miṣr, [1942].

Allāh: Kitāb fī Nash'at al-'Aqīdah al-Ilāhīyah [God: A Book concerning the Origin of Belief in the Divinity]. Cairo: Dār Nahḍat Miṣr, [1947].

Anā [Myself]. With a Foreword by Ṭāhir al-Ṭanāḥī. Cairo: Dār Nahḍat Miṣr, [1964].

Athar al-'Arab fī al-Ḥaḍārah al-Ūrubbīyah. 2d ed. Cairo: Dār Nahḍat Miṣr, [1st ed. 1946; 2d ed. n.d.]. English edition: *The Arab's Impact on European Civilisation.* 2d ed. Translated by Ismail Cashmiry and Muhammad al-Hadi. Revised by Shawki Sukkary. Cairo: Supreme Council for Islamic Affairs, n.d.

Dhū al-Nūrayn: 'Uthmān ibn 'Affān [The Possessor of the Two Lights]. Cairo: Dār Nahḍat Miṣr, [1954].

Al-Dīmūqrāṭīyah fī al-Islām [Democracy in Islam]. Cairo: Dār Nahḍat Miṣr, [1952].

Falsafat al-Ghazālī [The Philosophy of al-Ghazālī]. Maṭbū'āt al-Idārah al-'Āmmah lil-Thaqāfah al-Islāmīyah bi-al-Azhar [Publications of the General Office of Islamic Culture at al-Azhar (University)]. Cairo: Maṭba'at al-Azhar, 1960.

Fāṭimah al-Zahrā' wa-al-Fāṭimīyūn [Fāṭimah "the Shining One" and the Fāṭimids]. Cairo: Dār Nahḍat Miṣr, [1954].

Ḥaqā'iq al-Islām wa-Abāṭīl Khuṣūmihi [The Truths of Islam and the Lies of its Oppo-

nents]. Cairo: Dār Nahḍat Miṣr, [1957].
Ḥayāt Qalam [The Life of a Pen]. With a Foreword by Tāhir al-Ṭanāḥī. Cairo: Dār Nahḍat Miṣr, [1964].
Iblīs [Satan]. Cairo: Dār Nahḍat Miṣr, [1958].
Ibrāhīm: Abū al-Anbiyā' [Abraham: Father of the Prophets]. Cairo: Dār Nahḍat Miṣr, [1953].
Juḥā: al-Ḍāḥik al-Muḍḥik [Juḥā: the Laugher and the Jester]. Cairo: Dār Nahḍat Miṣr, [1956].
Khulāṣat al-Yawmīyah [Synopsis of a Diary]. Cairo: Maṭba'at al-Hilāl, [1911].
Mā Yuqāl 'an al-Islām [What is Being Said about Islam]. Cairo: Dār al-Rashād al-Ḥadīthah, [1963].
Maṭla' al-Nūr: Aw Ṭawāli' al-Ba'thah al-Muḥammadīyah [The Dawning of the Light: The Preliminaries that Gave Rise to the Message of Muḥammad]. Cairo: Dār Nahḍat Miṣr, [1955].
Mu'āwiyah ibn Abī Sufyān fī al-Mīzān [Mu'āwiyah ibn Abī Sufyān in the Balance]. Cairo: Dār Nahḍat Miṣr, [1956].
Raj'at Abī al-'Alā' [The Return of Abū al-'Alā']. Cairo: Dār Nahḍat Miṣr, [1939].
Sā'āt bayn al-Kutub: Al-Juz' al-Thānī [Hours among the Books: Part Two]. Cairo: Maktabat al-Nahḍah al-Miṣrīyah, 1945.
Sārah. Cairo: Dār Nahḍat Miṣr, [1960]. English edition: *Sara.* Translated by Moustafa Badawi. Cairo: General Egyptian Book Organization, 1978.
Al-Tafkīr: Farīḍah Islāmīyah [Reflection: A Duty of Islam]. Cairo: Dār Nahḍat Miṣr, [1961].
Yawmīyāt 1 [A Daily Chronicle, Part 1]. Cairo: Dār Nahḍat Miṣr, [1963].

Works by 'Abbās Maḥmūd al-'Aqqād — Collections

Al-'Abqarīyāt al-Islāmīyah [The Islamic "Genius" Series]. Beirut: Dār al-Ādāb, 1966.
Islāmīyāt [Islamic Studies]. Cairo: Dār al-Ma'ārif, 1969.
Al-Majmū'ah al-Kāmilah li-Mu'allifāt al-Ustādh 'Abbās Maḥmūd al-'Aqqād [The Complete Works of al-'Aqqād]. 26 vols. Beirut: Dār al-Kitāb al-Lubnānī, 1974-84.
Mawsū'at 'Abbās Maḥmūd al-'Aqqād al-Islāmīyah [The Islamic Encyclopedia of al-'Aqqād]. 7 vols. Beirut: al-Maktabah al-'Aṣrīyah, n.d.

Other Modern Works — Arabic

'Abd al-'Azīz, Manṣūr Ḥusayn. *Da'wat al-Ḥaqq aw al-Ḥaqīqah bayn al-Masīḥīyah wa-al-Islām* [The Call of Truth, or the Truth between Christianity and Islam]. Cairo: Al-Sharikah al-Miṣrīyah lil-Tibā'ah, 1963. 2d ed., Cairo: Maktabat 'Alā' al-Dīn, 1972.
'Abd al-Wahhāb, Aḥmad. *Al-Masīḥ fī Maṣādir al-'Āqā'id al-Masīḥīyah.* 2d ed. Cairo:

Maktabat Wahbah, 1988. English edition: Ahmed Abdel-Wahab Ali. *The Christ as Seen in the Sources of the Christian Beliefs.* 2d ed. Cairo: Wahba Book Shop, 1985.

'Abduh, Muḥammad. *Al-Islām wa-al-Naṣrānīyah ma' al-'Ilm wa-al-Madanīyah* [Islam and Christianity with regard to Science and Civilization]. Cairo: Maktabat wa-Maṭba'at Muḥammad 'Alī Ṣabīḥ, n.d.

________. *Risālat al-Tawḥīd* [Discourse on Unity]. Cairo: Dār al-Rashād al-Ḥadīthah, n.d. English edition: *The Theology of Unity.* Translated by Isḥāq Musa'ad and Kenneth Cragg. London: George Allen & Unwin, 1966.

Abū Rayyah, Maḥmūd. *Dīn Allāh Wāḥid: Muḥammad wa-al-Masīḥ Akhawān* [The Religion of God is One: Muḥammad and Christ are Brothers]. Cairo: Dār al-Karnak, [1963]. 2d ed. published as *Dīn Allāh Wāḥid: 'Alā Alsinat Jamī' al-Rusul* [The Religion of God is One: On the Tongues of All the Messengers]. Cairo: 'Alam al-Kutub, [1970].

Abū Zahrah, Muḥammad. *Muḥāḍarāt fī al-Naṣrānīyah* [Lectures on Christianity]. Cairo: Dār al-Fikr al-'Arabī, [1942].

Amīn, 'Uthmān. *Naẓarāt fī Fikr al-'Aqqād* [Reflections on the Thought of al-'Aqqād]. Cairo: Al-Maktabah al-Thaqāfīyah, 1966.

Ḍayf, Shawqī. *Ma' al-'Aqqād* [With al-'Aqqād]. 5th ed. Cairo: Dār al-Ma'ārif, 1988.

Diyāb, 'Abd al-Ḥayy. *Al-'Aqqād wa-Taṭawwuruhu al-Fikrī* [Al-'Aqqād and His Intellectual Development]. Salsalat al-Kutub al-Ḥadīthah [Modern Books Series], no. 28. Cairo: Al-Mu'assasah al-'Āmmah lil-Ṣaḥāfah wa-al-Ṭibā'ah, 1969.

Fahmī, Muḥammad 'Ārif Muṣṭafā. *Yasū' al-Masīḥ wa-al-Imām 'Alī, bayn al-Injīl wa-al-Qur'ān wa-al-'Aql* [Jesus Christ and Imām 'Alī in the Gospel and the Qur'ān and Reason]. Cairo: Maṭba'at al-Kīlānī, 1971.

al-Ḥalwajī, 'Abd al-Sattār 'Abd al-Ḥaqq. *'Abbās Maḥmūd al-'Aqqād: Nashrat Bibliyūjrāfīyah bi-Āthārihi al-Fikrīyah* [A Small Bibliography of His Scholarly Works]. Cairo: Maṭba'at Dār al-Kutub, 1964.

Haykal, Muḥammad Ḥusayn. *Ḥayāt Muḥammad.* Cairo: Maktabat al-Nahḍah al-Miṣrīyah, 1968. (First published in Cairo in 1935). English edition: *The Life of Muḥammad.* Translated from the 8th edition by Isma'īl Rāgī A. al-Fārūqī. N.p.: North American Trust Publications, 1976.

Ḥusayn, Muḥammad Kāmil. *Al-Dhikr al-Ḥakīm* [The Judicious Reminder]. Cairo: Maktabat al-Nahḍah al-Miṣrīyah, [1972].

________. *Qaryah Ẓālimah* [A Wrongful Village]. Cairo: Maktabat al-Nahḍah al-Miṣrīyah, [1954]. English edition: M. Kamel Hussein. *City of Wrong: A Friday in Jerusalem.* Translated by Kenneth Cragg. Amsterdam: Djambatan, 1959.

Isṭafānūs, 'Abd al-Masīḥ. *Taqdīm al-Kitāb al-Muqaddas li-Qāri' al-'Arabī: Tārīkhuhu, Ṣiḥḥatuhu, Tarjamātuhu, Dirāsatuhu* [Introduction to the Holy Bible: Its History, Veracity, Translation and Study]. N.p.: Dār al-Kitāb al-Muqaddas fī al-Sharq al-Awsaṭ, 1994.

al-Jabalāwī, Muḥammad Ṭāhir. *Min Dhikrīyāt fī Ṣuḥbat al-'Aqqād* [From the Memories of My Friendship with al-'Aqqād]. 2d ed. Maktabat al-Anjalū al-Miṣrīyah, 1967.

Kafāfī, 'Aṭā'. *Al-Naz'ah al-Nafsīyah fī Manhaj al-'Aqqād al-Naqdī* [The Psychological

Trend in al-'Aqqād's Critical Method]. Cairo: Hajr lil-Ṭabā'ah, 1987.

Khālid, Khālid Muḥammad. *Ma'an 'alā al-Ṭarīq: Muḥammad wa-al-Masīḥ* [Together on the Road: Muḥammad and Christ]. Cairo: Dār al-Kutub al-Ḥadīthah, 1958.

al-Khaṭīb, 'Abd al-Karīm. *Al-Masīḥ fī al-Qur'ān wa-al-Tawrāt wa-al-Injīl* [Christ in the Qur'ān, the Torah, and the Gospel]. Cairo: Dār al-Kutub al-Ḥadīthah, 1966.

Qumayḥah, Jābir. *Manhaj al-'Aqqād fī al-Tarājim al-Adabīyah* [Al-'Aqqād's Method in his Biographical Studies]. Cairo: Maktabat al-Nahḍah al-Miṣrīyah, 1980.

Riḍā, Rashīd. *Shubuhāt al-Naṣārā wa-Ḥujaj al-Islām* [The Ambiguities of the Christians and the Proofs of Islam]. Cairo: Dār al-Manār, [1928].

Riḍā, Rashīd, and Muḥammad 'Abduh. *Tafsīr al-Qur'ān al-Ḥakīm* [Commentary of the Judicious Qur'ān]. 12 vols. Cairo: Dār al-Manār, [1910].

al-Saḥḥār, 'Abd al-Ḥamīd Gūdah. *Al-Masīḥ 'Īsā bin Maryam* [The Messiah, Jesus the Son of Mary]. Cairo: Dār Miṣr lil-Ṭabā'ah, [1951].

al-Sakkūt, Ḥamdī. *'Abbās Maḥmūd al-'Aqqād.* A'lām al-Adab al-Mu'āṣir fī Miṣr [Leaders of Contemporary Literature in Egypt], no. 5. 2 vols. Cairo: Dār al-Kitāb al-Miṣrī, 1983.

Shalabī, Aḥmad. *Muqāranat al-Adyān* [The Religions in Comparison]. Vol. 2, *Al-Masīḥīyah* [Christianity]. Cairo: Maktabat al-Nahḍah al-Miṣrīyah, 1961.

al-Ṭayib, 'Abdullah. *Al-Murshid ilā Fahm Ash'ār al-'Arab wa-Ṣanā'atihā* [Guide to Understanding the Poetry of the Arabs and its Production]. 4th ed. 2 vols. Khartoum: Maṭba'at Jāmi'at al-Kharṭūm, 1991.

al-Tūnisī, Muḥammad Khalīfah. "Al-'Aqqād: Muḥāmī al-'Uẓamā'" [Advocate for the Eminent Personalities]. In *Al-'Aqqād: Darāsah wa Taḥīyah* [A Study and a Tribute], ed. Muḥammad Khalīfah al-Tūnisī, 164-85. Cairo: Maktabat al-Anjilū al-Miṣrīyah, n.d.

________, ed. *Fuṣūl min al-Naqd 'ind al-'Aqqād* [Passages from the Critical Writings of al-'Aqqād]. Cairo: Maktabat al-Khānijī bi-Miṣr, n.d.

'Uthmān, Fatḥī. *Ma' al-Masīḥ fī al-Anājīl al-Arba'ah* [With Christ in the Four Gospels]. 2d ed. Cairo: al-Dār al-Qawmīyah lil-Ṭibā'ah wa-al-Nashr, [1966].

al-Ziriklī, Khayr al-Dīn. *Al-A'lām: Qāmūs Tarājim lil-Ashhar al-Rijāl wa-al-Nisā' min al-'Arab wa-al-Musta'ribīn wa-al-Mustashriqīn* [The Eminent Ones: A Biographical Dictionary of the Best Known Men and Women among the Arabs, as well as Arabists and Orientalists]. 3d ed. 8 vols. Beirut: Dār al-'Ilm lil-Malāyīn, 1979.

Reference Dictionaries and Encyclopedias

The Anchor Bible Dictionary. Edited by David Noel Freedman. 6 vols. New York: Doubleday, 1992.

A Dictionary of Christian Ethics. Edited by John Macquarrie. London: SCM Press, 1967.

Dictionary of Jesus and the Gospels. Edited by Joel B. Green, Scot McKnight, and I. Howard Marshall. Downers Grove, IL: InterVarsity Press, 1992.

Encyclopaedia Biblica. Edited by T. K. Cheyne and J. Sutherland Black. 4 vols. New

York: Macmillan, 1903.

Encyclopaedia Judaica. Edited by Cecil Roth. 16 vols. Jerusalem: Keter Publishing House, 1971.

The Encyclopaedia of Islam, 1st ed. Edited by M. T. Houtsma et al. 8 vols. Leiden: E. J. Brill, 1913-36, with Supplement, 1938.

The Encyclopaedia of Islam, 2d ed. Edited by H. A. R. Gibb et al. 9 vols. to date. Leiden: E. J. Brill, 1960-.

The Encyclopedia of Religion. Edited by Mircea Eliade. 16 vols. New York: Macmillan, 1987.

The Oxford Classical Dictionary, 2d ed. Edited by N. G. L. Hammond and H. H. Scullard. Oxford: Clarendon Press, 1970.

The Oxford Dictionary of the Christian Church, 2d ed. Edited by F. L. Cross and E. A. Livingstone. Oxford: Oxford University Press, 1974.

New Catholic Encyclopedia. Edited by William J. McDonald. 14 vols. New York: McGraw-Hill, 1967.

Theological Dictionary of the Old Testament. Edited by G. Johannes Botterweck, Helmer Ringgren and Heinz-Josef Fabry. Translated by John T. Willis, et al. 9 vols. to date. Grand Rapids, MI: Wm. B. Eerdmans, 1974-.

Modern Works — Western Languages

'Abd al-Malik, Butrus. Review of *'Abqarīyat al-Masīḥ* [The Genius of Christ], by 'Abbās Maḥmūd al-'Aqqād. In *The Muslim World* 43 (1953): 218-19.

Adams, Charles D. *Islam and Modernism in Egypt: A Study of the Modern Reform Movement Inaugurated by Muḥammad 'Abduh.* The American University at Cairo Oriental Studies. London: Oxford University Press, 1933.

Ahmad, Ghulam. *Jesus in India: Being an Account of Jesus' Escape from Death on the Cross and of His Journey to India.* London: The London Mosque, 1978.

Alcalay, Reuben. *The Complete English-Hebrew Dictionary.* Tel Aviv: Massadah, 1962.

Allegro, John M. *The Dead Sea Scrolls.* Pelican Books. Harmondsworth, England: Penguin Books, 1956.

Anawati, G[eorges] C. "Deux livres récents sur le Christ." *La revue du Caire* 35 (August 1955): 163-73.

________. "La personne du Christ d'après deux livres récents d'auteurs musulmans." In *ATTI: dell'VIII Congresso Internazionale di Storia delle Religioni (Roma 17-23 Aprile 1955)* [ATTI: The Eighth International Congress for the History of Religions (Rome, April 17-23, 1955)], 443-46. Florence: G. C. Sansoni, 1956.

________. "Polémique, apologie et dialogue islamo-chrétiens: Positions classiques médiévales et positions contemporaines." *Euntes Docete* (Rome) 22 (1969): 375-451.

Anderson, A. A. *The Book of Psalms.* The New Century Bible, ed. Ronald E. Clements and Matthew Black. 2 vols. Grand Rapids, MI: Wm. B. Eerdmans, 1972; London:

Marshall, Morgan & Scott, 1972.

Arberry, Arthur J. *Modern Arabic Poetry: An Anthology with English Verse Translation.* Cambridge Oriental Series, no. 1. Cambridge: Cambridge University Press, 1950.

Aron, Robert. *Jesus of Nazareth: The Hidden Years.* Translated by Frances Frenaye. New York: William Morrow, 1961.

Ata ur-Rahim, Muhammad. *Jesus: Prophet of Islam.* Alexandra, Singapore: Omar Brothers, 1978.

Awad, Louis. *The Literature of Ideas in Egypt, Part I: Selection, Translation, and Introduction.* Vol. 3 in *Arabic Writing Today.* Studies in Near Eastern Culture and Society, no. 6. Atlanta: Scholars Press, 1986.

Ayoub, Mahmoud. "Islam and Christianity: A Study of Muhammad Abduh's View of the Two Religions." *Humaniora Islamica* 2 (1974): 121-37.

________. "Jesus the Son of God: A Study of the Terms *Ibn* and *Walad* in the Qur'an and Tafsīr Tradition." In *Christian-Muslim Encounters,* ed. Yvonne Yazbeck Haddad and Wadi Zaidan Haddad, 65-81. Gainsville, FL: University of Florida Press, 1995.

________. "The Miracle of Jesus: Muslim Reflections on the Divine Word." In *Christology in Dialogue,* ed. Robert F. Berkey and Sarah A. Edwards, 221-28. Cleveland: Pilgrim Press, 1993.

________. "Muslim Views of Christianity: Some Modern Examples." *Islamochristiana* 10 (1984): 49-70.

________. *The Qur'an and Its Interpreters.* Vol. 1. Albany: State University of New York Press, 1984.

________. *The Qur'an and Its Interpreters.* Vol. 2, *The House of 'Imrān.* Albany: State University of New York Press, 1992.

________. "Towards an Islamic Christology: An Image of Jesus in Early Shī'ī Muslim Literature." *The Muslim World* 66 (1976): 163-88.

________. "Towards an Islamic Christology, II: The Death of Jesus, Reality or Delusion (A Study of the Death of Jesus in Tafsīr Literature." *The Muslim World* 70 (1980): 91-121.

Badawi, M. M. *A Critical Introduction to Modern Arabic Poetry.* Cambridge: Cambridge University Press, 1975.

________. *Modern Arabic Literature and the West.* London: Ithaca Press, 1985.

Bauer, Walter. *A Greek-English Lexicon of the New Testament and Other Early Christian Literature.* Translated and edited by William F. Arndt and F. Wilbur Gingrich. 2d ed. revised and augmented by F. Wilbur Gingrich and Frederick W. Danker. Chicago: University of Chicago Press, 1979.

Beasley-Murray, George R. *John.* Word Biblical Commentary, ed. David A. Hubbard and Glenn W. Barker, vol. 36. Waco, TX: Word Books, 1987.

Beckwith, Roger T. *Calendar and Chronology, Jewish and Christian: Biblical, Intertestamental and Patristic Studies.* Arbeiten zur Geschichte des antiken Jundentums und des Urchristentums, no. 33. Leiden: E. J. Brill, 1996.

Beskow, Per. *Strange Tales about Jesus: A Survey of Unfamiliar Gospels.* Philadelphia:

Fortress Press, 1983.

Besterman, Theodore. *Voltaire.* 2d ed. Chicago: University of Chicago Press, 1976.

Bevan, Edwyn. *Stoics and Sceptics: Four Lectures Delivered in Oxford during Hilary Term 1913 for the Common University Fund.* Oxford: Clarendon Press, 1913.

Bijlefeld, Willem A. "Other Faith Images of Jesus: Some Muslim Contributions to the Christological Discussion." In *Christological Perspectives: Essays in Honor of Harvey K. McArthur,* ed. Robert F. Berkey and Sarah A. Edwards, 200-215, 293-302. New York: Pilgrim Press, 1982.

________. "A Prophet and More than a Prophet? Some Observations on the Qur'ānic Use of the Terms 'Prophet' and 'Apostle.'" *The Muslim World* 59 (1969): 1-28.

Borrmans, Maurice. *Jésus et les musulmans d'aujourd'hui.* Collection "Jésus et Jésus-Christ", ed. Joseph Doré, no. 69. Paris: Desclée, 1996.

Boyce, Mary. *Zoroastrians: Their Religious Beliefs and Practices.* London: Routledge & Kegan Paul, 1979.

Bradley, Keith R. *Slavery and Rebellion in the Roman World, 140 B.C.-70 B.C.* Bloomington and Indianapolis: Indiana University Press, 1989.

Bratcher, Robert G. "A Study of Isaiah 7:14: Its Meaning and Use in the Masoretic Text, the Septuagint and the Gospel of Matthew." *The Bible Translator* 9 (1958): 97-126.

Breasted, James Henry. *The Dawn of Conscience.* New York: Charles Scribner's Sons, 1933.

Bréhier, Émil. *The History of Philosophy.* Vol. 1, *The Hellenic Age.* Translated by Joseph Thomas. Chicago: University of Chicago Press, 1963.

________. *The History of Philosophy.* Vol. 2, *The Hellenistic and Roman Age.* Translated by Wade Baskin. Chicago: University of Chicago Press, 1965.

Brown, Colin. *Jesus in European Protestant Thought: 1778-1860.* Studies in Historical Theology 1, ed. David C. Steinmetz. Durham, NC: Labyrinth Press, 1985.

Brown, Francis, S. R. Driver, and Charles A. Briggs. *A Hebrew and English Lexicon of the Old Testament.* Oxford: Clarendon Press, 1907.

Brown, Raymond E. *The Birth of the Messiah: A Commentary on the Infancy Narratives in Matthew and Luke.* 2d ed. The Anchor Reference Library, ed. David Noel Freedman. New York: Doubleday, 1993.

________. *The Death of the Messiah: From Gethsemane to the Grave: A Commentary on the Passion Narratives in the Four Gospels.* The Anchor Reference Library, ed. David Noel Freedman. 2 vols. New York: Doubleday, 1994.

________. *The Gospel According to John: Introduction, Translation, and Notes.* The Anchor Bible, ed. William Foxwell Albright and David Noel Freedman, vols. 29 and 29A. Garden City, NY: Doubleday, 1966-70.

Brown, Raymond E., Karl P. Donfired, Joseph A. Fitzmyer, and John Reumann, eds. *Mary in the New Testament: A Collaborative Assessment by Protestant and Roman Catholic Scholars.* Philadelphia: Fortress Press, 1978; New York: Paulist Press, 1978.

Brownlee, William H. *Ezekiel 1-19.* Word Biblical Commentary, ed. David A. Hubbard and Glenn W. Barker, vol. 28. Waco, TX: Word Books, 1986.

Bruce, F. F. *The Acts of the Apostles: The Greek Text with Introduction and Commentary.* 3d ed. Grand Rapids, MI: William B. Eerdmans, 1990.

________. *History of the Bible in English: From the Earliest Versions.* 3d ed. Formerly *The English Bible.* New York: Oxford University Press, 1978.

________. *Jesus and Christian Origins Outside the New Testament.* Grand Rapids, MI: William B. Eerdmans, 1974.

________. *Paul: Apostle of the Heart Set Free.* Grand Rapids, MI: William B. Eerdmans, 1977.

Burkert, Walter. *Greek Religion: Archaic and Classical.* Translated by John Raffan. Cambridge: Harvard University Press, 1985.

Burrows, Millar. *The Dead Sea Scrolls.* New York: Viking Press, 1955.

________. *More Light on the Dead Sea Scrolls: New Scrolls and New Interpretations, with Translations of Important Recent Discoveries.* New York: Viking Press, 1958.

Buxbaum, Yitzhak. *The Life and Teachings of Hillel.* Northvale, NJ: Jason Aronson, 1994.

Cachia, Pierre. *An Overview of Modern Arabic Literature.* Islamic Surveys, ed. C. Hillenbrand. Edinburgh: Edinburgh University Press, 1990.

________. *Ṭāhā Ḥusayn: His Place in the Egyptian Literary Renaissance.* London: Luzac, 1956.

Cadoux, Cecil John. The Life of Jesus. Pelican Books. West Drayton, England: Penguin Books, 1948.

Campbell, R. J. *The Life of Christ.* Benn's Sixpenny Library, no. 128. London: Ernest Benn, 1927.

Carlyle, Thomas. *On Heroes, Hero-Worship and the Heroic in History.* Edited with an Introduction by Carl Niemeyer. Lincoln, NE: University of Nebraska Press, 1966.

Chadbourne, Richard M. *Ernest Renan.* Twayne's World Authors Series, ed. Sylvia E. Bowman, no. 34. New York: Twayne Publishers, 1968.

Chadwick, Henry. *The Early Church.* The Penguin History of the Church, ed. Owen Chadwick, vol. 1. London: Penguin Books, 1967.

Chambers, William, and Robert Chambers. *Carthage and the Carthaginians.* Chambers's Papers for the People, no. 20, vol. 3-4. Edinburgh: William and Robert Chambers, 1850.

Charlesworth, James H., ed. *The Messiah: Developments in Earliest Judaism and Christianity.* Minneapolis: Fortress Press, 1992.

Cook, S. A., F. E. Adcock, and M. P. Charlesworth. *The Cambridge Ancient History.* Vol. 9, *The Roman Republic: 133-44 B.C.* Cambridge: Cambridge University Press, 1932.

Cook, S. A., F. E. Adcock, and M. P. Charlesworth. *The Cambridge Ancient History.* Vol. 10, *The Augustan Empire: 44 B.C.-A.D. 70.* Cambridge: Cambridge University Press, 1934.

Cragg, Kenneth. *The Call of the Minaret.* 2d ed. London: Collins, 1985.

________. "'City of Wrong': A Muslim Studies the Cross, I & II." *The Muslim World*

46 (1956): 132-43, 225-36 (under the name 'Abd al-Tafāhum).

________. "'The Genius of Christ' — A Muslim Estimate." Review of *'Abqarīyat al-Masīḥ,* by 'Abbās Maḥmūd al-'Aqqād. In *The East and West Review* 20 (1954): 88-96.

________. *Jesus and the Muslim: An Exploration.* London: George Allen & Unwin, 1985.

________. "Jesus in Contemporary Islam." *The Listener* 63 (25 February 1960): 347, 349.

________. *The Pen and the Faith: Eight Modern Muslim Writers and the Qur'ān.* London: George Allen & Unwin, 1985.

Dajani, Zahia Ragheb. *Egypt and the Crisis of Islam.* American University Studies, series 9, vol. 56. New York: Peter Lang, 1990.

Daniel, Norman. *Islam and the West: The Making of an Image.* 2d ed. Oxford: Oneworld Publications, 1993.

Davies, W. D., and Dale C. Allison, Jr. *A Critical and Exegetical Commentary on the Gospel According to Saint Matthew.* The International Critical Commentary on the Holy Scriptures of the Old and New Testaments, ed. J. A. Emerton, C. E. B. Cranfield, and G. N. Stanton. 3 vols. Edinburgh: T & T Clark, 1988-97.

Deissmann, Adolf. *Light from the Ancient East.* London: Hodder and Stoughton, 1927.

de Matteo, Ignazio. "Taḥrīf or the Alteration of the Bible According to the Moslems." Abbreviated and translated by M. H. Ananikian. *The Moslem World* 14 (1924): 61-84.

el-Didi, Abdel-Fattah. *Jesus und der moderne Islam.* Arabische Kulture, no. 1. [Bonn]: n.p., [1956].

Donaldson, Dwight M. "Al-Ya'qūbī's Chapter about Jesus Christ." In *The MacDonald Presentation Volume,* ed. William G. Shellabear, Edwin E. Calverley, Elbert C. Lane, and Ruth S. Mackensen, 89-105. Princeton: Princeton University Press, 1933.

Dostoyevsky, Fyodor. *The Brothers Karamazov.* Translated by Constance Garnett. London: Heinemann, 1912. Translated by David McDuff. Penguin Classics. London: Penguin Books, 1993.

Dunn, James D. G. *Unity and Diversity in the New Testament: An Inquiry into the Character of Earliest Christianity.* 2d ed. London: SCM Press, 1990; Philadelphia: Trinity Press International, 1990.

Dupont-Sommer, A. *The Jewish Sect of Qumran and the Essenes: New Studies on the Dead Sea Scrolls.* Translated by R. D. Barnett. London: Vallentine, Mitchell & Co., 1954.

Elliot, J. K. *The Apocryphal New Testament: A Collection of Apocryphal Christian Literature in an English Translation.* Oxford: Clarendon Press, 1993.

Engineer, Asghar Ali. "Ḥaḍrat 'Īsā, Holy Qur'ān and Muslim Thinkers and Writers." *Journées Romaines* (Rome)18 (1991): 11-24.

Ewald, Heinrich. *The History of Israel.* 8 vols. 3d ed. London: Longmans, Green, 1876-86.

Fage, J. D., ed. *The Cambridge History of Africa.* Vol. 2, *From c. 500 BC to AD 1050.* Cambridge: Cambridge University Press, 1978.

Farès, Georges. "Le Christ et l'Islam contemporain." In *Mediterranée, carrefour des religions,* 31-52. Recherches et débats du centre catholique des intellectuels français, n.s. no. 28 (September 1959). Paris: Librairie Arthème Fayard, 1959.

Faris, Nabih Amin. "The Muslim Thinker and His Christian Relations." *The Muslim World* 47 (1957): 62-70.

Farrar, Frederic W. *The Life of Christ.* New York: H. M. Caldwell, 1874. "Popular Edition," London: Cassell, 1892.

Finegan, Jack. *Handbook of Biblical Chronology: Principles of Time Reckoning in the Ancient World and Problems of Chronology in the Bible.* Princeton: Princeton University Press, 1964.

________. *Light from the Ancient Past.* Princeton: Princeton University Press, 1946; 2d ed., 1959.

Fitzmyer, Joseph A. *The Gospel According to Luke.* The Anchor Bible, ed. William Foxwell Albright and David Noel Freedman, vols. 28 and 28A. Garden City, NY: Doubleday, 1981-85.

Ford, F. Peter, Jr. "Isma'il al-Faruqi on Muslim-Christian Dialogue: An Analysis from a Christian Perspective." *Islam and Christian-Muslim Relations* 4 (1993): 268-82.

________. "A Modern Muslim Assessment of Jesus: A Translation and Analysis of 'Abbās Maḥmūd al-'Aqqād's *The Genius of Christ.*" 2 vols. Ph.D. diss., Temple University, 1998.

________. "The Qur'ān as Sacred Scripture: An Assessment of Contemporary Christian Perspectives." *The Muslim World* 83 (1993): 142-64.

Freyne, Seán. *Galilee from Alexander the Great to Hadrian, 323 B.C.E. to 135 C.E.: A Study of Second Temple Judaism.* University of Notre Dame Center for the Study of Judaism and Christianity in Antiquity, no. 5. Wilmington, DE: Michael Glazier, Notre Dame: University of Notre Dame Press, 1980.

Furneaux, Rupert. *The Other Side of the Story: The Strange Story of Christianity, the Dark Spot of History.* London: Cassell, 1953.

Gardiner, Alan H. *The Admonitions of an Egyptian Sage.* Leipzig: J. C. Hinrichs, 1909.

Garrison, W[infred] E[rnest]. "Branch from 'The Golden Bough.'" Review of *King Jesus,* by Robert Graves. In *The Christian Century* 63 (1946): 1184-85.

________. "A Human Jesus." Review of *The Son of Man: The Story of Jesus,* by Emil Ludwig. In *The Christian Century* 45 (1928): 906-907.

Gaudeul, Jean-Marie. *Encounters and Clashes: Islam and Christianity in History.* 2 vols. Rome: Pontificio Istituto di Studi Arabi e Islamici, 1990.

Gaudeul, Jean-Marie, and Robert Casper. "Textes de la tradition musulmane concernant le taḥrīf (falsification) des écritures." *Islamochristiana* 6 (1980): 61-104.

Gibb, H[amilton] A. R. "Studies in Contemporary Arabic Literature, III: Egyptian Modernists." *Bulletin of the School of Oriental Studies, London Institute* 5 (1928-30): 445-66.

________. *Studies on the Civilization of Islam.* Edited by Stanford J. Shaw and William R. Polk. Beacon Books on World Affairs, ed. William R. Polk. Boston: Beacon Press,

1962.

Gill, Sam D. *Native American Religions: An Introduction.* Belmont, CA: Wadsworth, 1982.

Goddard, Hugh. "An Annotated Bibliography of Works about Christianity by Egyptian Muslim Authors (1940-1980)." *The Muslim World* 80 (1990): 251-77.

________. "Modern Pakistani and Indian Muslim Perceptions of Christianity." *Islam and Christian-Muslim Relations* 5 (1994): 165-88.

________. *Muslim Perceptions of Christianity.* CSIC Studies on Islam and Christianity. London: Grey Seal, 1996.

Goldingay, John E. *Daniel.* Word Biblical Commentary, ed. David A. Hubbard and Glenn W. Barker, vol. 30. Dallas: Word Books, 1989.

Goodenough, Erwin R. *By Light, Light: The Mystic Gospel of Hellenistic Judaism.* New Haven: Yale University Press, 1935.

Goodspeed, Edgar J. *Modern Apocrypha.* Boston: Beacon Press, 1956.

Grant, Michael. *Greek and Latin Authors: 800 B.C. - A.D. 1000.* New York: H. W. Wilson, 1980.

________. *Jesus: An Historian's Review of the Gospels.* New York: Charles Scribners' Sons, 1977.

________. *The Jews in the Roman World.* New York: Charles Scribners' Sons, 1973.

Graves, Robert. *King Jesus.* New York: Noonday Press (Farrar, Straus, Giroux), 1946; London: Cassell, 1946.

Graves, Robert, and Joshua Podro. *The Nazarene Gospel Restored.* Garden City, N.Y.: Doubleday, 1953; London: Cassell, [1953].

Grönbold, Günter. *Jesus in Indien: Das Ende einer Legende.* Munich: Kösel, 1985.

Gu, Xiaorong. "Resources, Choice, and Power: A Contemporary Study in Social Change and Ideological Transformation of Germany (1848-1914), Italy (1861-1963), and Egypt (1919-1983)." Ph.D. diss., Temple University, 1988.

Guillaume, Alfred. *The Traditions of Islam: An Introduction to the Study of the Hadith Literature.* Oxford: Clarendon Press, 1924.

Hagner, Donald A. *Matthew.* Word Biblical Commentary, ed. David A. Hubbard and Glenn W. Barker, vols. 33A and 33B. Dallas: Word Books, 1993-95.

Haywood, J. A. and H. M. Nahmad. *A New Arabic Grammar of the Written Language.* London: Lund Humphries, 1965.

Hick, John, ed. *The Myth of God Incarnate.* London: SCM, 1977.

Hodgson, Marshall G. S. *The Venture of Islam: Conscience and History in a World Civilization.* 3 vols. Chicago: University of Chicago Press, 1974.

Hook, Sidney. *The Hero in History: A Study in Limitation and Possibility.* London: Secker & Warburg, 1945.

Horne, Thomas Hartwell. *An Introduction to the Critical Study and Knowledge of the Holy Scriptures.* 7th ed. 2 vols. Philadelphia: Desilver, Thomas & Co., 1836.

Hourani, Albert. *Arabic Thought in the Liberal Age: 1798-1939.* Cambridge: Cambridge University Press, 1983.

al-Ḥusaynī, Isḥaq Mūsā. "Christ in the Qur'ān and in Modern Arabic Literature." *The Muslim World* 50 (1960): 297-302.

Husband, Richard Wellington. *The Prosecution of Jesus: Its Date, History and Legality.* Princeton: Princeton University Press, 1916.

Hyde, Walter Woodburn. *Paganism to Christianity in the Roman Empire.* Philadelphia: University of Pennsylvania Press, 1946.

Ibrahim, Ibrahim. "Aḥmad Amīn and 'Abbās Maḥmūd al-'Aqqād Between al-Qadīm and al-Jadīd: European Challenge and Islamic Response." In *Arab Civilization: Challenges and Responses: Studies in Honor of Constantine K. Zurayk,* ed. Ibrahim M. Oweiss, 208-230. Albany: State University of New York Press, 1988.

Japhet, Sara. *I & II Chronicles: A Commentary.* Old Testament Library. London: SCM Press, 1993.

Jeffery, Arthur. "A Collection of Anti-Christian Books and Pamphlets Found in Actual Use among the Mohammedans of Cairo." *The Moslem World* 15 (1925): 26-37.

Jeremias, Joachim. *Jesus' Promise to the Nations.* Philadelphia: Fortress Press, 1967.

________. *New Testament Theology: The Proclamation of Jesus.* Translated by John Bowden. New York: Charles Scribner's Sons, 1971.

Jessup, Henry Harris. *Fifty-Three Years in Syria.* 2 vols. New York: Revell, 1910.

Jomier, J. *Le commentaire coranique du Manar: Tendances modernes de l'exégèse coranique en Égypte.* Islam d'hier et d'aujourd'hui, no. 11. Paris: G.-P. Maisonneuve, 1954.

________. "Quatre ouvrages en arabe sur le Christ." *Mélanges de l'institute dominicain d'études orientales du Caire* (MIDEO, Cairo) 5 (1958): 367-86.

Kamel, Hisham Safwat. "Christ in Contemporary Arabic Literature." D.Missiology diss., Fuller Theological Seminary, 1990.

Keddie, Nikki R. *An Islamic Response to Imperialism: Political and Religious Writings of Sayyid Jamāl al-Dīn "al-Afghānī".* Berkeley: University of California Press, 1968.

Kennedy, Hugh. *The Prophet and the Age of the Caliphates: The Islamic Near East from the Sixth to the Eleventh Century.* A History of the Near East, ed. P. M. Holt. London: Longman, 1986.

Kerr, David A. "Christology in Christian-Muslim Dialogue." In *Christology in Dialogue,* ed. Robert F. Berkey and Sarah A. Edwards, 201-20. Cleveland: Pilgrim Press, 1993.

________. "The Problem of Christianity in Muslim Perspective: Implications for Christian Mission." *International Bulletin of Missionary Research* 5 (1981): 152-62.

al-Khaṭīb, 'Abd al-Karīm. "Christ in the Qur'ān, the Taurāt, and the Injīl: A Continuing Dialogue." Translated and edited by Kenneth E. Nolin. *The Muslim World* 61 (1971): 90-101.

Kilpatrick, Hilary. *The Modern Egyptian Novel: A Study in Social Criticism.* St. Anthony's Middle East Monographs, no. 1. London: Ithaca Press, 1974.

Klein, Ernest. *A Comprehensive Etymological Dictionary of the Hebrew Language for Readers of English.* New York: Macmillan, 1987.

Koch, Klaus. *The Prophets.* 2 vols. Philadelphia: Fortress Press, 1982-84.

Lacey, R. K. "An 11th Century Muslim's Syncretistic Perspective of Cosmology: Abū al-'Alā' al-Ma'arrī's Philosophical-Poetic Reflections in Luzūm Mā Lā Yalzam on the Make-up and Dynamics of the Universe." *The Muslim World* 85 (1995): 122-46.

Lane, E. W. *Arabic-English Lexicon.* 2 vols. Cambridge, England: Islamic Texts Society, 1984.

Lavan, Spencer. *The Ahmadiyah Movement: A History and Perspective.* Delhi: Manohar Book Service, 1974.

Leirvik, Oddbjørn. *Images of Jesus Christ in Islam: Introduction, Survey of Research, Issues of Dialogue.* Studia Missionalia Upsaliensia LXXVI. Uppsala: Swedish Institute of Missionary Research, 1999.

Levonian, Lootfy. "The Ikhwān al-Ṣafā' and Christ." *The Moslem World* 35 (1945): 27-31.

Liddell, Henry George, and Robert Scott. *A Greek-English Lexicon.* Revised and augmented by Henry Stuart Jones and Roderick McKenzie. 9th ed. with a Supplement, ed. E. A. Barber (1968). Oxford: Clarendon Press, 1940.

Long, Richard. *Tawfīq al-Ḥakīm: Playwright of Egypt.* London: Ithaca Press, 1979.

Ludwig, Emil. *Napoleon.* Translated by Eden and Cedar Paul. New York: Liveright, 1926.

________. *The Son of Man: The Story of Jesus.* Translated by Eden and Cedar Paul. New York: Boni & Liveright, 1928.

Mann, C. S. *Mark: A New Translation with Introduction and Commentary.* The Anchor Bible, ed. William Foxwell Albright and David Noel Freedman, vol. 27. Garden City, NY: Doubleday, 1986.

Manson, T. W. *The Teaching of Jesus.* Cambridge: Cambridge University Press, 1937.

McAuliffe, Jane Dammen. *Qur'ānic Christians: An Analysis of Classical and Modern Exegesis.* Cambridge: Cambridge University Press, 1991.

________. "The Qur'ānic Context of Muslim Biblical Scholarship." *Islam and Christian-Muslim Relations* 7 (1996): 141-58.

McKenzie, John L. *Second Isaiah: Introduction, Translation, and Notes.* The Anchor Bible, ed. William Foxwell Albright and David Noel Freedman, vol. 20. Garden City, NY: Doubleday, 1968.

McLachlan, H. John. Review of *The Nazarene Gospel Restored,* by Robert Graves and Joshua Podro. In *The Hibbert Journal* 52 (1954): 315-18.

Meier, John P. *A Marginal Jew: Rethinking the Historical Jesus.* The Anchor Reference Library, ed. David Noel Freedman. 2 vols., [vol. 3 forthcoming]. New York: Doubleday, 1991-94.

Merad, Ali. "Le Christ selon le Coran." *Revue de l'Occident musulman et de la Méditerranée* 5 (1968): 79-94. English translation as "Christ According to the Qur'an." In *Encounter: Documents for Muslim-Christian Understanding* (Rome) 69 (November, 1980): 1-17.

Metzger, Bruce M. *The Canon of the New Testament: Its Origin, Development, and Significance.* Oxford: Clarendon Press, 1987.

________. *The Early Versions of the New Testament: Their Origin, Transmission and Limitations.* Oxford: Clarendon Press, 1977.

________. *A Textual Commentary on the Greek New Testament.* London: United Bible Societies, 1971.

Michaels, J. Ramsey. *1 Peter.* Word Biblical Commentary, ed. David A. Hubbard and Glenn W. Barker, vol. 49. Waco, TX: Word Books, 1988.

Michel, Thomas F., ed. and trans. *A Muslim Theologian's Response to Christianity: Ibn Taymiyya's Al-Jawab al-Sahih.* Delmar, NY: Caravan Books, 1984.

Mitchell, Richard P. *The Society of the Muslim Brothers.* New York: Oxford University Press, 1969.

Morenz, Siegfried. *Egyptian Religion.* Translated by Ann E. Keep. Ithaca, NY: Cornell University Press, 1973.

Moule, C. F. D. *The Birth of the New Testament.* 3d ed. Black's New Testament Commentaries, ed. Henry Chadwick. London: Adam & Charles Black, 1981.

Mourad, Suleiman A. "A Twelfth-Century Muslim Biography of Jesus." *Islam and Christian-Muslim Relations* 7 (1996): 39-45.

Neill, Stephen, and Tom Wright. *The Interpretation of the New Testament: 1861-1986.* 2d ed. Oxford: Oxford University Press, 1988.

Nijim, Badie K. "'Abbās Maḥmūd al-'Aqqād: A Modern Muslim Apologist." M.A. thesis, Hartford Seminary, 1970.

Nolin, Kenneth E. Review of *Ma' al-Masīḥ fī al-Anājīl al-Arba'ah* [With Christ in the Four Gospels], by Fatḥī 'Uthmān. In *The Muslim World* 53 (1963): 252-54.

________. Review of *Al-Masīḥ fī al-Qur'ān wa-al-Tawrāt wa-al-Injīl* [Christ in the Qur'ān, the Torah, and the Gospel], by 'Abd al-Karīm al-Khaṭīb. In *The Muslim World* 59 (1969): 74-79.

________. "Truth: Christian-Muslim." *The Muslim World* 55 (1965): 237-45.

Nolland, John. Luke. Word Biblical Commentary, ed. David A. Hubbard and Glenn W. Barker, vols. 35A, 35B and 35C. Dallas: Word Books, 1989-93.

Notovitch, Nicolas. *La vie inconnue de Jésus-Christ.* Paris: M. Paul Ollendorf, 1894. English edition: *The Unknown Life of Jesus Christ.* Translated by Violet Crispe. London: Hutchinson, 1895.

al-Nowaihi, Mohamed. "The Religion of Islam: A Presentation to Christians." International Review of Mission 65 (1976): 216-25.

Pappas, Paul C. *Jesus' Tomb in India: The Debate on His Death and Resurrection.* Berkeley, CA: Asian Humanities Press, 1991.

Parrinder, Geoffrey. *Jesus in the Qur'ān.* London: Sheldon Press, 1965.

Patai, Raphael. *The Messiah Texts.* Detroit: Wayne State University Press, 1979.

Pellat, Charles. *The Life and Works of Jahiz: Translations of Selected Texts.* Translated by D. M. Hawke. The Islamic World Series, ed. G. E. von Grunebaum. Berkeley: University of California Press, 1969.

Pontificio Istituto di Studi Arabi. "Christ Seen by Contemporary Muslim Writers." Translated by Penelope Johnstone. *Encounter: Documents for Muslim-Christian Understand-*

ing (Rome) 87 (August, 1982): 1-14.

Portalié, Eugène. *A Guide to the Thought of Saint Augustine.* Translated by Ralph J. Bastian. Library of Living Catholic Thought. Chicago: Henry Regnery, 1960.

Pritchard, James B., ed. *Ancient Near Eastern Texts Relating to the Old Testament.* 3d ed. Princeton: Princeton University Press, 1969.

Rad, Gerhard von. *Genesis: A Commentary.* Translated by John H. Marks. 2d ed. Old Testament Library. Philadelphia: Westminster Press, 1961.

Ragg, Lonsdale, and Laura Ragg. *The Gospel of Barnabas, edited and translated from the Italian MS. in the Imperial Library at Vienna.* Oxford: The Clarendon Press, 1907. Reprinted as *The Gospel of Baranbas.* New Delhi: Idara Isha'at-e-Diniyat, n.d.

Renan, Ernest. *La vie de Jésus.* Paris: Michel Lévy Frères, 1863. English edition: *The Life of Jesus.* Everyman's Library, ed. Ernest Rhys, no. 805. London: J. M. Dent & Sons, 1927.

Review of *The Son of Man,* by Emil Ludwig. *The New Statesman* 31 (June 2, 1928): 262.

Ringgren, Helmer. *Religions of the Ancient Near East.* Translated by John Sturdy. Philadelphia: Westminster, 1973.

Robertson, E. H. *The New Translations of the Bible.* Studies in Ministry and Worship, ed. G. W. H. Lampe and David M. Paton. Naperville, IL: Alec R. Allenson, 1959.

Robinson, James M. *A New Quest of the Historical Jesus.* Studies in Biblical Theology, no. 25. London: SCM Press, 1959.

Robinson, Neal. *Christ in Islam and Christianity.* Albany: State University of New York Press, 1991.

________. "Creating Birds from Clay: A Miracle of Jesus in the Qur'ān and in Classical Muslim Exegesis." *The Muslim World* 79 (1989): 1-13.

Safrai, S., and M. Stern. *The Jewish People of the First Century: Historical Geography, Political History, Social, Cultural and Religious Life and Institutions.* 2 vols. Section 1 in Compendia Rerum Iudaicarum ad Novum Testamentum. Philadelphia: Fortress Press, 1974-76.

Safran, Nadav. *Egypt in Search of Political Community: An Analysis of the Intellectual and Political Evolution of Egypt, 1804-1952.* Harvard Middle Eastern Studies, no. 5. Cambridge: Harvard University Press, 1961.

Saliba, Issa A. "The Bible in Arabic: The 19th-Century Protestant Translation." *The Muslim World* 65 (1975): 254-63.

Sandbach, F. H. *The Stoics.* New York: W. W. Norton, 1975.

Sanders, E. P. *Jesus and Judaism.* Philadelphia: Fortress Press, 1985.

Sandmel, Samuel. *Philo of Alexandria: An Introduction.* New York: Oxford University Press, 1979.

al-Sayyid Marsot, Afaf Lutfi. *A Short History of Modern Egypt.* Cambridge: Cambridge University Press, 1985.

Schimmel, Annemarie. "Jesus and Mary as Poetical Images in Rūmī's Verse." In *Christian-Muslim Encounters,* ed. Yvonne Yazbeck Haddad and Wadi Zaidan Haddad, 143-57. Gainsville, FL: University of Florida Press, 1995.

Schneelmelcher, Wilhelm, ed. *New Testament Apocrypha.* English translation edited by R. McL. Wilson. 2d ed. 2 vols. Cambridge, England: James Clarke, 1991-92.

Schoonover, Kermit. "Contemporary Egyptian Authors." *The Muslim World* 45 (1955): 26-36.

________. "Some Observations on Modern Arabic Literature." *The Muslim World* 44 (1954): 20-30.

________. "A Survey of the Best Modern Arabic Books." *The Muslim World* 42 (1952): 48-55.

Schumann, Olaf H. *Der Christus der Muslime: Christologische Aspekte in der arabish-islamischen Literatur.* 2d ed. Kölner Veröffentlichungen zur Religionsgeschichte, ed. Michael Klöcker and Udo Tworuschka, no. 13. Cologne and Vienna: Böhlau Verlag, 1988.

________. "Pręsent-day Muslim Writers on Christ." *Al-Mushir* (Rawalpindi) 19 (1977): 31-43.

Schürer, Emil. *The History of the Jewish People in the Age of Jesus Christ (175 B.C. - A.D. 135).* Revised and edited by Geza Vermes and Fergus Millar. 2d ed. 3 vols. Edinburgh: T. & T. Clark, 1973-87.

Schweitzer, Albert. *The Quest of the Historical Jesus: A Critical Study of Its Progress from Reimarus to Wrede.* Translated by W. Montgomery. 3d ed. London: Adam & Charles Black, 1954.

Semah, David. *Four Egyptian Literary Critics.* Studies in Arabic Literature: Supplements to the Journal of Arabic Literature, ed. M. M. Badawi, P. Cachia, M. C. Lyons and J. N. Mattock, vol. 3. Leiden: E. J. Brill, 1974.

Shaban, M. A. *Islamic History: A New Interpretation.* 2 vols. Cambridge: Cambridge University Press, 1971-76.

Shanks, Hershel, ed. *Understanding the Dead Sea Scrolls: A Reader from the Biblical Archaeology Review.* New York: Random House, 1992.

Sharpe, Eric J. *Comparative Religion: A History.* 2d ed. La Salle, IL: Open Court, 1986.

Slomp, Jan. "The Gospel in Dispute: A Critical Evaluation of the First French Translation with the Italian Text and Introduction of the So-called Gospel of Barnabas." *Islamochristiana* 4 (1978): 67-111.

________. "The 'Gospel of Barnabas' in Recent Research," *Islamochristiana* 23 (1997): 81-109.

________. Review of *Der Christus der Muslime: Christologische Aspekte in der arabish-islamischen Literatur* (1st ed.), by Olaf H. Schumann. In *Al-Mushir* (Rawalpindi) 19 (1977): 88-90.

Sloyan, Gerard S. *Is Christ the End of the Law?* Biblical Perspectives on Current Issues, ed. Howard Clark Kee. Philadelphia: Westminster Press, 1978.

Smalley, Beryl. *The Study of the Bible in the Middle Ages.* 3d ed. Oxford: Basil Blackwell, 1983.

Smith, Charles D. "The 'Crisis of Orientation': The Shift of Egyptian Intellectuals to Islamic Subjects in the 1930's." *International Journal of Middle East Studies* 4 (1973):

382-410.

________. *Islam and the Search for Social Order in Modern Egypt: A Biography of Muhammad Husayn Haykal.* SUNY Series in Middle Eastern Studies, ed. Shahrough Akhavi. Albany: State University of New York Press, 1983.

Smith, Jane I., and Yvonne Y. Haddad. "The Virgin Mary in Islamic Tradition." *The Muslim World* 79 (1989): 161-87.

Smith, Ralph L. *Micah-Malachi.* Word Biblical Commentary, ed. David A. Hubbard and Glenn W. Barker, vol. 32. Waco, TX: Word Books, 1984.

Smith, Wilfred Cantwell. *Islam in Modern History.* Princeton: Princeton University Press, 1957.

________. Review of *City of Wrong: a Friday in Jerusalem,* by M. Kamel Hussein. In *The Muslim World* 51 (1961): 134-37.

Sox, David. *The Gospel of Barnabas.* London: George Allen & Unwin, 1984.

Stern, S. M. "'Abd al-Jabbār's Account of How Christ's Religion was Falsified by the Adoption of Roman Customs." *Journal of Theological Studies* n.s. 19 (1968): 128-85.

________. "Quotations from Apocryphal Gospels in 'Abd al-Jabbār." *Journal of Theological Studies* n.s. 18 (1967): 34-57.

Talley, Thomas J. *The Origins of the Liturgical Year.* 2d ed. Collegeville, MN: Liturgical Press, 1991.

Tarn, William. *Hellenistic Civilisation.* 3d ed. Revised by William Tarn and G. T. Griffith. London: Edward Arnold, 1952.

Teissier, Henri. "Des écrivains musulmans d'aujourd'hui nous parlent du Christ." *Cahiers religieux d'Afrique du Nord* (Algiers) 10 (January-March 1959): 28-36.

Thomas, David. "The Miracles of Jesus in Early Islamic Polemic." *Journal of Semitic Studies* 39 (1994): 221-43.

Thomas, Richard W. *A Workbook of Religion: English-Arabic.* Arabic title: *Dalīl al-Muṣṭalaḥāt al-Dīnīyah: Inklīzī-'Arabī.* Beirut: Rābiṭat al-Maṭbū'āt al-Masīḥīyah al-'Arabīyah, 1969.

Thompson, J. A. *The Book of Jeremiah.* The New International Commentary on the Old Testament, ed. R. K. Harrison. Grand Rapids, MI: William B. Eerdmans, 1980.

Tibawi, A. B. *American Interests in Syria, 1800-1901: A Study of Educational, Literary and Religious Work.* Oxford: Clarendon, 1966.

Torrey, Norman L. *Voltaire and the English Deists.* Oxford: Marston Press, 1963.

Troll, Christian W. *Sayyid Ahmad Khan: A Reinterpretation of Muslim Theology.* New Delhi: Vikas Publishing House, 1978.

Vanden Bossche, Chris R. *Carlyle and the Search for Authority.* Studies in Victorian Life and Literature. Columbus: Ohio State University Press, 1991.

Vermes, Geza. *The Complete Dead Sea Scrolls in English.* London: Allen Lane, The Penguin Press, 1997.

________. *Post-Biblical Jewish Studies.* Studies in Judaism in Late Antiquity, ed. Jacob Neusner, vol. 8. Leiden: E. J. Brill, 1975.

Vermes, Geza, and Martin D. Goodman, eds. *The Essenes According to the Classical*

Sources. Sheffield: JSOT Press, 1989.

Watt, W[illiam] Montgomery. "Carlyle on Muḥammad." *The Hibbert Journal* (1954-55): 247-54.

________. "The Christianity Criticized in the Qur'ān." *The Muslim World* 57 (1967): 197-201.

________. *Muslim-Christian Encounters: Perceptions and Misperceptions.* London: Routledge, 1991.

Wehr, Hans. *A Dictionary of Modern Written Arabic.* Edited by J Milton Cowan. Ithaca, NY: Cornell University Press, 1966.

Weigall, Arthur. *The Paganism in Our Christianity.* New York: G. P. Putnam's Sons, 1928.

Wessels, Antonie. *A Modern Arabic Biography of Muḥammad: A Critical Study of Muḥammad Ḥusayn Haykal's Hayāt Muhammad.* Leiden: E. J. Brill, 1972.

Wielandt, Rotraud. "'Abbās Maḥmūd al-'Aqqād (1889-1964): Nutzen und Nachteil religionsgeschichtlicher Studien für den Glauben." Chap. in *Offenbarung und Geschichte im Denken moderner Muslime.* Akademie der Wissenschaften und der Literatur, die orientalische Kommission, vol. 25. Wiesbaden: Franz Steiner, 1971.

Williamson, H. G. M. *Ezra, Nehemiah.* Word Biblical Commentary, ed. David A. Hubbard and Glenn W. Barker, vol. 16. Waco, TX: Word Books, 1985.

Wilson, Bryan R. *Magic and the Millennium: A Sociological Study of Religious Movements of Protest among Tribal and Third-World Peoples.* New York: Harper & Row, 1973.

Witherington, Ben, III. *The Jesus Quest: The Third Search for the Jew of Nazareth.* Downers Grove, IL: InterVarsity Press, 1995.

Woodberry, J. Dudley. "The Muslim Understanding of Jesus." *Word & World: Theology for Christian Ministry* 16 (1996): 173-78.

Wright, W. *A Grammar of the Arabic Language.* Revised by W. Robertson Smith and M. J. de Goeje. 3d ed. 2 vols. Cambridge: Cambridge University Press, 1955.

Yapp, M. E. *The Making of the Modern Near East: 1792-1923.* A History of the Near East, ed. P. M. Holt. London: Longman, 1987.

________. *The Near East Since the First World War.* A History of the Near East, ed. P. M. Holt. London: Longman, 1991.

Zaehner, R. C. *The Dawn and Twilight of Zoroastrianism.* New York: G. P. Putnam's Sons, 1961.

al-Zubaidi, A. M. K. "The Dīwān School." *Journal of Arabic Literature* 1 (1970): 36-48.

Index

Modern authors are included only when there is a direct reference to them by al-'Aqqād, or when their particular views are mentioned in the Introduction or Notes.